A HISTORY OF THE
CHRISTIAN CHURCH

A HISTORY OF THE CHRISTIAN CHURCH

BY

WILLISTON WALKER

TITUS STREET PROFESSOR OF ECCLESIASTICAL HISTORY
IN YALE UNIVERSITY

NEW YORK
CHARLES SCRIBNER'S SONS

TO MY WIFE

PREFATORY NOTE

In this history the writer has endeavored to treat the vast field of the story of the church so as to make evident, as far as he is able, the circumstances of its origin, its early development, the changes which led to the Reformation, as well as the course of that tremendous upheaval, and those influences which have resulted in the present situation and tendencies of the life of the church. As far as space would permit he has directed attention to the growth of doctrine and the modification of Christian thought.

In preparing the Bibliographical Suggestions at the end of this volume the author had primarily in mind the American reading public, and has there given the American places and dates of publication of many volumes which have also been issued in Great Britain. In particular the writings of Professors William Adams Brown, W. N. Clarke, A. B. Davidson, A. C. McGiffert, W. F. Adeney, T. M. Lindsay, James Moffatt, André Lagarde, Williston Walker, etc., there cited, are published in Edinburgh by Messrs. T. & T. Clark.

WILLISTON WALKER.

New Haven, May, 1919.

CONTENTS

CONTENTS

PERIOD VI. THE REFORMATION

PERIOD VII. THE TRANSITION TO THE MODERN RELIGIOUS SITUATION

MAPS

PERIOD I. FROM THE BEGINNINGS TO THE GNOSTIC CRISIS

SECTION I. THE GENERAL SITUATION

THE birth of Christ saw the lands which surrounded the Mediterranean in the possession of Rome. To a degree never before equalled, and unapproached in modern times, these vast territories, which embraced all that common men knew of civilized life, were under the sway of a single type of culture. The civilizations of India or of China did not come within the vision of the ordinary inhabitant of the Roman Empire. Outside its borders he knew only savage or semicivilized tribes. The Roman Empire and the world of civilized men were coextensive. All was held together by allegiance to a single Emperor, and by a common military system subject to him. The Roman army, small in comparison with that of a modern military state, was adequate to preserve the Roman peace. Under that peace commerce flourished, communication was made easy by excellent roads and by sea, and among educated men, at least in the larger towns, a common language, that of Greece, facilitated the interchange of thought. It was an empire that, in spite of many evil rulers and corrupt lower officials, secured a rough justice such as the world had never before seen; and its citizens were proud of it and of its achievements.

Yet with all its unity of imperial authority and military control, Rome was far from crushing local institutions. In domestic matters the inhabitants of the provinces were largely self-governing. Their local religious observances were generally respected. Among the masses the ancient languages and customs persisted. Even native rulers were allowed a limited sway in portions of the empire, as native states still persist under British rule in India. Such a land was Palestine at the time of Christ's birth. Not a little of the success of Rome as mistress of its diverse subject population was due to this considerate treatment of local rights and prejudices. The diver-

1

sity in the empire was scarcely less remarkable than its unity. This variety was nowhere more apparent than in the realm of religious thought.

Christianity entered no empty world. Its advent found men's minds filled with conceptions of the universe, of religion, of sin, and of rewards and punishments, with which it had to reckon and to which it had to adjust itself. Christianity could not build on virgin soil. The conceptions which it found already existing formed much of the material with which it must erect its structure. Many of these ideas are no longer those of the modern world. The fact of this inevitable inter- mixture compels the student to distinguish the permanent from the transitory in Christian thought, though the process is one of exceeding difficulty, and the solutions given by various scholars are diverse.

Certain factors in the world of thought into which Chris- tianity came belong to universal ancient religion and are of hoary antiquity. All men, except a few representatives of philosophical sophistication, believed in the existence of a power, or of powers, invisible, superhuman, and eternal, con- trolling human destiny, and to be worshipped or placated by prayer, ritual, or sacrifice. The earth was viewed as the cen- tre of the universe. Around it the sun, planets, and stars ran their courses. Above it was the heaven; below the abode of departed spirits or of the wicked. No conception of what is now called natural law had penetrated the popular mind. All the ongoings of nature were the work of invisible powers of good and evil, who ruled arbitrarily. Miracles were, therefore, to be regarded not merely as possible; they were to be expected whenever the higher forces would impress men with the im- portant or the unusual. The world was the abode of innu- merable spirits, righteous or malevolent, who touched human life in all its phases, and who even entered into such possession of men as to control their actions for good or ill. A profound sense of unworthiness, of ill desert, and of dissatisfaction with the existing conditions of life characterized the mass of man- kind. The varied forms of religious manifestation were evi- dences of the universal need of better relations with the spiritual and unseen, and of men's longing for help greater than any they could give one another.

Besides these general conceptions common to popular religion, the world into which Christianity came owed much to the specific influence of Greek thought. Hellenistic ideas dominated the intelligence of the Roman Empire, but their sway was extensive only among the more cultivated portion of the population. Greek philosophic speculation at first concerned itself with the explanation of the physical universe. Yet with Heraclitus of Ephesus (about B. C. 490), though all was viewed as in a sense physical, the universe, which is in constant flow, is regarded as fashioned by a fiery element, the all-penetrating reason, of which men's souls are a part. Here was probably the germ of the Logos (λόγος) conception which was to play such a rôle in later Greek speculation and Christian theology. As yet this shaping element was undistinguished from material warmth or fire. Anaxagoras of Athens (about B. C. 500–428) taught that a shaping mind (νοῦς) acted in the ordering of matter and is independent of it. The Pythagoreans, of southern Italy, held that spirit is immaterial, and that souls are fallen spirits imprisoned in material bodies. To this belief in immaterial existence they seem to have been led by a consideration of the properties of numbers—permanent truths beyond the realm of matter and not materially discerned.

To Socrates (B. C. 470?–399) the explanation of man himself, not of the universe, was the prime object of thought. Man's conduct, that is morals, was the most important theme of investigation. Right action is based on knowledge, and will result in the four virtues—prudence, courage, self-control, and justice—which, as the "natural virtues," were to have their eminent place in mediæval Christian theology. This identification of virtue with knowledge, the doctrine that to know will involve doing, was indeed a disastrous legacy to all Greek thinking, and influential in much Christian speculation, notably in the Gnosticism of the second century.

In Socrates's disciple, Plato (B. C. 427–347), the early Greek mind reached its highest spiritual attainment. He is properly describable as a man of mystical piety, as well as of the profoundest spiritual insight. To Plato the passing forms of this visible world give no real knowledge. That knowledge of the truly permanent and real comes from our acquaintance with the "ideas," those changeless archetypal, universal patterns which exist in the invisible spiritual world—the "intelligible" world, since known by reason rather than by the senses—and give whatever of reality is shared by the passing phenomena present to our senses. The soul knew these "ideas" in previous existence. The phenomena of the visible world call to remembrance these once known "ideas." The soul, existing before the body, must be independent of it, and not affected by its decay. This conception of immortality as an attribute of the soul, not shared by the body, was always influential in Greek thought and stood in sharp contrast to the Hebrew doctrine of resurrection. All "ideas" are not of equal worth. The highest are those of the true, the beautiful, and especially of the good. A clear perception of a personal God, as embodied in the "idea" of the good, was perhaps not attained by Plato; but he certainly approached closely to it. The good rules the world, not chance. It is the source of all lesser goods, and desires to be imitated in the actions of men. The realm of "ideas" is the true home of the soul, which finds its highest satisfaction in communion with them. Salvation is the recovery of the vision of the eternal goodness and beauty.

Aristotle (B. C. 384–322) was of a far less mystical spirit than Plato. To him the visible world was an unquestioned reality. He discarded Plato's sharp discrimination between "ideas" and phenomena. Neither exist without the other. Each existence is a substance, the result, save in the case of God, who is purely immaterial, of the impress of "idea," as the formative force, on matter which is the content. Matter in itself is only potential substance. It has always existed, yet never without form. Hence the world is eternal, for a realm of "ideas" antecedent to their manifestation in phenomena does not exist. The world is the prime object of knowledge, and Aristotle is therefore in a true sense a scientist. Its changes demand the initiation of a "prime mover," who is Himself unmoved. Hence Aristotle presents this celebrated argument for the existence of God. But the "prime mover" works with intelligent purpose, and God is, therefore, not only the beginning but the end of the process of the world's development. Man belongs to the world of substances, but in him there is not merely the body and sensitive "soul" of the animal; there is also a divine spark, a Logos (λόγος), which he shares with God, and which is eternal, though, unlike Plato's conception of spirit, essentially impersonal. In morals Aristotle held that happiness, or well-being, is the aim, and is attained by a careful maintenance of the golden mean.

Greek philosophy did not advance much scientifically beyond Plato and Aristotle, but they had little direct influence at the time of Christ. Two centuries and a half after His birth, a modified Platonism, Neo-Platonism, was to arise, of great importance, which profoundly affected Christian theology, notably that of Augustine. Aristotle was powerfully to influence the scholastic theology of the later Middle Ages. Those older Greek philosophers had viewed man chiefly in the light of his value to the state. The conquests of Alexander, who died B. C. 323, wrought a great change in men's outlook. Hellenic culture was planted widely over the Eastern world, but the small Greek states collapsed as independent political entities. It was difficult longer to feel that devotion to the new and vast political units that a little, independent Athens had, for instance, won from its citizens. The individual as an independent entity was emphasized. Philosophy had to be interpreted in terms of individual life. How could the individual make the most of himself? Two great answers were given, one of which was wholly foreign to the genius of Christianity, and could not be used by it; the other only partially foreign, and therefore destined profoundly to influence Christian theology. These were Epicureanism and Stoicism.

Epicurus (B. C. 342–270), most of whose life was spent in Athens, taught that mental bliss is the highest aim of man. This state is most perfect when passive. It is the absence of all that disturbs and annoys. Hence Epicurus himself does not deserve the reproaches often cast upon his system. Indeed, in his own life, he was an ascetic. The worst foes of mental happiness he taught are groundless fears. Of these the chief are dread of the anger of the gods and of death. Both are baseless. The gods exist, but they did not create nor do they govern the world, which Epicurus holds, with Democritus (B. C. 470?–380?), was formed by the chance and ever-changing combinations of eternally existing atoms. All is material, even the soul of man and the gods themselves. Death ends all, but is no evil, since in it there is no consciousness remaining. Hence, as far as it was a religion, Epicureanism was one of indifference. The school spread widely. The Roman poet Lucretius (B. C. 98?–55), in his brilliant *De Rerum Natura*, gave

expression to the worthier side of Epicureanism; but the influence of the system as a whole was destructive and toward a
sensual view of happiness.

Contemporarily with Epicurus, Euhemerus (about B. C. 300)
taught that the gods of the old religions were simply deified
men, about whom myths and tradition had cast a halo of
divinity.   He found a translator and advocate in the Roman
poet Ennius (B. C. 239?–170?).   Parallel with Epicureanism,
in the teaching of Pyrrho of Elis (B. C. 360?–270?), and his
followers, a wholly sceptical point of view was presented.   Not
merely can the real nature of things never be understood, but
the best course of action is equally dubious.   In practice
Pyrrho found, like Epicurus, the ideal of life one of withdrawal
from all that annoys or disturbs.   With all these theories
Christianity could have nothing in common, and they in turn
did not affect it.

The other great answer was that of Stoicism, the noblest
type of ancient pagan ethical thought, the nearest in some respects to Christianity, and in others remote from it.   Its leaders were Zeno (B. C. ?–264?), Cleanthes (B. C. 301?–232?), and
Chrysippus (B. C. 280?–207?).   Though developed in Athens, it
flourished best outside of Greece, and notably in Rome, where
Seneca (B. C. 3?–A. D. 65), Epictetus (A. D. 60?–?), and the
Emperor, Marcus Aurelius (A. D. 121–180), had great influence.
It was powerfully represented in Tarsus during the early life
of the Apostle Paul.   Stoicism was primarily a great ethical
system, yet not without claims to be considered a religion.
Its thought of the universe was curiously materialistic.   All
that is real is physical.   Yet there is great difference in the
fineness of bodies, and the coarser are penetrated by the finer.
Hence fine and coarse correspond roughly to the common distinctions between spirit and matter.   Stoicism approximated,
though it much modified, the view of Heraclitus.   The source
of all, and the shaping, harmonizing influence in the universe
is the vital warmth, from which all has developed by differing
degrees of tension, which interpenetrates all things, and to
which all will return.   Far more than Heraclitus's fire, which
it resembles, it is the intelligent, self-conscious world-soul, an all
indwelling reason, Logos (λόγος), of which our reason is a part.
It is God, the life and wisdom of all.   It is truly within us.
We can "follow the God within"; and by reason of it one can

say, as Cleanthes did of Zeus: "We too are thy offspring." The popular gods are simply names for the forces that stream out from God.

Since one wisdom exists in all the world, there is one natural law, one rule of conduct for all men. All are morally free. Since all are from God, all men are brothers. Differences in station in life are accidental. To follow reason in the place in which one finds oneself is the highest duty, and is equally praiseworthy whether a man is an Emperor or a slave. So to obey reason, the Logos, is the sole object of pursuit. Happiness is no just aim, though duty done brings a certain happiness purely as a by-product. The chief enemies of a perfect obedience are passions and lusts, which pervert the judgment. These must resolutely be put aside. God inspires all good acts, though the notion of God is essentially pantheistic.

The strenuous ascetic attitude of Stoicism, its doctrine of the all-pervading and all-ruling divine wisdom, Logos (λόγος), its insistence that all who do well are equally deserving, whatever their station, and its assertion of the essential brotherhood of all men, were profoundly to affect Christian theology. In its highest representatives the creed and its results were noble. It was, however, too often hard, narrow, and unsympathetic. It was for the few. It recognized that the many could never reach its standards. Its spirit was too often one of pride. That of Christianity is one of humility. Still it produced remarkable effects. Stoicism gave Rome excellent Emperors and many lesser officials. Though it never became a really popular creed, it was followed by many of high influence and position in the Roman world, and modified Roman law for the better. It introduced into jurisprudence the conception of a law of nature, expressed in reason, and above all arbitrary human statutes. By its doctrine that all men are by nature equal, the worst features of slavery were gradually ameliorated, and Roman citizenship widely extended.

One may say that the best educated thought in Rome and the provinces, by the time of Christ, in spite of wide-spread Epicureanism and Scepticism, inclined to pantheistic Monotheism, to the conception of God as good, in contrast to the non-moral character of the old Greek and Roman deities, to belief in a ruling divine providence, to the thought that true religion is not ceremonies but an imitation of the moral qualities of God, and toward a humaner attitude to men. The two elements lacking in this educated philosophy were those of certainty such as could only be given by belief in a divine revelation, and of that loyalty to a person which Christianity was to emphasize.

The common people, however, shared in few of these benefits. They lay in gross superstition. If the grip of the old religions of Greece and Rome had largely relaxed, they nevertheless believed in gods many and lords many. Every town had its patron god or goddess, every trade, the farm, the spring, the household, the chief events of life, marriage, childbirth. These views, too, were ultimately to appear in Christian history transmuted into saint-worship. Soothsayers and magicians drove a thriving trade among the ignorant, and none were more patronized than those of Jewish race. Above all, the common people were convinced that the maintenance of the historic religious cult of the ancient gods was necessary for the safety and perpetuity of the state. If not observed, the gods wreaked vengeance in calamities—an opinion that was the source of much later persecution of Christianity. These popular ideas were not vigorously opposed by the learned, who largely held that the old religions had a police value. They regarded the state ceremonies as a necessity for the common man. Seneca put the philosophical opinion bluntly when he declared that "the wise man will observe all religious usages as commanded by the law, not as pleasing to the gods." The lowest point in popular religious feeling in the Roman Empire corresponds roughly to the time of the birth of Christ.

The abler Emperors strove to strengthen and modify the ancient popular worships, for patriotic reasons, into worship of the state and of its head. This patriotic deification of the Roman state began, indeed, in the days of the republic. The worship of the "Dea Roma" may be found in Smyrna as early as B. C. 195. This reverence was strengthened by the popularity of the empire in the provinces as securing them better government than that of the republic. As early as B. C. 29, Pergamum had a temple to Rome and Augustus. This worship, directed to the ruler as the embodiment of the state, or rather to his "genius" or indwelling spirit, spread rapidly. It soon had an elaborate priesthood under state patronage, divided and organized by provinces, and celebrating not only worship but annual games on a large scale. It was probably the most highly developed organization of a professedly religious character under the early empire, and the degree to which it ultimately affected Christian institutions awaits further investigation. From a modern point of view there was much more of patriotism than of religion in this system. Christian missionaries in Japan have solved a similar, though probably less difficult, situation by holding reverence to the Emperor to be purely patriotic. But early Christian feeling regarded this worship of the Emperor as utterly irreconcilable with allegiance to Christ. The feeling is shown in the description of Pergamum in *Revelation* 2¹³. Christian refusal to render the worship seemed treasonable, and was the great occasion of the martyrdoms.

Men need a religion deeper than philosophy or ceremonies. Philosophy satisfies only the exceptional man. Ceremonies avail for more, but not those whose thoughts are active, or whose sense of personal unworthiness is keen. Some attempt was made to revive the dying older popular paganism. The earlier Emperors were, many of them, extensive builders and patrons of temples. The most notable effort to effect a revival and purification of popular religion was that of Plutarch (A. D. 46?–120?), of Chæronea in Greece, which may serve as typical of others. He criticised the traditional mythology. All that implied cruel or morally unworthy actions on the part of the gods he rejected. There is one God. All the popular gods are His attributes personified, or subordinate spirits. Plutarch had faith in oracles, special providences, and future retribution. He taught a strenuous morality. His attempt to wake up what was best in the dying older paganism was a hopeless task and won few followers.

The great majority of those who felt religious longings simply adopted Oriental religions, especially those of a redemptive nature in which mysticism or sacramentalism were prominent features. Ease of communication, and especially the great influx of Oriental slaves into the western portion of the Roman world during the later republic facilitated this process. The spread of these faiths independent of, and to a certain extent as rivals of, Christianity during the first three centuries of our era made that epoch one of deepening religious feeling throughout the empire, and, in that sense, undoubtedly facilitated the ultimate triumph of Christianity.

One such Oriental religion, of considerably extended appeal, though with little of the element of mystery, was Judaism, of which there will be occasion to speak more fully in another connection. The popular mind turned more largely to other Oriental cults, of greater mystery, or rather of larger redemptive sacramental significance. Their meaning for the religious development of the Roman world has been only recently appreciated at anything like its true value. The most popular of these Oriental religions were those of the Great Mother (Cybele) and Attis, originating in Asia Minor; of Isis and Serapis from Egypt; and of Mithras from Persia. At the same time there was much syncretistic mixture of these religions, one with another, and with the older religions of the lands to which they came. That of the Great Mother, which was essentially a primitive nature worship, accompanied by licentious rites, reached Rome in B. C. 204, and was the first to gain extensive foothold in the West. That of Isis and Serapis, with its emphasis on regeneration and a future life, was well established in Rome by B. C. 80, but had long to endure governmental opposition. That of Mithras, the noblest of all, though having an extended history in the East, did not become conspicuous at Rome till toward the year A. D. 100, and its great spread was in the latter part of the second and during the third centuries. It was especially beloved of soldiers. In the later years, at least of its progress in the Roman Empire, Mithras was identified with the sun—the *Sol Invictus* of the Emperors just before Constantine. Like other religions of Persian origin, its view of the universe was dualistic.

All these religions taught a redeemer-god. All held that the initiate shared in symbolic (sacramental) fashion the experiences of the god, died with him, rose with him, became partakers of the divine nature, usually through a meal shared symbolically with him, and participated in his immortality. All had secret rites for the initiated. All offered mystical (sacramental) cleansing from sin. In the religion of Isis and Serapis that cleansing was by bathing in sacred water; in those of the Great Mother and of Mithras by the blood of a bull, the *taurobolium*, by which, as recorded in inscriptions, the initiate was "reborn forever." All promised a happy future life for the faithful. All were more or less ascetic in their attitude toward the world. Some, like Mithraism, taught the brotherhood and essential equality of all disciples. There can be no doubt that the development of the early Christian doctrine of the sacraments was affected, if not directly by these religions, at least by the religious atmosphere which they helped to create and to which they were congenial.

In summing up the situation in the heathen world at the coming of Christ, one must say that, amid great confusion, and in a multitude of forms of expression, some of them very unworthy, certain religious demands are evident. A religion that should meet the requirements of the age must teach one righteous God, yet find place for numerous spirits, good and bad. It must possess a definite revelation of the will of God, as in Judaism, that is an authoritative scripture. It must inculcate a world-denying virtue, based on moral actions agreeable to the will and character of God. It must hold forth a future life with rewards and punishments. It must have a symbolic initiation and promise a real forgiveness of sins. It must possess a redeemer-god into union with whom men could come by certain sacramental acts. It must teach the brotherhood of all men, at least of all adherents of the religion. However simple the beginnings of Christianity may have been, Christianity must possess, or take on, all these traits if it was to conquer the Roman Empire or to become a world religion. It came "in the fulness of time" in a much larger sense than was formerly thought; and no one who believes in an overruling providence of God will deny the fundamental importance of this mighty preparation, even if some of the features of Christianity's early development bear the stamp and limitations of the time and have to be separated from the eternal.

SECTION II. THE JEWISH BACKGROUND

The external course of events had largely determined the development of Judaism in the six centuries preceding the birth of Christ. Judæa had been under foreign political control since the conquest of Jerusalem by Nebuchadrezzar, B. C. 586. It had shared the fortunes of the old Assyrian Empire and of its successors, the Persian and that of Alexander. After the break-up of the latter it came under the control of the Ptolemies of Egypt and then of the Seleucid dynasty of Antioch. While thus politically dependent, its religious institutions were practically undisturbed after their restoration consequent upon the Persian conquest of Babylonia; and the hereditary priestly families were the real native aristocracy of the land. In their higher ranks they came to be marked by political interest and religious indifference. The high-priesthood in particular became a coveted office by reason of its pecuniary and political influence. With it was associated, certainly from the Greek period, a body of advisers and legal interpreters, the Sanhedrim, ultimately seventy-one in number. Thus administered, the temple and its priesthood came to represent the more formal aspect of the religious life of the Hebrews. On the other hand, the feeling that they were a holy people living under Yahwe's holy law, their sense of religious separatism, and the comparative cessation of prophecy, turned the nation to the study of the law, which was interpreted by an ever-increasing mass of tradition. As in Mohammedan lands to-day, the Jewish law was at once religious precept and civil statute. Its interpreters, the scribes, became more and more the real religious leaders of the people. Judaism grew to be, in ever-increasing measure, the religion of a sacred scripture and its mass of interpretative precedent. For a fuller understanding and administration of the law, and for prayer and worship, the synagogue developed wherever Judaism was represented. Its origin is uncertain, going back probably to the Exile. In its typical form it was a local congregation including all Jews of the district presided over by a group of "elders," having often a "ruler" at its head. These were empowered to excommunicate and punish offenders. The services were very simple and could be led by any Hebrew, though usually under "a ruler of the synagogue." They included prayer, the reading of the law and the prophets, their translation and exposition (sermon), and the benediction. Because of the unrepresentative character of the priesthood, and the growing importance of the synagogues, the temple, though highly regarded, became less and less vital for the religious life of the people as the time of Christ is approached, and could be totally destroyed in A. D. 70, without any overthrow of the essential elements in Judaism.

Under the Seleucid Kings Hellenizing influences came strongly into Judæa, and divided the claimants for the high-priestly office. The forcible support of Hellenism by Antiochus IV, Epiphanes (B. C. 175–164), and its accompanying repression

of Jewish worship and customs, led, in B. C. 167, to the great
rebellion headed by the Maccabees, and ultimately to a period
of Judæan independence which lasted till the conquest by the
Romans in B. C. 63. This Hellenizing episode brought about
a profound cleft in Jewish life. The Maccabean rulers secured
for themselves the high-priestly office; but though the family
had risen to leadership by opposition to Hellenism and by religious zeal, it gradually drifted toward Hellenism and purely
political ambition. Under John Hyrcanus, the Maccabean
ruler from B. C. 135 to 105, the distinction between the religious parties of later Judaism became marked. The aristo-
cratic-political party, with which Hyrcanus and the leading
priestly families allied themselves, came to be known as Sadducees—a title the meaning and antiquity of which is uncertain. It was essentially a worldly party without strong religious conviction. Many of the views that the Sadducees
entertained were conservatively representative of the older
Judaism. Thus, they held to the law without its traditional
interpretation, and denied a resurrection or a personal immortality. On the other hand, they rejected the ancient notion of
spirits, good or bad. Though politically influential, they were
unpopular with the mass of the people, who opposed all foreign
influences and stood firmly for the law as interpreted by the
traditions. The most thoroughgoing representatives of this
democratic-legalistic attitude were the Pharisees, a name which
signifies the Separated, presenting what was undoubtedly a
long previously existing attitude, though the designation appears shortly before the time of John Hyrcanus. With his
reign the historic struggle of Pharisees and Sadducees begins.

As a whole, in spite of the fact that the Zealots, or men of
action, sprang from them, the Pharisees were not a political
party. Though they held the admiration of a majority of the
people, they were never very numerous. The ordinary working
Jew lacked the education in the minutiæ of the law or the leisure
to become a Pharisee. Their attitude toward the mass of Judaism was contemptuous.[1] They represented, however, views
which were widely entertained and were in many respects
normal results of Jewish religious development since the Exile.
Their prime emphasis was on the exact keeping of the law as
interpreted by the traditions. They held strongly to the ex-

---

[1] *John* 7[49].

istence of spirits, good and bad—a doctrine of angels and of
Satan that had apparently received a powerful impulse from
Persian ideas. They represented that growth of a belief in
the resurrection of the body, and in future rewards and punishments which had seen a remarkable development during the
two centuries preceding Christ's birth. They held, like the
people generally, to the Messianic hope. The Pharisees, from
many points of view, were deserving of no little respect. From
the circle infused with these ideas Christ's disciples were largely
to come. The most learned of the Apostles had been himself
a Pharisee, and called himself such years after having become
a Christian.[1] Their earnestness was praiseworthy. The great
failure of Pharisaism was twofold. It looked upon religion as
the keeping of an external law, by which a reward was earned.
Such keeping involved of necessity neither a real inward righteousness of spirit, nor a warm personal relation to God. It also
shut out from the divine promises those whose failures, sins,
and imperfect keeping of the law made the attainment of the
Pharisaic standard impossible. It disinherited the "lost sheep"
of the house of Israel. As such it received the well-merited
condemnation of Christ.

The Messianic hope, shared by the Pharisees and common
people alike, was the outgrowth of strong national consciousness and faith in God. It was most vigorous in times of national oppression. Under the earlier Maccabees, when a God-
fearing line had given independence to the people, it was little
felt. The later Maccabees, however, deserted their family
tradition. The Romans conquered the land in B. C. 63. Nor
was the situation really improved from a strict Jewish standpoint, when a half-Jewish adventurer, Herod, the son of the
Idumean Antipater, held a vassal kingship under Roman overlordship from B. C. 37 to B. C. 4. In spite of his undoubted
services to the material prosperity of the land, and his mag-
nificent rebuilding of the temple, he was looked upon as a tool
of the Romans and a Hellenizer at heart. The Herodians were
disliked by Sadducees and Pharisees alike. On Herod's death
his kingdom was divided between three of his sons, Archelaus
becoming "ethnarch" of Judæa, Samaria, and Idumea (B. C.
4–A. D. 6); Herod Antipas "tetrarch" of Galilee and Peræa
(B. C. 4–A. D. 39); and Philip "tetrarch" of the prevailingly

---

[1] *Acts* 23⁶.

heathen region east and northeast of the Sea of Galilee. Archelaus aroused bitter enmity, was deposed by the Emperor
Augustus, and was succeeded by a Roman procurator—the
occupant of this post from A. D. 26 to 36 being Pontius
Pilate.

With such hopelessly adverse political conditions, it seemed
as if the Messianic hope could be realizable only by divine aid.
By the time of Christ that hope involved the destruction of
Roman authority by supernatural divine intervention through
a Messiah; and the establishment of a kingdom of God in
which a freed and all-powerful Judaism should flourish under
a righteous Messianic King of Davidic descent, into which the
Jews scattered throughout the Roman Empire should be gathered, and by which a golden age would be begun. To the
average Jew it probably meant little more than that, by divine
intervention, the Romans would be driven out and the kingdom
restored to Israel. A wide-spread belief, based on *Malachi* 3[1],
held that the coming of the Messiah would be heralded by a
forerunner.

These hopes were nourished by a body of apocalyptic literature, pessimistic as to the present, but painting in brilliant
color the age to come. The writings were often ascribed to
ancient worthies. Such in the Old Testament canon is the
prophecy of *Daniel*, such without are the *Book of Enoch*, the
Assumption of Moses, and a number of others. A specimen of
this class of literature from a Christian point of view, but with
much use of Jewish conceptions, is *Revelation* in the New Testament. These nourished a forward-looking, hopeful religious
attitude that must have served in a measure to offset the strict
legalism of the Pharisaic interpretation of the law.

Other currents of religious life were moving also in Palestine,
the extent of which it is impossible to estimate, but the reality
of which is evident. In the country districts especially, away
from the centres of official Judaism, there was a real mystical
piety. It was that of the later Psalms and of the "poor in
spirit" of the New Testament, and the "Magnificat" and
"Benedictus"[1] may well be expressions of it. To this mystic
type belong also the recently discovered so-called *Odes of Solo-
mon*. From this simpler piety, in a larger and less mystical
sense, came prophetic appeals for repentance, of which those

[1] *Luke* 1[46-55, 68-79].

of John the Baptist are best known.   It was not Pharisaic, but far more vital.

One further conception of later Judaism is of importance by reason of its influence on the development of Christian theology. It is that of "wisdom," which is practically personified as existing side by side with God, one with Him, His "possession" before the foundation of the world, His agent in its creation.[1] It is possible that the influence of the Stoic thought of the all-pervading divine Logos (λόγος) is here to be seen; but a more ethical note sounds than in the corresponding Greek teaching. Yet the two views were easy of assimilation.

Palestine is naturally first in thought in a consideration of Judaism.   It was its home, and the scene of the beginnings of Christianity.   Nevertheless the importance of the dispersion of the Jews outside of Palestine, both for the religious life of the Roman Empire as a whole, and for the reflex effect upon Judaism itself of the consequent contact with Hellenic thought, was great.   This dispersion had begun with the conquests of the Assyrian and Babylonian monarchs, and had been furthered by many rulers, notably by the Ptolemies of Egypt, and the great Romans of the closing days of the republic and the dawning empire.   Estimates are at best conjectural, but it is not improbable that, at the birth of Christ there were five or six times as many Jews outside of Palestine as within its borders. They were a notable part of the population of Alexandria. They were strongly rooted in Syria and Asia Minor.   They were to be found, if in relatively small numbers, in Rome.   Few cities of the empire were without their presence.   Clannish and viewed with little favor by the heathen population, they prospered in trade, were valued for their good qualities by the rulers, their religious scruples were generally respected, and, in turn, they displayed a missionary spirit which made their religious impress felt.   As this Judaism of the dispersion presented itself to the surrounding heathen, it was a far simpler creed than Palestinian Pharisaism.   It taught one God, who had revealed His will in sacred Scriptures, a strenuous morality, a future life with rewards and punishments, and a few relatively simple commands relating to the Sabbath, circumcision, and the use of meats.   It carried with it everywhere the synagogue, with its unelaborate and non-ritualistic worship.   It appealed power-

[1] *Prov.* 3[19]; 8; *Psalms* 33[6].

fully to many heathens; and, besides full proselytes, the synagogues had about them a much larger penumbra of partially Judaized converts, the "devout men," who were to serve as a recruiting ground for much of the early Christian missionary propaganda.

In its turn, the Judaism of the dispersion was much influenced by Hellenism, especially by Greek philosophy, and nowhere more deeply than in Egypt. There, in Alexandria, the Old Testament was given to the reading world in Greek translation, the so-called Septuagint, as early as the reign of Ptolemy Philadelphus (B. C. 285–246). This made the Jewish Scriptures, heretofore locked up in an obscure tongue, widely accessible. In Alexandria, also, Old Testament religious ideas were combined with Greek philosophical conceptions, notably Platonic and Stoic, in a remarkable syncretism. The most influential of these Alexandrian interpreters was Philo (B. C. 20?–A. D. 42?). To Philo, the Old Testament is the wisest of books, a real divine revelation, and Moses the greatest of teachers; but by allegorical interpretation Philo finds the Old Testament in harmony with the best in Platonism and Stoicism. The belief that the Old Testament and Greek philosophy were in essential agreement was one of far-reaching significançe for the development of Christian theology. This allegorical method of Biblical explanation was greatly to influence later Christian study of the Scriptures. To Philo, the one God made the world as an expression of His goodness to His creation; but between God and the world the uniting links are a group of divine powers, viewed partly as attributes of God and partly as personal existences. Of these the highest is the Logos (λόγος), which flows out of the being of God Himself, and is the agent not merely through whom God created the world, but from whom all other powers flow. Through the Logos God created the ideal man, of whom actual man is a poor copy, the work of lower spiritual powers as well as of the Logos. Even from his fallen state man may rise to connection with God through the Logos, the agent of divine revelation. Yet Philo's conception of the Logos is far more philosophical than that of "wisdom" in *Proverbs*, of which mention has been made; and the source of the New Testament Logos doctrine is to be found in the Hebrew conception of "wisdom" rather than in the thought of Philo. He was, however, a great illustration of the manner in which Hellenic and Hebrew ideas might be united, and were actually to be united, in the development of later Christian theology. In no other portion of the Roman world was the process which Philo represented so fully developed as in Alexandria.

SECTION III.   JESUS AND THE DISCIPLES

The way was prepared for Jesus by John the Baptist, in the thought of the early Christians the "forerunner" of the Messiah. Ascetic in life, he preached in the region of the Jordan that the day of judgment upon Israel was at hand, that the Messiah was about to come; and despising all formalism in religion, and all dependence on Abrahamic descent, he proclaimed in the spirit of the ancient prophets their message: "repent, do justice." His directions to the various classes of his hearers were simple and utterly non-legalistic.[1] He baptized his disciples in token of the washing away of their sins; he taught them a special prayer. Jesus classed him as the last and among the greatest of the prophets. Though many of his followers became those of Jesus, some persisted independently and were to be found as late as Paul's ministry in Ephesus.[2]

While the materials are lacking for any full biography of Jesus such as would be available in the case of one living in modern times, they are entirely adequate to determine His manner of life, His character, and His teaching, even if many points on which greater light could be desired are left in obscurity. He stands forth clearly in all His essential qualities. He was brought up in Nazareth of Galilee, in the simple surroundings of a carpenter's home. The land, though despised by the more purely Jewish inhabitants of Judæa on account of a considerable admixture of races, was loyal to the Hebrew religion and traditions, the home of a hardy, self-respecting population, and particularly pervaded by the Messianic hope. Here Jesus grew to manhood through years of unrecorded experience, which, from His later ministry, must have been also of profound spiritual insight and "favor with God and man."

From this quiet life He was drawn by the preaching of John the Baptist. To him He went, and by him was baptized in

[1] *Luke* 3[2-14]; *Matt.* 3[1-12].   [2] *Acts,* 19[1-4].

the Jordan. In connection with this baptism there came to Him the conviction that He was the Messiah of Jewish hope, the chosen of God, the appointed founder of the divine kingdom. A struggle with temptations to interpret this Messiahship in terms of ordinary Jewish expectation, resulted in His rejection of all political or self-seeking methods of its realization as unworthy, and the unshakable conviction that His Messianic leadership was purely spiritual, and the kingdom solely a kingdom of God, He began at once to preach the kingdom and to heal the afflicted in Galilee, and soon had great popular following. He gathered about Him a company of intimate associates—the Apostles—and a larger group of less closely attached disciples. How long His ministry continued is uncertain, from one to three years will cover its possible duration. Opposition was aroused as the spiritual nature of His message became evident and His hostility to the current Pharisaism was recognized. Many of His first followers fell away. He journeyed to the northward toward Tyre and Sidon, and then to the region of Cæsarea Philippi, where He drew forth a recognition of His Messianic mission from His disciples. He felt, however, that at whatever peril He must bear witness in Jerusalem, and thither He went with heroic courage, in the face of growing hostility, there to be seized and crucified, certainly under Pontius Pilate (A. D. 26–36) and probably in the year 30. His disciples were scattered, but speedily gathered once more, with renewed courage, in the glad conviction that He still lived, having risen from the dead. Such, in barest outline, is the story of the most influential life ever lived. The tremendous impress of His personality was everywhere apparent.

In treating, however briefly, of the teaching and work of Jesus, it must be recognized, as Harnack has pointed out, that we have from the first a twofold Gospel—a Gospel of Jesus—His teachings; and a Gospel about Jesus—the impression that He made upon His disciples as to what He was. He began with what were the best possessions of contemporary Judaism, the kingdom of God and the Messianic hope. These had been the centre of John's message. The mysterious thing in Jesus' experience is that He felt Himself to be the Messiah, and, as far as can be judged, this conviction was no matter of deduction. It was a clear consciousness. He knew Himself to be the Messianic founder of the kingdom of God. Yet that kingdom was not earthly, Maccabean. It was always spiritual. But His conception of it enlarged. At first He seems to have regarded it as for Jews only.[1] As He went on, His conception of its inclusiveness grew, and He taught not merely that many "shall come from the east and west and from the north and south,"[2] but that the kingdom itself will be taken from the unbelieving Jews.[3] Jesus held Himself in a peculiar degree the friend of the sons and daughters of the kingdom whom Pharisaism had disinherited, the outcasts, publicans, harlots, and the poor. Their repentance was of value in the sight of God.

The kingdom of God, in Jesus' teaching, involves the recognition of God's sovereignty and fatherhood. We are His children. Hence we should love Him and our neighbors.[4] All whom we can help are our neighbors.[5] We do not so love now. Hence we need to repent with sorrow for sin, and turn to God; and this attitude of sorrow and trust (repentance and faith) is followed by the divine forgiveness.[6] The ethical standard of the kingdom is the highest conceivable. "Be ye therefore perfect, even as your Father which is in heaven is perfect."[7] It involves the utmost strenuousness toward self,[8] and unlimited forgiveness toward others.[9] Forgiveness of others is a necessary condition of God's forgiving us.[10] There are two ways in life: one broad and easy, the other narrow and hard. A blessed future or destruction are the ends.[11] Jesus was, like His age, strongly eschatological in His outlook. Though He felt that the kingdom is begun now,[12] it is to be much more powerfully manifested in the near future. The end of the present age seemed not far off.[13]

Most of these views and sayings can doubtless be paralleled in the religious thought of the age; but the total effect was revolutionary. "He taught them as one that had authority, and not as the scribes."[14] He could say that the least of His disciples is greater than John the Baptist;[15] and that heaven

---

[1] *Mark* 7²⁷; *Matt.* 10⁵⁻⁷, 15²⁴.   [2] *Luke* 13²⁹.   [3] *Mark* 12¹⁻¹².
[4] *Mark* 12²⁸⁻³⁴.   [5] *Luke* 10²⁵⁻³⁷.   [6] *Luke* 15¹¹⁻³².
[7] *Matt.* 5⁴⁸.   [8] *Mark* 9⁴³⁻⁵⁰.   [9] *Matt.* 18²¹, ²².
[10] *Mark* 11²⁵, ²⁶.   [11] *Matt.* 7¹³, ¹⁴.   [12] *Mark* 4¹⁻³²; *Luke* 17²¹.
[13] *Matt.* 10²³, 19²⁸, 24³⁴; *Mark* 13³⁰.
[14] *Mark* 1²².   [15] *Matt.* 11¹¹.

and earth should pass away before His words.[1] He called the
heavy-laden to Him and offered them rest.[2] He promised to
those who confessed Him before men that He would confess
them before His Father.[3] He declared that none knew the
Father but a Son, and he to whom the Son should reveal the
Father.[4] He proclaimed Himself lord of the Sabbath,[5] than
which, in popular estimate, there was no more sacred part of
the God-given Jewish law. He affirmed that He had power
to pronounce forgiveness of sins.[6] On the other hand, He
felt His own humanity and its limitations no less clearly. He
prayed, and taught His disciples to pray. He declared that
He did not know the day or the hour of ending of the present
world-age; that was known to the Father alone.[7] It was not
His to determine who should sit on His right hand and His
left in His exaltation.[8] He prayed that the Father's will, not
His own, be done.[9] He cried in the agony of the cross: "My
God, why hast Thou forsaken me?"[10] The mystery of His
person is in these utterances. Its divinity is no less evident
than its humanity. The *how* is beyond our experience, and
therefore beyond our powers of comprehension; but the church
has always busied itself with the problem, and has too often
practically emphasized one side to the exclusion of the other.

Jesus substituted for the external, work righteous, ceremonial religion of contemporary Judaism, the thought of piety
as consisting in love to God and to one's neighbor—to a God
who is a Father and a neighbor who is a brother—manifested
primarily in an attitude of the heart and inward life, the fruit
of which is external acts. The motive power of that life is
personal allegiance to Himself as the revelation of the Father,
the type of redeemed humanity, the Elder Brother, and the
King of the kingdom of God.

What Jesus taught and was gained immense significance
from the conviction of His disciples that His death was not the
end—from the resurrection faith. The *how* of this conviction
is one of the most puzzling of historical problems. The fact
of this conviction is unquestionable. It seems to have come
first to Peter,[11] who was in that sense at least the "rock" Apostle

---

[1] *Mark* 13[31].
[2] *Matt.* 11[28].
[3] *Matt.* 10[32].
[4] *Matt.* 11[27]; *Luke* 10[22].
[5] *Mark* 2[23-28].
[6] *Mark* 2[1-11].
[7] *Mark* 13[32].
[8] *Mark* 10[40].
[9] *Mark* 14[36].
[10] *Mark* 15[34].
[11] 1 *Cor.* 15[5].

on whom the church was founded. All the early disciples
shared it. It was the turning-point in the conversion of Paul.
It gave courage to the scattered disciples, brought them together again, and made them witnesses. Henceforth they had
a risen Lord, in the exaltation of glory, yet ever interested in
them. The Messiah of Jewish hope, in a profounder spiritual
reality than Judaism had ever imagined Him, had really lived,
died, and risen again for their salvation.

These convictions were deepened by the experiences of the
day of Pentecost. The exact nature of the pentecostal manifestation is, perhaps, impossible to recover. Certainly the conception of a proclamation of the Gospel in many foreign languages is inconsistent with what we know of speaking with
tongues elsewhere[1] and with the criticism reported by the
author of *Acts* that they were "full of new wine,"[2] which
Peter deemed worthy of a reply. But the point of significance
is that these spiritual manifestations appeared the visible and
audible evidence of the gift and power of Christ.[3] To these
first Christians it was the triumphant inauguration of a relation to the living Lord, confidence in which controlled much
of the thinking of the Apostolic Church. If the disciple visibly
acknowledged his allegiance by faith, repentance, and baptism,
the exalted Christ, it was believed, in turn no less evidently
acknowledged the disciple by His gift of the Spirit. Pentecost
was indeed a day of the Lord; and though hardly to be called
the birthday of the church, for that had its beginnings in Jesus'
association with the disciples, it marked an epoch in the proclamation of the Gospel, in the disciples' conviction of Christ's
presence, and in the increase of adherents to the new faith.

SECTION IV. THE PALESTINIAN CHRISTIAN COMMUNITIES

The Christian community in Jerusalem seems to have grown
rapidly. It speedily included Jews who had lived in the dispersion as well as natives of Galilee and Judæa, and even some
of the Hebrew priests. By the Christian body the name
"church" was very early adopted. The designation comes
from the Septuagint translation of the Old Testament, where
it had been employed to indicate the whole people of Israel as
a divinely called congregation. As such it was a fitting title

---

[1] See 1 *Cor.* 14[2-19].   [2] *Acts* 2[13].   [3] *Acts* 2[33].

for the true Israel, the real people of God, and such the early
Christians felt themselves to be. The early Jerusalem company were faithful in attendance at the temple, and in obedience to the Jewish law, but, in addition, they had their own
special services among themselves, with prayer, mutual exhortation, and "breaking of bread" daily in private houses.[1]
This "breaking of bread" served a twofold purpose. It was a
bond of fellowship and a means of support for the needy.
The expectation of the speedy coming of the Lord made the
company at Jerusalem a waiting congregation, in which the
support of the less well-to-do was provided by the gifts of the
better able, so that they "had all things common."[2] The act
was much more than that, however. It was a continuation
and a reminder of the Lord's Last Supper with His disciples
before His crucifixion. It had, therefore, from the first, a
sacramental significance.

Organization was very simple. The leadership of the Jerusalem congregation was at first that of Peter, and in a lesser
degree of John. With them the whole apostolic company was
associated in prominence, though whether they constituted so
fully a governing board as tradition affirmed by the time that
Acts was written may be doubted. Questions arising from the
distribution of aid to the needy resulted in the appointment
of a committee of seven,[3] but whether this action was the
origin of the diaconate or a temporary device to meet a particular situation is uncertain. The utmost that can be said is that
the duties thus intrusted resembled those later discharged
by deacons in the Gentile churches. At an early though
somewhat later period "elders" (πρεσβύτεροι) are mentioned,[4]
though whether these were simply the older members of the
church,[5] or were officers[6] not improbably patterned after those
of the Jewish synagogue, is impossible to determine.

The Jerusalem congregation was filled with the Messianic
hope, it would seem at first in a cruder and less spiritual form
than Jesus had taught.[7] It was devoted in its loyalty to the
Christ, who would soon return, but "whom the heaven must
receive until the times of restoration of all things." [8] Salvation it viewed as to be obtained by repentance, which included

---

[1] *Acts* 2[46].   [2] *Acts* 2[44].   [3] *Acts* 6[1-6].
[4] *Acts* 11[30].   [5] As *Acts* 15[23] might imply.   [6] *Acts* 14[23].
[7] See *Acts* 1[6].   [8] *Acts* 3[21].

sorrow for the national sin of rejecting Jesus as the Messiah as well as for personal sins. This repentance and acknowledgment of loyalty was followed by baptism in the name of Christ, as a sign of cleansing and token of new relationship, and was sealed with the divine approval by the bestowment of spiritual gifts.[1] This preaching of Jesus as the true Messiah, and fear of a consequent disregard of the historic ritual, led to an attack by Pharisaic Hellenist Jews, which resulted in the death of the first Christian martyr, Stephen, by stoning at the hands of a mob. The immediate consequence was a partial scattering of the Jerusalem congregation, so that the seeds of Christianity were sown throughout Judæa, in Samaria, and even in as remote regions as Cæsarea, Damascus, Antioch, and the island of Cyprus. Of the original Apostles the only one who is certainly known to have exercised a considerable missionary activity was Peter, though tradition ascribes such labors to them all. John may have engaged, also, in such endeavor, though the later history of this Apostle is much in dispute.

The comparative peace which followed the martyrdom of Stephen was broken for the Jerusalem church by a much more severe persecution about A. D. 44, instigated by Herod Agrippa I, who from 41 to his death in 44, was vassal-king over the former territories of Herod the Great. Peter was imprisoned, but escaped death, and the Apostle James was beheaded. In connection with the scattering consequent upon this persecution is probably to be found whatever truth underlies the tradition that the Apostles left Jerusalem twelve years after the crucifixion. At all events, Peter seems to have been only occasionally there henceforth; and the leadership of the Jerusalem church fell to James, "the Lord's brother," who even earlier had become prominent in its affairs.[2] This position, which he held till his martyr's death about 63, has often been called a "bishopric," and undoubtedly it corresponded in many ways to the monarchical bishopric in the Gentile churches. There is no evidence, however, of the application to James of the term "bishop" in his lifetime. When the successions of religious leadership among Semitic peoples are remembered, especially the importance attached to relationship to the founder, it seems much more likely that there was here a rudimentary caliphate. This interpretation is rendered the more

---

[1] *Acts* 2[37, 38].   [2] *Gal.* 1[19], 2[9]; *Acts* 21[18].

probable because James's successor in the leadership of the Jerusalem church, though not chosen till after the conquest of the city by Titus in 70, was Simeon, esteemed Jesus' kinsman.

Under the leadership of James the church in Jerusalem embraced two parties, both in agreement that the ancient law of Israel was binding on Christians of Jewish race, but differing as to whether it was similarly regulative for Christian converts from heathenism. One wing held it to be binding on all; the other, of which James was a representative, was willing to allow freedom from the law to Gentile Christians, though it viewed with disfavor such a mingling of Jews and Gentiles at a common table as Peter was disposed, for a time at least, to welcome.[1] The catastrophe which ended the Jewish rebellion in the year 70 was fateful, however, to all the Christian communities in Palestine, even though that of Jerusalem escaped the perils of the siege by flight. The yet greater overthrow of Jewish hopes under Hadrian, in the war of 132 to 135, left Palestinian Christianity a feeble remnant. Even before the first capture of the city, more influential *foci* of Christian influence were to be found in other portions of the empire. The Jerusalem church and its associated Palestinian communities were important as the fountain from which Christianity first flowed forth, and as securing the preservation of many memorials of Jesus' life and words that would otherwise have been lost, rather than as influencing, by direct and permanent leadership, the development of Christianity as a whole.

SECTION V. PAUL AND GENTILE CHRISTIANITY

As has already been mentioned, the persecution which brought about Stephen's martyrdom resulted in the planting of Christianity beyond the borders of Palestine. Missionaries, whose names have perished, preached Christ to fellow Jews. In Antioch a further extension of this propaganda took place. Antioch, the capital of Syria, was a city of the first rank, a remarkably cosmopolitan meeting-place of Greeks, Syrians, and Jews. There the new faith was preached to Greeks. The effect of this preaching was the spread of the Gospel among those of Gentile antecedents. By the populace they were nicknamed "Christians"—a title little used by the followers

---

[1] *Gal.* 2[12-16].

of Jesus themselves till well into the second century, though earlier prevalent among the heathen. Nor was Antioch the farthest goal of Christian effort. By 51 or 52, under Claudius, tumults among the Jews consequent upon Christian preaching by unknown missionaries attracted governmental attention in Rome itself. At this early period, however, Antioch was the centre of development. The effect of this conversion of those whose antecedents had been heathen was inevitably to raise the question of the relation of these disciples to the Jewish law. Should that rule be imposed upon Gentiles, Christianity would be but a Jewish sect; should Gentiles be free from it Christianity could become a universal religion, but at the cost of much Jewish sympathy. That this inevitable conflict was decided in favor of the larger doctrine was primarily the work of the Apostle Paul.

Paul, whose Hebrew name, Saul, was reminiscent of the hero of the tribe of Benjamin, of which he was a member, was born in the Cilician city of Tarsus, of Pharisaic parentage, but of a father possessed of Roman citizenship. Tarsus was eminent in the educational world, and at the time of Paul's birth was a seat of Stoic teaching. Brought up in a strict Jewish home, there is no reason to believe that Paul ever received a formal Hellenic education. He was never a Hellenizer in the sense of Philo of Alexandria. A wide-awake youth in such a city could not fail, however, to receive many Hellenic ideas, and to become familiar, in a measure at least, with the political and religious atmosphere of the larger world outside his orthodox Jewish home. Still, it was in the rabbinical tradition that he grew up, and it was as a future scribe that he went, at an age now unknown, to study under the famous Gamaliel the elder, in Jerusalem. How much, if anything, he knew of the ministry of Jesus other than by common report, it is impossible to determine. His devotion to the Pharisaic conception of a nation made holy by careful observance of the Jewish law was extreme, and his own conduct, as tried by that standard, was "blameless." Always a man of the keenest spiritual insight, however, he came, even while a Pharisee, to feel deep inward dissatisfaction with his own attainments in character. The law did not give a real inward righteousness. Such was his state of mind when brought into contact with Christianity. If Jesus was no true Messiah, He had justly suffered, and His disciples were justly objects of persecution. Could he be convinced that Jesus was the chosen of God, then He must be to him the first object of allegiance, and the law for opposition to the Pharisaic interpretation of which He died—and Paul recognized no other interpretation—must itself be abrogated by divine intervention.

Though the dates of Paul's history are conjectural, it may have been about the year 35 that the great change came—journeying to Damascus on an errand of persecution he beheld in vision the exalted Jesus, who called him to personal service. What may have been the nature of that experience can at best be merely conjectured; but of its reality to Paul and of its transforming power there can be no question. Henceforth he was convinced not only that Jesus was all that Christianity claimed Him to be, but he felt a personal devotion to his Master that involved nothing less than union of spirit. He could say: "I live, and yet no longer I, but Christ liveth in me."[1] The old legalism dropped away, and with it the value of the law. To Paul henceforth the new life was one of a new friendship. Christ had become his closest friend. He now viewed man, God, sin, and the world as through his friend's eyes. To do his friend's will was his highest desire. All that his friend had won was his. "If any man is in Christ, he is a new creature: the old things are passed away; behold they are become new."[2]

With an ardent nature such as Paul's this transformation manifested itself at once in action. Of the story of the next few years little is known. He went at first into Arabia—a region in the designation of that age not necessarily far south of Damascus. He preached in that city. Three years after his conversion he made a flying visit to Jerusalem, where he sojourned with Peter and met James, "the Lord's brother." He worked in Syria and Cilicia for years, in danger, suffering, and bodily weakness.[3] Of the circumstances of this ministry little is known. He can hardly have failed to preach to Gentiles; and, with the rise to importance of a mixed congregation at Antioch, he was naturally sought by Barnabas as one of judgment in the questions involved. Barnabas, who had been sent from Jerusalem, now brought Paul from Tarsus to Antioch, probably in the year 46 or 47. Antioch had become a great

[1] *Gal.* 2²⁰.   [2] 2 *Cor.* 5¹⁷.
[3] Some few incidents are enumerated in 2 *Cor.* 11 and 12.

focal point of Christian activity; and from it in obedience, as the Antiochian congregation believed, to divine guidance, Paul and Barnabas set forth for a missionary journey that took them to Cyprus and thence to Perga, Antioch of Pisidia, Iconium, Lystra, and Derbe—the so-called first missionary journey described in *Acts* 13 and 14. Apparently the most fruitful evangelistic endeavor thus far in the history of the church, it resulted in the establishment of a group of congregations in southern Asia Minor, which Paul afterward addressed as those of Galatia, though many scholars would find the Galatian churches in more northern and central regions of Asia Minor, to which no visit of Paul is recorded.

The growth of the church in Antioch and the planting of mixed churches in Cyprus and Galatia now raised the question of Gentile relation to the law on a great scale. The congregation in Antioch was turmoiled by visitors from Jerusalem who asserted: "Except ye be circumcised after the custom of Moses ye cannot be saved."[1] Paul determined to make a test case. Taking with him Titus, an uncircumcised Gentile convert, as a concrete example of non-legalistic Christianity, he went with Barnabas to Jerusalem and met the leaders there privately. The result reached with James, Peter, and John was a cordial recognition of the genuineness of Paul's work among the Gentiles, and an agreement that the field should be divided, the Jerusalem leaders to continue the mission to Jews, of course with maintenance of the law, while Paul and Barnabas should go with their free message to the Gentiles.[2] It was a decision honorable to both sides; but it was impossible of full execution. What were to be the relations in a mixed church? Could law-keeping Jews and law-free Gentiles eat together? That further question was soon raised in connection with a visit of Peter to Antioch.[3] It led to a public discussion in the Jerusalem congregation, probably in the year 49—the so-called Council of Jerusalem—and the formulation of certain rules governing mixed eating.[4] To Paul, anything but the freest equality of Jew and Gentile seemed impossible. To Peter and Barnabas the question of terms of common eating seemed of prime importance. Paul withstood them both. He must fight the battle largely alone, for Antioch seems to have held with Jerusalem in this matter of intercourse at table.

[1] *Acts* 15¹.   [2] *Gal.* 2¹⁻¹⁰.   [3] *Gal.* 2¹¹⁻¹⁶.   [4] *Acts* 15⁶⁻²⁹.

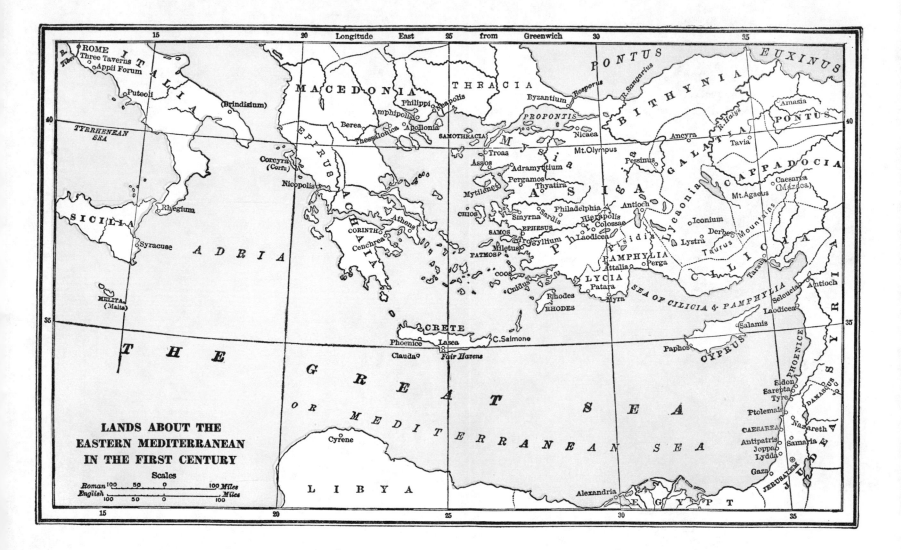

LANDS ABOUT THE
EASTERN MEDITERRANEAN
IN THE FIRST CENTURY

Scales

Roman 100   50   0   100 Miles
English 100   50   0   Miles
        100   50   0   100

Then followed the brief years of Paul's greatest missionary activity, and the period to which we owe all his epistles. Taking with him a Jerusalem Christian, of Roman citizenship, Silas by name, he separated from Barnabas by reason of dis-agreement regarding eating, and also by dissension regarding the conduct of Barnabas's cousin, Mark.[1] A journey through the region of Galatia brought him Timothy as an assistant. Unable to labor in western Asia Minor, Paul and his companions now entered Macedonia, founding churches in Philippi and Thessalonica, being coldly received in Athens, and spending eighteen months in successful work in Corinth (probably 51–53). Meanwhile the Judaizers had been undermining his apostolic authority in Galatia, and from Corinth he wrote to these churches his great epistle vindicating not merely his own ministry, but the freedom of Christianity from all obliga-tion to the Jewish law. It was the charter of a universal Christianity. To the Thessalonians he also wrote, meeting their peculiar difficulties regarding persecution and the ex-pected coming of Christ.

Taking Aquila and Priscilla, who had become his fellow la-borers in Corinth, with him to Ephesus, Paul left them there and made a hurried visit to Jerusalem and Antioch. On his return to Ephesus, where Christianity had already been planted, he began a ministry there of three years' duration (53?–56?). Largely successful, it was also full of opposition and of such peril that Paul "despaired even of life"[2] and ultimately had to flee. The Apostles' burdens were but increased during this stay at Ephesus by moral delinquencies, party strife, and consequent rejection of his authority in Corinth. These led not merely to his significant letters to the *Corinthians*, but on departure from Ephesus, to a stay of three months in Corinth itself. His authority was restored. In this Corinthian sojourn he wrote the greatest of his epistles, that to the *Romans*.

Meanwhile Paul had never ceased to hope that the breach between him and his Gentile Christians and the rank and file of the Jerusalem church could be healed. As a thank-offering for what the Gentiles owed to the parent community, he had been collecting a contribution from his Gentile converts. This, in spite of obvious peril, he determined to take to Jeru-salem. Of the reception of this gift and of the course of Paul's

---

[1] *Acts 15*[36-40].　　　　　　　　　　　[2] *2 Cor. 1*[8].

negotiations nothing is known; but the Apostle himself was speedily arrested in Jerusalem and sent a prisoner of the Roman Government to Cæsarea, doubtless as an inciter of rioting. Two years' imprisonment (57?–59?) led to no decisive result, since Paul exercised his right of appeal to the imperial tribunal at Rome, and were followed by his adventurous journey to the capital as a prisoner. At Rome he lived in custody, part of the time at least in his own hired lodging, for two years (60?–62?). Here he wrote to his beloved churches our *Ephesians, Colossians, Philippians,* and briefer letters to *Philemon* and to *Timothy* (the second epistle). Whether he was released from imprisonment and made further journeys is a problem which still divides the opinion of scholars, but the weight of such slight evidence as there is appears to be against it. There is no reason to doubt the tradition that he was beheaded on the Ostian way outside of Rome; but the year is uncertain. Tradition places his martyrdom in connection with the great Neronian persecution of 64. It was not conjoined in place with that savage attack, and may well have occurred a little earlier without being dissociated in later view from that event.

Paul's heroic battle for a universal, non-legalistic Christianity has been sufficiently indicated. His Christology will be considered in another connection.[1] Was he the founder or the remaker of Christian theology? He would himself earnestly have repudiated these imputations. Yet an interpretation by a trained mind was sure to present the simple faith of primitive Christianity in somewhat altered form. Though Paul wrought into Christian theology much that came from his own rabbinic learning and Hellenic experience, his profound Christian feeling led him into a deeper insight into the mind of Christ than was possessed by any other of the early disciples. Paul the theologian is often at variance with the picture of Christ presented by the Gospels. Paul the Christian is profoundly at one.

Paul's conception of freedom from the Jewish law was as far as possible from any antinomian undervaluation of morality. If the old law had passed away, the Christian is under "the law of the Spirit of life." He who has the Spirit dwelling in him, will mind "the things of the Spirit," and will "mortify

[1] Section VII.

the deeds of the body."[1] Paul evidently devoted much of his training of converts to moral instruction. He has a distinct theory of the process of salvation. By nature men are children of the first Adam, and share his inheritance of sin;[2] by adoption (a Roman idea) we are children of God and partakers of the blessings of the second Adam, Christ.[3] These blessings have special connection with Christ's death and resurrection. To Paul, these two events stand forth as transactions of transcendent significance. His attitude is well expressed in *Gal.* 6[14]: "Far be it from me to glory save in the cross of our Lord Jesus Christ"; and the reason for this glorying is twofold, that sin is thereby forgiven and redemption wrought,[4] and that it is the source and motive of the new life of faith and love.[5] This degree of emphasis on Christ's death was certainly new. To Paul the resurrection was no less important. It was the evidence that Jesus is the Son of God,[6] the promise of our own resurrection,[7] and the guarantee of men's renewed spiritual life.[8] Hence Paul preached "Jesus Christ and Him crucified,"[9] or "Jesus and the resurrection."[10]

The power by which men become children of the second Adam is a free gift of God through Christ. It is wholly undeserved grace.[11] This God sends to whom He will, and withholds from whom He will.[12] The condition of the reception of grace on man's part is faith.[13] "If thou shalt confess with thy mouth Jesus as Lord, and shalt believe in thy heart that God raised Him from the dead, thou shalt be saved."[14] This doctrine is of great importance, for it makes the essence of the Christian life not any mere belief about Christ, nor any purely forensic justification, as Protestants have often interpreted Paul, but a vital, personal relationship. The designation of Jesus as "Lord" was one, as Bousset has pointed out,[15] which had its rise in the Gentile churches of Syria, not impossibly in Antioch, and was the natural expression of those who had long been accustomed to employ it regarding their highest objects of veneration for their devotion to their new Master. To Paul,

---

[1] *Romans* 8[2, 5, 13]. [2] *Romans* 5[12-19]. [3] *Romans* 8[15-17]; 1 *Cor.* 15[45].
[4] *Romans* 3[24-26]. [5] *Gal.* 2[20]. [6] *Romans* 1[4].
[7] 1 *Cor.* 15[12-19]. [8] *Romans* 6[4-11]. [9] 1 *Cor.* 2[2].
[10] *Acts* 17[18]. [11] *Romans* 3[24]. [12] *Romans* 9[10-24].
[13] *Romans* 3[25-28]. [14] *Romans* 10[9]. [15] *Kyrios Christos*, Göttingen. 1913.

it is an epitome of his faith. Christ is the "Lord," himself the "slave." Nor is confidence in the resurrection less necessary, as the crowning proof of Christ's divine Sonship.[1]

The Christian life is one filled with the Spirit. All graces are from Him, all gifts and guidance. Man having the Spirit is a new creature. Living the life of the Spirit, he no longer lives that of the "flesh." But that all-transforming and indwelling Spirit is Christ Himself. "The Lord is the Spirit."[2] If Christ thus stands in such relation to the individual disciple that union with Him is necessary for all true Christian life, He is in no less vital association with the whole body of believers—the church. Paul uses the word church in two senses, as designating the local congregation, Philippi, Corinth, Rome, "the church that is in their house," and as indicating the whole body of believers, the true Israel. In the latter sense it is the body of Christ, of which each local congregation is a part.[3] From Christ come all officers and helpers, all spiritual gifts.[4] He is the source of the life of the church, and these gifts are evidence of His glorified lordship.[5]

Like the early disciples generally, Paul thought the coming of Christ and the end of the existing world-order near; though his views underwent some modification. In his earlier epistles he evidently believed it would happen in his lifetime.[6] As he came toward the close of his work he felt it likely that he would die before the Lord's coming.[7] Regarding the resurrection, Paul had the greatest confidence. Here, however, Hebrew and Greek ideas were at variance. The Hebrew conception was a living again of the flesh. The Greek, the immortality of the soul. Paul does not always make his position clear. *Romans* 8[11] looks like the Hebrew thought; but the great passage in 1 *Cor.* 15[35-54] points to the Greek. A judgment is for all,[8] and even among the saved there will be great differences.[9] The end of all things is the subjection of all, even Christ, to God the Father.[10]

[1] *Romans* 1[4].
[2] 2 *Cor.* 3[17].
[3] *Eph.* 1[22, 23]; *Col.* 1[18].
[4] *Eph.* 4[11]; 1 *Cor.* 12[4-11].
[5] *Eph.* 4[7-10].
[6] 1 *Thess.* 4[13-18].
[7] *Philippians* 1[23, 24]; 2 *Tim.* 4[6-8].
[8] 2 *Cor.* 5[10].
[9] 1 *Cor.* 3[10-15].
[10] 1 *Cor.* 15[20-28].

SECTION VI. THE CLOSE OF THE APOSTOLIC AGE

The history and fate of most of the Apostles is unknown. Though Peter cannot have been in Rome while Paul was writing his epistles thence, and some scholars of weight still hold the evidence insufficient to show that he was ever there at all, the cumulative force of such intimations as have survived make the conclusion probable that he was in Rome for a short time at least, and that his stay ended in martyrdom by crucifixion in the Neronian persecutions.[1] Such a stay, and especially such a death, would link him permanently with the Roman Church. On the other hand, a residence of John in Ephesus is much less assured.

The persecution under Nero was as fierce as it was local. A great fire in Rome, in July, 64, was followed by charges unjustly involving the Christians, probably at Nero's instigation, to turn popular rumor from himself. Numbers suffered death by horrible torture in the Vatican gardens, where Nero made their martyrdom a spectacle.[2] Thenceforth he lived in Christian tradition as a type of antichrist; but the Roman Church survived in strength. The destruction of Jerusalem at the close of the Jewish rebellion, in 70, was an event of more permanent significance. It almost ended the already waning influence of the Palestinian congregations in the larger concerns of the church. This collapse, and the rapid influx of converts from heathen antecedents soon made Paul's battle for freedom from law no longer a living question. Antioch, Rome, and before the end of the century, Ephesus, were now the chief centres of Christian development. The converts were mostly from the lower social classes,[3] though some of better position, notably women, were to be found among them. Such were Lydia of Philippi,[4] and, in much higher station, probably the consul, Flavius Clemens, and his wife, Flavia Domitilla, who suffered the one death and the other sentence of banishment in Rome under Domitian, in 95. To Domitilla, the Roman Church

---

[1] 1 *Peter* 5[13]; *John* 21[18, 19]; 1 *Clement*, 5, 6; Ignatius, *Romans*, 4[3]; Irenæus, *Against Heresies*, 3 : 1 : 1; Caius of Rome in Eusebius, *Church History*, 2 : 25 : 5–7.

[2] Tacitus, *Annals* 15[44]; Ayer, *A Source-Book for Ancient Church History*, p. 6.

[3] 1 *Cor.* 1[26-28]. [4] *Acts* 16[14].

owed one of its oldest catacombs. Of this persecution under
Domitian (81–96) few details are known, but it must have
been of severity in Rome and in Asia Minor.[1]

Yet though some gleanings can be recovered from this period,
the forty years from 70 to 110 remain one of the obscurest portions of church history. This is the more to be regretted because they were an epoch of rapid change in the church itself.
When the characteristics of the church can once more be clearly
traced its general conception of Christianity shows surprisingly
little of the distinctive stamp of Paul. Not only must many
now unknown missionaries have labored in addition to the great
Apostle, but an inrush of ideas from other than Christian
sources, brought undoubtedly by converts of heathen antecedents, modified Christian beliefs and practices, especially
regarding the sacraments, fastings, and the rise of liturgical
forms. The old conviction of the immediacy of the guidance
of the Spirit faded, without becoming wholly extinguished.
The constitution of the church itself underwent, in this period,
a far-reaching development, of which some account will be
given (p. 44).

An illustration of this non-Pauline Christianity, though
without evidence of the infiltration of heathen ideas, is to be
seen in the Epistle of James. Written late in the first century or early in the second, it is singularly poor in theological
content. Its directions are largely ethical. Christianity, in
the conception of the writer, is a body of right principles duly
practised. Faith is not, as with Paul, a new, vital, personal
relationship. It is intellectual conviction which must be supplemented by appropriate action. It is a new and simple
moral law.[2]

To this obscure period is due the composition of the Gospels. No subject in church history is more difficult. It would
appear, however, that at an early period, not now definitely
to be fixed, a collection of the sayings of Christ was in circulation. Probably not far from 75–80, and according to early
and credible tradition at Rome, *Mark's* Gospel came into
existence. Its arrangement was not purely historic, the selection of the materials being determined evidently by the importance attached to the doctrines and ecclesiastical usages
which they illustrated. With large use of the collection of

---

[1] 1 *Clement*, 1; *Rev.* 2[10, 13]; 7[13, 14].   [2] *James* 1[25]; 2[14-26].

sayings and of *Mark, Matthew* and *Luke's* Gospels came into being, probably between 80 and 95; the former probably having Palestine as its place of writing, and the latter coming, there is some reason to believe, from Antioch. The Johannine Gospel is distinctly individual, and may not unfairly be ascribed to Ephesus, and to the period 95–110. Other gospels were in circulation, of which fragments survive, but none which compare in value with the four which the church came to regard as canonical. There seems to have been little of recollections of Jesus extant at the close of the first century which was not gathered into the familiar Gospels. That this was the case may be ascribed to the great Jewish war and the decline of the Palestinian Hebrew congregations. To the Gospels the church owes the priceless heritage of its knowledge of the life of its Master, and a perpetual corrective to the one-sidedness of an interpretation, which, like even the great message of Paul, pays little attention to His earthly ministry.

SECTION VII. THE INTERPRETATION OF JESUS

An inevitable question of the highest importance which arose with the proclamation of Christianity, and must always demand consideration in every age of the church, is: What is to be thought of the Founder? The earliest Christology, as has been pointed out, was Messianic. Jesus was the Messiah of Jewish hope, only in a vastly more spiritual sense than that hope commonly implied. He had gone, but only for a brief time.[1] He was now in exaltation, yet what must be thought of His earthly life, that had so little of "glory" in it, as men use that term? That life of humiliation, ending in a slave's death, was but the fulfilment of prophecy. God had foreshadowed the things that "His Christ should suffer."[2] Early Jewish Christian thought recurred to the suffering servant of Isaiah, who was "wounded for our transgressions."[3] Christ is the "servant" or "child," ($\pi\alpha\hat{\iota}\varsigma$ $\Theta\epsilon o\hat{\upsilon}$), in the early Petrine addresses.[4] The glorification was at the resurrection. He is now "by the right hand of God exalted."[5] This primitive conception of the suffering servant exalted, persisted. It is that, in spite of a good deal of Pauline admixture, of the epistle

---

[1] *Acts* 3[21]. [2] *Acts* 3[18]. [3] *Isaiah* 53[5].
[4] *Acts* 3[13, 26]; 4[27, 30]. [5] *Acts* 2[32, 33]; 4[10, 12].

known as 1 *Peter* (3[18-22]). Clement, writing from Rome to the Corinthians, 93–97, also shares it.[1] It does not necessarily imply pre-existence. It does not make clear the relationship of Christ to God. It had not thought that problem out.

An obvious distinction soon was apparent. The disciples had known Christ in His life on earth. They now knew Him by His gifts in His exaltation. They had known Him after the flesh; they now knew Him after the spirit[2]—that is as the Jesus of history and the Christ of experience. To superficial consideration, at least, these two aspects were not easy of adjustment. The Jesus of history lived in a definite land, under human conditions of space and time. The Christ of experience is Lord of all His servants, is manifested as the Spirit at the same moment in places the most diverse, is omnipresent and omniscient. Paul regards it as a mark of Christianity that men call upon Him everywhere.[3] He prays to Him himself.[4] In his most solemn asseveration that his apostleship is not of any human origin, Paul classes God and Christ together as its source.[5] These attributes and powers of the Christ of experience are very like divine, it is evident; and they inevitably raised the question of Christ's relation to the Father as it had not been raised thus far, and in a mind of far subtler powers and greater training and education than that of any of the earlier disciples, that of Paul.

Paul knew Hebrew theology well, with its conception of the divine "wisdom" as present with God before the foundation of the world.[6] He also knew something of Stoicism, with its doctrine of the universal, omnipresent, fashioning divine intelligence, the Logos, that in many ways resembled the Hebrew wisdom. He knew the Isaian conception of the suffering servant. To Paul, therefore, the identification of the exalted Christ with the divine wisdom—Logos—was not only easy, but natural; and that wisdom—Logos—must be pre-existent and always with God. He is "the Spirit of God,"[7] the "wisdom of God."[8] "In Him dwelleth all the fulness of the Godhead bodily."[9] Even more, as in the Stoic conception of the Logos, He is the divine agent in creation; "all things have been created through Him and unto Him."[10] Though Paul

---

[1] 1 *Clement*, 16.   [2] *Romans* 1[3, 4].   [3] 1 *Cor.* 1[2].
[4] 2 *Cor.* 12[8, 9].   [5] *Gal.* 1[1].   [6] *Prov.* 8[22, 23].
[7] 1 *Cor.* 2[10, 11].   [8] *Ibid.*, 1[24].   [9] *Col.* 2[9].   [10] *Col.* 1[16].

probably never in set terms called Christ God,[1] he taught Christ's unity in character with God. He "knew no sin";[2] He is the full manifestation of the love of God, which is greater than any human love, and the motive spring of the Christian life in us.[3] It is plain, therefore, that though Paul often calls Christ man, he gives Him an absolutely unique position, and classes Him with God.

If the Christ of experience was thus pre-existent and post-existent in glory for Paul, how explain the Jesus of history? He was the suffering servant.[4] His humble obedience was followed, as in the earlier Petrine conception, by the great reward. "Wherefore also God highly exalted Him and gave unto Him the name which is above every name . . . that every tongue should confess that Jesus Christ is Lord." Paul looks upon the whole earthly life of Jesus as one of humiliation. It was indeed significant. "God was in Christ reconciling the world unto Himself." [5] Yet it was only "by the resurrection" that He was "declared to be the Son of God with power." [6] Paul's Christology combines, therefore, in a remarkable manner, Hebrew and Gentile conceptions. In it appear the suffering and exalted servant, the pre-existent divine wisdom, the divine agent in creation, and the redeemer power who for man's sake came down from heaven, died, and rose again.

Within half a generation of Paul's death, however, a differing interpretation appeared, probably representing an independent line of thought. It was that of the Gospel of Mark. The writer knew nothing of Paul's view of Christ's pre-existence. In his thought, Christ was from His baptism the Son of God by adoption.[7] That He was the Son of God thenceforth, in all His earthly lot, is the evangelist's endeavor to show. There was humiliation, indeed, but there was a glory also in His earthly life, of which Paul gives no hint. He had not to wait for the demonstration of the resurrection. The voice from heaven declared Him the Son at baptism. The man with an unclean spirit saluted Him at His first preaching as "the Holy One of God" (1[24]). The spirits of those possessed

---

[1] The translations, which imply that, in *Romans* 9[5] and *Titus* 2[13], are for various reasons to be rejected as Pauline.

[2] *2 Cor.* 5[21].   [3] *Romans* 8[39], 5[7, 8]; *Gal.* 2[20].   [4] *Philippians* 2[6-11].

[5] *2 Cor.* 5[19].   [6] *Romans* 1[4].   [7] *Mark* 1[9-11].

cried, "Thou art the Son of God" (3^{12}). He was transfigured before Peter, James, and John, while a heavenly voice proclaims: "This is my beloved Son" (9^{2-8}). The evangelist can only explain the lack of universal recognition in Christ's lifetime on earth by the declaration that He charged spirits and disciples not to make Him known (e. g. 1^{34}, 3^{12}, 5^{43}, 9^9). It is evident that this is a very different interpretation from that of Paul.

Mark's view was evidently unsatisfactory to his own age. It had no real theory of the incarnation. It does not trace back the sonship far enough. If that sonship was manifested in a portion of Christ's life, why not in all His life? That impressed the writers of the next two Gospels, *Matthew* and *Luke*. Like *Mark*, they have no trace of Paul's doctrine of pre-existence—their authors did not move in Paul's theological or philosophical realm. But they make the manifestation of Christ's divine sonship date from the very inception of His earthly existence. He was of supernatural birth. Like Mark, both regard His life as other than one of humiliation only.

Yet for minds steeped in the thoughts of Paul even these could not be satisfying interpretations. A fourth Gospel appeared about 95–110, probably in Ephesus, which sprang into favor, not only on account of its profoundly spiritual interpretation of the meaning of Christ, but because it combined in one harmonious presentation the divided elements of the Christologies which had thus far been current. In the Gospel which bears the name of John, the pre-existence and creative activity of Christ is as fully taught as by Paul. Christ is the Logos, the Word who "was with God, and the Word was God"; "All things were made by Him" ($1^{1, 3}$). There is no hint of virgin birth, as in *Matthew* and *Luke*, but a real, though unexplained, incarnation is taught: "The Word became flesh and dwelt among us" (1^{14}). The tendency of the earlier Gospels to behold glory, as well as humiliation, in Christ's earthly life is carried much further. That life is one primarily in which He "manifested His glory" (2^{11}, see 1^{14}). He declares to the woman of Samaria that He is the Messiah (4^{26}). He is regarded as "making Himself equal with God" (5^{18}). He remembers the glory of His pre-existence (17^5). He walks through life triumphantly conscious of His high divine mission. In the account of the Garden of Gethsemane no note

appears of the pathetic prayer that this cup pass from Him.[1]
In the story of the crucifixion there is no anguished cry: "My
God, why hast thou forsaken me";[2] rather, as with a sense of
a predetermined work accomplished, He dies with the words:
"It is finished."[3] Beyond question this Christology was
eminently satisfactory to the second century. It gave an
explanation, natural to the age, of that lordship which Christian feeling universally ascribed to Christ. It united the most
valued portions of the older Christologies. Though much dissent from it was to appear, it was formative of what was to
triumph as orthodoxy.

In spite of this Johannine Christology, traces of more naïve
and less philosophic interpretations survived. Such were those
of the obscure relics of extreme Judaizing Christianity, known
in the second century as Ebionites. To them, Jesus was the
son of Joseph and Mary, who so completely fulfilled the Jewish law that God chose Him to be the Messiah. He improved
and added to the law, and would come again to found a Messianic kingdom for the Jews. Such, in a very different way,
was Hermas of Rome (115–140), who strove to combine Paul's
doctrine of "the holy pre-existent Spirit which created the whole
creation,"[4] with that of the suffering and exalted servant.
The "servant," pictured as a slave in the vineyard of God,
is the "flesh in which the holy Spirit dwelt . . . walking honorably in holiness and purity, without in any way defiling the
Spirit."[5] As a reward, God chose the "flesh," i. e., Jesus,
"as a partner with the holy Spirit"; but this recompense is
not peculiar to Him. He is but a forerunner, "for all flesh,
which is found undefiled and unspotted, wherein the holy
Spirit dwelt, shall receive a reward."[6] This is, of course, in
a sense adoptionist. It was not easy for unphilosophic minds
to combine in one harmonious picture the Jesus of history
and the Christ of experience; and even in philosophic interpretations this contrast had much to do with the rise and wide
spread of Gnosticism in the second century.

The significance of the Gospel according to John in the development of Christology has been noted; its influence in the
interpretation of salvation was no less important. With it
are to be associated the Johannine Epistles. This literature

[1] 18[1-11]; compare Mark 14[32-42].   [2] Mark 15[34].   [3] John 19[30].
[4] Sim., 5[6].   [5] Ibid.   [6] Ibid.

probably had its rise in a region, Ephesus, where Paul long worked. Its position is Pauline, but developed in the direction of a much intenser mysticism. This mysticism centres about the thoughts of life and union with Christ, both of which are Pauline, and yet treated in a way unlike that of Paul. Life is the great word of the Johannine literature. He who knows the Christ of present experience has life. "This is life eternal, that they should know Thee, the only true God, and Him whom Thou didst send, even Jesus Christ."[1] For the writer, the world is divisible into two simple classes: "He that hath the Son hath the life, he that hath not the Son of God hath not the life."[2] By life, the author does not mean simple existence. To him it is blessed, purified immortality. "Now are we children of God, and it is not yet made manifest what we shall be. We know that if He shall be manifested we shall be like Him."[3] This life is based on union with Christ, and this union is a real sacramental participation. One can but feel that there is here the influence of ideas similar to those of the mystery religions. Paul had valued the Lord's Supper. To him it was a "communion" of the body and blood of Christ, a "remembrance" of Christ, through which: "Ye proclaim the Lord's death till He come."[4] The Johannine literature goes further: "Except ye eat the flesh of the Son of Man and drink His blood ye have not life in yourselves."[5] The Lord's Supper is already a mystical sacrament necessary for that union with Christ which is to procure a blessed immortality.

The Johannine literature stands on a spiritual plane of utmost loftiness. It is instructive to see how some of these problems looked to a contemporary of the same general school, an equally earnest Christian, but of far less spiritual elevation. Such a man is Ignatius of Antioch. Condemned as a Christian in his home city, in the last years of Trajan, 110–117, he was sent a prisoner to Rome to be thrown to the wild beasts. Of his history little is known, but from his pen seven brief letters exist, six of them written to the churches of Ephesus, Magnesia, Tralles, Rome, Philadelphia, and Smyrna; and one a personal note to Polycarp, bishop of Smyrna. They are full of gratitude for kindnesses shown on his journey, of warnings against spiri-

---

[1] *John* 17³; see also 3¹⁶, ³⁶, 6⁴⁷, 10²⁷, ²⁸, etc.
[2] 1 *John* 5¹²; compare *John* 3³⁶.   [3] 1 *John* 3².
[4] 1 *Cor.* 10¹⁶, 11²⁴, ²⁶.   [5] *John* 6⁵³.

tual perils, and of exhortations to unity. Their significance for the history of Christian institutions will be considered in Section IX. Ignatius has the same lofty Christology as the Johannine literature. Christ's sacrifice is "the blood of God." [1] He greets the Romans in "Jesus Christ our God." Yet he did not identify Christ wholly with the Father. "He is truly of the race of David according to the flesh, but Son of God by the divine will and power." [2] As in the Johannine literature, Ignatius held union with Christ necessary for life: "Christ Jesus, apart from whom we have not true life" [3]—and that life is ministered through the Lord's Supper. His conception of the Supper was, however, well-nigh magical. He says of it: "Breaking one bread which is the medicine of immortality and the antidote that we should not die but live forever in Jesus Christ." [4] Ignatius's most original thought was that the incarnation was the manifestation of God for the revelation of a new humanity. Before Christ the world was under the devil and death. Christ brought life and immortality.[5]

In the Johannine and the Ignatian writings alike, salvation was life, in the sense of the transformation of sinful mortality into blessed immortality. This thought had roots in Paul's teaching. Through the school of Syria and Asia Minor this became, in the Greek-speaking church, the conception of salvation. It was one that lays necessary emphasis on the person of Christ and the incarnation. The Latin conception, as will be seen, was that salvation consists in the establishment of right relations with God and the forgiveness of sins. This, too, had its Pauline antecedents. It necessarily lays prime weight on divine grace, the death of Christ, and the atonement. These conceptions are not mutually exclusive; but to these differences of emphasis is ultimately due much of the contrast in the later theological development of East and West.

SECTION VIII.   GENTILE CHRISTIANITY OF THE SECOND CENTURY

By the year 100 Christianity was strongly represented in Asia Minor, Syria, Macedonia, Greece, and Rome, and probably also in Egypt, though regarding its introduction into that

[1] *Eph.* 1.   [2] *Smyrn.*, 1.   [3] *Tral.*, 9.
[4] *Eph.* 20.   [5] *Eph.* 19, 20.

land there is no certain knowledge. It had extended very
slightly, if at all, to the more western portion of the empire.
Asia Minor was more extensively Christianized than any other
land. About 111–113 Pliny, the governor of Bithynia, could
report to Trajan that it was affecting the older temple worship.[1]
It was strongly missionary in spirit, and constantly extending.
Common Christianity, however, was far from representing,
or even understanding, the lofty theology of Paul or of the
Johannine literature. It moved in a much simpler range of
thought. Profoundly loyal to Christ, it conceived of Him
primarily as the divine revealer of the knowledge of the true
God, and the proclaimer of a "new law" of simple, lofty, and
strenuous morality. This is the attitude of the so-called
"Apostolic Fathers," with the exception of Ignatius, whose
thought has already been discussed.

These Christian writers were thus named because it was
long, though erroneously, believed that they were personal disciples of the Apostles. They include Clement of Rome (c. 93–
97); Ignatius of Antioch (c. 110–117); Polycarp of Smyrna
(c. 110–117); Hermas of Rome (c. 115–140); the author who
wrote under the name of Barnabas, possibly in Alexandria
(c. 131); and the anonymous sermon called Second Clement
(c. 160–170). To this literature should be added the Teaching
of the Twelve Apostles (c. 130–160, but presenting a survival
of very primitive conditions). The anonymous Epistle to Diognetus, often included among the writings of the Apostolic Fathers, is probably later than their period.

Christians looked upon themselves as a separated people,
a new race, the true Israel, whose citizenship was no longer
in the Roman Empire, though they prayed for its welfare and
that of its ruler, but in the heavenly Jerusalem.[2] They are
the church "which was created before the sun and moon,"
"and for her sake the world was framed."[3] The conception of
the church was not primarily that of the aggregate of Christians on earth, but of a heavenly citizenship reaching down
to earth, and gathering into its own embrace the scattered
Christian communities.[4] To this church the disciple is admitted by baptism. It is "builded upon waters."[5] That

---

[1] Letters, 10⁹⁶; Ayer, p. 20.   [2] 1 Clem., 61; Hermas, Sim., 1.
[3] Hermas, Vis., 2⁴; 2 Clem., 14.   [4] Teaching, 9.
[5] Hermas, Vis., 3³.

baptism implied antecedent belief in the truth of the Christian message, engagement to live the Christian life, and repentance.[1] Services were held on Sunday, and probably on other days.[2] These had consisted from the Apostles' time of two kinds: meetings for reading the Scriptures, preaching, song and prayer;[3] and a common evening meal with which the Lord's Supper was conjoined. By the time Justin Martyr wrote his *Apology* in Rome (153), the common meal had disappeared, and the Supper was joined with the assembly for preaching, as a concluding sacrament.[4] The Supper was the occasion for offerings for the needy.[5] The beginnings of liturgical forms are to be found before the close of the first century.[6]

Christian life was ascetic and legalistic. Wednesday and Friday were fasts, which were called "stations," as of soldiers of Christ on guard.[7] The Lord's Prayer was repeated thrice daily.[8] "Fasting is better than prayer, but almsgiving than both."[9] Second marriage was discouraged.[10] Simple repentance is not sufficient for forgiveness, there must be satisfaction.[11] A Christian can even do more than God demands—works of supererogation—and will receive a corresponding reward.[12] Great generosity was exercised toward the poor, widows, and orphans, some going so far as to sell themselves into slavery to supply the needy.[13] The rich were felt to be rewarded and helped by the prayers of the poor.[14] Wealthy congregations redeemed prisoners and sent relief to a distance, and in these works none was more eminent than that of Rome. On the other hand, though slaves were regarded as Christian brethren, their manumission was discouraged lest, lacking support, they fall into evil ways.[15] There is evidence, also, that the more well-to-do and higher stationed found the ideal of brotherhood difficult to maintain in practice.[16]

For Christians of heathen antecedents it was difficult to deny the existence of the old gods. They were very real to

---

[1] Justin, *Apology*, 61; Ayer, p. 33.   [2] Justin, *ibid.*, 67; Ayer, p. 35.
[3] Justin, *ibid.*, 67; see also Pliny, *Letters*, 10[96]; Ayer, pp. 21, 35.
[4] 65, 67; Ayer, pp. 33–35.   [5] Justin, *ibid.*, 67.
[6] 1 *Clem.*, 59–61, see also *Teaching*, 9, 10; Ayer, pp. 38, 39.
[7] *Teaching*, 8; Hermas, *Sim.*, 5[1]; Ayer, p. 38.
[8] *Teaching*, 8; Ayer, p. 38.   [9] 2 *Clem.*, 16.   [10] Hermas, *Mand.*. 4[4].
[11] *Ibid.*, *Sim.*, 7.   [12] *Ibid.*, *Sim.*, 5[2, 3]; Ayer, p. 48.
[13] 1 *Clem.*, 55.   [14] Hermas, *Sim.*, 2.
[15] *Ignatius to Polycarp*, 4.   [16] Hermas, *Sim.*, 9[20].

them, but were looked upon as demons, hostile to Christianity.[1] The Christians of the second century explained the resemblance between their own rites and those of the mystery religions, of which they were aware, as a parody by demons.[2] Fear, thus of demon influence was characteristic, and led to much use of exorcism in the name of Christ.[3] For all men there is to be a resurrection of the flesh, and a final judgment.[4]

SECTION IX. CHRISTIAN ORGANIZATION

No question in church history has been more darkened by controversy than that of the origin and development of church officers, and none is more difficult, owing to the scantiness of the evidence that has survived. It is probable that the development was diverse in different localities. Not all early Christian congregations had identical institutions at the same time. Yet a substantial similarity was reached by the middle of the second century. Something has already been said of the constitution of the Jewish Christian congregations.[5] The present discussion has to do with those on Gentile soil.

The earliest Gentile churches had no officers in the strict sense. Paul's letters to the Galatians, Corinthians, and Romans make no mention of local officers. Those to the Corinthians could hardly have avoided some allusion, had such officers existed. Their nearest approach[6] is only an exhortation to be in subjection to such as Stephanas, and does not imply that he held office. The allusion in 1 *Thess.* 5^{12} to those that "are over you in the Lord" is, at best, very obscure. Paul's earlier epistles show that all ministries in the church, of whatever sort, were looked upon as the direct gift of the Spirit, who inspires each severally for the service of the congregation.[7] It is fair to conclude that these bearers of the gifts of the Spirit might be different at different times, and many in the church might equally become vehicles of the charismatic inspiration. Paul, however, specifies three classes of leaders as in particular the gift of the Spirit—Apostles, prophets, teachers.[8] He himself regarded his Apostolate as charismatic.[9] If the Apostles' work was primarily that of founding Christian churches, those

---

[1] Justin, *Apology*, 5. [2] *Ibid.*, 62. [3] *Ibid.*, *Dialogue*, 85.
[4] 2 *Clem.*, 9, 16. [5] *Ante*, p. 23. [6] 1 *Cor.* 16$^{15, 16}$.
[7] 1 *Cor.* 12$^{4-11, 28-30}$, 14$^{26-33}$. [8] 1 *Cor.* 12^{28}. [9] *Gal.* 1$^{1, 11-16}$; 1 *Cor.* 14^{18}.

of the prophet and teacher were the proclamation or interpretation of the divinely inspired message. The exact shade of difference between prophet and teacher is impossible to discover. All, however, were charismatic men. The worst of sins was to refuse to hear the Spirit speaking through them.[1] Yet Paul undoubtedly exercised a real missionary superintendence over the churches founded by him, and employed his younger assistants in the work.[2] It is difficult to distinguish this from ordinary supervision such as any founder might employ.

It was inevitable, however, that such unlimited confidence as the earliest congregations possessed in charismatic gifts should be abused. The *Teaching of the Twelve Apostles* shows that self-seeking and fraudulent claimants to divine guidance were soon preying on the churches.[3] Tests had to be found to discriminate the true from the false. In the *Teaching*, and in *Hermas*[4] the touchstone is character. In 1 *John* 4[1-4] it is orthodoxy of teaching. The prophets long continued. They are to be found in Rome as late as the time of Hermas (115–140), to say nothing of the claims of those whom the church judged heretical, like Montanus and his followers even later. Such uncertain leadership could not, in the nature of things, continue unmodified. For his farewell message Paul called to Miletus the "elders" ($\pi\rho\epsilon\sigma\beta\acute{v}\tau\epsilon\rho o\iota$) of the church of Ephesus, exhorting them to "take heed unto yourselves and to all the flock in which the Holy Ghost hath made you bishops"— $\grave{\epsilon}\pi\acute{\iota}\sigma\kappa o\pi o\iota$—overseers.[5] These are in a certain sense charismatic men. They have been made bishops by the Holy Spirit. But they are recipients of a charism which makes them a definite group having particular duties to the congregation. In one of his latest letters Paul speaks of the "bishops and deacons" of the church in Philippi (1[1]). Even if this be held to mean the discharge of functions only—"those who oversee and those who serve"—the advance beyond the conditions of the Corinthian epistles is apparent. The gifts may be charismatic, but the recipients are beginning to be holders of a permanent official relation. Why these local officers developed is unknown; but the interests of good order and worship, and the example of the synagogue are probable suggestions. Absence

---

[1] *Teaching*, 11; Ayer, p. 40.
[2] *E. g.*, Timothy in 1 *Cor.* 4[17], 16[10].
[3] 11; Ayer, p. 40.   [4] *Mand.*, 11.   [5] *Acts* 20[17-29].

of prophets and teachers by whom worship could be conducted and the congregation led was certainly a cause in some
places. The *Teaching of the Twelve Apostles* directs: "Appoint for yourselves, therefore, bishops and deacons worthy
of the Lord, men who are meek and not lovers of money, and
true and approved; for unto you they also perform the service
of the prophets and teachers. Therefore despise them not;
for they are your honorable men along with the prophets and
teachers" (15). At Philippi, Ephesus, and in the *Teaching*,
these "bishops" are spoken of in the plural. This is also true
of Rome and of Corinth when Clement of Rome wrote in
93–97.[1] Clement speaks, also, of those against whom the
church in Corinth had rebelled as its "appointed presbyters" (54); and of "those who have offered the gifts of the
bishop's office" as presbyters (44). Polycarp of Smyrna,
writing to Philippi in 110–117, mentions only presbyters and
deacons and their duties. Hermas, 115–140, would seem to
imply that as late as his time there was this collegiate office at
Rome. It is "the elders (presbyters) that preside over the
church."[2] He speaks only of the duties of "deacons" and
"bishops."[3]

Ancient interpretation, such as that of Jerome, saw in these
collegiate bishops and presbyters the same persons, the names
being used interchangeably. That is the opinion of most
modern scholars, and seems the probable conclusion. The
view of the late Edwin Hatch, as developed by Harnack,
holds, however, that presbyters were the older brethren in the
congregation, from whom the collegiate bishops were taken.
A bishop would be a presbyter, but a presbyter not necessarily
a bishop. The subject is one of difficulty, the more so as the
word "presbyter," like the English "elder" is used in early
Christian literature both as a general designation of the aged,
and as a technical expression. Its particular meaning is hard
always to distinguish. It is evident, however, that till some
time after the year 100, Rome, Greece, and Macedonia had at
the head of each congregation a group of collegiate bishops,
or presbyter-bishops, with a number of deacons as their helpers. These were chosen by the church,[4] or at least "with the
consent of the whole church."[5]

---

[1] *1 Clem.*, 42, 44.   [2] *Vis.*, 2⁴.   [3] *Sim.*, 9²⁶, ²⁷.
[4] *Teaching*, 15; Ayer, p. 41.   [5] *1 Clem.*, 44; Ayer, p. 37.

Contemporary with the later portion of the literature just described, there is another body of writings which indicates the existence of a threefold ministry consisting of a single, monarchical bishop, presbyters, and deacons in each congregation of the region to which it applies. This would appear to be the intimations of 1 *Timothy* and *Titus*, though the treatment is obscure. Whatever Pauline elements these much disputed letters contain, their sections on church government betray a development very considerably beyond that of the other Pauline literature, and can scarcely be conceived as belonging to Paul's time. It is interesting to observe that the regions to which the letters are directed are Asia Minor and the adjacent island of Crete, the former being one of the territories in which the monarchical bishopric is earliest evident in other sources.

What is relatively obscure in these epistles is abundantly clear in those of Ignatius, 110–117. Himself the monarchical bishop of Antioch,[1] he exalts in every way the authority of the local monarchical bishop in the churches of Ephesus, Magnesia, Tralles, Philadelphia, and Smyrna. In four of these churches he mentions the bishop by name. Only when writing to the Romans he speaks of no bishop, probably for the sufficient reason that there was as yet no monarchical bishop at Rome. The great value to Ignatius of the monarchical bishop is as a rallying-point of unity, and as the best opponent of heresy. "Shun divisions as the beginning of evils. Do ye all follow your bishop, as Jesus Christ followed the Father, and the presbytery as the Apostles, and to the deacons pay respect." [2] The monarchical bishopric is not yet diocesan, it is the headship of the local church, or at most of the congregations of a single city; but Ignatius does not treat it as a new institution. He accepts it as established, though it evidently did not always command the obedience which he desired.[3] It is evident, however, that the monarchical bishopric must have come into being between the time when Paul summoned the presbyter-bishops to Miletus[4] and that at which Ignatius wrote.

[1] *Romans* 2.   [2] *Smyrn.*, 8.

[3] See *Phila.*, 7, where Ignatius declares it is by charismatic inspiration, and not by knowledge of divisions, that he exhorted: "Do nothing without the bishop."

[4] *Acts* 20[17-25].

How the monarchical bishopric arose is a matter of conjecture. Reasons that have been advanced by modern scholars are leadership in worship and the financial oversight of the congregation in the care of the poor and other obligations of charity. These are probable, the first-named perhaps the more probable. It is sufficient to observe, however, that leadership of a congregation by a committee of equals is unworkable for any protracted time. Some one is sure to be given headship.

One further observation of great importance is to be made. Clement of Rome (93–97), writing when Rome had as yet no monarchical bishop, traces the existence of church officers to apostolical succession.[1] It is no impeachment of the firmness of his conviction, though it militates against the historic accuracy of his view, that he apparently bases it on a misunderstanding of Paul's statement in 1 *Cor.* 16$^{15, 16}$. On the other hand, Ignatius, though urging in the strongest terms the value of the monarchical episcopate as the bond of unity, knows nothing of an apostolical succession. It was the union of these two principles, a monarchical bishop in apostolical succession, which occurred before the middle of the second century, that immensely enhanced the dignity and power of the bishopric. By the sixth decade of the second century monarchical bishops had become well-nigh universal. The institution was to gain further strength in the Gnostic and Montanist struggles; but it may be doubted whether anything less rigid could have carried the church through the crises of the second century.

SECTION X.   RELATIONS OF CHRISTIANITY TO THE ROMAN GOVERNMENT

Christianity was at first regarded by the Roman authorities as a branch of Judaism, which stood under legal protection.[2] The hostility of the Jews themselves must have made a distinction soon evident, and by the time of the Neronian persecution in Rome (64) it was plainly drawn. The Roman victims were not then charged, however, primarily with Christianity, but with arson—though their unpopularity with the multitude made them ready objects of suspicion. By the time that 1 *Peter* was written (*c.* 90), the mere fact of a Christian profession had become a cause for punishment (4^{16}). How much

[1] 1 *Cor.* 42, 44; Ayer, pp. 36, 37.   [2] *Acts* 18$^{14-16}$.

earlier "the name" had become a sufficient criminal charge it
is impossible to say.   Trajan's reply to Pliny, the governor of
Bithynia (111–113), presupposes that Christianity was already
viewed as criminal.   That already recognized, the Emperor
orders what must be deemed mild procedure from his point of
view.   Christians are not to be hunted out, and, if willing to
abjure by sacrifice, are to be acquitted.   Only in case of per-
sistence are they to be punished.[1]   From the standpoint of a
faithful Christian profession this was a test which could only be
met by martyrdom.   Trajan's immediate successors, Hadrian
(117–138), and Antoninus Pius (138–161) pursued the same
general policy, though discouraging mob accusations.   Marcus
Aurelius (161–180) gave renewed force to the law against strange
religions (176), and initiated a sharper period of persecution
which extended into the beginning of the reign of Commodus
(180–192).   Commodus, however, treated Christianity, on the
whole, with the toleration of indifference.   Always illegal, and
with extreme penalties hanging over it, the Christian profession
involved constant peril for its adherents; yet the number of
actual martyrs in this period appears to have been relatively
small compared with those of the third and fourth centuries.
No general persecution occurred before 250.

The charges brought against the Christians were atheism
and anarchy.[2]   Their rejection of the old gods seemed atheism;
their refusal to join in emperor-worship appeared treasonable.[3]
Popular credulity, made possible by the degree to which the
Christians held aloof from ordinary civil society, charged them
with crimes as revolting as they were preposterous.   A misunderstanding of the Christian doctrine of Christ's presence
in the Supper must be deemed the occasion of the common
accusation of cannibalism; and its celebration secretly in the
evening of that of gross licentiousness.[4]   Much of the governmental persecution of Christianity in this period had its incite-
ment in mob attacks upon Christians.   That was the case at
Smyrna when Polycarp suffered martyrdom in 156; while a
boycott, on the basis of charges of immoral actions, was the
immediate occasion of the fierce persecution in Lyons and
Vienne in 177.[5]   It is not surprising, therefore, that the major-

---

[1] Pliny's *Letters* 10[97]; Ayer, p. 22.   [2] Justin, *Apology*, 5, 6; 11, 12.
[3] *Martyrdom of Polycarp*, 3, 8–10.   [4] Justin, *Dialogue*, 10.
[5] Eusebius, *Church History*, 5[1].

ity of judicial proceedings against Christians in this period seem rather to have been under the general police power of magistrates to repress disturbance than by formal trial on the specific criminal charge of Christianity. Both procedures are to be found. To all these accusations the best answer of the Christians was their heroic constancy in loyalty to Christ, and their superior morality as judged by the standards of society about them.

SECTION XI. THE APOLOGISTS

These charges against Christians, and the hostile attitude of the Roman government, aroused a number of literary defenders, who are known as the Apologists. Their appearance shows that Christianity was making some conquest of the more intellectual elements of society. Their appeal is distinctly to intelligence. Of these Apologists the first was Quadratus, probably of Athens, who about 125 presented a defense of Christianity, now preserved only in fragments, to the Emperor Hadrian. Aristides, an Athenian Christian philosopher, made a similar appeal, about 140, to Antoninus Pius. Justin wrote the most famous of these defenses, probably in Rome, about 153. His disciple, Tatian, who combined the four Gospels into his famous *Diatessaron*, also belonged to the Apologists. With them are to be reckoned Melito, bishop of Sardis, who wrote between 169 and 180; and Athenagoras, of whom little is known personally, whose defense, which survives, was made about the year 177. Here also belongs the *Epistle to Diognetus*, often reckoned among the writings of the Apostolic Fathers.

There is no evidence that any of these Apologists greatly influenced heathen opinion, or that their appeal was seriously considered by the rulers whom it was their desire to persuade. Their work was deservedly valued in Christian circles, however, and undoubtedly strengthened Christian conviction of the nobility of the cause so earnestly defended. Several of the Apologists were from the ranks of the philosophers, and their philosophical interpretation aided in the development of theology. The most significant was Justin, and he may well stand as typical of the whole movement.

Justin, called the Martyr, from his heroic witness unto death in Rome under the prefect Rusticus, about 165, was born in Shechem, in the ancient Samaria, of heathen ancestry. He lived, for a time at least, in Ephesus, and it was in its vicinity probably that the conversion of which he gives a vivid account took place.[1] An eager student of philosophy, he accepted successively Stoicism, Aristotelianism, Pythagoreanism, and Platonism. While a Platonist his attention was directed to the Hebrew prophets, "men more ancient than all those who are esteemed philosophers." Theirs is the oldest and truest explanation "of the beginning and end of things and of those matters which the philosopher ought to know," since they were "filled with the holy Spirit." "They glorified the Creator, the God and Father of all things, and proclaimed His Son, the Christ." By his newly acquired conviction of the truth of their ancient prophetic message, Justin says: "straightway a flame was kindled in my soul; and a love of the prophets and of those men who are friends of Christ. . . . I found this philosophy alone to be safe and profitable." These quotations show the character of Justin's religious experience. It was not a profound and mystical union with a risen Lord, as with Paul. It was not a sense of forgiveness of sin. It was a conviction that in Christianity is the oldest, truest, and most divine of philosophies. Justin continued to look upon himself as a philosopher. He made his home in Rome and there wrote, about 153, his *Apology*, addressed to the Emperor Antoninus Pius and that sovereign's adopted sons, defending Christianity from governmental antagonism and heathen criticisms. A little later, perhaps on a visit to Ephesus, he composed his *Dialogue with Trypho*, similarly presenting the Christian case against Jewish objections. A second sojourn in Rome brought him to a martyr's death.

Justin's *Apology* (often called two Apologies, though the "second" is only an appendix) is a manly, dignified, and effective defense. Christians, if condemned at all, should be punished for definite proved crimes, not for the mere name without investigation of their real character. They are atheists only in that they count the popular gods demons unworthy of worship, not in respect to the true God. They are anarchists only to those who do not understand the nature of the kingdom that they seek. Justin then argues the truth of Christianity, especially from the fulfilment of Old Testament prophecy, and briefly explains Christian sacraments and worship.

[1] *Dialogue*, 2-8.

As a theologian, Justin's convictions were the result of his own experience. His central belief was that Christianity was the truest of philosophies, because taught by the prophets of the Old Testament, and by the divine Logos "our Teacher . . . who is both Son and Apostle of God the Father." [1] This divine Logos he conceives, in true Stoic fashion, as everywhere and always at work, teaching the Greeks, of whom he cites Socrates and Heraclitus, and the "barbarians," such as Abraham, so that these, and all who at any time obeyed the same guidance were really Christians. [2] His great advance on Stoicism is his conviction that this all-illuminating divine Logos became definitely incarnate in Christ, so that in Him is the full revelation of that which elsewhere is less distinctly seen. The content of the Christian message Justin conceives in terms very similar to those of the best contemporary heathen philosophy—knowledge of God, morality, the hope of immortality, and future rewards and punishments. Like common non-Pauline Christianity, he views the Gospel as a new law, teaching a somewhat ascetic moral life. Justin's emphasis is on the divine Logos, subordinate to God the Father, yet His Son, His agent, and one with Him in some true, though rather indefinite, sense. This emphasis is really at the expense of the historic Jesus, for though both are identified, the earthly life of Jesus has little interest for Justin save as the great historic instance of the incarnation of the Logos, and therefore the occasion on which the divine philosophy was most fully revealed. He does, indeed, speak of Christ's "cleansing by His blood those who believe on Him"; [3] but such thoughts are not primary. Hence the theology of Justin, faithful martyr though he was, was essentially rationalizing, with little of the profoundly religious content so conspicuous in Paul, the Johannine literature, or even in Ignatius. It marks, however, a conscious union of Christian thought with the Gentile philosophy, and therefore the beginnings of a "scientific" theology.

[1] *Apology*, 12.   [2] *Ibid.*, 46; Ayer, p. 72.   [3] *Ibid.*, 32.

PERIOD II. FROM THE GNOSTIC CRISIS TO CONSTANTINE

SECTION I. GNOSTICISM

THE later New Testament literature, and at least one of the Apostolic Fathers, strongly combat conceptions of Christ which it is evident must have been widely prevalent, especially in Asia Minor, in the opening years of the second century. These views denied His real humanity and His actual death. He had not come "in the flesh," but in ghost-like, Docetic appearance.[1] These opinions have generally been regarded as the beginnings of Gnosticism. It is true that this Docetic conception of Christ was a feature of much Gnostic teaching. It is more probable, however, that these early teachings were more largely based on an attempt to explain a seeming contradiction between the Jesus of history and the Christ of experience, than on purely Gnostic speculations. That earthly life of humiliation was so contrasted with His pre-existent and post-existent glory, that the simplest solution of the Christological problem may well have seemed to some the denial of the reality of His earthly life altogether. Christ did, indeed, appear. He taught His disciples; but all the time as a heavenly being, not one of flesh and blood.

Gnosticism, properly speaking, was something much more far-reaching. The height of its influence was from about 135 to 160, though it continued a force long after the latter date. It threatened to overwhelm the historic Christian faith, and by so doing brought upon the Christian Church its gravest crisis since the Pauline battle for freedom from law. Its spread and consequent peril were made possible by the relatively weakly organized, and doctrinally undefined state of the church at its beginning. The church overcame the danger; but at the cost of the development of a rigidity of organization, creed, and government which rendered the condition of the church at

---

[1] 1 *John* 1$^{1-3}$, 2^{22}, 4$^{2, 3}$; Ignatius, *Trallians*, 9–11; *Smyrn.*, 1–6.

the close of the second century a striking contrast to that of
its beginning.[1]

Gnosticism professed to be based on "knowledge" ($\gamma\nu\hat{\omega}\sigma\iota\varsigma$),
but not as that word is now commonly understood. Its knowl-
edge was always a mystical, supernatural wisdom, by which the
initiates were brought to a true understanding of the universe,
and were saved from this evil world of matter. It had a fundamental doctrine of salvation. In these respects it was akin
to the mystery religions. Its most prominent characteristic,
however, was its syncretism. It took unto itself many elements
from many sources, and assumed many forms. It is, therefore,
impossible to speak of a single type of Gnosticism. It was
prevailingly mystical, magical, or philosophical according to
the dominant admixture in its syncretism. Gnosticism was
pre-Christian in its origin, and was in existence before Christianity came into the world. There were Jewish and heathen
types. It is represented in the Hermetic literature of Egypt.
It had astral elements which may be traced back to Babylonian
religious conceptions, a dualistic view of the universe, Persian in origin, and a doctrine of emanations from God in the
"pleroma" or realm of spirit, which was probably Egyptian.
Perhaps its most fundamental conception, the wholly evil
character of the phenomenal world, was due to a combination
of the Platonic theory of the contrast between the real spiritual
sphere of "ideas," and this visible world of phenomena, interpreted in terms of Persian dualism—the one good and that to
which man strives to return, the other wholly bad and the
place of his imprisonment. The world of matter is evil. Its
creator and ruler is not, therefore, the high, good God, but an
inferior and imperfect being, the demiurge. Man, to be saved,
must be freed from this bondage to the visible world, and its
rulers, the planetary spirits; and the means of his freedom is
"knowledge" ($\gamma\nu\hat{\omega}\sigma\iota\varsigma$), a mystical, spiritual enlightenment for
the initiated which brings him into communion with the true
realm of spiritual realities.

Strongly syncretistic already, Gnosticism found much in
Christianity which it could use. In particular, the figure of
Christ was especially adapted to give a definite and concrete cen-
tre to its theory of a higher saving knowledge. He was the re-

[1] Useful selections regarding Gnosticism may be found in Ayer, pp.
76–102.

vealer of the hitherto unknown high and all-perfect God to men. By that illumination all "spiritual" men, who were capable of receiving it, would be led back to the realm of the good God. Since the material world is evil, Christ could not have had a real incarnation, and the Gnostics explained His appearance either as Docetic and ghostly, or as a temporary indwelling of the man Jesus, or as an apparent birth from a virgin mother without partaking of material nature. The God of the Old Testament, as the creator of this visible world, cannot be the high God whom Christ revealed, but the inferior demiurge. That all Christians did not possess the saving "knowledge," the Gnostics explained by holding it to be a secret teaching imparted by the Apostles to their more intimate disciples, a speaking "wisdom among the perfect." [1] It is true that while Paul was in no sense a Gnostic, there were many things in Paul's teachings of which Gnostics availed themselves. His sharp contrast between flesh and spirit;[2] his conception of Christ as victor over those "principalities and powers" which are the "world rulers of this darkness,"[3] and his thought of Christ as the Man from Heaven,[4] were all ideas which the Gnostics could employ. Paul was always to them the chief Apostle.

Gnosticism was divided into many sects and presented a great variety of forms. In all of them the high, good God is the head of the spiritual world of light, often called the "pleroma." From that world fragments have become imprisoned in this visible world of darkness and evil. In later Gnosticism this fallen element from the pleroma is represented as the lowest of a series of æons, or spiritual beings, emanating from the high God. To rescue this fallen portion, the seeds of light in the visible evil world, Christ came, bringing the true "knowledge." By His teaching those capable of receiving it are restored to the pleroma. They are at best few. Most Gnostics divided mankind into "spiritual," capable of salvation, and "material" who could not receive the message. Later Gnosticism, especially the school of Valentinus, taught a threefold division, "spiritual," who alone could attain "knowledge"; "psychical," capable of faith, and of a certain degree of salvation; and "material," who were hopeless.

Christian tradition represented the founder of Christian

---

[1] 1 *Cor.* 2⁶.

[2] *Romans* 8²²⁻²⁵; 1 *Cor.* 15⁵⁰.

[3] *Col.* 2¹⁵; *Eph.* 6¹².

[4] 1 *Cor.* 15⁴⁷.

Gnosticism to be Simon Magus,[1] but of his real relations to it little is known. More clearly defined leaders are Satornilus of Antioch, who labored before 150; Basilides, who taught in Alexandria about 130; and, above all, Valentinus, who was active in Rome from about 135 to 165, and who must be regarded as one of the most gifted thinkers of the age.

Gnosticism was an immense peril for the church. It cut out the historic foundations of Christianity. Its God is not the God of the Old Testament, which is the work of an inferior or even evil being. Its Christ had no real incarnation, death, or resurrection. Its salvation is for the few capable of spiritual enlightenment. The peril was the greater because Gnosticism was represented by some of the keenest minds in the church of the second century. The age was syncretistic, and in some respects Gnosticism was but the fullest accomplishment of that amalgamation of Hellenic and Oriental philosophical speculation with primitive Christian beliefs which was in greater or less degree in process in all Christian thinking.

SECTION II. MARCION

A special interest attaches to Marcion as one who was the first church reformer.[2] Born in Sinope, in Asia Minor, where he was a wealthy ship-owner, he came to Rome about 139, and joined the Roman congregation, making it a gift for its benevolent work equivalent to ten thousand dollars. He soon came to feel that Christianity was under the bondage of legalism, and, under the light of the Gnostic teaching of Cerdo, he saw the root of this evil in acceptance of the Old Testament and its God. Never more than partially a Gnostic, his prime interest was in church reform. Salvation, with him, was by right faith rather than by knowledge. To Marcion, Paul was the only Apostle who had understood the Gospel; all the rest had fallen into the errors of Judaism. The God of the Old Testament is a just God, in the sense of "an eye for an eye, and a tooth for a tooth." He created the world and gave the Jewish law. Christ, who was a Docetic manifestation, revealed the heretofore unknown good God of mercy. The God of the Old Testament opposed Him; but in Christ the authority of the Jewish law was done away, and the "just God" became un-

---

[1] *Acts* 8[9-24]; Irenæus, *Heresies*, 1[23]; Ayer, p. 79.

[2] See selections, Ayer, pp. 102–105.

just because of this unwarranted hostility to the revealer of the "good God." The Old Testament and its God are therefore to be rejected by Christians. Christ proclaimed a Gospel of love and of righteousness by faith, though, curiously enough, Marcion was extremely ascetic in his conception of the Christian life.

Marcion's endeavor to call the Roman Church back to what he deemed the Gospel of Christ and of Paul resulted in his own excommunication about 144. He now gathered followers into a separated church. For their use he compiled a canon of sacred books, composed of the epistles of Paul (omitting the Pastorals), and the Gospel of Luke, shorn of all passages which implied that Christ regarded the God of the Old Testament as His Father, or was in any way related to Him. As far as is known, this was the first attempt to form an authoritative collection of New Testament writings.

Marcion's movement was probably the most dangerous of those associated with Gnosticism. He sundered Christianity from its historic background as completely as had the more speculative Gnostic theories. He denied a real incarnation, and condemned the Old Testament and its God. All this was the more plausible because done in the name of a protest against growing legalism. For such a protest there was much justification. His churches spread extensively, in the Orient especially, and survived into the fifth century. His own later history is wholly unknown.

SECTION III. MONTANISM

Unlike Gnosticism, Montanism was a movement distinctly of Christian origin. In most of the churches of the second century the early hope of the speedy return of Christ was growing dim. The consciousness of the constant inspiration of the Spirit, characteristic of the Apostolic Churches, had also largely faded. With this declining sense of the immediacy of the Spirit's present work came an increasing emphasis on His significance as the agent of revelation. Paul had identified the Spirit and Christ.[1] That was not the general feeling half a century later. The Spirit had been the inspiration of prophecy in the Old Testament.[2] He guided the New Testament writers.[3] To

---

[1] 2 *Cor.* 3[17].

[2] *E. g.*, 1 *Clem.* 8, 13, 16; "the prophetic Spirit," Justin, *Apology*, 13.

[3] 1 *Clem.*, 47.

Christian thought at the beginning of the second century the Holy Spirit was differentiated from Christ, but was classed, like Him, with God. This appears in the Trinitarian baptismal formula,[1] which was displacing the older baptism in the name of Christ.[2] Trinitarian formulæ were frequently in use by the close of the first and beginning of the second century.[3] The Johannine Gospel represented Christ as promising the coming of the Holy Spirit to the disciples: "When the Comforter is come, whom I will send unto you from the Father, even the Spirit of Truth, which proceedeth from the Father, He shall bear Witness of Me," (15²⁶). The second century was convinced, therefore, not only that the Holy Spirit was in peculiar association with God the Father and Christ; but that Christ had promised the Spirit's coming in more abundant measure in the future.

It was this thought of the special dispensation of the Holy Spirit, combined with a fresh outburst of the early prophetic enthusiasm, and a belief that the end of the world-age was close at hand, that were represented in Montanism. To a considerable extent Montanism was, also, a reaction from the secular tendencies already at work in the church. Montanus, from whom the movement was named, was of Ardabau, near the region of Asia Minor known as Phrygia—long noted for its ecstatic type of religion.[4] A tradition, recorded by Jerome, affirmed that, before conversion, he had been a priest of Cybele. About 156 Montanus proclaimed himself the passive instrument through whom the Holy Spirit spoke. In this new revelation Montanus declared the promise of Christ fulfilled, and the dispensation of the Holy Spirit begun. To him were soon joined two prophetesses, Prisca and Maximilla. They now affirmed, as mouthpieces of the Spirit, that the end of the world was at hand, and that the heavenly Jerusalem was about to be established in Phrygia, whither believers should betake themselves. In preparation for the fast-approaching consummation the most strenuous asceticism should be practised, celibacy, fastings, and abstinence from meat. This vigorous attitude won response as a protest against the growing worldliness of the church at large, and to many was the most attractive feature of Montanism.

[1] *Matt.* 28¹⁹.　　[2] *Acts* 2³⁸.　　[3] *E. g.*, 1 *Clem.* 46, 58; Ignatius, *Eph.*, 9.
[4] See selections, Ayer, pp. 106–109.

The movement speedily attained considerable proportions. By the bishops of Asia Minor, who felt their authority threatened, one or more synods were held soon after 160, which have the distinction of being the earliest synods of church history, and in which Montanism was condemned. Its progress was not easily checked, even by the death of the last of its original prophets, Maximilla, in 179. Soon after 170 it was represented in Rome, and for years the Roman church was more or less turmoiled by it. In Carthage it won Tertullian, about 207, attracted chiefly by its ascetic demands, who thenceforth was the most eminent Montanist. Though gradually driven out of the dominant church, Montanism continued to be represented in the Orient till long after the acceptance of Christianity by the imperial government. In Carthage the followers of Tertullian persisted till the time of Augustine. In its ascetic demands Montanism represented a wide-spread tendency, and an asceticism as strict as anything Montanism taught was later to find a place in the great church in monasticism.

SECTION IV. THE CATHOLIC CHURCH

Neither Gnosticism nor Montanism, though extremely perilous, were ever embraced by a majority of Christians. The large church remained faithful to historic Christianity. By the latter third of the second century it was calling itself the "Catholic" Church. The word "Catholic" is first used of the church by Ignatius,[1] who employed it in the wholly untechnical sense of "universal." It is next to be found in the letter of the Church of Smyrna, describing the martyrdom of Polycarp (156), where it is difficult to decide whether the use is technical or not. Its employment as a technically descriptive adjective gradually became common, so that the strongly consolidated church that came out of the Gnostic and Montanist crises is now usually described as the "Old Catholic." This Old Catholic Church developed its distinguishing characteristics between 160 and 190. The hitherto relatively independent congregations were now knit into an effective union. The power of the bishops was greatly strengthened, a collection of authoritative New Testament Scripture recognized, and a creed formulated. Comparatively loosely organized Christianity

[1] *Smyrn.*, 8; Ayer, p. 42.

now became a rigid corporate body, having recognized official leaders and capable not merely of defining its faith, but of shutting out from its communion all who did not accept its creed or its officers. As a recent German writer has epitomized the change: "About 50, he was of the church who had received baptism and the Holy Spirit and called Jesus, Lord; about 180, he who acknowledged the rule of faith (creed), the New Testament canon, and the authority of the bishops."[1]

In a measure, the beginnings of this great change may be seen before the Gnostic and Montanist crises; but it was those struggles that brought it effectively into being. The characteristic answer of the Catholic Church to the Gnostics may be seen in the argument of Irenæus of Lyons.[2] Against Gnostic claims Irenæus, writing about 185, held that the Apostles did not preach before they had "perfect knowledge" of the Gospel. That preaching they recorded in the Gospels—*Matthew* and *John*, were written by Apostles themselves; while *Mark* reproduced the message of Peter and *Luke* that of Paul. Nothing Gnostic, Irenæus declares, is found in any of them. But the Gnostic may object that, besides this public apostolic teaching in the Gospels, there was a *viva voce* instruction, a speaking "wisdom among the perfect,"[3] of which Gnosticism was the heir. This Irenæus denied. He argued that, had there been such private teaching, the Apostles would have intrusted it to those, above all others, whom they selected as their successors in the government of the churches. In these churches of apostolic foundation the apostolic teaching had been fully preserved, and its transmission had been guaranteed by the orderly succession of their bishops. Go therefore to Rome, or to Smyrna, or Ephesus, and learn what is there taught, and nothing Gnostic will be found. Every church must agree with that of Rome, for there apostolical tradition has been faithfully preserved as in other Apostolic Churches.

It is difficult to see what more effective argument Irenæus could have advanced in the peculiar situation which confronted him; but it was an answer which greatly increased the significance of the churches of real or reputed apostolical foundation, and of their heads, the bishops. Irenæus went further. The church itself is the depository of Christian teach-

---

[1] Heussi, *Kompendium der Kirchengeschichte*, p. 44.
[2] *Heresies*, 3:1–4; Ayer, pp. 112–114.   [3] 1 *Cor.* 2⁶.

ing: "Since the Apostles, like a rich man in a bank, lodged in her hands most copiously all things pertaining to the truth."[1] This deposit is especially intrusted to "those who, together with the succession of the episcopate, have received the certain gift of truth,"[2] *i. e.* to the heads of the churches. To agree with the bishops is therefore a necessity. This argument was not peculiar to Irenæus, it was that of the leaders of Old Catholic teaching generally.

While the power of the episcopate and the significance of churches of apostolical foundation was thus greatly enhanced, the Gnostic crisis saw a corresponding development of creed, at least in the West. Some form of instruction before baptism was common by the middle of the second century.[3] At Rome this developed, apparently, between 150 and 175, and probably in opposition to Marcionite Gnosticism, into an explication of the baptismal formula of *Matt.* 28¹⁹—the earliest known form of the so-called Apostles' Creed. What antecedents in Asia Minor, if any, it may have had is still a question in scholarly dispute. Without symbolic authority in the Orient, all the Western churches received this creed from Rome, and it was regarded, by the time of Tertullian at least, as having apostolic authority, that is as a summary of apostolic teaching.[4] In its original form it read:

"I believe in God the Father Almighty; and in Christ Jesus, His only begotten Son, our Lord, who was born of the Holy Spirit and the Virgin Mary, crucified under Pontius Pilate and buried; the third day He rose from the dead, ascended into the heavens, being seated at the right hand of the Father, whence He shall come to judge the living and the dead; and in the Holy Spirit, holy church, forgiveness of sins, resurrection of the flesh."

The development of a canon of New Testament books was, also, the work of this period. By the church from the beginning the Old Testament was reckoned as Scripture. The Gospels and the letters of Paul were doubtless highly valued, but they did not, at first, have Scriptural authority. Clement of Rome (93–97), though constantly quoting the Old Testament as the utterance of God, was very free in his use of the words of the New Testament, and nowhere styled them divine.

---

[1] *Heresies*, 3 : 4¹.   [2] *Ibid.*, 4 : 26².

[3] Justin, *Apology*, 61.   [4] *Prescription*, 13, 36.

The earliest designation of a passage from the Gospels as "Scripture" was about 131, by the so-called Barnabas,[1] and of a quotation from Paul about 110–117, by Polycarp.[2]   By the time of Justin (153), the Gospels were read in the services in Rome, together with the Old Testament prophets.[3]   The process by which the New Testament writings came to Scriptural authority seems to have been one of analogy.   The Old Testament was everywhere regarded as divinely authoritative. Christians could think no less of their own fundamental books. The question was an open one, however, as to which were the canonical writings.   Works like Hermas and Barnabas were read in churches.   An authoritative list was desirable.   Marcion had prepared such a canon for his followers.   A similar enumeration was gradually formed, probably in Rome, by the Catholic party.   Apparently the Gospels were the first to gain complete recognition, then the letters of Paul.   By about 200, according to the witness of the Muratorian fragment, Western Christendom had a New Testament canon embracing *Matthew, Mark, Luke, John, Acts,* 1 and 2 *Corinthians, Ephesians, Philippians, Colossians, Galatians,* 1 and 2 *Thessalonians, Romans, Philemon, Titus,* 1 and 2 *Timothy, Jude,* 1 and 2 *John, Revelation,* and the so-called *Apocalypse of Peter.*[4]   In the Orient the development of a canon was not quite so rapid.   Certain books, like *Hebrews* and *Revelation* were disputed.   The whole process of canonical development into its precise present form was not completed in the West till 400, and in the East till even later.

By the year 200 the church of the western portion of the empire had, therefore, an authoritative collection of New Testament books, in the main like our own, to which to appeal. The East was not much behind.   The formation of the canon was essentially a process of selection from the whole mass of Christian literature, made originally by no council, but by the force of Christian opinion—the criterion being that the books accepted were believed to be either the work of an Apostle or of the immediate disciple of an Apostle, and thus to represent apostolic teaching.

Thus out of the struggle with Gnosticism and Montanism came the Old Catholic Church, with its strong episcopal organization, credal standard, and authoritative canon.   It differed

[1] *Barn.*, 4.   [2] *Phil.* 12.
[3] *Apology*, 66, 67.   [4] Ayer, pp. 117–120.

much from the Apostolic Church; but it had preserved historic Christianity and carried it through a tremendous crisis. It may be doubted whether a less rigid organization than that developed in this momentous second half of the second century could have achieved as much.

SECTION V. THE GROWING IMPORTANCE OF ROME

The Roman Church had been of prominence since the time of Paul. To it that Apostle wrote his most noteworthy letter. At Rome Paul, and probably Peter, died. The church endured the severest of early persecutions under Nero, and survived in vigor. Situated in the capital of the empire, it early developed a consciousness of strength and authority, which was doubtless increased by the fact that, by 100, it was, it would appear, the largest single congregation in Christendom. Even before the close of the first century Clement, writing anonymously to the Corinthians in the name of the whole Roman congregation (93–97), spoke as for those who expected to be obeyed.[1] The tone, if brotherly, was big-brotherly. This influence was increased by the well-known generosity of the Roman congregation.[2] Ignatius addressed it as "having the presidency of love."[3] The destruction of Jerusalem in the second Jewish war (135) ended any possible leadership of Christianity that might there have been asserted. The successful resistance to Gnosticism and Montanism strengthened it; and it reaped in abundance the fruits of that struggle. There the creed was formulated, there the canon formed. Above all, it was advantaged by the appeal of the opponents of Gnosticism to the tradition of the Apostolic churches, for Rome was the only church in the western half of the empire with which Apostles had had anything to do. Irenæus of Lyons, writing about 185, represented the general Western feeling of his time, when he not only pictures the Roman Church as founded by Peter and Paul, but declares "it is a matter of necessity that every church should agree with this church."[4] It was leadership in the preservation of the apostolic faith, not judicial supremacy, that Irenæus had in mind; but with such estimates

---

[1] 1 *Clem.*, 59, 63.
[2] Eusebius, *Church History*, 4 : 23[10]; Ayer, p. 24.
[3] *Romans.*   [4] *Heresies*, 3 : 3[2]; Ayer, p. 113.

wide-spread, the door was open for a larger assertion of Roman authority. Rather late in developing the monarchical episcopate, since Anicetus (154–165) seems to have been the first single head of the Roman Church, the prominence of its bishop grew rapidly in the Gnostic struggle, and with this growth came the first extensive assertion of the authority of the Roman bishop in the affairs of the church at large.

While Rome was thus gaining in strength Asia Minor was relatively declining. At the beginning of the second century Asia Minor and the adjacent portion of Syria had been the most extensively Christianized sections of the empire. That was probably, also, true at the century's close. Ephesus and Antioch had been, and were still, great Christian centres. Asia Minor had resisted Gnosticism, but it had been torn by Montanism and other sources of controversy, though the Montanists had been rejected. There is reason to think, however, that these disputes had borne hard on the united strength of its Christianity. The quarrel between Asia Minor and Rome arose over the time of the observance of Easter. While there is reason to suppose that Easter had been honored from early in Christian history, the first definite record of its celebration is in connection with a visit of Polycarp, bishop of Smyrna, to Anicetus, bishop of Rome, in 154 or 155. At that time the practice of Asia Minor, probably the more ancient, was to observe Easter with the Lord's Supper on the evening of the fourteenth of the month Nisan, like the Jewish Passover, regardless of the day of the week on which it might fall. The Roman custom, and that of some parts of the East, was to hold the Easter feast always on Sunday. The question was, therefore, should the day of the week or that of the month be the norm. Polycarp and Anicetus could not agree, but parted with mutual good-will, each adhering to his own practice.[1] The problem was further complicated by a dispute, about 167, in Laodicea, in Asia Minor itself, as to the nature of the celebration on the fourteenth of Nisan, some holding that Christ died on the fourteenth, as the fourth Gospel intimates, and others placing His death, as do the other Gospels, on the fifteenth. The latter treated the commemoration of the fourteenth of Nisan, therefore, as a Christian continuation of the Hebrew Passover.

---

[1] Eusebius, *Church History*, 5 : 24[16, 17]; Ayer, p. 164.

About 190 the problem became so acute that synods were held in Rome, Palestine, and elsewhere which decided in favor of the Roman practice. The churches of Asia Minor, led by Polycrates, bishop of Ephesus, refused conformity. Thereupon Victor, bishop of Rome (189–198), excommunicated the recalcitrant congregations. This high-handed action met with much protest, notably from Irenæus of Lyons, but it was a marked assertion of Roman authority.[1]

These embittered controversies were costly to Asia Minor, and any possible rivalry on equal terms of Ephesus and Rome was out of the question. The collapse of Jewish Christian leadership, the apparent lack at Antioch of men of eminence in the second century, and the decline of the influence of Asia Minor left Rome, by 200, the most eminent and influential centre of Christianity—a position of which the Roman bishops had the will and the ability to make full use. The rise of Alexandria and of Carthage to importance in the Christian thought and life of the third century could not rob Rome of its leadership. Their attainment of Christian significance was far younger than that of the capital of the empire.

SECTION VI. IRENÆUS

The earliest theological leader of distinction in the rising Old Catholic Church was Irenæus. His argument in defense of traditional Christianity against Gnosticism has already been outlined.[2] Born in Asia Minor, he was brought up in Smyrna, where he saw and heard Polycarp. The date of his birth has been most variously placed by modern scholars from about 115 to about 142, chiefly in the light of its possible bearing on traditions as to the authorship of the fourth Gospel. The later part of the period indicated has more probability than the earlier. From Asia Minor he removed to Lyons in what is now France, where he became a presbyter. The great persecution of 177, at Lyons, found him, fortunately, on an honorable mission to Rome; and, on his return, he was chosen bishop of Lyons, in succession to the martyred Pothinus. That post he continued to hold till his death (c. 200). Not far from 185 he wrote his chief work, *Against Heresies*, primarily

[1] Eusebius, *Church History*, 5 : 23, 24 ; Ayer, pp. 161–165.
[2] *Ante*, p. 60.

to refute the various Gnostic schools, but incidentally revealing his own theology.

Brought up in the tradition of Asia Minor and spending his later life in Gaul, Irenæus was a connecting-link not merely between distant portions of the empire, but between the older theology of the Johannine and Ignatian literature and the newer presentations which the Apologists and the "Catholic" movement of his own day were introducing. A man of deeply religious spirit, his interest was in salvation. In its explication he developed the Pauline and Ignatian conceptions of Christ as the new man, the renewer of humanity, the second Adam. God created the first Adam, He made him good and immortal; but both goodness and immortality were lost by Adam's disobedience. What man lost in Adam is restored in Christ, the incarnate Logos, who now completes the interrupted work. "I have shown that the Son of God did not then begin to exist [i. e. at Jesus' birth], being with the Father from the beginning; but when He became incarnate and was made man, He commenced afresh the long line of human beings, and furnished us, in a brief, comprehensive manner, with salvation; so that what we had lost in Adam—namely to be according to the image and likeness of God—that we might recover in Christ Jesus." [1] The work of Christ, thus described, Irenæus characterizes in a noble phrase. We follow "the only true and steadfast Teacher, the Word of God, our Lord Jesus Christ, who did through His transcendent love become what we are, that He might bring us to be even what He is Himself." [2] Christ is also the full revelation of God. [3] Our union with Him, following the teaching of Asia Minor and of Justin, Irenæus views as in some sense physical, through the Supper. [4] Irenæus's theory of Christ's new headship of humanity had added to it a suggestion of His mother as the second Eve. "The knot of Eve's disobedience was loosened by the obedience of Mary. For what the Virgin Eve had bound fast through unbelief, this did the Virgin Mary set free through faith." [5] In this curious ascription is one of the earliest evidences of that exaltation of the Virgin which was to play so large a part in Christian history. In some ways, even for his time, Irenæus was an old-fashioned man. The belief in Christ's speedy second com-

---

[1] *Heresies*, 3:18[1]; Ayer, pp. 137, 138.   [2] *Heresies*, 5; Preface.
[3] *Ibid.*, 4:20[7].   [4] *Ibid.*, 4:18[5]; Ayer, p. 138.   [5] *Ibid.*, 3:22[4].

ing had been growing faint, and the contest with Montanism was to extinguish it almost entirely With Irenæus it still burned brightly, and he looked eagerly for the time when the earth would be marvellously renewed.[1] For Irenæus the New Testament is as fully sacred Scripture as the Old.

SECTION VII. TERTULLIAN AND CYPRIAN

Tertullian was one of the most individual and remarkable personalities of the ancient church. Born (c. 150–155) of well-to-do heathen parentage in Carthage, he studied law and practised his profession in Rome. He was exceedingly well read in philosophy and history. Greek he had thoroughly mastered. About 190 to 195, he was converted to Christianity, probably in Rome, and now devoted himself with equal eagerness to the study of Christian literature, orthodox and heretical. Shortly after he returned to Carthage where he became a presbyter, and remained till his death (c. 222–225). At first in fellowship with the Roman Church, a wave of persecution that broke over North Africa in 202 under the Emperor Septimius Severus (193–211), strengthened his native Puritanism and brought him into sympathy with Montanism. Its ascetic and unworldly aspects most appealed to him. About 207 he broke with the "Catholic" Church, which he thenceforth bitterly criticised, and died in continuing protest, apparently, as the founder of a little sect of his own.

In 197 Tertullian began a career of literary activity in defense and explication of Christianity which lasted till 220. He was the first ecclesiastical writer of prominence to use Latin. Even the leaders of the Roman Church wrote in Greek till after his time. His style was vivid, satirical, readable. His method was often that of an advocate in the court-room. He was frequently unfair to opponents. He was not always consistent with himself. But he was of a fiery earnestness of spirit that makes what he wrote always impressive. He well deserves the title of father of Latin theology.

Tertullian was, primarily, no speculative theologian. His own thought was based on that of the Apologists, Irenæus, and to some extent on other bearers of the tradition of Asia Minor, and quite as much on Stoic teaching and legal conceptions.

---

[1] *Ibid.*. 5 : 33[3] : Ayer. p. 26.

He had the Roman sense of order and authority. All that he touched, however, he formulated with the clearness of definition of a trained judicial mind, and hence he gave precision, as none had before him, to many theological conceptions that had heretofore been vaguely apprehended.

For Tertullian Christianity was a great divine foolishness, wiser than the highest philosophical wisdom of men, and in no way to be squared with existing philosophical systems.[1] In reality he looked upon it largely through Stoic spectacles. Christianity is primarily knowledge of God. It is based on reason—"the soul by nature Christian"[2]—and authority. That authority is seated in the church, and only in the orthodox church, which alone has the truth, expressed in the creed, and alone has a right to use the Scriptures.[3] As with Irenæus, these valid churches are those that agree in faith with those founded by the Apostles, wherein the apostolic tradition has been maintained by the succession of bishops.[4] These are utterances of the still "Catholic" Tertullian. As with Justin and common Gentile Christianity of the second century, Christianity for Tertullian is a new law. "Jesus Christ . . . preached the new law and the new promises of the kingdom of heaven."[5] Admission to the church is by baptism, by which previous sins are removed. It is "our sacrament of water, in that by washing away the sins of our early blindness we are set free into eternal life."[6] Those who have received it are thenceforth "competitors for salvation in earning the favor of God."[7]

Tertullian had a deeper sense of sin than any Christian writer since Paul, and his teachings greatly aided the development of the Latin conceptions of sin and grace. Though not clearly worked out, and inconsistent with occasional expressions, Tertullian possessed a doctrine of original sin. "There is, then, besides the evil which supervenes on the soul from the intervention of the evil spirit, an antecedent, and in a certain sense natural evil, which arises from its corrupt origin."[8] But "the power of the grace of God is more potent indeed than nature."[9] The nature of grace he nowhere fully explains. It evidently included, however, not only "forgiveness of sins,"[10]

[1] *Prescription*, 7.   [2] *Apology*, 17.   [3] *Prescription*, 13–19.
[4] *Ibid.*, 32.   [5] *Ibid.*, 13.   [6] *Baptism*, 1.
[7] *Repentance*, 6.   [8] *Anima*, 41.   [9] *Ibid.*, 21.
[10] *Baptism*, 10.

but also "the grace of divine inspiration," by which power to do right is infused to give force to man's feeble, but free, will.[1] Loofs has shown that this latter conception, of the utmost significance for the theology of Western Christendom, is of Stoic origin.[2] But though salvation is thus based on grace, man has much to do. Though God forgives previous sins at baptism, satisfaction must be made for those committed thereafter by voluntary sacrifices, chiefly ascetic. The more a man punishes himself, the less God will punish him.[3]

Tertullian's most influential work was the definition of the Logos Christology, though he preferred to use the designation Son rather than Logos. If he advanced its content little beyond what had already been presented by the theologians of Asia Minor, and especially by the Apologists, his legal mind gave a clearness to its explanation such as had not before existed. Here his chief work was one written in his Montanist period—*Against Praxeas*. He defines the Godhead in terms which almost anticipate the Nicene result of more than a century later. "All are of one, by unity of substance; while the mystery of the dispensation is still guarded which distributes the unity into a Trinity, placing in their order the three, the Father, the Son, and the Holy Spirit; three, however . . . not in substance but in form; not in power but in appearance, for they are of one substance and one essence and one power, inasmuch as He is one God from whom these degrees and forms and aspects are reckoned under the name of the Father, and of the Son, and of the Holy Spirit."[4] He describes these distinctions of the Godhead as "persons,"[5] meaning by the word not our usage in the sense of personalities, but forms of manifestation. This unity of substance in Tertullian's thought is material, for he was sufficiently a Stoic to hold that "God is a body . . . for spirit has a bodily substance of its own kind."[6] With a similar precision, Tertullian distinguished between the human and divine in Christ. "We see His double state, not intermixed but conjoined in one person, Jesus, God and man."[7] Since both Son and Spirit are derived from the Father by emanation, both are

---

[1] *Patience*, 1.
[2] *Leitfaden zum Studium der Dogmengeschichte*, p. 164.
[3] *Repentance*, 2, 9.   [4] *Praxeas*, 2.   [5] *Ibid.*, 12.
[6] *Ibid.*, 7.   [7] *Ibid.*, 27.

subordinate to Him.[1] This doctrine of subordination, already taught in the Apologists, was to remain characteristic of the Logos Christology till the time of Augustine. These definitions were far more the work of a lawyer-like, judicial interpretation, than of philosophical consideration. As the first, also, to give technical usage to such expressions as *trinitas, substantia, sacramentum, satisfacere, meritum,* Tertullian left his permanent impress on Latin theology.

Cyprian was, in many ways, the intellectual heir of Tertullian, whom he called master. Born probably in Carthage, about 200, he spent all his life in that city. A man of wealth and education, he won distinction as a teacher of rhetoric. About 246 he was converted to the Christian faith, and two or three years later was chosen to the bishopric of Carthage. Here he showed high executive ability, and much practical good sense and kindliness of spirit without the touch of genius that characterized Tertullian. The persecution of 250 he escaped by flight; but in that of 258 he stood boldly forth and suffered as a martyr by beheading. Few leaders of the ancient church have been more highly regarded by subsequent ages.

In Cyprian's teaching the tendencies illustrated in the development of the "Catholic" Church received their full expression. The church is the one visible orthodox community of Christians. "There is one God, and Christ is one, and there is one church, and one chair (episcopate) founded upon the rock by the word of the Lord."[2] "Whoever he may be and whatever he may be, he who is not in the church of Christ is not a Christian."[3] "He can no longer have God for his Father, who has not the church for his mother."[4] "There is no salvation out of the church."[5] The church is based on the unity of its bishops, "whence ye ought to know that the bishop is in the church and the church in the bishop; and if any one be not with the bishop, that he is not in the church."[6] "The episcopate is one, each part of which is held by each one in its entirety."[7] This last quotation has its bearing on a controversy still alive as to whether Cyprian regarded all bishops as equal sharers in a common episcopal authority, the possession of each and of all; or held to the superiority of the bishop

---

[1] *Praxeas*, 7, 9.   [2] *Letters*, 39–43[5].   [3] *Ibid.*, 51–55[24].
[4] *Unity of the Church*, 6.   [5] *Letters*, 72–73[21].   [6] *Ibid.*, 68–66[8].
[7] *Unity of the Church*, 5; Ayer, p. 242.

of Rome. He certainly quoted *Matt.* 16[18, 19].[1] He looked upon Peter as the typical bishop. He referred to Rome as "the chief church whence priestly unity takes its source." [2] Rome was to him evidently the highest church in dignity; but Cyprian was not ready to admit a judicial authority over others in the Roman bishop, or to regard him as more than the first among equals.

Cyprian's significance as a witness to the full development of the doctrine that the Lord's Supper is a sacrifice offered by the priest to God will be considered in Section XIV. His conception of the Christian life, like that of Tertullian, was ascetic. Martyrdom is bringing forth fruit an hundredfold; voluntary celibacy, sixtyfold.[3]

SECTION VIII. THE TRIUMPH OF THE LOGOS CHRISTOLOGY
IN THE WEST

Though the "Catholic" Church was combating successfully the Gnostics, and though the Logos Christology was that of such formative minds as those of the writer of the fourth Gospel, Justin, Irenæus, and Tertullian, that Christology was not wholly regarded with sympathy by the rank and file of believers. Hermas had taught an adoptionist Christology at Rome as late as 140. The Apostles' Creed has no reference to any Logos doctrine. Tertullian says significantly of his own time (213–218): "The simple—I will not call them unwise or unlearned—who always constitute the majority of believers, are startled at the dispensation of the three in one, on the ground that their very rule of faith withdraws them from the world's plurality of gods to the one only true God." [4] It was difficult for them to see in trinitarian conceptions aught else but an assertion of tritheism. The last decade of the second and the first two of the third centuries were an important epoch, therefore, in Christological discussion, especially in Rome, where the question was in the balance.

To some extent this new Christological discussion seems to have been the indirect result of Montanism. That movement had made much of the fourth Gospel, proclaiming itself the inauguration of the dispensation of the Spirit, therein promised. Some opponents of Montanism in Asia Minor, in their reaction

---

[1] *E. g., Unity of the Church*, 4.   [2] *Letters*, 54–59[14].
[3] *Ibid.*, 76[6].   [4] *Praxeas*, 3.

from its teachings, went so far as to reject the fourth Gospel
and its doctrine of the Logos. Of these "Alogoi," as Epiphanius (?-403), writing much later, nicknamed them, little is
known in detail, but some of the critics of the Logos Christology
who now came into prominence were apparently influenced by
them. To these opponents in general the name Monarchians
is usually given—a title coined by Tertullian[1]—since they asserted the unity of God. The Monarchians fell into two very
unlike classes, those who held that Jesus was the Son of God
by adoption, the so-called Dynamic Monarchians; and those
who held that Christ was but a temporary form of manifestation of the one God, the party known as the Modalistic Monarchians. Thus, with the supporters of the Logos view, three
Christologies were contesting in Rome at the beginning of the
third century.

The first Dynamic Monarchian of prominence was Theodotus,
called the currier, or tanner, from Byzantium. He was a man of
learning, and is said to have been a disciple of the Alogoi, though,
unlike them, he accepted in some sense the fourth Gospel.
About 190 he came to Rome, and there taught that Jesus was
a man, born of the Virgin, of holy life, upon whom the divine
Christ (or the Holy Spirit) descended at His baptism. Some
of Theodotus's followers denied to Jesus any title to divinity;
but others held that He became in some sense divine at His
resurrection.[2] One is reminded of the Christology of Hermas
(*Ante*, p. 39). Theodotus was excommunicated by Bishop Victor of Rome (189–198); but his work there was continued by
Theodotus, "the money-changer," and Asclepiodorus, like their
master, probably from the Orient; but their effort to found a
rival communion outside the "Catholic" Church amounted to
little. The last attempt to present a similar theology in Rome
was that of a certain Artemon (230–40–270), but Dynamic
Monarchianism in the West was already moribund. Yet it
undoubtedly represented a type of Christology that was one
of the oldest in the Christian Church.

The Dynamic Monarchian party was stronger and more
persistent in the East. There it had its most famous representative in Paul of Samosata, the able and politically gifted
bishop of Antioch from *c.* 260 to 272. He represented the

---

[1] *Praxeas*, 3, 10.

[2] Hippolytus, *Refutation*, 7[23], 10[19]; Ayer, p. 172.

Logos, which he also described as the Son of God, as an impersonal attribute of the Father. This Logos had inspired Moses and the prophets. Jesus was a man, unique in that He was born of the Virgin, who was filled with the power of God, *i. e.*, by God's Logos. By this indwelling inspiration Jesus was united in will by love to God, but did not become in substance one with God. That union is moral, but inseparable. By reason of it Christ was raised from the dead, and given a kind of delegated divinity. Between 264 and 269 three synods considered Paul of Samosata's views, by the last of which he was excommunicated; but he kept his place till driven out by the Emperor Aurelian (p. 106).

Much more numerous than the Dynamic Monarchians were the Modalistic Monarchians, who made an appeal to the many for the reason already quoted from Tertullian (*ante*, p. 71), that in the presence of heathen polytheism, the unity of God seemed a prime article of the Christian faith, and any Logos conception or Dynamic Monarchianism seemed to them a denial of that unity. Cyprian coined for these Modalistic Monarchians the nickname Patripassians.[1] The leader of Modalistic Monarchianism was, like that of Dynamic Monarchianism, an Oriental Christian, Noetus, probably of Smyrna. The same controversies in Asia Minor may well have called forth both interpretations. Of Noetus little is known save that he taught in his native region in the period 180 to 200, "that Christ was the Father Himself, and that the Father Himself was born and suffered and died." [2] These views were transplanted to Rome, about 190, by a certain Praxeas, a follower of Noetus and an opponent of the Montanists, regarding whom Tertullian, then a Montanist and always a defender of the Logos Christology, said: "Praxeas did two works of the devil in Rome. He drove out prophecy and introduced heresy. He put to flight the Holy Spirit and crucified the Father." [3] A little later two other disciples of Noetus, Epigonus and Cleomenes, came to Rome and won, in large measure, the sympathy of Bishop Zephyrinus (198–217) for the Modalistic Monarchian position.

The most noted leader of the Modalistic school, whose name became permanently associated with this Christology, was Sa-

---

[1] *Letters*, 72–73[4].

[2] Hippolytus, *Against Noetus*, 1; Ayer, p. **177**.

[3] *Praxeas*, 1; Ayer, p. **179**.

bellius, of whose early life little is known, but who was teaching
in Rome about 215. His theology was essentially that of Noetus, but much more carefully wrought out, especially in that
it gave a definite place to the Holy Spirit as well as to the
Son. Father, Son, and Holy Spirit are all one and the same.
Each is a prosopon—πρόσωπον—(a word of large later orthodox use), that is a character or form of manifestation, of the
one God, who showed Himself in His character of creator as
the Father, in that of redeemer as the Son, and now as the
Holy Spirit. Sabellius, though soon excommunicated at Rome,
found large following for his views in the East, especially in
Egypt and Libya. Nor was he without considerable influence
on the development of what became the orthodox Christology.
His absolute identification of Father, Son, and Holy Spirit was
rejected; but it implied an equality which ultimately, as in
Augustine, triumphed over the subordination of Son and Spirit
characteristic of the Logos Christology both of Tertullian and
Athanasius.

The great advocate of the Logos Christology at this juncture
in Rome was Hippolytus (160-170—c. 235), the most learned
Christian writer then in the city, and the last considerable
theologian there to use Greek rather than Latin as his vehicle
of expression. As a commentator, chronicler, calculator of
Easter dates, Apologist, and opponent of heretics, he was held
in such high repute that his followers erected after his death
the earliest Christian portrait statue known. He opposed
vigorously the Monarchians of both schools. The fight in
Rome waxed hot. Bishop Zephyrinus (198-217) hardly knew
what to do, though he leaned toward the Monarchian side.
On his death he was succeeded by Kallistos (Calixtus, 217-222),
the most energetic and assertive bishop that Rome had yet
seen—a man who had been born a slave, had engaged unsuc-
cessfully in banking, and had, for a time, been a sufferer for his
Christian faith in the mines of Sardinia. Over Zephyrinus he
acquired great influence, and on his own attainment of the
bishopric, issued in his own name certain regulations as to the
readmission to the church of those repentant of sins of licentiousness, which show higher ecclesiastical claims than any heretofore advanced by a Roman bishop (see p. 101). Kallistos saw
that these disputes were hurting the Roman Church. He therefore excommunicated Sabellius (c. 217), and charged Hippolytus

with being a worshipper of two gods.[1] Hippolytus now broke with Kallistos, on this ground and on questions regarding discipline, and became the head of a rival communion in Rome —the first "counter-pope"—a position which he maintained till his banishment in the persecution of 235.

Kallistos tried to find a compromise formula in this Christological confusion. Father, Son and Logos, he held, are all names of "one indivisible spirit." Yet Son is also the proper designation of that which was visible, Jesus; while the Father was the spirit in Him. This presence of the Father in Jesus is the Logos. Kallistos was positive that the Father did not suffer on the cross, but suffered with the sufferings of the Son, Jesus; yet the Father "after He had taken unto Himself our flesh, raised it to the nature of deity, by bringing it into union with Himself, and made it one, so that Father and Son must be styled one God."[2] This is, indeed, far from logical or clear. One cannot blame Hippolytus or Sabellius for not liking it. Yet it was a compromise which recognized a pre-existent Logos in Christ, even if it identified that Logos with the Father; it insisted on the identity of that which indwelt Jesus with God; and it claimed a human Jesus, raised to divinity by the Father, and made one with Him, thus really showing a distinction between the Father and the Son, while denying in words that one exists. This compromise won the majority in Rome, and opened the door for the full victory of the Logos Christology there. That victory was determined by the able exposition of that Christology which came at the turning-point in this conflict (213–218) from the pen of Tertullian of Carthage—*Against Praxeas* (see *ante*, p. 69), with its clear definitions of a Trinity in three persons and of a distinction between the divine and human in Christ.

How completely this Christology won its way in Western Christendom is shown by the treatise on the *Trinity*, written by the Roman presbyter, Novatian, between 240 and 250. That eminent scholar was the first in the local Roman communion to use Latin rather than Greek. His quarrel with the dominant party in the church will be described later (p. 102). Novatian did little more than reproduce and expand Tertullian's views. But it is important that he treated this exposition as the only normal and legitimate interpretation of the "rule of truth"—the

---

[1] Hippolytus, *Refutation.* 9[6].   [2] *Ibid.*, 9[7].

"Apostles' Creed." That symbol had been silent regarding the
Logos Christology. To Novatian the Logos Christology is its
only proper meaning. Between Father and Son a "communion
of substance" exists.[1] The Latin equivalent of the later famous
Nicene Homoousion—ὁμοούσιον—was therefore current in Rome
before 250. Novatian has even a social Trinity. Comment-
ing on *John* 10[30], "I and the Father are one," he declares that
Christ "said one thing (*unum*). Let the heretics understand
that He did not say one person. For one placed in the neuter
intimates the social concord, not the personal unity." [2] The
most valuable thing in Novatian is that he emphasized what
was the heart of the conviction of the church in all this involved
Christological controversy, that Christ was fully God and
equally fully man.[3] Finally, about 262, the Roman bishop,
Dionysius (259–268), writing against the Sabellians, expressed
the Logos Christology in terms more nearly approximating to
what was to be the Nicene decision of 325 than any other third-
century theologian.[4] Thus the West had reached conclusions
readily harmonizable with the result at Nicæa, more than
sixty years before that great council. The East had attained
no such uniformity.

SECTION IX.   THE ALEXANDRIAN SCHOOL

Alexandria was, for more than six centuries, the second city
of the ancient world, surpassed only by Rome, and later by Constantinople, in importance. Founded by Alexander the Great
in B. C. 332, it was primarily a trading community, and as
such, attracted numbers of Greeks and Jews. Its intellectual
life was no less remarkable. Its library was the most famous
in the empire. In its streets East and West met. There Greek
philosophy entered into association, or competed in rivalry,
with Judaism and many other Oriental cults, while the influence
of ancient Egyptian thought persisted. It was the most
cosmopolitan city of the ancient world. There the Old Testament was translated into Greek, and there Philo reinterpreted
Judaism in terms of Hellenic philosophy. There Neo-Platonism
was to arise in the third century of our era. Of the introduction of Christianity into Alexandria, or into Egypt generally,

[1] *Trinity*, 31.   [2] *Ibid.*, 27.
[3] *Ibid.*, 11. 24.   [4] In Athanasius, *De Decretis*, 26.

nothing is known, but it must have been early, since when the veil of silence was lifted Christianity was evidently strongly rooted there. The Gnostic, Basilides, taught in Alexandria in the reign of Hadrian (117–138). There the various philosophical systems had their "schools," where instruction could be obtained by all inquirers, and it was but natural that Christian teachers should imitate this good example, though it would appear that the beginnings of this work were independent of the Alexandrian Church authorities.

By about 185 a famous catechetical school existed in Alexandria, then under the leadership of a converted Stoic philosopher, Pantænus. Whether it originated with him, or what his own theological position may have been, it is impossible to determine. With Clement of Alexandria (?–c. 215), Pantænus's pupil and successor, it comes into the light. The course of religious development in Alexandria had evidently differed from that in Asia Minor and the West. In the latter regions the contest with Gnosticism had bred a distrust of philosophy such that Tertullian could declare that there was no possible connection between it and Christianity. That contest had, also, immensely strengthened the appeal to apostolical tradition and consolidated organization. In Alexandria these characteristics of the "Old Catholic" Church had not so fully developed, while philosophy was regarded not as inconsistent with Christianity, but as its handmaid. Here a union of what was best in ancient philosophy, chiefly Platonism and Stoicism, was effected to a degree nowhere else realized in orthodox circles, and the result was a Christian Gnosticism. Clement of Alexandria was typical of this movement. At the same time he was a presbyter in the Alexandrian Church, thus serving as a connecting-link between the church and the school.

The more important of the works of Clement which have survived are three: his *Exhortation to the Heathen*, an apologetic treatise, giving incidentally no little information as to the mystery religions; his *Instructor*, the first treatise on Christian conduct, and an invaluable mine of information as to the customs of the age; and his *Stromata, or Miscellanies*, a collection of profound thoughts on religion and theology, arranged without much regard to system. Throughout he shows the mind of a highly trained and widely read thinker. Clement would interpret Christianity as Philo did Judaism, by philosophy, into scientific dogmatics. To him, as to Justin, whom he far surpassed in clearness of intellectual grasp, the divine Logos has always been the source of all the intelligence and morality of the human race—the teacher of mankind everywhere. "Our instructor is the holy God, Jesus, the Word who is the guide of all humanity."[1] He was the source of all true philosophy. "God is the cause of all good things; but of some primarily, as of the Old and the New Testament; and of others by consequence, as of philosophy. Perchance, too, philosophy was given to the Greeks directly and primarily, till the Lord should call the Greeks. For this was a schoolmaster to bring the Hellenic mind, as the law the Hebrews, to Christ."[2]

This training of humanity by the Logos has been, therefore, a progressive education. So it is, also, in the church. "Faith," that is simple, traditional Christianity, is enough for salvation; but the man who adds to his faith "knowledge," has a higher possession.[3] He is the true, Christian Gnostic. "To him that hath shall be given; to faith, knowledge; to knowledge, love; and to love, the inheritance."[4] The highest good to which knowledge leads—a good even greater than the salvation which it necessarily involves—is the knowledge of God. "Could we then suppose any one proposing to the Gnostic whether he would choose the knowledge of God or everlasting salvation; and if these, which are entirely identical, were separable, he would without the least hesitation choose the knowledge of God."[5] That highest good brings with it an almost Stoic absence of feeling, either of pleasure or of pain—a condition of blessedness in which Clement believes Christ stood, and to which the Apostles attained through His teaching.[6] One can readily comprehend that Clement, like Justin, had no real interest in the earthly life of Jesus. The Logos then became incarnate, indeed, but Clement's view of Christ's life is almost Docetic, certainly more so than that of any teacher of orthodox standing in the church of his own day.

Clement wrought out no complete theological system. That was to be the task of his even more celebrated pupil and successor in the headship of the Alexandrian catechetical school—Origen. Born of Christian parentage, probably in Alexandria, between 182 and 185, Origen grew up there into a

---

[1] *Instructor*, 1[7].   [2] *Stromata*, 1[5]; Ayer, p. 190.   [3] *Ibid.*, 1[6].
[4] *Ibid.*, 7[10].   [5] *Ibid.*, 4[22].   [6] *Ibid.*, 6[9].

familiarity with the Scriptures that was to render him the most fully acquainted with the Bible of any of the writers in the early church. His study of philosophy must also have been early begun. A youth of intense feeling and eager mental curiosity, he was as remarkable for his precocity as for the later ripeness of his scholarship. The persecution under Septimius Severus, in 202, cost the life of Origen's father, and he would have shared the same fate had not his mother frustrated his wishes by a stratagem. This persecution had driven Origen's teacher, Clement, from the city; and now, in 203, in spite of his youth, he gathered round himself inquirers with whom he reconstituted the catechetical school. This position he held with great success and with the approval of Bishop Demetrius, till 215, when the Emperor Caracalla drove all teachers of philosophy from Alexandria. His instruction had before been interrupted by visits to Rome (c. 211–212), where he met Hippolytus, and to Arabia (c. 213–214). His manner of life was ascetic in the extreme, and to avoid slander arising out of his relations with his numerous inquirers he emasculated himself, taking *Matt.* 19¹² as a counsel of perfection. The year 215 saw Origen in Cæsarea in Palestine, where he made friends of permanent value. Permitted to return to Alexandria, probably in 216, he resumed his instruction, and began a period of scholarly productivity the results of which were little short of marvellous.

Origen's labors in Alexandria were broken by a journey to Greece and Palestine in 230 or 231. He was still a layman; but, by friendly Palestinian bishops he was ordained a presbyter, in Cæsarea, probably that he might be free to preach. This ordination of an Alexandrian layman, Bishop Demetrius of Alexandria not unnaturally viewed as an intrusion on his jurisdiction, and jealousy of the successful teacher may have added to his resentment. At all events, Demetrius held synods by which Origen was banished from Alexandria, and as far as was in their power, deposed from the ministry. He now found a congenial home in friendly Cæsarea. Here he continued his indefatigable studies, his teaching, and to them he added frequent preaching. He made occasional journeys. He was surrounded by friends who held him in the highest esteem. With the great Decian persecution (see p. 86) of 250, this period of peace ended. He was imprisoned and tortured, and died either in Cæsarea or Tyre, probably in 251 (254?) as a consequence of the cruelties he had undergone. No man of purer spirit or nobler aims ornaments the history of the ancient church.

Origen was a man of many-sided scholarship. The field to which he devoted most attention was that of Biblical text-criticism and exegesis. Here his chief productions were his monumental _Hexapla_, giving the Hebrew and four parallel Greek translations of the Old Testament; and a long series of commentaries and briefer notes treating nearly the entire range of Scripture. It was the most valuable work that had yet been done by any Christian scholar. In the field of theology his _De Principiis_, written before 231, was not merely the first great systematic presentation of Christianity, but its thoughts and methods thenceforth controlled Greek dogmatic development. His _Against Celsus_, written between 246 and 248, in reply to the ablest criticism of Christianity that heathenism had produced—that of the Platonist Celsus (c. 177)—was the keenest and most convincing defense of the Christian faith that the ancient world brought forth, and one fully worthy of the greatness of the controversy. Besides these monumental undertakings he found time for the discussion of practical Christian themes, such as prayer and martyrdom, and for the preparation of many sermons. His was indeed a life of unwearied industry.

In Origen the process was complete which had long been interpreting Christian truths in terms of Hellenic thinking. He gave to the Christian system the fullest scientific standing, as tested by the science of that age, which was almost entirely comprised in philosophy and ethics. His philosophic standpoint was essentially Platonic and Stoic, with a decided leaning toward positions similar to those of the rising Neo-Platonism, the lectures of whose founder, Ammonius Saccas, he is said to have heard.[1] These philosophic principles he sought to bring into harmony with the Scriptures, as his great Hebrew fellow townsman, Philo, had done, by allegorical interpretation of the Bible. All normal Scripture, he held, has a threefold meaning. "The simple man may be edified by the 'flesh' as it were of the Scriptures, for so we name the obvious sense; while he who has ascended a certain way may be edified by the 'soul' as it were; the perfect man . . . may receive edifi-

[1] Eusebius, _Church History_, 6:19[6].

cation from the spiritual law, which has a shadow of good
things to come. For as man consists of body and soul and
spirit, so in the same way does Scripture."[1] This allegorical
system enabled Origen to read practically what he wished into
the Scriptures.

As a necessary foundation for his theological system, Origen
posited that "which differs in no respect from ecclesiastical
and apostolical tradition."[2] These fundamentals of traditional Christianity include belief (1) "in one God . . . the
Father of our Lord Jesus Christ, [who] Himself gave the law
and the prophets and the Gospels, being also the God of the
Apostles and of the Old and New Testaments"; (2) "that Jesus
Christ Himself . . . was born of the Father before all creatures
. . . became a man, and was incarnate although God, and
while made a man remained the God which He was . . . was
born of a Virgin . . . was truly born and did truly suffer and
. . . did truly die . . . did truly rise from the dead"; (3) "that
the Holy Spirit was associated in honor and dignity with the
Father and the Son"; (4) in the resurrection and in future rewards and punishments; (5) in free will; (6) in the existence
and opposition of the devil and his angels; (7) that the world
was made in time and will "be destroyed on account of its
wickedness"; (8) "that the Scriptures were written by the Spirit
of God"; (9) "that there are certain angels of God, and certain good influences which are His servants in accomplishing the
salvation of men."[3] These are essential beliefs for all Christians, learned and unlearned, as taught by the church; and on
them Origen proceeded to erect his mighty fabric of systematic
theology—that explanation of Christianity for him who would
add to his faith knowledge.

Origen's conception of the universe was strongly Platonic.
The real world is the spiritual reality behind this temporary,
phenomenal, visible world. In that world great transactions
have had their place. There, as with Plato, our spirits existed.
There sin first entered. There we fell, and thither the redeemed
will return. God, the uncreated, perfect Spirit, is the source of
all. From Him the Son is eternally generated. "His generation
is as eternal and everlasting as the brilliancy which is produced
from the sun."[4] Yet Christ is "a second God."[5] a "crea-

---

[1] *De Principiis*, 4 : 1[11]; Ayer, pp. 200, 201.   [2] *De Principiis*, Preface.
[3] All *ibid.*   [4] *De Principiis*, 1 : 2[4].   [5] *Celsus*. 5[39].

ture." Christ's position, as Loofs has pointed out, was viewed by Origen as the same as that of the *nous*—mind, thought—in the Neo-Platonic system. He is the "mediator" between God and His world of creatures, the being through whom they were made. Highest of these creatures is the Holy Spirit, whom Origen reckons to the Godhead, by reason of churchly tradition, but for whom he has no real necessity in his system.

All spiritual beings, including the spirits of men, were made by God, through the Son, in the true spiritual world. "He had no other reason for creating them than on account of Himself, *i. e.* His own goodness." [1] All were good, though their goodness, unlike that of God, was "an accidental and perishable quality." [2] All had free will. Hence some fell by sin in the invisible spiritual world. It was as a place of punishment and of reform that God created this visible universe, placing fallen spirits therein in proportion to the heinousness of their sins. The least sinful are angels and have as bodies the stars. Those of greater sinfulness are on the face of the earth, with animal souls, also, and mortal bodies. They constitute mankind. The worst are the demons, led by the devil himself.

Salvation was wrought by the Logos-Son becoming man, by uniting with a human soul that had not sinned in its previous existence and a pure body. While here Christ was God and man; but at the resurrection and ascension Christ's humanity was given the glory of His divinity, and is no longer human but divine. [3] That transformation Christ effects for all His disciples. "From Him there began the union of the divine with the human nature, in order that the human, by communion with the divine, might rise to be divine, not in Jesus alone, but in all those who not only believe but enter upon the life which Jesus taught." [4] Origen, more than any theologian since Paul, emphasized the sacrificial character of Christ's death; but he interpreted it in many ways, some of which were not very consistent with others. Christ suffered what was "for the good of the human race" as a representative and an example. [5] He was in some sense a propitiatory offering to God. He was a ransom paid to the powers of evil. [6] He conquered the demons. [7] He frustrated their expectation that they could hold

---

[1] *De Principiis*, 2 : 9[6].   [2] *Ibid.*, 1 : 6[2].   [3] *Celsus*, 3[41].
[4] *Ibid.*, 3[28]   [5] *Ibid.*, 7[17]; Ayer, p. 197.
[6] *Com. on Matt.*, 12[28], 16[8]; Ayer, p. 197.   [7] *Com. on John*, 6[37].

Him by the bonds of death and brought their kingdom to an end.[1] Those of mankind who are His disciples are received at death into Paradise; the evil find their place in hell. Yet, ultimately, not only all men, but even the devil and all spirits with him will be saved.[2] This will be the restoration of all things, when God will be all in all.

Origen's theological structure is the greatest intellectual achievement of the ante-Nicene Church. It influenced profoundly all after-thinking in the Orient. Yet it is easy to see how he could be quoted on either side in the later Christological controversies, and to understand, in the light of a later rigid orthodoxy, how he came to be regarded as a heretic, whose views were condemned by a synod in his native Alexandria in 399 or 400, by the Emperor Justinian in 543, and by the Fifth General Council in 553. His work was professedly for the learned, not for the common Christian. Because its science is not our science it seems strange to us. But it gave to Christianity full scientific standing in that age. In particular, the teachings of Clement and Origen greatly advanced the dominance of the Logos Christology in the Orient, though Sabellianism was still wide-spread there, and an adoptionist Christology had an eminent representative in the bishop of Antioch, Paul of Samosata, as late as 272.

Yet Origen was not without serious critics in the century in which he lived. Of these the most important, theologically, was Methodius, bishop of Olympus, in Lycia, who died about 311. Taking his stand on the tradition of Asia Minor, Methodius denied Origen's doctrines of the soul's pre-existence and imprisonment in this world, and affirmed the resurrection of the body. In ability he was not to be compared with Origen.

SECTION X. CHURCH AND STATE FROM 180 TO 260

The visible decline of the Roman Empire is usually reckoned from the death of Marcus Aurelius (180), though its causes go back much further. Population was diminishing. Trade and industry were fettered by heavy taxation. The leadership passed more and more from the hands of the cultivated classes. The army was largely recruited from the outlying provinces of the empire, and even from tribes beyond its borders. From the

---

[1] *Com. on Matt.*, 13⁹.   [2] *De Principiis*, 1 : 6¹⁻⁴; Ayer, p. 198.

death of Commodus (192), it dictated the choice of Emperors, who, in general, were very far from representing the higher type of Græco-Roman culture, as had the Antonines. The whole administrative machinery of the empire was increasingly inefficient, and the defense of its borders inadequate. From a military point of view, conditions grew steadily worse till the time of Aurelian (270–275), and were hardly securely bettered till that of Diocletian (284–305). In other respects no considerable pause was achieved in the decline. Yet this period was also one of increasing feeling of popular unity in the empire. The lines of distinction between the races were breaking down. In 212 the Roman citizenship was extended by Caracalla, not wholly from disinterested motives, to all free inhabitants of the empire. Above all, from a religious point of view, the close of the second and the whole of the third centuries were an age of syncretism, a period of deepening religious feeling, in which the mystery religions of the Orient—and Christianity also—made exceedingly rapid increase in the number of their adherents.

This growth of the church was extensive as well as intensive. To near the close of the second century it had penetrated little beyond those whose ordinary tongue was Greek. By the dawn of the third century the church was rapidly advancing in Latin-speaking North Africa and, though more slowly, in Spain and Gaul, and reaching toward, if it had not already arrived in, Britain. In Egypt Christianity was now penetrating the native population, while by 190 it was well represented in Syriac-speaking Edessa. The church was also reaching more extensively than earlier into the higher classes of society. It was being better understood; and though Tertullian shows that the old popular slanders of cannibalism and gross immorality were still prevalent in 197,[1] as the third century went on they seem to have much decreased, doubtless through growing acquaintance with the real significance of Christianity.

The relations of the state to the church during the period from 180 to 260 were most various, depending on the will of the several Emperors, but, on the whole, such as to aid rather than to hinder its growth till the last decade of this period. Legally, Christianity was condemned. It had no right to exist.[2] Practically, it enjoyed a considerable degree of tolera-

---

[1] Apology, 7.   [2] Tertullian, Apology, 4.

tion during most of this epoch. The persecution which had been begun under Marcus Aurelius continued into the reign of Commodus, but he soon neglected the church as he did about everything else not connected with his own pleasures. This rest continued till well into the reign of Septimius Severus (193–211); but was broken in 202 by a persecution of considerable severity, especially in Carthage and Egypt. Under Caracalla (211–217), persecution again raged in North Africa. Elagabalus (218–222), though an ardent supporter of sun-worship, was disposed to a syncretism which was not openly hostile to Christianity. Alexander Severus (222–235) was distinctly favorable. A syncretist who would unite many religions, he placed a bust of Christ in his private chapel along with images of leaders of other faiths; while his mother, Julia Mamæa, under whose influence he stood, heard lectures by Origen. He even decided a dispute as to whether a piece of property in Rome should be used by its Christian claimants, doubtless as a place of worship, or by their opponents as a cook-shop, in favor of the Christians. A change of policy came under Maximinus (235–238), by whom an edict against the Christians was issued, which, though not extensively enforced, thrust both the "Catholic" bishop, Pontianus, and his schismatic rival Hippolytus from Rome into the cruel slavery of the mines, where they soon lost their lives. In eastern Asia Minor and Palestine this persecution made itself felt. Under Gordian (238–244) and till near the end of the reign of Philip the Arabian (244–249) the church had rest. For that new outbreak Philip was in no way responsible. Indeed, an erroneous rumor declared him to be secretly a Christian. The number of martyrs in these persecutions was not large, as Origen testified, writing between 246 and 248,[1] and these outbreaks were local, if at times of considerable extent. Though Christians were deprived of all legal protection, the average believer must have thought that the condition of the church was approaching practical safety.

This growing feeling of security was rudely dispelled. The year 248 saw the celebration of the thousandth anniversary of the founding of Rome. It was a time of revival of ancient traditions and of the memories of former splendors. The empire was never more threatened by barbarian attack or torn

---

[1] *Celsus*, 3[8].

by internal disputes. The populace attributed these troubles to the cessation of persecution.[1] A fierce mob attack broke out in Alexandria before the death of Philip the Arabian. To the more observant heathens the growth of a rigidly organized church might well seem that of a state within the state, the more dangerous that Christians still largely refused army service or the duties of public office.[2] Nearer at hand lay the plausible, though fallacious, argument that as Rome had grown great when the old gods were worshipped by all, so now their rejection by a portion of the population had cost Rome their aid, and had caused the calamities evident on every hand. This was apparently the feeling of the new Emperor, Decius (249–251), and of a conservative Roman noble, Valerian, with whom Decius was intimately associated. The result was the edict of 250, which initiated the first universal and systematic persecution of Christianity.

The Decian persecution was by far the worst trial that the church as a whole had undergone—the more severe because it had principle and determination behind it. The aim was not primarily to take life, though there were numerous and cruel martyrdoms, but rather to compel Christians by torture, imprisonment, or fear to sacrifice to the old gods. Bishops Fabian of Rome and Babylas of Antioch died as martyrs. Origen and hosts of others were tortured. The number of these "confessors" was very great. So, also, was the number of the "lapsed"—that is, of those who, through fear or torture, sacrificed, burned incense, or procured certificates from friendly or venal officials that they had duly worshipped in the form prescribed by the state.[3] Many of these lapsed, when the persecution was over, returned to seek in bitter penitence readmission to the church. The question of their treatment caused a long, enduring schism in Rome, and much trouble elsewhere (see p. 101). Fierce as it was, the persecution under Decius and Valerian was soon over; but only to be renewed in somewhat milder form by Decius's successor, Gallus (251–253). In 253 Decius's old associate in persecution, Valerian, obtained possession of the empire (253–260). Though he at first left the Christians undisturbed, in 257 and 258 he renewed the attack with greater ferocity. Christian assemblies were forbid-

---

[1] Origen, *Celsus*, 3[15]; Ayer, p. 206. [2] Origen, *Celsus*, 8[73, 75].
[3] Ayer, p. 210, for specimens.

den; Christian churches and cemeteries confiscated; bishops, priests, and deacons ordered to be executed, and lay Christians in high places disgraced, banished, and their goods held forfeited.   Under this persecution Cyprian died in Carthage, Bishop Sixtus II and the Deacon Laurentius in Rome, and Bishop Fructuosus in Tarragona in Spain. It was a fearful period of trial, lasting, with intermissions indeed, from 250 to 259.

In 260 Valerian became a prisoner in the hands of the victorious Persians.   His son, associate Emperor and successor, Gallienus (260–268), a thoroughly weak and incompetent ruler, promptly gave up the struggle with Christianity. Church property was returned, and a degree of favor shown that has sometimes, though erroneously, been interpreted as a legal toleration.   That the act of Gallienus was not.   The old laws against Christianity were unrepealed.   Practically, however, a peace began which was to last till the outbreak of the persecution under Diocletian, in 303, though probably threatened by Aurelian just before his death in 275.   The church had come out of the struggle stronger than ever before.

SECTION XI.   THE CONSTITUTIONAL DEVELOPMENT OF THE CHURCH

The effect of the struggle with Gnosticism and Montanism upon the development of the bishoprics as centres of unity, witnesses to apostolical tradition, and bearers of an apostolical succession, has already been seen (Section IV).   The tendencies then developed continued to work in increasing power, with the result that, between 200 and 260, the church as an organization took on most of the constitutional features which were to characterize it throughout the period of the dominance of Græco-Roman culture.   Above all, this development was manifested in the increase of the power of the bishops.   The circumstances of the time, the contests with Gnostics and Montanists, the leadership of increasing masses of ignorant recent converts from heathenism, the necessities of uniformity in worship and discipline, all tended to centralize in the bishop the rights and authority which, in the first half of the second century had been the possession of the Christian congregation as a whole.   The "gifts of the Spirit," which had been very real to the thought of Christians of the apostolic and sub-apostolic ages, and which might be possessed by any one, were now a tradition rather than a vital reality. The contest with Montanism, among other causes, had led such claims to be regarded with suspicion. The tradition, however, remained, but it was rapidly changing into a theory of official endowment. These "gifts" were now the official possession of the clergy, especially of the bishops. The bishops were the divinely appointed guardians of the deposit of the faith, and therefore those who could determine what was heresy. They were the leaders of worship—a matter of constantly increasing importance with the growing conviction, wide-spread by the beginning of the third century, that the ministry is a priesthood. They were the disciplinary officers of the congregation—though their authority in this respect was not firmly fixed—able to say when the sinner needed excommunication and when he showed sufficient repentance for restoration. As given full expression by Cyprian of Carthage, about 250 (*ante*, p. 70), the foundation of the church is the unity of the bishops.

The Christians of a particular city had been regarded, certainly from the beginning of the second century, as constituting a single community, whether meeting in one congregation or many. As such they were under the guidance of a single bishop. Ancient civilization was strongly urban in its political constitution. The adjacent country district looked to its neighboring city. Christianity had been planted in the cities. By efforts going out from them, congregations were formed in the surrounding villages, which came at first into the city for their worship;[1] but as they grew larger must increasingly have met by themselves. Planted by Christians from the cities, they were under the oversight of the city bishop, whose immediate field of superintendence was thus growing, by the third century, into a diocese. In some rural portions of the East, notably Syria and Asia Minor, where city influence was relatively weak, country groups of congregations developed before the end of the third century, headed by a rural bishop, a *chorepiskopos* —χωρεπίσκοπος—but this system was not of large growth, nor were these country bishops deemed the equals in dignity of their city brethren. The system did not spread to the West at this time, though introduced there in the Middle Ages, only to prove unsatisfactory.

[1] Justin, *Apology*, 67; Ayer, p. 35.

To Cyprian, the episcopate was a unit, and each bishop a representative of all its powers, on an equality with all other bishops. Yet even in his time this theory was becoming impracticable. The bishops of the great, politically influential cities of the empire were attaining a superiority in dignity over others, which those of Rome even more than the rest were striving to translate into a superiority of jurisdiction. Rome, Alexandria, Antioch, Carthage, and Ephesus, with Jerusalem by reason of religious sentiment, had an outstanding eminence, and Rome most of all. Besides these greater posts, the bishop of the capital city of each province was beginning to be looked upon as having a certain superiority to those of lesser towns in his region; but the full development of the metropolitan dignity was not to come till the fourth century, and earlier in the East than in the West.

By the beginning of the third century clergy were sharply distinguished from laity. The technical use of the words *laikos* —λαικός—and *kleros*—κλῆρος—was a gradual development, as was the distinction which they implied. The earliest Christian employment of the former was by Clement of Rome.[1] The latter occurs in 1 *Peter* 5³, in wholly untechnical usage. But κλῆρος and its Latin equivalent, *ordo*, were the common expressions for the "orders" of magistrates and dignitaries of the Roman Empire. It is probably from such popular usage that they come into Christian employment. The letter of the churches of Lyons and Vienne, giving a description of the persecution of 177, spoke of the "order" of the martyrs—κλῆρον.[2] Tertullian wrote of "clerical order" and "ecclesiastical orders."[3] By his time the distinction had become practically fixed; even if Tertullian himself could recall, for purposes of argument, the early doctrine of the priesthood of all believers,[4] "are not even we laics priests?"[5]

Admission to clerical office was by ordination, a rite which certainly goes back to the earliest days of the church, at least as a sign of the bestowal of charismatic gifts, or separation for a special duty.[6] The ordinary process of the choice of a bishop by the middle of the third century was a nomination

[1] 93–97; in 1 *Clem.*, 40. [2] Eusebius, *Church History*, 5:1¹⁰.
[3] *Monogamy*, 12. [4] *Chastity*, 7.
[5] Compare 1 *Peter* 2⁵; *Rev.* 1⁶.
[6] *Acts* 6⁶, 13³; also 1 *Tim.* 4¹⁴, 5²²; 2 *Tim.* 1⁶.

by the other clergy, especially the presbyters, of the city; the approval of neighboring bishops, and ratification or election by the congregation.[1] Ordination followed at the hands of at least one already a bishop—a number of episcopal ordainers which had become fixed at a normal minimum of three by the end of the third century. The control of the choice of the presbyters, deacons, and lower clergy lay in the hand of their local bishop, by whom they were ordained.[2] The presbyters were the bishop's advisers. With his consent they administered the sacraments.[3] They preached. As congregations grew more numerous in a city, a presbyter would be placed in immediate charge of each, and their importance thereby enhanced, from its relative depression, immediately after the rise of the monarchical episcopate. There was no fixed limit to their number. The deacons were immediately responsible to the bishop, and were his assistants in the care of the poor and other financial concerns, in aiding in the worship and discipline. They often stood in closer practical relations to him than the presbyters. At Rome, the number of the deacons was seven, in remembrance of *Acts* 6[5]. When Bishop Fabian (236–250) adopted the civil division of the city as its fourteen charity districts, he appointed seven sub-deacons in addition to the seven deacons, that the primitive number might not be surpassed. Sub-deacons also existed in Carthage in the time of Cyprian, and quite generally at a little later period. In many parts of the church there was no fixed rule as to the number of deacons.

Bishops, presbyters, and deacons constituted the major orders. Below them there stood in the first half of the third century, the minor orders. In the general absence of all statistical information as to the early church, a letter of Bishop Cornelius of Rome, written about 251, is of high value as showing conditions in that important church. Under the single bishop in Rome there were forty-six presbyters and seven deacons. Below them, constituting what were soon to be known as the minor orders, were seven sub-deacons, forty-two acolytes. and fifty-two exorcists, readers, and janitors.[4] More

---

[1] Cyprian, *Letters*, 51–55[8] 66–68[2]. 67[4. 5]
[2] *Ibid.*, 23–29, 33–39[5], 34–40.
[3] Tertullian, *Baptism*, 17; Ayer, p. 16[1].
[4] Eusebius, *Church History*, 6 : 43[11].

than fifteen hundred dependents were supported by the church, which may have included thirty thousand adherents. Some of these offices were of very ancient origin. Those of readers and exorcists had originally been regarded as charismatic. Exorcists continued to be so viewed in the Orient, and were not there properly officers. By the time of Cyprian the reader's office was thought a preparatory step toward that of presbyter.[1] The exorcist's task was to drive out evil spirits, in whose prevalent working the age firmly believed. Of the duties of acolytes little is known save that they were assistants in service and aid. They were not to be found in the Orient. The janitors were especially important when it became the custom to admit none but the baptized to the more sacred parts of the service. In the East, though not in the West, deaconesses were to be found who were reckoned in a certain sense as of the clergy. Their origin was probably charismatic and was of high antiquity.[2] Their tasks were those of care for women, especially the ill. Besides these deaconesses there were to be found in the churches, both East and West, a class known as "widows," whose origin was likewise ancient.[3] Their duties were prayer and aid to the sick, especially of their own sex. They were held in high honor, though hardly to be reckoned properly as of the "clergy." All these were supported, in whole or in part, by the gifts of the congregation, which were of large amount, both of eatables and of money.[4] These gifts were looked upon, by the time of Cyprian, as "tithes," and were all at the disposal of the bishop.[5] By the middle of the third century the higher clergy were expected to give their whole time to the work of the ministry;[6] yet even bishops sometimes shared in secular business, not always of a commendable character. The lower clergy could still engage in trades. It is evident, however, that though the ancient doctrine of the priesthood of all believers might still occasionally be remembered, it had a purely theoretical value. In practical Christian life the clergy, by the middle of the third century were a distinct, close-knit spiritual rank, on whom the laity were religiously dependent, and who were in turn supported by laymen's gifts.

---

[1] *Letters*, 33[5].   [2] *Romans* 16[1].   [3] 1 *Tim.* 5[9, 10].

[4] *Teaching*, 13; Justin, *Apology*, 67; Tertullian, *Apology*, 39; Ayer, pp. 35, 41.

[5] *Letters*, 65-1[1].   [6] Cyprian, *Lapsed*, 6.

SECTION XII.   PUBLIC WORSHIP AND SACRED SEASONS

Already, by the time of Justin (153), the primitive division of worship into two assemblies, one for prayer and instruction and the other for the Lord's Supper in connection with a common meal had ceased. The Lord's Supper was now the crowning act of the service of worship and edification.[1] Its separation from the common meal was now complete. The course of development during the succeeding century was determined by the prevalence of ideas drawn from the mystery religions. There is no adequate ground to believe that there was intentional imitation. Christians of the last half of the second and the third centuries lived in an atmosphere highly charged with influences sprung from these faiths. It was but natural that they should look upon their own worship from the same point of view. It is probable that already existing tendencies in this direction were strongly reinforced by the great growth of the church by conversion from heathenism in the first half of the third century.

The church came to be more and more regarded as possessed of life-giving mysteries, under the superintendence and dispensation of the clergy. Inquirers were prepared for initiation by instruction—the catechumens. Such preparation, in some degree, had existed from the apostolic days. It was now systematized. Origen taught in an already celebrated school in Alexandria in 203. Cyprian shows that in Carthage, by about 250, such instruction was in charge of an officer designated by the bishop.[2] Instruction was followed by the great initiatory rite of baptism (see Section XIII), which granted admission to the propitiatory sacrifice of the life-giving mystery of the Lord's Supper (see Section XIV). As in the time of Justin, the other elements of worship consisted of Scripture reading, preaching, prayers, and hymns. These were open to all honest inquirers. The analogy of the mystery religions barred all but those initiate or about to be initiate from presence at baptism or the Lord's Supper, and led to a constant augmentation of the valuation placed on these rites as the most sacred elements of worship. Whether the custom had arisen by the third century of regarding these sacraments as a secret discipline, in which the exact words of the Creed and of the Lord's Prayer were for

[1] Justin, *Apology*, 67; Ayer, p. 35.   [2] *Letters*, 23–29.

the first time imparted to the baptized, and of which no mention was to be made to the profane, is uncertain. Such usages were wide-spread in the fourth and fifth centuries. Already in the third the forces were at work which were to lead to the practices.

Sunday was the chief occasion of worship, yet services were beginning to be held on week-days as well. Wednesday and Friday, as earlier (*ante*, p. 43), were days of fasting. The great event of the year was the Easter season. The period immediately before was one of fasting in commemoration of Christ's sufferings. Customs differed in various parts of the empire. In Rome a forty hours' fast and vigil was held in remembrance of Christ's rest in the grave. This was extended, by the time of the Council of Nicæa (325) to a forty days Lent. All fasting ended with the dawn of Easter morning, and the Pentecostal period of rejoicing then began. In that time there was no fasting, or kneeling in prayer in public worship.[1] Easter eve was the favorite season for baptism, that the newly initiate might participate in the Easter joy. Beside these fixed seasons, the martyrs were commemorated with celebration of the Lord's Supper annually on the days of their deaths.[2] Prayers for the dead in general, and their remembrance by offerings on the anniversaries of their decease, were in use by the early part of the third century.[3] Relics of martyrs had been held in high veneration since the middle of the second century.[4] The full development of saint-worship had not yet come; but the church was honoring with peculiar devotion the memory of the athletes of the Christian race who had not counted their lives dear unto themselves.

SECTION XIII.   BAPTISM

Baptism is older than Christianity. The rite gave to John, the "Forerunner," his name. He baptized Jesus. His disciples and those of Jesus baptized, though Jesus Himself did not.[5] The origin of the rite is uncertain; but it was probably

---

[1] Tertullian, *Corona*, 3.

[2] *Letter of the Church of Smyrna on Martyrdom of Polycarp*, 18; Cyprian, *Letters*, 33–39[3]; 36–12[2].

[3] Tertullian, *Corona*, 3; *Monogamy*, 10.

[4] *Letter of Smyrna*, as cited, 18.

[5] *John* 3[22], 4[1, 2].

a spiritualization of the old Levitical washings. Jewish teaching, traceable probably to a period as early as the time of Christ, required proselytes to the Hebrew faith not merely to be circumcised, but to be baptized.[1] It seems probable that John did not invent the rite, and simply used contemporary practice. It was a fitting symbol of the spiritual purification that followed the repentance that he preached. The mystery religions had equivalent rites (*ante*, p. 10); but so purely Jewish was that primitive Christianity to which baptism belongs, that it is inconceivable that they should have had any effect on the origin of the practice, though they were profoundly to influence its development on Gentile soil. Peter represents baptism as the rite of admission to the church, and to the reception of the Holy Spirit.[2] As the sacrament of admission baptism always stood till the religious divisions of post-Reformation days. It so stands for the vast majority of Christians at present.

With Paul, baptism was not merely the symbol of cleansing from sin,[3] it involved a new relation to Christ,[4] and a participation in His death and resurrection.[5] Though Paul apparently did not think baptism essential to salvation[6] his view approached that of the initiations of the mystery religions and his converts in Corinth, at least, held an almost magical conception of the rite, being baptized in behalf of their dead friends, that the departed might be benefited thereby.[7] Baptism soon came to be regarded as indispensable. The writer of the fourth Gospel represented Christ as declaring: "Verily, I say unto thee, except a man be born of water and the Spirit, he cannot enter the Kingdom of God."[8] The appendix to *Mark* pictured the risen Christ as saying: "He that believeth and is baptized shall be saved."[9] This conviction but deepened. To Hermas (115–140), baptism was the very foundation of the church, which "is builded upon waters."[10] Even to the philosophical Justin (153) baptism effected "regeneration" and "illumination."[11] In Tertullian's estimate it conveyed eternal life itself.[12]

---

[1] See Schürer, *Geschichte des Jüdischen Volkes*, 2[569-573].

[2] *Acts* 2[38]; see also 2[41]; 1 *Cor.* 12[13].   [3] 1 *Cor.* 6[11].   [4] *Gal.* 3[26, 27].

[5] *Romans* 6[4]; *Col.* 2[12].   [6] 1 *Cor.* 1[14-17].   [7] 1 *Cor.* 15[29].

[8] *John* 3[5].   [9] *Mark* 16[16].   [10] *Vis.*, 3[3].

[11] *Apology*, 61; Ayer, p. 33.   [12] *Baptism*, 1.

By the time of Hermas[1] and of Justin[2] the view was general that baptism washed away all previous sins. As in the mystery religions it had become the great rite of purification, initiation, and rebirth into the eternal life. Hence it could be received but once. The only substitute was martyrdom, "which stands in lieu of the fontal bathing, when that has not been received, and restores it when lost."[3] With the early disciples generally baptism was "in the name of Jesus Christ."[4] There is no mention of baptism in the name of the Trinity in the New Testament, except in the command attributed to Christ in *Matt.* 28[19]. That text is early, however. It underlies the Apostles' Creed, and the practice recorded in the *Teaching*,[5] and by Justin.[6] The Christian leaders of the third century retained the recognition of the earlier form, and, in Rome at least, baptism in the name of Christ was deemed valid, if irregular, certainly from the time of Bishop Stephen (254–257).[7]

Regarding persons baptized, the strong probability is that, till past the middle of the second century, they were those only of years of discretion. The first mention of infant baptism, and an obscure one, was about 185, by Irenæus.[8] Tertullian spoke distinctly of the practice, but discouraged it as so serious a step that delay of baptism was desirable till character was formed. Hence he doubted its wisdom for the unmarried.[9] Less earnest men than Tertullian felt that it was unwise to use so great an agency of pardon till one's record of sins was practically made up. A conspicuous instance, by no means solitary, was the Emperor Constantine, who postponed his baptism till his death-bed. To Origen infant baptism was an apostolic custom.[10] Cyprian favored its earliest possible reception.[11] Why infant baptism arose there is no certain evidence. Cyprian, in the letter just cited, argued in its favor from the doctrine of original sin. Yet the older general opinion seems to have held to the innocency of childhood.[12] More probable explanations are the feeling that outside the church there is no salvation, and the words attributed to Christ in *John* 3[5]. Christian par-

---

[1] *Man.*, 4[3].   [2] *Apology*, 61.   [3] Tertullian, *Baptism*, 16.
[4] *Acts* 2[38]; see also 8[16], 10[48], 19[5]; *Romans* 6[3]; *Gal.* 3[27].
[5] *Teaching*, 7; Ayer, p. 38.   [6] *Apology*, 61; Ayer, p. 33.
[7] Cyprian, *Letters*, 73–74[5].   [8] *Heresies*, 2:22[4].
[9] *Baptism*, 18.   [10] *Com. on Romans*, 5.
[11] *Letters*, 58–64[5].   [12] Tertullian, *Baptism*, 18.

ents would not have their children fail of entering the Kingdom of God. Infant baptism did not, however, become universal till the sixth century, largely through the feeling already noted in Tertullian, that so cleansing a sacrament should not be lightly used.

As to the method of baptism, it is probable that the original form was by immersion, complete or partial. That is implied in *Romans* 6[4] and *Colossians* 2[12]. Pictures in the catacombs would seem to indicate that the submersion was not always complete. The fullest early evidence is that of the *Teaching*: "Baptize in the name of the Father and of the Son and of the Holy Spirit in living [running] water. But if thou hast not living water, then baptize in other water; and if thou art not able in cold, then in warm. But if thou hast neither, then pour water upon the head thrice in the name of the Father and of the Son and of the Holy Spirit."[1] Affusion was, therefore, a recognized form of baptism. Cyprian cordially upheld it.[2] Immersion continued the prevailing practice till the late Middle Ages in the West; in the East it so remains. The *Teaching* and Justin show that fasting and an expression of belief, together with an agreement to live the Christian life were necessary prerequisites. By the time of Tertullian an elaborate ritual had developed. The ceremony began with the formal renunciation by the candidate of the devil and all his works. Then followed the threefold immersion. On coming from the fount the newly baptized tasted a mixture of milk and honey, in symbolism of his condition as a new-born babe in Christ. To that succeeded anointing with oil and the laying on of the hands of the baptizer in token of the reception of the Holy Spirit.[3] Baptism and what was later known as confirmation were thus combined. Tertullian also shows the earliest now known existence of Christian sponsors, *i. e.*, godparents.[4] The same customs of fasting and sponsors characterized the worship of Isis.

In the apostolic age baptism was administered doubtless not only by Apostles and other leaders, but widely by those charismatically eminent in the church. By 110–117 Ignatius, in the interest of unity, was urging, "it is not lawful apart

[1] 7; Ayer, p. 38.
[3] Tertullian, *Baptism*, 6–8; *Corona*. 3.
[2] *Letters*, 75–69[12].
[4] *Baptism*, 18.

from the bishop either to baptize or to hold a love-feast."[1] In Tertullian's time, "of giving it, the chief priest, who is the bishop, has the right; in the next place the presbyters and deacons . . . besides these even laymen have the right, for what is equally received can be equally given."[2] In the Greek and Roman Churches baptism still continues the only sacrament which any Christian, or indeed any seriously intending person, can administer in case of necessity.

The middle of the third century saw a heated discussion over the validity of heretical baptism. Tertullian had regarded it as worthless;[3] and his was undoubtedly the prevalent opinion of his time. After the Novatian schism (see p. 102) Bishop Stephen of Rome (254–257) advanced the claim that baptism, even by heretics, was effectual if done in proper form. His motives seem to have been partly the growing feeling that sacraments are of value in themselves, irrespective of the character of the administrant, and partly a desire to facilitate the return of the followers of Novatian. This interpretation was energetically resisted by Cyprian of Carthage, and Firmilian of Cæsarea in Cappadocia,[4] and led to certain important assertions of the authority of the Roman bishop. The deaths of Stephen and Cyprian gave a pause to the dispute; but the Roman view grew into general acceptance in the West. The East reached no such unanimity of judgment.

SECTION XIV. THE LORD'S SUPPER

Some account has been given of the early development of the doctrine of the Lord's Supper (*ante*, pp. 23, 40). It has been seen that "breaking of bread," in connection with a common meal, was a Christian practice from the beginning. From the time of Paul, certainly, it was believed to be by command of Christ Himself, and in peculiar remembrance of Him and of His death. Outside the New Testament three writers refer to the Lord's Supper before the age of Irenæus. Of these the account in the *Teaching*,[5] reflects the most primitive Christian conditions. It provides a simple liturgy of gratitude. Thou "didst bestow upon us spiritual food and drink and eternal life

---

[1] *Smyrna*, 8; Ayer, p. 42.
[2] *Baptism*, 17; Ayer, p. 167.
[3] *Baptism*, 15.
[4] Cyprian, *Letters*, 69–76.
[5] 9–11; Ayer, p. 38.

through Thy Son." From Christ come "life and knowledge."
A more mystical explanation of the Supper, however, began
early. *John* 6[47-58] teaches the necessity of eating the flesh and
drinking the blood of Christ to have "life." To Ignatius the
Supper "is the medicine of immortality, and the antidote that
we should not die but live forever." [1] Justin affirmed, "for
not as common bread and common drink do we receive these;
but in like manner as Jesus Christ our Saviour, having been
made flesh by the Word of God, had both flesh and blood for
our salvation, so likewise have we been taught that the food
which is blessed by the prayer of His Word, and from which
our blood and flesh by transmutation are nourished, is the flesh
and blood of that Jesus who was made flesh." [2] By Justin's
time (153) the Lord's Supper was already separated from the
common meal. Irenæus continued and developed the thought
of the fourth Gospel and of Ignatius that the Supper confers
"life." "For as the bread, which is produced from the earth,
when it receives the invocation of God, is no longer common
bread but the Eucharist, consisting of two realities, earthly and
heavenly; so also our bodies, when they receive the Eucharist,
are no longer corruptible, having the hope of the resurrection to eternity." [3] In how far these conceptions were due
to the mystery religions, with their teaching that sharing a
meal with the god is to become a partaker of the divine nature,
is difficult to decide; but they undoubtedly grew out of the
same habit of thought. It may be said that, by the middle
of the second century, the conception of a real presence of Christ
in the Supper was wide-spread. It was stronger in the West
than in the East, but ultimately it won its way also there.

In early Christian thought not only were believers themselves "a living sacrifice, holy, acceptable to God," [4] but all
actions of worship were sacrificial. The leaders of the church
"offered the gifts of the bishop's office." [5] All its membership
could "do good and communicate," "for with such sacrifices
God is well pleased." [6] In particular, the Lord's Supper was
a "sacrifice," [7] and this feeling was doubtless strengthened by
the circumstance that it was the occasion of the gifts of the

[1] *Eph.*, 20.
[2] *Apology*, 66; Ayer, p. 34.
[3] *Heresies*, 4: 18[5]; Ayer, pp. 138, 139.
[4] *Romans* 12[1].
[5] 1 *Clem.*, 44; Ayer, p. 37.
[6] *Heb.* 13:[6].
[7] *Teaching*, 14; Ayer, p. 41.

congregation for those in need.[1] As late a writer as Irenæus, while viewing the Lord's Supper as pre-eminently a "sacrifice," still held that all Christian actions are also of a sacrificial character.[2] Christianity, however, was in a world where sacrificial conceptions of a much more definite nature were familiar in the religions on every hand. Sacrifice demands a priest. With Tertullian the term *sacerdos* first comes into full use.[3]

With Cyprian the developed doctrine of the Lord's Supper as a sacrifice offered to God by a priest has been fully reached. "For if Jesus Christ, our Lord and God, is Himself the chief priest of God the Father, and has first offered Himself a sacrifice to the Father, and has commanded this to be done in commemoration of Himself, certainly that priest truly discharges the office of Christ, who imitates that which Christ did ; and he then offers a true and full sacrifice in the church when he proceeds to offer it according to what he sees Christ Himself to have offered." [4] The business of the Christian priest is "to serve the altar and to celebrate the divine sacrifices." [5] Already by Tertullian's time the Lord's Supper was held in commemoration of the dead.[6] Cyprian shows such "sacrifices" for martyrs.[7] The sense of the life-giving quality of the Supper led, also, to the custom of infant communion, of which Cyprian is a witness.[8] Here, as in the doctrine of Christ's physical presence, the conception of the Supper as a sacrifice to God was earlier in the West than in the East. It did not become general in the Orient much before 300. With it the "Catholic" conception of the Supper was evident as (*a*) a sacrament in which Christ is really present (the *how* of that presence was not to be much discussed till the Middle Ages), and in which the believer partakes of Christ, being thereby brought into union with Him and built up to the immortal life ; and (*b*) a sacrifice offered to God by a priest and inclining God to be gracious to the living and the dead. Much was still left obscure, but the essentials of the "Catholic" view were already at hand by 253.

---

[1] Justin, *Apology*, 67 ; Ayer, p. 35.
[2] *Heresies*, 4 : 17[5], 18[3].
[3] *Baptism*, 17 ; Ayer, p. 167.
[4] *Letters*, 62–63[14].
[5] *Ibid.*, 67[1].
[6] *Chastity*, 11.
[7] *Letters*, 33–39[3].
[8] *Lapsed*, 25.

SECTION XV.   FORGIVENESS OF SINS

The general view of early Christianity was that "if we confess our sins, He is faithful and righteous to forgive us our sins." [1]   But there were sins so bad that they could not be forgiven, they were "unto death." [2]   Just what this "sin unto death" might be, was uncertain.   It was one opinion that it was rejection of the Holy Spirit.   *Mark* represents Christ as saying: "Whosoever shall blaspheme against the Holy Spirit hath never forgiveness, but is guilty of an eternal sin" (3^{29}).   The *Teaching* held that "any prophet speaking in the Spirit, ye shall not try neither discern; for every sin shall be forgiven, but this sin shall not be forgiven." [3]   The general feeling was, however, that the unforgivable sins were idolatry or denial of the faith, murder, and gross licentiousness.   The first-named was specially hopeless.   No severer denunciations can be found in the New Testament than those directed by the writer of *Hebrews* toward such as "crucify to themselves the Son of God afresh" (6^{4-8}, 10^{26-31}).   To Tertullian the "deadly sins" were seven, "idolatry, blasphemy, murder, adultery, fornication, false-witness and fraud." [4]

While, by the time of Hermas (115–140), baptism was regarded as cleansing all previous sins, those committed after it, of the class just described, were "deadly."   But the tendency was toward some modification of this strictness.   The burden of Hermas was that, by exception, in view of the near end of the world, one further repentance had been granted after baptism. [5]   This extended even to adultery. [6]   Yet church practice was elsewhere milder, in the second century, than church theory.   Irenæus gives an account of the reclaiming of an adulteress, who "spent her whole time in the exercise of public confession." [7]   In Tertullian's time the feeling was that there was one repentance possible for deadly sins after baptism— "a second reserve of aid against hell"— "now once for all, because now for the second time, but never more." [8]   Restoration was to be, if at all, only after a humiliating public confession, an "exomologesis," "to feed prayers on fastings, to groan, to weep and make outcries unto the Lord your God; to bow

[1] 1 *John* 1^9.   [2] *Ibid.*, 5^{16}.   [3] 11; Ayer, p. 40.
[4] *Against Marcion*, 4^9.   [5] *Man.*, 4^3; Ayer, pp. 43, 44.
[6] *Ibid.*, 4^1.   [7] *Heresies*, 1 : 13^5.   [8] *Repentance*, 7, 12.

before the feet of the presbyters, and kneel to God's dear
ones." [1]   Yet practice was far from universally as rigorous as
Tertullian would imply.

The question inevitably arose as to when a sinner had done
enough to be restored.   The feeling appeared early that the
absolving power was divinely lodged in the congregation.[2]
This authority was also regarded as directly committed to
Peter, and, by implication, to church officers, when such developed.[3]   But, curiously, a double practice prevailed.   About to
be martyrs and confessors, *i. e.*, those who endured tortures
or imprisonment for their faith, were deemed also able to absolve because filled with the Spirit.[4]   This twofold authority
led to abuse.   Many of the confessors were lax.   Cyprian, in
particular, had trouble on this score.[5]   Naturally bishops tried
to repress this right of confessors; but it remained a popular
opinion till the cessation of persecution.   Absolution ultimately
raised the question of a scale of penance, a standard as to when
enough had been done to justify forgiveness, but that development is beyond the limits of the present period.   It is not to
be found till about 300.

These restorations, which were particularly of the licentious,[6]
were deemed exceptional, however common; and it came as
a shock, at least to a rigid Montanist ascetic like Tertullian,
when the aggressive Roman bishop, Kallistos (217–222), (*ante*,
p. 75), who had himself been a confessor, issued a declaration
in his own name, which is a landmark in the development of
papal authority, that he would absolve sins of the flesh on a
proper repentance.[7]   This was an *official* breach in the popular
list of "sins unto death," whatever actual breach earlier practice may have made.

In common judgment, denial of the faith was the worst of
these offenses, and not even Kallistos had promised pardon
for that.   The question was raised on a tremendous scale by
the Decian persecution.   Thousands lapsed and sought restoration after the storm was over.   In Rome, Bishop Fabian
died a martyr in 250.   The Roman Church was rent on the
question of their treatment.   A dispute beginning in personal
antipathies, not at first involving the lapsed, resulted in the

[1] *Repentance*, 9.   [2] *Matt.* 18[15-18].   [3] *Ibid.*, 16[18, 19].
[4] Tertullian, *Modesty*, 22.   [5] *Letters*, 17–26, 20–21, 21–22, 22–27.
[6] Tertullian, *Modesty*, 22.   [7] Tertullian, *Modesty*, 1.

choice by the majority of Cornelius, a comparative nobody, as bishop over Novatian, the most distinguished theologian in Rome (*ante*, p. 75). The minority supported Novatian. The majority soon advocated the milder treatment of the lapsed, while Novatian advanced to the rigorist position. Novatian began a schism that lasted till the seventh century, and founded protesting churches wide-spread in the empire. He renewed the older practice and denied restoration to all guilty of "sins unto death." His was a lost cause. Synods in Rome and Carthage in 251 and 253, representative of the majority, permitted the restoration of the lapsed, under strict conditions of penance. Though the question was to arise again in the persecution under Diocletian, which began in 303,[1] and though varied practice long continued in different parts of the church, the decision in Rome in 251 was ultimately regulative. All sins were thereby forgivable. The old distinction continued in name, but it was henceforth only between great sins and small.

SECTION XVI. THE COMPOSITION OF THE CHURCH AND THE HIGHER AND LOWER MORALITY

In apostolic times the church was undoubtedly conceived as composed exclusively of experiential Christians.[2] There were bad men who needed discipline in it,[3] but Paul could paint an ideal picture of the church as "not having spot or wrinkle or any such thing." [4] It was natural that this should be so. Christianity came as a new faith. Those who embraced it did so as a result of personal conviction, and at the cost of no little sacrifice. It was long the feeling that the church is a community of saved men and women. Even then, it was true that many were unworthy. This is Hermas's complaint. The oldest sermon outside the New Testament has a modern sound. "For the Gentiles when they hear from our mouth the oracles of God, marvel at them for their beauty and greatness; then, when they discover that our works are not worthy of the words which we speak, forthwith they betake themselves to blasphemy, saying that it is an idle story and a delusion." [5] Yet, in spite of the recognition of these facts the theory continued. But the

---

[1] The Melitian schism, Donatists.
[2] *Romans* 1⁷; 1 *Cor.* 1²; 2 *Cor.* 1¹; Col. 1².
[3] *E. g.,* 1 *Cor.* 5¹⁻¹³.   [4] *Eph.* 5²⁷.   [5] 2 *Clem.*, 13.

increasing age of Christianity forced a change of view. By the beginning of the third century there were many whose parents, possibly remoter ancestors, had been experiential Christians, but who, though they attended public worship, were Christians in little more than in name. What were they? They did not worship with the heathen. The public regarded them as Christians. Some of them had been baptized in infancy. Had the church a place for them? Their numbers were such that the church was compelled to feel that it had. Its own conception of itself was altering from that of a communion of saints to that of an agency for salvation. This change was evident in the teaching of Bishop Kallistos of Rome (217–222). He cited the parable of the tares and the wheat,[1] and compared the church to the ark of Noah in which were "things clean and unclean." [2] The earlier and later theories thus indicated divide the allegiance of modern Christendom to this day.

The rejection of the Montanists and the decay of the expectation of the speedy end of the world undoubtedly greatly favored the spread of worldliness in the church—a tendency much increased by its rapid growth from heathen converts between 202 and 250. As common Christian practice became less strenuous, however, asceticism grew as the ideal of the more serious. Too much must not be expected of common Christians. The *Teaching*, in the first half of the second century, had exhorted: "If thou art able to bear the whole yoke of the Lord, thou shalt be perfect; but if thou art not able, do that which thou art able" (6). Hermas (115–140) had taught that a man could do more than God commanded, and would receive a proportionate reward.[3] These tendencies but increased. They were, however, greatly furthered by a distinction between the "advice" and the requirements of the Gospel, which was clearly drawn by Tertullian[4] and Origen.[5]

While the requirements of Christianity are binding on all Christians, the advice is for those who would live the holier life. On two main phases of conduct the Gospel was thought to give such counsels of perfection. Christ said to the rich young man: "If thou wouldest be perfect, go, sell that thou hast, and give to the poor, and thou shalt have treasure in heaven." [6]

---

[1] *Matt.* 13[24-30].
[2] Hippolytus, *Refutation*, 9[7].
[3] *Sim.*, 5[2, 3].
[4] *To his Wife*. 2[1].
[5] *Com. on Romans*, 3[3].
[6] *Matt.* 19[21].

He also declared that some are "eunuchs for the kingdom of heaven's sake," and that, "in the resurrection they neither marry nor are given in marriage, but are as angels."[1] Paul said "to the unmarried and to widows, it is good for them if they abide even as I."[2] Voluntary poverty and voluntary celibacy were, therefore, deemed advice impossible of fulfilment by all Christians, indeed, but conferring special merit on those who practised them. About these two conceptions all early Christian asceticism centred, and they were to be the foundation stones of monasticism when that system arose at the close of the third century. As the clergy should set a specially good example, not only was second marriage discouraged from the sub-apostolic age;[3] but, by the beginning of the third century, marriage after entering on office was deemed unallowable.[4] The life of celibacy, poverty, and contemplative retirement from the activities of the world was admired as the Christian ideal, and was widely practised, though as yet without separation from society. The road to full monasticism had been fairly entered. Probably the most unfortunate aspect of this double ideal was that it tended to discourage the efforts of the ordinary Christian.

SECTION XVII. REST AND GROWTH, 260–303

The end of the period of persecution affected by the edict of Gallienus, in 260, was followed by more than forty years of practical peace. Legally, the church had no more protection than before, and the able Emperor Aurelian (270–275) is said to have intended a renewal of persecution when prevented by death. Even with him it apparently did not come to the proclamation of a new hostile edict. The chief feature of this epoch was the rapid growth of Christianity. By 300 Christianity was effectively represented in all parts of the empire. Its distribution was very unequal, but it was influential in the central provinces of political importance, in Asia Minor, Macedonia, Syria, Egypt, northern Africa, central Italy, southern Gaul and Spain. Nor was its upward progress in the social

---

[1] *Matt.*, 19[12], 22[30].   [2] 1 *Cor.* 7[8].

[3] 1 *Tim.* 3[2], see also Hermas, *Man.*, 4[4], against second marriage of Christians in general.

[4] Hippolytus, *Refutation*, 9[7].

scale less significant. During this period it won many officers
of government and imperial servants. Most important of all,
it began now to penetrate the army on a considerable scale.
As late as 246–248 the best that Origen could say in reply to
Celsus's criticism that Christians failed of their duty to the
state by refusal of army service, was that Christians did a
better thing by praying for the success of the Emperor.[1] Origen
also expresses and defends Christian unwillingness to assume
the burdens of governmental office.[2] Even then Christians had
long been found in the Roman armies;[3] but Origen undoubtedly voiced prevalent Christian feeling in the middle of the
third century. By its end both Christian feeling and practice
had largely changed.

This period of rapid growth was one of greatly increasing
conformity to worldly influences also. How far this sometimes
went a single illustration may show. The Council of Elvira,
now Granada, in Spain (c. 313), provided that Christians who
as magistrates wore the garments of heathen priesthood could
be restored after two years' penance, provided they had not
actually sacrificed or paid for sacrifice.[4]

As compared with the first half of the third century, its
latter portion was a period of little literary productivity or
theologic originality in Christian circles. No names of the
first rank appeared. The most eminent was that of Dionysius,
who held the bishopric of Alexandria (247–264), a pupil of Origen
and like him for a time head of the famous catechetical school.
Through his writings the influence of Origen was extended,
and the great theologian's thoughts were in general dominant
in that period in the East. Dionysius combated the wide-
spread Eastern Sabellianism. He also began the practice of
sending letters to his clergy, notifying them of the date of
Easter—a custom soon largely developed by the greater bishoprics, and made the vehicle of admonition, doctrinal definition, and controversy. Beside the Sabellianism, which Dionysius combated, Dynamic Monarchianism was vigorously represented in Antioch by Paul of Samosata till 272 (ante, p. 72).
This administratively gifted bishop held a high executive position under Zenobia, Queen of Palmyra, to whom Antioch belonged for a period before her overthrow by the Emperor

---

[1] *Celsus*, 8⁷³.   [2] *Ibid.*, 8⁷⁵.
[3] *E. g.*, Tertullian, *Corona*, 1.   [4] *Canon*, 55.

Aurelian. Paul's opponents, being unable to deprive him of possession of the church building, appealed to Aurelian, who decided that it rightfully belonged to "those to whom the bishops of Italy and of the city of Rome should adjudge it." [1] Doubtless Aurelian was moved by political considerations in this adjudication, but this Christian reference to imperial authority, and the Emperor's deference to the judgment of Rome were significant.

With Antioch of this period is to be associated the foundation of a school of theology by Lucian, of whom little is known of biographical detail, save that he was a presbyter, held aloof from the party in Antioch which opposed and overcame Paul of Samosata, taught there from c. 275 to c. 303, and died a martyr's death in 312. Arius and Eusebius of Nicomedia were his pupils, and the supposition is probable that his views were largely reproduced in them. Like Origen, he busied himself with textual and exegetical labors on the Scriptures, but had little liking for the allegorizing methods of the great Alexandrian. A simpler, more grammatical and historical method of treatment both of text and doctrine characterized his teaching.

SECTION XVIII.   RIVAL RELIGIOUS FORCES

The latter half of the third century was the period of the greatest influence of Mithraism in the empire. As the *Sol Invictus*, Mithras was widely worshipped, and this cult was popular in the army and favored by the Emperors who rose from its ranks. Two other forces of importance arose in the religious world. The first was Neo-Platonism. Founded in Alexandria by Ammonius Saccas (?–c. 245), its real developer was Plotinus (205–270), who settled in Rome about 244. From him, the leadership passed to Porphyry (233–304). Neo-Platonism was a pantheistic, mystical interpretation of Platonic thoughts. God is simple, absolute existence, all perfect, from whom the lower existences come. From Him the Nous (νοῦς) emanates like the Logos in the theology of Origen. From the Nous the world-soul derives being, and from that individual souls. From the world-soul the realm of matter comes. Yet each stage is inferior in the amount of being it possesses to the one above—

[1] Eusebius, *Church History*, 7 : 30[19].

has less of reality—reaching in gradations from God, who is all-perfect, to matter which, as compared with Him, is negative. The morals of Neo-Platonism, like those of later Greek philosophy generally, were ascetic, and its conception of salvation was that of a rising of the soul to God in mystic contemplation, the end of which was union with the divine. Neo-Platonism was much to influence Christian theology, notably that of Augustine. Its founders were not conspicuously organizers, however, and it remained a way of thinking for the relatively few rather than an inclusive association of the many.

Far otherwise was it with a second movement, that of Manichæism. Its founder, Mani, was born in Persia in 215 or 216, began his preaching in Babylon in 242, and was crucified in 276 or 277. Strongly based on the old Persian dualism, Manichæism was also exceedingly syncretistic. It received elements from Zoroastrianism, Buddhism, Judaism, and Christianity. Light and darkness, good and evil are eternally at war. Its conception of the relations of spirit and matter, and of salvation, in many ways resembled those of Gnosticism. Man is essentially a material prison house of the realm of evil, in which some portion of the realm of light is confined. Hence salvation is based on right knowledge as to the nature of this bondage, and desire to return to the realm of light, coupled with extreme ascetic rejection of all that belongs to the sphere of darkness, especially the physical appetites and desires. Its worship was as simple as its asceticism was strict. Its membership was in two classes, the perfect, always relatively few, who practised its full austerities; and the hearers, who accepted its teachings, but with much less strictness of practice—a distinction not unlike that between monks and ordinary Christians in the church. Its organization was fairly centralized and rigid. In Manichæism Christianity had a real rival. Its spread was rapid in the empire, and it absorbed not only many of the followers of Mithraism, but the remnants of Christian-Gnostic sects, and other early heresies. Its great growth was to be in the fourth and fifth centuries, and its influence was to be felt till the late Middle Ages through sects which were heirs of its teachings, like the Cathari.

In 284 Diocletian became Roman Emperor.   A man of the humblest origin, probably of slave parentage, he had a distinguished career in the army, and was raised to the imperial dignity by his fellow soldiers.   Though a soldier-emperor, he was possessed of great abilities as a civil administrator, and determined to reorganize the empire so as to provide more adequate military defense, prevent army conspiracies aiming at a change of Emperors, and render the internal administration more efficient.   To these ends he appointed an old companion-in-arms, Maximian, regent of the West, in 285, with the title of Augustus, which Diocletian himself bore.   In further aid of military efficiency he designated, in 293, two "Cæsars"—one, Constantius Chlorus, on the Rhine frontier, and the other, Galerius, on that of the Danube.   Each was to succeed ultimately to the higher post of "Augustus."   All was held in harmonious working by the firm hand of Diocletian.

In internal affairs the changes of Diocletian were no less sweeping.   The surviving relics of the old republican empire, and of senatorial influence, were now set aside.   The Emperor became an autocrat in the later Byzantine sense.   A new division of provinces was effected; and Rome was practically abandoned as the capital, Diocletian making the more conveniently situated Nicomedia, in Asia Minor, his customary residence. In character Diocletian was a rude but firm supporter of heathenism of the cruder camp type.

To such a man of organizing abilities, the closely knit, hierarchically ordered church presented a serious political problem. It must have seemed a state within the state over which he had no control.   Though there had never been a Christian uprising against the empire, and Christianity had held aloof from politics to a remarkable degree, the church was rapidly growing in numbers and strength.   Two courses lay open for a vigorous ruler, either to force it into submission and break its power, or to enter into alliance with it and thus secure political control of the growing organism.   The latter was to be the method of Constantine; the former the attempt of Diocletian.   No other course could be expected from a man of his religious outlook. The Eastern Cæsar, Galerius, was even more hostile to Christianity, and had much influence over Diocletian.   To him the suggestions of persecution may have been due. The growth of Christianity, moreover, was uniting all the forces of threatened heathenism against it; while Diocletian and Galerius were disposed to emphasize emperor-worship and the service of the old gods.

Diocletian moved slowly, however. A cautious effort to rid the army and the imperial palace service of Christians was followed, beginning in February, 303, by three great edicts of persecution in rapid succession. Churches were ordered destroyed, sacred books confiscated, clergy imprisoned and forced to sacrifice by torture. In 304 a fourth edict required all Christians to offer sacrifices. It was a time of fearful persecution. As in the days of Decius there were many martyrs, and many who "lapsed." Popular feeling was, however, far less hostile than in previous persecutions. The Christians had become better known. The severity of the persecution varied with the attitude of the magistrates by whom its penalties were enforced. Cruel in Italy, North Africa, and the Orient, the friendly "Cæsar," Constantius Chlorus, made apparent compliance in Gaul and Britain by destroying church edifices, but left the Christians themselves unharmed. He thereby gained a popularity with those thus spared that was to redound to the advantage of his son.

The voluntary retirement of Diocletian, and the enforced abdication of his colleague, Maximian, in 305, removed the strong hand of the only man able to master the complex governmental situation. Constantius Chlorus and Galerius now became "Augusti," but in the appointment of "Cæsars," the claims of the sons of Constantius Chlorus and Maximian were passed over in favor of two protégés of Galerius, Severus and Maximinus Daia. Persecution had now practically ceased in the West. It continued in increased severity in the East. Constantius Chlorus died in 306, and the garrison in York acclaimed his son Constantine as Emperor. On the strength of this army support, Constantine forced from Galerius his own recognition as "Cæsar," with charge of Gaul, Spain, and Britain. Soon after Maximian's son, Maxentius, defeated Severus and made himself master of Italy and North Africa. The next trial of strength in the struggle for the empire to which Constantine had set himself must be with Maxentius. Its outcome would determine the mastery of the whole West. Licinius, a protégé of Galerius, succeeded to a portion of the former possessions of Severus.

Before the decisive contest for the West took place, however, Galerius, in conjunction with Constantine and Licinius, issued in April, 311, an edict of toleration to Christians "on condition that nothing is done by them contrary to discipline." [1] This was, at best, a grudging concession, though why it was granted at all by the persecuting Galerius, who was its main source, is not wholly evident. Perhaps he had become convinced of the futility of persecution. Perhaps the long and severe illness which was to cost him his life a few days later may have led him to believe that some help might come from the Christians' God. The latter supposition is given added probability because the edict exhorts Christians to pray for its authors.

The death of Galerius in May, 311, left four contestants for the empire. Constantine and Licinius drew together by mutual interest; while Maximinus Daia and Maxentius were united by similar bonds. Daia promptly renewed persecution in Asia and Egypt. Maxentius, while not a persecutor, was a pronounced partisan of heathenism. Christian sympathy naturally flowed toward Constantine and Licinius. Constantine availed himself to the full of its advantages. To what extent he was now a personal Christian it is impossible to say. He had inherited a kindly feeling toward Christians. He had joined in the edict of 311. His forces seemed scarcely adequate for the great struggle with Maxentius. He doubtless desired the aid of the Christians' God in the none too equal conflict— though it is quite probable that he may not then have thought of Him as the only God. Constantine's later affirmation that he saw a vision of the cross with the inscription, "in this sign conquer," was a conscious or unconscious legend. But that he invaded Italy, as in some sense a Christian, is a fact. A brilliant march and several successful battles in northern Italy brought him face to face with Maxentius at Saxa Rubra, a little to the north of Rome, with the Mulvian bridge across the Tiber between his foes and the city. There, on October 28, 312, occurred one of the decisive struggles of history, in which Maxentius lost the battle and his life. The West was Constantine's. The Christian God, he believed, had given him the victory, and

[1] Eusebius, *Church History*, 8 : 17[9]; Ayer, p. 262.

every Christian impulse was confirmed. He was, thenceforth, in all practical respects a Christian, even though heathen emblems still appeared on coins, and he retained the title of Pontifex Maximus.

Probably late in 312 Constantine and Licinius published in Milan the great edict which gave complete freedom to Christianity, though it has been preserved only in the form addressed by Licinius to the Eastern officers.[1] It was no longer, as in 311, one of toleration; nor did it make Christianity the religion of the empire. It proclaimed absolute freedom of conscience, placed Christianity on a full legal equality with any religion of the Roman world, and ordered the restoration of all church property confiscated in the recent persecution. A few months after the edict was issued, in April, 313, Licinius decisively defeated the persecutor, Maximinus Daia, in a battle not far from Adrianople, which seemed to the Christians a second Mulvian bridge. Two Emperors were, however, one too many. Licinius, defeated by Constantine in 314, held scarcely more than a quarter of the empire. Estranged from Constantine, the favor shown by the latter to Christianity Licinius increasingly resented. His hostility grew to persecution. It was, therefore, with immense satisfaction that the Christians witnessed his final defeat in 323. Constantine was at last sole ruler of the Roman world. The church was everywhere free from persecution. Its steadfastness, its faith, and its organization had carried it through its perils. But, in winning its freedom from its enemies, it had come largely under the control of the occupant of the Roman imperial throne. A fateful union with the state had begun.

[1] Eusebius, *Church History*, 10 : 5; Ayer, p. 263.

PERIOD III. THE IMPERIAL STATE CHURCH

SECTION I. THE CHANGED SITUATION

To Constantine's essentially political mind Christianity was the completion of the process of unification which had long been in progress in the empire. It had one Emperor, one law, and one citizenship for all free men. It should have one religion. Constantine moved slowly, however. Though the Christians were very unequally distributed and were much more numerous in the East than in the West, they were but a fraction of the population when the Edict of Milan granted them equal rights. The church had grown with great rapidity during the peace in the last half of the third century. Under imperial favor its increase was by leaps and bounds. That favor Constantine promptly showed. By a law of 319 the clergy were exempted from the public obligations that weighed so heavily on the well-to-do portion of the population.[1] In 321 the right to receive legacies was granted, and thereby the privileges of the church as a corporation acknowledged.[2] The same year Sunday work was forbidden to the people of the cities.[3] In 319 private heathen sacrifices were prohibited.[4] Gifts were made to clergy, and great churches erected in Rome, Jerusalem, Bethlehem, and elsewhere under imperial auspices. Above all, Constantine's formal transferrence of the capital to the rebuilt Byzantium, which he called New Rome, but which the world has named in his honor, Constantinople, was of high significance. Undoubtedly political and defensive in its motives, its religious consequences were far-reaching. From its official foundation, in 330, it established the seat of empire in a city of few heathen traditions or influences, situated in the most strongly Christianized portion of the world. It left the bishop of Rome, moreover, the most conspicuous man

[1] *Codex Theodosianus*, 16 : 2²; Ayer, *Source Book*, p. 283.
[2] *Ibid.*, 16 : 2⁴; Ayer, p. 283.
[3] *Codex Justinianus*, 3 : 12³; Ayer, p. 284.
[4] *Codex Theodosianus*, 9 : 16²; Ayer, p. 286.

in the ancient capital, to which the Latin-speaking West still looked with reverence—in a conspicuity which was the more possible of future importance because it was wholly unintended by Constantine, and was spiritual rather than political. Great as were the favors which Constantine showed to the church, they were only for that strong, close-knit, hierarchically organized portion that called itself the "Catholic." The various "heretical" sects, and they were still many, could look for no bounty from his hands.

If Christianity was to be a uniting factor in the empire, the church must be one. Constantine found that unity seriously threatened. In North Africa the persecution under Diocletian had led to a schism, somewhat complicated and personal in its causes, but resembling that of Novatian in Rome, half a century earlier (*ante*, p. 102). The church there was divided. The strict party charged that the new bishop of Carthage, Cæcilian, had received ordination in 311, from the hands of one in mortal sin, who had surrendered copies of the Scriptures in the recent persecution. That ordination it held invalid, and chose a counterbishop, Majorinus. His successor, in 316, was the able Donatus the Great, from whom the schismatics received the name, Donatists. In 313 Constantine made grants of money to the "Catholic" clergy of North Africa.[1] In these the Donatists did not share, and appealed to the Emperor. A synod held in Rome the same year decided against them, but the quarrel was only the more embittered. Constantine thereupon mapped out what was to be henceforth the imperial policy in ecclesiastical questions. He summoned a synod of his portion of the empire to meet, at public expense, in Arles, in southern Gaul. The church itself should decide the controversy, but under imperial control. Here a large council assembled in 314. The Donatist contentions were condemned. Ordination was declared valid even at the hands of a personally unworthy cleric. Heretical baptism was recognized, and the Roman date of Easter approved.[2] The Donatists appealed to the Emperor, who once more decided against them, in 316; and as they refused to yield, now proceeded to close their churches and banish their bishops. The unenviable spectacle of the persecution of Christians by Christians was exhibited. North Africa was in turmoil. Con-

---

[1] Eusebius, *Church History*, 10:6; Ayer, p. 281.
[2] See Ayer, p. 291.

stantine was, however, dissatisfied with the results, and in 321 abandoned the use of force against these schismatics. They grew rapidly, claiming to be the only true church possessed of a clergy free from "deadly sins" and of the only valid sacraments. Not till the Mohammedan conquest did the Donatists disappear.

SECTION II. THE ARIAN CONTROVERSY TO THE DEATH OF CONSTANTINE

A much more serious danger to the unity of the church than the Donatist schism which Constantine encountered was the great Arian controversy. It has already been pointed out that while the West, thanks to the work of Tertullian and Novatian, had reached practical unanimity regarding the unity of substance between Christ and the Father (*ante*, pp. 69–76), the East was divided. Origen, still its most dominating theological influence, could be quoted in opposing senses. If he had taught the eternal generation of the Son, he had also held Him to be a second God and a creature (*ante*, p. 81). Adoptionist tendencies persisted, also, about Antioch; while Sabellianism was to be found in Egypt. The East, moreover, was vastly more interested in speculative theology than the West, and therefore more prone to discussion; nor can there be any doubt that, in the fourth century, much more of intellectual ability was to be found in the Greek-speaking than in the Latin-speaking portion of the empire.

The real cause of the struggle was these varying interpretations; but the actual controversy began in Alexandria, about 320, in a dispute between Arius and his bishop, Alexander (312?–328). Arius, a pupil of Lucian of Antioch (*ante*, p. 106), was presbyter in charge of the church known as Baucalis. He was advanced in years and held in high repute as a preacher of learning, ability, and piety. Monarchian influences imbibed in Antioch led him to emphasize the unity and self-contained existence of God. In so far as he was a follower of Origen, he represented the great Alexandrian's teaching that Christ was a created being. As such He was not of the substance of God, but was made like other creatures of "nothing." Though the first-born of creatures, and the agent in fashioning the world, He was not eternal. "The Son has a beginning, but . . . God is without beginning."[1] Christ was, indeed, God in a certain sense to Arius, but a lower God, in no way one with the Father in essence or eternity.   In the incarnation, this Logos entered a human body, taking the place of the human reasoning spirit.   To Arius's thinking, Christ was neither fully God nor fully man, but a *tertium quid* between.   This is what makes his view wholly unsatisfactory.

Bishop Alexander was influenced by the other side of Origen's teaching.   To him the Son was eternal, like in essence to the Father, and wholly uncreated.[2]   His view was, perhaps, not perfectly clear, but its unlikeness to that of Arius is apparent. Controversy arose between Arius and Alexander, apparently on Arius's initiative.   It soon grew bitter, and about 320 or 321 Alexander held a synod in Alexandria by which Arius and a number of his sympathizers were condemned. Arius appealed for help to his fellow pupil of the school of Lucian, the power-ful bishop, Eusebius of Nicomedia, and soon found a refuge with him.   Alexander wrote widely to fellow bishops, and Arius defended his own position, aided by Eusebius.   The Eastern ecclesiastical world was widely turmoiled.

Such was the situation when Constantine's victory over Licinius made him master of the East as well as of the West. The quarrel threatened the unity of the church which he deemed essential.   Constantine therefore sent his chief ecclesi-astical adviser, Bishop Hosius of Cordova, in Spain, to Alex-andria with an imperial letter, counselling peace and describing the issue involved as "an unprofitable question."[3]   The well-meant, but bungling effort was vain.   Constantine, therefore, proceeded to employ the same device he had already made use of at Arles in the Donatist dispute.   He called a council of the entire church.   That of Arles had been representative of all the portion of the empire then ruled by Constantine. Constantine was now master of all the empire, and therefore bishops of all the empire were summoned.   The principle was the same, but the extent of Constantine's enlarged jurisdiction made the gathering in Nicæa the First General Council of the church.

The council, which assembled in Nicæa in May, 325, has

---

[1] Arius to Eusebius, Theodoret, *Church History*, 1[4]; Ayer, p. 302.
[2] Letter of Alexander, in Socrates, *Church History*, 1[6].
[3] Letter in Eusebius, *Life of Constantine*, 2[64-72].

always lived in Christian tradition as the most important in the history of the church. To it the bishops were summoned at government expense, accompanied by lower clergy, who did not, however, have votes in its decisions. The East had the vast preponderance. Of about three hundred bishops present only six were from the West. It included three parties. A small section, led by Eusebius of Nicomedia, were thorough-going Arians. Another small group were equally strenuous supporters of Alexander. The large majority, of whom the church historian, Eusebius of Cæsarea, was a leader, were not deeply versed in the question at issue. Indeed, the majority, as a whole, were described by an unsympathetic writer as "simpletons." [1] As far as they had any opinion, they stood on the general basis of the teachings of Origen. Conspicuous in the assembly was the Emperor himself, who, though not baptized, and therefore not technically a full member of the church, was far too eminent a personage not to be welcomed enthusiastically.

Almost at the beginning of the council a creed presented by the Arians was rejected. Eusebius of Cæsarea then offered the creed of his own church. It was a sweet-sounding confession, dating from before the controversy, and was, therefore, wholly indefinite as to the particular problems involved. This Cæsarean creed was now amended most significantly by the insertion of the expressions, "begotten, not made," "of one essence (*homoousion*, ὁμοούσιον) with the Father"; and by the specific rejection of Arian formulæ such as "there was when He was not" and "He was made of things that were not." The later technically unlike words essence, substance (οὐσία), and hypostasis (ὑπόστασις) were here used as equivalent expressions. Loofs has shown conclusively[2] that the influences which secured these changes were Western, doubtless above all that of Hosius of Cordova, supported by the Emperor. In particular, the test word, *homoousion*, had long been orthodox in its Latin equivalent, and had been in philosophic usage in the second century, though rejected by a synod in Antioch in the proceedings against Paul of Samosata (*ante*, p. 73). Indeed, it was used very sparingly by Athanasius himself in his earlier defense of the Nicene faith. It is easy to understand Constantine's atti-

[1] Socrates, *Church History*, 1⁸.
[2] *Realencyklopädie für prot. Theol. u. Kirche*, 2¹⁴, ¹⁵.

tude. Essentially a politician, he naturally thought a formula that would find no opposition in the Western half of the empire, and would receive the support of a portion of the East, more acceptable than one which, while having only a part of the East in its favor, would be rejected by the whole West. To Constantine's influence the adoption of the Nicene definition was due. That he ever understood its shades of meaning is more than doubtful; but he wanted a united expression of the faith of the church on the question in dispute, and believed that he had found it. Under his supervision, all but two of the bishops present signed it. These, and Arius, Constantine sent into banishment. The imperial politics had apparently secured the unity of the church, and had given it what it had never before possessed, a statement which might be assumed to be a universally recognized creed.

Besides this action in thus formulating the creed, the Council of Nicæa issued a number of important canons regulating church discipline, paved the way for the return of those in Egypt who had joined the Melitian schism over the treatment of the lapsed, made easy the readmission of Novatians, and ordered a uniform date in the observation of Easter.

It is not strange, in view of the manner in which the Nicene creed was adopted, that soon after the council ended great opposition to its test word, *homoousion*, was manifested in the East. To the defeated Arians it was, of course, obnoxious. They were few. To the large middle party of disciples of Origen it was scarcely less satisfactory, for to them it seemed Sabellian. Though Eusebius of Nicomedia and his Arian sympathizer, Theognis of Nicæa, had signed, their evident hostility was such that Constantine sent both bishops into exile. By 328, however, they were home again, possibly through the favor of the Emperor's sister, Constantia. Eusebius soon acquired a greater influence over Constantine than any other ecclesiastic of the East, and used it to favor the cause of Arius. With such elements of opposition to the Nicene result, the real battle was not in the council but in the more than half a century which followed its conclusion.

Meanwhile the great defender of the Nicene faith had come fully on the scene. Athanasius was born in Alexandria about 295. In the early stages of the Arian controversy he was a deacon, and served as private secretary to Bishop Alexander.

As such he accompanied his bishop to Nicæa, and on Alexander's death, in 328, was chosen in turn to the Alexandrian bishopric —a post which he was to hold, in spite of attack and five banishments, till his own demise in 373. Not a great speculative theologian, Athanasius was a great character. In an age when court favor counted for much, he stood like a rock for his convictions, and that the Nicene theology ultimately conquered was primarily due to him, for the Nicene West possessed no able theologian. To him, the question at issue was one of salvation, and that he made men feel it to be so was a main source of his power. The Greek conception of salvation had been, since the beginnings of the tradition of Asia Minor, the transformation of sinful mortality into divine and blessed immortality—the impartation of "life" (*ante*, p. 40). Only by real Godhead coming into union with full manhood in Christ could the transformation of the human into the divine be accomplished in Him, or be mediated by Him to His disciples. As Athanasius said: "He [Christ] was made man that we might be made divine."[1] To his thinking the great error of Arianism was that it gave no basis for a real salvation. Well was it for the Nicene party that so moderate, yet determined, a champion stood for it, since the two other prominent defenders of the Nicene faith, Bishops Marcellus of Ancyra and Eustathius of Antioch, were certainly far from theologically impeccable, and were accused, not wholly rightly, of opinions decidedly Sabellian.

Eusebius of Nicomedia soon saw in Athanasius the real enemy. Constantine would not desert the Nicene decision, but the same practical result could be achieved, Eusebius thought, by striking its defenders. Political and theological differences were cleverly used to secure the condemnation of Eustathius in 330. The Eusebians determined to secure the discomfiture of Athanasius and the restoration of Arius. The latter, who had returned from banishment even before Eusebius, now presented to Constantine a creed carefully indefinite on the question at issue.[2] To Constantine's untheological mind this seemed a satisfactory retraction, and an expression of willingness to make his peace. He directed Athanasius to restore Arius to his place in Alexandria. Athanasius refused. Charges of overbearing

---

[1] *Incarnation*, 54³.
[2] Socrates, *Church History*, 1²⁶; Ayer, p. 307.

and disloyal conduct were brought against Athanasius. Constantine was finally persuaded that the main obstacle in the path of peace was Athanasius's stubbornness. The bishops assembled for the dedication of Constantine's just completed church in Jerusalem, met in Tyre, and then in Jerusalem, under Eusebian influences, and decided in favor of Arius's restoration in 335, and near the end of the year Constantine banished Athanasius to Gaul. Shortly after the same forces procured the deposition of Marcellus of Ancyra for heresy. The leading defenders of the Nicene creed being thus struck down, the Eusebians planned the restoration of Arius himself to church fellowship; but on the evening before the formal ceremony should take place Arius suddenly died (336). An aged man, the excitement may well have been fatal.

The Nicene faith seemed thus not officially overthrown, but practically undermined, when Constantine died on May 22, 337. Shortly before his demise he was baptized at the hands of Eusebius of Nicomedia. The changes which his life had witnessed, and he had largely wrought, in the status of the church were enormous; but they were not by any means wholly advantageous. If persecution had ceased, and numbers were rapidly growing under imperial favor, doctrinal discussions that earlier would have run their course were now political questions of the first magnitude, and the Emperor had assumed a power in ecclesiastical affairs which was ominous for the future of the church. Yet in the existing constitution of the Roman Empire such results were probably inevitable, once the Emperor himself should become, like Constantine, an adherent of the Christian faith.

SECTION III.   CONTROVERSY UNDER CONSTANTINE'S SONS

The death of Constantine was succeeded by the division of the empire among his three sons, with some intended provisions for other relatives that were frustrated by a palace intrigue and massacre. Constantine II, the eldest, received Britain, Gaul, and Spain; Constantius, Asia Minor, Syria, and Egypt; while the intermediate portion came to the youngest, Constans. Constantine II died in 340, so that the empire was speedily divided between Constans in the West, and Constantius in the East. Both Emperors showed themselves, from the

first, more partisan in religious questions than their father had
been. A joint edict of 346 ordered temples closed, and forbade sacrifice on pain of death.[1] The law was, however, but
slightly enforced. The Donatist controversy in North Africa
had greatly extended, and that land, in consequence, was the
scene of much agrarian and social agitation. The Donatists
were, therefore, attacked in force by Constans, and though
not wholly crushed, were largely rooted out.

The most important relationship of the sons of Constantine
to the religious questions of the age was to the continuing
Nicene controversy. Under their rule it extended from a
dispute practically involving only the East, as under Constantine, to an empire-wide contest. At the beginning of their
joint reigns the Emperors permitted the exiled bishops to return. Athanasius was, therefore, once more in Alexandria before the close of 337. Eusebius was, however, still the most
influential party leader in the East, and his authority was but
strengthened when he was promoted, in 339, from the bishopric
of Nicomedia to that of Constantinople, where he died about
341. Through the influence of Eusebius Athanasius was forcibly driven from Alexandria in the spring of 339, and an Arian
bishop, Gregory of Cappadocia, put in his place by military
power. Athanasius fled to Rome, where Marcellus of Ancyra
soon joined him.

East and West were now under different Emperors, and
Constans held to the Nicene sympathies of his subjects. Not
merely was the empire divided, but Bishop Julius of Rome
could now interfere from beyond the reach of Constantius.
He welcomed the fugitives and summoned their opponents to
a synod in Rome, in 340, though the Eusebians did not appear.
The synod declared Athanasius and Marcellus unjustly deposed.
The Eastern leaders replied not merely with protests against
the Roman action, but with an attempt to do away with the
Nicene formula itself, in which they had the support of Constantius. Two synods in Antioch, in 341, adopted creeds,
far, indeed, from positively Arian in expression, but from which
all that was definitely Nicene was omitted. In some respects
they represented a pre-Nicene orthodoxy. The death of Eusebius, now of Constantinople, at this juncture cost the opponents of the Nicene decision his able leadership. The two

---

[1] *Codex Theodosianus*, 16 · 10⁴; Ayer, p. 323.

brother Emperors thought that the bitter quarrel could best
be adjusted by a new General Council, and accordingly such a
body gathered in Sardica, the modern Sofia, in the autumn of
343. General Council it was not to be. The Eastern bishops,
finding themselves outnumbered by those of the West, and
seeing Athanasius and Marcellus in company with them, withdrew. By the Westerners Athanasius and Marcellus were
once more approved, though the latter was a considerable burden to their cause by reason of his dubious orthodoxy. East
and West seemed on the point of ecclesiastical separation.

The Council of Sardica had completely failed in its object
of healing the quarrel, but the Westerners there assembled
passed several canons, under the leadership of Hosius of Cordova, that are of great importance in the development of the
judicial authority of the bishop of Rome. What they did was
to enact the actual recent course of proceedings regarding
Athanasius and Marcellus into a general rule. It was decided
that in case a bishop was deposed, as these had been, he might
appeal to Bishop Julius of Rome, who could cause the case to
be retried by new judges, and no successor should be appointed
till the decision of Rome was known.[1] They were purely
Western rules and seem to have aroused little attention, even
in Rome, at the time, but were important for the future.

The two imperial brothers were convinced that the controversy was assuming too serious aspects. At all events, Constans favored Athanasius, and the rival bishop, Gregory, having
died, Constantius permitted Athanasius to return to Alexandria
in October, 347, where he was most cordially welcomed by the
overwhelming majority of the population, which had always
heartily supported him. The situation seemed favorable for
Athanasius, but political events suddenly made it worse than
it had ever been. A rival Emperor arose in the West in the
person of Magnentius, and in 350 Constans was murdered.
Three years of struggle brought victory over the usurper to
Constantius, and left him sole ruler of the empire (353).

Constantius, at last in full control, determined to end the
controversy. To his thinking Athanasius was the chief enemy.
The leadership against Athanasius was now in the hands of
Bishops Ursacius of Singidunum, and Valens of Mursa. At
synods held in Arles in 353, and in Milan in 355, Constantius

[1] See Ayer, pp. 364–366.

forced the Western bishops to abandon Athanasius, and to resume communion with his Eastern opponents. For resistance to these demands Liberius, bishop of Rome, Hilary of Poitiers, the most learned bishop of Gaul, and the aged Hosius of Cordova were sent into banishment. Athanasius, driven from Alexandria by military force in February, 356, began his third exile, finding refuge for the next six years largely among the Egyptian monks. At a synod held in Sirmium, the Emperor's residence, in 357, *ousia* (substance) in any of its combinations was forbidden as unscriptural.[1] This, so far as the influence of the synod went, was an abolition of the Nicene formula. Hosius signed it, though he absolutely refused to condemn Athanasius. The declaration of Sirmium was strengthened by an agreement secured by Constantius at the little Thracian town of Nice, in 359, in which it was affirmed "we call the Son like the Father, as the holy scriptures call Him and teach."[2] The Emperor and his episcopal favorites, notably Valens of Mursa, now secured its acceptance by synods purporting to represent East and West, held in Rimini, Seleucia, and Constantinople. The Old-Nicene formula was set aside, and the whole church had, theoretically, accepted the new result. The proper term, the only one allowed in court circles, was "the Son is like the Father"—*homoios*—hence those who supported its use were known as the Homoion ("like") party. Apparently colorless, the history of its adoption made it a rejection of the Nicene faith, and opened the door to Arian assertions. The Arians had triumphed for the time being, and that success was largely aided by the fact that its Homoion formula appealed to many who were heartily tired of the long controversy.

Really, however, the Arian victory had prepared the way for the ruin of Arianism, though that result was not immediately apparent. The opposition to the Nicene formula had always been composed of two elements: a small Arian section, and a much larger conservative body, which stood mainly on positions reached by Origen, to which Arianism was obnoxious, but which looked upon *homoousios*, the Nicene phrase, as an unwarranted expression already condemned in Antioch, and of Sabellian ill-repute. Both elements had worked together to resist the Nicene formula, but their agreement went no further. Extreme Arians were raising their heads in Alexandria

[1] Hilary of Poitiers, *De Synodis*, 11; Ayer, p. 317.   [2] Ayer, p. 319.

and elsewhere. The conservatives were even more hostile to them than to the Nicene party. They would not say *homoousios* —of one substance—but they were willing to say *homoiousios* —not in the sense of like substance, as the natural translation would be, but of equality of attributes. They were also beginning to draw a distinction between *ousia*—substance, essence—and *hypostasis*—now using the latter in the sense of "subsistence," instead of making them equivalent, as in the Nicene symbol. This enabled them to preserve the Origenistic teaching of "three hypostases," while insisting on the community of attributes. The newly formed middle party came first into evidence with a synod at Ancyra, in 358, and its chief early leaders were Bishops Basil of Ancyra, and George of Laodicea. They have usually been called the Semi-Arians, but the term is a misnomer. They rejected Arianism energetically. They really stood near to Athanasius. He recognized this approach, and Hilary of Poitiers furthered union by urging that the conservatives meant by *homoiousios* what the Nicene party understood by *homoousios*.[1] The ultimate Nicene victory was to come about through the fusion of the Nicene and the "Semi-Arian" parties. In that union the tradition of Asia Minor, and the interpretations of Origen were to combine with those of Alexandria. It was a slow process, however, and in its development the earlier Nicene views were to be considerably modified into the New-Nicene theology.

SECTION IV. THE LATER NICENE STRUGGLE

Constantius died in 361 as he was preparing to resist his cousin, Julian, whom the soldiers in Paris had declared Emperor. His death left the Roman world to Julian. Spared on account of his youth at the massacre of his father and other relatives on the death of Constantine, he looked upon Constantius as his father's murderer. Brought up in peril of his life, and forced to strict outward churchly observance, he came to hate everything which Constantius represented, and was filled with admiration for the literature, life, and philosophy of the older Hellenism. He was not an "apostate," in the sense of a turncoat. Though necessarily concealed from the public, his heathenism had long been real, when his campaign against Constan-

[1] *De Synodis*, 88; Ayer, p. 319.

tius enabled him publicly to declare it. It was heathenism of a mystical, philosophical character. On his accession he attempted a heathen revival. Christianity was everywhere discouraged, and Christians removed from office. Bishops banished under Constantius were recalled, that the quarrels of Christians might aid in the heathen reaction. Athanasius was thus once more in Alexandria in 362, but before the year was out was exiled for the fourth time by Julian, who was angered by his success in making converts from heathenism. Julian's reign was soon over. In 363 he lost his life in a campaign against the Persians. In him Rome had its last heathen Emperor.

The reign of Julian showed the real weakness of the Arianizing elements which Constantius had supported. Athanasians and Semi-Arians drew together. Furthermore, the Nicene debate was broadening out to include a discussion of the relations of the Holy Spirit to the Godhead. Since the time of Tertullian, in the West, Father, Son, and Holy Spirit had been regarded as three "persons," of one substance (*ante*, p. 69). The East had reached no such unanimity. Even Origen had been uncertain whether the Spirit was "created or uncreated," or "a son of God or not."[1] There had not been much discussion of the theme. Now that it had come forward, the *homoousia* of the Holy Spirit with the Father, seemed to Athanasius and his friends a corollary from the *homoousia* of the Son. At a synod held in Alexandria in 362, by the just returned Athanasius, terms of union were drawn up for rival parties in Antioch. It would be sufficient "to anathematize the Arian heresy and confess the faith confessed by the holy Fathers at Nicæa, and to anathematize also those who say that the Holy Ghost is a creature and separate from the essence of Christ."[2] The employment of the terms "three hypostases" and "one hypostasis" the synod regarded as indifferent, provided "three" was not used in the sense of "alien in essence," and "one" in that of Sabellian unity. The door was thus opened by Athanasius himself not only for the full definition of the doctrine of the Trinity, but for the New-Nicene orthodoxy, with its Godhead in one essence (substance) and three hypostases.

The death of Julian was succeeded by the brief reign of

---

[1] *De Principiis*, Preface.
[2] *Tomus ad Antiochenos*, 3 ; Ayer, p. 350.

Jovian. The empire had once more a Christian ruler, and happily, one who interfered little in ecclesiastical politics. Athanasius promptly returned from his fourth exile. Jovian's rule ended in 364, and he was succeeded by Valentinian I (364–375), who, finding the imperial defense too great a task, took charge of the West, giving to his brother, Valens (364–378) the sovereignty of the East. Valentian interfered little with churchly affairs. Valens came under the influence of the Arian clergy of Constantinople, and both Homoousian and Homoiousian sympathizers shared his dislike—a situation which helped to bring these parties nearer together. He condemned Athanasius to a fifth and final exile, in 365; but it was brief, and the aged bishop did not have to go far from the city. Valens was, however, no such vigorous supporter of Arianism as Constantius had been. Athanasius died in Alexandria, in 373, full of years and honors.

At the death of Athanasius the leadership in the struggle was passing into the hands of new men, of the New-Nicene party. Chief of these were the three great Cappadocians, Basil of Cæsarea in Cappadocia, Gregory of Nazianzus, and Gregory of Nyssa. Born of a prominent Cappadocian family about 330, Basil received the best training that Constantinople and Athens could yield, in student association with his life-long friend Gregory of Nazianzus. About 357 he yielded to the ascetic Christian tendencies of the age, and gave up any idea of a career of worldly advancement, living practically as a monk. He visited Egypt, then the home of the rising monastic movement, and became the great propagator of monasticism in Asia Minor. He was, however, made for affairs and not for the cloister. Deeply versed in Origen, and in sympathy with the Homoiousian party, he belonged to the section which gradually came into fellowship with Athanasius, and like Athanasius he supported the full consubstantiality of the Holy Spirit. To the wing of the Homoiousian party which refused to regard the Spirit as fully God—the so-called Macedonians—he offered strenuous opposition. It was a far-reaching victory for his cause when Basil became bishop of the Cappadocian Cæsarea, in 370. The post gave him ecclesiastical authority over a large section of eastern Asia Minor, which he used to the full till his early death, in 379, to advance the New-Nicene cause. He sought also to promote a good under-

standing between the opponents of Arianism in the East and
the leaders of the West.

Gregory of Nyssa was Basil's younger brother. An orator
of ability, and a writer of even greater skill and theological
clearness than Basil, he had not Basil's organizing and administrative gifts. His title was derived from the little Cappadocian town—Nyssa—of which he became bishop in 371 or
372. He lived till after 394, and ranks among the four great
Fathers of the Oriental Church.

Gregory of Nazianzus (329?–389?) had his title from the
town of his birth, where his father was bishop. Warmly befriended with Basil from student days, like Basil he felt strongly
the monastic attraction. His ability as a preacher was greater
than that of either of his associates, but was exercised in most
varying stations. As a priest he aided his father, from about
361. By Basil he was made bishop of the village of Sasima.
About 378 he went to Constantinople to oppose the Arianism
which was the faith of the vast majority of its inhabitants.
The accession of the zealously Nicene Emperor, Theodosius,
in 379, gave him the needed support, and he preached with
such success that he gained the repute of having turned the
city to the Nicene faith. By Theodosius he was made bishop
of Constantinople in 381. But the frictions of party strife
and the inclination to ascetic retirement which had several
times before driven him from the world, caused him speedily
to relinquish this most exalted ecclesiastical post. As a writer
he ranked with Gregory of Nyssa. Like him he is reckoned
one of the Eastern Fathers, and the later Orient has given him
the title, the "Theologian."

To the three Cappadocians, more than to any others, the
intellectual victory of the New-Nicene faith was due. To the
men of that age their work seemed the triumph of the Nicene
formula. What modifications they really made have been well
expressed by a recent German writer:[1]

Athanasius (and Marcellus) taught the one God, leading a
threefold personal life, who reveals Himself as such. The Cappadocians think of three divine hypostases, which, as they manifest
the same activity, are recognized as possessing one nature and the
same dignity. The mystery for the former lay in the trinity; for

[1] Seeberg, *Text-Book of the History of Doctrines*, Eng. tr., 1:232.

the latter, in the unity. . . . The Cappadocians interpreted the doctrine of Athanasius in accordance with the conceptions and underlying principles of the Logos-Christology of Origen. They paid, however, for their achievement a high price, the magnitude of which they did not realize—the idea of the personal God. Three personalities and an abstract, impersonal essence, are the resultant.

The original Nicene success and the temporary triumph of Arianism had been made possible by imperial interference. The same force was to give victory to the New-Nicene orthodoxy. The death of Valens in the great Roman defeat by the West Goths, near Adrianople, in 378, left his nephew, Gratian, the sole surviving ruler. Gratian preferred the care of the West, and wisely appointed as Emperor for the East an able general and administrator, Theodosius, who became ultimately, for a brief period, the last sole ruler of the Roman Empire. Born in Spain, he grew up in full sympathy with the theology of the West, and shared to the utmost its devotion to the Nicene faith. In 380, in conjunction with Gratian, he issued an edict that all should "hold the faith which the holy Apostle Peter gave to the Romans," which he defined more particularly as that taught by the existing bishops, Damasus of Rome, and Peter of Alexandria.[1] This edict constitutes a reckoning point in imperial politics and ecclesiastical development. Henceforth there was to be but one religion in the empire, and that the Christian. Moreover, only that form of Christianity was to exist which taught one divine essence in three hypostases, or, as the West would express it in supposedly similar terms, one substance in three persons.

In 381 Theodosius held an Eastern synod in Constantinople, which ultimately gained repute as the Second General Council, and obtained an undeserved credit as the supposed author of the creed which passed into general use as "Nicene." Of its work little is known. It undoubtedly rejected, however, that wing of the Homoiousian party—the Macedonian—which refused to accept the consubstantiality of the Holy Spirit, and approved the original Nicene creed. Personal differences continued between East and West, and between Eastern parties; but the forcible way in which the Emperor now drove out the

---

[1] *Codex Theodosianus*, 16¹; Ayer, p. 367.

Arians decided the fate of Arianism in the empire, in spite of a brief toleration of Arianism in northern Italy by Gratian's successor, Valentinian II, influenced by his mother, against which Ambrose of Milan had to strive.   Here, too, the authority of Theodosius was potent after her death, about 388.   Arianism in the empire was a lost cause, though it was to continue for several centuries among the Germanic invaders, thanks to the missionary work of Ulfila (see Section V).

Yet even when the synod of 381 met, the Nicene creed, as adopted in 325, failed to satisfy the requirements of theologic development in the victorious party.   It said nothing regarding the consubstantiality of the Holy Spirit, for instance.   A creed more fully meeting the state of discussion was desirable, and actually such a creed came into use, and by 451 was regarded as adopted by the General Council of 381.   It ultimately took the place of the genuine Nicene creed, and is that known as the "Nicene" to this day.   Its exact origin is uncertain, but it is closely related to the baptismal creed of Jerusalem, as reconstructible from the teaching of Cyril, afterward bishop of that city, about 348; and also to that of Epiphanius of Salamis, about 374.[1]

On reviewing this long controversy, it may be said that it was a misfortune that a less disputed phrase was not adopted at Nicæa, and doubly a misfortune that imperial interference played so large a part in the ensuing discussions.   In the struggle the imperial church came into existence, and a policy of imperial interference was fully developed.   Departure from official orthodoxy had become a crime.

Theodosius's attitude was no less strenuous toward remaining heathenism than in regard to heretical Christian parties. In 392 he forbade heathen worship under penalties similar to those for lese-majesty and sacrilege.[2]   It was the old weapon of heathenism against Christianity now used by Christian hands against heathenism.   Constantine's toleration had fully disappeared.   Nevertheless, heathen worship persisted, and only slowly died out.

---

[1] Ayer, *Source Book*, pp. 354–356.
[2] *Codex Theodosianus*, 16[10, 12]; Ayer, p. 347.

SECTION V.   ARIAN MISSIONS AND THE GERMANIC INVASIONS

Throughout the history of the empire the defense of the frontiers of the Rhine and the Danube against the Teutonic peoples beyond had been an important military problem. Under Marcus Aurelius a desperate, but ultimately successful war had been waged by the Romans on the upper Danube (167–180). Considerable shifting of tribes and formations of confederacies took place behind the screen of the Roman frontier; but by the beginning of the third century the group known as the Alemans had formed across the upper Rhine, and half a century later, that of the Franks on the lower right side of that river. Between these two developments, about 230–240, the Goths completed their settlement in what is now southern Russia. In 250 and 251 the Roman hold in the Balkans was seriously threatened by a Gothic invasion, in which the persecuting Emperor, Decius, lost his life. The Goths effected a settlement in the region north of the lower Danube. They invaded the empire, and the peril was not stayed till the victories of Claudius (269), from which he derived his title, "Gothicus." The stronger Emperors, Aurelian, Diocletian, and Constantine, held the frontiers of the Rhine and the Danube effectively; but the danger of invasion was always present. By the fourth century the Goths north of the Danube, who were most in contact with Roman civilization of any of the Germanic tribes, were known as the Visigoths, while their kinsmen in southern Russia were called Ostrogoths. The exact meaning of these names is uncertain, though they are generally regarded as signifying West and East Goths.

There was, indeed, much interchange between Romans and Germans, especially from the time of Aurelian onward. Germans served, in increasing numbers, in the Roman armies. Roman traders penetrated far beyond the borders of the empire. Germans settled in the border provinces and adopted Roman ways. Prisoners of war, taken probably in the raid of 264, from Cappadocia, had introduced the germs of Christianity among the Visigoths before the close of the third century, and even a rudimentary church organization in certain places. The Visigoths, as a nation, had not been converted. To that work Ulfila was to contribute. Born about 310, of parentage sprung, in part at least, from the captives just mentioned, he was of Christian origin, and became a "reader" in the services of the little Christian Gothic circle. In 341 he accompanied a Gothic embassy, and was ordained bishop by the Arian Eusebius of Nicomedia, then bishop of Constantinople, whether in the latter city, or in Antioch where the synod (*ante*, p. 120) was then sitting, is uncertain. His theology, which seems to have been very simple, was thenceforth anti-Nicene, and after the formation of the new Homoion party he was to be reckoned one of its adherents. For the next seven years he labored in his native land, till persecution compelled him and his fellow Christians to seek refuge on Roman soil, living and laboring for many years near the modern Plevna, in Bulgaria. His great work was the translation of the Scriptures, or at least of the New Testament, into the Gothic tongue. In 383 he died on a visit to Constantinople. Unfortunately, the complete oblivion into which these Arian labors fell, owing to their unorthodox character in the view of the following age, allows no knowledge of Ulfila's associates, nor a judgment as to how far the credit of turning the Visigoths to Christianity belonged to him, or to the Gothic chieftain Fritigern, about 370.

But, however brought about, the Visigoths, in spite of heathen persecution, rapidly accepted Arian Christianity. Not only they, but their neighbors the Ostrogoths, the Vandals in part, and remoter Germanic tribes, such as the Burgundians and Lombards, had embraced the Arian faith before invading the empire. Indeed, so widely had Christianity penetrated that it seems not improbable that, had the invasions been a couple of generations delayed, all might have entered the empire as Christians. As it was, those tribes only which were the farthest removed from the influences going out from the Visigoths —those of northwestern Germany, of whom the chief were the Franks and the Saxons—remained overwhelmingly heathen at the time of the invasions. Such rapid extension of Christianity shows that the hold of native paganism must have been slight, and that many, whose names have utterly perished, shared in the work of conversion. It was of the utmost significance that when the walls of the empire were broken the Germans came, for the most part, not as enemies of Christianity. Had the Western empire fallen, as well it might, a century before, the story of Christianity might have been vastly different.

Pressed by an invasion of Huns from western Central Asia, the Visigoths sought shelter across the frontier of the lower Danube in 376. Angered by ill-treatment from Roman officials, they crossed the Balkans and annihilated the Roman army near Adrianople, in 378, in a battle in which the Emperor Valens lost his life. The strong hand of Theodosius (379–395) restrained their further attacks; but on his death the empire, divided between his son of eighteen, Arcadius, in the East, and his eleven-year-old son, Honorius, in the West, was no longer able to resist the attack. Under Alaric, the Visigoths plundered almost to the walls of Constantinople, and thence moved into Greece, penetrating as far as Sparta. By 401 the Visigoths were pressing into northern Italy, but were resisted for the next few years by Theodosius's able Vandal general, Stilicho, whom he had left as guardian for the young Honorius. Stilicho's murder, in 408, opened the road to Rome, and Alaric promptly marched thither. It was not till 410, however, that the Visigothic chieftain actually captured the city. The poppular impression of this event was profound. The old mistress of the world had fallen before the barbarians. Alaric, desirous of establishing a kingdom for himself and of securing Roman Africa, the granary of Italy, marched at once for southern Italy, and there died before the close of 410. Under Ataulf the Visigothic host marched northward, invading southern Gaul in 412. Here the Goths settled by 419, developing ultimately a kingdom that included half of modern France, to which they added most of Spain by conquest during the course of the century. The Roman inhabitants were not driven out, but they were subjected to their Germanic conquerors, who appropriated much of the land, and placed its older occupants in a distinctly inferior position. Commerce was hampered, the life of the cities largely broken down, and civilization crippled.

While these events were in progress, the tribes across the Rhine had seen their opportunity. The Arian Vandals and heathen Alans and Suevi invaded Gaul at the close of 406, ultimately pushing their way into Spain, where they arrived before the Visigoths. The Franks had pressed into northern Gaul and the Burgundians conquered the region around Strassburg, and thence gradually the territory of eastern Gaul which still bears their name. Britain, involved in this collapse of

Roman authority, was increasingly invaded by the Saxons,
Angles, and Jutes, who had been attacking its coasts since the
middle of the fourth century.   There Roman civilization had
a weaker grasp than on the continent, and as Germanic conquest slowly advanced, it drove the Celtic element largely
westward, and made much of Britain a heathen land.   The
Vandals from Spain, having entered Africa by 425, invaded it
in full force in 429, under Gaiseric.   They soon established there
the most powerful of the early Germanic kingdoms, whose piratical ships speedily dominated the western Mediterranean.
A Vandal raid sacked Rome in 455.   A fearful invasion of
Gaul in 451, by the Huns under Attila, was checked in battle
near Troyes by the combined forces of the Romans and Visigoths.   The next year Attila carried his devastations into Italy,
and was barely prevented from taking Rome by causes which
are now obscure, but among which the efforts of its bishop,
Leo I, were believed to have been determinative.

Though the rule of the Emperors was nominally maintained
in the West, and even the Germanic conquerors, who established
kingdoms in Gaul, Spain, and Africa were professedly their dependents, the Emperors became the tools of the chiefs of the
army.   On the death of Honorius, in 423, the empire passed
to Valentinian III.   His long reign, till 455, was marked by the
quarrels of Boniface, count of Africa, and Aetius, the count
of Italy, which permitted the Vandal conquest of North Africa.
Aetius won, indeed, about the last victory of the empire when,
with the Visigoths, he defeated Attila in 451.   Between 455 and
476 no less than nine Emperors were set up and deposed in the
West.   The real ruler of Italy was the head of the army.   From
456 to 472 this post was held by Ricimer, of Suevic and Visigothic descent.   After his death the command was taken by
a certain Orestes, who conferred the imperial title on his son,
Romulus, nicknamed Augustulus.   The army in Italy was
recruited chiefly from smaller Germanic tribes, among them the
Rugii and Heruli.   It now demanded a third of the land.
Orestes refused, and the army rose in mutiny in 476 under the
Germanic general Odovakar, whom it made King.   This date
has usually been taken as that of the close of the Roman Empire.   In reality it was without special significance.   Romulus
Augustulus was deposed.   There was no further Emperor in
the West till Charlemagne.   But Odovakar and his contem-

poraries had no thought that the Roman Empire was at an end. He ruled in Italy as the Visigoths ruled in southern France and Spain, a nominal subject of the Roman Emperor, who sat on the throne in Constantinople.

Odovakar's sovereignty in Italy was ended in 493 in the struggle against new Germanic invaders of Italy, the Ostrogoths, led by Theodoric. Under that successful conqueror a really remarkable amalgamation of Roman and Germanic institutions was attempted. His capital was Ravenna, whence he ruled till his death in 526. The Ostrogothic kingdom in Italy was brought to an end by the long wars under the Emperor Justinian, which were fought, from 535 to 555, by Belisarius and Narses, who restored a ravaged Italy to the empire. Contemporaneously (534) the imperial authority was re-established in North Africa and the Vandal kingdom brought to an end. Italy was not long at peace. Between 568 and 572 a new Germanic invasion, that of the Lombards, founded a kingdom that was to last for two centuries. Masters of northern Italy, to which region they gave their name, the Lombards did not, however, win Rome and the southern part of the peninsula, nor did they gain Ravenna, the seat of the imperial exarch, till the eighth century. Rome remained, therefore, connected with the empire which had its seat in Constantinople, but so distant and so close to the Lombard frontier that effective control from Constantinople was impossible— a condition extremely favorable for the growth of the political power of its bishop.

Contemporaneously with the earlier of the events just described, changes of the utmost significance were in process in Gaul. The Franks, of whom mention has been made, had long been pressing into the northern part of the ancient provinces. Divided into several tribes, the King of the Salic Franks, from about 481, was Clovis. A chieftain of great energy, he soon extended his sovereignty as far as the Loire. He and his people were still heathen, though he treated the church with respect. In 493 he married Clotilda, a Burgundian, but, unlike most of her fellow countrymen, a "Catholic," not an Arian. After a great victory over the Alemans, in 496, he declared for Christianity, and was baptized with three thousand of his followers in Rheims, on Christmas of that year. His was the first Germanic tribe, therefore, to be con-

verted to the orthodox faith. Visigoths, Ostrogoths, Vandals,
Burgundians, and Lombards were Arians. This agreement in
belief won for Clovis not only the good-will of the old Roman
population and the support of the bishops whom he, in turn,
favored but, added to his own abilities, enabled him before his
death, in 511, to take from the Visigoths most of their possessions north of the Pyrenees and to become so extensive a ruler
that he may well be called the founder of France, his territories
stretching even beyond the Rhine. That the Franks were
"Catholic" was ultimately, though not immediately, to bring
connections between them and the papacy of most far-reaching
consequences.

The conversion of the Franks had also much influence on
the other Germanic invaders, though the example of the native
population among whom they were settled worked even more
powerfully. The Burgundians abandoned Arianism in 517,
and in 532 became part of the Frankish kingdom. The imperial conquests of Justinian ended the Arian kingdoms of the
Vandals and Ostrogoths. The rivalry of the creeds was ter-
minated in Spain by the renunciation of Arianism by the Visigothic King, Recared, in 587, and confirmed at the Third Council of Toledo, in 589. About 590 the gradual conversion of
the Lombards to Catholicism began—a process not completed
till about 660. Thus all Arianism ultimately disappeared.

SECTION VI. THE GROWTH OF THE PAPACY

To the distinction already attaching to the Roman Church
and its bishop the period of the invasions brought new eminence. Believed to be founded by Peter, situated in the ancient capital, the guardian of apostolical tradition, the largest
and most generous church of the West, it had stood orthodox
in the Arian controversy, and in the ruin of the Germanic invasions it seemed the great surviving institution of the ancient
world which they were unable to overthrow. While most of
the bishops of Rome in this period were men of moderate
abilities, several were the strongest leaders of the West, and to
them great advancement in the authority of the Roman bishop
—the development of a real papacy—was due. Such a leader
of force was Innocent I (402–417). He claimed for the Roman
Church not only custody of apostolical tradition and the founda-

tion of all Western Christianity, but ascribed the decisions of
Sardica (*ante*, p. 121) to the Council of Nicæa, and based on
them a universal jurisdiction of the Roman bishop.[1] Leo I
(440–461) greatly served Rome, in the judgment of the time,
during the invasions of the Huns and Vandals, and largely
influenced the result of the Council of Chalcedon (p. 151). He
emphasized the primacy of Peter among the Apostles, both in
faith and government, and taught that what Peter possessed had
passed to Peter's successors.[2] These claims Leo largely made
good. He ended the attempt to create an independent Gallic
see in Arles; he exercised authority in Spain and North Africa.
In 445 he procured an edict from the Western Emperor, Valentinian III, ordering all to obey the Roman bishop, as having
the "primacy of Saint Peter."[3] On the other hand, the Council of Chalcedon, in 451, by its twenty-eighth canon placed
Constantinople on a practical equality with Rome.[4] Against
this action Leo at once protested; but it foreshadowed the ultimate separation, far more political than religious, between the
churches of East and West.

In the struggle with Monophysitism (p. 154), the bishops of
Rome resisted the efforts of the Emperor Zeno (474–491) and
the Patriarch Acacius of Constantinople to modify the results
of Chalcedon by the so-called *Henoticon*,[5] with the result that
Pope Felix III (483–492) excommunicated Acacius, and a
schism began between East and West which ended in 519 in
a papal triumph. During this controversy Pope Gelasius (492–
496) wrote a letter to Zeno's successor, the Eastern Emperor
Anastasius, in which he declared "there are . . . two by whom
principally this world is ruled: the sacred authority of the
pontiffs and the royal power. Of these the importance of the
priests is so much the greater, as even for Kings of men they
will have to give an account in the divine judgment."[6] In
502 Bishop Ennodius of Pavia urged that the Pope can be
judged by God alone.[7] The later claims of the mediæval
papacy were, therefore, sketched by the beginning of the
sixth century. Circumstances prevented their development
in full practice in the period immediately following. The rise
of the Ostrogothic kingdom in Italy and the reconquest of

[1] *Letters*, 2, 25; Mirbt, *Quellen zur Geschichte des Papsttums*, 54, 55.
[2] *Sermons*, 3[2, 3]; Ayer, p. 477.   [3] Mirbt, p. 65.   [4] Ayer, p. 521.
[5] Ayer, p. 527.   [6] Ayer, p. 531.   [7] Mirbt, p. 70.

Italy by the Eastern empire, diminished the independence of the papacy. Outside of Italy the growth of a new Catholic power, the Franks, and the gradual conversion of Arian Germanic rulers, brought about a harmony between the new sovereigns and their bishops that gave to the latter extensive independence of Roman claims, though accompanied by great dependence on the Germanic sovereigns. The full realization of the papal ideal, thus early established, was to be a task of centuries, and was to encounter many vicissitudes.

SECTION VII.   MONASTICISM

It has been pointed out that ascetic ideals and a double standard of Christian morality had long been growing in the church before the time of Constantine (*ante*, pp. 103, 104). Their progress was aided by the ascetic tendencies inherent in the better philosophies of the ancient world.   Origen, for instance, who was permeated with the Hellenistic spirit, was distinguished for his asceticism.   Long before the close of the third century the holy virgins were a conspicuous element in the church, and men and women, without leaving their homes, were practising asceticism.   Nor is asceticism, or even monasticism, peculiar to Christianity.   Its representatives are to be found in the religions of India and among Jews, Greeks, and Egyptians.

Certain causes led to its increased development contemporary with the recognition of Christianity by the state.   The low condition of the church, emphasized by the influx of vast numbers in the peace from 260 to 303, and after the conversion of Constantine, led to enlarged valuation of the ascetic life by serious-minded Christians.   The cessation of martyrdoms left asceticism the highest Christian achievement attainable.   The world was filled with sights that offended Christian morality, from which it seemed well to flee.   The mind of antiquity regarded the practice of contemplation as more estimable than the active virtues.   Above all, the extreme formalism and rigidity of public worship, as developed by the close of the third century, led to a desire for a freer and more individual approach to God.   Monasticism was soon to become formal enough; but in its initiation it was a breach with the limitations of conventional Christian worship and service.   It was in origin a layman's movement.

Anthony, the founder of Christian monasticism, was born in Koma, in central Egypt, about 250, of native (Coptic) stock. Impressed with Christ's words to the rich young man,[1] he gave up his possessions, and about 270 took up the ascetic life in his native village. Some fifteen years later he went into the solitude, becoming a hermit. Here he is said to have lived till 356 (?). He believed himself tormented by demons in every imaginable form. He fasted. He practised the strictest self-denial. He prayed constantly. He would draw near to God by overcoming the flesh. Anthony soon had many imitators, some of whom lived absolutely alone, others in groups, of which the largest were in the deserts of Nitria and Scetis. Whether singly or in groups, these monks were as far as possible hermit-like. Their worship and their self-denials were largely of their own devising.

The first great improver of monasticism was Pachomius. Born about 292, he became a soldier, and was converted from heathenism to Christianity when perhaps twenty years old. At first he adopted the hermit life, but dissatisfied with its irregularities, he established the first Christian monastery in Tabennisi, in southern Egypt, about 315–320. Here all the inmates were knit into a single body, having assigned work, regular hours of worship, similar dress, and cells close to one another—in a word, a life in common under an abbot. This was a vastly more healthful type of monasticism. It was also one possible for women, for whom Pachomius established a convent. At his death, in 346, there were ten of his monasteries in Egypt.

The two types, the hermit form of Anthony and the cenobite organization of Pachomius, continued side by side in Egypt, and both were carried from that land to the rest of the empire. Syria saw a considerable development early in the fourth century. There the hermit form took extravagant expression, of which an example, a little later, is that of the famous Simeon Stylites, who dwelt for thirty years, till his death in 459, on the top of a pillar, situated east of Antioch. Monasticism in Asia Minor, on the other hand, continued the tradition of Pachomius, chiefly owing to the efforts of its great popularizer, Basil (*ante*, p. 125), who labored for its spread from about 360 to his death in 379. The Rule which bears

[1] *Matt.* 19[21].

his name, whether his actual composition or not, was even more that of a life in common than that of Pachomius. It emphasized work, prayer, and Bible reading. It taught that monks should aid those outside by the care of orphans, and similar good deeds. It discouraged extreme asceticism. Basil's Rule is, in a general way, a basis of the monasticism of the Greek and Russian Churches to the present day, though with much less weight laid than by him on work and helpfulness to others.

The introduction of monasticism into the West was the work of Athanasius. By the closing years of the fourth century the exhortations and examples of Jerome, Ambrose, and Augustine brought it much favor, though it also encountered no little opposition. In France its great advocate was Martin of Tours, who established a monastery near Poitiers about 362. Soon monasticism, both in its cenobite and in its hermit forms, was to be found throughout the West. The earliest monks, as in the East, were laymen; but Eusebius, bishop of Vercelli in Italy, who died in 371, began the practice of requiring the clergy of his cathedral to live the monastic life. Through the influence of this example it gradually became the custom for monks to receive priestly ordination. Such clerical consecration became, also, the rule ultimately in the East.

Western monasticism was long in a chaotic condition. Individual monasteries had their separate rules. Asceticism, always characteristic in high degree of Eastern monasticism, found many disciples. On the other hand, many monasteries were lax. The great reformer of Western monasticism was Benedict of Nursia. Born about 480, he studied for a brief time in Rome, but, oppressed by the evils of the city, he became a hermit (c. 500) in a cave of the mountains at Subiaco, east of Rome. The fame of his sanctity gathered disciples about him, and led to the offer of the headship of a neighboring monastery, which he accepted only to leave when he found its ill-regulated monks unwilling to submit to his discipline. At some uncertain date, traditionally 529, he now founded the mother monastery of the Benedictine order, on the hill of Monte Cassino, about half-way between Rome and Naples. To it he gave his Rule, and in it he died; the last certain event of his life, his meeting with the Ostrogothic King, Totila, having taken place in 542.

Benedict's famous Rule[1] exhibited his profound knowledge of human nature and his Roman genius for organization. His conception of a monastery was that of a permanent, self-contained and self-supporting garrison of Christ's soldiers. At its head was an abbot, who must be implicitly obeyed, yet who was bound in grave matters of common concern to consult all the brethren, and in minor questions the elder monks. None was to become a monk without having tried the life of the monastery for a year; but, once admitted, his vows were irrevocable. To Benedict's thinking, worship was undoubtedly the prime duty of a monk. Its daily common observance occupied at least four hours, divided into seven periods. Almost as much emphasis was laid on work. "Idleness is the enemy of the soul." Hence Benedict prescribed manual labor in the fields and reading. Some fixed time must be spent in reading each day, varying with the seasons of the year; and in Lent books must be assigned, with provision to insure their being read. These injunctions made every Benedictine monastery, at all true to the founder's ideal, a centre of industry, and the possessor of a library. The value of these provisions in the training of the Germanic nations and the preservation of literature was inestimable. Yet they were but secondary to Benedict's main purpose, that of worship. In general, Benedict's Rule was characterized by great moderation and good sense in its requirements as to food, labor, and discipline. It was a strict life, but one not at all impossible for the average earnest man.

In the Benedictine system early Western monasticism is to be seen at its best. His Rule spread slowly. It was carried by Roman missionaries to England and Germany. It did not penetrate France till the seventh century; but by the time of Charlemagne it had become well-nigh universal. With the Rule of Benedict the adjustment between monasticism and the church was complete. The services of its monks as missionaries and pioneers were of inestimable value. In troubled times the monastery afforded the only refuge for peace-loving souls. The highest proof of its adaption to the later Roman Empire and the Middle Ages was that not only the best men supported the institution; they were to be found in it. Its

---

[1] Extracts in Ayer, pp. 631–641; practically in full in Henderson, *Select Historical Documents of the Middle Ages*, pp. 274–314.

great faults, from a modern point of view, were its emphasis on a distinction between higher and lower morality, and its discredit of the life of the Christian family; but both were inheritances from Christian conditions and ideals in the Roman Empire antecedent to the development of monasticism. Monasticism was their product, not their cause.

SECTION VIII. AMBROSE AND CHRYSOSTOM

The contrast between East and West is in many ways illustrated by the unlike qualities and experiences of Chrysostom and Ambrose. Ambrose was born in Trier, now in western Germany, where his father held the high civil office of prætorian prefect of Gaul, about 337–340. Educated in Rome for a civil career, his talents, integrity, and likableness led to his appointment, about 374, as governor of a considerable part of northern Italy, with his residence in Milan, then practically an imperial capital. The death of the Arian bishop, Auxentius, in 374, left the Milanese see vacant. The two factions were soon in bitter struggle as to the theological complexion of his successor. The young governor entered the church to quiet the throng, when the cry was raised, "Ambrose Bishop!" and he found himself, though unbaptized, elected bishop of Milan. To Ambrose, this was a call of God. He gave up his wealth to the poor and the church. He studied theology. He became a most acceptable preacher. Above all, he possessed to the full the Roman talent for administration, and he soon became the first ecclesiastic of the West. Strongly attached to the Nicene faith, Ambrose would make no compromise with the Arians, and resisted all their attempts to secure places of worship in Milan—an effort in which they were aided by the Empress Justina, mother of the youthful Valentinian II. In the same spirit he opposed successfully the efforts of the heathen party in Rome to obtain from Valentinian II the restoration of the Altar of Victory in the Senate chamber, and other privileges for the older worship. His greatest triumph was in the case of the Emperor Theodosius. That quick-tempered ruler, angered by the murder of the governor of Thessalonica, in 390, caused a punitive massacre of its inhabitants. Ambrose, with rare moral courage, called on the Emperor to manifest his public repentance.[1] It throws a

[1] Ayer, pp. 390, 391.

pleasing light on the character of Theodosius that he obeyed
the admonition.

Ambrose was a theological writer of such reputation that
the Roman Church reckons him as one of its "Doctors"—or
authoritative teachers. His work, however, in this field was
largely a reproduction of the thoughts of Greek theologians,
though with a deeper sense of sin and grace than they. "I
will not glory because I am righteous, but I will glory because
I am redeemed. I will not glory because I am free from sin,
but because my sins are forgiven." [1] Ambrose's bent was
practical. He wrote on Christian ethics, in full sympathy with
the ascetic movement of the time. He contributed much to
the development of Christian hymnology in the West. Forceful and sometimes overbearing, he was a man of the highest
personal character and of indefatigable zeal—a true prince of the
church. Such men were needed in the shock of the collapsing
empire if the church was to survive in power. He died in 397.

Very different was the life of Chrysostom. John, to whom
the name Chrysostom, "golden-mouthed," was given long after
his death, was born of noble and well-to-do parents in Antioch about 345–347. Losing his father shortly after his birth,
he was brought up by his religious-minded mother, Anthusa,
and early distinguished himself in scholarship and eloquence.
About 370, he was baptized and probably ordained a "reader."
He now practised extreme asceticism, and pursued theological
studies under Diodorus of Tarsus, one of the leaders of the
later Antiochian school. Not satisfied with his austerities, he
became a hermit (c. 375), and so remained till ill-health compelled his return to Antioch, where he was ordained a deacon
(c. 381). In 386 he was advanced to the priesthood. Then
followed the happiest and most useful period of his life. For
twelve years he was the great preacher of Antioch—the ablest
that the Oriental Church probably ever possessed. His sermons were exegetical and eminently practical. The simple,
grammatical understanding of the Scriptures, always preferred
in Antioch to the allegorical interpretation beloved in Alexandria, appealed to him. His themes were eminently social—the
Christian conduct of life. He soon had an enormous following.

Such was Chrysostom's fame that, on the see of Constantinople falling vacant, he was practically forced by Eutropius,

---

[1] *De Jacob et vita beata*, 1 : 6[21].

the favorite of the Emperor Arcadius, to accept the bishopric of the capital in 398. Here he soon won a popular hearing like that of Antioch. From the first, however, his way in Constantinople was beset with foes. The unscrupulous patriarch of Alexandria, Theophilus, desired to bring Constantinople into practical subjection. Himself the opponent of Origen's teaching, he charged Chrysostom with too great partiality for that master. Chrysostom's strict discipline, for which there was ample justification, was disliked by the loose-living clergy of Constantinople. Worst of all, he won the hostility of the vigorous Empress Eudoxia, by reasons of denunciations of feminine extravagance in dress, which she thought aimed at herself. Chrysostom was certainly as tactless as he was fearless in denouncing offenses in high places. All the forces against him gathered together. A pretext for attack soon arose. In his opposition to Origen, Theophilus had disciplined certain monks of Egypt. Four of these, known as the "tall brothers," fled to Chrysostom, by whom they were well received. Theophilus and Chrysostom's other enemies now secured a synod, at an imperial estate near Constantinople known as "The Oak," which, under the leadership of Theophilus, condemned and deposed Chrysostom in 403. The Empress was as superstitious as she was enraged, and an accident in the palace—later tradition pictured it probably mistakenly as an earthquake—led to Chrysostom's recall shortly after he had left the capital. Peace was of brief duration. A silver statue of the Empress, erected hard by his cathedral, led to denunciations by Chrysostom of the ceremonies of its dedication. The Empress saw in him more than ever a personal enemy. This time, in spite of warm popular support, he was banished to the miserable town of Cucusus, on the edge of Armenia. Pope Innocent I protested, but in vain. Yet from this exile Chrysostom continued so to influence his friends by letter that his opponents determined to place him in deeper obscurity. In 407 he was ordered to Pityus, but he never reached there, dying on the journey.

The fate of this most deserving, if not most judicious, preacher of righteousness illustrates the seamy side of imperial interference in ecclesiastical affairs, and the rising jealousies of the great sees of the East, from whose mutual hostility the church and the empire were greatly to suffer.

SECTION IX.   THE CHRISTOLOGICAL CONTROVERSIES

The Nicene result determined that Christ is fully God, and "was made man." On the common basis of Nicene orthodoxy, however, the further question arose as to the relations of the divine and human in Him. Regarding that problem the Nicene creed was silent, and even the great Nicene champion, Athanasius, had not paid much attention to it. Only in the West had a general formula come into extensive use. As the Nicene decision had been largely anticipated by Tertullian, with the result that the West had been united when the East was divided, so thanks to the clear definitions of that great African writer, the West had a conception of full deity and full manhood existing in Christ, without confusion, and without diminution of the qualities appropriate to each. In the new struggle, as in that of Nicæa, the Western view was to triumph. Yet neither in its conception of "one substance in three persons," nor in that of "one person, Jesus, God, and man" (*ante*, p. 69), had the West any wrought-out philosophical theory. What Tertullian had given it were clear-cut judicial definitions of traditional beliefs rather than philosophically thought-out theology. It was the advantage of the West once more, as in the Nicene struggle, that it was now united, even if its thought was not so profound as that of the divided East, when the East fairly began to wrestle with the intellectual problems involved.

It was possible to approach the Christological problem from two angles. The unity of Christ might be so emphasized as to involve a practical absorption of His humanity into divinity; or the integrity of each element, the divine and the human, maintained in such fashion as to give color to the interpretation that in Him were two separate beings. Both tendencies were manifested in the controversy—the first being that toward which the theological leaders of Alexandria leaned, and the latter being derivable from the teachings of the school of Antioch.

The first and one of the ablest of those who undertook a really profound discussion of the relation of the human and the divine in Christ was Apollinaris, bishop of Laodicea in Syria (?–c. 390). A hearty supporter of the Nicene decision, he enjoyed for a considerable time at least the friendship of Athanasius. His intellectual gifts were such as to command respect even from his opponents. Moreover, as with Athanasius, Apollinaris's interest was primarily religious. To both, Christ's work for men was the transformation of our sinful mortality into divine and blessed immortality. This salvation, Apollinaris thought with Athanasius, could be achieved only if Christ was completely and perfectly divine. But how, Apollinaris argued, could Christ be made up of a perfect man united with complete God? Was that not to assert two Sons, one eternal, and the other by adoption?[1] Nor could Apollinaris explain Christ's sinlessness or the harmony of His wills, if Christ was complete man joined with full God.[2] To him, the best solution seemed akin to that of Arius, whom he otherwise opposed, that in Jesus the place of the soul was taken by the Logos, and only the body was human. That view having been condemned, though without mention of his name, by a synod in Alexandria in 362,[3] Apollinaris apparently altered his theory so as to hold that Jesus had the body and animal soul of a man, but that the reasoning spirit in Him was the Logos.[4] At the same time he held that the divine so made the human one with it—so absorbed it—that "God has in His own flesh suffered our sorrows."[5] These opinions seemed to do special honor to Christ's divinity, and were destined to be widely and permanently influential in Oriental Christian thinking, but they really denied Christ's true humanity, and as such speedily called down condemnation on their author. Rome decided against him in 377 and 382, Antioch in 378, and finally the so-called Second Ecumenical Council—that of Constantinople —in 381.[6]

Apollinaris was strongly oppposed by Gregory of Nazianzus and by the school of Antioch. The founder of the latter, in its later stage, was Diodorus (?–394), long a presbyter of Antioch, and from 378 to his death bishop of Tarsus. Its roots, indeed, ran back into the earlier teaching of Paul of Samosata (*ante*, p. 72) and Lucian (*ante*, p. 106); but the extreme positions which they represented, and their leadership, were rejected, and the school stood on the basis of the Nicene orthodoxy. It was marked by a degree of literalism in its exegesis of Scripture quite in contrast to the excessive use of allegory

---

[1] Ayer, p. 495.　　　　　　　　　　　　　　　　[2] *Ibid.*
[3] Athanasius, *Tomus ad Antiochenos*, 7.
[4] Ayer, p. 495　　　　　[5] *Ibid.*, p. 496.　　　　　　[6] *Canon*, 1.

by the Alexandrians. Its philosophy showed the influence of Aristotle as theirs that of Plato. Its thought of Christ was more influenced by the tradition of Asia Minor, of the "second Adam," and by the ancient distinction between the Jesus of history and the Christ of experience than was Alexandria. Antioch, therefore, laid more weight of teaching on the earthly life and human nature of Jesus than was the tendency in Alexandria. In this attempt to give true value to Christ's humanity, Diodorus approached the view that in Christ were two persons in moral rather than essential union. Since the Logos is eternal and like can only bear like, that which was born of Mary was the human only. The incarnation was the indwelling of the Logos in a perfect man, as of God in a temple. These views are reminiscent of the adoptionist Christology, which had found one of its latest avowed defenders in Paul of Samosata in Antioch a century earlier. They were out of touch with the Greek conception of salvation—the making divine of the human.

Among the disciples of Diodorus were Chrysostom (*ante*, p. 141), Theodore of Mopsuestia, and Nestorius. Theodore, a native of Antioch, who held the bishopric for which he is named for thirty-six years, till his death in 428, was the ablest exegete and theologian of the Antiochian school. Though he maintained that God and man in Christ constituted one person—*prosopon, πρόσωπον*—he had difficulty in making that contention real, and held theories practically identical with those of Diodorus.[1]

Nestorius, a presbyter and monk of Antioch, held in high repute there as a preacher, was made patriarch of Constantinople in 428. Recent discoveries, especially of his own autobiographical work, *The Treatise of Heraclides of Damascus*, have immensely broadened knowledge of his real theological position, as well as of the facts of his later life. His dogmatic standpoint was essentially that of the school of Antioch; yet he would not admit that there were in Christ two persons— the doctrine with which he was charged. "With the one name Christ we designate at the same time two natures. . . . The essential characteristics in the nature of the divinity and in the humanity are from all eternity distinguished."[2] Perhaps his furthest departure from the current Greek conception of salvation is to be seen in such an expression as: "God the Word

---

[1] Ayer, pp. 498–501.   [2] *Ibid.*, p. 502.

is also named Christ because He has always conjunction with Christ. And it is impossible for God the Word to do anything without the humanity, for all is planned upon an intimate conjunction, not on the deification of the humanity." [1] Nestorius would emphasize the reality and completeness of the human in the Christian's Lord.

Opposed to Nestorius, and to be his bitterest enemy, was Cyril, the patriarch of Alexandria (412–444), the nephew and successor of the patriarch who had had so unworthy a part in the downfall of Chrysostom. In him unscrupulous ambition combined with the jealousy of Constantinople long entertained in Alexandria—and it must be admitted, reciprocated—and with the hostility of the rival schools of Alexandria and Antioch. Yet it is but just to Cyril to note that there was more in his opposition to Nestorius than mere jealousy and rivalry, however prominent those unlovely traits may have been. Cyril, following the Alexandrian tradition, and in consonance with the Greek conception of salvation, saw in Christ the full making divine of the human. Though he rejected the view of Apollinaris and held that Christ's humanity was complete in that it possessed body, soul, and spirit, he really stood very near to Apollinaris. His emphasis on the divine in Christ was such that, though he described the union in Him as that of "two natures," the only personality in Christ was that of the Logos. The Logos "took flesh," He clothed Himself with humanity. The human element had no personality apart from the Logos. Jesus was not an individual man. Yet while Cyril held to an interchange of qualities between the divine and the human, each is a complete nature. "From two natures, one"; and that one personality is the divine. For Cyril it was, therefore, God made flesh, who was born, who died, of whom we partake in the Supper, and whose making divine of humanity is the proof and means that we, too, shall be made partakers of the divine nature.[2] If the school of Antioch came near such a separation of the divine and the human as to leave Christ only the Son of God by adoption, that of Cyril allowed Him little more than an impersonal humanity absorbed in divinity.

An ancient designation of the Mother of Jesus was "Mother of God"—*Theotokos*, Θεοτόκος. It had been used by Alexander of Alexandria, Athanasius, Apollinaris, and Gregory of Nazianzus.

[1] Ayer, p. 502.   [2] See Ayer, pp. 505–507.

To Cyril it was, of course, a natural expression. Everywhere in the East it may be said to have been in good usage, save where the school of Antioch had influence, and even Theodore of Mopsuestia of that school was willing to employ the expression, if carefully guarded.[1] Nestorius found it current coin in Constantinople. To his thinking it did not sufficiently distinguish the human from the divine in Christ. He therefore preached against it, at the beginning of his bishopric, declaring the proper form to be "Mother of Christ"—"for that which is born of flesh is flesh."[2] Yet even he expressed himself a little later as willing to say *Theotokos*, in the guarded way in which Theodore would employ it. "It can be endured in consideration of the fact that the temple, which is inseparably united with God the Word, comes of her."[3] In preaching against this expression Nestorius had touched popular piety and the rising religious reverence for the Virgin on the quick. Cyril saw his opportunity to humiliate the rival see of Constantinople and the school of Antioch at one blow, while advancing his own Christology. Cyril promptly wrote to the Egyptian monks defending the disputed phrase, and there soon followed an exchange of critical letters between Cyril and Nestorius. It speedily came to an open attack on the patriarch of Constantinople.

Cyril now brought every influence at his command to his aid in one of the most repulsive contests in church history. He appealed to the Emperor and Empress, Theodosius II and Eudocia, and to the Emperor's sister, Pulcheria, representing that Nestorius's doctrines destroyed all basis of salvation. He presented his case to Pope Celestine I (422–432). Nestorius, in his turn, also wrote to the Pope. Celestine promptly found in favor of Cyril, and ordered, through a Roman synod in 430, that Nestorius recant or be excommunicated. The action of the Pope is hard to understand. The letter of Nestorius agreed more nearly in its definition of the question at issue with the Western view than did the theory of Cyril. Nestorius declared his faith in "both natures which by the highest and unmixed union are adored in the one person of the Only Begotten."[4] Politics were probably the determining factor. Rome and Alexandria had long worked together against the

---

[1] Ayer, p. 500. [2] *Ibid.*, p. 501. [3] *Ibid.*
[4] In Loofs, *Nestoriana*, p. 171.

rising claims of Constantinople. Nestorius was less respectful in his address to the Pope than Cyril. Moreover, without being a Pelagian, Nestorius had given some degree of favor to the Pelagians whom the Pope opposed (see p. 187). Nestorius's attack on the much-prized *Theotokos* was also displeasing to Celestine.

The empire being now widely involved in the dispute, the two Emperors, Theodosius II of the East, and Valentinian III in the West, called a general council to meet in Ephesus in 431. Cyril and his followers were early on hand, as was Nestorius, but the friends of Nestorius were slow in arriving. Cyril and Memnon, bishop of Ephesus promptly organized such of the council as were present and they could secure. Nestorius was condemned and deposed in a single day's session.[1] A few days later Nestorius's friends, led by John, the patriarch of Antioch, arrived. They organized and, in turn, condemned and deposed Cyril and Memnon.[2] Cyril's council, meanwhile, had been joined by the papal delegates, and added John to its list of deposed, at the same time condemning Pelagianism (see p. 188), doubtless to please the West. The Emperor Theodosius II was at a loss as to what course to pursue. Nestorius retired to a monastery. Theodosius imprisoned Cyril and Memnon as trouble-makers, but politics inclined to their side and they were soon allowed to return to their sees. The real victim was Nestorius, and worse was to follow.

Antioch and Alexandria were now in hostility more than ever, but both, under imperial pressure, were made willing to compromise. Antioch would sacrifice Nestorius, and Cyril concede something to Antioch in creedal formula. Accordingly, in 433, John of Antioch sent to Cyril a creed composed, it is probable, by Theodoret of Cyrus, then the leading theologian of the school of Antioch. This creed was more Antiochian than Alexandrian, though it could be interpreted in either direction. "We therefore acknowledge our Lord Jesus Christ . . . complete God and complete man. . . . A union of the two natures has been made, therefore we confess one Christ. . . . The holy Virgin is *Theotokos*, because God the Word was made flesh and became man, and from her conception united with Himself the temple received from her."[3]

---

[1] Ayer. p. 507.   [2] *Ibid.*, 509.   [3] *Ibid.*, pp. 510, 511.

Cyril now signed this creed, though without retracting any of his former utterances. By so doing he made irrevocable the overthrow of Nestorius. Yet Nestorius could have signed it even more willingly than he. This agreement enabled Cyril to secure general recognition in the East for his council of 431, in Ephesus—in the West the participation of papal representatives had always accredited it as the Third General Council.

Nestorius himself was banished to upper Egypt. There he lived a miserable existence. and there he wrote, certainly as late as the autumn of 450, his remarkable *Treatise of Heraclides of Damascus*. Whether he survived the Council of Chalcedon is uncertain. There is some reason to think that he did. At all events he rejoiced in the steps which led to it, and felt himself in sympathy with the views which were then proclaimed orthodox.

Not all of Nestorius's sympathizers shared in his desertion. Ibas, the leading theologian of the Syrian school of Edessa, supported his teaching. Persecuted in the empire, Nestorianism found much following even in Syria, and protection in Persia. There it developed a wide missionary activity. In the seventh century it entered China, and about the same time southern India. Nestorian churches still exist in the region where Turkey and Persia divide the territory between Lake Urumia and the upper Tigris, and also in India.

The agreement of 433 between Antioch and Alexandria was, in reality, but a truce. The division of the two parties but increased. Cyril undoubtedly represented the majority of the Eastern Church, with his emphasis on the divine in the person of Christ, at the expense of reducing the human to an impersonal humanity. Though he vigorously rejected Apollinarianism, his tendency was that of Apollinaris. It had the sympathy of the great party of monks; and many, especially in Egypt, went further than Cyril, and viewed Christ's humanity as practically absorbed in His divinity, so that He possessed one nature only, and that divine. Cyril died in 444, and was succeeded as patriarch of Alexandria by Dioscurus, a man of far less intellectual acumen and religious motive, but even more ambitious, if possible, to advance the authority of the Alexandrian see. Two years later, 446, a new patriarch, Flavian, took the bishop's throne in Constantinople. Though little is known of his early history, it seems probable that his sympathies were with the school of Antioch. From the first, Flavian's course promised to be stormy. He had the opposition not only of Dioscurus, but of the imperial favorite minister, Chrysaphius, who had supplanted Pulcheria in the counsels of Theodosius II. Chrysaphius was a supporter of the Alexandrians.

Occasion for quarrel soon arose. Dioscurus planned an attack on the remaining representatives of the Antiochian school as Nestorian heretics. In sympathy with this effort, and as a leader of the monastic party, on the help of which Dioscurus counted, stood the aged abbot or "archimandrite," Eutyches of Constantinople, a man of little theological ability, a partisan of the late Cyril, and influential not only by reason of his popularity, but by the friendship of Chrysaphius. Eutyches was now charged with heresy by Bishop Eusebius of Dorylæum. Flavian took up the case with reluctance, evidently knowing its possibilities of mischief; but at a local synod in Constantinople, late in 448, Eutyches was examined and condemned. His heresy was that he affirmed: "I confess that our Lord was of two natures before the union [i. e., the incarnation], but after the union one nature."[1]

Rome had now one of the ablest of its Popes in the person of Leo I (440–461) (see ante, p. 135), and to Leo both Eutyches and Flavian speedily presented the case.[2] To Flavian, whom he heartily supported, Leo wrote his famous letter of June, 449, usually called the Tome,[3] in which the great Pope set forth the view which the West had entertained since the time of Tertullian, that in Christ were two full and complete natures, which, "without detracting from the properties of either nature and substance, came together in one person." What may be said, chiefly in criticism of Leo's letter is that, while representing clearly and truly the Western tradition, it did not touch the intellectual depths to which the subtler Greek mind had carried its speculations. Probably it was well that it did not.

Meanwhile Dioscurus was moving actively in Eutyches's defense and the extension of his own claims. At his instance the Emperor called a general council to meet in Ephesus in August, 449. At Ephesus Dioscurus was supreme. Eutyches was rehabilitated, Flavian and Eusebius of Dorylæum con-

---

[1] Ayer, pp. 513, 514.   [2] Letters of Leo, 20–28.
[3] Ibid., 28; extracts, Ayer, p. 515.

demned. Leo's *Tome* was denied a reading. It was a stormy meeting, but probably not more so than that of Ephesus, in 431, or Chalcedon, in 451. Flavian died shortly after, and rumor had it in consequence of physical violence at the council. The report seems unfounded. Dioscurus had achieved a great victory, but at the fatal cost of a rupture of the ancient alliance between Alexandria and Rome. Leo promptly denounced the council as a "synod of robbers"; but the Emperor, Theodosius II, gave it his hearty support and a sympathizer with Dioscurus became patriarch of Constantinople.

Leo had no success with Theodosius II, but much with the Emperor's sister, Pulcheria; and the situation was profoundly altered when the accidental death of Theodosius in July, 450, put Pulcheria and her husband, Marcian, on the throne. The new sovereigns entered at once into relations with Leo. The Pope wished a new council in Italy, where his influence would have been potent, but this did not satisfy imperial politics. The new General Council was called to meet in Nicæa, in the autumn of 451. Imperial convenience led to the change of place to Chalcedon, opposite Constantinople, and there some six hundred bishops, all but the papal delegates and two others from the Orient, assembled in what has ever since been known as the Fourth Ecumenical Council (that of Ephesus, in 449, being rejected).

The council proceeded rapidly with its work. Dioscurus was deposed and sent into exile by imperial authority, where he died three years later. After imperial pressure had been exerted, a commission was appointed, of which the papal delegates were members, to draw up a creed. Its production was promptly ratified by the council. The result was, indeed, a Western triumph. Rome had given the decision to the question at issue, and in so doing had made a compromise between the positions of Antioch and Alexandria that was wholly satisfactory to neither. The result was a lengthy document, reciting the so-called Nicæno-Constantinopolitan creed (*ante*, p. 128), approving Leo's *Tome*, and condemning previous heresies.[1] Its essential part—the creed of Chalcedon—is as follows:

We, then, following the holy Fathers, all with one consent, teach men to confess one and the same Son, our Lord Jesus Christ,

---

[1] Ayer, pp. 517–521.

the same perfect in Godhead and also perfect in manhood; truly God and truly man, of a reasonable soul and body; consubstantial (ὁμοούσιον) with the Father according to the Godhead, and consubstantial with us according to the manhood, in all things like unto us, without sin; begotten before all ages of the Father according to the Godhead, and in these latter days, for us and for our salvation, born of the Virgin Mary, the Mother of God (*Theotokos*), according to the manhood; one and the same Christ, Son, Lord, Only-begotten, in two natures, inconfusedly, unchangeably, indivisibly, inseparably, the distinction of natures being by no means taken away by the union, but rather the property of each nature being preserved, and concurring in one person (*prosopon*) and one subsistence (*hypostasis*), not parted or divided into two persons, but one and the same Son and Only-begotten, God the Word, the Lord Jesus Christ; as the prophets from the beginning have declared concerning Him, and the Lord Jesus Christ Himself has taught us, and the creed of the holy Fathers has handed down to us.

Such is the creed that has ever since been regarded in the Greek, Latin, and most Protestant Churches as the "orthodox" solution of the Christological problem. It is easy to criticise it. Its adoption was greatly involved in ecclesiastical politics. It solved few of the intellectual difficulties regarding Christology which had been raised in the East. It did not even heal the Christological quarrels. But, when all is admitted, it must be said that its formulation was fortunate and its consequences useful. It established a norm of doctrine in a field in which there had been great confusion. More important than that, it was true to the fundamental conviction of the church that in Christ a complete revelation of God is made in terms of a genuine human life.

If a coincidence of imperial and Roman interests had secured a great dogmatic victory for Rome, the imperial authority was determined that the victory should not be one of Roman jurisdiction. By a canon, against which Leo protested, the council exalted the claims of Constantinople to a dignity like that of Rome (*ante*, p. 135). Nor was the downfall of Alexandria less damaging. Alexandrian rivalry of Constantinople had been Rome's advantage in the East. Now successful rivalry was at an end, for the consequences of the Chalcedonian decision crippled Alexandria permanently. By the council the historic distribution of the Orient was completed, Jerusalem being given the patriarchal standing which it had long claimed, side by side with the three older patriarchates, Constantinople, Alexandria, and Antioch.

SECTION X. THE EAST DIVIDED

The creed of Chalcedon was now the official standard of the empire. Its Western origin and spirit made it unacceptable, however, to a large portion of the East. To many Orientals it seemed "Nestorian." This was especially true in those regions which shared most strongly in the Alexandrian tendency to emphasize the divine in Christ at the expense of the fully human, and these elements of opposition included most of the monks, the old native stock of Egypt generally, and a large portion of the population of Syria and Armenia. Undoubtedly the tendencies which the "orthodox" Cyril and his heretical successor, Dioscurus, had represented were consonant with the Greek conception of salvation, and seemed to do special honor to Christ. These rejecters of the creed of Chalcedon included many shades of opinion, but as a whole they showed little departure from Cyril. Their chief difference from Chalcedon and the West was one of emphasis. They rejected Eutyches, yet most of them would say "of two natures," provided it was understood that the human and divine were united in the incarnation into one nature, and that essentially divine, with human attributes. As with Cyril, this humanity was impersonal, and, perhaps, even more than with him it was transformed into divinity, so that without ceasing, in a certain sense, to be human, it was properly describable as one divine nature. Hence the opponents of Chalcedon were called Monophysites—believers in one nature.

Immediately after the Council of Chalcedon Palestine and, next, Egypt were in practical revolution, which the government was able only slowly to master. By 457 the see of Alexandria was in possession of a Monophysite, Timothy, called by his enemies the Cat; by 461, Peter the Fuller, of the same faith, held that of Antioch. These captures were not to be permanent, but the native populations of Egypt and Syria were throwing off the dominance of Constantinople and largely sympathized with the Monophysite protest. In Antioch Peter the Fuller caused fresh commotion by adding to the *Trisagion,* so that the ascription ran: "Holy God, holy Strong, holy Immortal, *who was crucified for us.*"

The empire found itself grievously threatened, politically no less than religiously, by these disaffections; and much of the imperial policy for more than two centuries was devoted to their adjustment, with slight permanent success. In the contest between Zeno and Basilicus for the imperial throne, the latter made a direct bid for Monophysite support by issuing, in 476, an *Encyclion*, in which he anathematized "the so-called *Tome* of Leo, and all things done at Chalcedon" in modification of the Nicene creed.[1] For such a reversal the East was not yet ready, and this action of Basilicus was one of the causes that led to his overthrow by Zeno. Zeno, however, probably induced by the patriarch Acacius of Constantinople, made a new attempt to heal the schism. In 482 he published his famous *Henoticon*.[2] In it the results of the Councils of Nicæa and Constantinople were confirmed, Nestorius and Eutyches condemned, and Cyril's "twelve chapters"[3] approved. It gave a brief Christological statement, the exact relationship of which to that of Chalcedon was not, and was not intended to be, clear. Its chief significance was in the declaration: "These things we write, not as making an innovation upon the faith, but to satisfy you; and every one who has held or holds any other opinion, either at the present or at another time, whether at Chalcedon or in any synod whatever, we anathematize." This left it free to hold the Chalcedonian creed to be erroneous. The consequence was not peace but confusion. While many Monophysites accepted it, the Monophysite extremists would have nothing to do with the *Henoticon*. On the other hand, the Roman see, feeling its honor and its orthodoxy attacked by this practical rejection of Chalcedon, excommunicated Acacius and broke off relations with the East, the schism continuing till 519, when the Emperor Justin renewed the authority of Chalcedon, under circumstances that increased the prestige of the papacy,[4] but only alienated Egypt and Syria the more.

Justin's successor, the great Justinian (527-565), more fully than any other of the Eastern Emperors, succeeded in making himself master of the church. His conspicuous military suc-

---

[1] Ayer, pp. 523–526.
[3] *Ibid.*, pp. 505–507.
[2] *Ibid.*, pp. 527–529.
[4] *Ante*, p. 135; see Ayer, p. 536.

cesses restored to the empire for a time control of Italy and
North Africa. The church was now practically a department
of the state. Heathenism was suppressed and persecuted as
never before. While Justinian himself was, at first, strongly
Chalcedonian in his sympathies, his Empress, Theodora, leaned
to the Monophysite side. He soon gave up the persecution of
Monophysites with which his reign began. Himself one of the
ablest theological minds of the age, he sought to develop an
ecclesiastical policy that would so interpret the creed of Chalcedon that, while leaving it technically untouched, would exclude any possible Antiochian or "Nestorian" construction,
thus bringing its significance fully into accord with the theology of Cyril of Alexandria. By this means he hoped to placate the Monophysites, and also to satisfy the wishes of the
East generally, whether "orthodox" or Monophysite, without
offending Rome and the West too deeply by an actual rejection
of the Chalcedonian decision. Hence the establishment of a
Cyrillic-Chalcedonian orthodoxy was Justinian's aim. It was
a difficult task. As far as concerned a satisfaction of the Monophysites in general it failed. In its effort to render the Cyrillic interpretation of the creed of Chalcedon the only "orthodox" view it succeeded. Any form of Antiochianism was permanently discredited. By this result Justinian undoubtedly
satisfied the wishes of the overwhelming majority of the
"orthodox" East.

Justinian was greatly aided in his task by the rise of a fresh
interpretation of the Chalcedonian creed, in the teaching of a
monastic theologian, Leontius of Byzantium (c. 485–543). The
age was witnessing a revival of the Aristotelian philosophy,
and Leontius applied Aristotelian distinctions to the Christological problems. The feeling of much of the East, both
"orthodox" and Monophysite, was that the affirmation of
two natures in Christ could not be interpreted without involving two hypostases—subsistences—and therefore being "Nestorian." An explanation without these "Nestorian" consequences was what Leontius now gave. The natures might be
"intra-hypostatic"—ἐνυπόστατος—that is, there might be such
a hypostatic union that while the peculiarities of one nature
remained, it might find its hypostasis in the other. In Christ
this one hypostasis, which is that of both natures, is that of
the Logos. Thus Leontius would interpret the creed of Chal-

cedon in terms wholly consonant with the aim, if not with the exact language, of Cyril. The human in Christ is real, but is so subordinated that the ultimate reality is the divine.

Such an interpretation seemed, at the time, a quite possible basis of reunion with the more moderate Monophysites, who constituted their majority. The large section led by Severus, Monophysite patriarch of Antioch (512–518), who, till his death in 538, found a refuge in Egypt, held essentially the same position as Leontius. Their chief difference was that they regarded the Chalcedonian Council and its creed with greater suspicion. With the more radical Monophysites, led by Julian of Halicarnassus (d. after 518), the prospect of union was less auspicious. They went so far as to hold that Christ's body was incorruptible from the beginning of the incarnation, and incapable of suffering save so far as Christ Himself permitted it. Its enemies charged the theory of Julian with Docetic significance.

To meet this situation by establishing an anti-Antiochian, Cyrillic interpretation of the creed of Chalcedon, and winning, if possible, the moderate Monophysites, was the aim of Justinian. He came to favor the so-called "Theopaschite" (i. e., "suffering God") formula of the Scythian monks, "one of the Trinity suffered in the flesh," after a controversy lasting from 519 to 533. Because of monastic quarrels in Palestine, and also because the Emperor's theological sympathies, like those of his age, were exceedingly intolerant, Justinian condemned the memory and teachings of Origen in 543.[1]

Justinian's great effort to further his theological policy was the occasion of the discussion known as that of the "Three Chapters." In 544 Justinian, defining the issue by his own imperial authority, condemned the person and writings of Theodore of Mopsuestia, now more than a century dead, but once the revered leader of the school of Antioch (ante, p. 145), the writings of Theodoret of Cyrus in criticism of Cyril (ante, p. 148), and a letter of Ibas of Edessa to Maris the Persian (ante, p. 149). Theodoret and Ibas had been approved by the Council of Chalcedon. The action of the Emperor nominally left the creed of Chalcedon untouched, but made it impossible of interpretation in any but a Cyrillic sense, condemned the school of Antioch, and greatly disparaged the authority of the Council of Chalcedon. The edict aroused not a little opposi-

[1] Ayer, pp. 542, 543.

tion. Pope Vigilius (537–555) disliked it, but the imperial reconquest of Italy had placed the Popes largely in the power of the Emperor. Between his knowledge of the feeling of the West and his fear of Justinian, Vigilius's attitude was vacillating and utterly unheroic.[1] To carry out his will, Justinian now convened the Fifth General Council, which met in Constantinople in 553. By it the "Three Chapters," i. e., Theodore and the writings just described, were condemned, the "Theopaschite" formula approved, and Origen once more reckoned a heretic.[2] Pope Vigilius, though in Constantinople, refused to share in these proceedings, but such was the imperial pressure that within less than a year he acceded to the decision of the council. The Cyrillic interpretation of the creed of Chalcedon was now the only "orthodox" understanding. The action of the council was resisted for a few years in North Africa; and the yielding attitude of the Pope led to a schismatic separation of northern Italy from Rome which lasted till the time of Gregory the Great, and in the neighboring Illyricum and Istria even longer. One main purpose of the condemnation of the "Three Chapters"—the reconciliation of the Monophysites—failed. In Egypt and Syria Monophysitism remained the dominant force, the real reason being that these provinces were developing a native national consciousness antagonistic to the empire, for which theological differences were the excuse more than the cause.

Under Justinian's successors, Justin II (565–578), and Tiberius II (578–582), alternate severe persecution of the Monophysites and vain attempts to win them occurred. These efforts were now of less significance as the Monophysite groups were now practically separated national churches. The native Monophysite body of Egypt can hardly be given fixed date for its origin. From the Council of Chalcedon the land was increasingly in religious rebellion. That church, the Coptic, is still the main Christian body of Egypt, numbering more than six hundred and fifty thousand adherents, strongly Monophysite to this day in doctrine, under the rule of a patriarch who still takes his title from Alexandria, though his seat has long been in Cairo. Its services are still chiefly in the ancient Coptic, though Arabic has to some extent replaced it. The most conspicuous daughter of the Coptic Church is the Abys-

[1] See Ayer, pp. 544–551.　　　　　[2] Ayer, pp. 551, 552.

sinian. When Christianity was introduced into "Ethiopia" is uncertain. There is some reason to think that its first missionary was Frumentius, ordained a bishop by Athanasius, about 330. The effective spread of Christianity there seems to have been by Egyptian monks, about 480. The Abyssinian Church stands to the present day in dependent relations to that of Egypt, its head, the *Abuna*, being appointed by the Coptic patriarch of Alexandria. It is Monophysite, and differs little from that of Egypt, save in the backwardness of its culture, and the great extent to which fasting is carried. It is probably the lowest in civilization of any existing church.

While Egypt presented the spectacle of a united Monophysite population, Syria was deeply divided. Part of its inhabitants inclined to Nestorianism (*ante,* p. 149). Some were orthodox, and many Monophysite. The great organizer of Syrian Monophysitism, after its persecution in the early part of the reign of Justinian, was Jacob, nicknamed Baradæus (?-578). Born near Edessa, he became a monk and enjoyed the support of Justinian's Monophysite-disposed Empress, Theodora. In 541 or 543 he was ordained bishop of Edessa, and for the rest of his life served as a Monophysite missionary, ordaining, it is said, eighty thousand clergy. To him Syrian Monophysitism owed its great growth, and from him the Syrian Monophysite Church, which exists to the present day, derives the name given by its opponents, Jacobite. Its head calls himself patriarch of Antioch, though his seat has for centuries been in the Tigris Valley, where most of his flock are to be found. They number about eighty thousand.

Armenia during the first four centuries of the Roman Empire was a vassal kingdom, never thoroughly Romanized, maintaining its own language and peculiarities under its own sovereigns. Christian beginnings are obscure; but the great propagator of Christianity in the land was Gregory, called the Illuminator, who labored in the closing years of the third century. By him King Tiridates (*c.* 238–314) was converted and baptized—Armenia thus becoming the first country to have a Christian ruler, since this event antedated the Christian profession of Constantine. Armenian Christianity grew vigorously. Never very closely bound to the Roman world, Armenia was in part conquered by Persia in 387. In the struggles of the next century hatred of Persia seems to have turned

Armenia in the Monophysite direction, since Persia favored Nestorianism (*ante*, p. 149). By an Armenian council, held in Etchmiadzin (Valarshabad), in 491, the Council of Chalcedon and the *Tome* of Leo were condemned, and the Armenian or Gregorian Church—so named from its founder—has been ever since Monophysite. Armenians at present are wide-spread throughout the Turkish empire and the adjacent portions of Russia. Armenians are believed to number not less than two millions nine hundred thousand, of whom the greater part are Gregorians. The Gregorian Church is now far the most important and vigorous of these ancient separated churches of the East.

The effect of the Christological controversies was disastrous to church and state. By the close of the sixth century the Roman state church of the East had been rent, and separated churches, Nestorian and Monophysite had been torn from it. Egypt and Syria were profoundly disaffected toward the government and religion of Constantinople—a fact that largely accounts for the rapid conquest of those lands by Mohammedanism in the seventh century.

SECTION XI.   CATASTROPHES AND FURTHER CONTROVERSIES IN
THE EAST

Justinian's brilliant restoration of the Roman power was but of brief duration. From 568, the Lombards were pressing into Italy. Without conquering it wholly, they occupied the north and a large portion of the centre. The last Roman garrisons were driven out of Spain by the Visigoths in 624. The Persians gained temporary control of Syria, Palestine, and Egypt between 613 and 629, and overran Asia Minor to the Bosphorus. On the European side the Avars, and the Slavic Croats and Serbs, conquered the Danube lands and most of the Balkan provinces, largely annihilating Christianity there, penetrating in 623 and 626 to the defenses of Constantinople itself. That the empire did not then perish was due to the military genius of the Emperor Heraclius (610–642), by whom the Persians were brilliantly defeated, and the lost eastern provinces restored. Before his death, however, a new power, that of Mohammedanism, had arisen. Its prophet died in Medina in 632, but the conquest which he had planned was carried out by the Caliphs Omar and Othman. Damascus fell in 635, Jerusalem and Antioch in 638, Alexandria in 641. In 651, the Persian kingdom was brought to an end. By 711, the Mohammedan flood crossed the Strait of Gibraltar into Spain, bringing the Visigothic monarchy to a close, and swept forward into France, where its progress was permanently checked by the Franks, under Charles Martel, in the great battle of 732, between Tours and Poitiers. In the East, Constantinople successfully resisted it, in 672–678, and again in 717–718. Syria, Egypt, and North Africa were permanently taken by the Mohammedans.

Under such circumstances, before the final catastrophe, efforts were naturally made to secure unity in the threatened portions of the empire. After negotiations lasting several years, in which the patriarch Sergius of Constantinople was the leader, a union policy was inaugurated by the Emperor Heraclius, on the basis of a declaration that in all that He did Christ acted by "one divine-human energy." Cyrus, the "orthodox" patriarch of Alexandria, set up a formula of union, of which this was the substance, in Egypt, in 633, with much apparent success in conciliating Monophysite opinion.[1] Opposition arose, led by a Palestinian monk, Sophronius, soon to be patriarch of Jerusalem. Sergius was alarmed and now tried to stop any discussion of the question. He now wrote, in that sense, to Pope Honorius (625–638), who advised against the expression "energy" as unscriptural, and said, rather incidentally, that Christ had one will. Heraclius now, in 638, issued his *Ekthesis*, composed by Sergius, in which he forbade discussion of the question of one or two energies and affirmed that Christ had one will.

It was easier to start a theological controversy than to end it. Pope John IV (640–642) condemned the doctrine of one will in Christ—or Monothelite heresy as it was called—in 641. Heraclius died that year, and was succeeded by Constans II (642–668), who issued, in 648, a *Typos*, in which he forbade discussion of the question of Christ's will or wills.[2] The holder of the papacy was the ambitious Martin I (649–655), who saw in the situation an opportunity not only to further an interpretation of the theological problem consonant with the views of the West, which had always held that Christ's

---

[1] Ayer, pp. 661, 662.   [2] *Ibid.*, pp. 662–664.

natures were each perfect and entire, but also to assert papal authority in the Orient. He therefore assembled a great synod in Rome in 649, which proclaimed the existence of two wills in Christ—human and divine—and not only condemned Sergius and other patriarchs of Constantinople, but the *Ekthesis* and the *Typos*.[1] This was flat defiance of the Emperor. Constans had Pope Martin arrested and brought a prisoner to Constantinople in 653, where he was treated with great brutality. Martin had the courage of his convictions. He was exiled to the Crimea, where he died. Strained relations between Rome and Constantinople followed. Constans II was succeeded by Constantine IV (668–685). By that time, the Monophysite provinces, the retention of which had been the source of the discussion, had been taken by the Mohammedans. It was more important to placate Italy than to favor them. The Emperor entered into negotiations with Pope Agatho (678–681), who issued a long letter of definition as Leo I had once set forth his *Tome*. Under imperial auspices a council, the Sixth General Council, was held in Constantinople in 680 and 681. By it Christ was declared to have "two natural wills or willings . . . not contrary one to the other . . . but His human will follows, not as resisting or reluctant, but rather as subject to His divine and omnipotent will." It also condemned Sergius and other of his successors in the patriarchate of Constantinople, Cyrus of Alexandria and Pope Honorius.[2] For the third time Rome had triumphed over the divided East in theological definition. Nicæa, Chalcedon, and Constantinople had all been Roman victories. It must be said, also, that a human will was necessary for that complete and perfect humanity of Christ as well as perfect divinity, for which the West had always stood. The doctrine, thus defined, was the logical completion of that of Chalcedon. With its definition, the Christological controversies were ended in so far as doctrinal determination was concerned.

While the Sixth General Council was thus a Western success, it had a sort of appendix which was, in a sense, a Western defeat. Like the council of the "Three Chapters" (553), it had formulated no disciplinary canons. A council to do this work was summoned by Justinian II (685–695, 704–711), to meet in Constantinople in 692, and is called from the domed

---

[1] Extracts, Ayer, pp. 664, 865.   [2] Ayer, pp. 665–672.

room in which it assembled—which was that in which the
council of 680 and 681 had met—the Second Trullan Council,
or *Concilium Quini-sextum*, as completing the Fifth and Sixth
General Councils. It was entirely Eastern in its composition,
and is looked upon by the Oriental Church as the completion
of the council of 680 and 681, though its validity is not accepted
by that of Rome. Many ancient canons were renewed; but
several of the new enactments directly contradicted Western
practice. It enacted, in agreement with Chalcedon, that
"the see of Constantinople shall enjoy equal privilege with the
see of Old Rome." It permitted marriage to deacons and presbyters, and condemned the Roman prohibition of such marriages. The Greek Church still maintains this permission. It
forbade the Roman custom of fasting on Saturdays in Lent.
It prohibited the favorite Western representation of Christ
under the symbol of a lamb, ordering instead the depiction of
a human figure.[1] Though not very important in themselves,
these enactments are significant of the growing estrangement in
feeling and practice between East and West.

The apparent collapse of the Eastern empire in the seventh
century was followed by a very considerable renewal of its
strength under the able Leo III, the Isaurian (717–740), to
whose military and administrative talents its new lease of life
was due. A forceful sovereign, he would rule the church in
the spirit of Justinian. He desired to make entrance as easy
as possible for Jews, Moslems, and the representatives of the
stricter Christian sects, such as the remaining Montanists.
They charged the church with idolatry, by reason of the wide-
spread veneration of pictures. In 726, Leo forbade their further
employment in worship. The result was religious revolt.
The monks and common people resisted, partly from veneration
of images, partly in the interest of the freedom of the church
from imperial dictation. Leo enforced his decree by the army.
In most of the empire he had his will. Italy was too remote,
and there Popes and people resisted him. Under Pope Gregory
III (731–741), a Roman synod of 731 excommunicated the
opponents of pictures. The Emperor answered by removing
all of Sicily and such portions of Italy as he could from the
Pope's jurisdiction. Leo's able and tyrannous son, Constantine V (740–775), pursued the same policy even more relent-

[1] Ayer, pp. 673–679.

lessly. A synod assembled by him in Constantinople in 754 condemned pictures and approved his authority over the church. In this struggle the papacy sought the help of the Franks and tore itself permanently from dependence on the Eastern Emperors. A change of imperial policy came, however, with the accession of Constantine VI (780–797), under the dominance of his mother, Irene, a partisan of pictures. By imperial authority, and with the presence of papal delegates, the Seventh and, in the estimate of the Greek Church, the last, General Council now assembled in Nicæa in 787. By its decree pictures, the cross, and the Gospels "should be given due salutation and honorable reverence, not indeed that true worship, which pertains alone to the divine nature. . . . For the honor which is paid to the image passes on to that which the image represents, and he who shows reverence to the image shows reverence to the subject represented in it." [1] The council seems to have been unconscious that much the same thing could have been said by heathenism for its images.

Among the vigorous supporters of image-reverence was John of Damascus (700?–753?), the most honored of the later theologians of the Eastern portion of the ancient church. Born in the city from which he took his name, the son of a Christian high-placed in the civil service of the Mohammedan Caliph, he succeeded to his father's position, only to abandon it and become a monk of the cloister of St. Sabas near Jerusalem. His chief work, *The Fountain of Knowledge,* is a complete, systematic presentation of the theology of the church of the East. With little of originality, and much use of extracts from earlier writers, he presented the whole in clear and logical form, so that he became the great theological instructor of the Greek Church, and, thanks to a Latin translation of the twelfth century, influenced the scholasticism of the West. His philosophical basis is an Aristotelianism largely influenced by Neo-Platonism. In the Christological discussion he followed Leontius (*ante,* p. 155), in an interpretation of the Chalcedonian symbol consonant with the views of Cyril. To him the death of Christ is a sacrifice offered to God, not a ransom to the devil. The Lord's Supper is fully the body and blood of Christ, not by transubstantiation, but by a miraculous transformation wrought by the Holy Spirit.

[1] Ayer, pp. 694–697.

John of Damascus summed up the theological development of the Orient, and beyond the positions which he represented the East made practically no progress. Its contribution to the intellectual explanation of Christianity was completed.

SECTION XII. THE CONSTITUTIONAL DEVELOPMENT OF THE CHURCH

The acceptance of Christianity as the religion of the empire gave to the Emperors a practical authority over the church. By the time of Justinian, the Emperor declared, on his own initiative, what was sound doctrine, and to a considerable extent regulated churchly administration.[1] The Emperors largely controlled appointment to high ecclesiastical office, especially in the East. This imperial power was limited, however, by the necessity, which even Emperors as powerful as Justinian felt, of securing the approval of the church through general councils for statements of faith and canons of administration. The imperial support of these edicts and decisions of general councils made heresy a crime, and must seriously have limited freedom of Christian thought. It was a very narrow path both in doctrinal opinion and in administration, that a bishop of Constantinople, for instance, had to walk. If conditions were more favorable for the papacy (*ante*, pp. 134–136), it was largely a consequence of the general ineffectiveness of imperial control in Italy, though cases were not lacking where the Popes felt the heavy hands of the Emperors.

As in the third century, the bishops continued to be the centres of local ecclesiastical administration, and their power tended to increase. By them the other clergy were not merely ordained, but the pay of those below them was in their hands. The First Council of Nicæa provided that other clergy should not remove from a diocese without the bishop's consent.[2] In each of the provinces the bishop of the capital city was the metropolitan, who, according to the synod of Antioch (341), should "have precedence in rank . . . that the other bishops do nothing extraordinary without him."[3] The ancient custom of local synods, for the consideration of provincial questions was extended, the First Council of Nicæa requiring them to be held

---

[1] *E. g.*, Ayer, pp. 542, 555.　　　　[2] Ayer. p. 361.
[3] *Ibid.*, p. 363.

twice a year.[1] This metropolitan arrangement was fully introduced into the East by the middle of the fourth century. In the West it was about half a century later in development, and was limited in Italy by the dominance of the papacy. Nevertheless it won its way in northern Italy, Spain, and Gaul. Above the metropolitans stood the bishops of the great capitals of the empire, the patriarchs, whose prominence antedated the rise of the metropolitan system. These were the bishops, or patriarchs, of Rome, Constantinople (by 381), Alexandria, Antioch, and, by 451, Jerusalem.

By Constantine, the clergy were made a privileged class and exempted from the public burdens of taxation (319).[2] The government, anxious not to lose its revenues through the entrance into clerical office of the well-to-do, ordered that only those "of small fortune" should be ordained (326).[3] The result of this policy was that, though the ordination of slaves was everywhere discouraged, and was forbidden in the East by the Emperor Zeno in 484, the clergy were prevailingly recruited from classes of little property or education. The brilliant careers of some men of talent and means, of whom Ambrose is an example, show the possibilities then before those of high ability who passed these barriers. The feeling, which had long existed, that the higher clergy, at least, should not engage in any worldly or gainful occupation, grew, and such works were expressly forbidden by the Emperor Valentinian III in 452. Such exclusive devotion to the clerical calling demanded an enlarged support. The church now received not merely the gifts of the faithful, as of old; but the income of a rapidly increasing body of landed estates presented or bequeathed to it by wealthy Christians, the control of which was in the hands of the bishops. An arrangement of Pope Simplicius (468-483) provided that ecclesiastical income should be divided into quarters, one each for the bishop, the other clergy, the up-keep of the services and edifices, and for the poor.

The feeling was natural that the clergy should be moral examples to their flocks. Celibacy had long been prized as belonging to the holier Christian life. In this respect the West was stricter than the East. Pope Leo I (440-461) held that even sub-deacons should refrain from marriage,[4] though it was

---

[1] Ayer, p. 360.
[3] *Ibid.*, p. 280.
[2] *Ibid.*, p. 283.
[4] *Letters*, 14[5].

to be centuries before this rule was universally enforced in the Western Church. In the East, the practice which still continues was established by the time of Justinian, that only celibates could be bishops, while clergy below that rank could marry before ordination. This rule, though not without advantages, has had the great disadvantage of blocking promotion in the Eastern Church, and leading to the choice of bishops prevailingly from the ranks of the monks.

While the bishop's power was thus extensive, the growth of the church into the rural districts about the cities, and of many congregations in the cities themselves, led to the formation of congregations in charge of presbyters, and thus to a certain increase in the importance of the presbyterial office. These congregations still belonged, in most regions, to the undivided city church, ruled by the bishop; but by the sixth century the parish system made its appearance in France. There the priest (presbyter) in charge received two-thirds of the local income, paying the rest to the bishop.

The incoming of masses from heathenism into the church led, at first, to an emphasis on the catechumenate. Reception to it, with the sign of the cross and laying on of hands, was popularly regarded as conferring membership in the church, and was as far as the great multitude of less earnest Christians went in Christian profession, save in possible danger of death. The growth of generations of exclusively Christian ancestry, and, in the West, the spread of Augustinian doctrines of baptismal grace, brought this half-way attitude to an end. The catechumenate lost its significance when the whole population had become supposedly Christian.

In one important respect East and West fell asunder in this period regarding rites connected with baptism. As already described, by the time of Tertullian (*ante*, p. 96), baptism proper was followed by anointing and laying on of hands in token of the reception of the Holy Spirit. In Tertullian's age both baptism and laying on of hands were acts of the bishop, save in case of necessity, when baptism could be administered by any Christian (*ante*, p. 97). With the growth of the church, presbyters came to baptize regularly in East and West. With regard to the further rite the two regions differed. The East saw its chief significance in the anointing, and allowed that to be performed, as it does to-day, by the presbyter with oil consecrated by the bishop. The West viewed the laying on of hands as the all-important matter, and held that that could be done by the bishop alone[1] as successor to the Apostles. The rites therefore became separated in the West. "Confirmation" took place often a considerable time after baptism, when the presence of the bishop could be secured, though it was long before the age of the candidate was fixed in the Western Church.

SECTION XIII. PUBLIC WORSHIP AND SACRED SEASONS

Public worship in the fourth and fifth centuries stood wholly under the influence of the conception of secret discipline, the so-called *disciplina arcani*, derived, it is probable, from conceptions akin to or borrowed from the mystery religions. Its roots run back apparently into the third century. Under these impulses the services were divided into two parts. The first was open to catechumens and the general public, and included Bible reading, singing, the sermon, and prayer. To the second, the true Christian mystery, none but the baptized were admitted. It had its crown in the Lord's Supper, but the creed and the Lord's Prayer were also objects of reserve from those uninitiated by baptism. With the disappearance of the catechumenate in the sixth century, under the impression that the population was all now Christian, the secret discipline came to an end.

The public portion of Sunday worship began with Scripture reading, interspersed with the singing of psalms. These selections presented three passages, the prophets, *i. e.*, Old Testament, the epistles, the Gospels, and were so read as to cover the Bible in the course of successive Sundays. The desirability of reading appropriate selections at special seasons, and of some abbreviation led, by the close of the fourth century, to the preparation of lectionaries. In the Arian struggle the use of hymns other than psalms grew common, and was furthered in the West with great success by Ambrose of Milan.

The latter part of the fourth and the first half of the fifth centuries was above all others an age of great preachers in the ancient church. Among the most eminent were Gregory of Nazianzus, Chrysostom, and Cyril of Alexandria in the East,

---

[1] *Acts* 8[14-17].

and Ambrose, Augustine, and Leo I in the West. This preaching was largely expository, though with plain application to the problems of daily life. In form it was often highly rhetorical, and the hearers manifested their approval by applause. Yet, while this preaching was probably never excelled, preaching was by no means general, and in many country districts. or even considerable cities, few sermons were to be heard. Prayer was offered before and after the sermon in liturgical form. The benediction was given by the bishop, when present, to the various classes for whom prayer was made, and the non-baptized then dismissed.

The private portion of the service—the Lord's Supper— followed. Both East and West held that, by divine power, the miracle of the presence of Christ was wrought, but differed as to when in the service it took place. In the judgment of the East it was during the prayer known as the invocation, *epiklesis*. This was undoubtedly the view in the West till late in the sixth century. There, however, it was replaced, probably under Roman influence, by the conviction that the Eucharistic miracle occurred when the words of institution were recited, culminating in "This is My body . . . this is the new covenant in My blood." To Gregory of Nyssa and Cyril of Alexandria the Supper is the repetition of the incarnation, wherein Christ takes the elements into union with Himself as once He did human flesh. The Lord's Supper was at once a sacrifice and a communion. It was possible to emphasize one aspect or the other. The East put that of communion in the foreground. Consonant with its theory of salvation, the Supper was viewed as primarily a great, life-giving mystery, wherein the partaker received the transforming body and blood of his Lord, and thereby became, in a measure at least, a partaker of the divine nature, built up to the immortal and sinless life. This view was far from denied in the West. It was held to be true. But the Western conception of salvation as coming into right relations with God, led the West to emphasize the aspect of sacrifice, as inclining God to be gracious to those in whose behalf it was offered. The Western mind did not lend itself so readily as the Eastern to mysticism. In general, the Oriental administration of the Lord's Supper tended to become a mystery-drama, in which the divine and eternal manifested itself in life-giving energy.

Beside the Sunday worship, daily services of a briefer character were now very common, and had widely developed into morning and evening worship.

The older festivals of the Christian year, Easter and Pentecost, were, as earlier, great periods of religious observance. Easter was preceded by a forty days' fast, though the method of reckoning this lenten period varied. The Roman system became ultimately that of the whole West, and continues to the present. The whole of Holy Week was now a time of special penitential observance, passing over to the Easter rejoicing. By the fourth century the observance of Ascension was general. The chief addition to the festivals of the church which belongs to this period is that of Christmas. Apparently no feast of Christ's nativity was held in the church till into the fourth century. By the second century, January 6 had been observed by the Gnostic disciples of Basilides as the date of Jesus' baptism. At a time not now apparent, but probably about the beginning of the fourth century, this was regarded in the East as the time of Christ's birth also, by reason of an interpretation of *Luke* 3²³, which made Him exactly thirty years old at His baptism. Other factors were at work, however. It was an opinion in the third century that the universe was created at the vernal equinox, reckoned in the Julian calendar as March 25. Similar habits of thought would make the beginning of the new creation, the inception of the incarnation, fall on the same day, and therefore Christ's birth on the winter solstice, December 25. That that date, when the sun begins to turn, was the birthday of the Mithraic *Sol Invictus*, was not probably the reason of the choice, though it may well have commended it as substituting a great Christian for a popular heathen festival. At all events, the celebration of December 25 as Christmas appears first in Rome, apparently in 353 or 354, though it may date from 336. From Rome it spread to the East, being introduced into Constantinople, probably by Gregory of Nazianzus, between 378 and 381. A sermon of Chrysostom, preached in Antioch in 388, declares that the celebration was then not ten years old in the East, and the discourse was delivered, it would appear, on the first observance of December 25 in the Syrian capital. It reached Alexandria between 400 and 432.¹ From its inauguration,

---

¹ Kirsopp Lake, in Hastings's *Encyclopædia of Religion and Ethics*, 3⁶⁰¹⁻⁸.

Christmas became one of the great festivals of the church, comparable only with Easter and Pentecost.

SECTION XIV.   LOWER CHRISTIANITY

The beginnings of veneration of martyrs and of their relics run back to the middle of the second century. Their deaths were regularly commemorated with public services (*ante*, p. 93). With the conversion of Constantine, however, and the accession to the church of masses fresh from heathenism, this reverence largely increased. Constantine himself built a great church in honor of Peter in Rome. His mother, Helena, made a pilgrimage to Jerusalem, where the true cross was thought to be discovered. Men looked back on the time of persecution with much reason, as a heroic age, and upon its martyrs as the athletes of the Christian race. Popular opinion, which had long sanctioned the remembrance of the martyrs in prayer and worship, had passed over, before the close of the fourth century, to the feeling that they were to be prayed to as intercessors with God,[1] and as able to protect, heal, and aid those who honored them. There arose thus a popular Christianity of the second rank, as Harnack has well called it. The martyrs, for the masses, took the place of the old gods and heroes. To the martyrs, popular feeling added distinguished ascetics, church leaders, and opponents of heresy. There was, as yet, no regular process of weighing claims to sainthood. Inclusion in its ranks was a matter of common opinion. They were guardians of cities, patrons of trades, curers of disease. They are omnipresent. As Jerome expressed it: "They follow the Lamb, whithersoever He goeth. If the Lamb is present everywhere, the same must be believed respecting those who are with the Lamb."[2] They were honored with burning tapers.[3]

Chief of all these sacred personages was the Virgin Mary. Pious fancy busied itself with her early. To Irenæus she was the second Eve (*ante*, p. 66). Yet, curiously enough, she did not stand out pre-eminent till well into the fourth century, at least in the teaching of the intellectual circles in the church though popular legend, as reflected for instance in the apocry-

[1] Augustine, *Sermons*, 159[1].   [2] *Against Vigilantius*, 6.
[3] *Ibid.*, 7.

phal *Protevangelium of James*, had made much of her. Ascetic feeling, as illustrated in Tertullian and Clement of Alexandria, asserted her perpetual virginity. With the rise of monasticism, the Virgin became a monastic ideal. The full elevation of Mary to the first among created beings came with the Christological controversies, and the complete sanction of the description "Mother of God," in the condemnation of Nestorius and the decision of the Councils of Ephesus and Chalcedon. Thenceforth the Virgin was foremost among all saints in popular and official reverence alike. To her went out much of that feeling which had found expression in the worship of the mother goddesses of Egypt, Syria, and Asia Minor, though in a far nobler form. Above that was the reverence rightfully her due as the chosen vehicle of the incarnation. All that martyr or Apostle could do for the faithful as intercessor or protector, she, as blessed above them, could dispense in yet more abundant measure. In proportion, also, as the Cyrillic interpretation of the Chalcedonian creed and Monophysitism tended to emphasize the divine in Christ at the expense of the human, and therefore, however unintentionally, put Him afar from men, she appeared a winsome sympathizer with our humanity. In a measure, she took the place of her Son, as mediator between God and man.

The roots of angel-worship are to be found in apostolic times,[1] yet though made much of in certain Gnostic systems, and playing a great rôle, for instance, in the speculations of an Origen, angels were not conspicuously objects of Christian reverence till late in the fourth century. They were always far less definite and graspable by the common mind than the martyrs. Reverence for angels was given great furtherance by the Neo-Platonic Christian mystic work composed in the last quarter of the fifth century in the name of Dionysius the Areopagite,[2] and called that of Pseudo-Dionysius. Of all angelic beings, the Archangel Michael was the most honored. A church in commemoration of him was built a few miles from Constantinople by Constantine, and one existed in Rome early in the fifth century. When the celebration of his festival on Michaelmas, September 29—one of the most popular of mediæval feast-days in the West—was instituted, is uncertain.

It has already been pointed out that reverence for relics

---

[1] *Col.* 2:18.　　　　　　　　　　　　　　　　　[2] *Acts* 17:34.

began early. By the fourth century it was being developed to an enormous extent, and included not merely the mortal remains of martyrs and saints, but all manner of articles associated, it was believed, with Christ, the Apostles, and the heroes of the church. Their wide-spread use is illustrated by the statute of the Seventh General Council (787): "If any bishop from this time forward is found consecrating a temple without holy relics, he shall be deposed as a transgressor of the ecclesiastical traditions."[1] Closely connected with this reverence for relics was the valuation placed on pilgrimages to places where they were preserved, and above all to the Holy Land, or to Rome.

Reverence for pictures was slower in gaining a foothold. It seemed too positively connected with the ancient idolatry. By the time of Cyril of Alexandria, however, it was rapidly spreading in the Eastern Church, where it became, if anything, more prevalent than in the West. The struggles ending in the full authorization of pictures by the Seventh General Council have already been narrated (*ante*, p. 163). Christian feeling was that representation on a flat surface only, paintings, and mosaics, not statues, should be allowed, at least in the interior of churches, and this remains the custom of the Greek Church to the present, though this restriction was not a matter of church law.

This Christianity of the second rank profoundly affected the life of the people, but it had also its heartiest supporters in the monks, and it was furthered rather than resisted by the great leaders of the church, certainly after the middle of the fifth century. It undoubtedly made the way from heathenism to Christianity easier for thousands, but it largely heathenized the church itself.

SECTION XV. SOME WESTERN CHARACTERISTICS

While East and West shared in the theological development already outlined, and Western influences contributed much to the official decisions in the Arian and Christological controversies, there was a very appreciable difference in the weight of theological interest in the two portions of the empire. The West produced no really conspicuous theological leader between

[1] *Canon* 7.

Cyprian (*d.* 258) and Ambrose (340?–397). Even Hilary of Poitiers (300?–367) was not sufficiently eminent as an original thinker to make a real exception. Both Hilary and Ambrose were devoted students of the Greek Fathers—the latter especially of the great Cappadocians. Though Tertullian was personally discredited by his Montanism, his influence lived on in the greatly valued Cyprian. While, therefore, Greek elements entered largely into Western thinking, it developed its own peculiarities.

The western part of the empire was disposed, like Tertullian, to view Christianity under judicial rather than, like the East, under philosophical aspects. Its thought of the Gospel was that primarily of a new law. While the West did not deny the Eastern conception that salvation is a making divine and immortal of our sinful mortality, that conception was too abstract for it readily to grasp. Its own thought was that salvation is getting right with God. Hence, in Tertullian, Cyprian, and Ambrose there is a deeper sense of sin, and a clearer conception of grace than in the East. Religion in the West had a closer relation to the acts of every-day life than in the East. It was more a forgiveness of definitely recognized evil acts, and less an abstract transformation of nature, than in the East —more an overcoming of sin, and less a rescue from earthiness and death. In the West, through the teaching of Tertullian, Cyprian, and Ambrose, sin was traced to an inherited vitiation of human nature in a way that had no corresponding parallel in the East. There can be no doubt, also, that this Western estimate of sin and grace, imperfectly worked out though it yet was, combined with the firmer ecclesiastical organization of the West, gave the Western Church a stronger control of the daily life of the people than was achieved by that of the East. All these Western peculiarities were to come to their full fruition in the work of Augustine.

SECTION XVI.   JEROME

Jerome was the ablest scholar that the ancient Western Church could boast. Born about 340 in Strido in Dalmatia, he studied in Rome, where he was baptized by Pope Liberius in 360. Aquileia he made his headquarters for a while, where he became the friend of Rufinus (?–410), the translator of

Origen, like Jerome to be a supporter of monasticism and a
monk in Palestine, but with whom he was to quarrel over
Origen's orthodoxy.   Jerome had a restless desire to know the
scholarly and religious world.   From 366 to 370 he visited the
cities of Gaul.   The next three years saw him again in Aquileia.
Then came a journey through the Orient to Antioch, where he
was overtaken with a severe illness in which he believed Christ
Himself appeared and reproached him for devotion to the
classics.   He now turned to the Scriptures, studying Hebrew,
and living as a hermit from 373 to 379, not far from Antioch.
Ordained a presbyter in Antioch, in 379, he studied in Constantinople under Gregory Nazianzus.   The year 382 saw him in
Rome, where he won the hearty support of Pope Damasus
(366–384), and preached in season and out of season the merits
of the monastic life.   Soon he had a large following, especially
among Roman women of position ; but also much enmity, even
among the clergy, for monasticism was not as yet popular in
the West, and Jerome himself was one of the most vindictive
of disputants.   The death of Damasus made Jerome's position
so uncomfortable in Rome that he retired, in 385, to Antioch,
whither a number of his Roman converts to monastic celibacy,
led by Paula and her daughter, Eustochium, soon followed him.
With them he journeyed through Palestine and to the chief
monastic establishments of Egypt, returning to Bethlehem in
386, where Paula built nunneries and a monastery for men.
Here, as head of the monastery, Jerome made his headquarters
till his death, in 420.

Jerome's best use of his unquestionable learning was as a
translator of the Scriptures.   The older Latin versions were
crude, and had fallen into much corruption.   Pope Damasus
proposed to Jerome a revision.   That he completed for the
New Testament about 388.   The Old Testament he then translated in Bethlehem, with the aid of Jewish friends.   It is a
proof of Jerome's soundness of scholarship that, in spite even
of the wishes of Augustine, he went back of the Septuagint to
the Hebrew.   The result of Jerome's work was the *Vulgate*,
still in use in the Roman Church.   It is his best monument.
Jerome had, also, no small deserts as a historian.   He continued the *Chronicle* of Eusebius.   His *De Viris Inlustribus* is
a biographical dictionary of Christian writers to and including
himself.   He was an abundant commentator on the Scriptures.

He urged by treatise and by letter the advantages of celibacy and of the monastic life. As a theologian he had little that was original to offer. He was an impassioned defender of tradition and of Western popular usage. A controversialist who loved disputation, he attacked opponents of asceticism like Jovinianus, critics of relic-reverence like Vigilantius, and those who, like Helvidius, held that Mary had other children than our Lord. He condemned Origen, whom he had once admired. He wrote in support of Augustine against the Pelagians. In these controversial writings Jerome's littleness of spirit is often painfully manifest. Though deserving to be reckoned, as he is by the Roman Church, one of its "Doctors," by reason of the greatness of his learning and the use which he made of it, the title "saint" seems more a tribute to the scholar than to the man.

SECTION XVII. AUGUSTINE

In Augustine the ancient church reached its highest religious attainment since apostolic times. Though his influence in the East was to be relatively slight, owing to the nature of the questions with which he was primarily concerned, all Western Christianity was to become his debtor. Such superiority as Western religious life came to possess over that of the East was primarily his bequest to it. He was to be the father of much that was most characteristic in mediæval Roman Catholicism. He was to be the spiritual ancestor, no less, of much in the Reformation. His theology, though buttressed by the Scriptures, philosophy, and ecclesiastical tradition, was so largely rooted in his own experience as to render his story more than usually the interpretation of the man.

Africa gave three great leaders to Latin Christianity, Tertullian, Cyprian, and Augustine. Augustine was born in Tagaste, in Numidia, now Suk Ahras in the Department of Constantine in Algeria, on November 13, 354. His father, Patricius, was a heathen of good position but of small property, an easy-going, worldly character, who did not embrace Christianity till near the end of life. His mother, Monnica, was a Christian woman of high worth, eagerly ambitious for her son, though the full radiance of her Christian life was to be manifested in her later years, developed through Ambrose and

Augustine himself. In Augustine there were two natures, one passionate and sensuous, the other eagerly high-minded and truth-seeking. It may not be wrong to say that father and mother were reflected in him. From Tagaste he was sent for the sake of schooling to the neighboring Madaura, and thence to Carthage, where he pursued the study of rhetoric. Here, when about seventeen, he took a concubine, to whom he was to hold for at least fourteen years, and to them a son, Adeodatus, whom he dearly loved, was born in 372. If the sensuous Augustine was thus early aroused, the truth-seeking Augustine was speedily awakened. When nineteen, the study of Cicero's now almost completely lost *Hortensius* "changed my affections, and turned my prayers to Thyself, O Lord." [1] This imperfect conversion caused Augustine to desire to seek truth as that alone of value. He began to study the Scriptures, "but they appeared to me unworthy to be compared with the dignity of Cicero." [2] He now turned for spiritual and intellectual comfort to the syncretistic, dualistic system known as Manichæism (*ante*, p. 107). He was willing to pray "Grant me chastity and continence, but not yet." [3]

For nine years Augustine remained a Manichæan, living partly in Carthage and partly in Tagaste, engaged in study and teaching. He was crowned at Carthage for a theatrical poem.[4] He gathered friends about him, of whom Alypius was to prove the closest. As he went on he began to doubt the intellectual and moral adequacy of Manichæism. His associates urged him to meet the highly respected Manichæan leader, Faustus. The inadequacy of Faustus's expositions completed his mental disillusion. Though he remained outwardly a Manichæan, Augustine was now inwardly a sceptic. By the advice of Manichæan friends Augustine removed to Rome in 383, and by their aid, in 384, he obtained from the prefect, Symmachus, a government appointment as teacher of rhetoric in Milan—then the Western capital of the empire.

Here in Milan, Augustine came under the powerful preaching of Ambrose, whom he heard as an illustration of pulpit eloquence rather than with approval of the message, since he was now under the sway of the sceptical philosophy of the New Academy. Here Monnica and Alypius joined him. At

---

[1] *Confessions*, 3[4].   [2] *Ibid.*, 3[5].
[3] *Ibid.*, 8[7].   [4] *Ibid.*, 4[2, 3].

his mother's wish he now became betrothed as befitted his station in life, though marriage was postponed on account of the youth of the woman. He dismissed regretfully his faithful concubine and entered on an even less creditable relation with another.[1] It was the lowest point of his moral life. At this juncture Augustine came in contact with Neo-Platonism, (*ante*, p. 106), through the translations of Victorinus. It was almost a revelation to him. Instead of the materialism and dualism of Manichæism, he now saw in the spiritual world the only real world, and in God the source not only of all good, but of all reality. Evil was no positive existence, as with the Manichæans. It was negative, a lack of good, an alienation of the will from God. To know God is the highest of blessings. This new philosophy, which always colored Augustine's teachings, made it possible for him to accept Christianity. He was impressed by the authority of the church, as a hearer of Ambrose might well have been. As he said later, "I should not believe the Gospel except as moved by the authority of the Catholic Church." [2]

A crisis in Augustine's experience was now at hand. He had never felt more painfully the cleft between his ideals and his conduct. He was impressed by learning of the Christian profession made in old age, some years before, by the Neo-Platonist Victorinus, whose writings had so recently influenced him.[3] A travelled African, Pontitianus, told him and Alypius of the monastic life of Egypt. He was filled with shame that ignorant men like these monks could put away temptations which he, a man of learning, felt powerless to resist.[4] Overcome with self-condemnation, he rushed into the garden and there heard the voice of a child from a neighboring house, saying: "Take up and read." He reached for a copy of the epistles that he had been reading, and his eyes fell on the words: "Not in rioting and drunkenness, not in chambering and wantonness, not in strife and envying; but put ye on the Lord Jesus Christ, and make not provision for the flesh to fulfil the lusts thereof." [5] From that moment Augustine had the peace of mind and the sense of divine power to overcome his sins which he had thus far sought in vain. It may be that it was, as it

---

[1] *Confessions*, 6[15].   [2] *Against the Epistle of Manichæus*, 5; Ayer, p. 455.
[3] *Confessions*, 8[2]; Ayer, pp. 431–433.   [4] *Confessions*, 8[8].
[5] *Romans* 13[13, 14]; *Confessions*, 8[12]; Ayer, pp. 435–437.

has been called, a conversion to monasticism. If so, that was but its outward form. In its essence it was a fundamental Christian transformation of nature.

Augustine's conversion occurred in the late summer of 386. He resigned his professorship partly on account of illness, and now retired with his friends to the estate named Cassisiacum, to await baptism. He was far from being the master in theology as yet. His most characteristic tenets were undeveloped. He was still primarily a Christianized Neo-Platonist; but the type of his piety was already determined. At Cassisiacum the friends engaged in philosophical discussion, and Augustine wrote some of the earliest of his treatises. At the Easter season of 387 he was baptized, with Adeodatus and Alypius, by Ambrose in Milan. Augustine now left Milan for his birthplace. On the journey Monnica died in Ostia. The story of her death, as told by Augustine, is one of the noblest monuments of ancient Christian literature.[1] His plans thus changed, he lived for some months in Rome, but by the autumn of 388 was once more in Tagaste. Here he dwelt with a group of friends, busied in studies much as at Cassisiacum. During this period in Tagaste his brilliant son, Adeodatus, died. Augustine thought to found a monastery, and to further this project went to Hippo, near the modern Bona, in Algeria, early in 391. There he was ordained to the priesthood, almost forcibly. Four years later he was ordained colleague-bishop of Hippo. When his aged associate, Valerius, died is unknown, but Augustine probably soon had full episcopal charge. In Hippo he founded the first monastery in that portion of Africa, and made it also a training-school for the clergy. He died on August 28, 430, during the siege of Hippo by the Vandals.

Almost from the time of his baptism Augustine wrote against the Manichæans. With his entrance on the ministry, and especially as bishop, he was brought into conflict with the Donatists (ante, p. 113), then wide-spread in northern Africa. This discussion led Augustine to a full consideration of the church, its nature and its authority. By the early years of his episcopate he had reached his characteristic opinions on sin and grace. They were not the product of the great Pelagian controversy which occupied much of his strength from 412 onward, though that struggle clarified their expression.

[1] *Confessions*, 9¹⁰⁻¹².

The secret of much of Augustine's influence lay in his mystical piety. Its fullest expression, though everywhere to be found in his works, is perhaps in the remarkable *Confessions*, written about 400, in which he gave an account of his experiences to his conversion. No other similar spiritual autobiography was written in the ancient church, and few at any period in church history. It has always stood a classic of religious experience. "Thou hast formed us for Thyself, and our hearts are restless till they find their rest in Thee" (1[1]). "It is good, then, for me to cleave unto God, for if I remain not in Him, neither shall I in myself; but He, remaining in Himself, reneweth all things. And Thou art the Lord my God, since Thou standest not in need of my goodness" (7[11]). "I sought a way of acquiring strength sufficient to enjoy Thee; but I found it not until I embraced that 'Mediator between God and man, the man Christ Jesus,' 'who is over all God blessed forever' calling me" (7[18]). "My whole hope is only in Thy exceeding great mercy. Give what Thou commandest, and command what Thou wilt" (10[29]). "I will love Thee, O Lord, and thank Thee, and confess unto Thy name, because Thou hast put away from me these so wicked and nefarious acts of mine. To Thy grace I attribute it, and to Thy mercy, that Thou hast melted away my sin as it were ice" (2[7]). Here is a deeper note of personal devotion than the church had heard since Paul, and the conception of religion as a vital relationship to the living God was one the influence of which was to be permanent, even if often but partially comprehended.

Augustine's first thought of God was thus always one of personal connection with a being in whom man's only real satisfaction or good is to be found; but when he thought of God philosophically, it was in terms borrowed from Neo-Platonism. God is simple, absolute being, as distinguished from all created things which are manifold and variable. He is the basis and source of all that really exists. This conception led Augustine to emphasize the divine unity, even when treating of the Trinity. His doctrine he set forth in his great work *On the Trinity*. It became determinative henceforth of Western thinking. "Father, Son, and Holy Spirit, one God, alone, great, omnipotent, good, just, merciful, creator of all things visible and invisible." [1] "Father, Son, and Holy Spirit, of one and the same substance,

[1] *Trinity*, 7 : 6[12].

God the creator, the omnipotent Trinity, work indivisibly" (4^{21}).
"Neither three Gods, nor three goods, but one God, good, omnipotent, the Trinity itself."[1]   Tertullian, Origen, and Athanasius had taught the subordination of the Son and Spirit to
the Father.   Augustine so emphasized the unity as to teach
the full equality of the "persons."   "There is so great an
equality in that Trinity, that not only the Father is not greater
than the Son, as regards divinity, but neither are the Father and
the Son together greater than the Holy Spirit." [2]   Augustine
was not satisfied with the distinction "persons"; but it was
consecrated by usage, and he could find nothing more fitting:
"When it is asked, what are the three? human language labors
under great poverty of speech.   Yet we say, three 'persons,'
not in order to express it, but in order not to be silent." [3]   It
is evident that, though Augustine held firmly to the ecclesiastical tradition, his own inclinations, and his Neo-Platonic philosophy inclined toward the Modalistic Monarchian position.
It would, however, be wholly unjust to call him a Modalist.
He attempted to illustrate the Trinity by many comparisons,
such as memory, understanding, will,[4] or the even more famous
lover, loved, and love.[5]

This sense of unity and equality made Augustine hold that
"God the Father alone is He from whom the Word is born,
and from whom the Holy Spirit principally proceeds.   And
therefore I have added the word principally, because we find
that the Holy Spirit proceeds from the Son also."[6]   Eastern
remains of subordinationism and feeling that the Father is
the sole source of all, taught that the Holy Spirit proceeds from
the Father alone, but Augustine had prepared the way for that
filioque, which, acknowledged in Spain, at the Third Council
of Toledo, in 589, as a part of the so-called Nicene creed, spread
over the West, and remains to this day a dividing issue between
the Greek and Latin Churches.

In the incarnation Augustine emphasized the human as
strongly as the divine.   "Christ Jesus, the Son of God, is both
God and man; God before all worlds; man in our world. . . .
Wherefore, so far as He is God, He and the Father are one; so
far as He is man, the Father is greater than He." [7]   He is the

---

[1] *Trinity*, 8, Preface.   [2] *Ibid.*   [3] *Ibid.*, 5^9.
[4] *Ibid.*, 10^{12}.   [5] *Ibid.*, 9^2.   [6] *Ibid.*, 15^{17}.
[7] *Enchiridion*, 35.

only mediator between God and man, through whom alone there is forgiveness of sins. "It [Adam's sin] cannot be pardoned and blotted out except through the one mediator between God and man, the man, Christ Jesus."[1] Christ's death is the basis of that remission. As to the exact significance of that death, Augustine had not thought to consistent clearness. He viewed it sometimes as a sacrifice to God, sometimes as an endurance of our punishment in our stead, and sometimes as a ransom by which men are freed from the power of the devil. To a degree not to be found in the Greek theologians, Augustine laid stress on the significance of the humble life of Jesus. That humility was in vivid contrast to the pride which was the characteristic note in the sin of Adam. It is an example to men. "The true mediator, whom in Thy secret mercy Thou hast pointed out to the humble, and didst send, that by His example also they might learn the same humility."[2]

Man, according to Augustine, was created good and upright, possessed of free will, endowed with the possibility of not sinning and of immortality.[3] There was no discord in his nature. He was happy and in communion with God.[4] From this state Adam fell by sin, the essence of which was pride.[5] Its consequence was the loss of good.[6] God's grace was forfeited, the soul died, since it was forsaken of God.[7] The body, no longer controlled by the soul, came under the dominion of "concupiscence," of which the worst and most characteristic manifestation is lust. Adam fell into a state of total and hopeless ruin, of which the proper ending is eternal death.[8] This sin and its consequences involved all the human race; "for we were all in that one man [Adam] when we were all that man who fell into sin."[9] "The Apostle, however, has declared concerning the first man that 'in him all have sinned.'"[10] Not only were all men sinners in Adam, but their sinful state is made worse since all are born of "concupiscence."[11] The result is that the whole human race, even to the youngest infant is a "mass of perdition,"[12] and as such deserves the wrath of God. From this hopeless state of original sin "no one, no,

---

[1] *Enchiridion*, 48.   [2] *Confessions*, 10[43].   [3] *Rebuke and Grace*, 33.
[4] *City of God*, 14[26].   [5] *Nature and Grace*, 33.   [6] *Enchiridion*, 11.
[7] *City of God*, 13[2].   [8] *Ibid.*, 14[15].   [9] *Ibid.*, 13[14]; Ayer, p. 439.
[10] *Romans* 5[12]; *Forgiveness of Sins*, 1[11].   [11] *Marriage*, 1[27].
[12] *Original Sin*. 34.

not one, has been delivered, or is being delivered, or ever will be delivered, except by the grace of the Redeemer." [1]

Salvation comes by God's grace, which is wholly undeserved, and wholly free. "Wages is paid as a recompense for military service. It is not a gift; wherefore he says 'the wages of sin is death,' to show that death was not inflicted undeservedly, but as the due recompense of sin. But a gift, unless it is wholly unearned, is not a gift at all. We are to understand, then, that man's good deserts are themselves the gift of God, so that when these obtain the recompense of eternal life, it is simply grace given for grace." [2] This grace comes to those to whom God chooses to send it. He therefore predestinates whom He will, "to punishment and to salvation." [3] The number of each class is fixed. [4] Augustine had held, in the period immediately following his conversion, that it is in man's power to accept or reject grace, but even before the Pelagian controversy, he had come to the conclusion that grace is irresistible. The effect of this saving grace is twofold. Faith is instilled, and sins, both original and personal, are forgiven at baptism: "The faith by which we are Christians is the gift of God." [5] As such it is immediate justification. But grace does much more. As with Tertullian (*ante*, p. 69), it is the infusion of love by the Holy Spirit. It frees the enslaved will to choose that which is pleasing to God, "not only in order that they may know, by the manifestation of that grace, what should be done, but moreover in order that, by its enabling, they may do with love what they know." [6] It is a gradual transformation of nature, a sanctification. Through us, God does good works, which He rewards as if they were men's own and to which He ascribes merit. No man can be sure of his salvation in this life. He may have grace now, but, unless God adds the gift of perseverance, he will not maintain it to the end. [7] It would seem that Augustine may have been led to this conclusion largely by the doctrine of baptismal regeneration. It is evident that if men receive grace at baptism, many do not keep it.

This doctrine of grace was coupled in Augustine with a high valuation of the visible Catholic Church, as that only in which the true infusion of love by the Holy Spirit may be found

---

[1] *Original Sin,* 34   [2] *Enchiridion,* 107.   [3] *Ibid.,* 100; Ayer, p. 442
[4] Ayer, p. 442.   [5] *Predestination,* 3.   [6] *Rebuke and Grace,* 3.
[7] *Gift of Perseverance,* 1.

Replying to the Donatists, who were thoroughly "orthodox" in doctrine and organization, and yet rejected the Catholic Church as impure, because allowing the sacraments to be administered by men who may have been guilty of "deadly" sins, Augustine said: "Those are wanting in God's love who do not care for the unity of the Church; and consequently we are right in understanding that the Holy Spirit may be said not to be received except in the Catholic Church . . . whatever, therefore, may be received by heretics and schismatics, the charity which covereth the multitude of sins is the especial gift of Catholic unity." [1] Sacraments are the work of God, not of men. They do not, therefore, depend on the character of the administrator. Hence baptism or regular ordination need not be repeated on entering the Catholic Church. But while those outside have thus the true and valid form of the sacraments, it is only in the Catholic Church that the sacraments attain their appropriate fruition, for there only can that love be found to which they witness, and which is of the essence of the Christian life. Even in the Catholic Church, not all are in the way of salvation. That is a mixed company, of good and bad. "It is not by different baptisms, but by the same, that good Catholics are saved, and bad Catholics or heretics perish." [2]

To Augustine, sacraments include all the holy usages and rites of the church. They are the visible signs of the sacred things which they signify. Thus, he names as sacraments, exorcism, ordination, marriage, and even the salt given to catechumens. Baptism and the Lord's Supper are pre-eminently sacraments. By the sacraments the church is knit together. "There can be no religious society, whether the religion be true or false, without some sacrament or visible symbol to serve as a bond of union." [3] Furthermore, the sacraments are necessary for salvation. "The churches of Christ maintain it to be an inherent principle, that without baptism and partaking of the Supper of the Lord it is impossible for any man to attain either to the kingdom of God or to salvation and everlasting life." [4] Yet, by reason of his doctrines of grace and predestination, the sacraments for Augustine are signs of spiritual realities, rather than those realities themselves. They are essential; but the verities to which they witness are, whenever received, the work of divine

[1] *Baptism*, 3[16, 21].
[2] *Ibid.*, 5[28, 39].
[3] *Reply to Faustus*, 19[11].
[4] *Forgiveness of Sins*, 1[34].

grace. He who does not "obstruct faith" may expect, however, to receive the benefit of the sacrament.[1] The problem was not yet wrought out as it was to be in the Middle Ages; but Augustine may be called the father of the doctrine of the sacraments in the Western Church.

Augustine's greatest treatise was his *City of God*, begun in 412, in the dark days after the capture of Rome by Alaric, and finished about 426. It was his philosophy of history, and his defense of Christianity against the heathen charge that neglect of the old gods under whom Rome had grown great was the cause of its downfall. He showed that the worship of the old gods had neither given Rome strength, virtue, nor assurance of a happy future life. The loss of the old gods, that the worship of the one true God should come, was not a loss, but a great gain. Augustine then discusses the creation and the origin and consequences of evil. That brings him to his great theory of history. Since the first rebellion against God "two cities have been formed by two loves: the earthly by love of self, even to the contempt of God; the heavenly by the love of God, even to the contempt of self."[2] These had their representatives in Cain and Abel. Of the City of God, all have been members who have confessed themselves strangers and pilgrims on the earth. The Earthly City has as its highest representatives heathen Babylon and Rome, but all other civil states are its embodiment. It is a relative good. To it peace and civil order are due. In a world of sin, though having love of self as its principle, it represses disorder and secures to each his own. But it must pass away as the City of God grows. Those who make up the City of God are the elect whom God has chosen to salvation. These are now in the visible church, though not all in that church are elect. "Therefore the church even now is the kingdom of Christ, and the kingdom of heaven. Accordingly, even now His saints reign with Him, though otherwise than as they shall reign hereafter; and yet, though the tares grow in the church along with the wheat, they do not reign with Him."[3] The visible, hierarchically organized church it is, therefore, that is the City of God, and must more and more rule the world. In this teaching of Augustine lay much of the philosophic basis of the theory of the mediæval papacy.

---

[1] *Letters*, 98[10]; Ayer, p. 450.   [2] *City of God*, 14[28].   [3] *Ibid.*, 20[c].

It is evident that, clear as was the system of Augustine in many respects, it contained profound contradictions, due to the intermingling of deep religious and Neo-Platonic thoughts and popular ecclesiastical traditionalism. Thus, he taught a predestination in which God sends grace to whom He will, yet he confined salvation to the visible church endowed with a sacramental ecclesiasticism. He approached the distinction made at the Reformation between the visible and the invisible church, without clearly reaching it. His heart piety, also, saw the Christian life as one of personal relation to God in faith and love, yet he taught no less positively a legalistic and monastic asceticism. The Middle Ages did not advance in these respects beyond Augustine. It did not reconcile his contradictions. It is by reason of them that most various later movements could draw inspiration from him.

SECTION XVIII.   THE PELAGIAN CONTROVERSY

Augustine's most famous controversy, and that in which his teachings on sin and grace came to clearest expression, was with Pelagius and that teacher's disciples. Pelagius was a British, or perhaps an Irish monk, of excellent repute, much learning, and great moral earnestness, who had settled in Rome about the year 400, when probably well on in years. He seems to have been shocked at the low tone of Roman morals and to have labored earnestly to secure more strenuous ethical standards. Instead of being an innovator, his teaching in many ways represented older views than those of Augustine. With the East generally, and in agreement with many in the West, he held to the freedom of the human will. "If I ought, I can," well expresses his position. His attitude was that of the popular Stoic ethics. "As often as I have to speak of the principles of virtue and a holy life, I am accustomed first of all to call attention to the capacity and character of human nature and to show what it is able to accomplish; then from this to arouse the feelings of the hearer, that he may strive after different kinds of virtue." [1] He, therefore, denied any original sin inherited from Adam, and affirmed that all men now have the power not to sin. Like the Stoics generally, he recognized that the mass of men are bad. Adam's sin set them an ill example,

[1] Ayer, pp. 458, 459.

which they have been quick to follow. Hence they almost all
need to be set right. This is accomplished by justification by
faith alone, through baptism, by reason of the work of Christ.
No man between Paul and Luther so emphasized justification
by faith alone. After baptism, man has full power and duty
to keep the divine law.

Pelagius won a vigorous follower in the much younger
Cœlestius, a lawyer, and possibly a Roman though he has been
claimed as an Irishman. About 410, the two went to North
Africa and called on Augustine in Hippo, without finding him.
Pelagius then journeyed to the East, while Cœlestius remained
in Carthage and sought to be ordained a presbyter by Bishop
Aurelius. That bishop now received from Paulinus, a deacon
of Milan, a letter charging Cœlestius with six errors. (1)
"Adam was made mortal and would have died whether he had
sinned or had not sinned. (2) The sin of Adam injured himself alone, and not the human race. (3) New-born children are
in that state in which Adam was before his fall. (4) Neither
by the death and sin of Adam does the whole race die, nor by
the resurrection of Christ does the whole race rise. (5) The
law leads to the kingdom of heaven as well as the Gospel.
(6) Even before the coming of the Lord there were men without sin." [1] This was an unfriendly statement, but Cœlestius
did not reject it; and it probably represents his views, which
may have been somewhat more radical than those of Pelagius.
An advisory synod in Carthage, in 411, decided against his
ordination. Cœlestius then journeyed to Ephesus, where he
apparently received the desired consecration.

Augustine had not been present in Carthage, but he soon
heard of the matter, and at once began his long-continued
literary polemic against Pelagianism, which he found had
many supporters. Augustine's own religious experience was
deeply wounded. He believed that he had been saved by
irresistible divine grace from sins which he could never have
overcome by his own strength. He held Pelagius in error as
denying original sin, rejecting salvation by infused grace, and
affirming human power to live without sin. Pelagius did not
reject grace, but to him grace was remission of sins in baptism
and general divine teaching. To Augustine the main work of
grace was that infusion of love by which character is gradually

---

[1] Ayer, p. 461.

transformed. Pelagius found support in the East. Early in 415, Augustine sent Orosius to Jerome, then in Palestine, to interest him for the Augustinian cause. By Jerome, Pelagius was accused before Bishop John of Jerusalem, but was approved by the bishop; and before the year was out, a synod held in Diospolis (Lydda in Palestine) declared Pelagius orthodox.

In this situation Augustine and his friends caused two North African synods to be held in 416, one for its local district in Carthage and the other for Numidia in Mileve. These condemned the Pelagian opinions and appealed to Pope Innocent I (402–417) for confirmation. Innocent was undoubtedly pleased at this recognition of papal authority, and did as the African synods wished. Innocent died shortly after, and was succeeded by Zosimus (417–418), a Greek, and therefore naturally no special sympathizer with the distinctive Augustinian positions. To Zosimus, Cœlestius now appealed in person. The new Pope declared that the African synods had been too hasty, and seems to have regarded Cœlestius as orthodox. A new synod met in Carthage early in 418, but the Africans made a more effective move. In April, 418, at their instance the Western Emperor, Honorius, issued a rescript condemning Pelagianism and ordering the exile of its adherents. In May a large council was held in Carthage, which held that Adam became mortal by sin, that children should be baptized for the remission of original sin, that grace was necessary for right living, and that sinlessness is impossible in this life. Moved by these actions, Zosimus now issued a circular letter condemning Pelagius and Cœlestius.

Pelagius now disappears. He probably died before 420. A new and able champion of his opinions now appeared in the person of Bishop Julian of Eclanum, in southern Italy. An edict of the Emperor Honorius, in 419, required the bishops of the West to subscribe a condemnation of Pelagius and Cœlestius. Julian and eighteen others in Italy refused. Several of them were driven into exile and sought refuge in the East. In Julian, Augustine found an able opponent, and Pelagianism its chief systematizer; but a defender who was much more of a rationalist than Pelagius. About 429 Julian and Cœlestius found some support from Nestorius in Constantinople, though Nestorius was not a Pelagian. This favor worked to Nestorius's disadvantage in his own troubles, and together with the wish

of the Pope led to the condemnation of Pelagianism by the
so-called Third General Council in Ephesus in 431 (*ante*, p.
148). Pelagianism, thus officially rejected in the West and the
East, nevertheless lived on in less extreme forms, and has always represented a tendency in the thinking of the church.

SECTION XIX.   SEMI-PELAGIANISM

Augustine's fame as the great teacher of the Western Church
was secure even before his death in 430. By no means all accepted, however, the more peculiar portions of his theology,
even where Pelagianism was definitely rejected. Thus, Jerome
ascribed to the human will a share in conversion, and had no
thought of an irresistible divine grace, though deeming grace
essential to salvation. Northern Africa, which had led the
Western Church intellectually since the time of Tertullian, was
now devastated by the Vandals. Its pre-eminence in leadership now passed to southern France, and it was there that the
chief controversy over Augustinian principles arose. John
Cassianus, probably from Gaul, but who had journeyed to the
East, visited Egypt, and had served as deacon under Chrysostom, founded a monastery and a nunnery in Marseilles about
415, and died there about 435. Not far from 429 he wrote his
Collationes, in the form of conversations with Egyptian monks.
In his opinion "the will always remains free in man, and it
can either neglect or delight in the grace of God." [1]

In 434 Vincent, a monk of Lérins, wrote a *Commonitorium,*
in which, without attacking Augustine by name, his design
was to do so really, by representing Augustine's teachings on
grace and predestination as novelties without support in
Catholic tradition. "Moreover, in the Catholic Church itself
all possible care should be taken that we hold that faith which
has been believed everywhere, always and by all." [2] These
men and their associates were called in the sixteenth century
"Semi-Pelagians," though Semi-Augustinians would be more
correct, since they agreed in most points with Augustine,
though rejecting his essential doctrines of predestination and
irresistible grace. These were earnest men who sincerely feared
that Augustine's doctrines would cut the nerve of all human

---

[1] 12; Ayer, p. 469.

[2] *Quod ubique, quod semper, quod ab omnibus,* 2[4]; Ayer, p. 471.

effort after righteousness of life, especially that righteousness as sought in monasticism. Predestination and irresistible grace seemed to deny human responsibility.

This dissent from Augustine appeared in still more positive form in the writings of Faustus, abbot of Lérins, and afterward bishop of Riez. In his treatise on *Grace*, of about 474, he recognized original sin, but held that men still have "the possibility of striving for salvation." Grace is the divine promise and warning which inclines the weakened but still free will to choose the right rather than, as with Augustine, an inward transforming power. God foresees what men will do with the invitations of the Gospel. He does not predestinate them. Though Faustus rejected Pelagius, he really stood closer to him than to Augustine.

A more Augustinian direction was given to the thought of southern France by the able and devoted Cæsarius (469?–542), for a time a monk of Lérins, and from 502 onward bishop of Arles. In 529 he held a little synod in Orange, the canons of which received a much larger significance because approved by Pope Boniface II (530–532). They practically ended the Semi-Pelagian controversy, though Semi-Pelagian positions have always largely been maintained in the church.[1] It was affirmed by this synod that man is not only under original sin, but has lost all power to turn to God, so that "it is brought about by the infusion of the Holy Spirit and His operation in us that we wish to be set free." It is "by the free gift of grace, that is, by the inspiration of the Holy Spirit," that we have "the desire of believing" and "come to the birth of holy baptism." All good in man is the work of God. Thus many of the main thoughts of Augustine were approved; but with a decided weakening of emphasis. The irresistibility of grace is nowhere affirmed. On the contrary, those in error are said to "resist that same Holy Spirit." Predestination to evil is condemned. But, most marked of all, the reception of grace is so bound to baptism that the sacramental quality of grace and the merit of good works are put in the foreground. "We also believe this to be according to the Catholic faith, that grace having been received in baptism, all who have been baptized, can and ought, by the aid and support of Christ, to perform those things which belong to the salvation of the soul, if they

[1] Ayer, pp. 472–476.

labor faithfully." [1] Augustinianism was approved, but with undoubted modification in the direction of popular "Catholic" religious conceptions. Its sharp points were blunted.

The tendencies toward a blunted, ecclesiastically and sacramentally emphasized presentation of Augustinianism, which have already been noted, characterized the thinking of Gregory the Great, the interpreter of Augustine to the Middle Ages. A teacher of little originality, he presented the theological system already developed in the West, in essential harmony with the popular Christianity of his age. His influence was thus far-reaching. He is reckoned with Ambrose, Augustine, and Jerome one of the Doctors of the Latin Church. In administrative abilities and achievements Gregory was one of the greatest of the Popes, and Latin Christianity generally had in him a leader of broad vision and permanent accomplishment.

Gregory was born in Rome of a senatorial Christian family about 540. Before 573 he was made prefect, or governor, of the city by the Emperor Justin II. The monastic life attracted him from civil distinctions, and by 574 he had devoted his wealth to the founding of monasteries and to the poor, and become a member of the monastery of St. Andrew in what had formerly been his own home on the Cælian hill. Gregory always retained his interest in monasticism, and did much for the regulation and extension of the monastic life. His own temperament was too active for the cloister, and in 579 Pope Pelagius II (579–590) sent him as papal ambassador to the court of Constantinople, where he served with ability, though, curiously, without acquiring a knowledge of Greek. About 586 he was once more in Rome as the abbot of St. Andrew. In 590 he was chosen Pope, being the first monk to attain that office. He died on March 12, 604.

The time of Gregory's papacy was propitious for an able Pope. The papacy, which had risen high under Innocent I (402–417) and Leo I (440–461), had sunk in power after Justinian had conquered the Ostrogoths and restored the imperial authority in Italy. Since 568, however, the control of the Emperors in Italy had more and more waned before the Lom-

---

[1] Ayer, p. 475.

bards, who threatened Rome itself. Though nominally subject to the Emperor, Gregory was the real leader against Lombard aggression. He raised troops, defended Rome by force
and by tribute, even made a peace with the Lombards on his
own authority, and succeeded, after infinite effort and confused struggles both with the Lombards and the imperial representatives, in keeping Rome unconquered throughout his
pontificate. He was the strongest man in Italy, and must
have seemed to the Romans and to the Lombards alike far
more a real sovereign than the distant and feeble Emperor.

The support of the papacy as well as the source of much of
the food of Rome was in its large estates, the Patrimony of
Peter, in Sicily, Italy, and even in southern France and northern Africa. Of these Gregory showed himself an energetic but
kindly landlord. Their management took much of his attention. Their revenues increased, and Gregory employed this
income liberally not only in the maintenance of the clergy and
public worship, and in the defense of Rome, but in charitable
foundations and good works of all kinds.

Gregory was convinced that "to all who know the Gospel
it is apparent that by the Lord's voice the care of the whole
church was committed to the holy Apostle and prince of all
the Apostles, Peter." [1] He would exercise a jurisdiction over
the church as Peter's successor. As such, he protested against
certain acts of ecclesiastical discipline inflicted by the patriarch
of Constantinople, John the Faster; and announced that he
would receive an appeal. In the acts sent for his inspection
Gregory found John described as "universal bishop." Against
this claim for Constantinople he raised vigorous protest.[2] His
own practice was the employment of the title still borne by the
Roman bishops, "servant of the servants of God." He exercised judicial authority with greater or less success in the
affairs of the churches of Ravenna and Illyria. He attempted
to interfere in the almost independent life of the church of
France, re-establishing the papal vicariate in Arles, in 595,
coming into friendly relations with the Frankish court, and attempting to remove abuses in French ecclesiastical administration.[3] Here his success was small. With some good fortune he asserted the papal authority in Spain, where the
Visigothic sovereign, Recared, had renounced Arianism in 587.

---

[1] *Letters*, 5[20].   [2] Ayer, pp. 592–595.   [3] *Ibid.*, pp. 591–592.

Even more significant for the future was Gregory's far-reaching missionary campaign for the conversion of England, inaugurated in 596, of which some account will be given (p. 198). It not only advanced markedly the cause of Christianity, but was the initiation of a closer relationship of England, and ultimately of Germany, with the papacy than had yet been achieved elsewhere. Nearer home, among the Arian Lombards, Gregory inaugurated ultimately successful efforts to turn them to the Catholic faith, especially through the aid of Theodelinda, who was successively the Queen of Kings Authari (584–591) and Agilulf (592–615).

Tradition has ascribed to Gregory a great work in the reformation of church music—the "Gregorian chants"—and in the development of the Roman liturgy; but the absence of contemporary reference makes it probable that his services in both these respects were relatively inconspicious. On the other hand, his abilities as a preacher were undoubted. As a writer three of his works maintained high popularity throughout the Middle Ages—his exposition of Job, or *Moralia*, his treatise on the character and duties of the pastoral office, the *Regula Pastoralis*, and his credulous *Dialogues on the Life and Miracles of the Italian Fathers*.

Gregory's theology is Augustinian, but with another emphasis than that of Augustine. He developed all of Augustine's ecclesiastical tendencies, and that mass of material from popular Christianity which Augustine took up into his system. Miracles, angels, and the devil have an even greater part in Gregory's system than in that of Augustine. While Gregory held that the number of the elect is fixed, and depends upon God, he had no such interest in predestination as had Augustine. He often speaks as if predestination is simply divine foreknowledge. His interests were practical. Man is fettered in original sin, the evidence of which is his birth through lust. From this condition he is rescued by the work of Christ, received in baptism; but sins committed after baptism must be satisfied. Works of merit wrought by God's assisting grace make satisfaction. "The good that we do is both of God and of ourselves; of God by prevenient grace, our own by good will following." [1] Penance is the proper reparation for sins after baptism. It involves recognition of the evil of the sin, con-

---

[1] *Moralia*, 33²¹.

trition, and satisfaction. The church has many helps for him
who would seek merit or exercise penance. Of these the greatest is the Lord's Supper, which Gregory viewed as a repetition
of the sacrifice of Christ, available for the living and the dead.
There is also the aid of the saints. "Those who trust in no
work of their own should run to the protection of the holy
martyrs." [1] For those who, while really disciples of Christ,
make an insufficient use of these opportunities to achieve works
of merit, fail to do penance, or avail themselves inadequately
of the helps offered in the church, there remain the purifying
fires of purgatory.

The thought of purgatory was not new with Gregory. The
first faint intimation may be found in Hermas of Rome.[2]
With Cyprian it is more evident, and he cites in this connec-
tion *Matt.* 5^{26}.[3] Augustine, on the basis of 1 *Cor.* 3^{11-15}, argued
that purgatory was not improbable, though he felt no absolute
certainty regarding it.[4] Cæsarius of Arles held more definitely
to the conception. To him it was a fact. Gregory now taught
purgatory as a matter essential to the faith. "It is to be believed that there is a purgatorial fire before the judgment for
certain light sins." [5] Though the Eastern Church held that an
intermediate state exists between death and the judgment,
and souls can be helped therein by prayer and sacrifice, its
conception of purgatory has always been vague compared with
that of the West.

Thus, in all departments of ecclesiastical activity Gregory
stood forth the most conspicuous leader of his time. In him
the Western Church of the Middle Ages already exhibited its
characteristic traits, whether of doctrine, life, worship, or organization. Its growth was to be in the directions in which
Gregory had moved.

Contemporary with Gregory in part, and of significance as
the transmitter of much of the theological leaning of the ancient church to the Middle Ages, was Isidore, the head of the
Spanish church from about 600 to 636, as bishop of Seville.
His *Book of Sentences*—brief statements of doctrine—was to
be the theological text-book of the Western Church till the
twelfth century. His *Origins or Etymologies* embraced well-
nigh the round of learning of his age, ecclesiastical and secular,

---

[1] *Moralia*, 16^{51}.   [2] *Vis.*, 3^7.   [3] *Letters*, $51-55^{20}$.
[4] *Enchiridion*, 69; *City of God*, 21^{26}.   [5] *Dialogues*, 4^{33}.

and was a main source of knowledge in the Middle Ages of the thought of antiquity. His value as a historian of the Goths and Vandals was great. In him, as the most learned man of his age, all the earlier Middle Ages were to find a teacher of little originality but of remarkable breadth of learning.

PERIOD IV. THE MIDDLE AGES TO THE CLOSE OF THE INVESTITURE CONTROVERSY

SECTION I.   MISSIONS IN THE BRITISH ISLANDS

THE spread of Arianism among the Germanic tribes, the conversion of the Franks to the Roman faith, and the gradual acceptance of Catholic orthodoxy by the Germanic invaders have already been noted (*ante*, pp. 129–134).   Much, however, remained to be done.   There is no more striking proof of the vitality of the church in the collapsing empire and the opening Middle Ages than the vigor and success with which it undertook the extension of Christianity.

Christianity had some foothold in the British Isles before the conversion of Constantine.   Bishops of York, London, and probably Lincoln, were present at the Council of Arles in 314. Yet it survived the downfall of the Roman Empire but feebly among the Celtic population, while much of the soil of southern and eastern England was won for heathenism by the Anglo-Saxon invaders.   Some slight Christian beginnings were to be found chiefly in the south of Ireland before the time of Patrick; but he so advanced the cause of the Gospel in that island and so organized its Christian institutions, that he deserves the title of the Apostle of Ireland.

Born about 389, possibly in southern Wales, Patrick was the son of a deacon and the grandson of a priest.   His training was therefore Christian.   Seized in a raid about 405, he was for six years a slave in Ireland.   Escaped to the Continent, Patrick was for a considerable time an inmate of the monastery of Lérins, off the southern coast of France.   In 432 he was ordained a missionary bishop by Bishop Germanus of Auxerre, and began the work in Ireland which ended with his death in 461.   Most of Patrick's missionary labors were in northeastern Ireland, though not without some efforts in the south and wilder west.   Few facts survive; but of his zeal there can be no question, and as little of his conspicuous abilities as an organizer under whom the hitherto scattered Christianity of

Ireland was systematized and made great advance. He brought the island in some measure into association with the Continent and with Rome.

It seems certain that Patrick introduced the diocesan epis-copate into Ireland; but that institution was soon modified by the clan system of the island, so that there were, instead, many monastic and tribal bishops. Monasticism was favored by Patrick; but the great developer of the peculiar Irish monasticism was Finian of Clonard (470?–548), under whose leadership a strongly missionary and, for the time, a notably learned group of Irish monasteries came into being. The monastic schools of Ireland were justly famous in the sixth and seventh centuries. The glory of this Irish monasticism was its missionary achievement.

The beginnings of Christianity in Scotland are very obscure. Ninian is said to have labored there in the fourth century and the early years of the fifth, but of his date and real work little can be said. Kentigern, or Mungo (527?–612?), who spread Christianity in the neighborhood of Glasgow, is almost as dim a figure. It would seem probable that the northern Irish settlers who founded, about 490, the kingdom of Dalriada, em-bracing the modern Argyleshire, came as Christians. The great missionary to Scotland was Columba (521–597), a man closely related with some of the most powerful tribal families of Ireland, and a pupil of Finian of Clonard. Distinguished already as a monk and a founder of monasteries in Ireland, he transferred his labors, in 563, to Scotland, establishing himself with twelve companions on the island of Iona or Hy, under the protection of his fellow countryman and relative, the King of Dalriada. There Columba developed a most flourishing monas-tery, and thence he went forth for missionary labors among the Picts, who occupied the northern two-thirds of Scotland. By Columba and his associates the kingdom of the Picts was won for the Gospel. As in Ireland, Christian institutions were largely monastic. There were no dioceses, and even the bishops were under the authority, save in ordination, of Co-lumba, who was a presbyter, and of his successors as abbots of Iona.

These Irish missionary efforts were carried to northern Eng-land, among the Anglo-Saxons of Northumbria. There, on the island of Lindisfarne, off the extreme northeastern coast of

England, a new Iona was established by Aidan, a monk from
Iona, in 634. Thence Christianity was widely spread in the
region by him till his death in 651, and afterward by his
associates. Nor was the missionary zeal of these Celtic monks
by any means confined to the British Islands. Columbanus,
or Columba the Younger (543?–615), became a monk of the
celebrated Irish monastery of Bangor, which was founded in
558 by Comgall, a leader in learning and missionary zeal.
From Bangor, Columbanus set forth, about 585, with twelve
monastic companions, and settled in Anegray, in Burgundy,
near which he planted the monastery of Luxeuil. Driven
forth about 610, in consequence of his prophet-like rebuke of
King Theuderich II and the King's grandmother, Brunhilda,
Columbanus worked for a brief time in northern Switzerland,
where his Irish companion and disciple, Gallus, was to live as
an anchorite, and to give his name to, rather than to found, the
later monastery of St. Gall. Columbanus made his way to
northern Italy, and there established in 614, in the Appenines,
the monastery of Bobbio, in which he died a year later.

Columbanus was only one of the earlier of a number of Irish
monks who labored on the Continent—many of them in what
is now central and southern Germany. Thus, Kilian wrought
in Würzburg and Virgil in Salzburg. One modification of Christian practice, of great later importance, was introduced on the
Continent by these Irish monks, notably by Columbanus.
The entrance of thousands into the church when Christianity
was accepted by the state had largely broken down the old
public discipline. There had grown up the custom of private
confession among the monks of East and West. Basil had
strongly favored it in the East. Nowhere had it more hearty
support than among the Irish monks, and by them it was extended to the laity, as was indeed the case, to some extent, by
the monks of the East. The Irish on the Continent were the
introducers of private lay confession. In Ireland, also, grew
up the first extensive penitential books, in which appropriate
satisfactions were assessed for specific sins—though these books
had their antecedents in earlier canons of councils. These
penitential treatises the Irish monks made familiar on the Continent.

Meanwhile, a work of the utmost significance for the religious
history of Britain and the papacy had been undertaken by

Pope Gregory the Great. Moved by a missionary impulse which he had long felt, and taking advantage of the favorable situation afforded by the marriage of Æthelberht, "King" of Kent and overlord of much of southeastern England, to a Frankish Christian princess, Berhta, Gregory sent a Roman friend, Augustine, the prior of his beloved monastery on the Cælian hill, with a number of monastic companions, to attempt the conversion of the Anglo-Saxons. The expedition left Rome in 596, but its courage was small, and all the persuasive power of Gregory was required to induce it to proceed. It was not till the spring of 597 that the party, reinforced by Frankish assistants, reached Canterbury. Æthelberht and many of his followers soon accepted Christianity. Gregory looked upon the struggle as already won. Augustine received episcopal consecration from Vergilius of Arles in November, 597, and, by 601, Gregory appointed Augustine metropolitan with authority to establish twelve bishops under his jurisdiction. When northern England should be converted a similar metropolitanate was to be established in York. London and York were to be the ecclesiastical capitals. The British bishops, over whom Gregory had no recognized jurisdiction, the Pope committed to the superintendency of Augustine.[1] The task in reality was to prove much more arduous than it seemed to Gregory's sanguine vision, and the greater part of a century was to pass before Christianity was to be dominant in England. Yet the movement, thus inaugurated, was vastly to strengthen the papacy. The Anglo-Saxons owed their conversion chiefly to the direct efforts of Rome, and they in turn displayed a devotion to the papacy not characteristic of the older lands, like France and Spain, where Christianity had been otherwise introduced. Anglo-Saxon Christianity was to produce, moreover, some of the most energetic of missionaries by whom the Gospel and papal obedience were alike to be advanced on the Continent.

England was not brought to the acceptance of Christianity without much vicissitude. The hegemony of Kent was waning before the death of Æthelberht, and with it the first Christian triumphs were eclipsed. Northumbria gradually gained leadership. It was a success when Edwin, King of North-

[1] Gee and Hardy, *Documents Illustrative of English Church History*, pp. 9, 10.

umbria, was converted through the work of Paulinus, soon to be bishop of York, in 627. The heathen King, Penda of Mercia, however, defeated and slew Edwin in 633, and a heathen reaction followed in Northumbria. Under King Oswald, who had become a Christian when an exile in Iona, Christianity was re-established in Northumbria, chiefly through the aid of Aidan (*ante*, p. 197). It was of the Irish, or as it is often called, the "Old British" type. Penda once more attacked, and in 642 Oswald was killed in battle. Oswald's brother, Oswy, like him a convert of Iona, after much struggle secured all of Northumbria by 651, and a widely recognized overlordship besides. English Christianity was becoming firmly established.

From the first coming of the Roman missionaries there had been controversy between them and their Irish or Old British fellow Christians. The points of difference seem of minor importance. An older system of reckoning, discarded in Rome, resulted in diversity as to the date of Easter. The forms of tonsure were unlike. Some variations, not now recoverable, existed in the administration of baptism. Furthermore, as has been pointed out, Roman Christianity was firmly organized and diocesan, while that of the Old British Church was monastic and tribal. · While the Old British missionaries looked upon the Pope as the highest dignitary in Christendom, the Roman representatives ascribed to him a judicial authority which the Old British did not fully admit. Southern Ireland accepted the Roman authority about 630. In England the decision came at a synod held under King Oswy at Whitby in 664. There Bishop Colman of Lindisfarne defended the Old British usages, while Wilfrid, once of Lindisfarne, but won for Rome on a pilgrimage, and soon to be bishop of York, opposed. The Roman custom regarding Easter was approved, and with it the Roman cause in England won the day. By 703 northern Ireland had followed the same path, and by 718, Scotland. In Wales the process of accommodation was much slower, and was not completed till the twelfth century. In England this strengthening of the Roman connection was much furthered by the appointment, in 668, by Pope Vitalian, of a Roman monk, Theodore, a native of Tarsus in Cilicia, as archbishop of Canterbury. An organizer of ability, he did much to make permanent the work begun by his predecessors.

The two streams of missionary effort combined to the advan-

tage of English Christianity.   If that from Rome contributed
order, the Old British gave missionary zeal and love of learning.
The scholarship of the Irish monasteries was transplanted to
England, and was there strengthened by frequent Anglo-
Saxon pilgrimages to Rome.   Of this intellectual movement a
conspicuous illustration was Bede, generally called the "Venerable" (672?–735).   An almost life-long member of the joint
monastery of Wearmouth and Jarrow in Northumbria, his learning, like that of Isidore of Seville, a century earlier, embraced
the full round of knowledge of his age, and made him a teacher
of generations to come.   He wrote on chronology, natural phenomena, the Scriptures, and theology.   Above all, he is remembered for his *Ecclesiastical History of the English Nation,* a
work of great merit and the chief source of information regarding the Christianization of the British Islands.

SECTION II.   CONTINENTAL MISSIONS AND PAPAL GROWTH

With the conversion of Clovis to orthodox Christianity
(496) (*ante,* p. 133), a close relationship of church and state began in the Frankish dominions.   To a large extent it was true
that Frankish conquest and Christianization were two sides
of the same shield.   Under the descendants of Clovis—the
Merovingian Kings—the internal condition of the Frankish
church sank, however, to a low ebb.   Bishops and abbots were
appointed for political considerations, much church land was
confiscated or put in secular hands.   Even the efforts of Gregory I to gain more effective papal control in France and to
effect reform had little lasting result.

The political collapse of the Merovingians, led to the rise to
power of the Carolingian house, originally "mayors of the palace," which was accomplished when Pippin, called, not wholly
correctly, of Heristal, won the battle of Tertry in 687.   The
Merovingian Kings continued in name, but the real authority
was exercised by Pippin as "duke of the Franks."   After his
death in 714, his illegitimate son Charles Martel (715–741) exercised all the powers of a King.   By him the Mohammedan
advance in western Europe was permanently stayed, by the
great battle between Tours and Poitiers in 732.   He saw the
advantage of churchly aid, and supported missionary effort in
western Germany and the Netherlands, where he wished to ex-

tend his political control.   Yet neither Pippin "of Heristal" nor Charles Martel were more helpful to the church of their own territories than the Merovingians.   They exploited it for political reasons, confiscated its lands, and did little to check its disorders.   Nevertheless, under Charles Martel a great missionary and reformatory work was initiated that was to Christianize large sections of western Germany, reform the Frankish church, and bring the papacy and the Franks into relations of the utmost consequence to both.

Willibrord (657?–739), a Northumbrian, began missionary work in Frisia with the support of Pippin of Heristal, and, in 695, was consecrated a missionary bishop by Pope Sergius I— an action which resulted in the establishment of the see of Utrecht.   His work had scanty success, and was taken up by one of the ablest and most remarkable men of the period— Winfrid or Boniface (680?–754).   An Anglo-Saxon of Devonshire by birth, Winfrid became a monk of Nutcell near Winchester.   In 716, he began missionary labors in Frisia, but with such ill success that he returned to England.   In 718 and 719, he was in Rome, where he received from Pope Gregory II (715–731) appointment to labor in Germany.   From 719 to 722, he worked in Frisia and Hesse, going once more to Rome in the year last named, and receiving consecration as a missionary bishop, swearing allegiance to the Pope.[1]   The next ten years witnessed a great success in Hesse and Thuringia.   Not only were heathen converted, but the Irish monks were brought largely into obedience to Rome.   Gregory III (731–741) made Boniface an archbishop in 732, with authority to found new sees. After a third journey to Rome, in 738, he thus organized the church of Bavaria, and a little later that of Thuringia.   In 744, he aided his disciple, Sturm, in the foundation of the great Benedictine monastery of Fulda, destined to be a centre of learning and priestly education for all western-central Germany.   Between 746 and 748, Boniface was made archbishop of Mainz, which thus became the leading German see.   In all this Boniface strengthened the causes of order and discipline and increased papal authority.   His work was greatly aided by the considerable numbers of men and women who came as fellow workers from his native England, and for whom he found place in monastic and other Christian service.

[1] Robinson, *Readings in European History*, 1: 105–111.

The death of Charles Martel in 741 saw his authority divided between his sons Carloman (741–747), and Pippin the Short (741–768). Both were far more churchly than their father, and Carloman ultimately retired from power to become a monk. While neither would abandon authority over the Frankish church, both supported Boniface in the abolition of its worst irregularities and abuses, and in a closer connection with Rome. In a series of synods held under Boniface's leadership, beginning in 742, the worldliness of the clergy was attacked, wandering bishops censured, priestly marriage condemned, and stricter clerical discipline enforced. At a synod held in 747 the bishops assembled recognized the jurisdiction of the papacy, though, as the civil rulers were not present, these conclusions lacked the force of Frankish law. The Frankish church, thanks to the work of Boniface, was vastly bettered in organization, character, and discipline, while, what was equally valued by him, the authority of the papacy therein was very decidedly increased, even though that of the mayor of the palace continued the more potent.

As Boniface drew toward old age his thoughts turned toward the mission work in Frisia, with which he had begun. He secured the appointment of his Anglo-Saxon disciple, Lull, as his successor in the see of Mainz. In 754 he went to Frisia, and there was murdered by the heathen, thus crowning his active and widely influential life with a death of witness to his faith. His work had been one for order, discipline, and consolidation, as well as Christian advancement, and these were the chief needs of the age.

SECTION III. THE FRANKS AND THE PAPACY

It has already been pointed out (*ante*, p. 162) that the papacy, and Italy generally, opposed the iconoclastic efforts of the Emperor Leo III, going so far as to excommunicate the opponents of pictures in a Roman synod held under Gregory III, in 731. The Emperor answered by removing southern Italy and Sicily from papal jurisdiction, and placing these regions under the see of Constantinople—a matter long a thorn in the side of the papacy. In Rome and northern Italy the imperial power exercised from Constantinople was too feeble to control papal action. The imperial representative was the exarch of Ravenna, under whom stood a duke of Rome for military affairs, though the Pope was in many respects the Emperor's representative in the civil concerns of the city. The papacy was now in practical rebellion against the rulers who had their seat in Constantinople. It was, however, in a most dangerous position. The Lombards were pressing, and were threatening the capture of Rome. The disunion consequent on the iconoclastic dispute made it necessary, if the papacy was to maintain any considerable independence in Rome, to find other protection against the Lombards than that of the Emperor. This the Popes sought, and at last obtained, from the Franks.

In 739 Gregory III appealed to Charles Martel for aid against the Lombards, but in vain. With Pippin the Short it was otherwise. He was more ecclesiastically minded, and greater plans than even his father had entertained now moved him. Pippin and the papacy could be of mutual assistance each to the other. The new Lombard King, Aistulf (749–756), conquered Ravenna from the Emperor in 751 and was grievously pressing Rome itself. Pippin desired the kingly title as well as the kingly power in France. He had determined upon a revolution which should relegate the last of the feeble Merovingians, Childeric III, to a monastery, and place Pippin himself on the throne. For this change he desired not only the approval of the Frankish nobility, but the moral sanction of the church. He appealed to Pope Zacharias (741–752). The Pope's approval was promptly granted, and before the close of 751, Pippin was formally in the kingly office. To this he was anointed and crowned, but whether by Boniface, as has usually been supposed, is uncertain.

This transaction, which seems to have been simple at the time, was fraught with the most far-reaching consequences. From it might be drawn the conclusion that it was within the Pope's power to give and withhold kingdoms. All unseen in it, were wrapped up the re-establishment of the empire in the West, the Holy Roman Empire, and that interplay of papacy and empire which forms so large a part of the history of the Middle Ages. From this point of view it was the most important event of mediæval history.

If the Pope could thus help Pippin, the latter could be no less serviceable to the Pope. Aistulf and his Lombards continued to press Rome. Stephen II, therefore, went to Pippin himself, crowning and anointing Pippin and his sons afresh in the church of St. Denis near Paris, in 754, and confirming to them the indefinite title of "Patricians of the Romans"—all the more useful, perhaps, because implying a relation to Rome that was wholly undefined. It had been borne by the imperial exarch in Ravenna. Soon after this crowning, Pippin fulfilled his reciprocal obligation. At the head of a Frankish army, late in 754, or early in 755, he invaded Italy and compelled Aistulf to agree to surrender to the Pope Ravenna and the other recent Lombard conquests. A second campaign, in 756, was necessary before the Lombard King made good his promise. The Exarchate of which Ravenna was the capital and the Pentapolis were now the possessions of the Pope. The "States of the Church" were begun—that temporal sovereignty of the papacy which was to last till 1870. Yet, as far as can now be judged, in thus granting the Exarchate to Pope Stephen, Pippin regarded himself as overlord. Rome itself, Pippin did not give to the Pope. It was not his to give. Legally, the status of Rome would have been hard to define. Though the Popes had practically broken with the Emperor at Constantinople, Rome had not been conquered from him. Indeed the papacy recognized the sovereignty of the Eastern Emperor in the style of its public documents till 772. Pippin had the wholly nebulous rights that might be included in the title "Patrician of the Romans." Actually, Rome was in the possession of the Pope.

Though the Pope was thus now a territorial ruler, the extent of his possessions was far from satisfying papal ambition, if one may judge by a curious forgery, the authorship of which is unknown, but which seems to date from this period—the so-called "Donation of Constantine." [1] In charter form, and with an expression of a creed, and a fabulous account of his conversion and baptism, Constantine ordered all ecclesiastics to be subject to Pope Sylvester and successive occupants of the Roman see, and transferred to them "the city of Rome and all the provinces, districts, and cities of Italy or of the Western regions." This meant a sovereignty over the Western half of the empire—at least an overlordship. Discredited by a few of the wiser men of the Middle Ages, the "Donation" was gen-

[1] Henderson, *Select Historical Documents*, pp. 319–329.

erally believed, till its falsity was demonstrated by Nicholas of Cues in 1433 and Lorenzo Valla in 1440.

SECTION IV. CHARLEMAGNE

Pippin the Short died in 768. A strong ruler, his fame has been unduly eclipsed by that of his greater son, who, in general, simply carried further what the father had begun. Pippin had divided his kingdom between his two sons, Charles and Carloman. Ill will existed between the brothers, but the situation was relieved by the death of Carloman in 771. With that event the real reign of Charles, to whom the world has so ascribed the title "Great" as to weave it indissolubly with his name—Charlemagne—began.

Charlemagne, perhaps more than any other sovereign in history, was head over all things to his age. A warrior of great gifts, he more than doubled his father's possessions. When he died his sway ruled all of modern France, Belgium, and Holland, nearly half of modern Germany and Austria-Hungary, more than half of Italy, and a bit of northeastern Spain. It was nearer imperial size than anything that had been seen since the downfall of the Western Roman Empire. Conquest was but part of his work. His armies, by extending the frontier, gave rest and time for consolidation to the central portion of his territories. He was the patron of learning, the kindly master of the church, the preserver of order, to whom nothing seemed too small for attention or too great for execution.

A quarrel with Desiderius, King of the Lombards, resulted in the conquest and extinction of that kingdom by Charlemagne in two campaigns in the years 774 to 777. Pippin's grants to the papacy were renewed, but the situation was practically altered. The papacy was no longer separated as it had been from the main Frankish territories by the intervening Lombard kingdom. Charlemagne's connection with Rome was a much more effective overlordship than that of his father, and he thenceforth treated the Pope as the chief prelate of his realm, rather than as an independent power, though he did not go so far as to dictate the choice of the Popes, as he did that of the bishops of his kingdom.

Highly important for the extension of Christianity was Charlemagne's conquest of the Saxons, then occupying what is now northwestern Germany—a result achieved only after a series of campaigns lasting from 772 to 804. His forcible imposition of Christianity was made permanent by the more peaceful means of planting bishoprics and monasteries throughout the Saxon land. By this conversion the last considerable Germanic tribe, and one of the most gifted and energetic, was brought into the Christian family of Europe to its permanent advantage. Frisia, also, now became a wholly Christian land. Charlemagne's contests with the rebellious duke, Tassilo, of already Christianized Bavaria, led not only to the full absorption of the Bavarian bishoprics in the Frankish ecclesiastical system, but to successful wars against the Avars and the extension of Christianity into much of what is now Austria.

Such a ruler, devoted equally to the extension of political power and of Christianity, and controlling the greater part of Western Christendom, was, indeed, a figure of imperial proportions. It is not surprising, therefore, that Pope Leo III (795–816), who was greatly indebted to Charlemagne for protection from disaffected Roman nobles, placed on the head of the Frankish King the Roman imperial crown as the latter knelt in St. Peter's Church on Christmas day, 800. To the thinking of the Roman populace who applauded, as to the West generally, it was the restoration of the empire to the West, that had for centuries been held by the ruler in Constantinople. It placed Charlemagne in the great succession from Augustus. It gave a theocratic stamp to that empire. Unexpected, and not wholly welcome at the time to Charlemagne, it was the visible embodiment of a great ideal. The Roman Empire, men thought, had never died, and now God's consecration had been given to a Western Emperor by the hands of His representative. It was not, necessarily, a rejection of the imperial title of the ruler in Constantinople. The later empire had frequently seen two Emperors, East and West. Leo V (813–820), the Emperor in Constantinople, later, formally recognized the imperial title of his Western colleague. For the West and for the papacy the coronation was of the utmost consequence. It raised questions of imperial power and of papal authority that were to be controverted throughout the Middle Ages. It emphasized the feeling that church and state were but two sides of the same shield, the one leading man to temporal happiness, the other to eternal blessedness,

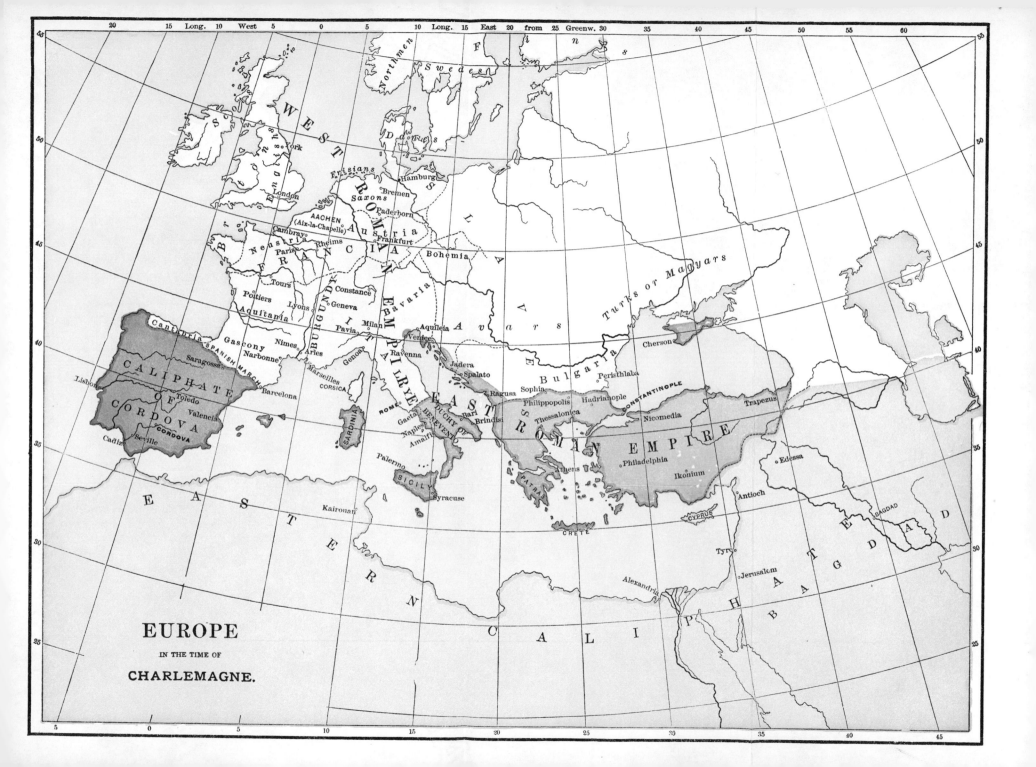

EUROPE

IN THE TIME OF

CHARLEMAGNE.

and both closely related and owing mutual helpfulness. It made more evident than ever the deep-seated religious and political cleavage between East and West. To the great Emperor himself it seemed the fulfilment of the dream of Augustine's *City of God* (*ante*, p. 184)—the union of Christendom in a kingdom of God, of which he was the earthly head. His pcwer was never greater than when he died, in 814.

At Charlemagne's accession no schools were so flourishing in Western Europe as those to be found in connection with the monasteries of the British Islands. It was from England that this many-sided monarch procured his chief intellectual and literary assistant. Alcuin (735?–804) was probably a native, and certainly a student of York. From 781 to his death, with some interruptions, he was Charlemagne's main aid in a real renaissance of classical and Biblical learning, that rendered the reign bright compared with the years before, and raised the intellectual life of the Frankish state. Charlemagne himself, though without becoming much of a scholar, set the example as an occasional pupil in this "school of the palace." In 796 Charlemagne made Alcuin the head of the monastery of St. Martin in Tours, which now became under his leadership a centre of learning for the whole Frankish realm. Others helped in this intellectual revival, like the Lombard, Paul the Deacon (720?–795), the Frank, Einhard (770?–840), or the Visigoth, Theodulf (760?–821). The mere mention of these various national relationships shows the care which Charlemagne exhibited to secure from any portion of Western Europe those who could raise the intellectual standards of his empire.

With this growth of learning came theological discussion. The Spanish bishops, Elipandus of Toledo and Felix of Urgel, taught an adoptionist Christology—that Christ, though in His divine nature the Son of God, was in His human nature only a son by adoption. Under Charlemagne's leadership these opinions were condemned in synods held in Regensburg (792) and Frankfort (794). In this work Charlemagne regarded himself as the theological guide no less than the protector of the church. In similar fashion, at the synod of Frankfort just mentioned, Charlemagne had the conclusions of the General Council of 787, in Nicæa (*ante*, p. 163), condemned, rejected its approval of picture reverence, and caused the *Libri Carolini*, defending his position, to be issued. In 8C9, at a synod in Aachen, Charlemagne approved the Spanish addition *filioque* (*ante*, p. 180) to the so-called Nicene-Constantinopolitan creed. All these acts were in consultation with the bishops and theologians of his realm, but with no special deference to the Pope or reference of the matters to papal judgment.

SECTION V.   ECCLESIASTICAL INSTITUTIONS

Roman political institutions were based on the cities, on which the surrounding country was dependent, and Christian organization followed the same rule. The country districts were dependent upon and were cared for by the city bishops and their appointees, save where, in the East, there were "country bishops." The Germanic invasions altered this situation. By the sixth century the beginnings of the parish system were to be found in France (*ante*, p. 166). There it rapidly grew, and it was stimulated by the custom of the foundation of churches by large landowners. The founders and their heirs retained the right of nominating the incumbent. This situation left episcopal control uncertain. Charlemagne, therefore, provided that besides the right of ordination of all parish priests, the bishop should have visitorial and disciplinary power throughout his diocese. The churchly status was further strengthened by the full legal establishment of tithes. Long favored by the clergy through Old Testament example, they were demanded by a Frankish synod in Macon, in 585. By Pippin they were treated as a legal charge, and full legal sanction was given them by Charlemagne. They were to be collected not only by bishops, but by and for the use of the incumbent of each parish. Moreover, constant gifts of lands to the church had raised ecclesiastical possessions, by the time of the early Carolingians, to a third of the soil of France. The great holdings were a constant temptation in the financial need of a Charles Martel, who appropriated much, but under the friendly government of Charlemagne they were respected, if earlier confiscations were not restored.

Under Charlemagne, preaching was encouraged and books of sermons prepared. Confession was favored, though not yet obligatory. Every Christian was expected to be able to repeat the Lord's Prayer and the Apostles' Creed.

Charlemagne renewed and extended the metropolitan system.

which had fallen into abeyance. At the beginning of his reign there was but one metropolitan in the Frankish kingdom. At its end there were twenty-two. These were now generally known as archbishops—a title which goes back to the time of Athanasius, though long loosely used. In Carolingian theory the archbishop was the judge and disciplinary officer of the bishops of his province, possessed of powers which the growth of papal jurisdiction was soon to curtail. It was also his duty to call frequent synods to consider the religious problems of the archdiocese, or as it was usually styled, the province.

For the better regulation of his immediate clerical assistants, Bishop Chrodegang of Metz introduced, about 760, a semi-monastic life in common, which was favored and spread by Charlemagne. From the designation of this life as the *vita canonica*, the name "canons" for the clergy attached to a cathedral or collegiate church arose. Their place of meeting was called the *capitulum*, or chapter—a title soon applied to the canons themselves. By this means the life and work of the bishop and his immediately associated clergy was largely regulated. Charlemagne himself designated the bishops of his realm.

In all these changes, save that of personal authority over episcopal appointments, Charlemagne was but carrying further the reforms begun by Boniface. Much that he completed his father, Pippin, had commenced. At Charlemagne's death, the Frankish church was in a far better state of education, discipline, and efficiency than it had been under the later Merovingians and early Carolingians.

SECTION VI. COLLAPSING EMPIRE AND RISING PAPACY

Charlemagne's great power was personal. Scarcely had he died when the rapid decline of his empire began. His son and successor, Louis the Pious (814–840), was of excellent personal character, but wholly unequal to the task left by Charlemagne, or even to the control of his own sons, who plotted against him and quarrelled with one another. After his death they divided the empire between them by the Treaty of Verdun in 843. To Lothair (843–855) came Frankish Italy and a strip of territory including the valley of the Rhone and the region lying immediately west of the Rhine, together with the imperial title. To

Louis (843–875) was given the region east of the Rhine, whence he acquired the nickname, "the German." To Charles the Bald (843–877) came most of modern France and ultimately the imperial crown. This Treaty of Verdun is usually regarded as the point whence France and Germany go their separate ways.

These rulers proved utterly inadequate for unity or defense. France suffered grievously from attacks by the Scandinavian Normans, who pushed up its rivers and burned its towns, ultimately (911) establishing themselves permanently in Normandy. Italy was a prey to Saracen raids, in one of which (841) St. Peter's itself, in Rome, was plundered. A little later, with the beginning of the tenth century, the raids of the Hungarians brought devastation to Germany and Italy. Under these circumstances, when national unity or defense was impossible, feudalism developed with great rapidity. Its roots run back to the declining days of the Roman Empire, but with the death of Charlemagne it was given great impetus. It was intensely divisive, substituting for any strong central government many local seats of authority, jealous one of another and engaged in constant struggle. Churches and monasteries became largely the prey of local nobles, or defended their rights with difficulty as parts of the feudal system. This social and political form of organization was to dominate Europe till the thirteenth century, and largely to make possible the growth of the mediæval papacy.

The impulse given to learning by Charlemagne did not immediately die. At the court of Charles the Bald, John Scotus (?–877?), to whom the name Erigena was much later added, held somewhat the same position that Alcuin had occupied under Charlemagne. He translated the much admired writings of the Pseudo-Dionysius (*ante*, p. 171), and developed his own Neo-Platonic philosophy, which his age was too ignorant to judge heretical or orthodox. In Germany, Hrabanus Maurus (776?–856), abbot of Fulda and archbishop of Mainz, a pupil of Alcuin, attained a deserved reputation as a teacher, commentator on the Scriptures, furtherer of clerical education and author of what was well-nigh an encyclopædia. In Hincmar (805?–882), archbishop of Rheims, France possessed not only a prelate of great assertiveness and influence, but a theological controversialist of decided gift.

The renewed study of Augustine which this intellectual

revival effected led to two doctrinal controversies. The first was regarding the nature of Christ's presence in the Supper. About 831 Paschasius Radbertus, a monk of the monastery of Corbie, near Amiens, of remarkable learning in Greek as well as in Latin theology, set forth the first thoroughgoing treatise on the Lord's Supper, *De corpore et sanguine Domini*. In it he taught with Augustine, that only those who partake in faith receive the virtue of the sacrament, and with the Greeks, that it is the food of immortality; and also, that by divine miracle the substance is made the very body and blood of Christ. That was transubstantiation, though the word was not to be coined before the twelfth century. To Radbertus, Hrabanus Maurus replied; but a more elaborate answer was that of a fellow monk of Corbie, Ratramnus, about 844. Yet his view agreed in much with that of Radbertus. The body and blood of Christ are mysteriously present; yet they are not identical with the body that suffered on the cross. The controversy was not decided at the time, but the future, in the Roman Church, was with Radbertus.

The second controversy was aroused by Gottschalk (808?–868?). A monk of Fulda, made so by parental dedication, his efforts for release from his bonds were frustrated by Hrabanus Maurus. He then turned to the study of Augustine, and his hard fate, perhaps, led him to emphasize a double divine predestination—to life or to death. He was attacked by Hrabanus Maurus and Hincmar, but found vigorous defenders. Condemned as a heretic at a synod in Mainz in 848, he spent the next twenty years in monastic imprisonment, persecuted by Hincmar, and refusing to retract. The controversy was a fresh flaring up of the old dispute between thoroughgoing Augustinianism and the semi-Pelagianism which was the actual theory of a large portion of the church.

As the collapse of Charlemagne's empire grew more complete, however, these controversies and the intellectual life out of which they sprang faded. By 900 a renewed barbarism had largely extinguished the light which had shone brightly a century before. One great exception to this general condition existed. In England, Alfred the Great (871–901?), distinguished as the successful opponent of the Danish conquerors, in a spirit like that of Charlemagne gathered learned men about him, and encouraged the education of the clergy.

The collapsing empire of Charlemagne led to the rise of a churchly party in France, which despairing of help from the state, looked toward the papacy as the source of unity and hope. This party regarded with suspicion also any control of the church by the sovereigns or nobility, and it represented the jealousy of the ordinary bishops and lower clergy toward the great archbishops with their often arbitrary assertions of authority, of whom Hincmar was a conspicuous example. The aim of the movement was not the exaltation of the papacy for its own sake; rather its exaltation as a means of checking secular control and that of the archbishops, and of maintaining ecclesiastical unity. From this circle, between 847 and 852, and probably from Hincmar's own region of Rheims, came one of the most remarkable of forgeries—the so-called Pseudo-Isidorian Decretals—purporting to be collected by a certain Isidore Mercator, by whom Isidore of Seville (*ante*, p. 193) and Marius Mercator were doubtless intended. It consisted of decisions of Popes and councils from Clement of Rome in the first century to Gregory II in the eighth, part genuine and part forged. The "Donation of Constantine" (*ante*, p. 204) is included. The early Popes therein claim for themselves supreme jurisdiction. All bishops may appeal directly to papal authority. Intervening archiepiscopal rights are limited, and neither papacy nor bishops are subject to secular control. With its origin the papacy had nothing to do; but it was to be used mightily to the furtherance of papal claims. The age was uncritical. It passed immediately as genuine, and was not exposed till the Reformation had awakened historical study.

With the decline of imperial power, the independence of the papacy rapidly rose. The Popes showed themselves the strongest men in Italy. Leo IV (847–855), aided by south Italian cities, defeated the Saracens and surrounded the quarter of St. Peter's in Rome with a wall—the "Leonine City." In Nicholas I (858–867) the Roman see had its ablest and most assertive occupant between Gregory the Great and Hildebrand. He sketched out a programme of papal claims, hardly surpassed later, but which the papacy was to be centuries in achieving. Nicholas attempted to realize the ideals of Augustine's *City of God*. In his thought, the church is superior to all earthly powers, the ruler of the whole church is the Pope, and the bishops are his agents. These conceptions he was able to make effective in two notable cases, in which he had also the advantage of choosing the side on which right lay. The first was that of Thietberga, the injured wife of Lothair II of Lorraine. Divorced that that sovereign might marry his concubine, Waldrada, she appealed to Nicholas, who declared void the sanctioning decision of a synod held in Metz, in 863, and excommunicated the archbishops of Trier and Cologne who had supported Lothair. The Pope had defended helpless womanhood, he none the less humbled two of the most powerful German prelates and thwarted a German ruler. In the second case, Nicholas received the appeal of the deposed Bishop Rothad of Soissons, who had been removed by the overbearing Archbishop Hincmar of Rheims, and forced his restoration. Here Nicholas appeared as the protector of the bishops against their metropolitans and the defender of their right to appeal to the Pope as the final judge. In this quarrel the Pseudo-Isidorian Decretals were first employed in Rome.

In a third case, Nicholas, though having right on his side, was less successful. The Emperor in Constantinople, Michael III, "the Drunkard," was ruled by his uncle, Bardas, a man of unsavory reputation. The patriarch, Ignatius, refused Bardas the sacrament, and was deposed. In his place, Bardas procured the appointment of one of the most learned men of the later Greek world, Photius (patriarch 858-867, 878-886), then a layman. Ignatius, thus injured, appealed to Nicholas, who sent legates to Constantinople. They joined in approval of Photius. The Pope repudiated their action, and, in 863, declared Photius deposed. Photius now accused the Western Church of heresy for admitting the *filioque* clause to the creed, fasting on Saturdays, using milk, butter, and cheese in Lent, demanding priestly celibacy, and confining confirmation to the bishops. At a synod under his leadership in Constantinople, in 867, the Pope was condemned. Nicholas failed in his attempt to exercise his authority over the Eastern Church. The ill feeling between East and West was but augmented, which was to lead, in 1054, to the complete separation of the churches,

During this period following the death of Charlemagne important missionary efforts were begun. Ansgar (801 ?-865), a monk of Corbie, entered Denmark in 826, but was driven out the next year. In 829 and 830 he labored in Sweden. In 831 he was appointed archbishop of the newly constituted see of Hamburg, with prospective missionary jurisdiction over Denmark, Norway, and Sweden. The destruction of Hamburg by the Danes, in 845, resulted in Ansgar's removal to Bremen, which was united ecclesiastically with Hamburg. Ansgar's efforts were backed by no Frankish military force, and his patient labors accomplished little. The full Christianization of Scandinavia was yet in the future.

Larger success attended missions in the East. The Bulgars, originally a Turanian people, from eastern Russia, had conquered a large territory in the Balkan region in the seventh century, and, in turn, had adopted the manners and speech of their Slavic subjects. Under their King, Boris (852–884), Christianity was introduced, Boris being baptized in 864. For some time undecided between Constantinople and Rome, Boris finally chose spiritual allegiance to the former, since the patriarch of Constantinople was willing to recognize a self-governing Bulgarian church. This adhesion was of immense consequence in determining the future growth of the Greek Church in Eastern Europe. The most celebrated missionaries among the Slavs were, however, the brothers Cyril (?–869) and Methodius (?–885). Natives of Thessalonica, they had attained high position in the Eastern empire. On the request of Rostislav, duke of Moravia, the Eastern Emperor, Michael III, sent the brothers thither in 864. There they labored with great success. A struggle of several years between the papacy and Constantinople for possession of this new-won territory resulted in the ultimate victory of Rome. The use of a Slavic liturgy was permitted by Pope John VIII (872–882), though soon withdrawn, but from this source its worship came ultimately to the Russian church. From Moravia, Christianity in its Roman form came to Bohemia about the close of the ninth century.

SECTION VII.   PAPAL DECLINE AND RENEWAL BY THE REVIVED EMPIRE

It may seem strange that the papacy which showed such power under Nicholas I should within twenty-five years of his death have fallen into its lowest degradation. The explanation is the growing anarchy of the times. Up to a certain point the collapse of the empire aided the development of papal

authority; that passed, the papacy became the sport of the
Italian nobles and ultimately of whatever faction was in control of Rome, since the Pope was chosen by the clergy and
people of the city.   The papacy could now appeal for aid to no
strong outside political power as Zacharias had to Pippin against
the Lombards.

At the close of the ninth century the papacy was involved
in the quarrels for the possession of Italy.   Stephen V (885–
891) was overborne by Guido, duke of Spoleto, and compelled
to grant him the empty imperial title.   Formosus (891–896)
was similarly dependent, and crowned Guido's son, Lambert,
Emperor in 892.   From this situation Formosus sought relief
in 893 by calling in the aid of Arnulf, whom the Germans had
chosen King in 887.   In 895 Arnulf captured Rome, and was
crowned Emperor by Formosus the next year.   A few months
later Lambert was in turn master of Rome, and his partisan,
Stephen VI (896–897), had the remains of the lately deceased
Formosus disinterred, condemned in a synod, and treated
with extreme indignity.   A riot, however, thrust Stephen VI
into prison, where he was strangled.

Popes now followed one another in rapid succession, as the
various factions controlled Rome.   Between the death of
Stephen VI (897) and the accession of John XII (955) no less
than seventeen occupied the papal throne.   The controlling
influences in the opening years of the tenth century were those
of the Roman noble Theophylact, and his notorious daughters, Marozia and Theodora.   The Popes were their creatures.
From 932 to his death in 954 Rome was controlled by Marozia's
son Alberic, a man of strength, ability, and character, who did
much for churchly reforms in Rome, but nevertheless secured
the appointment of his partisans as Popes.   On his death he
was succeeded as temporal ruler of Rome by his son Octavian,
who had few of the father's rough virtues.   Though without
moral fitness for the office, Octavian secured his own election
as Pope in 955, choosing as his name in this capacity John XII
(955–964), being one of the earliest Popes to take a new name
on election.   He altered the whole Roman situation and introduced a new chapter in the history of the papacy, by calling
for aid upon the able German sovereign, Otto I, against the
threatening power of Berengar II, who had gained control of
a large part of Italy.

The line of Charlemagne came to an end in Germany, in 911, with the death of Louis the Child. With the disintegration of the Carolingian empire and the growth of feudalism, Germany threatened to fall into its tribal divisions, Bavaria, Swabia, Saxony, Franconia, and Lorraine. The most powerful men were the tribal dukes. The necessities of defense from the Northmen and Hungarians forced a degree of unity, which was aided by the jealousy felt by the bishops of the growing power of the secular nobility. In 911 the German nobles and great clergy, therefore, chose Conrad, duke of Franconia, as King (911–918). He proved inadequate, and in 919 Henry the Fowler, duke of Saxony, was elected his successor (919–936). His ability was equal to the situation. Though having little power, save in Saxony, he secured peace from the other dukes, fortified his own territories, drove back the Danes, subdued the Slavs east of the Elbe, and finally, in 933, defeated the Hungarian invaders. The worst perils of Germany had been removed, and the foundations of a strong monarchy laid, when he was succeeded as King by his even abler son, Otto I (936–973).

Otto's first work was the consolidation of his kingdom. He made the semi-independent dukes effectively his vassals. In this work he used above all the aid of the bishops and great abbots. They controlled large territories of Germany, and by filling these posts with his adherents, their forces, coupled with his own, were sufficient to enable Otto to control any hostile combination of lay nobles. He named the bishops and abbots, and under him they became, as they were to continue to the Napoleonic wars, lay rulers as well as spiritual prelates. The peculiar constitution of Germany thus arose, by which the imperial power was based on control of ecclesiastical appointments—a situation which was to lead to the investiture struggle with the papacy in the next century. As Otto extended his power he founded new bishoprics on the borders of his kingdom, partly political and partly missionary in aim, as Brandenburg and Havelberg among the Slavs, and Schleswig, Ripen, and Aarhus for the Danes. He also established the archbishopric of Magdeburg.

Had Otto confined his work to Germany it would have been for the advantage of that land, and for the permanent upbuilding of a strong central monarchy. He was, however, attracted by Italy, and established relations there of the utmost historic importance, but which were destined to dissipate the strength of Germany for centuries. A first invasion in 951 made him master of northern Italy. Rebellion at home (953) and a great campaign against the Hungarians (955) interrupted his Italian enterprise; but in 961 he once more invaded Italy, invited by Pope John XII, then hard pressed by Berengar II (*ante*, p. 215). On February 2, 962, Otto was crowned in Rome by John XII as Emperor—an event which, though in theory continuing the succession of the Roman Emperors from Augustus and Charlemagne, was the inauguration of the Holy Roman Empire, which was to continue in name till 1806. Theoretically, the Emperor was the head of secular Christendom, so constituted with the approval of the church expressed by coronation by the papacy. Practically, he was a more or less powerful German ruler, with Italian possessions, on varying terms with the Popes.

John XII soon tired of Otto's practical control, and plotted against him. Otto, of strong religious feeling, to whom such a Pope was an offense, doubtless was also moved by a desire to strengthen his hold on the German bishops by securing a more worthy and compliant head of the church. In 963 Otto compelled the Roman people to swear to choose no Pope without his consent, caused John XII to be deposed, and brought about the choice of Leo VIII (963–965). The new Pope stood solely by imperial support. On Otto's departure John XII resumed his papacy, and on John's death the Roman factions chose Benedict V. Once more Otto returned, forced Benedict into exile, restored Leo VIII, and after Leo's speedy demise, caused the choice of John XIII (965–972). Otto had rescued the papacy, for the time being, from the Roman nobles, but at the cost of subserviency to himself.

Otto's son and successor, Otto II (973–983), pursued substantially the same policy at home, and regarding the papacy, as his father, though with a weaker hand. His son, Otto III (983–1002), went further. The Roman nobles had once more controlled the papacy in his minority, but in 996 he entered Rome, put them down, and caused his cousin Bruno to be made Pope as Gregory V (996–999)—the first German to hold the papal office. After Gregory's decease Otto III placed on the papal throne his tutor, Gerbert, archbishop of Rheims, as Silvester II (999–1003)—the first French Pope, and the most learned man of the age.

The death of Otto III ended the direct line of Otto I, and the throne was secured by Henry II (1002–1024), duke of Bavaria and great-grandson of Henry the Fowler. A man filled with sincere desire to improve the state of the church, he yet felt himself forced by the difficulties in securing and maintaining his position to exercise strict control over ecclesiastical appointments. His hands were too fully tied by German affairs to interfere effectually in Rome. There the counts of Tusculum gained control of the papacy, and secured the appointment of Benedict VIII (1012–1024), with whom Henry stood on good terms, and by whom he was crowned. Henry even persuaded the unspiritual Benedict VIII at a synod in Pavia in 1022, at which both Pope and Emperor were present, to renew the prohibition of priestly marriage and favor other measures which the age regarded as reforms.

With the death of Henry II the direct line was once more extinct, and the imperial throne was secured by a Franconian count, Conrad II (1024–1039), one of the ablest of German rulers, under whom the empire gained great strength. His thoughts were political, however, and political considerations determined his ecclesiastical appointments. With Rome he did not interfere. There the Tusculan party secured the papacy for Benedict VIII's brother, John XIX (1024–1032), and on his death for his twelve-year-old nephew, Benedict IX (1033–1048), both unworthy, and the latter one of the worst occupants of the papal throne. An intolerable situation arose at Rome, which was ended (see p. 221) by Conrad's able and far more religious son, Henry III, Emperor from 1039 to 1056.

SECTION VIII.   REFORM MOVEMENTS

Charlemagne himself valued monasticism more for its educational and cultural work than for its ascetic ideals. Those ideals appealed, however, in Charlemagne's reign to a soldier-nobleman of southern France, Witiza, or as he was soon known, Benedict (750?–821) called of Aniane, from the monastery founded by him in 779. Benedict's aim was to secure everywhere the full ascetic observation of the "Rule" of Benedict of Nursia (*ante*, p. 139). The educational or industrial side of monasticism appealed little to him.   He would raise monasticism to greater activity in worship, contemplation, and self-denial.   Under Louis the Pious Benedict became that Emperor's chief monastic adviser, and by imperial order, in 816 and 817, Benedict of Aniane's interpretation of the elder Benedict's Rule was made binding on all monasteries of the empire. Undoubtedly a very considerable improvement in their condition resulted.   Most of these benefits were lost, however, in the collapse of the empire, in which monasticism shared in the common fall.

The misery of the times itself had the effect of turning men's minds from the world, and of magnifying the ascetic ideal. By the early years of the tenth century a real ascetic revival of religion was beginning that was to grow in strength for more than two centuries.   Its first conspicuous illustration was the foundation in 910 by Duke William the Pious, of Aquitaine, of the monastery of Cluny, not far from Macon in eastern France.[1]   Cluny was to be free from all episcopal or worldly jurisdiction, self-governing, but under the protection of the Pope.   Its lands were to be secure from all invasion or secularization, and its rule that of Benedict, interpreted with great ascetic strictness.   Cluny was governed by a series of abbots of remarkable character and ability.   Under the first and second of these, Berno (910–927) and Odo (927–942), it had many imitators, through their energetic work.   Even the mother Benedictine monastery of Monte Cassino, in Italy, was reformed on Cluny lines, and, favored by Alberic, a monastery, St. Mary on the Aventine hill, was founded which represented Cluny ideas in Rome.   By the death of Odo the Cluny movement was wide-spread in France and Italy.

It was no part of the original purpose of Cluny to bring other monasteries into dependence on it, or to develop far-reaching churchly political plans.   Its aim was a monastic reformation by example and influence.   Yet even at the death of the first abbot five or six monasteries were under the control of the abbot of Cluny.   Under the fifth abbot, Odilo (994–1048), however, Cluny became the head of a "congregation," since he brought all monasteries founded or reformed by Cluny into dependence on the mother house, their heads being appointed by and responsible to the abbot of Cluny himself.

[1] Henderson, *Select Historical Documents*, pp. 329–333.

This was new in monasticism, and it made Cluny practically an order, under a single head, with all the strength and influence that such a constitution implies. It now came to have a force comparable with that of the Dominicans or Jesuits of later times. With this growth came an enlargement of the reformatory aims of the Cluny movement. An illustration is the "Truce of God." Though not originated by Cluny, it was taken up and greatly furthered by Abbot Odilo from 1040 onward. Its aim was to limit the constant petty wars between nobles by prescribing a closed season in memory of Christ's passion, from Wednesday evening till Monday morning, during which acts of violence should be visited with severe ecclesiastical punishments. Its purpose was excellent; its success but partial.

As the Cluny movement grew it won the support of the clergy, and became an effort, not for the reform of monasticism, as at first, but for a wide-reaching betterment of clerical life. By the first half of the eleventh century the Cluny party, as a whole, stood in opposition to "Simony"[1] and "Nicolaitanism."[2] By the former was understood any giving or reception of a clerical office for money payment or other sordid consideration. By the latter, any breach of clerical celibacy, whether by marriage or concubinage. These reformers desired a worthy clergy, appointed for spiritual reasons, as the age understood worthiness. While many of the Cluny party, and even abbots of Cluny itself, had apparently no criticism of royal ecclesiastical appointments, if made from spiritual motives, by the middle of the eleventh century a large section was viewing any investiture by a layman as simony, and had as its reformatory ideal a papacy strong enough to take from the Kings and princes what it deemed their usurped powers of clerical designation. This was the section that was to support Hildebrand in his great contest.

Elsewhere than in the Cluny movement ascetic reform was characteristic of the tenth and eleventh centuries. In Lorraine and Flanders a monastic revival of large proportions was instituted by Gerhard, abbot of Brogne (?–959). In Italy, Romuald of Ravenna (950?–1027) organized settlements of hermits, called "deserts," in which the strictest asceticism was practised, and from which missionaries and preachers went

[1] *Acts* 8[18-24].　　　　　　　　[2] *Rev.* 2[6, 14, 15].

forth. The most famous "desert," which still exists and gave
its name to the movement, is that of Camaldoli, near Arezzo.
Even more famous was Peter Damiani (1007?–1072), likewise
of Ravenna, a fiery supporter of monastic reform, and opponent of simony and clerical marriage, who was, for a time,
cardinal bishop of Ostia, and a leading ecclesiastical figure in
Italy in the advancement of Hildebrandian ideas, preceding
Hildebrand's papacy.

It is evident that before the middle of the eleventh century
a strong movement for churchly reform was making itself
felt. Henry II had, in large measure, sympathized with it
(*ante*, p. 218). Henry III (1039–1056) was even more under
its influence. Abbot Hugh of Cluny (1049–1109) was a close
friend of that Emperor, while the Empress, Agnes, from Aquitaine, had been brought up in heartiest sympathy with the
Cluny party, of which her father had been a devoted adherent.
Henry III was personally of a religious nature, and though he
had no hesitation in controlling ecclesiastical appointments
for political reasons as fully as his father, Conrad II, he would
take no money for so doing, denounced simony, and appointed
bishops of high character and reformatory zeal.

The situation in Rome demanded Henry III's interference,
for it had now become an intolerable scandal. Benedict IX,
placed on the throne by the Tusculan party, had proved so
unworthy that its rivals, the nobles of the Crescenzio faction,
were able to drive him out of Rome, in 1044, and install their
representative as Silvester III in his stead. Benedict, however,
was soon back in partial possession of the city, and now, tiring
temporarily of his high office, and probably planning marriage,
he sold it in 1045 for a price variously stated as one or two thousand pounds of silver. The purchaser was a Roman archpriest
of good repute for piety, John Gratian, who took the name
Gregory VI. Apparently the purchase was known to few.
Gregory was welcomed at first by reformers like Peter Damiani.
The scandal soon became public property. Benedict IX refused to lay down the papacy, and there were now three Popes
in Rome, each in possession of one of the principal churches,
and each denouncing the other two. Henry III now interfered. At a synod held by him in Sutri in December, 1046,
Silvester III was deposed, and Gregory VI compelled to resign
and banished to Germany. A few days later, a synod in Rome,

under imperial supervision, deposed Benedict IX. Henry III immediately nominated and the overawed clergy and people of the city elected a German, Suidger, bishop of Bamberg, as Clement II (1046–1047). Henry III had reached the high-water mark of imperial control over the papacy. So grateful did its rescue from previous degradation appear that the reform party did not at first seriously criticise this imperial domination; but it could not long go on without raising the question of the independence of the church. The very thoroughness of Henry's work soon roused opposition.

Henry III had repeated occasion to show his control of the papal office. Clement II soon died, and Henry caused another bishop of his empire to be placed on the papal throne as Damasus II. The new Pope survived but a few months. Henry now appointed to the vacant see his cousin Bruno, bishop of Toul, a thoroughgoing reformer, in full sympathy with Cluny, who now journeyed to Rome as a pilgrim, and after merely formal canonical election by the clergy and people of the city—for the Emperor's act was determinative—took the title of Leo IX (1049–1054).

SECTION IX. THE REFORM PARTY SECURES THE PAPACY

Leo IX set himself vigorously to the task of reform. His most effective measure was a great alteration wrought in the composition of the Pope's immediate advisers—the cardinals. The name, cardinal, had originally been employed to indicate a clergyman permanently attached to an ecclesiastical position. By the time of Gregory I (590–604), its use in Rome was, however, becoming technical. From an uncertain epoch, but earlier than the conversion of Constantine, in each district of Rome a particular church was deemed, or designated, the most important, originally as the exclusive place for baptisms probably. These churches were known as "title" churches, and their presbyters or head presbyters were the "cardinal" or leading priests of Rome. In a similar way, the heads of the charity districts into which Rome was divided in the third century were known as the "cardinal" or leading deacons. At a later period, but certainly by the eighth century, the bishops in the immediate vicinity of Rome, the "suburbi-carian" or suburban bishops, were called the "cardinal bishops." This division of the college of cardinals into "cardinal bishops," "cardinal priests," and "cardinal deacons" persists to the present day. As the leading clergy of Rome and vicinity, they were, long before the name "cardinal" became exclusively or even primarily attached to them, the Pope's chief aids and advisers.

On attaining the papacy Leo IX found the cardinalate filled with Romans, and so far as they were representative of the noble factions which had long controlled the papacy before Henry III's intervention, with men unsympathetic with reform. Leo IX appointed to several of these high places men of reformatory zeal from other parts of Western Christendom. He thus largely changed the sympathies of the cardinalate, surrounded himself with trusted assistants, and in considerable measure rendered the cardinalate thenceforth representative of the Western Church as a whole and not simply of the local Roman community. It was a step of far-reaching consequence. Three of these appointments were of special significance. Humbert, a monk of Lorraine, was made cardinal bishop, and to his death in 1061 was to be a leading opponent of lay investiture and a force in papal politics. Hugh the White, a monk from the vicinity of Toul, who was to live till after 1098, became a cardinal priest, was long to be a supporter of reform, only to become for the last twenty years of his life the most embittered of opponents of Hildebrand and his successors. Finally, Hildebrand himself, who had accompanied Leo IX from Germany, was made a sub-deacon, charged with the financial administration, in some considerable measure, of the Roman see. Leo IX appointed other men of power and reformatory zeal to important, if less prominent, posts in Rome and its vicinity.

Hildebrand, who now came into association with the cardinalate, is the most remarkable personality in mediæval papal history. A man of diminutive stature and unimpressive appearance, his power of intellect, firmness of will, and limitlessness of design made him the outstanding figure of his age. Born in humble circumstances in Tuscany, not far from the year 1020, he was educated in the Cluny monastery of St. Mary on the Aventine in Rome, and early inspired with the most radical of reformatory ideals. He accompanied Gregory VI to Germany on that unlucky Pope's banishment (*ante,*

p. 221), and thence returned to Rome with Leo IX.   Probably he was already a monk, but whether he was ever in Cluny itself is doubtful.   He was, however, still a young man, and to ascribe to him the leading influence under the vigorous Leo IX is an error.   Leo was rather his teacher.

Leo IX entered vigorously on the work of reform.   He stood in cordial relations with its chief leaders, Hugo, abbot of Cluny, Peter Damiani, and Frederick of Lorraine.   He made extensive journeys to Germany and France, holding synods and enforcing papal authority.   At his first Easter synod in Rome, in 1049, he condemned simony and priestly marriage in the severest terms.   A synod held under his presidency in Rheims the same year affirmed the principle of canonical election, "no one shall be promoted to ecclesiastical rulership without the choice of the clergy and people."   By these journeys and assemblies the influence of the papacy was greatly raised.

In his relations with southern Italy and with Constantinople Leo IX was less fortunate.   The advancing claims of the Normans, who since 1016 had been gradually conquering the lower part of the peninsula, were opposed by the Pope, who asserted possession for the papacy.   Papal interference with the churches, especially of Sicily, which still paid allegiance to Constantinople, aroused the assertive patriarch of that city, Michael Cerularius (1043–1058), who now, in conjunction with Leo, the metropolitan of Bulgaria, closed the churches of the Latin rite in their regions and attacked the Latin Church in a letter written by the latter urging the old charges of Photius (*ante*, p. 213), and adding a condemnation of the use of unleavened bread in the Lord's Supper—a custom which had become common in the West in the ninth century.   Leo IX replied by sending Cardinal Humbert and Frederick of Lorraine, the papal chancellor, to Constantinople in 1054, by whom an excommunication of Michael Cerularius and all his followers was laid on the high altar of St. Sofia.   This act has been usually regarded as the formal separation of the Greek and Latin Churches.   In 1053 Leo's forces were defeated and he himself captured by the Normans.   He did not long survive this catastrophe, dying in 1054.

On the death of Leo IX, Henry III appointed another German, Bishop Gebhard of Eichstädt, as Pope.   He took the title of Victor II (1055–1057).   Though friendly to the reform party, Victor II was a devoted admirer of his imperial patron, and on the unexpected death of the great Emperor in 1056, did much to secure the quiet succession of Henry III's son Henry IV, then a boy of six, under the regency of the Empress Mother, Agnes. Less than a year later Victor II died.

SECTION X.   THE PAPACY BREAKS WITH THE EMPIRE

Henry III's dominance was undoubtedly displeasing to the more radical reformers, who had endured it partly of necessity, since it was not apparent how the papacy could otherwise be freed from the control of the Roman nobles, and partly because of Henry's sympathy with many features of the reform movement. Henry himself had been so firmly intrenched in his control of the German church, and of the papacy itself, that the logical consequences of the reform movement appear not to have been clear to him. Now he was gone. A weak regency had taken his place. The time seemed ripe to the reformers for an advance which should lessen imperial control, or, if possible, end it altogether.

On Victor II's death the Romans, led by the reform clergy, chose Frederick of Lorraine Pope as Stephen IX (1057–1058) without consulting the German regent. A thoroughgoing reformer, the new Pope was the brother of Duke Godfrey of Lorraine, an enemy of the German imperial house, who by his marriage with the Countess Beatrice of Tuscany had become the strongest noble in northern Italy. Under Stephen, Cardinal Humbert now issued a programme for the reform party in his *Three Books Against the Simoniacs*, in which he declared all lay appointment invalid and, in especial, attacked lay investiture, that is the gift by the Emperor of a ring and a staff to the elected bishop in token of his induction into office. The victory of these principles would undermine the foundations of the imperial power in Germany. Their strenuous assertion could but lead to a struggle of gigantic proportions. Nevertheless, Stephen did not dare push matters too far. He, therefore, sent Hildebrand and Bishop Anselm of Lucca, who secured the approval of the Empress Agnes for his papacy. Scarcely had this been obtained when Stephen died in Florence.

Stephen's death provoked a crisis. The Roman nobles reasserted their old authority over the papacy and chose their own partisan, Benedict X, only a week later. The reform cardinals had to flee. Their cause seemed for the moment lost. The situation was saved by the firmness and political skill of Hildebrand. He secured the approval of Godfrey of Tuscany and of a part of the people of Rome for the candidacy of Gerhard, bishop of Florence, a reformer and, like Godfrey, a native of Lorraine. A representative of this Roman minority obtained the consent of the regent, Agnes. Hildebrand now gathered the reform cardinals in Siena, and Gerhard was there chosen as Nicholas II (1058–1061). The military aid of Godfrey of Tuscany soon made the new Pope master of Rome. Under Nicholas II the real power was that of Hildebrand, and in lesser degree of the cardinals Humbert and Peter Damiani.

The problem was to free the papacy from the control of the Roman nobles without coming under the overlordship of the Emperor. Some physical support for the papacy must be found. The aid of Tuscany could be counted as assured. Beatrice and her daughter, Matilda, were to be indefatigable in assistance. Yet Tuscany was not sufficient. Under the skilful guidance of Hildebrand, Nicholas II entered into cordial relations with the Normans, who had caused Leo IX so much trouble, recognized their conquests, and received them as vassals of the papacy. With like ability, intimate connections were now established, largely through the agency of Peter Damiani and Bishop Anselm of Lucca, with the democratic party in Lombardy known as the Pataria, opposed to the anti-reformatory and imperialistic higher clergy of that region. Strengthened by these new alliances, Nicholas II at the Roman synod of 1059 expressly forbad lay investiture under any circumstances.

The most significant event of the papacy of Nicholas II was the decree of this Roman synod of 1059 regulating choice to the papacy—the oldest written constitution now in force, since, in spite of considerable modification, it governs the selection of Popes to this day. In theory, the choice of the Pope had been, like that of other bishops, by the clergy and people of the city of his see. This was termed a canonical election. In practice, such election had meant control by whatever political power was dominant in Rome. The design of the new constitution was to remove that danger. In form, it put into law the circumstances of Nicholas's own election.[1] Its chief author seems to have been Cardinal Humbert. It provided that, on the death of a Pope, the cardinal bishops shall first consider as to his successor and then advise with the other cardinals. Only after their selection has been made should the suffrages of the other clergy and people be sought. In studiously vague language, the document guards "the honor and reverence due to our beloved son Henry"—that is the youthful Henry IV—but does not in the least define the Emperor's share in the choice. The evident purpose was to put the election into the hands of the cardinals, primarily of the cardinal bishops. It was, furthermore, provided that the Pope might come from anywhere in the church, that the election could be held elsewhere than in Rome in case of necessity, and that the Pope chosen should possess the powers of his office immediately on election wherever he might be. This was, indeed, a revolution in the method of choice of the Pope, and would give to the office an independence of political control not heretofore possessed.

Scarcely had these new political and constitutional results been achieved than they were imperilled by the death of Nicholas II in 1061. That of the energetic Cardinal Humbert also occurred the same year. Hildebrand became more than ever the ruling force in the reform party. Within less than three months of Nicholas's death, Hildebrand had secured the election of his friend Anselm, bishop of Lucca, as Alexander II (1061-1073). The German bishops were hostile, however, to the new method to papal election, the Lombard prelates disliked the papal support of the Pataria, and the Roman nobles resented their loss of control over the papacy. These hostile elements now united, and at a German assembly held in Basel in 1061 procured from the Empress-regent the appointment as Pope of Cadalus, bishop of Parma, who took the name of Honorius II. In the struggle that followed, Honorius nearly won; but a revolution in Germany in 1062 placed the chief power in that realm and the guardianship of the young Henry IV in the hands of the ambitious Anno, archbishop of Cologne. Anno wished to stand well with the reform party, and threw his influence on the side of Alexander, who was declared the rightful Pope at a synod of German and Italian prelates held

[1] Text in Henderson, *Select Historical Documents*, pp. 361–365. The so-called "Papal Version" is in all probability the original.

in Mantua in 1064.   Thus Hildebrand's bold policy triumphed over a divided Germany.

Alexander II, with Hildebrand's guidance, advanced the papal authority markedly.   Anno of Cologne and Siegfried of Mainz, two of the most powerful prelates of Germany, were compelled to do penance for simony.   He prevented Henry IV from securing a divorce from Queen Bertha.   He lent his approval to William the Conqueror's piratical expedition which resulted in the Norman conquest of England in 1066, and further aided William's plans by the establishment of Norman bishops in the principal English sees.   He gave his sanction to the efforts of the Normans of southern Italy which were to result in the conquest of Sicily.   Meanwhile Henry IV came of age in 1065. Far from being a weak King, he soon showed himself one of the most resourceful of German rulers.   It was inevitable that the papal policy regarding ecclesiastical appointments should clash with that historic control by German sovereigns on which their power in the empire so largely rested.   The actual dispute came over the archbishopric of Milan—a post of the first importance for the control of northern Italy.   Henry had appointed Godfrey of Castiglione, whom Alexander had charged with simony.   The Pataria of Milan chose a certain Atto, whom Alexander recognized as rightful archbishop.   In spite of that act, Henry now secured Godfrey's consecration, in 1073, to the disputed post.   The struggle was fully on. The contest involved the power of the imperial government and the claims of the radical papal reform party.   Alexander looked upon Henry as a well-intentioned young man, misled by bad advice, and he therefore excommunicated not Henry himself, but Henry's immediate counsellors as guilty of simony. Within a few days thereafter Alexander II died, leaving the great dispute to his successor.

SECTION XI.   HILDEBRAND AND HENRY IV

Hildebrand's election came about in curious disregard of the new constitution established under Nicholas II.   During the funeral of Alexander II, in St. John Lateran, the crowd acclaimed Hildebrand Pope, and carried him, almost in a riot, to the church of St. Peter in Chains, where he was enthroned.   He took the name of Gregory VII (1073–1085).   In his accession the extremest interpretation of the principles of Augustine's *City of God* had reached the papal throne. The papacy he viewed as a divinely appointed universal sovereignty, which all must obey, and to which all earthly sovereigns are responsible, not only for their spiritual welfare, but for their temporal good government. Though Cardinal Deusdedit, rather than Hildebrand, was probably the author of the famous *Dictatus*, it well expresses Hildebrand's principles: "That the Roman Church was founded by God alone." "That the Roman pontiff alone can with right be called universal." "That he alone can depose or reinstate bishops." "That he alone may use [*i. e.*, dispose of] the imperial insignia." "That it may be permitted him to depose Emperors." "That he himself may be judged of no one." "That he may absolve subjects from their fealty to wicked men."[1] It was nothing less than an ideal of world-rulership. In view of later experience it may be called impracticable and even unchristian; but neither Hildebrand nor his age had had that experience. It was a great ideal of a possible regenerated human society, effected by obedience to commanding spiritual power, and as such was deserving of respect in those who held it, and worthy of that trial which alone could reveal its value or worthlessness.

The opening years of Hildebrand's pontificate were favorable for the papacy. A rebellion against Henry IV by his Saxon subjects, who had many grievances, and the discontent of the nobles of other regions kept Henry fully occupied. In 1074 he did penance in Nuremberg before the papal legates, and promised obedience. At the Easter synod in Rome in 1075, Hildebrand renewed the decree against lay investiture, denying to Henry any share in creating bishops. A few months later Henry's fortunes changed. In June, 1075, his defeat of the Saxons made him apparently master of Germany, and his attitude toward the papacy speedily altered. Henry once more made an appointment to the archbishopric of Milan. Hildebrand replied, in December, 1075, with a letter calling Henry to severe account.[2] On January 24, 1076, Henry, with his nobles and bishops, held a council in Worms, at which the turncoat cardinal, Hugh the White, was forward with personal

---

[1] Henderson, *Select Historical Documents*, pp. 366, 367; extracts in Robinson, *Readings in European History*, 1 : 274.

[2] Henderson, pp. 367–371; Robinson, 1 : 276–279.

charges against Hildebrand.   There a large portion of the **Ger-man** bishops joined in a fierce denunciation of Hildebrand and a rejection of his authority as Pope[1]—an action for which the approval of the Lombard prelates was speedily secured.

Hildebrand's reply was the most famous of mediæval papal decrees.   At the Roman synod of February 22, 1076, he ex-communicated Henry, forbad him authority over Germany and Italy, and released all Henry's subjects from their oaths of allegiance.[2]   It was the boldest assertion of papal authority that had ever been made.   To it Henry replied by a fiery letter addressed to Hildebrand, "now no pope, but a false monk," in which he called on Hildebrand to "come down, to be damned throughout all eternity."[3]

Had Henry IV had a united Germany behind him the result might easily have been Hildebrand's overthrow.   Germany was not united.   The Saxons and Henry's other political enemies used the opportunity to make him trouble.   Even the bishops had regard for the authority of a Pope they had nominally rejected.   Henry was unable to meet the rising opposition. An assembly of nobles in Tribur, in October, 1076, declared that unless released from excommunication within a year he would be deposed, and the Pope was invited to a new assembly to meet in Augsburg, in February, 1077, at which the whole Ger-man political and religious situation should be considered. Henry was in great danger of losing his throne.   It became a matter of vital importance to free himself from excommunica-tion.   Hildebrand refused all appeals; he would settle the ques-tions at Augsburg.

Henry IV now resolved on a step of the utmost dramatic and political significance.   He would meet Hildebrand before the Pope could reach the assembly in Augsburg and wring from him the desired absolution.   He crossed the Alps in the winter and sought Hildebrand in northern Italy, through which the Pope was passing on his way to Germany.   In doubt whether Henry came in peace or war, Hildebrand sought refuge in the strong castle of Canossa, belonging to his ardent supporter, the Countess Matilda of Tuscany, the daughter of Beatrice (*ante,*

---

[1] Henderson, pp. 373–376.

[2] Henderson, pp. 376, 377 ; Robinson, 1 : 281, 282.

[3] Henderson, pp. 372, 373 ; Robinson, 1 : 279–281.   The letter seems to belong here, rather than to January, 1076, to which it is often assigned.

p. 226). Thither Henry went, and there presented himself before the castle gate on three successive days, barefooted as a penitent. The Pope's companions pleaded for him, and on January 28, 1077, Henry IV was released from excommunication. In many ways it was a political triumph for the King. He had thrown his German opponents into confusion. He had prevented a successful assembly in Augsburg under papal leadership. The Pope's plans had been disappointed. Yet the event has always remained in men's recollection as the deepest humiliation of the mediæval empire before the power of the church.[1]

In March, 1077, Henry's German enemies, without Hildebrand's instigation, chose Rudolf, duke of Swabia, as counter-King. Civil war ensued, while the Pope balanced one claimant against the other, hoping to gain for himself the ultimate decision. Forced at last to take sides, Hildebrand, at the Roman synod in March, 1080, a second time excommunicated and deposed Henry.[2] The same political weapons can seldom be used twice effectively. Sentiment had crystallized in Germany, and this time the Pope's action had little effect. Henry answered by a synod in Brixen in June, 1080, deposing Hildebrand,[3] and choosing one of Hildebrand's bitterest opponents, Archbishop Wibert of Ravenna, as Pope in his place. Wibert called himself Clement III (1080–1100). The death of Rudolf in battle, in October following, left Henry stronger in Germany than ever before. He determined to be rid of Hildebrand. In 1081 Henry invaded Italy, but it was three years before he gained possession of Rome. Pressed upon by the overwhelming German and Lombard forces, Hildebrand's political supporters proved too weak to offer permanently effective resistance. The Roman people, and no less than thirteen of the cardinals, turned to the victorious German ruler and his Pope. In March, 1084, Wibert was enthroned, and crowned Henry Emperor. Hildebrand, apparently a beaten man, still held the castle of San Angelo, and absolutely refused any compromise. In May a Norman army came to Hildebrand's relief, but these rough supporters so burned and plundered Rome, that he had to with-

---

[1] The best account is that of Hildebrand himself. Henderson, pp. 385–387; Robinson, 1 : 282–283.

[2] Henderson, pp. 388–391.

[3] *Ibid.*, pp. 391–394.

draw with them, and after nearly a year of this painful exile, he died in Salerno, on May 25, 1085.

Hildebrand's relations to other countries have been passed by in the account of his great struggle with Germany. It may be sufficient to say that his aims were similar, though so engrossed was he in the conflict with Henry IV that he never pushed matters to such an extreme with the Kings of England and France. He attempted to bring the high clergy everywhere under his control. He caused extensive codification of church law to be made. He enforced clerical celibacy as not only the theoretical but the practical rule of the Roman Church. If his methods were worldly and unscrupulous, as they undoubtedly were, no misfortune ever caused him to abate his claims, and even in apparent defeat he won a moral victory. The ideals that he had established for the papacy were to live long after him.

SECTION XII.   THE STRUGGLE ENDS IN COMPROMISE

On the death of Hildebrand, the cardinals faithful to him chose as his successor Desiderius, the able and scholarly abbot of Monte Cassino, who took the name of Victor III (1086–1087). So discouraging was the outlook that he long refused the doubtful honor. When at last he accepted it, he quietly dropped Hildebrand's extremer efforts at world-rulership, though renewing the prohibition of lay investiture with utmost vigor. He was, however, able to be in Rome but a few days. That city remained in the hands of Wibert, and before the end of 1087 Victor III was no more. The situation of the party of Hildebrand seemed well-nigh hopeless. After much hesitation, a few of the reform cardinals met in Terracina, and chose a French Cluny monk, who had been appointed a cardinal bishop by Hildebrand, Odo of Lagary, as Pope Urban II (1088–1099). A man of Hildebrandian convictions, without Hildebrand's genius, Urban was far more conciliatory and politically skilful. He sought with great success to create a friendly party among the German clergy, aided thereto by the monks of the influential monastery of Hirschau. He stirred up disaffection for Henry IV, often by no worthy means. Yet it was not till the close of 1093 that Urban was able to take effective possession of Rome and drive out Wibert. His rise in power was thence rapid.   At a great synod held in Piacenza in March, 1095, he sounded the note of a crusade.   At Clermont in November of the same year he brought the Crusade into being (p. 239).   On the flood of the crusading movement Urban rose at once to a position of European leadership.   Henry IV and Wibert might oppose him, but the papacy had achieved a popular significance compared with which they had nothing to offer.

Though men were weary of the long strife, the next Pope, Paschal II (1099–1118), made matters worse rather than better.   Henry IV's last days were disastrous.   A successful rebellion, headed by his son, Henry V (1106–1125), forced his abdication in 1105.   His death followed the next year.   Henry V's position in Germany was stronger than his father's ever had been, and he was more unscrupulous.   His assertion of his rights of investiture was as insistent as that of his father.   In 1110 Henry V marched on Rome in force.   Paschal II was powerless and without the courage of a Hildebrand.   The Pope and Henry now agreed (1111) that the King should resign his right of investiture, provided the bishops of Germany should relinquish to him all temporal lordships.[1]   That would have been a revolution that would have reduced the German church to poverty, and the protest raised on its promulgation in Rome, in February, 1111, showed it impossible of accomplishment.   Henry V then took the Pope and the cardinals prisoners.   Paschal weakened.   In April, 1111, he resigned to Henry investiture with ring and staff, and crowned him Emperor.[2]   The Hildebrandian party stormed in protest.   At the Roman synod of March, 1112, Paschal withdrew his agreement, which he could well hold was wrung from him by force.   A synod in Vienne in September excommunicated Henry and forbad lay investiture, and this action the Pope approved.

Yet the basis of a compromise was already in sight.   Two French church leaders, Ivo, bishop of Chartres, and Hugo of Fleury, in writings between 1099 and 1106, had argued that church and state each had their rights of investiture, the one with spiritual, the other with temporal authority.   Anselm, the famous archbishop of Canterbury, a firm supporter of reform principles (1093–1109), had refused investiture from Henry I

[1] Henderson, pp. 405–407; Robinson, 1: 290–292.
[2] Henderson, pp. 407, 408.

of England (1100–1135), and led to a contest which ended in the resignation by the King of investiture with ring and staff, while retaining to the crown investiture with temporal possession by the reception of an oath of fealty. These principles and precedents influenced the further course of the controversy. The compromise came in 1122, in the Concordat of Worms, arranged between Henry V and Pope Calixtus II (1119–1124). By mutual agreement, elections of bishops and abbots in Germany were to be free and in canonical form, yet the presence of the Emperor at the choice was allowed, and in case of disputed election he should consult with the metropolitan and other bishops of the province. In other parts of the empire, Burgundy and Italy, no mention was made of the imperial presence. The Emperor renounced investiture with ring and staff, *i. e.*, with the symbols of spiritual authority. In turn, the Pope granted him the right of investiture with the temporal possessions of the office by the touch of the royal sceptre, without demand of payment from the candidate. This imperial recognition was to take place in Germany before consecration, and in the other parts of the empire within six months thereafter.[1] The effect was that in Germany at least a bishop or abbot must be acceptable both to the church and to the Emperor. In Italy the imperial power, which had rested on control of churchly appointments, was greatly broken. It was an outcome of the struggle which would but partially have satisfied Hildebrand. Yet the church had won much. If not superior to the state, it had vindicated its equality with the temporal power.

SECTION XIII.   THE GREEK CHURCH AFTER THE PICTURE
CONTROVERSY

The Isaurian dynasty in Constantinople (717–802), witnessed the severe internal conflicts caused by the picture-worshipping controversy, which was in a measure a struggle for the freedom of the church from imperial control (*ante*, p. 162). It beheld the loss of Rome and of the Exarchate, and the rise of the renewed Western empire under Charlemagne. The periods of the Phrygian (820–867) and Macedonian dynasties (867–1057) were marked by a notable revival of learning, so that, intellectually, the East was decidedly superior to the West. The pa-

[1] Henderson, pp. 408, 409; Robinson, 1 : 292, 293.

triarch, Photius, whose quarrel with Nicholas I has already been noted, was of eminent scholarship. His *Myriobiblon* is of permanent worth, as preserving much of ancient classical authors otherwise lost. Symeon "Metaphrastes" compiled his famous collection of the lives of the Eastern saints in the tenth century. In Symeon, "the New Theologian" (?–1040?), the Greek Church had its noblest mystic, who believed that the revelation of the divine light—the very vision of God—is possible of attainment and is of grace, bringing peace, joy, and justification. Theologically, the Greek world had nothing new to offer. It held with intensity to the traditions of the past.

The chief religious controversy in the East of this epoch was that caused by the Paulicians. The origin and history of the movement is obscure. They called themselves Christians simply, their nickname being apparently due to their reverence for Paul the Apostle, rather than as sometimes claimed to any real connection with Paul of Samosata. The movement appears to have begun with a Constantine-Silvanus, of Mananalis, near Samosata, about 650–660. In it ancient heretical beliefs, akin to and perhaps derived from the Marcionites and Gnostics, reappeared. Though the Paulicians repudiated Manichæism, they were dualists, holding that this world is the creation of an evil power, while souls are from the kingdom of the good God. They accepted the New Testament, with the possible exception of the writings ascribed to Peter, as the message of the righteous God. They viewed Christ as an angel sent by the good God, and hence Son of God by adoption. His work was primarily that of instruction. They rejected monasticism, the external sacraments, the cross, images, and relics. Their ministry was that of wandering preachers and "copyists." The Catholic hierarchy they repudiated. They opposed the externalism of current orthodox religious life.

The Paulicians seem to have spread rapidly in the Eastern empire, and to have taken strong root in Armenia. Persecuted by the orthodox, their military powers procured them considerable respect. Constantine V transplanted colonies of them to the Balkan peninsula in 752, as a defense against the Bulgarians —a process which was repeated on a larger scale by the Emperor, John Tzimiskes, in 969. There they seem to have given origin to the very similar Bogomiles, who in turn were to be influential in the development of the Cathari of southern France

(p. 249).   Driven to seek refuge among the Saracens, some sections of the Paulicians harassed the borders of the empire in the ninth century, and even penetrated deeply into it, till their military success, though not their religious activity, was permanently checked by the Emperor, Basil I, in 871.

The latter half of the ninth and the tenth centuries was a period of revived military power for the Eastern empire, especially under John Tzimiskes (969–976) and Basil II (976–1025). By the latter, Bulgaria and Armenia were conquered.   Internal dissensions and a fear of usurping militarism weakened the empire in the eleventh century, so that the rise of the Seljuk Turks found it unprepared.   In 1071 the Turks conquered a large part of Asia Minor, and in 1080 established themselves in Nicæa, less than a hundred miles from Constantinople.   This great loss to Christianity was to be one of the causes leading to the Crusades.

SECTION XIV.   THE SPREAD OF THE CHURCH

The tenth and eleventh centuries were an epoch of large extension of Christianity.   Ansgar's work in the Scandinavian lands (*ante*, p. 213) had left few results.   Scandinavian Christianization was a slow and gradual process.   Unni, archbishop of Hamburg (918–936), imitated Ansgar, but without great success.   The work was carried forward by Archbishop Adaldag (937–988).   Under his influence, King Harold Bluetooth of Denmark accepted Christianity, and Danish bishoprics were established.   Under Harold's son, Sweyn, heathenism was again in power; but he was brought to favor the church in 995, and the work was completed in Denmark by King Canute the Great (1015–1035), who also ruled England and, for a time, Norway.

The story of Norway is similar.   Some Christian beginnings were made under Hakon I (935–961), and missionaries were sent by Harold Bluetooth of Denmark.   Christianity in Norway was not permanently established till the time of Olaf I (995–1000), who brought in English preachers.   The work was now extended to the Orkneys, Shetland, Hebrides, Faroe, Iceland, and Greenland, then in Scandinavian possession. Olaf II (1015–1028) enforced Christianity in Norway with such extreme measures that he was deposed and Canute gained control; yet he lives in tradition as St. Olaf. Magnus I (1035–1047) completed the work.

In Sweden, after many beginnings from the time of Ansgar, Christianity was effectively established by King Olaf Skött-konung (994–1024), who was baptized in 1008. Yet the work was slow, and heathenism was not fully overthrown till about 1100. Finland and Lapland were not reached till two centuries later.

After various efforts in the tenth century, Christianity was effectively established in Hungary by King Stephen I (997–1038), the organizer of the Hungarian monarchy, who lives in history as St. Stephen. The Polish duke, Mieczyslaw, accepted Christianity in 967, and in 1000 King Boleslaus I (992–1025) organized the Polish church with an archbishopric in Gnesen. Pomerania was not Christianized till 1124–1128.

The movements just considered were the work of the Latin Church. The great extension of the Greek Church lies in this period and was accomplished by the conversion of Russia. Its beginnings are obscure. Efforts for the spread of Christianity in Russia seem to have been made as early as the time of the patriarch of Constantinople Photius (866). The Russian Queen, Olga, received baptism on a visit to Constantinople in 957. The work was at last definitely established by Grandduke Vladimir I (980–1015), who received baptism in 988, and compelled his subjects to follow his example. A metropolitan, nominated by the patriarch of Constantinople, was placed at the head of the Russian church, with his see speedily in Kiev, from which it was transferred in 1299 to the city of Vladimir, and in 1325 to Moscow.

PERIOD V. THE LATER MIDDLE AGES

SECTION I. THE CRUSADES

THE Crusades are in many ways the most remarkable of the phenomena of the Middle Ages. Their causes were many. The historian who emphasizes economic influences may well claim the unusually trying conditions of the eleventh century as a main source. Between 970 and 1040 forty-eight famine years were counted. From 1085 to 1095 conditions were even worse. Misery and unrest prevailed widely. The more settled conditions of the age made impossible such migrations of nations as had been exhibited in the Germanic invasions at the downfall of the Western empire. The same desire to change environment was, however, felt.

Stimulated by these economic conditions, doubtless, the whole eleventh century was a period of deepening religious feeling. Its manifestations took monastic and ascetic forms. It was characterized by a strong sense of "other-worldliness," of the misery of earth and the blessedness of heaven. This increasing religious zeal had been the force which had reformed the papacy, and had supported antagonism to simony and Nicolaitanism, and nerved the long struggle with the empire. Those regions where the reform movement had shone brightest, or which had come into closest relations with the reforming papacy, France, Lorraine, and southern Italy, were the recruiting-grounds of the chief crusading armies. The piety of the time placed great value on relics and pilgrimages, and what more precious relic could there be, or what nobler pilgrimage shrine, than the land hallowed by the life, death, and resurrection of Christ? That land had been an object of pilgrimage since the days of Constantine. Though Jerusalem had been in Moslem possession since 638, pilgrimages had been, save for brief intervals, practically uninterrupted. They had never been more numerous than in the eleventh century, till the conquest of much of Asia Minor, from 1071 onward, and the capture of Jerusalem, by the Seljuk Turks, made pilgrimages almost impossible and desecrated the holy places.

It was to an age profoundly impressed with the spiritual advantage of pilgrimages that the news of these things came. The time, moreover, was witnessing successful contests with Mohammedanism. Between 1060 and 1090 the Normans of southern Italy had wrested Sicily from the Moslems. Under Ferdinand I of Castile (1028–1065) the effective Christian reconquest of Spain from the Mohammedans had begun. The later eleventh century is the age of the Cid (1040?–1099). The feeling was wide-spread that Christianity could dispossess Mohammedanism. Love of adventure, hopes for plunder, desire for territorial advancement and religious hatred, undoubtedly moved the Crusaders with very earthly impulses. We should wrong them, however, if we did not recognize with equal clearness that they thought they were doing something of the highest importance for their souls and for Christ.

The first impulse to the Crusades came from an appeal of the Eastern Emperor, Michael VII (1067–1078), to Hildebrand for aid against the Seljuks. That great Pope, to whom this seemed to promise the reunion of Greek and Latin Christendom, took the matter up in 1074, and was able to report to Henry IV of Germany that fifty thousand men were ready to go under the proper leadership. The speedy outbreak of the investiture struggle frustrated the plan. It was effectively to be revived by Urban II, the heir in so many directions of Hildebrand.

Alexius I (1081–1118), a stronger ruler than his immediate predecessors in Constantinople, felt unable to cope with the perils which threatened the empire. He, therefore, appealed to Urban II for assistance. Urban received the imperial messengers at the synod in Piacenza, in northern Italy, in March, 1095, and promised his help. At the synod held in Clermont, in eastern France, in the following November, Urban now proclaimed the Crusade in an appeal of almost unexampled consequence. The enterprise had magnified in his conception from that of aid to the hard-pressed Alexius to a general rescue of the holy places from Moslem hands. He called on all Christendom to take part in the work, promising forgiveness of sins to all and eternal life to those who should fall in the enterprise. The message found immediate and enthusiastic response. Among the popular preachers who took it up none was more famous than Peter the Hermit, a monk

from Amiens or its vicinity. Early legend attributed to him
the origin of the Crusade itself, of which he was unquestionably
one of the most effective proclaimers. He does not deserve
the distinction thus attributed to him, nor was his conduct on
the Crusade, once it had started, such as to do credit to his
leadership or even to his courage.

Such was the enthusiasm engendered, especially in France,
that large groups of peasants, with some knights among them,
set forth in the spring of 1096, under the lead of Walter the
Penniless; a priest, Gottschalk, and Peter the Hermit himself.
By some of these wild companies many Jews were massacred
in the Rhine cities. Their own disorderly pillage led to savage
reprisals in Hungary and the Balkans. That under Peter
reached Constantinople, but was almost entirely destroyed by
the Turks in an attempt to reach Nicæa. Peter himself did
not share this catastrophe, joined the main crusading force,
and survived the perils of the expedition.

The real work of the First Crusade was accomplished by
the feudal nobility of Europe. Three great armies were raised.
That from Lorraine and Belgium included Godfrey of Bouillon,
the moral hero of the Crusade, since he commanded the respect
due to his single-minded and unselfish devotion to its aims,
though not its ablest general. With Godfrey were his brothers,
Baldwin and Eustace. Other armies from northern France
were led by Hugh of Vermandois and Robert of Normandy.
From southern France came a large force under Count Rai-
mond of Toulouse, and from Norman Italy a well-equipped
army led by Bohemund of Taranto and his nephew Tancred.
The earliest of these forces started in August, 1096. No single
commander led the hosts. Urban II had appointed Bishop
Ademar of Puy his legate; and Ademar designated Constantinople as the gathering place. Thither each army made its
way as best it could, arriving there in the winter and spring
of 1096–1097, and causing Alexius no little difficulty by their
disorder and demands.

In May, 1097, the crusading army began the siege of Nicæa.
Its surrender followed in June. On July 1 a great victory
over the Turks near Dorylæum opened the route across Asia
Minor, so that Iconium was reached, after severe losses through
hunger and thirst, by the middle of August. By October the
crusading host was before the walls of Antioch. That city

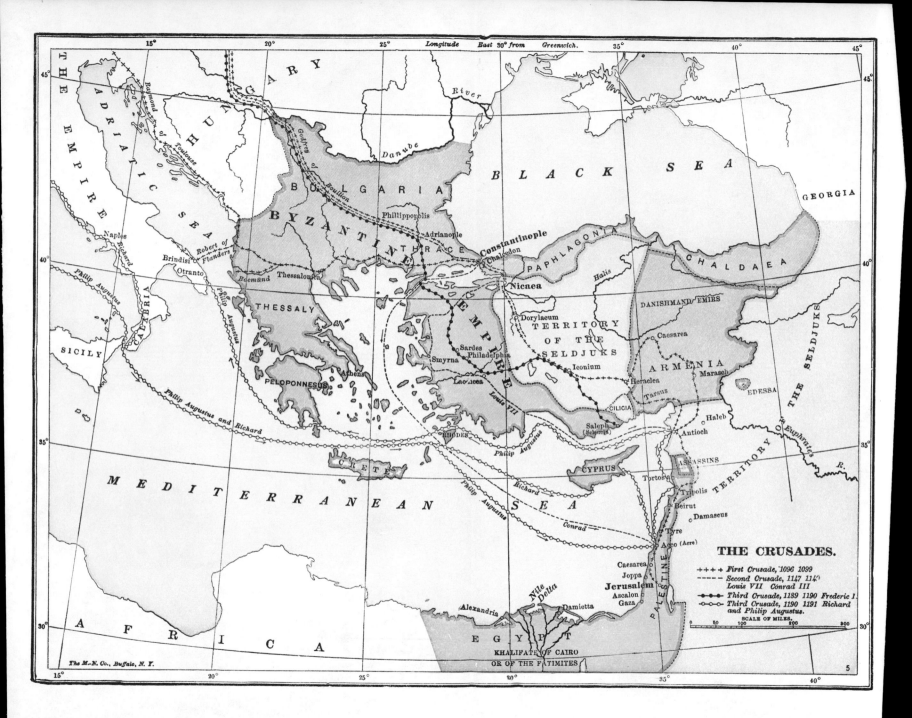

THE CRUSADES.

Longitude   East 30° from   Greenwich.

THE EMPIRE

ADRIATIC SEA

HUNGARY

Naples
Brindisi
Otranto

CALABRIA

SICILY

AFRICA

Raymond of Toulouse
Robert of Flanders
Boemund
Thessalonica

THESSALY

Philip Augustus

PELOPONNESUS

Athens

MEDITERRANEAN   SEA

CRETE

Danube

BULGARIA

BYZANTINE

THRACE

Phillippopolis
Adrianople

Constantinople
Chalcedon

Nicaea

EMPIRE

Smyrna   Sardes
Philadelphia

Laodicea

RHODES

Philip Augustus

BLACK   SEA

PAPHLAGONIA

Halis

Dorylaeum

TERRITORY
OF   THE
SELDJUKS

Iconium

Heraclea
Tarsus
CILICIA

Saleph
(Seleucia)

CYPRUS

Richard

Conrad

Nile
Delta

Alexandria

Damietta

EGYPT

KHALIFATE OF CAIRO
OR OF THE FATIMITES

GEORGIA

CHALDAEA

DANISHMAND EMIRS

Caesarea

ARMENIA
Marasch

EDESSA

THE   SELDJUKS

R. Euphrates

Antioch
Haleb

ASSASSINS

Tortosa
Tripolis
Beirut   Damascus

Tyre

Acco (Acre)

Caesarea
Joppa

Jerusalem
Ascalon
Gaza

PALESTINE

TERRITORY   OF

THE CRUSADES.

++++ *First Crusade, 1096 1099*
- - - - *Second Crusade, 1147 1149*
     Louis VII   Conrad III
●━●━● *Third Crusade, 1189 1190 Frederic I.*
○━○━○ *Third Crusade, 1190 1191 Richard
     and Philip Augustus*

SCALE OF MILES.
0   50   100   150   200   250

The M.-N. Co., Buffalo, N. Y.

5

it captured only after a difficult siege, on June 3, 1098. Three days later the Crusaders were besieged in the city by the Turkish ruler Kerbogha of Mosul. The crisis of the Crusade was this time of peril and despair; but on June 28 Kerbogha was completely defeated. Yet it was not till June, 1099, that Jerusalem was reached, and not till July 15 that it was captured and its inhabitants put to the sword. The complete defeat of an Egyptian relieving army near Ascalon on August 12, 1099, crowned the success of the Crusade.

On the completion of the work, Godfrey of Bouillon was chosen Protector of the Holy Sepulchre. He died in July, 1100, and was succeeded by his abler brother, who had established a Latin county in Edessa, and now took the title of King Baldwin I (1100–1118). The Crusaders were from the feudal West, and the country was divided and organized in full feudal fashion. It included, besides the Holy Land, the principality of Antioch, and the counties of Tripoli and Edessa, which were practically independent of the King of Jerusalem. In the towns important Italian business settlements sprang up; but most of the knights were French. Under a patriarch of the Latin rite in Jerusalem, the country was divided into four archbishoprics and ten bishoprics, and numerous monasteries were established.

The greatest support of the kingdom soon came to be the military orders. Of these, that of the Templars was founded by Hugo de Payens in 1119, and granted quarters near the site of the temple—hence their name—by King Baldwin II (1118–1131). Through the hearty support of Bernard of Clairvaux the order received papal approval in 1128, and soon won wide popularity in the West. Its members took the usual monastic vows and pledged themselves, in addition, to fight for the defense of the Holy Land and to protect pilgrims. They were not clergy, but laymen. In some respects the order was like a modern missionary society. Those who sympathized with the Crusade, but were debarred by age or sex from a personal share in the work, gave largely that they might be represented by others through the order. Since property was mostly in land, the Templars soon became great landholders in the West. Their independence and wealth made them objects of royal jealousy, especially after their original purpose had been frustrated by the end of the Crusades, and led to their brutal suppression in France in 1307 by King Philip IV (1285–1314). While the Crusades lasted they were a main bulwark of the kingdom of Jerusalem.

Much the same thing may be said of the great rivals of the Templars, the Hospitallers or Knights of St. John. Charlemagne had founded a hospital in Jerusalem, which was destroyed in 1010. Refounded by citizens of Amalfi, in Italy, it was in existence before the First Crusade, and was named for the church of St. John the Baptist, near which it stood. This foundation was made into a military order by its grand master, Raymond du Puy (1120–1160?), though without neglecting its duties to the sick. After the crusading epoch it maintained a struggle with the Turks from its seat in Rhodes (1310–1523), and then from Malta (1530–1798). A third and later order was that of the Teutonic Knights, founded by Germans in 1190. Its chief work, however, was not to be in Palestine but, from 1229 onward, in Prussia, or as it is now known, East Prussia, where it was a pioneer in civilization and Christianization.

In spite of feudal disorganization the kingdom of Jerusalem was fairly successful till the capture of Edessa by the Mohammedans in 1144 robbed it of its northeastern bulwark. Bernard of Clairvaux, now at the height of his fame, proclaimed a new Crusade and enlisted Louis VII of France (1137–1180) and the Emperor Conrad III (1138–1152) from Germany in 1146. In 1147 the Second Crusade set forth; but it showed little of the fiery enthusiasm of its predecessor, its forces largely perished in Asia Minor, and such as reached Palestine were badly defeated in an attempt to take Damascus, in 1148. It was a disastrous failure, and its collapse left a bitter feeling in the West toward the Eastern empire, to whose princes that failure, rightly or wrongly, was charged.

One reason of the success of the Latin kingdom had been the quarrels of the Mohammedans. In 1171 the Kurdish general, Saladin, made himself master of Egypt; by 1174 he had secured Damascus, and by 1183 Saladin's territories surrounded the Latin kingdom on the north, east, and south. A united Mohammedanism had now to be met. Results soon followed. At Hattin the Latin army was defeated in July, 1187. The loss of Jerusalem and of most of the Holy Land speedily followed. The news of this catastrophe roused Europe to the

Third Crusade (1189–1192). None of the Crusades was more elaborately equipped. Three great armies were led by the Emperor Frederick Barbarossa (1152–1190), the first soldier of his age, by King Philip Augustus of France (1179–1223), and by King Richard "Cœur de Lion" of England (1189–1199). Frederick was accidentally drowned in Cilicia. His army, deprived of his vigorous leadership, was utterly ineffective. The quarrels between the Kings of France and England, and Philip's speedy return to France to push his own political schemes, rendered the whole expedition almost abortive. Acre was recovered, but Jerusalem remained in Moslem possession.

The Fourth Crusade (1202–1204) was a small affair as far as numbers engaged, but of important political and religious consequences. Its forces were from the districts of northern France known as Champagne and Blois, and from Flanders. Men had become convinced that the true route to the recovery of Jerusalem was the preliminary conquest of Egypt. The Crusaders therefore bargained with the Venetians for transportation thither. Unable to raise the full cost, they accepted the proposition of the Venetians that, in lieu of the balance due, they stop on their way and conquer Zara from Hungary for Venice. This they did. A much greater proposal was now made to them. They should stop at Constantinople, and assist in dethroning the imperial usurper, Alexius III (1195–1203). Alexius, son of the deposed Isaac II, promised the Crusaders large payment and help on their expedition provided they would overthrow the usurper, and crafty Venice saw bright prospects of increased trade. Western hatred of the Greeks contributed. Though Pope Innocent III forbad this division of purpose, the Crusaders were persuaded. Alexius III was easily driven from his throne; but the other Alexius was unable to keep his promises to the Crusaders, who now with the Venetians, in 1204, captured Constantinople, and plundered its treasures. No booty was more eagerly sought than the relics in the churches, which now went to enrich the places of worship of the West. Baldwin of Flanders was made Emperor, and a large portion of the Eastern empire was divided, feudal fashion, among Western knights. Venice obtained a considerable part and a monopoly of trade. A Latin patriarch of Constantinople was appointed, and the Greek Church made subject to the Pope. The Eastern empire still continued, though it was not to regain Constantinople till 1261. This Latin conquest was disastrous. It greatly weakened the Eastern empire, and augmented the hatred between Greek and Latin Christianity.

A melancholy episode was the so-called "Children's Crusade" of 1212. A shepherd boy, Stephen, in France, and a boy of Cologne, in Germany, Nicholas, gathered thousands of children. Straggling to Italy, they were largely sold into slavery in Egypt. Other crusading attempts were made. An expedition against Egypt, in 1218–1221, had some initial success, but ended in failure. It is usually called the Fifth Crusade. The most curious was the Sixth (1228–1229). The free-thinking Emperor Frederick II (1212–1250), had taken the cross in 1215, but showed no haste to fulfil his vows. At last, in 1227, he started, but soon put back. He seems to have been really ill, but Pope Gregory IX (1227–1241), believing him a deserter, and having other grounds of hostility, excommunicated him. In spite of the ban, Frederick went forward in 1228, and the next year secured, by treaty with the Sultan of Egypt, possession of Jerusalem, Bethlehem, Nazareth and a path to the coast. Jerusalem was once more in Christian keeping till 1244, when it was permanently lost. The crusading spirit was now well-nigh spent, though Louis IX of France (St. Louis, 1226–1270) led a disastrous expedition against Egypt in 1248–1250, in which he was taken prisoner, and an attack on Tunis in 1270, in which he lost his life. The last considerable expedition was that of Prince Edward, soon to be Edward I of England (1272–1307), in 1271 and 1272. In 1291, the last of the Latin holdings in Palestine was lost. The Crusades were over, though men continued to talk of new expeditions for nearly two centuries more.

Viewed from the aspect of their purpose the Crusades were failures. They made no permanent conquest of the Holy Land. It may be doubted whether they greatly retarded the advance of Mohammedanism. Their cost in lives and treasure was enormous. Though initiated in a high spirit of devotion, their methods at best were not those which modern Christianity regards as illustrative of the Gospel, and their conduct was disgraced throughout by quarrels, divided motives, and low standards of personal conduct. When their indirect results are examined, however, a very different estimate is to be made of their worth. Civilization is the result of so complex factors

that it is hard to assign precise values to single causes. Europe
would have made progress during this period had there been no
Crusades. But the changes wrought are so remarkable that
the conclusion is unavoidable that the largest single influence
was that of the Crusades.

By the commerce which the Crusades stimulated the cities
of northern Italy and of the great trade route over the Alps
and down the Rhine rose to importance. By the sacrifices of
feudal lands and property which they involved, a new political
element, that of the towns—a "third estate"—was greatly
stimulated, especially in France. The mental horizon of the
Western world was immeasurably extended. Thousands who
had grown up in the densest ignorance and narrow-mindedness
were brought into contact with the splendid cities and ancient
civilization of the East. Everywhere there was intellectual
awakening. The period witnessed the highest theological
development of the Middle Ages—that of Scholasticism. It
beheld great popular religious movements, in and outside of
the church. It saw the development of the universities. In it
the study of Roman law became a transforming influence.
Modern vernacular literature began to flourish. A great artistic development, the national architecture of northern France,
misnamed the Gothic, now ran its glorious career. The Europe
of the period of the Crusades was awake and enlightened compared with the centuries which had gone before. Admitting
that the Crusades were but one factor in this result, they were
worth all their cost.

SECTION II.   NEW RELIGIOUS MOVEMENTS

The epoch of the First Crusade was one of increasing religious
earnestness, manifesting itself in other-worldliness, asceticism,
mystical piety, and emphasis on the monastic life. The long
battle against simony and Nicolaitanism had turned popular
sympathies from the often criticised "secular," or ordinary
clergy, to the monks as the true representatives of the religious
ideal. Cluny had, in a measure, spent its force. Its very
success had led to luxury of living. New religious associations
were arising, of which the most important was that of the
Cistercians—an order which dominated the twelfth century
as Cluny had the eleventh.

Like Cluny, the Cistercians were of French origin. A Benedictine monk, Robert, of the monastery of Montier, impressed with the ill-discipline of contemporary monasticism, founded a monastery of great strictness in Citeaux, not far from Dijon, in 1098. From the first, the purpose of the foundation of Citeaux was to cultivate a strenuous, self-denying life. Its buildings, utensils, even the surroundings of worship, were of the plainest character. In food and clothing it exercised great austerity. Its rule was that of Benedict, but its self-denial was far beyond that of Benedictines generally. Under its third abbot, Stephen Harding (1109–1134), an Englishman, the significance of Citeaux rapidly grew. Four affiliated monasteries were founded by 1115, under his leadership. Thenceforth its progress was rapid throughout all the West. By 1130, the Cistercian houses numbered thirty; by 1168, two hundred and eighty-eight, and a century later six hundred and seventy-one. Over all these the abbot of Citeaux had authority, assisted by a yearly assembly of the heads of the affiliated monasteries. Much attention was devoted to agriculture, relatively little to teaching or pastoral work. The ideals were withdrawal from the world, contemplation, and imitation of "apostolic poverty."

Not a little of the early success of the Cistercians was due to the influence of Bernard (1090–1153), the greatest religious force of his age, and, by common consent, deemed one of the chief of mediæval saints. Born of knightly ancestry in Fontaines, near Dijon, he inherited from his mother a deeply religious nature. With some thirty companions, the fruit of his powers of persuasion, he entered the monastery of Citeaux, probably in 1112. Thence he went forth in 1115 to found the Cistercian monastery of Clairvaux, abbot of which he remained, in spite of splendid offers of ecclesiastical preferment, till his death. A man of the utmost self-consecration, his prime motive was a love to Christ, which in spite of extreme monastic self-mortification, found so evangelical an expression as to win the hearty approval of Luther and Calvin. The mystic contemplation of Christ was his highest spiritual joy. It determined not merely his own type of piety, but very largely that of the age in its nobler expressions. Above all, men admired in Bernard a moral force, a consistency of character, which added weight to all that he said and did.

Bernard was far too much a man of action to be confined

to the monastery. The first preacher of his age, and one of the greatest of all ages, he moved his fellows profoundly, from whatever social class they might come. He conducted a vast correspondence on the problems of the time. The interests of the church, of which he was regarded as the most eminent ornament, led to wide journeyings. In particular, the healing of the papal schism which resulted in the double choice by the cardinals in 1130 of Innocent II (1130–1143) and Anacletus II (1130–1138) was Bernard's work. His dominating part in organizing the unfortunate Second Crusade has already been considered (*ante*, p. 242). His influence with the papacy seemed but confirmed when a former monk of Clairvaux was chosen as Eugene III (1145–1153), though many things that Eugene did proved not to Bernard's liking. Convinced that his own views were the only orthodox conceptions, he persuaded others, also, and secured the condemnation of Abelard (p. 265) by the synod of Sens in 1141, and its approval by the Pope. In 1145 Bernard preached, with some temporary success, to the heretics of southern France. In 1153 he died, the best known and the most widely mourned man of his age.

Bernard's ascetic and other-worldly principles were represented, curiously, in a man whom he bitterly opposed—Arnold of Brescia (?–1155). With all his devotion to "apostolic poverty," Bernard had no essential quarrel with the hierarchical organization of his day, or hostility to its exercise of power in worldly matters. Arnold was much more radical. Born in Brescia, a student in France, he became a clergyman in his native city. Of severe austerity, he advanced the opinion that the clergy should abandon all property and worldly power. So only could they be Christ's true disciples. In the struggle between Innocent II and Anacletus II he won a large following in Brescia, but was compelled to seek refuge in France, where he became intimate with Abelard, and was joined with him in condemnation, at Bernard's instigation, by the synod of Sens (1141). Bernard secured Arnold's expulsion from France. In 1143 the Roman nobles had thrown off the temporal control of the papacy and established what they believed to be a revival of the Senate. To Rome Arnold went. He was not a political leader so much as a preacher of "apostolic poverty." In 1145 Eugene III restored Arnold to church fellowship, but by 1147, Arnold and the Romans had driven Eugene out of the city. There Arnold remained influential till the accession of the vigorous Hadrian IV (1154–1159)—the only Englishman who has ever occupied the papal throne. Hadrian, in 1155, compelled the Romans to expel Arnold by proclaiming an interdict forbidding religious services in the city; and bargained with the new German sovereign, Frederick Barbarossa (1152–1190), for the destruction of Arnold as the price of imperial coronation. In 1155 Arnold was hanged and his body burned. Though charged with heresy, these accusations are vague and seem to have had little substance. Arnold's real offense was his attack upon the riches and temporal power of the church.

Far more radical had been a preacher in southern France, in the opening years of the twelfth century—Peter of Bruys, of whose origin or early life little is known. With a strict asceticism he combined the denial of infant baptism, the rejection of the Lord's Supper in any form, the repudiation of all ceremonies and even of church buildings, and the rejection of the cross, which should be condemned rather than honored as the instrument through which Christ had suffered. Peter also opposed prayers for the dead. Having burned crosses in St. Gilles, he was himself burned by the mob at an uncertain date, probably between 1120 and 1130. Reputed to be Peter's disciple, but hardly so to be regarded was Henry, called "of Lausanne," once a Benedictine monk, who preached, with large following, from 1101 till his death after 1145, in western and especially southern France. Above all, a preacher of ascetic righteousness, he denied in ancient Donatist spirit the validity of sacraments administered by unworthy priests. His test of worthiness was ascetic life and apostolic poverty. By this standard he condemned the wealthy and power-seeking clergy. Arnold, Peter, and Henry have been proclaimed Protestants before the Reformation. To do so is to misunderstand them. Their conception of salvation was essentially mediæval. They carried to a radical extreme a criticism of the worldly aspects of clerical life which was widely shared and had its more conservative manifestation in the life and teachings of Bernard.

SECTION III. ANTICHURCHLY SECTS. CATHARI AND WAL-
DENSES. THE INQUISITION

The Manichæism of the later Roman Empire, of which Augustine was once an adherent (*ante*, pp. 107, 176), seems never absolutely to have died out in the West. It was stimulated by the accession of Paulicians and Bogomiles (*ante*, p. 235) whom the persecuting policy of the Eastern Emperors drove from Bulgaria, and by the new intercourse with the East fostered by the Crusades. The result was a new Manichæism. Its adherents were called Cathari, as the "Pure," or Albigenses, from Albi, one of their chief seats in southern France. With the ascetic and enthusiastic impulse which caused and accompanied the Crusades, the Cathari rose to great activity. Though to be found in many parts of Europe, their chief regions were southern France, northern Italy, and northern Spain. In southern France, Bernard himself labored in vain for their conversion. With the criticism of existing churchly conditions consequent upon the disastrous failure of the Second Crusade (*ante*, p. 242), they multiplied with great rapidity. In 1167 they were able to hold a widely attended council in St. Felix de Caraman, near Toulouse; and before the end of the century they had won the support of a large section, possibly a majority, of the population of southern France and the protection of its princes. In northern Italy they were very numerous. The Cathari in Florence alone in 1228 counted nearly one-third of the inhabitants. By the year 1200 they were an exceeding peril for the Roman Church. In the movement the ascetic spirit of the age found full expression, and criticism of the wealth and power of the church saw satisfaction in complete rejection of its clergy and claims.

Like the ancient Manichæs, the Cathari were dualists. The Bogomiles and many of the Cathari of Italy held that the good God had two sons, Satanel and Christ—of whom the elder rebelled and became the leader of evil. The Cathari of France generally asserted two eternal powers, the one good, the other malign. All agreed that this visible world is the work of the evil power, in which souls, taken prisoners from the realm of the good God, are held in bondage. The greatest of sins, the original sin of Adam and Eve, is human reproduction, whereby the number of prison-houses is increased. Salvation is by repentance, asceticism, and the "consolation." This rite, like baptism in the church, works forgiveness of sins and restoration to the kingdom of the good God. It is conferred by laying on of hands by one who has received it, together with placing the Gospel of John on the head of the candidate. It is the true apostolical succession. One who has received the "consolation" becomes perfect, a *perfectus;* but lest he lose the grace, he must henceforth eschew marriage, avoid oaths, war, possession of property, and the eating of meat, milk, or eggs, since they are the product of the sin of reproduction. The "perfect," or, as they were called in France, the *bons hommes*—good men— were the real clergy of the Cathari, and there are notices of "bishops" and even of a "Pope" among them, though exactly what the gradations in authority were it is impossible to say. By a convenient belief the majority of adherents, the *credenti* or "believers," were allowed to marry, hold property, and enjoy the good things of this world, even outwardly to conform to the Roman Church, assured that, should they receive the "consolation" before death, they would be saved. Those who died unconsoled would, in the opinion of most of the Cathari, be reincarnated in human, or even animal, bodies till at last they, too, should be brought to salvation. The "believers" seem not always to have been fully initiated into the tenets of the system.

The Cathari made great use of Scripture, which they translated and in which they claimed to find their teachings. Some rejected the Old Testament entirely as the work of the evil power, others accepted the Psalms and the prophets. All believed the New Testament to come from the good God. Since all things material are of evil, Christ could not have had a real body or died a real death. They therefore rejected the cross. The sacraments, with their material elements, were evil. The good God is dishonored by the erection of churches built and ornamented with material creations of the evil power. The services of the Cathari were simple. The Scriptures were read, especially the Gospel of John, as the most spiritual of all. A sermon was preached. The "believers" then knelt and adored the "perfect" as those indwelt with the divine Spirit. The "perfect," in turn, gave their blessing. Only the Lord's Prayer was used in the service. A common meal, at which the bread was consecrated, was held in many places

once a month, as a kind of Lord's Supper. The student of the
movement will find in it extremely interesting survivals of
ancient Christian rites and ceremonies, orthodox and heretical.
In general, the "perfect" seem to have been men and women
of uprightness, moral earnestness, and courageous steadfastness in persecution. Of their effectiveness in gaining the allegiance of thousands, especially from the humbler walks of life,
there can be no question.

Unlike the Cathari, the Waldenses originated in no conscious
hostility to the church and, had they been treated with skill,
would probably never have separated from it. In 1176 Valdez,
or Waldo, a rich merchant of Lyons, impressed by the song of
a wandering minstrel recounting the sacrifices of St. Alexis,
asked a master of theology "the best way to God." The clergyman quoted that golden text of monasticism: "If thou wouldst
be perfect, go, sell that thou hast, and give to the poor, and thou
shalt have treasure in heaven; and come, follow Me."[1] Valdez put this counsel literally into practice. Providing modestly
for his wife and daughters, he gave the rest of his means to the
poor. He determined to fulfil the directions of Christ to the
Apostles[2] absolutely. He would wear the raiment there designated. He would live by what was given him. To know his
duty better he procured a translation of the New Testament.
His action made a deep impression on his friends. Here, they
thought, was true "apostolic poverty." By 1177 he was
joined by others, men and women, and the little company
undertook to carry further Christ's directions by preaching
repentance. They called themselves the "Poor in Spirit."[3]
They now appealed to the Third Lateran Council, in 1179, for
permission to preach. The council did not deem them heretical. It thought them ignorant laymen, and Pope Alexander
III (1159–1181) refused consent. This led to decisive action.
Valdez, who appears in what is known of his later history as
determined, not to say obstinate, felt that this refusal was the
voice of man against that of God. He and his associates continued preaching. As disobedient, they were, therefore, excommunicated, in 1184, by Pope Lucius III (1181–1185).

These unwise acts of the papacy not only forced the Waldenses out of the church against their will, they brought to
them a considerable accession. The Humiliati were a company

[1] *Matt.* 19²¹.　　[2] *Matt.* 10.　　[3] Probably from *Matt.* 5³.

of lowly folk who had associated themselves for a common life of penance in and about Milan. These, too, were forbidden to hold separate meetings, or to preach, by Alexander III, and were excommunicated in 1184 for disobedience. A very considerable part of these Lombard Humiliati now joined the Waldenses, and came under the control of Valdez. The early characteristics of the Waldenses now rapidly developed. Chief of all was the principle that the Bible, and especially the New Testament, is the sole rule of belief and life. Yet they read it through thoroughly mediæval spectacles. It was to them a book of law—of minute prescriptions, to be followed to the letter. Large portions were learned by heart. In accordance with what they believed to be its teachings they went about, two by two, preaching, clad in a simple woollen robe, barefooted or wearing sandals, living wholly on the gifts of their hearers, fasting on Mondays, Wednesdays, and Fridays, rejecting oaths and all shedding of blood, and using no prayers but the Lord's and a form of grace at table. They heard confessions, observed the Lord's Supper together, and ordained their members as a ministry. As unbiblical, they rejected masses and prayers for the dead, and denied purgatory. They held the sacraments invalid if dispensed by unworthy priests. They believed prayer in secret more effective than in church. They defended lay preaching by men and women. They had bishops, priests, and deacons, and a head, or rector, of the society. The first was Valdez himself; later appointment was by election. Besides this inner circle, the society proper, they soon developed a body of sympathizers, "friends" or "believers," from whom the society was recruited, but who remained outwardly in communion with the Roman Church. Most of this development seems to have been immediately subsequent to their excommunication in 1184. Much of it was due to Catharite example, yet they opposed the Cathari and justly regarded themselves as widely different.

Certain conflicts of opinion, and a feeling that the government of Valdez was arbitrary, led to the secession of the Lombard branch by 1210—a breach that attempts at reunion in 1218, after Valdez's death, failed to heal. The two bodies remained estranged. The able Pope, Innocent III (1198–1216), improved these disputes by countenancing in 1208 the organization of *pauperes catholici*, which allowed many of the practices of the Waldenses under strict churchly oversight. Considerable numbers were thus won back to the church. Nevertheless, the Waldensian body spread. Waldenses were to be found in northern Spain, in Austria and Germany, as well as in their original homes. They were gradually repressed, till their chief seat came to be the Alpine valleys southwest of Turin, where they are still to be found. At the Reformation they readily accepted its principles, and became fully Protestant. Under modern religious freedom they are laboring with success in many parts of Italy. Their story is one of heroic endurance of persecution—a most honorable history—and they are the only mediæval sect which still survives, though with wide modification of their original ideals and methods.

By the opening of the thirteenth century the situation of the Roman Church in southern France, northern Italy, and northern Spain was dubious. Missionary efforts to convert Cathari and Waldenses had largely failed. It was felt that sharper measures were needed. A crusade was ordered as early as 1181 by Pope Alexander III (1159–1181), against the viscount of Béziers as a supporter of the Cathari, but it accomplished little. Under Innocent III (1198–1216) the storm broke. After having vainly tried missionary efforts, the murder of the papal legate, Peter of Castelnau, in 1208, induced Innocent to proclaim a crusade against the heretics of southern France. The attack was agreeable to the French monarchy, which had found the nobles of the region too independent vassals. These combined interests of Pope and King led to twenty years of destructive warfare (1209–1229), in which the power of the southern nobles was shattered and cities and provinces devastated. The defenders of the Cathari were rendered impotent or compelled to join in their extermination.

The termination of the struggle was followed by a synod of much importance held in Toulouse in 1229. The Cathari and Waldenses had made much use of the Bible. The synod, therefore, forbad the laity to possess the Scriptures, except the psalter and such portions as are contained in the breviary, and especially denounced all translations. The decree was, indeed, local, but similar considerations led to like prohibitions in Spain and elsewhere. No universal denial of Bible reading by the laity was issued during the Middle Ages.

A second act of significance which marked the synod of Tou-

louse was the beginning of a systematic inquisition. The question of the punishment of heretics had been undetermined in
the earlier Middle Ages. There had been a good many instances
of death, generally by fire, at the hands of rulers, churchmen,
or the mob, but ecclesiastics of high standing had opposed.
The identification of the Cathari with the Manichæans, against
whom the later Roman Emperors had denounced the death
penalty, gave such punishment the sanction of Roman law.
Peter II of Aragon, in 1197, ordered the execution of heretics
by fire. Pope Innocent III (1198–1216) held that heresy, as
treason against God, was of even greater heinousness than
treason against a King. The investigation of heresy was not
as yet systematized. That task the synod of Toulouse undertook. Its work was speedily perfected by Pope Gregory IX
(1227–1241), who intrusted the discovery of heresy to inquisitors chosen chiefly from the Dominican order—a body formed
with very different aims. As speedily developed, the inquisition became a most formidable organ. Its proceedings were
secret, the names of his accusers were not given to the prisoner,
who, by a bull of Innocent IV, in 1252, was liable to torture.
The confiscation of the convict's property was one of its most
odious and economically destructive features, and, as these
spoils were shared by the lay authorities, this feature undoubtedly kept the fires of persecution burning where otherwise they
would have died out. Yet, thanks to the inquisition, and other
more praiseworthy means shortly to be described, the Cathari
were utterly rooted out in the course of a little more than a
century, and the Waldenses greatly repressed. This earlier
success accounts, in large measure, for the tenacity with which
the Roman Church clung to the inquisition in the Reformation
age.

SECTION IV. THE DOMINICANS AND FRANCISCANS

The Cathari and Waldenses profoundly affected the mediæval church. Out of an attempt to meet them by preachers
of equal devotion, asceticism, and zeal, and of greater learning,
grew the order of the Dominicans. In the same atmosphere
of "apostolic poverty" and literal fulfilment of the commands
of Christ in which the Waldenses flourished, the Franciscans
had their birth. In these two orders mediæval monasticism

had its noblest exemplification.   In Francis of Assisi mediæval piety had its highest and most inspiring representative.

Dominic was a native of Calaroga, in Castile, and was born in 1170.   A brilliant student in Palencia, and a youth of deep religious spirit, he became a canon of Osma, about ninety miles northeast of Madrid.   From 1201 he enjoyed the friendship of a kindred spirit, Diego of Acevedo, the bishop of Osma. The two journeyed on political business in 1203 through southern France, where the Cathari were then in the height of their power.   There they found the Roman missionaries treated with contempt.   At a meeting with these missionary leaders in Montpellier, in 1204, Diego urged a thorough reform of method.   Only by missionaries as self-denying, as studious of "apostolic poverty," and as eager to preach as the "perfect" of the Cathari, could these wanderers be won back to the Roman fold.   Moved by the bishop's exhortation, the missionaries endeavored to put his advice into practice.   A nunnery, chiefly for converted Catharite women, was established in 1206, in Prouille, not far from Toulouse.   Thus far Diego seems to have been the leader, but he had to return to his diocese, and died in 1207.   Thenceforward Dominic carried on the work.   The storm of the great anti-Cathari war made it most discouraging. Dominic was tempted by the offer of bishoprics to leave so thankless a task, but he persisted.   He would take the Apostle Paul as his model.   He would win the people by preaching. Gradually he gathered like-minded men about him.   In 1215 friends presented them a house in Toulouse.   The same year Dominic visited the Fourth Lateran Council in Rome, seeking papal approval for a new order.   It was refused, though his efforts were commended, and he now adopted the so-called "Rule" of St. Augustine.   Recognition amounting to the practical establishment of the order was, however, obtained from Pope Honorius III (1216–1227) in 1216.

Even in 1217, when the new association numbered but a few, Dominic determined to send his preachers widely.   With a view to influencing future leaders, he directed them first to the great centres of education, Paris, Rome, and Bologna. The order grew with amazing rapidity.   Its first general chapter was held in Bologna in 1220.   Here, under the influence of Franciscan example, it adopted the principle of mendicancy— the members should beg even their daily food.   By this chapter, or that of the following year, the constitution of the "Order of Preachers," or Dominicans, as they were popularly called, was developed. At the head was a "master-general," chosen by the general chapter, originally for life. The field was divided into "provinces," each in charge of a "provincial prior," elected for a four-year term by the provincial chapter. Each monastery chose a "prior," also for four years. The general chapter included the "master-general," the "provincial priors," and an elected delegate from each province. The system was one, therefore, that combined ingeniously authority and representative government. It embraced monasteries for men, and nunneries for women, though the latter were not to preach, but ultimately developed large teaching activities.

Dominic died in 1221. The order then numbered sixty houses, divided among the eight provinces of Provence, Toulouse, France, Lombardy, Rome, Spain, Germany, and England, and for years thereafter it increased rapidly. Always zealous for learning, it emphasized preaching and teaching, sought work especially in university towns, and soon became widely represented on the university faculties. Albertus Magnus and Thomas Aquinas, the theologians; Eckhart and Tauler, the mystics; Savonarola, the reformer, are but a few of the great names that adorn the catalogue of Dominicans. Their learning led to their employment as inquisitors—a use that formed no part of Dominic's ideal. The legends which represent him as an inquisitor are baseless. He would win men, as did his example, Paul, by preaching. To achieve that result he would undergo whatever sacrifice or asceticism that would make his preachers acceptable to those whom they sought. Yet it is evident that lowly, self-sacrificing and democratic as were Dominic's aims, the high intellectualism of his order tended to give it a relatively aristocratic flavor. It represented, however, an emphasis on work for others, such as had appeared in the Waldenses. Its ideal was not contemplation apart from the world, but access to men in their needs.

Great as was the honor paid to Dominic and the Dominicans, it was exceeded by the popular homage given to the Franciscans, and especially to their founder. The austere preacher, of blameless youth, planning how he may best reach men, and adopting poverty as a means to that end, is not so winsome a figure as that of the gay, careless young man who sacrifices all for Christ and his fellows, and adopts poverty not as a recommendation of his message, but as the only means of being like his Master. In Francis of Assisi is to be seen not merely the greatest of mediæval saints, but one, who through his absolute sincerity of desire to imitate Christ in all things humanly possible, belongs to all ages and to the church universal.

Giovanni Bernadone was born in 1181 or 1182, the son of a cloth merchant of Assisi, in central Italy. To the boy the nickname Francesco—Francis—was given, and soon supplanted that bestowed on him in baptism. His father, a serious man of business, was little pleased to see the son leading in the mischief and revelry of his young companions. A year's experiences as a prisoner of war in Perugia, following a defeat in which he had fought on the side of the common people of Assisi, against the nobles, wrought no change in his life. A serious illness began to develop another side of his character. He joined a military expedition to Apulia, but withdrew, for what reason is not evident. His conversion was a gradual process. "When I was yet in my sins it did seem to me too bitter to look upon the lepers, but the Lord Himself did lead me among them, and I had compassion upon them. When I left them, that which had seemed to me bitter had become sweet and easy." [1] This note of Christ-like compassion was that to which Francis's renewed nature first responded. On a pilgrimage to Rome he thought he heard the divine command to restore the fallen house of God. Taking it literally, he sold cloth from his father's warehouse to rebuild the ruined church of St. Damian, near Assisi. Francis's father, thoroughly disgusted with his unbusinesslike ways, now took him before the bishop to be disinherited; but Francis declared that he had henceforth no father but the Father in heaven. This event was probably in 1206 or 1207.

For the next two years Francis wandered in and about Assisi, aiding the unfortunate, and restoring churches, of which his favorite was the Portiuncula, in the plain outside the town. There, in 1209, the words of Christ to the Apostles,[2] read in the service, came to him, as they had to Valdez, as a trumpet-call to action. He would preach repentance and the kingdom of

---

[1] *Testament of Francis.* Highly illuminative as to his spirit and purposes. Robinson, *Readings* 1 : 392–395.

[2] *Matt.* 10[7-14].

God, without money, in the plainest of garments, eating what
might be set before him. He would imitate Christ and obey
Christ's commands, in absolute poverty, in Christ-like love, and
in humbled deference to the priests as His representatives.
"The Most High Himself revealed to me that I ought to live
according to the model of the holy Gospel." Like-minded associates gathered about him. For them he drafted a "Rule,"
composed of little besides selections from Christ's commands,
and with it, accompanied by eleven or twelve companions, he
applied to Pope Innocent III for approval. It was practically
the same request that Valdez had preferred in vain in 1179.
But Innocent was now trying to win some of the Waldenses for
the church, and Francis was not refused. The associates now
called themselves the Penitents of Assisi, a name for which, by
1216, Francis had substituted that of the Minor, or Humbler,
Brethren, by which they were henceforth to be known.

Francis's association was a union of imitators of Christ, bound
together by love and practising the utmost poverty, since only
thus, he believed. could the world be denied and Christ really
followed. Two by two, they went about preaching repentance,
singing much, aiding the peasants in their work, caring for the
lepers and outcasts. "Let those who know no trade learn one,
but not for the purpose of receiving the price of their toil, but
for their good example and to flee idleness. And when we are
not given the price of our work, let us resort to the table of the
Lord, begging our bread from door to door." [1] Soon wide-
reaching missionary plans were formed, which the rapid growth
of the association made possible of attempting. Francis himself, prevented by illness from reaching the Mohammedans
through Spain, went to Egypt in 1219, in the wake of a crusading
expedition, and actually preached before the Sultan.

Francis himself was little of an organizer. The free association was increasing enormously. What were adequate rules
for a handful of like-minded brethren were soon insufficient for
a body numbering several thousands. Change would have
come in any event. It was hastened, however, by the organizing talents of Cardinal Ugolino of Ostia, the later Pope Gregory IX (1227–1241), who had befriended Francis, and whose
appointment Francis secured as "protector" of the society.
Under Ugolino's influence, and that of Brother Elias of Cortona,

---

[1] *Testament.*

the transformation of the association into a full monastic order went rapidly forward. From the time of Francis's absence in Egypt and Syria in 1219 and 1220, his real leadership ceased. A new rule was adopted in 1221, and a third in 1223. In the latter, emphasis was no longer laid on preaching, and begging was established as the normal, not the exceptional, practice. Already, in 1219, provinces had been established, each in charge of a "minister." Papal directions, in 1220, had prescribed obedience to the order's officers, established a novitiate, a fixed costume, and irrevocable vows.

Probably most of these changes were inevitable. They were unquestionably a grief to Francis, though whether so deeply as has often been contended is doubtful. He was always deferential to ecclesiastical authority, and seems to have regarded these modifications more with regret than with actual opposition. He withdrew increasingly from the world. He was much in prayer and singing. His love of nature, in which he was far in advance of his age, was never more manifest. Feeble in body, he longed to be present with Christ. He bore what men believed to be the reproduction of Christ's wounds. How they may have been received is an unsolved, and perhaps insoluble, problem. On October 3, 1226, he died in the church of Portiuncula. Two years later he was proclaimed a saint by Pope Gregory IX. Few men in Christian history have more richly deserved the title.

In organization, by Francis's death, the Franciscans were like the Dominicans. At the head stood a "minister general" chosen for twelve years. Over each "province" was a "provincial minister," and over each group a "custos," for, unlike the Dominicans, the Franciscans did not at first possess houses. As with the Dominicans, provincial and general chapters were held by which officers were chosen and legislation achieved. Like the Dominicans, also, the Franciscans had almost from the first, their feminine branch—the so-called "second order." That of the Franciscans was instituted by Francis himself, in 1212, through his friend and disciple, Clara Sciffi of Assisi (1194–1253). The growth of the Franciscans was extremely rapid, and though they soon counted many distinguished scholars, they were always more democratic, more the order of the poor, than the Dominicans.

The Dominicans and Franciscans, known respectively as

Black Friars and Gray Friars in England, soon exercised an almost unbounded popular influence. Unlike the older orders, they labored primarily in the cities. There can be no doubt that their work resulted in a great strengthening of religion among the laity. At the same time they undermined the influence of the bishops and ordinary clergy, since they were privileged to preach and absolve anywhere. They thus strengthened the power of the papacy by diminishing that of the ordinary clergy. One chief influence upon the laity was the development of the "Tertiaries" or "third orders"—a phenomenon which first appeared in connection with the Franciscans, though the tradition which connects it with Francis himself is probably baseless. The "third order" permitted men and women, still engaged in ordinary occupations, to live a semi-monastic life of fasting, prayer, worship, and benevolence. A conspicuous illustration is St. Elizabeth of Thuringia (1207–1231). Ultimately all the mendicant orders developed Tertiaries. As time went on the system tended to become an almost complete monasticism, from which the married were excluded. It must be regarded as a very successful attempt to meet the religious ideals of an age which regarded the monastic as the true Christian life.

The piety of the twelfth and thirteenth centuries found many expressions other than through the Dominicans and Franciscans. One important manifestation, especially in the Netherlands, Germany, and France, was through the Beguines—associations of women living in semi-monastic fashion, but not bound by irrevocable vows. They seem to have received their name from those hostile to them in memory of the preacher of Liége, Lambert le Bègue, who was regarded as having been a heretic; and the Beguine movement undoubtedly often sheltered anti-churchly sympathizers. It was in the main orthodox, however, and spread widely, existing in the Netherlands to the present. Its loose organization made effective discipline difficult, and, in general, its course was one of deterioration. A parallel, though less popular, system of men's associations was that of the Beghards.

The divisions in the Franciscan order, which had appeared in Francis's lifetime between those who would emphasize a simple life of Christ-like poverty and those who valued numbers, power, and influence, were but intensified with his death. The stricter party found a leader in Brother Leo, the looser in Elias of Cortona. The papal policy favored the looser, since ecclesiastical politics would be advanced by the growth and consolidation of the order along the lines of earlier monasticism. The quarrel became increasingly embittered. The use of gifts and buildings was secured by the laxer party on the claim that they were held not by the order itself but by "friends." Pope Innocent IV (1243–1254), in 1245, allowed such use, with the reservation that it was the property of the Roman Church, not of the order. These tendencies the stricter party vigorously opposed. But that party itself fell into dubious orthodoxy. Joachim of Floris, in extreme southern Italy (1145?–1202), a Cistercian abbot who had been reputed a prophet, had divided the history of the world into three ages, those of the Father, the Son, and the Holy Spirit. That of the Spirit was to come in full power in 1260. It was to be an age of men who understood "the eternal Gospel"—not a new Gospel, but the old, spiritually interpreted. Its form of life was to be monastic. In the sixth decade of the thirteenth century many of the stricter Franciscans adopted these views and were persecuted not merely by the laxer element, but by the moderates, who obtained leadership when Bonaventura was chosen general minister in 1257. These stricter friars of prophetic faith were nicknamed "Spirituals." Under Pope John XXII (1316–1334) some of the party were burned by the inquisition in 1318. During his papacy a further quarrel arose as to whether the poverty of Christ and the Apostles was complete. John XXII decided in 1322 in favor of the laxer view, and imprisoned the great English schoolman, William of Occam, and other asserters of Christ's absolute poverty. The quarrel was irreconcilable, and finally Pope Leo X (1513–1521) formally recognized the division of the Franciscans in 1517 into "Observant," or strict, and "Conventual," or loose sections, each with its distinct officers and general chapters.

SECTION V. EARLY SCHOLASTICISM

The educational work of cathedral and monastic schools has already been noted in connection with Bede, Alcuin, and Hrabanus Maurus (*ante*, pp. 200, 207, 210). It was long simply imitative and reproductive of the teaching of the Church Fathers, especially of Augustine and Gregory the Great. Save in the case of John Scotus Erigena (*ante*, p. 210), it showed little that was original. Schools, however, increased, especially in France in the eleventh century, and with their multiplication came an application of the methods of logic, or of dialectics, to the discussion of theological problems which resulted in fresh and fertile intellectual development. Since it originated in the schools, the movement was known as "Scholasticism." Most of the knowledge of dialectic method was at first derived from scanty translations of portions of Aristotle's writings and of Porphyry's *Isagoge*, both the work of Boetius (480?–524).

The development of Scholasticism was inaugurated and accompanied by a discussion as to the nature of "universals" —that is as to the existence of genera and species—a debate occasioned by Porphyry's *Isagoge*. Three positions might be taken. The extreme "realists," following Platonic influences (*ante*, p. 3), asserted that universals existed apart from and antecedent to the individual objects—*ante rem, i. e.*, the genus man was anterior to and determinative of the individual man. The moderate "realists," under the guidance of Aristotle (*ante*, p. 4), taught that universals existed only in connection with individual objects—*in re*. The "nominalists," following Stoic precedent, held that universals were only abstract names for the resemblances of individuals, and had no other existence than in thought—*post rem*. The only real existence for them was the individual object. This quarrel between "realism" and "nominalism" continued throughout the scholastic period and profoundly influenced its theological conclusions.

The first considerable scholastic controversy was a renewal of the dispute once held between Paschasius Radbertus and Ratramnus as to the nature of Christ's presence in the Lord's Supper (*ante*, p. 211). Berengar (?–1088), head of the cathedral school in Tours about 1049, attacked the prevalent conception that the elements are changed as to substance into the actual body and blood of Christ. His position was essentially nominalist. Berengar was immediately opposed by Lanfranc (?–1089), then prior of the monastery of Bec in Normandy, and to be William the Conqueror's celebrated archbishop of Canterbury. Berengar was condemned at the Roman synod of 1050. He conformed and was restored in 1059. About ten years later he reasserted his opinions, but once more withdrew them in 1079, only to declare them again. The discussion showed that the view soon to be known as "transubstantiation" had become the dominant opinion in Latin Christendom. It was to have full approval at the Fourth Lateran Council in 1215, where it was given the highest dogmatic standing.

Berengar's dialectic methods were employed, with very dissimilar results, by Anselm, who has often been called the Father of the Schoolmen. Born in Aosta in northern Italy about 1033, Anselm became a monk under Lanfranc in Bec, whom he succeeded as prior. Under him the school of Bec attained great distinction. In 1093 he became archbishop of Canterbury—having a stormy episcopate by reason of his Hildebrandian principles. He died in office in 1109. As a theologian, Anselm was an extreme realist, and was moreover convinced of the full capacity of a proper dialectic to prove the truths of theology. His famous ontological demonstration of the existence of God is at once realistic and Neo-Platonic. As set forth in his *Proslogion*, God is the greatest of all beings. He must exist in reality as well as in thought, for if He existed in thought only, a yet greater being, existing in reality as well as in thought, could be conceived; which is impossible. This proof, which aroused the opposition of Gaunilo, a monk of Marmoutiers, in Anselm's lifetime, seems to most a play on words, though its permanent validity has not lacked defenders.

Anselm next directed his attention to Roscelin, a canon of Compiègne, who, under nominalistic influence, had asserted that either the Father, Son, and Spirit are identical or are three Gods. At a synod held in Soissons in 1092 Roscelin was compelled to abjure tritheism. Anselm now declared that nominalism was essentially heretical, and that view was the prevalent one for the next two centuries.

Anselm's most influential contribution to theology was his discussion of the atonement in his *Cur Deus-homo*, the ablest treatment that had yet appeared. Anselm totally rejected any thought, such as the early church had entertained, of a ransom paid to the devil. Man, by sin, has done dishonor to God. His debt is to God alone. Anselm's view is feudal. God's nature demands satisfaction. Man, who owes obedience at all times, has nothing wherewith to make good past disobedience. Yet, if satisfaction is to be made at all, it can be rendered only by one who shares human nature, who is Himself man, and yet as God has something of infinite value to offer. Such a being is the God-man. Not only is His sacrifice a satisfaction, it deserves a reward. That reward is the eternal blessedness of His brethren. Anselm's widely influential theory rests ultimately on the realistic conviction that there is such an objective existence as humanity which Christ could assume.

Anselm was of devout spirit, fully convinced that dialectic explanation could but buttress the doctrines of the church. "I believe, that I may understand," is a motto that expresses his attitude. The same high realist position was maintained by William of Champeaux (1070?–1121), who brought the school of St. Victor, near Paris, into great repute, and died as bishop of Chalons.

The ablest use of the dialectic method in the twelfth century was made by Abelard (1079–1142), a man of irritating method, vanity, and critical spirit, but by no means of irreligion. Born in Pallet, in Brittany, he studied under Roscelin and William of Champeaux, both of whom he opposed and undoubtedly far surpassed in ability. On the vexed question of the universals he took a position intermediate between the nominalism of one teacher and the realism of the other, though leaning rather to the nominalist side. Only individuals exist, but genera and species are more than names. Hence he is usually called a "conceptualist," though he gave universals greater value than mere mental conceptions.

Abelard's life was stormy. By the age of twenty-two he was teaching with great following in Melun, near Paris. By 1115 he was a canon of Notre Dame, with a following in Paris such as no lecturer had yet enjoyed. He fell in love with Heloise—the niece of his fellow canon, Fulbert—a woman of singular devotion of nature. With her he entered into a secret marriage. The enraged uncle, believing his niece deceived, revenged himself by having Abelard emasculated, and thus barred from clerical advancement. Abelard now became a monk. To teach was his breath of life, however, and he soon resumed lecturing. A reply to Roscelin's tritheism leaned so far in the other direction that his enemies charged him with

Sabellianism, and his views were condemned at a synod in Soissons in 1121. His criticisms of the traditional career of St. Denis made the monastery of St. Denis an uncomfortable place of abode, and he now sought a hermit's life. Students gathered about him and founded a little settlement which he called the Paraclete. His criticisms had aroused, however, the hostility of that most powerful religious leader of the age, the orthodox traditionalist Bernard, and he now sought refuge as abbot of the rough monastery in Rhuys, in remote Brittany. Yet he left this retreat to lecture for a while in Paris, and engaged in a correspondence with Heloise, who had become the head of a little nunnery at the Paraclete, which is the most interesting record of affection—especially on the part of Heloise —which the Middle Ages has preserved. Bernard procured his condemnation at the synod of Sens in 1141, and the rejection of his appeal by Pope Innocent II. Abelard was now a broken man. He made submission and found a friend in Peter, the abbot of Cluny. In 1142 he died in one of the monasteries under Cluny jurisdiction.

Abelard's spirit was essentially critical. Without rejecting the Fathers or the creeds, he held that all should be subjected to philosophical examination, and not lightly believed. His work, *Sic et non—Yes and No*—setting against each other contrary passages from the Fathers on the great doctrines, without attempt at harmony or explanation, might well arouse a feeling that he was a sower of doubts. His doctrine of the Trinity was almost Sabellian. His teaching that man has inherited not guilt but punishment from Adam was contrary to the Augustinian tradition. His ethical theory that good and evil inhere in the intention rather than in the act, disagreed with current feeling. His belief that the philosophers of antiquity were sharers of divine revelation, however consonant with ancient Christian opinion, was not that of his age. Nor was Abelard less individual, though decidedly modern, in his conception of the atonement. Like Anselm, he rejected all ransom to the devil; but he repudiated Anselm's doctrine of satisfaction no less energetically. In Abelard's view the incarnation and death of Christ are the highest expression of God's love to men, the effect of which is to awaken love in us. Abelard, though open to much criticism from the standpoint of his age, was a profoundly stimulating spirit. His direct followers were few, but his indirect influence was great, and the impulse given by him to the dialectic method of theological inquiry far-reaching.

A combination of a moderate use of the dialectic method with intense Neo-Platonic mysticism is to be seen in the work of Hugo of St. Victor (1097?–1141). A German by birth, his life was uneventful. About 1115 he entered the monastery of St. Victor, near Paris, where he rose to be head of its school. A quiet, modest man, of profound learning and piety, his influence was remarkable. He enjoyed the intimate friendship of Bernard. Probably his most significant works were his commentary on the *Celestial Hierarchy* of Pseudo-Dionysius the Areopagite (*ante*, p. 171) and his treatise *On the Mysteries of the Faith*. In true mystic fashion he pictured spiritual progress as in three stages—cogitation, the formation of sense-concepts; meditation, their intellectual investigation; contemplation, the intuitive penetration into their inner meaning. This last attainment is the true mystical vision of God, and the comprehension of all things in Him.

No original genius, like Abelard and Hugo, but a man of great intellectual service to his own age, and held in honor till the Reformation, was Peter Lombard, "the Master of the Sentences" (?–1160?). Born in humble circumstances in northern Italy, Peter studied in Bologna and Paris, in part at least aided by the generosity of Bernard. In Paris he became ultimately teacher of theology in the school of Notre Dame, and near the close of his life, in 1159, bishop of the Parisian see. Whether he was ever a pupil of Abelard is uncertain; but he was evidently greatly influenced by Abelard's works. Under Hugo of St. Victor he certainly studied, and owed that teacher much. Between 1147 and 1150 he wrote the work on which his fame rests—the *Four Books of Sentences*. After the well-accustomed fashion, he gathered citations from the creeds and the Fathers on the several Christian doctrines. What was fresh was that he proceeded to explain and interpret them by the dialectic method, with great moderation and good sense, and with constant reference to the opinions of his contemporaries. He showed the influence of Abelard constantly, though critical of that thinker's extremer positions. He was even more indebted to Hugo of St. Victor. Under the four divisions, God, Created Beings, Salvation, Sacraments and the Last Things, he discussed the whole round of theology. The result was a handbook which so fully met the needs of the age that it remained till the Reformation the main basis of theological instruction.

With the middle of the twelfth century the first period of Scholasticism was over. The schools continued in increasing activity, but no creative geniuses appeared. The last half of the century was distinguished, however, by the introduction to the West, which had thus far had little of Aristotle, of the greater part of his works and of much Greek philosophy besides, by the Jews of Spain and southern France, who, in turn, derived them from the Arabs. The Latin conquest of Constantinople, in 1204 (*ante*, p. 243), led ultimately to direct translations from the originals. The result was to be a new and greater outburst of scholastic activity in the thirteenth century.

SECTION VI. THE UNIVERSITIES

Cathedral and monastic schools were never more flourishing than in the twelfth century. Teachers were multiplying and gathering about them students. Anselm, Abelard, William of Champeaux, Hugo of St. Victor, and Peter Lombard were simply the most eminent of a host. Students flocked to them in large numbers from all parts of Europe. Paris and Oxford were famed for theology, Bologna for church and civil law, Salerno for medicine. Under these circumstances the universities developed in a manner which it is difficult exactly to date. The change which they implied was not the establishment of teaching where none had been before, but the association of students and teachers into a collective body, after the fashion of a trade guild, primarily for protection and good order, but also for more efficient management and the regulation of admission to the teaching profession. In its educational capacity such a group was often called a *studium generale*. The beginnings of university organization—which must be distinguished from the commencement of teaching—may be placed about the year 1200.

By the close of the twelfth century there were in Bologna two "universities," or mutual protective associations of students. The organization in Paris became normal, however, for northern Europe. Its earliest rules date from about 1208, and its recognition as a legal corporation from a letter of Pope Innocent III of about 1211. In Paris there was a single "university," originally formed by the union of the cathedral school and the more private schools of the city, and divided for instruction into four faculties—one preparatory, that of the "arts," in which the *trivium* (grammar, rhetoric, and logic) and the *quadrivium* (astronomy, arithmetic, geometry, and music) were taught; and the three higher faculties of theology, canon law, and medicine. Over each faculty a dean presided. Besides this educational organization students and professors were also grouped, for mutual aid, in "nations," each headed by a proctor. These varied in number in the several institutions. In Paris they were four—the French, the Picards, the Normans, and the English.

Teaching was principally by lecture and by constant debate, a method which, whatever its shortcomings, rendered the student ready master of his knowledge, and brought talent to light. The first degree, that of bachelor, was similar to an admission to apprenticeship in a guild. The second degree, that of master or doctor, resembling the master workman in a guild, carried with it full authority to teach in the institution where it was conferred, and soon, for the graduates of the larger universities, to teach anywhere. The use of Latin as the sole language of the classroom made possible the assembly of students from all parts of Europe, and they flocked to the more famous universities in immense numbers.

The needs of these students, many of whom were of extreme poverty, early aroused the interest of benefactors. One of the most influential and oldest foundations thus established was that formed in Paris by Robert de Sorbon (1201–1274) in 1252. It provided a home and special teaching for poor students, under the guidance of "fellows" of the house. Such establishments, soon known as "colleges," rapidly multiplied, and gave shelter to the great majority of students, rich and poor. The system still survives in the English universities. So prominently was the Sorbonne identified with theological instruction that its name came to be popularly, though erroneously, attached to the faculty of theology in Paris. That university ranked till the Reformation as the leader of Europe, especially in the theological studies.

Universities, many of which were short-lived, sprang up

with great rapidity. In general, they were regarded as ecclesiastical—authorization by the Pope being almost essential. The most conspicuous early lay approval was that of Naples, in 1225, by the Emperor Frederick II.

SECTION VII. HIGH SCHOLASTICISM AND ITS THEOLOGY

The recovery of the whole of Aristotle, the rise of the universities, and the devotion of the mendicant orders to learning, ushered in a new period of Scholasticism in the thirteenth century, and marked the highest intellectual achievement of the Middle Ages. The movement toward this "modern theology," as it was called, was not without much opposition, especially from traditionalists and adherents to the Augustinian Neo-Platonic development. Aristotle met much hostility. A series of great thinkers, all from the mendicant orders, made his victory secure. Yet even they, while relying primarily on Aristotle, made much use of Plato as reflected in Augustine and the Pseudo-Dionysius (*ante*, pp. 171, 266).

To Alexander of Hales (?–1245), an Englishman and ultimately a Franciscan, who taught in Paris, was due the treatment of theology in the light of the whole of Aristotle. Yet to him the Scripture is the only final truth. With this new period of Scholasticism a broader range of intellectual interest is apparent than in the earlier, though the old problem between realism and nominalism continued its pre-eminence. Alexander was a moderate realist. Universals exist *ante rem* in the mind of God, *in re* in the things themselves, and *post rem* in our understanding. In this he was followed by Albertus Magnus and Aquinas.

Albertus Magnus (1206?–1280), a German and a Dominican, studied in Padua, and taught in many places in Germany, but principally in Cologne. He served as provincial prior for his order, and was, for a few years, bishop of Regensburg. The most learned man of his age, his knowledge of science was really remarkable. His acquaintance not merely with Aristotle, but with the comments of Arabian scholars, was profounder than that of Alexander of Hales. He was, however, a great compiler and commentator rather than an original theological genius. That which he taught was brought to far clearer expression by his pupil, Thomas Aquinas.

Thomas Aquinas (1225?–1274) was a son of Landulf, count of Aquino, a small town about half-way between Rome and Naples. Connected with the German imperial house of Hohenstaufen and with that of Tancred, the Norman Crusader, it was against the wishes of his parents that Thomas entered the Dominican order in 1243. His spiritual superiors were aware of his promise, and sent him to Cologne to study under Albertus Magnus, who soon took his pupil to Paris. On receiving the degree of bachelor of divinity, Thomas returned to Cologne in 1248, and now taught as subordinate to Albertus Magnus. These were years of rapid intellectual growth. Entrance into the Paris faculty was long refused him on account of jealousy of the mendicant orders, but in 1257 he was given full standing there. From 1261 for some years he taught in Italy, then once more in Paris, and finally, from 1272, in Naples. He died, on his way to the Council of Lyons, in 1274. In these crowded years of teaching Thomas was constantly consulted on important civil and ecclesiastical questions, and was active in preaching; yet his pen was busy with results as voluminous as they were important. His great *Summa Theologiæ* was begun about 1265, and not fully completed at his death. Personally he was a simple, deeply religious, prayerful man. Intellectually his work was marked by a clarity, a logical consistency, and a breadth of presentation that places him among the few great teachers of the church. In the Roman communion his influence has never ceased. By declaration of Pope Leo XIII (1878–1903), in 1879, his work is the basis of present theological instruction.

Closely associated with Aquinas in friendship and for a time in teaching activities in the University of Paris, was John Fidanza (1221–1274), generally known as Bonaventura. Born in Bagnorea, in the States of the Church, he entered the Franciscan order in 1238, rising to become its "general" in 1257. A year before his death he was made a cardinal. Famed as a teacher in Paris, he was even more distinguished for his administration of the Franciscan order and for his high character. Much less an Aristotelian than Aquinas, he was especially influenced by the Neo-Platonic teachings of Augustine and Pseudo-Dionysius. He was essentially a mystic. By meditation and prayer one may rise into that union with God which brings the highest knowledge of divine truth. Yet, though a mystic, Bonaven-

tura was a theologian of dialectic ability whose work, more
conservative and less original than that of Aquinas, nevertheless commanded high respect.

According to Aquinas, in whom Scholasticism attained its
noblest development, the aim of all theological investigation is
to give knowledge of God and of man's origin and destiny.
Such knowledge comes in part by reason—natural theology—
but the attainments of reason are inadequate. They must be
augmented by revelation. That revelation is contained in the
Scriptures, which are the only final authority; but they are to
be understood in the light of the interpretations of the councils
and the Fathers—in a word, as comprehended by the church.
The truths of revelation cannot be attained by reason, but they
are not contrary to reason, and reason can show the inadequacy of objections to them. Aquinas is thus far from sharing
Anselm's conviction that all truths of Christianity are philosophically demonstrable; but he holds that there can be no
contradiction between philosophy and theology, since both are
from God.

In treating of God Aquinas combined Aristotelian and Neo-
Platonic conceptions. He is the first cause. He is pure ac-
tivity. He is also the most real and perfect of existences.
He is the absolute substance, the source and end of all things.
As perfect goodness, God does always that which He sees to
be right. Regarding the Trinity and the person of Christ,
Aquinas stood essentially on the basis of Augustine and the
Chalcedonian formula (*ante*, p. 151).

God needs nothing, and therefore the creation of the world
was an expression of the divine love which He bestows on the
existences He thus called into being. God's providence ex-
tends to all events, and is manifested in the predestination of
some to everlasting life, and in leaving others to the consequences of sin in eternal condemnation. Aquinas's position is
largely determinist. Man has, indeed, in a certain sense, freedom. His will acts; but that does not preclude the determining or permissive providence of God. The divine permission
of evil results in the higher good of the whole. Though sin is
no less sinful, its existence permits the development of many
virtues which go to make strength of character in those who
resist.

Aquinas abandoned the ancient distinction between "soul"

and "spirit." The soul of man is a unit, possessing intellect and will. It is immaterial. Man's highest good is the vision and enjoyment of God. As originally created man had, in addition to his natural powers, a superadded gift which enabled him to seek that highest good and practise the three Christian virtues—faith, hope, and love. This Adam lost by sin, which also corrupted his natural powers, so that his state became not merely a lack of original righteousness, but a positive turning toward lower aims. Sin is, therefore, more than merely negative. In this fallen state it was impossible for Adam to please God, and this corruption was transmitted to all his posterity. Man still has the power to attain the four natural virtues, prudence, justice, courage, and self-control; but these, though bringing a certain measure of temporal honor and happiness, are not sufficient to enable their possessor to attain the vision of God.

Man's restoration is possible only through the free and unmerited grace of God, by which man's nature is changed, his sins forgiven, and power to practise the three Christian virtues infused. No act of his can win this grace. While God could conceivably have forgiven man's sins and granted grace without the sacrifice of Christ—here Aquinas differed from Anselm— the work of Christ was the wisest and most efficient method God could choose, and man's whole redemption is based on it. That work involved satisfaction for man's sin, and Christ won a merit which deserves a reward. It also moves men to love. Aquinas thus developed and combined views presented by Anselm and Abelard. Christ's satisfaction superabounds man's sin, and the reward which Christ cannot personally receive, since as God He needs nothing, comes to the advantage of His human brethren. Christ does for men what they cannot do for themselves.

Once redeemed, however, the good works that God's grace now enables man to do deserve and receive a reward. Man now has power to fulfil not only the precepts but the counsels of the Gospel (*ante*, p. 103). He can do works of supererogation, of which the chief would be the faithful fulfilment of the monastic life. He can not merely fit himself for heaven; he can add his mite to the treasury of the superabundant merits of Christ and the saints. Yet all this is made possible only by the grace of God. Aquinas thus finds full room for the two dominating conceptions of mediæval piety—grace and merit.

Grace does not come to men indiscriminately. It has its definite channels and these are the sacraments, and the sacraments alone. Here Scholasticism attained far greater clearness of definition than had previously existed. The ancient feeling that all sacred actions were sacraments was still alive in the twelfth century, but Hugo of St. Victor and Abelard clearly placed five in a more conspicuously sacramental category than others, and Peter Lombard defined the sacraments as seven. Whether this reckoning was original with him is still an unsolved problem; nor was it at once universally accepted. The influence of his *Sentences* ultimately won the day. As enumerated by Peter Lombard, the sacraments are baptism, confirmation, the Lord's Supper, penance, extreme unction, ordination, and matrimony. All were instituted by Christ, directly or through the Apostles, and all convey grace from Christ the head to the members of His mystical body, the church. Without them there is no true union with Christ.

Every sacrament consists of two elements which are defined in Aristotelian terms of form and matter (*ante*, p. 4)—a material portion (water, bread, and wine, etc.) ; and a formula conveying its sacred use ("I baptize thee," etc.). The administrant must have the intention of doing what Christ and the church appointed, and the recipient must have, at least in the case of those of years of discretion, a sincere desire to receive the benefit of the sacrament. These conditions fulfilled, the sacrament conveys grace by the fact of its reception—that is *ex opere operato*. Of this grace God is the principal cause; the sacrament itself is the instrumental cause. It is the means by which the virtue of Christ's passion is conveyed to His members.

By baptism the recipient is regenerated, and original and previous personal sins are pardoned, though the tendency to sin is not obliterated. Man is now given the grace, if he will use it, to resist sin, and the lost power to attain the Christian virtues. Infant baptism had become the universal practice, but in the time of Aquinas immersion was still the more prevalent form, and had his approval.

The sole recognized theory regarding Christ's presence in the Supper was that which had been taught by Paschasius Radbertus (*ante*, p. 211) and Lanfranc (*ante*, p. 262), and had

been known since the first half of the twelfth century as transubstantiation. It had been given full dogmatic authority by the
Fourth Lateran Council in 1215. Aquinas but added clearness of definition. At the words of consecration by the priest
the miracle is wrought by the power of God, so that while the
"accidents" (shape, taste, and the like) remain unaltered, the
"substance" is transformed into the very body and blood of
Christ.

Aquinas also accepted and developed the view that the whole
body and blood of Christ is present in either element. It was
far from original with him, but had grown with the increasing
custom of the laity to partake of the bread only. A withdrawal
of the cup instigated by the clergy did not take place. The
abandonment of the cup was rather a layman's practice due to
fear of dishonoring the sacrament by misuse of the wine. Such
anxiety had manifested itself as early as the seventh century
in the adoption of the Greek custom of dipping the bread in
the wine—a practice repeatedly disapproved by ecclesiastical
authority, but supported by lay sentiment. By the twelfth
century the laity were avoiding the use of the wine altogether,
apparently first of all in England. By the time of Aquinas
lay communion in the bread alone had become prevalent.
Similar considerations led to the general abandonment by the
Western Church, in the twelfth and thirteenth centuries of the
practice of infant communion, which had been universal, and
which continues in the Greek Church to the present.

Mediæval piety and worship reach their highest point in the
Lord's Supper. It is the continuation of the incarnation, the
repetition of the passion, the source of spiritual upbuilding to
the recipient, the evidence of his union with Christ, and a sacrifice well pleasing to God, inclining Him to be gracious to those
in need on earth and in purgatory.

Penance, though not reckoned a sacrament of equal dignity
with baptism or the Lord's Supper, was really of great, if not
prime, importance in mediæval practice. Mediæval thought
regarding the personal religious life centred about the two
conceptions of grace and merit. Baptism effected the forgiveness of previous sins; but for those after baptism penance was
necessary. The Latin mind has always been inclined to view
sin and righteousness in terms of definite acts rather than as
states, and therefore to look upon man's relations to God under

the aspects of debt and credit—though holding that the only basis of credit is the effect of God's grace. These tendencies were never more marked than in the scholastic period. They represented wide-spread popular views which the schoolmen explained theologically, rather than originated.

According to Aquinas, penance involves four elements, contrition, confession, satisfaction, and absolution. Contrition is sincere sorrow for the offense against God and a determination not to repeat it. Yet Aquinas holds that, as all sacraments convey grace, a penance begun in "attrition," that is, in fear of punishment, may by infused grace become a real contrition.

Private confession to the priest had made gradual progress since its advocacy by the old British missionaries (*ante*, p. 197). Abelard and Peter Lombard were of opinion that a true contrition was followed by divine forgiveness, even without priestly confession, though they thought such confession desirable. The Fourth Lateran Council, in 1215, required confession to the priest at least once a year of all laymen of age of discretion. Such confession thereby became church law. Alexander of Hales argued its necessity, and Aquinas gave it more logical exposition. It must be made to the priest as the physician of the soul, and include all "deadly" sins—the catalogue of which was now much larger than in the early church (*ante*, p. 100).

Though God forgives the eternal punishment of the penitent, certain temporal penalties remain as a consequence of sin. This distinction was clearly made by Abelard and became the current property of the schoolmen. These temporal penalties satisfy the sinner's offense against God so far as it is in his power to do so. They also enable him to avoid sin in the future. They are the "fruits of repentance." It is the business of the priest to impose these satisfactions, which, if not adequate in this life, will be completed in purgatory.

On evidence thus of sorrow for sin, confession, and a willingness to give satisfaction, the priest, as God's minister or agent, pronounces absolution. Here, then, was the great control of the priesthood over the laity till the Reformation, and in the Roman Church to the present. Without priestly pardon no one guilty after baptism of a "deadly" sin has assurance of salvation.

A great modification of these satisfactions was, however, rapidly growing in the century and a half before Aquinas. A remission of a portion or of all of these "temporal" penalties could be obtained. Such remission was called an "indulgence." Bishops had long exercised the right to abridge satisfactions in cases where circumstances indicated unusual contrition. Great services to the church were held to deserve such consideration. Peter Damiani (1007?–1072) regarded gifts of land for a monastery or a church as affording such occasions. These did not constitute the full indulgence system, however. That seems to have originated in southern France, and the earliest, though not undisputed, instance is about the year 1016. Their first conspicuous employment was by a French Pope, Urban II (1088–1099), who promised full indulgence to all who engaged in the First Crusade, though Pope Alexander II had given similar privileges on a smaller scale for battle against the Saracens in Spain about 1063. Once begun, the system spread with great rapidity. Not only Popes but bishops gave indulgences, and on constantly easier terms. Pilgrimages to sacred places or at special times, contributions to a good work, such as building a church or even a bridge or a road, were deemed deserving of such reward. The financial possibilities of the system were soon perceived and exploited. Since "temporal" penalties included those of purgatory, the value of an indulgence was enormous, though undefined, and the tendency to substitute it for a real penance was one to which human nature readily responded.

Such was the practice to which Aquinas now gave the classic interpretation. Following Alexander of Hales, he taught that the superabundant merits of Christ and of the saints form a treasury of good works from which a portion may be transferred by the authority of the church, acting through its officers, to the needy sinner. It can, indeed, avail only for those who are really contrite, but for such it removes, in whole or in part, the "temporal" penalties here and in purgatory. Indulgences were never a license to commit sin. They were an amelioration of penalties justly due to sins already committed and regretted. But, however interpreted, there can be no doubt as to the moral harmfulness of the system, or that it grew worse till the Reformation, of which it was an immediately inducing cause.

At their deaths, according to Aquinas, the wicked pass immediately to hell, which is endless, and from which there is no release. Those who have made full use of the grace offered in the church go at once to heaven. The mass of Christians who have but imperfectly availed themselves of the means of grace must undergo a longer or shorter purification in purgatory.

The church is one, whether in heaven, on earth, or in purgatory. When one member suffers, all suffer; when one does well, all share in his good work. On this unity of the church Aquinas bases prayers to the saints and for those in purgatory. The visible church requires a visible head. To be subject to the Roman Pontiff is necessary for salvation. To the Pope, also, belongs the right to issue new definitions of faith, and Aquinas implies the doctrine of papal infallibility.

It was Aquinas's good fortune that his philosophy and his theology alike found a hearty disciple in the greatest of mediæval poets, Dante Alighieri (1265–1321), whose *Divina Commedia* moves, in these respects, almost wholly in Aquinas's realm of thought.

Aquinas was a Dominican, and their natural rivalry soon drew upon his system the criticism of Franciscan scholars, many of whom were of English birth. Such a critic was Richard of Middletown (?–1300?); but the most famous of all, and one of the greatest of the schoolmen, was John Duns Scotus (1265?–1308). In spite of his name he appears to have been an Englishman. Educated in Oxford, where he became its most famous teacher, he removed to Paris in 1304. Four years later the general of the order sent him to Cologne, where he died just as his work there had begun. The keenest critic and the ablest dialectician of all the schoolmen, he attacked the work of Aquinas with the utmost acumen. He attained a position as authoritative teacher in the Franciscan order similar to that of Aquinas in the Dominican, and the theological rivalries of the Thomists and Scotists continued to rage till the Reformation.

Aquinas had held that the essence of God is being. To Scotus, it is arbitrary will. The will in God and man is free. Aquinas held that God did what He saw to be right. To Scotus what God wills is right by the mere fact of willing. Though, like Aquinas, Scotus was a modified realist, he laid emphasis on the individual rather than on the universal. To him the individual is the more perfect form.

Since God is absolute will, the sacrifice of Christ has the value which God puts upon it. Any other act would have been sufficient for salvation had God seen fit so to regard it. Nor can we say, with Aquinas, that Christ's death was the wisest way of salvation. That would be to limit God's will. All we can affirm is that it was the way chosen by God. Similarly, Scotus minimized the repentance necessary for salvation. Aquinas has demanded contrition or an "attrition"—fear of punishment—that by the infusion of grace became contrition. Scotus held that "attrition" is sufficient by divine appointment to secure fitness for pardon. It is followed by forgiveness, and that by the infusion of grace by which a man is enabled to do certain acts to which God has been pleased to attach merit. The sacraments do not of themselves convey grace, but are the conditions appointed by God upon which, if fulfilled, grace is bestowed.

The most fundamental difference between Aquinas and Scotus is one of attitude. To Aquinas there could be no real disagreement between theology and philosophy, however inadequate the latter to reach all the truths of the former. To Duns much in theology is philosophically improbable, yet must be accepted on the authority of the church. The breakdown of Scholasticism had begun, for its purpose had been to show the reasonableness of Christian truth.

The dispute which roused the loudest controversy between Thomists and Scotists was regarding the "immaculate conception" of the Virgin Mary. Aquinas had taught that she shared in the original sin of the race. Scotus held that she was free from it—a doctrine that was to be declared that of the church by Pope Pius IX (1846–1878) in 1854.

Yet more radical in his divorce of philosophy from theology was Scotus's pupil, William of Occam (?–1349?). An English Franciscan of the most earnest type, he studied in Oxford, taught in Paris, defended the complete poverty of Christ and the Apostles against Pope John XXII (ante, p. 261), suffered imprisonment, only to escape in 1328 and find refuge with Louis of Bavaria, then in quarrel with the Pope. For the rest of his life he defended the independence of the state from ecclesiastical authority with the utmost steadfastness.

Occam attacked any form of "realism" fiercely. Only individual objects exist. Any association in genera or species is purely mental, having no objective reality. It is simply a

use of symbolic "terms." Hence, Occam was called a "termi-
nist." His system was a far more vigorous and destructive
nominalism than that of Roscelin (*ante*, p. 263). Yet actual
knowledge of things in themselves men do not have, only of
mental concepts. This denial led him to the conclusion that
no theological doctrines are philosophically provable. They
are to be accepted—and he accepted them—simply on authority. That authority he made in practice that of the church;
though in his contest with what he deemed a derelict papacy
he taught that Scripture, and not the decisions of councils and
Popes, is alone binding on the Christian. No wonder that
Luther, in this respect, could call him "dear master."

Occam's philosophical views gained increasing sway after his
death. From thence onward till just before the Reformation
nominalism was the dominant theological position. It was the
bankruptcy of Scholasticism. While it undoubtedly aided investigation by permitting the freest (philosophical) criticism of
existing dogma, it based all Christian belief on arbitrary authority. That was really to undermine theology, for men do
not long hold as true what is intellectually indefensible. It
robbed of interest the great speculative systems of the older
Scholasticism. Men turned increasingly, in the fourteenth
and fifteenth centuries, to mysticism, or returned to Augustine
for the intellectual and religious comfort which Scholasticism
was unable longer to afford.

SECTION VIII. THE MYSTICS

Besides the intellectual, the mystical tendency was strongly
represented in many of the schoolmen. Hugo of St. Victor
and Bonaventura may as rightly be reckoned to the mystics
as to the scholastics. Aquinas showed marked mystic leanings,
derived from Augustine and the Pseudo-Dionysius. Aristotle
never wholly conquered Neo-Platonic influences. Neo-Platonism itself enjoyed a measure of revival in the twelfth and thirteenth centuries, partly through the strongly Neo-Platonizing
Arabian commentaries on Aristotle, but even more through
the widely read *Liber de Causis*, falsely ascribed to Aristotle, but
containing excerpts from the Neo-Platonic philosopher, Proclus (410–485), and ultimately by translations directly from
Proclus's accredited works.

An important representative of this mystical spirit was "Meister" Eckhart (1260–1327), a German Dominican, who studied in Paris, served as provincial prior of the Saxon district, lived for a time in Strassburg, and taught in Cologne. At the close of his life Eckhart was under trial for heresy. He himself declared his readiness to submit his opinions to the judgment of the church, but two years after his death a number of his teachings were condemned by Pope John XXII. In true Neo-Platonic fashion Eckhart taught that that which is real in all things is the divine. In the soul of man is a spark of God. That is the true reality in all men. All individualizing qualities are essentially negative. Man should, therefore, lay them aside. His struggle is to have God born in his soul, that is to enter into full communion with and to come under the control of the indwelling God. In this effort Christ is the pattern and example, in whom Godhead dwelt in humanity in all fulness. With God dominant the soul is filled with love and righteousness. Churchly observances may be of some value, but the springs of the mystic life are far deeper and its union with God more direct. Good works do not make righteous. It is the soul already righteous that does good works. The all-important matter is that the soul enters into its full privilege of union with God.

Perhaps the most eminent of Eckhart's disciples was John Tauler (?–1361), a Dominican preacher who worked long in Strassburg, of which he was probably a native, in Cologne and in Basel. The times in Germany were peculiarly difficult. The long contest for the empire between Frederick of Austria and Louis of Bavaria, and papal interferences therein, wrought religious as well as political confusion. The bubonic plague of 1348–1349, known in England as the "black death," devastated the population. To his distressed age Tauler was a preacher of helpfulness, whose sermons have been widely read ever since. In them are many "evangelical" thoughts, which aroused the admiration of Luther, and have often led to the claim that he was a Protestant before Protestantism. He emphasized the inward and the vital in religion, and condemned dependence on external ceremonies and dead works. His real position was that of a follower of Eckhart, with similar mystic emphasis on union with the divine, on "God being born within," though he avoided the extreme statements which had led to churchly condemnation of Eckhart's opinions. A less practical but widely influential representative of the same tendencies was the ascetic Dominican, Henry Suso (?–1366), whose writings did much to further this mystic point of view.

Through these influences a whole group of mystic sympathizers was raised up in southwestern Germany and Switzerland, who called themselves "Friends of God." These included not only many of the clergy, but nuns and a considerable number of laity. Among the laymen, Rulman Merswin, of Strassburg (1307–1382), was the most influential. Originally a banker and merchant, he was intimate with Tauler, whose views he shared, and devoted all the latter part of his life to religious labors. He mystified his contemporaries and posterity by letters and books which he set forth purporting to come from a "great Friend of God" in the Highlands (*i. e.,* Switzerland), whose existence was long believed real, but now is practically proved to have been a fiction of Merswin himself. The most important work of these Friends of God was the "German Theology," written late in the fourteenth century by an otherwise unknown and unnamed priest of the *Deutsch-Herrn Haus* of Frankfort, which was to influence Luther, and to be printed by him in 1516 and 1518.

These German mystics all leaned strongly toward pantheism. They all, however, represented a view of the Christian life which saw its essence in a transforming personal union of the soul with God, and they all laid little weight on the more external methods of ordinary churchly life.

This mystical movement was furthered in the Netherlands by John of Ruysbroeck (1294–1381), who was influenced by Eckhart's writings and enjoyed the personal friendship of Tauler and other of the Friends of God. Ruysbroeck's friend, in turn, was Gerhard Groot (1340–1384)—a brilliant scholar, who upon his conversion, about 1374, became the most influential popular preacher of the Netherlands. A more conservative churchly thinker than Ruysbroeck, Groot was much less radical in his mysticism. A man of great practical gifts, Groot's work led shortly after his death to the foundation by his disciple, Florentius Radewyn (1350–1400), of the Brethren of the Common Life. This association, of which the first house was established in Deventer, grew out of the union of Groot's converts for a warmer religious life. They grouped themselves in houses of brethren and of sisters, who lived essentially a monastic life under common rules, but without permanent vows, engaged in religious exercises, copying books of edification, and especially in teaching. Work was required of all. These houses were wide-spread in the Netherlands and in Germany, and did much to promote popular piety in the fifteenth century.

The Brethren of the Common Life were non-monastic in the matter of vows. Groot's preaching led to an influential movement for those who preferred the monastic life, though it, also, did not take full form till shortly after his death. This was the foundation of the famous monastery of Windesheim, which soon gathered a number of affiliated convents about it, and became a reformatory influence of power in the monastic life of the Netherlands and Germany. In both these movements the mystic influence was strongly present, though in a much more churchly form than among the immediate disciples of Eckhart.

The noblest product of this simple, mystical, churchly piety is the *Imitation of Christ*—a book the circulation of which has exceeded that of any other product of the Middle Ages. Though its authorship has been the theme of heated controversy, it was unquestionably the work of Thomas à Kempis (1380?–1471). A pupil of the Brethren of the Common Life in Deventer, most of his long life was spent in the monastery of Mount St. Agnes, near Zwolle. This foundation was a member of the Windesheim congregation, of which Thomas's older brother, John, was one of the founders. Thomas's life was outwardly the most uneventful conceivable; but few have understood, as did he, the language of simple, mystical devotion to Christ.

The mystical movement had its reverse side in a pantheism which broke with all churchly and even all moral teaching. Such was that of Amalrich of Bena (?–1204), a teacher in Paris, who was led by the writings of John Scotus Erigena (*ante*, p. 210) and the extreme Neo-Platonic opinions of the Spanish Mohammedan expositor of Aristotle, Averroes (1126–1198), to the conclusions that God is all, that He is incarnate in the believer as in Christ, and that the believer cannot sin. He also held that as the Jewish law and ritual had been abolished by the coming of Christ, so that of earlier Christianity was now done away with by the coming of the Holy Spirit. Amalrich was compelled to recant by Pope Innocent III, but he left a number of followers.

Similar extravagances kept cropping out in the regions of Germany and the Netherlands, where the mysticism already described had its chief following. In many ways it was simply that mysticism carried to a pantheistic extreme. It was usually quietist, believing that the soul could become one with God by contemplation, and in consequence of that union its acts could no longer be sinful, since it is controlled by God. All sacraments and penances, even prayer, become superfluous. These views were not united into a compact system, nor did their holders constitute a sect, though they have often been so regarded and named the "Brethren and Sisters of the Free Spirit." Undoubtedly, however, such notions were rather frequently to be found in monasteries and nunneries, where mysticism was practised extravagantly, and among the Beguines, whom they brought into doubtful repute. They were not only repressed by the inquisition, but were opposed by the greater mystic leaders of whom an account has been given.

SECTION IX. MISSIONS AND DEFEATS

The period between the Crusades and the Reformation was one of gains and losses for Christendom. In Spain the Christian forces struggled with increasing success against the Mohammedans. Gradually, four Christian states dominated the peninsula. Castile conquered Toledo in 1085, defeated the Moslems at Las Navas de Tolosa in 1212, and united with Leon into a strong state in 1230. Little Navarre stretched on both sides of the Pyrenees. Meanwhile Aragon on the east and Portugal on the west were winning their independence, so that by 1250 Mohammedan power on the peninsula was confined to the kingdom of Granada, whence it was to be driven in 1492. The Spanish Christian kingdoms were weak. The real power of Spain was not to be manifest till the joint reign of Ferdinand and Isabella united Castile and Aragon in 1479.

In the East the great Mongol empire, which began with the conquest of northern China in 1213, stretched across northern Asia, conquering most of what is now European Russia between 1238 and 1241, and reaching the borders of Palestine in 1258.

By this devastation the flourishing Nestorian Church in central Asia (*ante*, p. 149) was almost annihilated. Yet after the first rush of conquest was over, central Asia under Mongol control was accessible as it had never been before and was not to be till the nineteenth century. About 1260 two Venetian merchants, Nicolo and Maffeo Polo, made the long journey by land to Peking, where they were well received by the Mongol Khan, Kublai. Returning in 1269, they started again in 1271, taking Nicolo's more famous son, Marco, who entered the Khan's service. It was not till 1295 that the Polos were back in Venice. Even before their return an Italian Franciscan, John of Monte Corvino, had started in 1291 for Peking, where he established a church about 1300. Christianity flourished for a time. Pope Clement V (1305–1314) appointed John an archbishop with six bishops under him. The work came to an end, however, when the Mongols and other foreigners were expelled from China by the victorious native Ming dynasty in 1368.

Efforts were made to reach the Mohammedans, but with little success. Francis of Assisi himself preached to the Sultan in Egypt in 1219 (*ante*, p. 258). More famous as a missionary was Raimon Lull (1235?–1315), a native of the island of Majorca. From a wholly worldly life he was converted in 1266, and now studied Arabic, as a missionary preparation, writing also his *Ars Major*, which he intended as an irrefutable demonstration of Christianity. In 1291 he began missionary work in Tunis, only to be expelled at the end of a year. He labored to induce the Pope to establish schools for missionary training. He went once more to Africa and was again driven out. His eloquence persuaded the Council of Vienne in 1311 to order teaching in Greek, Hebrew, Chaldee, and Arabic, in Avignon, Paris, Salamanca, Bologna, and Oxford, though this remained a pious wish. Back to Tunis he went as a missionary in 1314, and met a martyr's death by stoning the next year. He had little to show of missionary achievement, but much of missionary inspiration.

The prevailing characteristic of this period was the loss of once Christian territories. The last of the conquests of the Crusaders in Palestine passed out of their hands in 1291. A new Mohammedan force was arising in the Ottoman Turks. Sprung from central Asia, they attained an independent position in Asia Minor in 1300. In 1354 they invaded the European portion of the Eastern empire, capturing Adrianople in 1361, and gradually spreading their rule over the Balkan lands. But a fragment of the empire remained till 1453, when Constantinople fell and the Eastern empire was at an end. The victorious career of the Turks was to carry them, in the Reformation age, nearly half across Europe. Christians ruled by them were deprived of political rights, though Christian worship and organization continued, under conditions of much oppression. The Greek Church, which had stood higher in culture than the Latin, certainly till the thirteenth century, was now largely robbed of significance. Its daughter in Russia was not conquered, however, and was growing rapidly in strength and importance. With it lay the future of the Eastern Church.

SECTION X.   THE PAPACY AT ITS HEIGHT AND ITS DECLINE

The contest between papacy and empire was by no means ended by the Concordat of Worms (*ante*, p. 234). The religious interest in the struggle was thereafter far less. Hildebrand's quarrel had involved a great question of church purification. The later disputes were plain contests for supremacy.

Frederick "Barbarossa" (1152–1190), of the house of Hohenstaufen, was one of the ablest of the Holy Roman Emperors. His model was Charlemagne, and he aspired to a similar control of churchly affairs. A vigorous ruler at home, no sovereign had been more thoroughly master of Germany than he. In spite of the Concordat of Worms he practically controlled the appointment of German bishops. On the other hand, his claims met with energetic resistance from the cities of northern Italy, which were growing strong on the commerce induced by the Crusades. This hostility he at first successfully overcame. With Alexander III (1159–1181) Frederick's most able enemy mounted the papal throne. The cardinals were divided in the choice, and an imperialistic minority elected a rival Pope, who called himself Victor IV, and whom Frederick and the German bishops promptly supported. Alexander's position was long difficult. In 1176, however, Frederick was defeated at Legnano by the Lombard league of Italian cities, and was forced to recognize Alexander. Frederick's attempt to control the papacy had been shattered, but his authority over the German bishops was scarcely diminished.[1] Frederick won a further success over the papacy, in 1186, by the marriage of his son Henry with the heiress of Sicily and southern Italy, thus threatening the papal states from north and south.

Alexander III also won at least an apparent success over Henry II (1154–1189), one of the ablest of English Kings. That monarch, in order to strengthen his hold over the English church, secured the election of his apparently complaisant chancellor, Thomas Becket, as archbishop of Canterbury, in 1162. Once in office, Becket showed himself a determined upholder of ecclesiastical claims. Henry now, in 1164, secured the enactment of the Constitutions of Clarendon[2], limiting the right of appeal to Rome in ecclesiastical cases, restricting the power of excommunication, subjecting the clergy to civil courts, and putting the election of bishops under the control of the King, to whom they must do homage. Becket now openly broke with the King. In 1170 a truce was brought about, but it was of short duration, and a hasty expression of anger on the part of Henry led to Becket's murder just at the close of the year. Alexander used the deed skilfully. In 1172 Becket was canonized, and continued till the Reformation one of the most popular of English saints. Henry was forced to abandon the Constitutions of Clarendon, and do penance at Becket's grave. Yet in spite of this apparent papal victory, Henry continued his control of English ecclesiastical affairs much as before.

Frederick "Barbarossa" died in 1190, on the Third Crusade. He was succeeded by his son, Henry VI (1190–1197), who, in 1194, obtained full possession of his wife's inheritance in Sicily and southern Italy, and developed ambitious plans of greatly extending his imperial sway. The papacy, with both ends of Italy in the possession of the German sovereign, was in great political danger; but the situation was relieved by the early death of Henry VI in 1197, and the accession to the papacy in 1198 of one of its ablest mediæval representatives, Innocent III (1198–1216).

Innocent III was unquestionably a man of personal humility and piety, but no Pope ever had higher conceptions of the papal

---

[1] See "Peace of Venice," Henderson, *Select Historical Documents*, pp. 425–430.

[2] Gee and Hardy, *Documents Illustrative of English Church History*, pp. 68–73.

office and under him the papacy reached its highest actual power. The death of Henry VI saw Germany divided. One party supported the claims of Henry's brother, Philip of Swabia, the other those of Otto of Brunswick, of the rival house of Welf (Guelph). Out of this confused situation Innocent strove with great skill to bring advantage to the papacy. He secured large concessions in Italy and Germany from Otto, yet when Philip gradually gained the upper hand, Innocent secured an agreement that the rival claims should be submitted to the judgment of a court controlled by the Pope. The murder of Philip in 1208 frustrated this plan, and put Otto IV once more to the fore. Innocent now obtained from Otto the desired guarantee of the extent of the papal states, and a promise to abandon control of German episcopal elections, and on the strength of these concessions crowned Otto Emperor in 1209. Otto promptly forgot all his promises. The angered Pope now put forward Frederick II (1212–1250), the young son of the late Emperor, Henry VI, who was chosen to the German throne by the elements opposed to Otto, in 1212, and renewed all Otto's broken promises. In 1214 Otto was wholly defeated by the French King, Philip II (1179–1223) on the field of Bouvines, and Frederick was assured of the empire. Thus, Innocent III seemed wholly to have defended papal claims and to have dictated the imperial succession. The world supremacy of the papacy appeared realized.

Nor was Innocent III less successful in humbling the sovereigns of other lands. He compelled the powerful Philip II of France, by the prohibition of religious services—an interdict —to take back the Queen, Ingeborg, whom Philip had unjustly divorced. He separated King Alfonso IX of Leon from a wife too closely related. King Peter of Aragon received his kingdom as a fief from the Pope. Innocent's greatest apparent victory was, however, in the case of England. The cruel and unpopular King John (1199–1216), in a divided election tried to secure his candidate as archbishop of Canterbury. The dispute was appealed to Rome. The King's choice was set aside and Innocent's friend, Stephen Langton, received the prize. John resisted. Innocent laid England under an interdict. The King drove out his clerical opponents. The Pope now excommunicated him, declared his throne forfeited and proclaimed a crusade against him. The defeated King not merely made a humiliating submission to the Pope, in 1213, but acknowledged his kingdom a fief of the papacy, agreeing to pay a feudal tax to the Pope of a thousand marks annually.[1] Yet when the barons and clergy wrung *Magna Charta* from John in 1215, Innocent denounced it as an injury to his vassal.

In the internal affairs of the church Innocent's policy was strongly centralizing. He claimed for the papacy the right of decision in all disputed episcopal elections. He asserted sole authority to sanction the transfer of bishops from one see to another. His crusade against the Cathari has already been noted (*ante*, p. 253). The great Fourth Lateran Council of 1215, at which transubstantiation was declared an article of faith, and annual confession and communion required, was also a papal triumph. The conquest of Constantinople by the Fourth Crusade (*ante*, p. 243), though not approved by Innocent, seemed to promise the subjection of the Greek Church to papal authority.

In Innocent III the papacy reached the summit of its worldly power. The succeeding Popes continued the same struggle, but with decreasing success. The Emperor Frederick II, ruler of Germany, as well as of northern and southern Italy and Sicily, a man of much political ability and of anything but mediæval piety, though put in office largely by Innocent III, soon proved the chief opponent of the world pretensions of the papacy. Under Gregory IX (1227–1241), the organizer of the inquisition and the patron of the Franciscans (*ante*, pp. 254, 258), and Innocent IV (1243–1254) the papal contest was carried on against Frederick II, with the utmost bitterness and with very worldly weapons. Frederick was excommunicated, and rivals were raised up against him in Germany by papal influence. The papacy seemed convinced that only the destruction of the Hohenstaufen line, to which Frederick belonged, would assure its victory. On Frederick's death in 1250 it pursued his son, Conrad IV (1250–1254), with the same hostility, and gave his heritage in southern Italy and Sicily to Edmund of England, son of King Henry III. A new influence, that of France, was making itself felt in papal counsels. Urban IV (1261–1264) was a Frenchman and appointed French cardinals. He now gave, in 1263, southern Italy and Sicily to Charles of Anjou, brother of King Louis IX of France (1226–1270). This was a turning-

---

[1] Henderson, pp. 430–432.

point in papal politics, and with it the dependence of the papacy
on France really began.   The next Pope was also a Frenchman,
Clement IV (1265–1268).   During his papacy Conradin, the
young son of Conrad IV, asserted his hereditary claims to
southern Italy and Sicily by force of arms.   He was excommunicated by Clement IV and defeated by Charles of Anjou,
by whose orders he was beheaded in Naples, in 1268.   With
him ended the line of Hohenstaufen, which the Popes had so
strenuously opposed, though there is no reason to think that
the Pope was responsible in any way for Conradin's execution.

These long quarrels and the consequent confusion had
greatly enfeebled the power of the Holy Roman Empire.
Thenceforward, to the Reformation, it was far more a group of
feeble states than an effective single sovereignty.   It was able
to offer little resistance to papal demands.   Other forces were,
however, arising that would inevitably make impossible such
a world sovereignty as Innocent III had exercised.   One such
force was the new sense of nationality, which caused men to
feel that, as Frenchmen or Englishmen, they had common interests against all foreigners, even the Pope himself.   Such a
sense of unity had not existed in the earlier Middle Ages.   It
was rapidly developing, especially in France and England in
the latter half of the thirteenth century.   A second cause was
the rise in intelligence, wealth, and political influence of the
middle class, especially in the cities.   These were restive under
ecclesiastical interference in temporal affairs.   Closely associated with this development was the growth of a body of lay
lawyers and the renewed study of the Roman law.   These
men were gradually displacing ecclesiastics as royal advisers,
and developing the effectiveness of the royal power by precedents from a body of law—the Roman—which knew nothing of
mediæval ecclesiastical conditions.   There was also a growing
conviction among thoughtful and religious men that such
worldly aims as the recent papacy had followed were inconsistent with the true interests of the church.   These were
growing forces with which the papacy must reckon.   The weakness of the papacy, from a worldly point of view, was that it
had no adequate physical forces at its disposal.   It must balance off one competitor against another, and the wreck wrought
in Germany left the door open to France without forces which
could be matched against her.

Papal interference in Germany continued. Pope Gregory X (1271–1276) ordered the German electors, in 1273, to choose a King, under threat that the Pope himself would make the appointment if they failed. They chose Rudolf I, of Habsburg (1273–1291), who promptly renewed the concessions to the papacy which had been once made by Otto IV and Frederick II.

Quite otherwise was it speedily with France. The power of that monarchy had been rapidly growing, and in Philip IV, "the Fair" (1285–1314), France had a King of absolute unscrupulousness, obstinacy, and high conceptions of royal authority. In Boniface VIII (1294–1303) the papacy was held by a man of as lofty aspirations to world-rule as had ever there been represented. Neither participant in the struggle commands much sympathy. War had arisen between France, Scotland, and England which compelled the English King, Edward I (1272–1307), to rally the support of all his subjects by inviting the representatives of the Commons to take a place in Parliament, in 1295, thus giving them a permanent share in the English national councils. The struggle also induced the Kings of France and England to tax their clergy to meet its expenses. The clergy complained to Pope Boniface, who, in 1296 issued the bull *Clericis laicos*,[1] inflicting excommunication on all who demanded or paid such taxes on clerical property without papal permission. Philip replied by prohibiting the export of money from France, thus striking at the revenues of the Pope and of the Italian bankers. The latter moved Boniface to modify his attitude so that the clergy could make voluntary contributions, and even allowed that, in great necessities, the King could lay a tax. It was a royal victory.

Comparative peace prevailed between Philip and Boniface for a few years. In 1301 the struggle again began. Philip had Bernard Saisset, bishop of Pamiers, whom the Pope had recently sent to him as nuntius, arrested and charged with high treason. The Pope ordered Bernard's release and cited the French bishops, and ultimately King Philip himself, to Rome. In reply, Philip summoned the first French States-General, in which clergy, nobles, and commoners were represented. This body, in 1302, sustained the King in his attitude of resistance. The Pope answered with the famous bull,

[1] Henderson, pp. 432–434; Robinson, 1: 488–490.

Unam sanctam,[1] the high-water mark of papal claim to supremacy over civil powers. It affirmed that temporal powers are subject to the spiritual authority, which is judged in the person of the Pope by God alone. It declared, following the opinion of Aquinas (*ante*, p. 277), "that it is altogether necessary to salvation for every human being to be subject to the Roman pontiff"—an affirmation the exact scope of which has led to much subsequent discussion. Philip answered with a new assembly, where the Pope was charged with an absurd series of crimes, involving heresy and moral depravity, and appeal was issued for a general council of the church before which the Pope might be tried. Philip was determined that this should be no mere threat. He would force the Pope to consent. He therefore sent his able jurist vice-chancellor, William Nogaret, who joined to himself Boniface's ancient family enemy, Sciarra Colonna. Together they gathered a force and made Boniface a prisoner in Anagni, just as he was about to proclaim Philip's excommunication, in 1303. Boniface was courageous. He would make no concessions. His friends soon freed him, but a month later he died.

These events were a staggering blow to the temporal claims of the papacy. It was not primarily that Philip's representatives had held Boniface for a short time a prisoner. A new force had arisen, that of national sentiment, to which the King had appealed successfully, and against which the spiritual weapons of the papacy had been of little avail. The papal hope of world-rulership in temporal affairs had proved impossible of permanent realization.

Worse for the papacy was speedily to follow. After the death of Boniface's successor, the excellent Benedict XI (1303–1304), the cardinals chose a Frenchman, Bertrand de Gouth, who took the title of Clement V (1305–1314). A man of weakness of character and grave moral faults, he was fully under the influence of King Philip IV, of France. He declared Philip innocent of the attack on Boniface VIII, and cancelled Boniface's interdicts and excommunications, modifying the bull *Unam sanctam* to please the King. An evidence of French domination that was patent to all the world was the removal of the seat of the papacy, in 1309, to Avignon—on the river Rhone—a town not belonging indeed to the French kingdom,

---

[1] Henderson, pp. 435–437; Robinson, 1 : 346–348.

but in popular estimate amounting to the establishment of the papacy in France. Undoubtedly the troubled state of Italian politics had something to do with this removal. At Avignon the papacy was to have its seat till 1377—a period so nearly equal to the traditional exile of the Jews as to earn the name of the Babylonish Captivity. Nor was the cup of Clement's humiliation yet filled. The cold-blooded King compelled him to join in the cruel destruction of the Templars (*ante*, p. 242).

Clement V's pontificate is interesting as marking the conclusion, to the present, of the official collections of church or "canon" law. That great body of authority was the product of the history of the church since the early councils, and embraced their decisions, the decrees of synods and of Popes. The Middle Ages had seen many collections, of which the most famous was that gathered, probably in 1148, by Gratian, a teacher of canon law in Bologna. Pope Gregory IX (1227–1241) caused an official collection to be formed, in 1234, including new decrees up to his time. Pope Boniface VIII (1294–1303), published a similar addition in 1298, and Clement V (1305–1314) enlarged it in 1314, though his work was not published till 1317, under his successor, John XXII (1316–1334). The great structure, thus laboriously erected through the centuries, is a mass of ecclesiastical jurisprudence embracing all domains of ecclesiastical life. Though official collections ceased from Clement V to the twentieth century, the creation of church law has continued in all ages, and the recent Pope, Pius X (1903–1914), in 1904 ordered the codification and simplification of the whole body of canon law by a special commission.

SECTION XI.   THE PAPACY IN AVIGNON, CRITICISM. THE SCHISM

The Popes, while the papacy was in Avignon, were all Frenchmen. It seemed as if the papacy had become a French institution. This association caused greatly increased restlessness in view of papal claims, especially in nations which, like England, were at war with France during much of this period, or Germany on which the still continuing interference of the papacy bore hard. The ablest of the Avignon Popes was unquestionably John XXII (1316–1334). The double imperial election in Germany, in 1314, had divided that land between supporters of Louis the Bavarian (1314–1347), and Frederick of Austria.   John XXII, supported by King Philip V of France (1316–1322), thought the occasion ripe to diminish German influence in Italy for the benefit of the States of the Church.   He declined to recognize either claimant, and declared that the Pope had right to administer the empire during vacancies.   When Louis interfered in Italian affairs the Pope excommunicated him, and a contest with the papacy ensued which lasted till Louis's death.   In its course the German electors issued the famous declaration of 1338, in Rense, which was confirmed by the Reichstag in Frankfort the same year, that the chosen head of the empire needs no approval from the papacy whatever for full entrance on or continuation in the duties of his office.

These attacks upon the state aroused literary defenders of considerable significance.   One of these was the great Italian poet, Dante Alighieri (1265–1321).   His Latin treatise, _On Monarchy_, is not surely dated, but was composed between 1311 and 1318.   Dante holds that peace is the best condition of mankind.   It is most effectively secured by an Emperor. The power of empire rightfully came to Rome.   It is as necessary for man's temporal happiness as the papacy is to guide men to eternal blessedness.   Each is directly from God, and neither should interfere in the province of the other.   Dante carefully controverts the papal interpretation of the Bible texts and historical instances on which claims to control over the state were based.   All this is the more impressive since Dante was no free-thinker but theologically of most impeccable orthodoxy.

Much more radical than Dante, and vastly influential on later political theories were several treatises produced in France. The Dominican, John of Paris (1265?–1306), taught that both papal and royal powers are based on the sovereignty of the people, and neither has a right to interfere with the sphere of the other.   The most important of these works was the _Defensor Pacis_ of Marsilius of Padua (?–1342?) and John of Jandun (?–1328).   It is the most startlingly modern treatise that the age produced.   Its principal author, Marsilius, was long a teacher in Paris, where he was rector of the university in 1313, and was regarded as learned in medicine.   The _Defensor Pacis_ was written in 1324, in the controversy between Pope John XXII and the Emperor Louis the Bavarian. Its radical views caused its authors to seek protection from the Emperor, which they enjoyed, though with some hesitation, for the rest of their lives. They were excommunicated by John XXII in 1327, and Pope Clement VI declared, in 1343, that he had never read a worse heretical book.

According to Marsilius, who was deeply versed in Aristotle, the basis of all power is the people; in the state the whole body of citizens; in the church the whole body of Christian believers. They are the legislative power; by them rulers in church and state are appointed, and to them these executive officers are responsible. The only final authority in the church is the New Testament; but priests have no power of physical force to compel men to obey it. Their sole duty is to teach, warn, and reprove. The New Testament teaches that bishops and priests are equivalent designations, yet it is well, as a purely human constitution, to appoint some clergy superintendents over others. This appointment gives no superior spiritual power, nor has one bishop spiritual authority over another, or the Pope over all. Peter had no higher rank than the other Apostles. There is no New Testament evidence that he was ever in Rome. The New Testament gives no countenance to the possession of earthly lordships and estates by clergymen. No bishop or Pope has authority to define Christian truth as contained in the New Testament, or make binding laws. These acts can be done only by the legislative body of the church—the whole company of Christian believers, represented in a general council. Such a council is the supreme authority in the church. Since the Christian state and the Christian church are coterminous, the executive of the Christian state, as representing a body of believers, may call councils, appoint bishops, and control church property.[1] Here were ideas that were to bear fruit in the Reformation, and even in the French Revolution; but they were too radical greatly to impress their age. Their time was later, and something was lacking in Marsilius himself. He was a cool thinker rather than a man who could translate theory into action in such fashion as to create large leadership.

Because of a zeal which Marsilius lacked, and of ideas not

[1] See, for some extracts, Robinson, 1: 491–497.

too much in advance of the age, a greater authority was wielded by William of Occam, whose theological influence and energetic defense of the extremer Franciscan doctrine of the absolute poverty of Christ and the Apostles has been noted (*ante*, pp. 261, 278). Occam, like Marsilius, found a refuge with Louis the Bavarian. To him, as to Dante, papacy and empire are both founded by God, and neither is superior to the other. Each has its own sphere. The church has purely religious functions. Its final authority is the New Testament.

Voices were raised in defense of papal claims. One of the most celebrated, though typical rather than original, was that of the Italian Augustinian monk, Augustinus Triumphus (1243–1328). In his *Summa de potestate ecclesiastica*, written about 1322, he holds that all princes rule as subject to the Pope, who can remove them at pleasure. No civil law is binding if disapproved by him. The Pope can be judged by none; nor can one even appeal from the Pope to God, "since the decision and court of God and the Pope are one." Yet should the Pope fall into heresy, his office is forfeited.

These opinions of the papal supporters were far from being shared by Germans engaged in a struggle against the papacy for the political autonomy of the empire, or by Englishmen at war with France, who believed the Avignon papacy the tool of the French sovereign. Pope Clement V (1305–1314) had asserted the right of the papacy to appoint to all ecclesiastical office. Such appointees were called "provisors," and the intrusion of papal favorites in England aroused King and Parliament in 1351 to enact the Statute of Provisors. Elections to bishoprics and other ecclesiastical posts should be free from papal interference. In case appointment was made by the regular authorities, and also by the Pope, the provisor was to be imprisoned till he resigned his claim. This law inevitably led to disputes between papal and royal authority, and a further statute of 1353, known as that of *Præmunire* forbade appeals outside of the kingdom under penalty of outlawry.[1] In enforcement these statutes were largely dead letters, but they show the growth of a spirit in England which was further illustrated when Parliament, in 1366, refused longer to recognize the right of King John to subject his kingdom, in 1213, to the Pope as a fief (*ante*, p. 288).

[1] Gee and Hardy, *Documents*, pp. 103, 104, 113–119.

No feature of the Avignon papacy contributed to its criticism so largely as its offensive taxation of church life. The Crusades had been accompanied by a much readier circulation of money, and a great increase in commerce. Europe was passing rapidly from barter to money payments. Money taxes, rather than receipts in kind, were everywhere increasing. It was natural that this change should take place in church administration also; but the extent to which taxation was pushed by the Popes of the thirteenth and fourteenth centuries was a scandal, and it was much aggravated when the removal of the papacy to Avignon largely cut off the revenues from the papal estates in Italy without diminishing the luxury or expensiveness of the papal court. This period saw the extensive development, in imitation of secular feudal practice, of the annates, that is a tax of one year's income, more or less, from each new appointment. Since the reservation of posts to exclusive papal appointment was at the same time immensely extended, this became a large source of revenue. The income of vacant benefices, also, became a significant source of papal receipts. Taxes for bulls and other papal documents, also rose rapidly in amount and productivity. These were but a portion of the papal exactions, and the total effect was the impression that the papal administration was heavily and increasingly burdensome on the clergy, and through them on the people. This feeling was augmented by the ruthless manner in which churchly censures, such as excommunication, were imposed on delinquent taxpayers. The papacy seemed extravagant in expenditure and offensive in taxation, and its repute in both respects was to grow worse till the Reformation.

The collapse of the imperial power in Italy, for which the papacy was largely responsible, and the transfer to Avignon, left Italy to the wildest political confusion. Nowhere was the situation worse than in Rome. In 1347 Cola di Rienzi headed a popular revolution against the nobles and established a parody of the ancient republic. He was soon driven out, but in 1354 was in power again, only to be murdered in the partisan struggles. Innocent VI (1352–1362) sent the Spanish cardinal Albornoz (?–1367) as his legate to Italy. By Albornoz's military and diplomatic abilities the papal interests in Rome and Italy generally were much improved, so that Urban V (1362–1370) actually returned to the Eternal City in 1367.

The death of Albornoz deprived him of his chief support, and in 1370 the papacy was once more in Avignon. Urban V was succeeded by Gregory XI (1370–1378), whom St. Catherine of Siena (1347–1380) urged in the name of God to return to Rome. The distracted state of the city also counselled his presence if papal interests were to be preserved. Accordingly he transferred the papacy to Rome in 1377, and there died the next year.

The sudden death of Gregory XI found the cardinals in Rome. A majority were French, and would gladly have returned to Avignon. The Roman people were determined to keep the papacy in Rome, and to that end to have an Italian Pope. Under conditions of tumult the cardinals chose Bartolommeo Prignano the archbishop of Bari, who took the name Urban VI (1378–1389). A tactless man, who desired to terminate French influence over the papacy, and effect some reforms in the papal court, he soon had the hostility of all the cardinals. They now got together, four months after his election, declared their choice void since dictated by mob violence, and elected Cardinal Robert of Geneva as Pope Clement VII (1378–1394). A few months later Clement VII and his cardinals were settled in Avignon. There had been many rival Popes before, but they had been chosen by different elements. Here were two Popes, each duly elected by the same body of cardinals. The objection that Urban VI had been chosen out of fear had little force, since the cardinals had recognized him without protest for several months; but they had done all they could to undo the choice. Europe saw two Popes, each condemning the other. There was no power that could decide between them, and the several countries followed the one or the other as their political affinities dictated. The Roman Pope was acknowledged by northern and central Italy, the greater part of Germany, Scandinavia, and England. To the Pope in Avignon, France, Spain, Scotland, Naples, Sicily, and some parts of Germany adhered. It was a fairly equal division. The great schism had begun. Europe was pained and scandalized, while the papal abuses, especially of taxation, were augmented, and two courts must now be maintained. Above all, the profound feeling that the church must be visibly one was offended. The papacy sank enormously in popular regard.

In Rome Urban VI was succeeded by Boniface IX (1389–

1404), and he by Innocent VII (1404–1406), who was followed
by Gregory XII (1406–1415). In Avignon Clement VII was
followed by a Spaniard, Peter de Luna, who took the name
Benedict XIII (1394–1417).

SECTION XII.   WYCLIF AND HUSS

The English opposition to the encroachments of the Avignon
papacy has already been noted (*ante*, p. 295).   Other forces
were also working in the island.   Of these that of Thomas
Bradwardine (?–1349) was one of the most potent in the intellectual realm.   Bradwardine, who was long an eminent theologian in Oxford, and died archbishop of Canterbury, was a
leader in the revival of the study of Augustine, which marked
the decline of Scholasticism, and was to grow in influence till
it profoundly affected the Reformation.   He taught predestination in most positive form; like Augustine, he conceived religion as primarily a personal relationship of God and the soul,
and emphasized grace in contrast to merit.   There were now,
therefore, other intellectual traditions besides those of later
nominalistic Scholasticism in the Oxford of Wyclif's student
days.

John Wyclif (?–1384) was born in Hipswell in Yorkshire.
Few details of his early life are known.   He entered Balliol
College, Oxford, of which he became ultimately for a short
time "master."   In Oxford he rose to great scholarly distinction, lecturing to large classes, and esteemed the ablest theologian of its faculty.   Philosophically he was a realist, in contrast to the prevailing nominalism of his age.   He was deeply
influenced by Augustine, and through Augustine by Platonic
conceptions.   Wyclif gradually became known outside of Oxford.   In 1374 he was presented, by royal appointment, to
the rectory of Lutterworth, and the same year was one of the
King's commissioners—probably theological adviser—to attempt in Bruges with the representatives of Pope Gregory XI
an adjustment of the dispute regarding "provisors" (*ante*,
p. 295).   In how far these appointments were due to the powerful son of King Edward III, John of Gaunt, Duke of Lancaster, is uncertain, though he probably regarded Wyclif as likely
to be useful in his designs on church property; but Wyclif's
opinions, if entertained in 1374, cannot then have been widely

known. There is no evidence that the Pope yet looked on him with distrust, and recent investigation has shown that his reformatory work did not begin in 1366, as formerly supposed.

By 1376, however, it was the wealth of the church and clerical interference, especially that of the Popes, in political life, that aroused his opposition. He lectured that year in Oxford *On Civil Lordship.* Wyclif's view of ecclesiastical office and privilege was curiously feudal. God is the great overlord. He gives all positions, civil and spiritual, as fiefs, to be held on condition of faithful service. They are lordships, not property. God gives the use but not the ownership. If the user abuses his trust he forfeits his tenure. Hence a bad ecclesiastic loses all claim to office, and the temporal possessions of unworthy clergy may well be taken from them by the civil rulers, to whom God has given the lordship of temporal things, as He has that of things spiritual to the church. This doctrine, advanced in all simplicity and sincerity, was undoubtedly pleasing to John of Gaunt and his hungry crew of nobles who hoped for enrichment from church spoliation. It was no less satisfactory to many commoners, who had long been critical of the wealth, pretensions, and too often lack of character of the clergy. It was not displeasing to the mendicant orders, who had always, in theory at least, advocated "apostolic poverty."

Wyclif's teaching aroused the opposition of the high clergy, the property-holding orders, and of the papacy. In 1377 he was summoned to answer before the bishop of London, William Courtenay. The protection of John of Gaunt and other nobles rendered the proceeding abortive. The same year Pope Gregory XI issued five bulls ordering Wyclif's arrest and examination.[1] Yet Wyclif enjoyed the protection of a strong party at court and much popular favor, so that further proceedings against him by the archbishop of Canterbury and the bishop of London were frustrated in 1378.

Wyclif was now rapidly developing his reformatory activities in a flood of treatises in Latin and English. The Scriptures, he taught, are the only law of the church. The church itself is not, as the common man imagined, centred in the Pope and the cardinals. It is the whole company of the elect. Its only certain head is Christ, since the Pope may not be one of the elect. Wyclif did not reject the papacy. The church may

[1] Gee and Hardy, pp. 105–108.

well have an earthly leader, if such a one is like Peter, and strives for the simple conditions of early Christianity. Such a Pope would be presumably one of the elect. But a Pope who grasps worldly power and is eager for taxes is presumptively non-elect, and therefore antichrist. With his deeper knowledge of the Bible, Wyclif now attacked the mendicant orders, which had supported him in his assertion of apostolic poverty, regarding them as without Scriptural warrant and the main pillars of the existing papacy. He was now fighting current churchly conditions all along the line.

Wyclif now proceeded to more constructive efforts. Convinced that the Bible is the law of God, Wyclif determined to give it to the people in the English tongue. Between 1382 and 1384 the Scriptures were translated from the Vulgate. What share Wyclif had in the actual work is impossible to say. It has been usually thought that the New Testament was from his pen, and the Old from that of Nicholas of Hereford. At all events, the New Testament translation was vivid, readable, and forceful, and did a service of fundamental importance for the English language—to say nothing of English piety. The whole was revised about 1388, possibly by Wyclif's disciple, John Purvey. Its circulation was large. In spite of severe repression in the next century, at least one hundred and fifty manuscripts survive.

To bring the Gospel to the people Wyclif began sending out his "poor priests." In apostolic poverty, barefoot, clad in long robes, and with staff in the hand, they wandered two by two, as had the early Waldensian or Franciscan preachers. Unlike the latter, they were bound by no permanent vows. Their success was great.

But events soon lamed the Lollard movement, as the following of Wyclif was popularly called. Convinced that the elect are a true priesthood, and that all episcopal claims are unscriptural, Wyclif saw in the priestly power of exclusive human agency in the miracle of transubstantiation a main buttress of what he deemed erroneous priestly claim. He therefore attacked this doctrine in 1381. His own view of Christ's presence seems to have been essentially that later known as consubstantiation. It was not his positive assertions, but his attack, however, that aroused resentment, for to oppose transubstantiation was to touch one of the most popularly cherished beliefs of the later Middle Ages.   That attack cost Wyclif many followers and roused the churchly authorities to renewed action. This tide of opposition was strengthened by events in 1381, for which Wyclif was in no way responsible.   The unrest of the lower orders, which had been growing since the dislocation of the labor market by the "black death" of 1348–1350, culminated in 1381 in a great peasant revolt, which was with difficulty put down.   This bloody episode strengthened the party of conservatism.   In 1382 the archbishop of Canterbury held a synod in London by which twenty-four Wyclifite opinions were condemned.[1]   Wyclif was no longer able to lecture in Oxford. His "poor priests" were arrested.   He was too strong in popular and courtly support, however, to be attacked personally, and he died still possessed of his pastorate in Lutterworth on the last day of 1384.

No small element in Wyclif's power was that he was thought to have no scholastic equal in contemporary England.   Men hesitated to cross intellectual swords with him.   Equally conspicuous were his intense patriotism and his deep piety.   He voiced the popular resentment of foreign papal taxation and greed, and the popular longing for a simpler, more Biblical faith.   It was his misfortune that he left no follower of conspicuous ability to carry on his work in England.   Yet throughout the reign of Richard II (1377–1399) the Lollard movement continued to grow.   With the accession of the usurping house of Lancaster in the person of Henry IV (1399–1413), the King, anxious to placate the church, was persuaded to secure the passage in 1401 of the statute *De hæretico comburendo*,[2] under which a number of Lollards were burned.   Henry IV spared Lollards in high lay station.   Not so his son, Henry V (1413–1422).   Under him their most conspicuous leader, Sir John Oldcastle, Lord Cobham, a man of the sternest religious principles, whom tradition and dramatic license transformed into the figure of Falstaff, was condemned, driven into rebellion, and executed in 1417.   With his death the political significance of Lollardy in England was at an end, though adherents continued in secret till the Reformation.   Wyclif's chief influence was to be in Bohemia rather than in the land of his birth.

Bohemia had undergone a remarkable intellectual and political development in the fourteenth century.   The Holy Roman

---

[1] Gee and Hardy, pp. 108–110.   [2] *Ibid.*, pp. 133–135.

Emperor, Charles IV (1346–1378) was also King of Bohemia, and did much for that land. In 1344 he secured the establishment of Prague as an archbishopric, releasing Bohemia from ecclesiastical dependence on Mainz. Four years later he procured the foundation of a university in Prague. In no country of Europe was the church more largely a landholder, or the clergy more worldly than in Bohemia. Charles IV was not unfriendly to moral reform. During and following his reign a series of preachers of power stirred Bohemia, attacking the secularization of the church. Such were Conrad of Waldhausen (?–1369), Milicz of Kremsier (?–1374), Matthias of Janov (?–1394), and Thomas of Stitny (1331–1401). These all opposed clerical corruption, emphasized the Scriptures as the rule of life, and sought a more frequent participation in the Lord's Supper. Milicz and Matthias taught that antichrist was at hand, and was manifest in an unworthy clergy. These men had little direct influence on Huss, but they stirred Bohemia to a readiness to accept his teachings.

Bohemia was torn, furthermore, by intense rivalry between the Germanic and the Slavonic (Czech) elements of the population. The latter was marked by a strong desire for racial supremacy and Bohemian autonomy.

Curiously, also, Bohemia, hitherto so little associated with England, was brought into connection with that country by the marriage of the Bohemian princess, Anna, to King Richard II, in 1383. Bohemian students were attracted to Oxford, and thence brought Wyclif's doctrines and writings into their native land, especially to the University of Prague. The great propagator of Bohemian Wyclifism was to be John Huss, in whom, also, all Czech national aspirations were to have an ardent advocate. It was this combination of religious and patriotic zeal that gave Huss his remarkable power of leadership.

John Huss was born, of peasant parentage, in Husinecz, whence he derived his name by abbreviation, about the year 1373. His studies were completed in the University of Prague, where he became Bachelor of Theology in 1394, and Master of Arts two years later. In 1401 he was ordained to the priesthood, still maintaining a teaching connection with the university, of which he was "rector" in 1402. Meanwhile Huss had become intimately acquainted with Wyclif's philosophical treatises, with the "realism" of which he sympathized. Wyclif's religious works, known by Huss certainly from 1402, won his approbation, and henceforth Huss was, theologically, a disciple of Wyclif. More conservative than his master, he did not deny transubstantiation; but like him he held the church to consist of the predestinate only, of whom the true head is not the Pope, but Christ, and of which the law is the New Testament, and its life that of Christ-like poverty. Though the publication of Huss's commentary on the *Sentences* of Peter Lombard has led to a higher estimate of his scholarly gifts than formerly prevailed, it is certain that in his sermons and treatises Huss usually reproduced not only the thoughts but the language of Wyclif.

In 1402 Huss became preacher at the Bethlehem chapel, in Prague, and soon gained immense popular following through his fiery sermons in the Bohemian language. Though Wyclifite views were condemned by the majority of the university in 1403 Huss's preaching had, at first, the support of the archbishop, Zbynek (1403–1411); but his criticisms of the clergy gradually turned this favor into opposition, which was increased as Huss's essential agreement with Wyclif constantly became more evident. New causes of dissent speedily arose. In the schism Bohemia had held to the Roman Pope, Gregory XII (1406–1415). As a step toward the healing of the breach King Wenzel of Bohemia now favored a policy of neutrality between the rival Popes. Huss and the Bohemian element in the university supported Wenzel. Archbishop Zbynek, the German clergy, and the German portion of the university clung to Gregory XII. Wenzel therefore, in 1409, arbitrarily changed the constitution of the university, giving the foreign majority one vote in its decisions and the Bohemians three, thus completely reversing the previous proportion. The immediate result was the secession of the foreign elements and the foundation, in 1409, of the University of Leipzig. This Bohemian nationalist victory, of doubtful permanent worth or right, Huss fully shared. Its immediate consequences were that he became the first "rector" of the newly regulated university, and enjoyed a high degree of courtly favor. His views were now spreading widely in Bohemia.

Meanwhile the luckless Council of Pisa had run its course (1409) (see p. 307). Zbynek now supported its Pope, Alexander V (1409–1410), to whom he complained of the spread of Wyc-

lifite opinions in Bohemia, and by whom he was commissioned
to root them out. Huss protested, and was excommunicated
by Zbynek in 1410. The result was great popular tumult in
Prague, where Huss was more than ever a national hero.
King Wenzel supported him. In 1412 Alexander V's successor,
Pope John XXIII (1410–1415), promised indulgence to all who
should take part in a crusade against King Ladislaus of Naples.
Huss opposed, holding that the Pope had no right to use physical force, that money payments effected no true forgiveness,
and, unless of the predestinate, the indulgence could be of no
value to a man. The result was an uproar. The Pope's bull
was burned by the populace. Huss, however, lost many
strong supporters in the university and elsewhere, and was
once more excommunicated, while Prague was placed under
papal interdict. Wenzel now persuaded Huss, late in 1412, to
go into exile from Prague. To this period of retirement is
due the composition of his chief work—essentially a reproduction of Wyclif—the *De Ecclesia (On the Church)*. In 1413 a
synod in Rome formally condemned Wyclif's writings.

The great Council of Constance (see p. 308) was approaching,
and the confusion in Bohemia was certain to demand its consideration. Huss was asked to present himself before it, and
promised a "safe-conduct," afterward received, by the Holy
Roman Emperor, Sigismund. Huss, though he felt his life in
grave peril, determined to go, partly believing it his duty to
bear witness to what he deemed the truth, and partly convinced
that he could bring the council to his way of thinking. Shortly
after his arrival in Constance he was imprisoned. Sigismund
disregarded his promised safe-conduct. His Bohemian enemies
laid bitter charges against him. On May 4, 1415, the council
condemned Wyclif, and ordered his long-buried body burned.
Huss could hope for no favorable hearing. Yet, in the end,
the struggle resolved itself into a contest of principles. The
council maintained that every Christian was bound to submit
to its decisions. Only by so holding could it hope to end the
papal schism which was the scandal of Christendom. It insisted on Huss's complete submission. The Bohemian reformer
was of heroic mould. He would play no tricks with his conscience. Some of the accusations he declared false charges.
Other positions he could not modify unless convinced of their
error. He would not submit his conscience to the overruling

judgment of the council.   On July 6, 1415, he was condemned and burned, meeting his death with the most steadfast courage.

While Huss was a prisoner in Constance his followers in Prague began administering the cup to the laity in the Lord's Supper—an action which Huss approved and which soon became the badge of the Hussite movement.   The news of Huss's death aroused the utmost resentment in Bohemia, to which fuel was added when the Council of Constance forbade the use of the cup by laymen, and caused Huss's disciple, Jerome of Prague, to be burned in 1416.   Bohemia was in revolution. Two parties speedily developed there—an aristocratic, having its principal seat in Prague, and known as the Utraquists (communion in both bread and wine), and a radical, democratic, called from its fortress, the Taborites.

The Utraquists would forbid only those practices which they deemed prohibited by the "law of God," *i. e.*, the Bible.   They demanded free preaching of the Gospel, the cup for the laity, apostolic poverty, and strict clerical life.   The Taborites repudiated all practices for which express warrant could not be found in the "law of God."   Fierce quarrel existed between these factions, but both united to resist repeated crusades directed against Bohemia.   Under the leadership cf the blind Taborite general, John Zizka, all attempts to crush the Hussites were bloodily defeated.   Church property was largely confiscated.   Nor were the opponents of the Hussites more successful after Zizka's death in 1424.   Under Prokop the Great the Hussites carried the war beyond the borders of Bohemia.   Some compromise seemed unavoidable.   The Council of Basel (see p. 310), after long negotiation, therefore, met the wishes of the Utraquists part way in 1433, granting the use of the cup, and in a measure the other demands outlined above.   The Taborites resisted and were almost swept away by the Utraquists, in 1434, at the battle of Lipau, in which Prokop was killed.   The triumphant Utraquists now came to an agreement with the Council of Basel, in 1436, and on these terms were nominally given place in the Roman communion. Yet, in 1462 Pope Pius II (1458–1464) declared this agreement void.   The Utraquists, nevertheless, held their own, and the Bohemian Parliament, in 1485 and 1512, declared their full equality with the Catholics.   At the Reformation a considerable portion welcomed the newer ideas; others then returned to the Roman Church.

The real representatives of Wyclifite principles were the Taborites rather than the Utraquists. Out of the general Hussite movement, with elements drawn from Taborites, Utraquists, and Waldenses, rather than exclusively from the Taborites there grew, from about 1453, the *Unitas Fratrum,* which absorbed much that was most vital in the Hussite movement, and became the spiritual ancestor of the later Moravians (see pp. 502, 503).

Wyclif and Huss have often been styled forerunners of the Reformation. The designation is true if regard is had to their protest against the corruption of the church, their exaltation of the Bible, and their contribution to the sum total of agitation that ultimately resulted in reform. When their doctrines are examined, however, they appear to belong rather to the Middle Ages. Their conception of the Gospel was that of a "law." Their place for faith was no greater than in the Roman communion. Their thought of the church was a one-sided development of Augustinianism. Their conception of the relation of the clergy to property is that common to the Waldenses and the founders of the great mendicant orders. Their religious earnestness commands deep admiration, but in spite of Luther's recognition of many points of agreement with Huss, the Reformation owed little to their efforts.

SECTION XIII. THE REFORMING COUNCILS

The papal schism was the scandal of Christendom, but its termination was not easy. The logic of mediæval development was that no power exists on earth to which the papacy is answerable. Yet good men everywhere felt that the schism must be ended, and that the church must be reformed "in head and members"—that is, in the papacy and clergy. The reforms desired were moral and administrative. Doctrinal modifications were as yet unwished by Christendom as a whole. A Wyclif might proclaim them in England, but he was generally esteemed a heretic. Foremost among those who set themselves seriously to the task of healing the schism were the teachers of the age, especially those of the University of Paris. Marsilius of Padua had there proclaimed the supremacy of a general coun-

cil in his *Defensor Pacis* of 1324.   The necessities of the situation rather than his arguments were rapidly leading to the same
conclusion.   It was presented first with clearness by a doctor
of canon law, then in Paris, Conrad of Gelnhausen (1320?–
1390), who advised King Charles V of France (1364–1380), in
written treatises of 1379 and 1380, to unite with other princes
in calling a council, if necessary, without the consent of the
rival Popes.   Conrad went no further than to hold that such
a council was justified by the necessities of an anomalous
situation.   Conrad's proposal was reinforced, in such fashion
as to rob him of the popular credit of its origination, by the
treatise of another German scholar at the University of Paris,
Heinrich of Langenstein (1340?–1397), set forth in 1381.

The thought of a general council as the best means of healing
the schism, thus launched, made speedy converts, not only in
the University of Paris, but in the great school of canon law in
Bologna, and even among the cardinals.   To call a council
presented many difficulties, however, and the leaders at Paris,
Peter of Ailli (Pierre d'Ailli) (1350–1420) and John Gerson
(Jean Charlier de Gerson) (1363–1429), famed for their mastery
of nominalistic theology, and the latter eminent among Christian mystics, were slow to adopt the conciliar plan.   Efforts
were vainly made for years to induce the rival Popes to resign.
France withdrew from the Avignon Pope, without recognizing
the Roman, from 1398 to 1403, and again in 1408; but its example found slight following elsewhere.   By 1408 d'Ailli and
Gerson had come to see in a council the only hope, and were
supported by Nicholas of Clémanges (1367–1437), a former
teacher of the Parisian university who had been papal secretary
in Avignon from 1397 to 1405, to whom one great source of
evil in the church seemed the general neglect of the Scriptures.

The cardinals of both Popes were now convinced of the
necessity of a council.   Meeting together in Leghorn, in 1408,
they now issued a call in their own names for such an assembly
in Pisa, to gather on March 25, 1409.   There it met with an
attendance not only of cardinals, bishops, the heads of the great
orders, and leading abbots, but also of doctors of theology and
canon law, and the representatives of lay sovereigns.   Neither
Pope was present or acknowledged its rightfulness.   Both were
declared deposed.   This was a practical assertion that the
council was superior to the papacy.   Its action, however, was

too hasty, for instead of ascertaining, as d'Ailli advised, whether the person of the proposed new Pope would be generally acceptable, the cardinals now elected Peter Philargès, archbishop of Milan, who took the name Alexander V (1409–1410). The council then dissolved, leaving the question of reform to a future council.

In some respects the situation was worse than before the Council of Pisa met. Rome, Naples, and considerable sections of Germany clung to Gregory XII. Spain, Portugal, and Scotland supported Benedict XIII. England, France, and some portions of Germany acknowledged Alexander V. There were three Popes where before there had been two. Yet, though mismanaged, the Council of Pisa was a mark of progress. It had shown that the church was one, and it increased the hope that a better council could end the schism. This assembly had been called by the cardinals. For such invitation history had no precedent. A summons by the Emperor, if possible with the consent of one or more of the Popes, would be consonant with the practice of the early church. To that end those supporting the council idea now labored.

The new Holy Roman Emperor-elect, Sigismund (1410–1437), was convinced of the necessity of a council. He recognized as Pope John XXIII (1410–1415), one of the least worthy of occupants of that office, who had been chosen successor to Alexander V in the Pisan line. Sigismund used John's difficulties with King Ladislaus of Naples, to secure from him joint action by which Emperor-elect and Pope called a council to meet in Constance on November 1, 1414. There the most brilliant and largely attended gathering of the Middle Ages assembled. As in Pisa, it included not only cardinals and bishops, but doctors of theology and representatives of monarchs, though the lay delegates were without votes. Sigismund was present in person, and also John XXIII.

John XXIII hoped to secure the indorsement of the council. To this end he had brought with him many Italian bishops. To neutralize their votes the council organized by "nations," the English, German, and French, to which the Italians were forced to join as a fourth. Each "nation" had one vote, and one was assigned also to the cardinals. Despairing of the council's approval, John XXIII attempted to disrupt its session by flight, in March, 1415. Under Gerson's vigorous leadership the council, however, declared on April 6, 1415, that as "representing the Catholic Church militant [it] has its power immediately from Christ, and every one, whatever his position or rank, even if it be the papal dignity itself, is bound to obey it in all those things which pertain to the faith, to the healing of the schism, and to the general reformation of the Church of God."[1] On May 29 the council declared John XXIII deposed. On July 4 Gregory XII resigned. The council had rid the church of two Popes by its successful assertion of its supreme authority over all in the church. It is easy to see why its leaders insisted on a full submission from Huss, whose trials and martyrdom were contemporary with these events (*ante*, p. 304).

Benedict XIII proved more difficult. Sigismund himself, therefore, journeyed to Spain. Benedict he could not persuade to resign, and that obstinate pontiff asserted himself till death, in 1422 or 1423, as the only legitimate Pope. What Sigismund was unable to effect with Benedict he accomplished with the Spanish kingdoms. They and Scotland repudiated Benedict. The Spaniards joined the council as a fifth "nation," and, on July 26, 1417, Benedict, or Peter de Luna, as he was once more called, was formally deposed. The careful action of the council, in contrast to the haste in Pisa, had made it certain that no considerable section of Christendom would support the former Popes.

One main purpose of the council had been moral and administrative reform. Here the jealousies of the several interests prevented achievement of real importance. The cardinals desired no changes that would materially lessen their revenue. Italy, on the whole, profited by the existing situation. England had relative self-government already in ecclesiastical affairs, thanks to its Kings. France was at war with England, and indisposed to unite with that land. So it went, with the result that the council finally referred the question of reforms to the next Pope "in conjunction with this holy council or with the deputies of the several nations"—that is each nation was left to make the best bargain it could. The council enumerated a list of subjects for reform discussion, which relate almost entirely to questions of appointment, taxation, or administration.[2] As a reformatory instrument the Council of Constance

[1] Robinson, 1 : 511.   [2] *Ibid.*, 1 : 513.

was a bitter disappointment. Its one great achievement was that it ended the schism. In November, 1417, the cardinals, with six representatives from each nation, elected a Roman cardinal, Otto Colonna, as Pope. He took the name Martin V (1417–1431). Roman Christendom had once more a single head. In April, 1418, the council ended, the new Pope promising to call another in five years, in compliance with the decree of the council.[1]

The Council of Constance was a most interesting ecclesiastical experiment. It secured the transformation of the papacy from an absolute into a constitutional monarchy. The Pope was to remain the executive of the church, but was to be regulated by a legislative body, meeting at frequent intervals and representing all interests in Christendom.

It seemed that this great constitutional change had really been accomplished. Martin V called the new council to meet in Pavia in 1423. The plague prevented any considerable attendance. The Pope would gladly have had no more of councils. The Hussite wars distressed Europe, however (*ante*, p. 305), and such pressure was brought to bear on him that in January, 1431, Martin V summoned a council to meet in Basel, and appointed Cardinal Giuliano Cesarini his legate to conduct it. Less than two months later Martin V was dead and Eugene IV (1431–1447) was Pope. The council opened in July, 1431, but in December Eugene ordered it adjourned, to meet in Bologna in 1433. The council refused, and re-enacted the declaration of Constance that it was superior to the Pope. Thus, almost from the first, bad feeling existed between the Council of Basel and the papacy. Mindful that jealousies between "nations" had frustrated the reform plans in Constance, the council rejected such groupings, and instead organized four large committees, on reform, doctrine, public peace, and general questions. It began its work with great vigor and promise of success. It made an apparent reconciliation with the moderate Hussites in 1433 (*ante*, p. 305). Roman unity seemed restored. The Pope found little support and, before the close of 1433, formally recognized the council. Its future seemed assured.

The Council of Basel now proceeded to those administrative and moral reforms which had failed of achievement at Con-

[1] Robinson, 1 : 512.

stance.   It ordered the holding of a synod in each diocese annually, and in each archbishopric every two years, in which
abuses should be examined and corrected.   It provided for a
general council every ten years.   It reasserted the ancient
rights of canonical election against papal appointments.   It
limited appeals to Rome.   It fixed the cardinals at twenty-four
in number, and ordered that no nation should be represented
by more than a third of the college.   It cut off the annates and
the other more oppressive papal taxes entirely.   All this was
good, but the spirit in which it was done was increasingly a
vindictive attitude toward Pope Eugene.   The taxes by which
the papacy had heretofore been maintained were largely abolished, but no honorable support of the papacy was provided in
their stead.   This failure not only increased the anger of the
papacy but caused division in the council itself.   At this point
a great opportunity presented itself, of which Eugene IV made
full use, and regarding which the council so put itself in the
wrong as to ruin its prospects.

The Eastern empire was now hard pressed in its final struggles with the conquering Turks.   In the hope of gaining help
from the West the Emperor, John VIII (1425–1448), with the
patriarch of Constantinople, Joseph II (1416–1439) and Bessarion (1395–1472), the gifted archbishop of Nicæa, were ready
to enter into negotiation for the union of the Greek and Latin
Churches.   Both Pope and council were disposed to use this
approach for their several advantage.   The majority of the
council would have the Greeks come to Avignon.   The Pope
offered an Italian city, which the Greeks naturally preferred.
The council divided on the issue in 1437, the minority seceding,
including Cesarini.   The Pope now announced the transferrence
of the council to Ferrara to meet the Greeks.   Thither the
minority went, and there in March, 1438, the Eastern Emperor,
with many Oriental prelates, arrived.   The Pope had practically won.   An event so full of promise as the reunion of
Christendom robbed the still continuing Council of Basel of
much of its interest.

The Council of Ferrara, which was transferred to Florence
in 1439, witnessed protracted discussion between Greeks and
Latins, in which as a final result the primacy of the Pope was
accepted in vague terms, which seemed to preserve the rights
of the Eastern patriarchs, the Greeks retained their peculiarities

of worship and priestly marriage, while the disputed *filioque* clause of the creed was acknowledged by the Greeks, though with the understanding that they would not add it to the ancient symbol.   Mark, the vigorous archbishop of Ephesus, refused agreement, but the Emperor and most of his ecclesiastical following approved, and the reunion of the two churches was joyfully proclaimed in July, 1439.   An event so happy greatly increased the prestige of Pope Eugene IV.   The hollowness of the achievement was not at once apparent.   Reunions with the Armenians, and with certain groups of Monophysites and Nestorians, were also announced in Florence or speedily after the council.   The reconciliation of the Armenians in 1439 was the occasion of a famous papal bull defining the mediæval doctrine of the sacraments.   Yet from the first the Oriental monks were opposed.   On the Greeks' return Mark of Ephesus became the hero of the hour.   Bessarion, whom Eugene had made a cardinal, had to fly to Italy, where he was to have a distinguished career of literary and ecclesiastical service.   No efficient military help came to the Greeks from the West, and the capture of Constantinople by the Turks in 1453 permanently frustrated those political hopes which had inspired the union efforts of 1439.

Meanwhile the majority in Basel proceeded to more radical action under the leadership of its only remaining cardinal, the able and excellent but dictatorial Louis d'Allemand (1380?–1450).   In 1439 it voted Eugene IV deposed, and chose as his successor a half-monastic layman, Duke Amadeus of Savoy, who took the name Felix V.   By this time, however, the Council of Basel was fast losing its remaining influence.   Eugene IV had won, and was succeeded in Rome by Nicholas V (1447–1455).   Felix V laid down his impossible papacy in 1449.   The council put the best face on its defeat by choosing Nicholas V his successor, and ended its troubled career.   Though the council idea still lived and was to be powerful in the Reformation age, the fiasco in Basel had really ruined the hope of transforming the papacy into a constitutional monarchy or of effecting needed reform through conciliar action.

Yet if the council thus failed, individual nations profited by its quarrel with the papacy, notably France, where the monarchy was coming into new power through effective resistance to England under impulses initiated by Joan of Arc (1410?–

1431). In 1438 King Charles VII (1422–1461), with the clergy and nobles, adopted the "pragmatic sanction" of Bourges, by which the greater part of the reforms attempted in Basel were enacted into law for France. France therefore secured relief from the most pressing papal taxes and interferences, and this freedom had not a little to do with the attitude of the land previous to the Reformation age.

Not so fortunate was Germany. There the nobles in the Reichstag in Mainz of 1439 adopted an "acceptation" much resembling the French "pragmatic sanction"; but the divisions and weakness of the country gave room to papal intrigue, so that its provisions were practically limited by the Concordat of Aschaffenburg of 1448. Certain privileges were granted to particular princes; but Germany, as a whole, remained under the weight of the papal taxation.

Throughout the period of the councils a new force was manifesting itself—that of nationality. The Council of Constance had voted by nations. It had authorized the nations to make terms with the papacy. Bohemia had dealt with its religious situation as a nation. France had asserted its national rights. Germany had tried to do so. With the failure of the councils to effect administrative reform, men began asking whether what they had sought might not be secured by national action. It was a feeling that was to increase till the Reformation, and greatly to influence the course of that struggle.

SECTION XIV.   THE ITALIAN RENAISSANCE AND ITS POPES

The most remarkable intellectual event contemporary with the story of the papacy in Avignon and the schism was the beginning of the Renaissance. That great alteration in mental outlook has been treated too often as without mediæval antecedents. It is coming to be recognized that the Middle Ages were not uncharacterized by individual initiative, that the control of the church was never such as to make other-worldliness wholly dominant, and that the literary monuments of Latin antiquity, at least, were widely known. The revival of Roman law had begun contemporaneously with the Crusades, and had attracted increasing attention to that normative feature of ancient thought, first in Italy and later in France and Germany. Yet when all these elements are recognized, it remains true that the Renaissance involved an essentially new outlook on the world, in which emphasis was laid on its present life, beauty, and satisfaction—on man as man—rather than on a future heaven and hell, and on man as an object of salvation or of loss. The means by which this transformation was wrought was a reappreciation of the spirit of classical antiquity, especially as manifested in its great literary monuments.

The Renaissance first found place in Italy. Its rise was favored by many influences, among which three, at least, were conspicuous. The two great dominating powers of the Middle Ages, the papacy and empire, were suddenly lamed, as far as Italy was concerned, by the collapse of the imperial power in the latter part of the thirteenth century and the removal of the papacy to Avignon early in the fourteenth. The commerce of Italy, fostered by the Crusades and continuing after their close, had led to a higher cultural development in the peninsula than elsewhere in Europe. The intense division of Italian politics gave to the cities a quality of life not elsewhere existent, rendering local recognition of talent easy, and tending to emphasize individualism.

The earliest Italian in whom the Renaissance spirit was a dominating force was Petrarch (1304–1374). Brought up in Avignon, and in clerical orders, his real interest was in the revival of Latin literature, especially the writings of Cicero. A diligent student, and above all a man of letters, he was the friend of princes, and a figure of international influence. Scholasticism he despised. Aristotle he condemned. Though really religious in feeling, however lacking in practice, his point of view was very unlike the mediæval. He had, moreover, that lack of profound seriousness, that egotistical vanity and that worship of form rather than of substance which were to be characteristic of much of Italian humanism; but he aroused men to a new interest in antiquity and a new world-outlook. Petrarch's friend and disciple was Boccaccio (1313–1375), now chiefly remembered for his *Decameron,* but greatly influential in his own age in promoting the study of Greek, in unlocking the mysteries of classical mythology, and in furthering humanistic studies in Florence and Naples.

Greek may never have died out in southern Italy, but its humanistic cultivation began when, in 1360, Boccaccio brought Leontius Pilatus to Florence. About 1397 Greek was taught, under the auspices of the government of the same city, by Manuel Chrysoloras (1355?–1415), who translated Homer and Plato. The Council of Ferrara and Florence (1438–1439) (*ante*, p. 311) greatly fostered this desire to master the treasures of the East by bringing Greeks and Latins together. Bessarion (*ante*, p. 312) thenceforth aided the work. To the influence of Gemistos Plethon (1355–1450), another Greek attendant on this reunion council, was due the founding of the Platonic Academy, about 1442, by Cosimo de' Medici (1389–1464), the real ruler of Florence. There the study of Plato was pursued ardently, later, under the leadership of Marsilio Ficino (1433–1499). Ficino, who became a priest, combined an earnest Christianity with his platonic enthusiasm. He believed a return to the Christian sources the chief need of the time—a feeling not shared by the majority of Italian humanists, but to be profoundly influential beyond the Alps, as propagated by his admirers, Jacques Le Fèvre in France and John Colet in England. Colet, in turn, transmitted it to Erasmus. Almost as influential was Pico della Mirandola (1463–1494), whose zeal for Hebrew and knowledge of the Kabala were to influence Reuchlin.

Historical criticism was developed by Lorenzo Valla (1405–1457), who exposed the falsity of the Donation of Constantine (*ante*, p. 204) about 1440, and denied the composition of the Apostles' Creed by the Apostles. He criticised the rightfulness of monastic vows, and laid the foundation of New Testament studies, in 1444, by a comparison of the Vulgate with the Greek.

An examination of the dates just given will show that the Renaissance movement in Italy was in full development before the fall of Constantinople, in 1453. By the middle of the fifteenth century it was dominating the educated class in Italy. In general, its attitude toward the church was one of indifference. It revived widely a pagan point of view, and sought to reproduce the life of antiquity in its vices as well as its virtues. Few periods in the world's history have been so boastfully corrupt as that of the Italian Renaissance.

The Renaissance movement was given wings by a great invention, about 1440–1450—that of printing from movable type. Whether Mainz or Strassburg, in Germany, or Haarlem in Holland was its birthplace is still a matter of learned dispute. The art spread with rapidity, and not only rendered the possession of the many the books which had heretofore been the property of the few, but, from the multiplication of copies, made the results of learning practically indestructible. More than thirty thousand publications were issued before 1500.

No mention of the Renaissance could fail to note its services to art. Beginnings of better things had been made, indeed, in Italy before its influence was felt. Cimabue (1240?-1302?), Giotto (1267?-1337), and Fra Angelico (1387-1455) belong to the pre-Renaissance epoch, remarkable as is their work. With Masaccio (1402-1429), Filippo Lippi (1406-1469), Botticelli (1444-1510), and Ghirlandajo (1449-1494), painting advanced through truer knowledge of perspective, greater anatomical accuracy, and more effective grouping to the full noonday of a Leonardo da Vinci (1452-1519), a Raphael Sanzio (1483-1520), a Michelangelo Buonarroti (1475-1564), and their mighty associates. Sculpture received a similar impulse in the work of Ghiberti (1378-1455), and Donatello (1386-1466); while architecture was transformed by Brunelleschi (1379-1446), Bramante (1444?-1514), and Michelangelo. Most of the work of these great artists, however classical in motive, was wrought in the service of the church.

The most conspicuous early seat of the Italian Renaissance was Florence, though it was influential in many cities. With the papacy of Nicholas V (1447-1455), it found, for the first time, a mighty patron in the head of the church, and Rome became its chief home. To him the foundation of the Vatican library was due. The next Pope, Alfonso Borgia, a Spaniard, who took the name Calixtus III (1455-1458), was no friend of humanism, and was earnestly though fruitlessly, intent on a crusade that should drive the Turks from the recently conquered Constantinople. In Enea Silvio Piccolomini, who ruled as Pius II (1458-1464), the papacy had a remarkable occupant. In early life a supporter of the conciliar movement, and active at the Council of Basel, he had won distinction as a humanistic writer of decidedly unclerical tone. Reconciled to Eugene IV, he became a cardinal, and ultimately Pope, now opposing all the conciliar views that he had once supported, and forbidding future appeals to a general council. His efforts to stir Europe against the Turks were unavailing. Yet, in spite of his changing and self-seeking attitude, he had the most worthy conception of the duties of the papal office of any Pope of the latter half of the fifteenth century. The succeeding Popes, till after the dawn of the Reformation, were patrons of letters and artists, great builders who adorned Rome and felt the full impulse of the Renaissance.

Meanwhile a change had come over the ideals and ambitions of the papacy. The stay in Avignon and the schism had rendered effective control in the States of the Church impossible. They were distracted by the contests of the people of Rome, and especially by the rivalries of the noble houses, notably those of the Colonna and the Orsini. Italy had gradually consolidated into five large states, Venice, Milan, Florence, Naples, or the Kingdom of the Two Sicilies, as it was called, and the States of the Church, though many smaller territories remained outside these larger groups, and were objects of contest. The politics of Italy became a kaleidoscopic effort to extend the possessions of the larger powers, and to match one against the other, in which intrigue, murder, and duplicity were employed to an almost unexampled extent.

Into this game of Italian politics the papacy now fully plunged. Its desire was to consolidate and increase the States of the Church and maintain political independence. Its ambitions and its aims were like those of other Italian rulers. The papacy became secularized as at no other period in its history, save possibly the tenth century. Martin V (1417–1431), the Pope chosen at the Council of Constance, himself a Colonna, succeeded, in a measure, in restoring papal authority in Rome. His successor, Eugene IV (1431–1447), was not so fortunate, and spent a large part of his pontificate in Florence. Nicholas V (1447–1455), the humanist, effectively controlled Rome and strengthened the papal authority—a policy which was continued by Calixtus III (1455–1458), Pius II (1458–1464), and Paul II (1464–1471). With Sixtus IV (1471–1484) political ambition took almost complete control of the papacy. He warred with Florence, he sought to enrich and advance his relatives, he aimed to extend the States of the Church. A patron of learning, he built extensively. The Sistine Chapel preserves his name. All these endeavors required money, and he increased papal taxation and the financial abuses of the curia. He made into an article of faith the wide-spread belief that indulgences are available for souls in purgatory by a bull of 1476.[1]

[1] Kidd, *Documents Illustrative of the Continental Reformation*, p. 3.

The next Pope, Innocent VIII (1484–1492), was of weak and pliant nature, notorious through the open manner in which he sought to advance the fortunes of his children, his extravagant expenditures, and his sale of offices. He even received a pension from Sultan Bayazid II for keeping the latter's brother and rival, Jem, a prisoner. Innocent's successor, Alexander VI (1492–1503), a nephew of Calixtus III, and a Spaniard (Rodrigo Borgia), obtained the papacy not without bribery, and was a man of unbridled immorality, though of considerable political insight. His great effort was to advance his bastard children, especially his daughter, Lucrezia Borgia, by advantageous marriages, and his unscrupulous and murderous son, Cesare Borgia, by aiding him to carve a principality out of the States of the Church. His reign saw the beginning of the collapse of Italian independence through the invasion of Charles VIII of France (1483–1498), in 1494, in an attempt to assert the French King's claim to the throne of Naples. In 1499 Louis XII of France (1498–1515), conquered Milan, and in 1503 Ferdinand the Catholic, of Spain (1479–1516), secured Naples. Italy became the wretched battleground of French and Spanish rivalries.

Under such circumstances to increase the temporal power of the papacy was not easy; but the task was achieved by the most warlike of the Popes, Julius II (1503–1513), nephew of Sixtus IV. The Orsini and Colonna were reconciled, Cesare Borgia driven from Italy, the cities of Romagna freed from their Venetian conquerors, the various nations in Europe grouped in leagues, with the result that the French were, for the time, expelled from Italy. In this contest Louis XII secured a parody of a general council in Pisa, which Pope Julius answered by calling the Fifth Lateran Council in Rome. It met from 1512 to 1517, and though reforms were ordered it accomplished nothing of importance. Julius II was undoubtedly a ruler of great talents, who led his soldiers personally, and was animated by a desire to strengthen the temporal power of the papacy, rather than to enrich his relatives. As a patron of art and a builder he was among the most eminent of the Popes.

Julius II was succeeded by Giovanni de' Medici, who took the name Leo X (1513–1521). With all the artistic and literary tastes of the great Florentine family of which he was a member, he combined a love of display and extravagant expenditure.

Far less warlike than Julius II, and free from the personal vices of some of his predecessors, he nevertheless made his prime interests the enlargement of the States of the Church, and the balancing of the various factions of Italy, domestic and foreign, for the political advantage of the papacy. He strove to advance his relatives. In 1516 he secured by a "concordat" with Francis I of France (1515–1547) the abolition of the "Pragmatic Sanction" (*ante,* p. 313) on terms which left to the King the nomination of all high French ecclesiastics and the right to tax the clergy, while the annates and other similar taxes went to the Pope. The next year a revolt began in Germany, the gravity of which Leo never really comprehended, which was to tear half of Europe from the Roman obedience.

Such Popes represented the Italian Renaissance, but they in no sense embodied the real spirit of a church which was to millions the source of comfort in this life and of hope for that to come. A revolution was inevitable. Nor did such a papacy represent the real religious life of Italy. The Renaissance affected only the educated and the upper classes. The people responded to appeals of preachers and the example of those they believed to be saints, though unfortunately seldom with lasting results save on individual lives.

Such a religious leader, when the Renaissance was young, was St. Catherine (1347–1380), the daughter of a dyer of Siena. A mystic, the recipient as she believed of divinely sent visions, she was a practical leader of affairs, a healer of family quarrels, a main cause in persuading the papacy to return from Avignon to Rome, a fearless denouncer of clerical evils, and an ambassador to whom Popes and cities listened with respect. Her correspondence involved counsel of almost as much political as religious value to many of the leaders of the age in church and state alike.

Even more famous in the later period of the Renaissance was Girolamo Savonarola of Florence (1452–1498). A native of Ferrara, intended for the medical profession, a refusal of marriage turned his thoughts to a monastic life. In 1474 he became a Dominican in Bologna. Eight years later his work in Florence began. At first little successful as a preacher, he came to speak with immense popular effectiveness, that was heightened by the general conviction which he himself shared that he was a divinely inspired prophet. He was in no sense a Protestant.

His religious outlook was thoroughly mediæval. The French invasion of 1494 led to a popular revolution against the Medici, and Savonarola now became the real ruler of Florence, which he sought to transform into a penitential city. A semi-monastic life was adopted by many of the inhabitants. At the carnival seasons of 1496 and 1497, masks, indecent books and pictures were burned. For the time being the life of Florence was radically changed. But Savonarola aroused enemies. The adherents of the deposed Medici hated him, and above all, Pope Alexander VI, whose evil character and misrule Savonarola denounced. The Pope excommunicated him and demanded his punishment. Friends sustained him for a while, but the fickle populace turned against him. In April, 1498, he was arrested, cruelly tortured, and on May 23 hanged and his body burned by the city government. Not the least of Alexander VI's crimes was his persecution of this preacher of righteousness, though Savonarola's death was due quite as much to Florentine reaction against him as to the hostility of the Pope.

SECTION XV. THE NEW NATIONAL POWERS

The half-century from 1450 to 1500 saw a remarkable growth in royal authority and national consciousness in the western kingdoms of Europe. France, which had seemed well-nigh ruined by the long wars with England, from 1339 to 1453, came out of them with the monarchy greatly strengthened, since these struggles had been immensely destructive to the feudal nobility. Louis XI (1461–1483), by intrigue, arms, and tyranny, with the aid of commoners, broke the power of the feudal nobility and secured for the crown an authority it had not hitherto possessed. His son, Charles VIII (1483–1498), was able to lead the now centralized state into a career of foreign conquest in Italy that was to open a new epoch in European politics and give rise to rivalries that were to determine the political background of the whole Reformation age. What these Kings had attempted in centralization at home, and in conquest abroad, was carried yet further by Louis XII (1498–1515), and by the brilliant and ambitious Francis I (1515–1547). France was now a strong, centralized monarchy. Its church was largely under royal control, and to a considerable degree relieved of the worst papal abuses, thanks to the "Pragmatic Sanction" of 1438 (*ante*, p. 313); and the custom which grew up with the strengthening of the monarchy in the fifteenth century that appeals could be taken from church courts to those of the King. The control of the monarchy over clerical appointments, clerical taxation, and clerical courts was increased by the "concordat" of 1516 (*ante*, p. 319), which gave to the Pope in turn desired taxes. By the dawn of the Reformation the church of France was, in many respects, a state church.

In England the Wars of the Roses, between Yorkists and Lancastrians, from 1455 to 1485, resulted in the destruction of the power of the high nobility to the advantage of the crown. Parliament survived. The King must rule in legal form; but the power of a Henry VII (1485–1509), the first of the house of Tudor, was greater than that of any English sovereign had been for a century, and was exercised with almost unlimited absolutism, though in parliamentary form, by his even abler son, Henry VIII (1509–1547). The English sovereigns had attained, even before the Reformation, a large degree of authority in ecclesiastical affairs, and, as in France, the church in England was largely national at the close of the fifteenth century.

This nationalizing process was nowhere in so full development as in Spain, where it was taking on the character of a religious awakening, which was to make that land a pattern for the conception of reform, often, though not very correctly, called the Counter-Reformation—a conception that was to oppose the Teutonic ideal of revolution, and was ultimately able to hold the allegiance of half of Europe to a purified Roman Church. The rise of Spain was the political wonder of the latter part of the fifteenth century. Aside from the main currents of mediæval European life, the history of the peninsula had been a long crusade to throw off the Mohammedan yoke, which had been imposed in 711. Nowhere in Europe were patriotism and Catholic orthodoxy so interwoven. The struggle had resulted, by the thirteenth century, in the restriction of the Moors to the kingdom of Granada, and in the formation of four Christian kingdoms, Castile, Aragon, Portugal, and Navarre. These states were weak, and the royal power limited by the feudal nobility. A radical change came when the prospective rulership of the larger part of the peninsula was united, in 1469, by the marriage of Ferdinand, heir of Aragon (King, 1479–1516) with Isabella, heiress of Castile (Queen, 1474–1504). Under their joint sovereignty Spain took a new place in European life. The disorderly nobles were repressed. The royal authority was asserted. In 1492 Granada was conquered and Mohammedanism overcome. The same year witnessed the discovery of a new world by Columbus, under Spanish auspices, which speedily became a source of very considerable revenue to the royal treasury. The French invasions of Italy led to Spanish interference, which lodged Spain firmly in Naples by 1503, and soon rendered Spanish influence predominant throughout Italy. On Ferdinand's death, in 1516, these great possessions passed to his grandson, already heir of Austria and the Netherlands, and to wear the imperial title as Charles V. Spain had suddenly become the first power in Europe.

The joint sovereigns, Ferdinand and Isabella, devoted themselves no less energetically to the control of the church than to the extension of their temporal authority. The "Spanish awakening" was in no sense unique. It did not differ in principle from much that had been attempted elsewhere in the later Middle Ages. No nation with a history like that of Spain could desire doctrinal change. It was intensely devoted to the system of which the papacy was the spiritual head. But it believed that papal aggressions in administrative affairs should be limited by royal authority, and that an educated, moral, and zealous clergy could, by the same power, be encouraged and maintained. It was by reason of the success with which these results were accomplished that the Spanish awakening became the model of the "Counter-Reformation."

No more conscientious or religiously minded sovereign ever ruled than Isabella, and if Ferdinand was primarily a politician, he was quick to see the political advantages of a policy that would place the Spanish church in subjection to the crown. In 1482 the joint sovereigns forced Pope Sixtus IV to agree to a concordat placing nomination to the higher ecclesiastical posts in the royal control. The policy thus begun was speedily extended by the energetic sovereigns. Papal bulls now required royal approval for promulgation. Church courts were supervised. The clergy were taxed for the benefit of the state.

Ferdinand and Isabella now proceeded to fill the important stations in the Spanish church not only with men devoted to the royal interests, but of strenuous piety and disciplinary zeal. In this effort they had the aid of many men of ability, but chief among them stood Gonzalez (or Francisco) Ximenes de Cisneros (1436–1517), in whom the Spanish awakening had its typical representative.

Born of a family of the lower nobility, Ximenes went to Rome after studies in Alcalá and Salamanca.   On his return, in 1465, after six years in the seat of the papacy, he showed great ability in church business and much talent as a preacher.   About 1480 he was appointed vicar-general of the diocese by Mendoza, then bishop of Siguenza.   In the full tide of success Ximenes now renounced all his honors and became a Franciscan monk of the strictest observance.   Not content with these austerities, he adopted the hermit's life.   In 1492, however, on recommendation of Mendoza, now become archbishop of Toledo, Queen Isabella appointed Ximenes her confessor, and consulted him in affairs of state as well as questions of conscience.   Queen and confessor worked in harmony, and under their vigorous action a thoroughgoing reform of discipline was undertaken in the disorderly monasteries of the land.   Ximenes's influence was but increased when, in 1495, on Isabella's insistence, and against his own protests, he became Mendoza's successor in the archbishopric of Toledo, not only the highest ecclesiastical post in Spain, but one with which the grand-chancellorship of Castile was united.   Here he maintained his ascetic life.   Supported by the Queen, he turned all the powers of his high office to rid Spain of unworthy clergy and monks. No opposition could thwart him, and more than a thousand monks are said to have left the peninsula rather than submit to his discipline.   The moral character and zeal of the Spanish clergy were greatly improved.

Ximenes, though no great scholar, saw the need of an educated clergy.   He had encountered Renaissance influences in Rome, and would turn them wholly to the service of the church. In 1498 he founded the University of Alcalá de Henares, to which he devoted a large part of his episcopal revenues, and where he gathered learned men, among them four professors of Greek and Hebrew.   A quarter of a century later Alcalá counted seven thousand students.   Though opposed to general reading of the Bible by the laity, Ximenes believed that the Scriptures should be the principal study of the clergy.   The noblest monument of this conviction is the Complutensian Polyglot (Alcalá = Complutum), on which he directed the labor from 1502 to 1517. The Old Testament was presented in Hebrew, Greek, and Latin, with the Targum on the Pentateuch; the New Testament in Greek and Latin. The New Testament was in print by 1515. To Ximenes belongs the honor, therefore, of first printing the New Testament in Greek, though as papal permission for publication could not be obtained till 1520, the Greek Testament, issued in 1516, by Erasmus, was earlier on the market.

The less attractive side of Ximenes's character is to be seen in his willingness to use force for the conversion of the Mohammedans. In affairs of state his firmness and wisdom were of vast service to Isabella, Ferdinand, and Charles V, till his death in 1517.

The intellectual impulse thus inaugurated by Ximenes led ultimately to a revival of the theology of Aquinas, begun by Francisco de Vittoria (?–1546) in Salamanca, and continued by Vittoria's disciples, the great Roman theologians of the early struggle with Protestantism, Domingo de Soto (1494–1560) and Melchior Cano (1525–1560).

Characteristic of the Spanish awakening was the reorganization of the inquisition. The Spanish temper viewed orthodoxy and patriotism as essentially one, and regarded the maintenance of their religions by Jews and Mohammedans, or relapse by such of those dissenters as had embraced Christianity, as perils to church and state alike. Accordingly, in 1480, Ferdinand and Isabella established the inquisition, entirely under royal authority, and with inquisitors appointed by the sovereign. It was this national character that was the distinguishing feature of the Spanish inquisition, and led to protests by Pope Sixtus IV, to which the sovereigns turned deaf ears. Supported by the crown, it speedily became a fearful instrument, under the leadership of Tomas Torquemada (1420–1498). Undoubtedly its value in breaking the independence of the nobles and replenishing the treasury by confiscation commended it to the sovereigns, but its chief claim to popular favor was its repression of heresy and dissent.

Spain had, therefore, at the close of the fifteenth century, the most independent national church of any nation in Europe, in which a moral and intellectual renewal—not destined to be permanent—was in more vigorous progress than elsewhere; yet a church intensely mediæval in doctrine and practice, and fiercely intolerant of all heresy.

In Germany the situation was very different. The empire lacked all real unity. The imperial crown, in theory elective, was worn by members of the Austrian house of Habsburg from 1438 to 1740, but the Emperors had power as possessors of their hereditary lands, rather than as holders of imperial authority. Under Frederick III (1440–1493) wars between the princes and cities and the disorder of the lower nobility, who lived too often by what was really highway robbery, kept the land in a turmoil which the Emperor was powerless to suppress. Matters were somewhat better under Maximilian I (1493–1519), and an attempt was made to give stronger central authority to the empire by frequent meetings of the old feudal Reichstag, the establishment of an imperial supreme court (1495), and the division of the empire into districts for the better preservation of public peace (1512). Efforts were made to form an imperial army and collect imperial taxes. These reforms had little vitality. The decisions of the court could not be enforced nor the taxes collected. The Reichstag was, indeed, to play a great rôle in the Reformation days, but it was a clumsy parliament, meeting in three houses, one of the imperial electors, the second of lay and spiritual princes, and the third of delegates from the free imperial cities. The lower nobles and the common people had no share in it.

The imperial cities were an important element in German life, owning no superior but the feeble rule of the Emperor. They were industrious and wealthy, but they were far from democratic in their government, and were thoroughly self-seeking as far as the larger interests of Germany were concerned. Their commercial spirit led them to resist the exactions of clergy and princes alike.

In no country of Europe was the peasantry in a state of greater unrest, especially in southwestern Germany, where insurrections occurred in 1476, 1492, 1512, and 1513. The peasants were serfs—a condition that had passed away in England, and largely in France. Their state had been made rapidly worse by the substitution of the Roman law—a law made largely for slaves—for the old legal customs, and by the close of the fifteenth century they were profoundly disaffected.

Yet if German national life as a whole was thus disordered and dissatisfied, the larger territories of Germany were growing stronger, and developing a kind of semi-independent local national life in themselves. This was notably true of Austria, electoral and ducal Saxony, Bavaria, Brandenburg, and Hesse. The power of their rulers was increasing, and they were beginning to exercise a local authority in churchly affairs, controlling the nomination of bishops and abbots, taxing the clergy, and limiting to some extent ecclesiastical jurisdiction. This local territorial churchmanship had not gone far, but that it existed was of the utmost importance in giving a framework which the Reformation was rapidly to develop when Roman obedience was rejected.

The years preceding the Reformation witnessed two marriages by the Habsburg rulers of Austria of the utmost importance for the political background of the Reformation age. In 1477 the death of Charles the Bold, the ambitious duke of Burgundy, left the heirship of his Burgundian territories and the Netherlands to his daughter, Mary. Her marriage that year, with Maximilian I, to the dissatisfaction of Louis XI of France, who seized upper Burgundy, sowed the seeds of quarrel between the Kings of France and the Habsburg line which were largely to determine the politics of Europe till 1756. Philip, the son of Maximilian and Mary, in turn married Juana, heiress of Ferdinand and Isabella of Spain. So it came about that Philip and Juana's son, Charles, became possessor of Austria, the Netherlands, and the wide-extended Spanish territories in Europe and the New World—a larger sovereignty than had been held by a single ruler since Charlemagne—to which the imperial title was added in 1519. Charles V became heir also to the rivalry between the Habsburg line to which he belonged and the Kings of France. That rivalry and the struggle for religious reform were to interplay throughout the Reformation age, constantly modifying each other.

SECTION XVI. RENAISSANCE AND OTHER INFLUENCES NORTH OF THE ALPS

Though the fifteenth century was a notable period of university foundation in Germany—no less than twelve coming into existence between 1409 and 1506—these new creations did not owe their existence to the Renaissance. They grew partly out of a strong desire for learning, but even more from the ambition of the larger territorial rulers to possess such schools in their own lands. An influence favorable to the ultimate triumph of humanism was the revival of the older realistic mediæval theology, and a tendency to go back of even the earlier schoolmen to Augustine, and to Neo-Platonic rather then Aristotelian conceptions. These revivals were strongly represented in the University of Paris by the last quarter of the fifteenth century, and spread thence to German universities with considerable following. They made for many the bridge to humanism, and they rendered possible that dominance of Augustinian conceptions which was to be characteristic of the Reformation age.

The Renaissance beyond the Alps was inaugurated by contact with Italian humanists at the Councils of Constance and Basel, but it did not become a powerful influence till near the close of the fifteenth century. Its conquests were earlier in Germany than in France, England, or Spain. Some considerable impulse was given by the learned mathematician and philosopher, Nicholas of Cues (1401–1464), who collected a notable library. He died a cardinal and bishop of Brixen. Many of its earlier representatives in Germany were little fitted, however, to commend it to the serious-minded. German students brought home from Italy the love of the classics, and also the loose living too often characteristic of the Italian Renaissance. Such were men like the vagabond poet, Peter Luder, who passed from university to university, a disreputable exponent of the new learning, from 1456 to 1474. A very different teacher, who had studied in Italy, was Rudolf Agricola (1443–1485), who closed his life as professor in Heidelberg. A man of worth and influence, he did much to further classical education in the fitting schools. Through Agricola's disciple, Alexander Hegius, who dominated the school in Deventer from 1482 to 1498, that foundation became a centre of classical instruction, of which Erasmus was to be the most famous pupil. By the close of the fifteenth century a great improvement in the teaching of Latin had taken place in the secondary schools of Germany.

Humanism found footing in the universities, not without severe struggle. Its earliest conquest was the University of

Vienna, where the semi-pagan Latin poet, Conrad Celtes (1459–1508), enjoyed the patronage of the humanistically inclined Emperor, Maximilian I. By the first decade of the sixteenth century, humanism was pressing into the Universities of Basel, Tübingen, Ingolstadt, Heidelberg, and Erfurt. It also found many patrons in the wealthy commercial cities, notably in Nuremberg, Strassburg, and Augsburg. So numerous were its sympathizers by the close of the fifteenth century that learned circles were being formed, like the Rhenish Literary Association, organized by Celtes in Mainz, in 1491, the members of which corresponded, circulated each other's works, and afforded mutual assistance. By 1500 humanism was becoming a vital factor in Germany.

German humanism presented many types, but was, in general, far less pagan and more serious-minded than that of Italy. Many of its leaders were sincere chruchmen, anxious to reform and purify religious life. It is to be seen at its best in its two most famous representatives, Reuchlin and Erasmus.

Born in humble circumstances, in Pforzheim, in 1455, Johann Reuchlin early gained local reputation as a Latinist, and was sent as companion to the young son of the margrave of Baden to the University of Paris, about 1472. Here, in Paris, he began the study of Greek, instruction in which had been offered there since 1470. In 1477 he received the master's degree in Basel, and there taught Greek. Even before his graduation he published a Latin dictionary (1475–1476). He studied law in Orléans and Poitiers, and in later life was much employed in judicial positions; but his interests were always primarily scholarly. The service of the count of Württemberg took him to Florence and Rome in 1482—cities which he visited again in 1490 and 1498. At Florence, even on his first visit, his acquaintance with Greek commanded admiration. There he met and was influenced by the scholars of the Platonic Academy (*ante*, p. 315), and from Pico della Mirandola (*ante*, p. 315) he acquired that strange interest in Kabalistic doctrines that added much to his fame in Germany. Reuchlin was regarded as the ablest Greek scholar of the closing years of the fifteenth century in Germany, and his influence in promotion of Greek studies was most fruitful.

Reuchlin had the Renaissance desire to return to the sources, and this led him first of non-Jewish scholars in Germany, to make a profound study of Hebrew that he might the better understand the Old Testament. The fruit of twenty years of this labor was the publication in 1506 of a Hebrew grammar and lexicon—*De Rudimentis Hebraicis*—which unlocked the treasures of that speech to Christian students. The bitter quarrel into which the peace-loving scholar was drawn by reason of these Hebrew studies, and with him all educated Germany, will be described in treating of the immediate antecedents of the Lutheran revolt. Reuchlin was no Protestant. He refused approval to the rising Reformation, which he witnessed till his death in 1522. But he did a service of immense importance to Biblical scholarship, and his intellectual heir was to be his grandnephew, that scholar among the reformers, Philip Melanchthon.

Desiderius Erasmus was born out of wedlock in Rotterdam, or Gouda, probably in 1466. The school in Deventer awakened his love of letters (*ante*, p. 327). His poverty drove him into an Augustinian monastery in Steyn, but he had no taste for the monastic life, nor for that of the priesthood, to which he was ordained in 1492. By 1495 he was studying in Paris. The year 1499 saw him in England, where he made the helpful friendship of John Colet, who directed him toward the study of the Bible and the Fathers. A few years of studious labors, chiefly in France and the Netherlands, saw him once more in England, in 1505, then followed a three years' sojourn in Italy. In 1509 he again returned to England, and now taught in the University of Cambridge, enjoying the friendship of many of the most distinguished men of the kingdom. The years 1515–1521 were spent for the most part in the service of Charles V in the Netherlands. From 1521 to his death in 1536 Basel, where he could have ample facilities for publication, was his principal home. He may thus be called a citizen of all Europe.

Erasmus was not an impeccable Latinist. His knowledge of Greek was rather superficial. He was, above all, a man of letters, who touched the issues of his time with consummate wit and brilliancy of expression; set forth daring criticism of clergy and civil rulers, and withal was moved by deep sincerity of purpose. Convinced that the church of his day was overlaid with superstition, corruption, and error, and that the monastic life was too often ignorant and unworthy, he had yet no wish to break with the church that he so freely criticised. He was too primarily intellectual to have sympathy with the Lutheran revolution, the excesses of which repelled him. He was too clear-sighted not to see the evils of the Roman Church. Hence neither side in the struggle that opened in the latter part of his life understood him, and his memory has been condemned by polemic writers, Protestant and Catholic. His own thought was that education, return to the sources of Christian truth, and flagellation of ignorance and immorality by merciless satire would bring the church to purity. To this end he labored. His *Handbook of the Christian Soldier* of 1502 was a simple, earnest presentation of an unecclesiastical Christianity, largely Stoic in character. His *Praise of Folly* of 1509 was a biting satire on the evils of his age in church and state. His *Familiar Colloquies* of 1518 were witty discussions in which fastings, pilgrimages, and similar external observances were the butts of his brilliant pen. His constructive work was of the highest importance. In 1516 came the first edition of his Greek Testament, the pioneer publication of the Greek text, for that of Ximenes was still inaccessible (*ante*, p. 324). This was followed by a series of the Fathers—Jerome, Origen, Basil, Cyril, Chrysostom, Irenæus, Ambrose, and Augustine, not all wholly from his pen, but all from his impulse, which placed scholarly knowledge of early Christianity on a new plane, and profoundly aided a Reformation, the deeper religious springs of which Erasmus never understood. Erasmus rendered a service for the Christian classics, much like that of the Italian humanists for the pagan writers of Greece and Rome.

Yet Erasmus did something more than revive a knowledge of Christian sources. In a measure, he had a positive theology. To him Christianity was but the fullest expression through Christ, primarily in the Sermon on the Mount, of universal, essentially ethical religion, of which the philosophers of antiquity had also been bearers. He had little feeling for the sacramental or for the deeply personal elements in religion. A universal ethical theism, having its highest illustration in Christ, was his idea. His way of thinking was to have little influence on the Reformation as a whole, though much on Socinianism, and is that represented in a great deal of modern theology, of which he was thus the spiritual ancestor.

Though Germany was more largely influenced by the Renaissance at the beginning of the sixteenth century than any other land beyond the Alps, the same impulses were stirring elsewhere. The efforts of Ximenes in Spain have already been noted (*ante*, p. 324). In England John Colet (1467?–1519) was introducing educational reforms and lecturing on the epistles of Paul in Oxford and London. His influence in turning Erasmus to Biblical studies was considerable (*ante*, p. 329). He rejected all allegorical interpretation of the Scriptures, criticised clerical celibacy and auricular confession, and desired to better the education and morals of the clergy. As the sixteenth century dawned humanism was gaining constantly increasing following in England, and King Henry VIII (1509–1547) was deemed its patron.

The situation in France was similar. The chief representative of a churchly reformatory humanism was Jaques Le Fèvre, of Etaples (1455–1536), most of whose active years were spent in or near Paris. A modest, kindly little man, of mystical piety, he published a Latin translation and commentary on Paul's epistles in 1512, which denied the justifying merits of good works and held salvation a free gift from God. He never perceived, however, any fundamental difference between himself and the Roman Church; but he gathered round himself a body of devoted pupils, destined to most unlike participation in the Reformation struggle, Guillaume Briçonnet, to be bishop of Meaux; Guillaume Budé, eminent in Greek and to be instrumental in founding the Collège de France; Louis de Berquin, to die a Protestant martyr; and Guillaume Farel, to be the fiery reformer of French-speaking Switzerland.

To all these religious-minded humanists the path of reform seemed similar. Sound learning, the study and preaching of the Bible and the Fathers, and the correction of ignorance, immorality, and glaring administrative abuses would make the church what it should be. This solution did not meet the deep needs of the situation; but the humanists rendered an indispensable preparation for the Reformation. They led men to study Christian sources afresh. They discredited the later scholastic theology. They brought in new and more natural methods of exegesis. To a large degree they looked on life from another standpoint than the mediæval. They represented a release of the mind, in some considerable measure, from mediæval traditionalism.

Partly as a result of the Renaissance emphasis on the sources, but even more in consequence of the invention of printing, the latter half of the fifteenth century witnessed a wide distribution of the Bible in the Vulgate and in translation. No less than ninety-two editions of the Vulgate were put forth before 1500. Eighteen editions of a German version were printed before 1521. The New Testament was printed in French in 1477; the whole Bible ten years later; 1478 saw the publication of a Spanish translation; 1471 the printing of two independent versions in Italian. In the Netherlands the *Psalms* were seven times published between 1480 and 1507. The Scriptures were printed in Bohemian in 1488. If England had no printed Bible before the Reformation, many manuscripts of Wyclif's translation were in circulation.

Efforts were made to restrict the reading of the Bible by the laity, since its use seemed the source of mediæval heresies; but there can be no doubt that familiarity with it much increased among the less educated priesthood and among laymen. Yet the real question of the influence of this Bible reading is the problem of Biblical interpretation. The Middle Ages never denied the final authority of the Bible. Augustine and Aquinas so regarded it. It was the Bible interpreted, however, by the Fathers, the teachers, and the councils of the church. Should that churchly right to interpret be denied, there remained only the right of private interpretation; but the voices from Bohemia and the mediæval sects which denied the interpreting authority of the church, found no general response as yet. The commanding word had yet to be spoken. The mere reading of the Bible involved no denial of mediæval ideals. Only when those ideals were rejected could the interpreting authority which supported them be denied and the Bible become the support of the newer conceptions of salvation and of the church. The Bible was not so much the cause of Protestantism as was Protestantism a new interpretation of the Scriptures.

The closing years of the fifteenth century were, as has been seen, a period of religious betterment in Spain. No such corresponding revival of interest in religion is to be traced in France or England; but Germany was undergoing a real and pervasive religious quickening in the decades immediately preceding the Reformation. Its fundamental motive seems to

have been fear. Much in the popular life of Germany tended
to increase the sense of apprehension. The witchcraft delusion,
though by no means new, was rapidly spreading. A bull of
Pope Innocent VIII in 1484 declared Germany full of witches,
and the German inquisitors, Jakob Sprenger and Heinrich
Krämer, published their painfully celebrated *Malleus Malefi-
carum* in 1489. It was a superstition that added terror to
popular life, and was to be shared by the reformers no less
than by their Roman opponents. The years from 1490 to
1503 were a period of famine in Germany. The Turkish peril
was becoming threatening. The general social unrest has already been noted (*ante*, p. 325). All these elements contributed
to the development of a sense of the reality and nearness of
divine judgments, and the need of propitiating an angry God.
Luther's early religious experiences were congenial to the spirit
of this pervasive religious movement.

The religious spirit of Germany at the close of the fifteenth
century found expression in pilgrimages. A few of the more
wealthy journeyed to the Holy Land, more went to Rome,
but the most popular foreign pilgrimage shrine was that of
St. James at Compostella in Spain. German pilgrim shrines
were thronged, and great collections of relics were made, notably by the Saxon Elector, Frederick the Wise (1486–1525), to
be Luther's protector, who placed them in the castle church, to
the door of which Luther was to nail his famous Theses. The
intercession of Mary was never more sought, and Mary's
mother, St. Anna, was but little less valued. Christ was popularly regarded as a strict judge, to be placated with satisfactions or absolutions.

Yet side by side with this external and work-trusting religious
spirit, Germany had not a little of mystic piety, that saw the
essence of religion in the relation of the individual soul to God;
and a good deal of what has been called "non-ecclesiastical
religion," which showed itself not only in simple, serious lives,
like that of Luther's father, but in increasing attempts of lay
princes to improve the quality of the clergy, of towns to regulate beggary, to control charitable foundations, which had
been in exclusive ecclesiastical hands, and in various ways to
vindicate for laymen, as such, a larger share in the religious
life of the community. The active life was asserting its claims
against the contemplative. Theology, as such, had largely

lost its hold on popular thought, discredited by nominalism, despised by humanism, and supplanted by mysticism.

It was no dead age to which Luther was to speak, but one seething with unrest, vexed with multitudinous unsolved problems and unfulfilled longings.

PERIOD VI. THE REFORMATION

SECTION I. THE LUTHERAN REVOLUTION

THE religious and economic situation of Germany at the beginning of the sixteenth century was in many respects critical. Papal taxation and papal interference with churchly appointments were generally deemed oppressive. The expedition of clerical business by the papal curia was deemed expensive and corrupt. The clergy at home were much criticised for the unworthy examples of many of their number in high station and low. The trading cities were restive under clerical exemptions from taxation, the prohibition of interest, the many holidays, and the churchly countenance of beggars. Monasteries were in many places in sore need of reform, and their large landed possessions were viewed with ill favor, both by the nobles who would gladly possess them, and the peasantry who labored on them. The peasantry in general were in a state of economic unrest, not the least of their grievances being the tithes and fees collected by the local clergy Added to these causes of restlessness were the intellectual ferment of rising German humanism and the stirrings of popular religious awakening, manifested in a deepening sense of terror and concern for salvation. It is evident that, could these various grievances find bold expression in a determined leader, his voice would find wide hearing.

In the intellectual world of Germany, moreover, division was being greatly intensified by a quarrel involving one of the most peace-loving and respected of humanists, Reuchlin (*ante*, p. 328), and uniting in his support the advocates of the new learning. Johann Pfefferkorn (1469–1522), a convert from Judaism, procured an order from the Emperor, Maximilian, in 1509, confiscating Jewish books as doing dishonor to Christianity. The archbishop of Mainz, to whom the task of inquiry was intrusted, consulted Reuchlin and Jakob Hochstraten (1460–1527), the Dominican inquisitor in Cologne. They took opposite sides. Hochstraten supported Pfefferkorn, while Reuchlin defended Jewish literature as with slight exceptions desirable, urged a fuller knowledge of Hebrew, and the substitution of friendly discussion with the Jews for the confiscation of their books.   A storm of controversy was the result.   Reuchlin was accused of heresy and put on trial by Hochstraten.   The case was appealed to Rome, and dragged till 1520, when it was decided against Reuchlin.   The advocates of the new learning, however, looked upon the whole proceeding as an ignorant and unwarranted attack on scholarship, and rallied to Reuchlin's support.

From this humanistic circle came, in 1514 and 1517, one of the most successful satires ever issued—the *Letters of Obscure Men*.   Purporting to be written by opponents of Reuchlin and the new learning, they aroused wide-spread ridicule by their barbarous Latinity, their triviality, and their ignorance, and undoubtedly created the impression that the party opposed to Reuchlin was hostile to learning and progress.   Their authorship is still uncertain, but Crotus Rubeanus (1480?–1539?) of Dornheim and Ulrich von Hutten (1488–1523) certainly had parts in it.   Hutten, vain, immoral, and quarrelsome, but brilliantly gifted as a writer of prose and verse, and undoubtedly patriotic, was to give support of dubious worth to Luther in the early years of the Reformation movement.   The effect of the storm raised over Reuchlin was to unite German humanists, and to draw a line of cleavage between them and the conservatives, of whom the Dominicans were the most conspicuous.

It was while this contest was at its height that a protest against an ecclesiastical abuse, made, in no unusual or spectacular fashion, by a monastic professor in a recently founded and relatively inconspicuous German university, on October 31, 1517, found immediate response and launched the most gigantic revolution in the history of the Christian Church.

Martin Luther, from whom this protest came, is one of the few men of whom it may be said that the history of the world was profoundly altered by his work.   Not a great scholar, an organizer or a politician, he moved men by the power of a profound religious experience, resulting in unshakable trust in God, and in direct, immediate and personal relations to Him, which brought a confident salvation that left no room for the elaborate hierarchical and sacramental structures of the Middle Ages.   He spoke to his countrymen as one profoundly of them

in aspirations and sympathies, yet above them by virtue of a
vivid and compelling faith, and a courage, physical and spiritual,
of the most heroic mould. Yet so largely was he of his race,
in his virtues and limitations, that he is understood with difficulty, to this day, by a Frenchman or an Italian, and even
Anglo-Saxons have seldom appreciated that fulness of sympathetic admiration with which a German Protestant speaks
his name. But whether honored or opposed, none can deny
his pre-eminent place in the history of the church.

Luther was born on November 10, 1483, in Eisleben, where
his father was a peasant miner. His father and mother were
of simple, unecclesiastical piety. The father, more energetic
and ambitious than most peasants, removed to Mansfeld a
few months after Martin's birth, where he won respect and a
modest competence, and was fired with ambition to give his
son an education fitting to a career in the law. After preparatory schooling in Mansfeld, Magdeburg, and Eisenach, Martin
Luther entered the University of Erfurt in 1501, where he was
known as an earnest, companionable, and music-loving student.
The humanistic movement beginning to be felt in Erfurt had
little influence upon him. His interest was rather in the later,
nominalistic scholastic philosophy, representative of the school
of Occam, though he read fairly widely in the Latin classics.

Luther felt strongly that deep sense of sinfulness which was
the ground note of the religious revival of the age in Germany.
His graduation as master of arts in 1505, made it necessary
then to begin his special preparation in law. He was profoundly moved, however, by the sudden death of a friend and
by a narrow escape from lightning, and he therefore broke off
his career, and, in deep anxiety for his soul's salvation, entered the monastery of Augustinian hermits in Erfurt, in July,
1505. The "German congregation" of Augustinians, recently
reformed by Andreas Proles (1429–1503), and now under the
supervision of Johann von Staupitz (?–1524), enjoyed deserved
popular respect and represented mediæval monasticism at its
best. Thoroughly mediæval, in general, in its theological position, it made much of preaching, and included some men
who were disposed to mystical piety and sympathetic with
the deeper religious apprehensions of Augustine and Bernard.
To Staupitz, Luther was to owe much. In the monastic life
Luther won speedy recognition. In 1507 he was ordained to

the priesthood. The next year saw him in Wittenberg, at the command of his superiors, preparing for a future professorship in the university which had been there established by the Saxon Elector, Frederick III, "the Wise" (1486–1525), in 1502. There he graduated bachelor of theology in 1509, but was sent back the same year to Erfurt, possibly to study for the degree of sententiarius, or licensed expounder of that great mediæval text-book of theology, the "Sentences" of Peter Lombard (*ante*, p. 266). On business of his order he made a memorable journey to Rome, probably in 1510. Back once more in Wittenberg, which was thenceforth to be his home, he became a doctor of theology in 1512 and began at once to lecture on the Bible, treating the *Psalms* from 1513 to 1515, then *Romans* till late in 1516, and thereupon *Galatians*, *Hebrews*, and *Titus*. His practical abilities were recognized by his appointment, in 1515, as district vicar in charge of eleven monasteries of his order, and he began, even earlier, the practice of preaching in which, from the first, he displayed remarkable gifts. In his order he bore the repute of a man of singular piety, devotion, and monastic zeal.

Yet, in spite of all monastic strenuousness, Luther found no peace of soul. His sense of sinfulness overwhelmed him. Staupitz helped him by pointing out that true penitence began not with fear of a punishing God, but with love to God. But if Luther could say that Staupitz first opened his eyes to the Gospel, the clarifying of his vision was a slow and gradual process. Till 1509 Luther devoted himself to the later scholastics, Occam, d'Ailli, and Biel. To them he owed permanently his disposition to emphasize the objective facts of revelation, and his distrust of reason. Augustine, however, was opening new visions to him by the close of 1509, and leading him to a rapidly growing hostility toward the dominance of Aristotle in theology. Augustine's mysticism and emphasis on the salvatory significance of the human life and death of Christ fascinated him. Anselm and Bernard helped him. By the time that Luther lectured on the *Psalms* (1513–1515), he had become convinced that salvation is a new relation to God, based not on any work of merit on man's part, but on absolute trust in the divine promises, so that the redeemed man, while not ceasing to be a sinner, yet is freely and fully forgiven, and from the new and joyous relationship to God in Christ, the new life of willing conformity to God's will flows.   It was a re-emphasis of a most important side of the Pauline teaching.   Yet it was not wholly Pauline.   To Paul the Christian is primarily a renewed moral being.   To Luther he is first of all a forgiven sinner ; but Luther, like Paul, made salvation in essence a right personal relationship to God.   The ground and the pledge of this right relationship is the mercy of God displayed in the sufferings of Christ in man's behalf.   Christ has borne our sins.   We, in turn, have imputed to us His righteousness.   The German mystics, especially Tauler, now helped Luther to the conclusion that this transforming trust was not, as he had supposed, a work in which a man had a part, but wholly the gift of God.   The work preparatory to his lectures on *Romans* (1515–1516) but intensified these convictions.   He now declared that the common opinion that God would infallibly infuse grace into those who did what was in their power was absurd and Pelagian. The basis of any work-righteousness had been overthrown for Luther.

While thus convinced as to the nature and method of salvation, Luther's own peace of soul was not yet secured.   He needed the further conviction of certainty of his own personal justification.   That certainty he had, with Augustine, denied. Yet as he labored on the latter part of his lectures on *Romans*, and even more clearly in the closing months of 1516, his confidence that the God-given nature of faith involved personal assurance became conviction.   Thenceforth, in his own personal experience the sum of the Gospel was the forgiveness of sins.   It was "good news," filling the soul with peace, joy, and absolute trust in God.   It was absolute dependence on the divine promises, on God's "word."

Luther had not, thus far, consciously worked out a new system of theology.   He had had a deep, vital experience. It was an experience, however, in no way to be squared with much of current theories of salvation in which acts, penances, and satisfactions had a prominent part.   No theoretic considerations made Luther a reformer.   He was driven by the force of a profound inward experience to test the beliefs and institutions which he saw about him.   The profundity and nobility of Luther's experience cannot be doubted.   Yet its applicability as a universal test may be questioned.   To him faith was a vital, transforming power, a new and vivifying personal relationship. Many men, however, while sincerely desirous of serving God and their generation, have no such sense of personal forgiveness, no such soul-stirring depth of feeling, no such childlike trust. They desire, with God's aid, to do the best they can. For them "justification by faith alone" is either well-nigh meaningless, or becomes an intellectual assent to religious truth. To enter into the experience of Luther or of Paul is by no means possible for all.

By 1516 Luther did not stand alone. In the University of Wittenberg his opposition to Aristotelianism and Scholasticism and his Biblical theology found much sympathy. His colleagues, Andreas Bodenstein of Karlstadt (1480?–1541), who, unlike Luther, had represented the older Scholasticism of Aquinas, and Nikolaus von Amsdorf (1483–1565), now became his hearty supporters.

In 1517 Luther had an opportunity to apply his new conception of salvation to a crying abuse. Pope Leo X had decided in favor of the claims of Albrecht of Brandenburg to hold at the same time the archbishopric of Mainz, the archbishopric of Magdeburg, and the administration of the bishopric of Halberstadt, an argument moving thereto being a large financial payment. To indemnify himself, Albrecht secured as his share half the proceeds in his district of the indulgences that the papacy had been issuing, since 1506, for building that new church of St. Peter which is still one of the ornaments of Rome. A commissioner for this collection was Johann Tetzel (1470–1519), a Dominican monk of eloquence, who, intent on the largest possible returns, painted the benefits of indulgences in the crassest terms.[1] To Luther, convinced that only a right personal relation with God would bring salvation, such teaching seemed destructive of real religion. As Tetzel approached—he was not allowed to enter electoral Saxony—Luther preached against the abuse of indulgences and, on October 31, 1517, posted on the door of the castle church, in Wittenberg, which served as the university bulletin board, his ever memorable Ninety-five Theses.[2]

Viewed in themselves, it may well be wondered why the

[1] See extracts in Kidd, *Documents Illustrative of the Continental Reformation*, pp. 12–20.

[2] Kidd, pp. 21–26; English tr. Wace and Buchheim, *Luther's Primary Works*, pp. 6–14.

Ninety-five Theses proved the spark which kindled the explosion. They were intended for academic debate. They do not deny the right of the Pope to grant indulgences. They question the extension of indulgences to purgatory, and make evident the abuses of current teaching—abuses which they imply the Pope will repudiate when informed. Yet though they are far from expressing the full round of Luther's thought, certain principles are evident in them which, if developed, would be revolutionary of the churchly practice of the day. Repentance is not an act, but a life-long habit of mind. The true treasury of the church is God's forgiving grace. The Christian seeks rather than avoids divine discipline. "Every Christian who feels true compunction has of right plenary remission of pain and guilt, even without letters of pardon." In the restless condition of Germany it was an event of the utmost significance that a respected, if humble, religious leader had spoken boldly against a great abuse, and the Theses ran the length and breadth of the empire.

Luther had not anticipated the excitement. Tetzel answered at once,[1] and stirred Konrad Wimpina (?–1531) to make reply. A more formidable opponent was the able and disputatious Johann Maier of Eck (1486–1543), professor of theology in the University of Ingolstadt, who answered with a tract circulated in manuscript and entitled *Obelisci*. Luther was charged with heresy. He defended his position in a sermon on "Indulgence and Grace" ;[2] he replied to Eck. By the beginning of 1518, complaints against Luther had been lodged in Rome by Archbishop Albrecht of Mainz and the Dominicans. The result was that the general of the Augustinians was ordered to end the dispute and Luther was summoned before the general chapter of the order met in Heidelberg, in April. There Luther argued against free will and the control of Aristotle in theology and won new adherents, of whom one of the most important was Martin Butzer (Bucer). At about the same time Luther put forth a more elaborate defense of his position on indulgences, the *Resolutiones*.

Luther had desired no quarrel with the papacy. He seems to have believed that the Pope might see the abuses of indulgences as he did, but the course of events was leading to no choice save the sturdy maintenance of his views or submission.

[1] Kidd, pp. 30, 31.   [2] *Ibid.*, p. 29.

In June, 1518, Pope Leo X issued a citation to Luther to appear in Rome, and commissioned his censor of books, the Dominican Silvestro Mazzolini of Prierio, to draw up an opinion on Luther's position. The summons and the opinion reached Luther early in August. Prierio asserted that "the Roman Church is representatively the college of cardinals, and moreover is virtually the supreme pontiff," and that "He who says that the Roman Church cannot do what it actually does regarding indulgences is a heretic." [1] Luther's case would apparently have speedily ended in his condemnation had he not had the powerful protection of his prince, the Elector Frederick, "the Wise." In how far Frederick sympathized with Luther's religious beliefs at any time is a matter of controversy; but, at all events he was proud of his Wittenberg professor, and averse to an almost certain condemnation in Rome. His political skill effected a change of hearing from the Roman court to the papal legate at the Reichstag in Augsburg, the learned commentator on Aquinas, Cardinal Thomas Vio (1469–1534), known from his birthplace (Gaeta) as Cajetanus. Cajetanus was a theologian of European repute and seems to have thought the matter rather beneath his dignity. He ordered Luther to retract, especially criticisms of the completeness of papal power of indulgence. Luther refused,[2] and, on October 20, fled from Augsburg, having appealed to the Pope "to be better informed."[3] Not satisfied with this, Luther appealed from Wittenberg, in November, 1518, to a future general council.[4] How little chance of a favorable hearing he had in Rome is shown by the bull issued the same month by Leo X defining indulgences in the sense which Luther had criticised.[5] Luther had no real hope of safety. If his courage was great, his danger was no less so; but he was rescued from immediate condemnation by the favorable turn of political events.

Meanwhile the summer of 1518 had seen the installation as professor of Greek in Wittenberg of a young scholar, a native of Bretten and grandnephew of Reuchlin, Philip Melanchthon (1497–1560), who was to be singularly united with Luther in their after work. Never was there a greater contrast. Melanchthon was timid and retiring; but he was without a superior in scholarship, and under the strong impress of Luther's per-

[1] Kidd, pp. 31, 32.   [2] Ibid., pp. 33–37.   [3] Ibid., pp. 37–39.
[4] Ibid., p. 40.   [5] Ibid., p. 39.

sonality, he devoted his remarkable abilities, almost from his arrival in Wittenberg, to the furtherance of the Lutheran cause.

The Emperor, Maximilian, was now visibly nearing the end of his life, which was to come in January, 1519, and the turmoil of a disputed election was impending. Pope Leo X, as an Italian prince, looked with disfavor on the candidacy of Charles of Spain, or Francis of France, as increasing foreign influence in Italy, and sought the good-will of the Elector Frederick, whom he would gladly have seen chosen. It was no time to proceed against Frederick's favored professor. Leo, therefore, sent his chamberlain, the Saxon Karl von Miltitz, as his nuncio, with a golden rose, a present expressive of high papal favor, to the Elector. Miltitz flattered himself that he could heal the ecclesiastical quarrel and went far beyond his instructions. On his own motion he disowned Tetzel, and held an interview with Luther, whom he persuaded to agree to keep silent on the questions in dispute, to submit the case, if possible, to learned German bishops, and to write a humble letter to the Pope.[1]

Any real agreement was impossible. Luther's Wittenberg colleague, Andreas Bodenstein of Karlstadt (1480?–1541), had argued in 1518, in opposition to Eck, that the text of the Bible is to be preferred even to the authority of the whole church. Eck demanded a public debate, to which Karlstadt agreed, and Luther soon found himself drawn into the combat, proposing to contend that the supremacy of the Roman Church is unsupported by history or Scripture. In June and July, 1519, the great debate was held in Leipzig. Karlstadt, who was an unready disputant, succeeded but moderately in holding his own against the nimble-witted Eck. Luther's earnestness acquitted itself much better; but Eck's skill drove Luther to the admission that his positions were in some respects those of Huss, and that in condemning Huss the revered Council of Constance had erred. To Eck this seemed a forensic triumph, and he believed victory to be his, declaring that one who could deny the infallibility of a general council was a heathen and a publican.[2] It was, indeed, a momentous declaration into which Luther had been led. He had already rejected the final authority of the Pope, he now admitted the fallibility of councils. Those steps implied a break with the whole authoritative

---

[1] Kidd, pp. 41–44. [2] *Ibid.*, pp. 44–51.

system of the Middle Ages, and allowed final appeal only to the Scriptures, and to the Scriptures, moreover, interpreted by the individual judgment. Eck felt that the whole controversy might now be speedily ended by a papal bull of condemnation, which he now set himself to secure and which was issued on June 15, 1520.[1]

Luther was now, indeed, in the thick of the battle. His own ideas were rapidly crystallizing. Humanistic supporters, like Ulrich von Hutten, were now rallying to him as one who could lead in a national conflict with Rome. Luther himself was beginning to see his task as a national redemption of Germany from a papacy which, rather than the individual Pope, he was coming to regard as antichrist. His doctrine of salvation was bearing larger fruitage. In his little tract, *On Good Works*, of May, 1520, after defining "the noblest of all good works" to be "to believe in Christ," he affirmed the essential goodness of the normal trades and occupations of life, and denounced those who "limit good works so narrowly that they must consist in praying in church, fasting or giving alms."[2] This vindication of the natural human life as the best field for the service of God, rather than the unnatural limitations of asceticism, was to be one of Luther's most important contributions to Protestant thought, as well as one of his most significant departures from ancient and mediæval Christian conceptions.

Luther's great accomplishment of the year 1520 and his completion of his title to leadership were the preparation of three epoch-making works. The first of these treatises was published in August, entitled *To the Christian Nobility of the German Nation*.[3] Written with burning conviction, by a master of the German tongue, it soon ran the breadth of the empire. It declared that three Roman walls were overthrown by which the papacy had buttressed its power. The pretended superiority of the spiritual to the temporal estate is baseless, since all believers are priests. That truth of universal priesthood casts down the second wall, that of exclusive papal right to interpret the Scriptures; and the third wall, also, that a reformatory council can be called by none but the Pope. "A true, free council" for the reform of the church should be sum-

---

[1] Kidd, pp. 74–79.   [2] Robinson, *Readings*, 2: 66–68.
[3] Translated in full in Wace and Buchheim's, *Luther's Primary Works*, pp. 17–92.

moned by the temporal authorities. Luther then proceeded
to lay down a programme for reformatory action, his suggestions being practical rather than theological. Papal misgovernment, appointments, and taxation are to be curbed;
burdensome offices abolished; German ecclesiastical interests
should be placed under a "Primate of Germany"; clerical marriage permitted; the far too numerous holy days reduced in
the interest of industry and sobriety; beggary, including that
of the mendicant orders, forbidden; brothels closed; luxury
curbed; and theological education in the universities reformed.
No wonder the effect of Luther's work was profound. He had
voiced what earnest men had long been thinking.

Two months later Luther put forth in Latin his *Babylonish
Captivity of the Church*,[1] in which questions of the highest theological import were handled and the teaching of the Roman
Church unsparingly attacked. The sole value of a sacrament,
Luther taught, is its witness to the divine promise. It seals or
attests the God-given pledge of union with Christ and forgiveness of sins. It strengthens faith. Tried by the Scripture
standard, there are only two sacraments, baptism and the
Lord's Supper, though penance has a certain sacramental value
as a return to baptism. Monastic vows, pilgrimages, works of
merit, are a man-made substitute for the forgiveness of sins
freely promised to faith in baptism. Luther criticised the denial
of the cup to the laity, doubted transubstantiation, for which
he would substitute a theory of consubstantiation derived from
d'Ailli, and especially rejected the doctrine that the Supper is
a sacrifice to God. The other Roman sacraments, confirmation, matrimony, orders, and extreme unction, have no sacramental standing in Scripture.

It is one of the marvels of Luther's stormy career that he was
able to compose and issue, contemporaneously with these
intensely polemic treatises, and while the papal bull was being
published in Germany, his third great tractate of 1520, that *On
Christian Liberty*.[2] In calm confidence he presented the para-
dox of Christian experience: "A Christian man is the most
free lord of all, and subject to none; a Christian man is the
most dutiful servant of all, and subject to every one." He is
free, since justified by faith, no longer under the law of works

---

[1] *Luther's Primary Works*, pp. 141–245.
[2] *Ibid.*,, pp. 95–137.

and in new personal relationship with Christ. He is a servant because bound by love to bring his life into conformity to the will of God and to be helpful to his neighbor. In this tract, in an elsewhere unmatched measure, the power and the limitations of Lutheranism are evident. To Luther the essence of the Gospel is the forgiveness of sins, wrought through a faith, which, as with Paul, is nothing less than a vital, personal transforming relationship of the soul with Christ. It is unquestionably the highest of Christian experiences. Its limitation, as already pointed out, is that this experience, if regarded as the sole type of true religion, is one beyond the practical attainment of many earnest men. To this tract Luther prefaced a letter to Pope Leo X, which is a most curious document, breathing good-will to the Pontiff personally, but full of denunciation of the papal court and its claims for the papacy, in which the Pope is represented as "sitting like a lamb in the midst of wolves." Though Luther's vision was to clarify hereafter regarding many details, his theological system was thus practically complete in its main outlines by 1520.

Meanwhile Eck and Girolamo Aleander (1480–1542) had come with the papal bull, as nuncios, to Germany. In Wittenberg its publication was refused, and its reception in large parts of Germany was lukewarm or hostile, but Aleander secured its publication in the Netherlands, and procured the burning of Luther's books in Louvain, Liége, Antwerp, and Cologne. On December 10, 1520, Luther answered by burning the papal bull and the canon law, with the approving presence of students and citizens of Wittenberg, and without opposition from the civil authorities. It was evident that a considerable section of Germany was in ecclesiastical rebellion, and the situation demanaded the cognizance of the highest authorities of the empire.

On June 28, 1519, while the Leipzig disputation was in progress, the imperial election had resulted in the choice of Maximilian's grandson Charles V (1500–1558). Heir of Spain, the Netherlands, the Austrian territories of the house of Habsburg, master of a considerable portion of Italy, and of newly discovered territories across the Atlantic, his election as Holy Roman Emperor made him the head of a territory vaster than that of any single ruler since Charlemagne. It was an authority greatly limited, however, in Germany by the territorial powers of the local princes. As yet Charles was young and unknown, and both sides in the religious struggles of the day had strong hope of his support. In reality he was an earnest Roman Catholic, of the type of his grandmother, Isabella of Castile, sharing her reformatory views, desirous of improvement in clerical morals, education, and administration, but wholly unsympathetic with any departure from the doctrinal or hierarchical system of the Middle Ages. He had at last come to Germany, and partly to regulate his government in that land, partly to prepare for the war about to break out over the rival claims of France and Spain in Italy, had called a Reichstag to meet in Worms in November, 1520. Though there was much other business, all felt the determination of Luther's case of high importance. The papal nuncio, Aleander, pressed for a prompt condemnation, especially after the final papal bull against Luther was issued on January 2, 1521. Since Luther was already condemned by the Pope, the Reichstag had no duty, Aleander urged, but to make that condemnation effective. On the other hand, Luther had wide popular support, and his ruler, the Elector Frederick the Wise, a master of diplomatic intrigue, was, fortunately for Luther, of the opinion that the condemned monk had never had an adequate trial. Frederick, and other nobles, believed that he should be heard before the Reichstag previous to action by that body. Between the two counsels the Emperor wavered, convinced that Luther was a damnable heretic, but politician enough not to oppose German sentiment too sharply, or to throw away the possible advantage of making the heretic's fate a lever in bringing the Pope to the imperial side in the struggle with France.

The result was that Luther was summoned to Worms under the protection of an imperial safe-conduct. His journey thither from Wittenberg was well-nigh a popular ovation. On April 17, 1521, Luther appeared before the Emperor and Reichstag. A row of his books was pointed out to him and he was asked whether he would recant them or not. Luther requested time for reflection. A day was given him, and on the next afternoon he was once more before the assembly. Here he acknowledged that, in the heat of controversy, he had expressed himself too strongly against persons, but the substance of what he had written he could not retract, unless convinced of its wrongfulness by Scripture or adequate argument. The

Emperor, who could hardly believe that such temerity as to
deny the infallibility of a general council was possible, cut the
discussion short. That Luther cried out, "I cannot do otherwise. Here I stand. God help me, Amen," is not certain,
but seems not improbable. The words at least expressed the
substance of his unshaken determination. He had borne a
great historic witness to the truth of his convictions before the
highest tribunal of his nation. Of his dauntless courage he
had given the completest proof. The judgment of his hearers
was divided, but if he alienated the Emperor and the prelates
by his strong and, as it seemed to them, self-willed assertion,
he made a favorable impression on many of the German nobility and, fortunately, on the Elector Frederick. That prince,
though he thought Luther too bold, was confirmed in his determination that no harm should come to the reformer. Yet
the result seemed a defeat for Luther. A month after Luther
had started on his homeward journey he was formally put under
the ban of the empire, though not till after many of the members of the Reichstag had left. He was to be seized for punishment and his books burned.[1] This ban was never formally
abrogated, and Luther remained the rest of his life under imperial condemnation.

Had Germany been controlled by a strong central authority
Luther's career would soon have ended in martyrdom. Not
even an imperial edict, however, could be executed against the
will of a vigorous territorial ruler, and Frederick the Wise
proved once more Luther's salvation. Unwilling to come out
openly as his defender, perhaps somewhat afraid to do so, he
had Luther seized by friendly hands, as the reformer journeyed
homeward from Worms, and carried secretly to the Wartburg
Castle, near Eisenach. For months Luther's hiding-place was
practically unknown; but that he lived and shared in the fortunes of the struggle his ready pen made speedily apparent.
His attacks on the Roman practice grew more intense, but the
most lasting fruit of this period of enforced retirement was his
translation of the New Testament, begun in December, 1521,
and published in September of the following year. Luther
was by no means the first to translate the Scriptures into German, but the earlier versions had been made from the Vulgate,
and were hard and awkward in expression. Luther's work

[1] Kidd, *Documents*, pp. 79–89.

was not merely from the Greek, for which the labors of Erasmus gave the basis, it was idiomatic and readable. It largely determined the form of speech that should mark future German literature—that of the Saxon chancery of the time—wrought and polished by a master of popular expression. Few services greater than this translation have ever been rendered to the development of the religious life of a nation. Nor, with all his deference to the Word of God, was Luther without his own canons of criticism. These were the relative clearness with which his interpretation of the work of Christ and the method of salvation by faith is taught. Judged by these standards, he felt that *Hebrews, James, Jude,* and *Revelation* were of inferior worth. Even in Scripture itself there were differences in value.

The month which saw the beginning of Luther's work as a translator—December, 1521—witnessed the publication in Wittenberg of a small volume by Melanchthon, the *Loci Communes,* meaning Cardinal Points of Theology. With it the systematic presentation of Lutheran theology may be said to have begun.[1] It was to be enlarged, developed, and modified in many later editions.

SECTION II. SEPARATIONS AND DIVISIONS

Luther's sojourn in the Wartburg left Wittenberg without his powerful leadership; but there were not wanting many there to continue the ecclesiastical revolution. To his earlier associates in the university, Karlstadt, Melanchthon, and Nikolaus von Amsdorf (1483–1565), there had been added, in the first half of the year 1521, Johann Bugenhagen (1485–1558) and Justus Jonas (1493–1555). Of these, Karlstadt had unquestionably greatest natural leadership, but was rash, impulsive, and radical. Luther had as yet made no changes in public worship or in monastic life. Yet it was inevitable that demand for such changes should come. Luther's fiery fellow monk, Gabriel Zwilling (1487?–1558), by October, 1521, was denouncing the mass and urging the abandonment of clerical vows. He soon had a large following, especially in the Augustinian monastery of Wittenberg, many of the inmates of which now renounced their profession. With equal zeal Zwilling was soon attacking images. At Christmas, 1521, Karlstadt celebrated

---

[1] Extracts in Kidd, *Documents,* pp. 90–94.

the Lord's Supper in the castle church, without priestly garb, sacrificial offering, elevation of the host, and with the cup offered to the laity.   Auricular confession and fasts were abandoned.   Karlstadt taught that all ministers should marry, and, in January, 1522, took to himself a wife.   He was soon opposing the use of pictures, organs, and the Gregorian chanting in public worship.   Under his leadership the Wittenberg city government broke up the ancient religious fraternities and confiscated their property, decreed that the services should be in German, condemned pictures in the churches, and forbad beggary, ordering that really needy cases be aided from the city treasury.   The public commotion was augmented by the arrival, on December 27, 1521, of three radical preachers from Zwickau, chief of whom were Nikolaus Storch and Markus Thomä Stübner.   These men claimed immediate divine inspiration, opposed infant baptism, and prophesied the speedy end of the world.   Melanchthon was somewhat shaken by them at first, though their influence in general has been exaggerated.   They undoubtedly added something to a state of turmoil.[1]

These rapid changes, followed by a popular attack on images, were highly displeasing to Elector Frederick the Wise, and they drew forth the warning protests of German princes and the imperial authorities.   Though Luther was to further, within the next three or four years, most of the changes which Karlstadt and Zwilling had made, he now felt that his cause was in peril through a dangerous radicalism.   The city government appealed to Luther to return.   The Elector nominally forbad him, out of political considerations, but on March 6, 1522, Luther was once more in Wittenberg, which thenceforth was to be his home.   Eight days of preaching showed his power. The Gospel, he declared, consisted in the knowledge of sin, in forgiveness through Christ, and in love to one's neighbor. The alterations, which had raised the turmoil, had to do with externals.   They should be effected only in a spirit of consideration of the weak.   Luther was master of the situation. Karlstadt lost all influence and had to leave the city.   Many of the changes were, for the moment, undone, and the old order of worship largely re-established.   Luther thus showed a decidedly conservative attitude.   He opposed not merely

---

[1] Kidd, pp. 94–104.

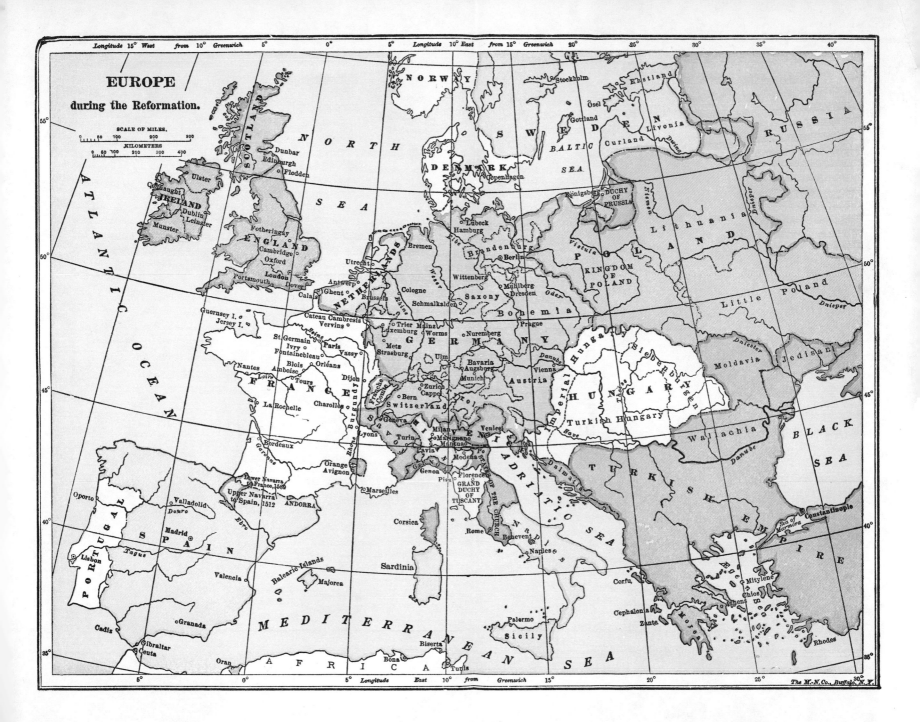

EUROPE
during the Reformation.

SCALE OF MILES.

0   50   100   200   300

KILOMETERS

0   50   200   300   400

Longitude 15° West   from 10° Greenwich   5°   0°   5°   Longitude 10° East   from 15° Greenwich   20°   25°   30°   35°   40°

ATLANTIC OCEAN

NORTH SEA

NORWAY

SWEDEN

Stockholm

Öland

Gotland

Ehstland

Livonia

Curland

Düna

RUSSIA

BALTIC SEA

DENMARK

Copenhagen

Königsberg

DUCHY OF PRUSSIA

Niemen

Lithuania

POLAND

Lübeck

Hamburg

Bremen

Elbe

Brandenburg

Berlin

Vistula

KINGDOM OF POLAND

Little Poland

Dnieper

Dnieper

SCOTLAND

Dunbar

Edinburgh

Flodden

Fotheringay

ENGLAND

Cambridge

Oxford

London

Portsmouth

Dover

Calais

Connaught

IRELAND

Ulster

Dublin

Leinster

Munster

Guernsey I.

Jersey I.

Cateau Cambresis

Vervins

Antwerp

Ghent

Brussels

NETHERLANDS

Utrecht

Weser

Wittenberg

Cologne

Müllberg

Dresden

Saxony

Schmalkalden

Oder

Bohemia

Prague

Seine

St. Germain

Ivry

Fontainebleau

Paris

Vassy

Nantes

Loire

Blois

Amboise

Tours

Orléans

Dijon

Trier

Mainz

Luxemburg

Worms

Metz

Strasburg

GERMANY

Nuremberg

Ulm

Bavaria

Augsburg

Munich

Danube

Vienna

Austria

Imperial Hungary

Siebenburgen

Moldavia

Jedisan

Dniester

FRANCE

La Rochelle

Charolles

Bourgogne

Rhône

Franche Comté

Savoy

Zurich

Cappel

Bern

Geneva

Lyons

Switzerland

Turin

Milan

Marignano

Mantua

Venice

Po

Pavia

Modena

Genoa

ADRIATIC SEA

Dalmatia

HUNGARY

Turkish Hungary

Save

Wallachia

Danube

TURKISH

BLACK SEA

Bordeaux

Garonne

Orange

Avignon

Marseilles

Lower Navarra to France, 1589

Upper Navarra to Spain, 1512

ANDORRA

Florence

GRAND DUCHY OF TUSCANY

Pisa

GRAND DUCHY OF THE CHURCH

Rome

Benevent

Naples

EMPIRE

Constantinople

Sea of Marmora

Oporto

PORTUGAL

Lisbon

Tagus

Cadiz

Gibraltar

Ceuta

SPAIN

Valladolid

Madrid

Duero

Ebro

Valencia

Granada

Balearic Islands

Majorca

Corsica

Sardinia

MEDITERRANEAN SEA

Palermo

Sicily

Naples

Corfu

Cephalonia

Zante

Morea

Mitylene

Chios

Athens

Rhodes

Oran

AFRICA

Biserta

Bona

Tunis

Longitude   East   10°   from   Greenwich   15°   20°   25°   30°

The M.-N.Co., Buffalo, N.Y.

the Romanists, as heretofore, but those of the revolution who would move, as he believed, too rapidly. The separations in the reform party itself had begun. Yet there can be no doubt as to Luther's wisdom. His action caused many of the German rulers to look upon him with kindliness, as one who, though condemned at Worms, was really a force for order in troublous times, and continued especially that favor of his Elector without which his cause would even now have made speedy shipwreck.

Meanwhile the Emperor's hands were tied by the great war with France for the control of Italy, which was to keep him absent from Germany from 1522 to 1530. Effective interference on his part with the Reformation was impossible. Pope Leo X had closed his splendor-loving reign in December, 1521, and had been succeeded by Charles V's old Netherlandish tutor as Adrian VI—a man of strict mediæval orthodoxy, but fully conscious of the need of moral and administrative reform in the papal court, whose brief papacy of twenty months was to be a painfully fruitless effort to check the evils for which he believed Luther's heretical movement to be a divine punishment. Sympathy with Luther was rapidly spreading, not merely throughout Saxony, but in the cities of Germany. To the Reichstag, which met in Nuremberg in November, 1522, Adrian now sent, demanding the enforcement of the edict of Worms against Luther, while admitting that much was amiss in ecclesiastical administration. The Reichstag replied by declaring the edict impossible of enforcement, and by demanding a council for churchly reform, to meet within a year in Germany, while, pending its assembly, only the "true, pure, genuine, holy Gospel" was to be preached. The old complaints against papal misgovernment were renewed by the Reichstag. Though not in form, it was in reality a victory for Luther and his cause. It looked as if the Reformation might gain the support of the whole German nation.[1]

Under these favorable circumstances Evangelical congregations were rapidly forming in many regions of Germany, as yet without any fixed constitution or order of service. Luther now was convinced that such associations of believers had full power to appoint and depose their pastors. He held, also, however, that the temporal rulers, as in the positions of chief

[1] Kidd, pp. 105–121.

power and responsibility in the Christian community, had a prime duty to further the Gospel. The experiences of the immediate future, and the necessities of actual church organization within extensive territories, were to turn Luther from whatever sympathy he now had with this free-churchism to a strict dependence on the state. To meet the demands of the new Evangelical worship, Luther issued, in 1523, his *Ordering of Worship*, in which he emphasized the central place of preaching; his *Formula of the Mass*, in which, though still using Latin, he did away with its sacrificial implications, recommended the cup for lay usage, and urged the employment of popular hymns by the worshippers; and his *Taufbüchlein*, in which he presented a baptismal service in German. The abandonment of private masses and masses for the dead, with their attendant fees, raised a serious problem of ministerial support, which Luther proposed to solve by salaries from a common chest maintained by the municipality. Luther held that great freedom was permissible in details of worship, as long as the "Word of God" was kept central. The various reformed congregations, therefore, soon exhibited considerable variety, and the tendency to the use of German rapidly increased, Luther himself issuing a *German Mass* in 1526. Confession Luther regarded as exceedingly desirable as preparing the undeveloped Christian for the Lord's Supper, but not as obligatory. Judged by the development of the Reformation elsewhere, Luther's attitude in matters of worship was strongly conservative, his principle being that "what is not contrary to Scripture is for Scripture and Scripture for it." He therefore retained much of Roman usage, such as the use of candles, the crucifix, and the illustrative employment of pictures.[1]

Thus far the tide had been running strongly in directions favorable to Luther, but with the years 1524 and 1525 separations began, the effects of which were to limit the Reformation movement, to make Luther a party rather than a national leader, to divide Germany, and to throw Luther into the arms of the temporal princes. The first of these separations was from the humanists. Their admired leader, Erasmus, had little sympathy with Luther's doctrine of justification by faith alone. To his thinking reform would come by education, the rejection of superstition and a return to the "sources" of

[1] Kidd, 121–133.

Christian truth.   The stormy writings of Luther and the popular tumult were becoming increasingly odious to him.   In common with humanists generally, he was alarmed by the great decline in attendance on the German universities, which set in universally with the rise of the religious controversy, and the fading of interest in purely scholarly questions.   Though frequently urged, he was long reluctant to attack Luther, however; but at last, in the autumn of 1524, he challenged Luther's denial of free will.   To Erasmus Luther replied, a year later, with the stiffest possible assertion of determinism and predestination, though Melanchthon was soon to move in the opposite direction.   The breach between Luther and Erasmus was incurable.   Most of the humanists deserted Luther, though among the disciples of Melanchthon a younger school of Lutheran humanists slowly developed.[1]

To some in Germany Luther seemed but a half-way reformer. Such a radical was his old associate Karlstadt, who, having lost all standing in Wittenberg, went on to yet more radical views and practices and, securing a large following in Orlamünde, practically defied Luther and the Saxon government.   He denied the value of education, dressed and lived like the peasantry, destroyed images, and rejected the physical presence of Christ in the Supper.   Even more radical was Thomas Münzer, who asserted immediate revelation and attacked Romanists and Lutherans alike for their dependence on the letter of the Scripture.   A man of action, he led in riotous attacks on monasteries, and preached battle against the "godless."   These and men like them Luther strongly opposed, naming them Schwärmer, i. e., fanatics; but their presence indicated a growing rift in the forces of reform.

Yet more serious was a third separation—that caused by the peasants' revolt.   The state of the German peasantry had long been one of increasing misery and consequent unrest, especially in southwestern Germany, where the example of better conditions in neighboring Switzerland fed the discontent.   With the peasant revolt Lutheranism had little directly to do.   Its strongest manifestations were in regions into which the reform movement had but slightly penetrated.   Yet the religious excitement and radical popular preaching were undoubtedly contributing, though not primary, causes.   Begun

[1] Kidd, pp. 171–174.

in extreme southwestern Germany in May and June, 1524, the insurrection was exceedingly formidable by the spring of the following year. In March, 1525, the peasants put forth twelve articles,[1] demanding the right of each community to choose and depose its pastor, that the great tithes (on grain) be used for the support of the pastor and other community expenses, and the small tithes abolished, that serfdom be done away, reservations for hunting restricted, the use of the forests allowed to the poor, forced labor be regulated and duly paid, just rents fixed, new laws no longer enacted, common lands restored to communities from which they had been taken, and payments for inheritance to their masters abolished. To modern thinking these were moderate and reasonable requests. To that age they seemed revolutionary.

Other groups of peasants, one of which had Thomas Münzer as a leader, were far more radical. Luther at first attempted to mediate, and was disposed to find wrong on both sides; but as the ill-led rising fell into greater excesses he turned on the peasants with his savage pamphlet, *Against the Murderous and Thieving Rabble of the Peasants*, demanding that the princes crush them with the sword. The great defeat of Francis I of France, near Pavia by the imperial army on February 24, 1525, had enabled the princes of Germany to master the rising. The peasant insurrection was stamped out in frightful bloodshed.

Of the separations, that occasioned by the peasants' war was undoubtedly the most disastrous. Luther felt that his Gospel could not be involved in the social and economic demands of the disorderly peasants. But the cost was great. Popular sympathy for his cause among the lower orders of southern Germany was largely forfeited, his own distrust of the common man was augmented, his feeling that the reform must be the work of the temporal princes greatly strengthened. His opponents, moreover, pointed to these risings as the natural fruitage of rebellion against the ancient church.

Meanwhile the mediæval, though in his way reformatory, Adrian VI had died, and had been succeeded in the papacy, in November, 1523, by Giulio de' Medici as Clement VII (1523–1534)—a man of respectable character but with little sense of the importance of religious questions, and primarily in policy an Italian worldly prince. To the new Reichstag assembled in

[1] Kidd, pp. 174–179.

Nuremberg in the spring of 1524, Clement sent as his legate the skilful cardinal, Lorenzo Campeggio (1474–1539). With the Reichstag Campeggio could effect little. It promised to enforce the Edict of Worms against Luther "as far as possible," and demanded a "general assembly of the German nation" to meet in Speier, in the following autumn. This gathering the absent Emperor succeeded in frustrating. Campeggio's real success was, however, outside the Reichstag. Through his efforts a league to support the Roman cause was formed in Regensburg, on July 7, 1524, embracing the Emperor's brother, Ferdinand, the dukes of Bavaria, and a number of south German bishops. A fifth of the ecclesiastical revenues was assigned to the lay princes, regulations to secure a more worthy clergy enacted, clerical fees lightened, the number of saints' days to be observed as holidays diminished, and preaching to be in accordance with the Fathers of the ancient church rather than the schoolmen.[1] It was the beginning of a real Counter-Reformation; but its effect was to increase the separation of parties in Germany, and to strengthen the line of demarcation on the basis of the possessions of rival territorial princes. The nation was in hopeless division.

While Rome was thus strengthened in southern Germany Luther's cause received important accessions. Chief of these was the adhesion, in 1524, of the far-sighted landgrave Philip of Hesse (1518–1567), the ablest politician among the Lutheran princes. At the same time Albert of Prussia, grand master of the Teutonic Knights, George of Brandenburg, Henry of Mecklenburg, and Albert of Mansfeld were showing a decided interest in the Evangelical cause. The important cities, Magdeburg, Nuremberg, Strassburg, Augsburg, Esslingen, Ulm, and others of less moment had also been won by 1524.

It was in the dark days of the peasant revolt that Luther's cautious protector, Frederick the Wise, died (May 5, 1525), and was succeeded by his brother John "the Steadfast" (1525–1532). The change was favorable to Luther, for the new Elector was a declared and active Lutheran. In these months falls, also, Luther's marriage to Katherine von Bora (1499–1552), on June 13, 1525, a union which was to manifest some of the most winsome traits of the reformer's character. The marriage was rather suddenly arranged, and the charge sometimes made

[1] Kidd, pp. 133–151.

that desire for matrimony had any share in Luther's revolt from Rome is palpably absurd; but, though this repudiation of clerical celibacy was undoubtedly favorable in its ultimate results, it was, at the time, an added cause of division, and the union of an ex-monk and a former nun seemed to give point to the bitter jibe of Erasmus that the Reformation, which had appeared a tragedy, was really a comedy, the end of which was a wedding.[1]

The suppression of the peasant revolt had left the princes and the cities the real ruling forces in Germany, and political combinations were now formed for or against the Reformation. Such a league of Catholics was instituted by Duke George of Saxony and other Catholic princes met in Dessau in July, 1525; and as a reply Philip of Hesse and the new Elector John of Saxony organized a Lutheran league in Torgau. The great imperial victory of Pavia in the previous February had resulted in the captivity of the defeated King of France, Francis I. The war had gone decisively in favor of the Emperor, and its results seemed to be garnered by the Treaty of Madrid of January, 1526, by which Francis gained his release. Both monarchs pledged themselves to combined efforts to put down heresy.[2] The prospects of Lutheranism were indeed dark. From this peril the Lutheran cause owed its rescue primarily to the Pope. Clement VII, always more an Italian prince than a churchman, was thoroughly alarmed at the increase of imperial power in Italy. He formed an Italian league against the Emperor, which was joined by the French King in May, 1526. Francis I repudiated the Treaty of Madrid, and now the League of Cognac ranged France, the Pope, Florence, and Venice against the Emperor. The results of Pavia seemed lost. The war must be fought over again. The Emperor's hands were too full to interfere in the religious struggles of Germany.[3]

So it came about that when the new Reichstag met in Speier in the summer of 1526, though the imperial instructions forbad alterations in religion and ordered the execution of the Edict of Worms, the Lutherans were able to urge that the situation had changed from that contemplated by the Emperor when his commands were issued from Spain. The terrifying advance of the Turks, which was to result in the Hungarian disas-

[1] Kidd, pp. 179, 180.   [2] *Ibid.*, p. 180.   [3] *Ibid.*, p. 182.

ter of Mohacz on August 29, 1526, also counselled military unity. The Reichstag, therefore, enacted that, pending a "council or a national assembly," each of the territorial rulers of the empire is "so to live, govern, and carry himself as he hopes and trusts to answer it to God and his imperial majesty." [1]

This was doubtless a mere *ad interim* compromise; but the Lutheran princes and cities speedily interpreted it as full legal authorization to order their ecclesiastical constitutions as they saw fit. Under its shelter the organization of Lutheran territorial churches was now rapidly accomplished. Some steps had been taken toward such territorial organization even before the Reichstag of 1526. Beyond the borders of the empire Albert of Brandenburg (1511–1568), the grand master of the Teutonic Knights in East Prussia, transformed his office into a hereditary dukedom under the overlordship of Poland, in 1525, and vigorously furthered the Lutheranization of the land. [2] In electoral Saxony itself, Elector John was planning a more active governmental control of ecclesiastical affairs, and Luther had issued his *German Mass and Order of Divine Service,* of 1526, before the Reichstag. [3] The decree of the Reichstag now greatly strengthened these tendencies. In Hesse, Landgrave Philip caused a synod to be held in Homberg, in October, 1526, where a constitution was adopted largely through the influence of Francis Lambert (1487–1530), a pupil of Luther. In each community the faithful communicants were to constitute the governing body by which pastor should be chosen and discipline administered. Representatives from these local bodies, a pastor and a lay brother from each, should constitute an annual synod for all Hesse, of which the landgrave and high nobles should also be members. [4] Here was an organization proposed which was consonant, in large measure, with Luther's earlier views. But Luther had changed. He had come to distrust the common man, and on his advice the landgrave rejected the proposals and adopted instead the procedure of electoral Saxony.

In Saxony, which became the norm in a general way for the creation of territorial churches, "visitors" were appointed by the Elector to inquire into clerical doctrine and conduct on the basis of articles drawn up by Melanchthon in 1527, and

---

[1] Kidd, pp. 183–185.
[3] *Ibid.,* pp. 193–202.
[2] *Ibid.,* pp. 185–193.
[4] *Ibid.,* pp. 222–230.

enlarged the following year.[1] The old jurisdiction of bishops was cast off, the land was divided into districts, each under a "superintendent" with administrative, but not spiritual, superiority over the parish minister, and in turn responsible to the Elector. Unworthy or recalcitrant clergy were driven out, similarity of worship secured, and monastic property, altar endowment and similar foundations confiscated, in part for the benefit of parish churches and schools, but largely for that of the electoral treasury. In a word, a Lutheran state church, coterminous with the electoral territories, and having all baptized inhabitants as its members, was substituted for the old bishop-ruled church. Other territories of Evangelical Germany were similarly organized. To aid in popular religious instruction, which the confusion of a decade had reduced to a deplorable condition, Luther prepared two catechisms in 1529, of which the *Short Catechism* is one of the noblest monuments of the Reformation.[2]

That this development of territorial churches could take place was due to favoring political conditions. The Emperor had a tremendous war to wage with domination in Italy as its prize. His brother, Ferdinand, was crowned King of Hungary on November 3, 1527, and thenceforth was in struggle with the Turks. Effective interference in Germany was impossible. But fortune favored the Emperor. On May 6, 1527, an imperial army containing many German Lutheran recruits, captured Rome, shut up Pope Clement VII in the castle of San Angelo, and subjected the city to every barbarity. Though fortune seemed to turn toward the French in the early part of 1528, before the end of that year the imperial forces had asserted their mastery. The Pope was compelled to make his peace with the Emperor, at Barcelona, on June 29, 1529,[3] and France gave up the struggle by the Peace of Cambrai, on the 5th of the following August. The great war which had raged since 1521 was over, and Charles V could now turn his attention to the suppression of the Lutheran revolt. Nor had the Lutheran leaders been wholly fortunate. Deceived by a forgery by Otto von Pack, an official of ducal Saxony, the Landgrave Philip of Hesse and the Elector John of Saxony had been convinced that the Catholics intended to attack them. Philip determined to anticipate the alleged plot, and was arm-

---

[1] Kidd, pp. 202–205. [2] *Ibid.*, pp. 205–222. [3] *Ibid.*, p. 246.

ing for that purpose in 1528, when the forgery was discovered. The effect of the incident was to embitter the relations of the two great ecclesiastical parties.

Under these circumstances it was inevitable that when the next Reichstag met in Speier, in February, 1529, the Catholic majority should be strongly hostile to the Lutheran innovators. That Reichstag now ordered, by a majority decision, that no further ecclesiastical changes should be made, that Roman worship should be permitted in Lutheran lands, and that all Roman authorities and orders should be allowed full enjoyment of their former rights, property, and incomes. This would have been the practical abolition of the Lutheran territorial churches. Unable to defeat this legislation, the Lutheran civil powers represented in the Reichstag, on April 19, 1529, entered a formal protest of great historic importance since it led to the designation of the party as "Protestant." It was supported by John of electoral Saxony, Philip of Hesse, Ernst of Lüneburg, George of Brandenburg-Ansbach, Wolfgang of Anhalt, and the cities Strassburg, Ulm, Constance, Nuremberg, Lindau, Kempten, Memmingen, Nördlingen, Heilbronn, Isny, St. Gallen, Reutlingen, Weissenburg, and Windsheim.[1]

The Protestant prospects were dark, and the situation demanded a defensive union, which Philip of Hesse undertook to secure. At this critical juncture the Reformation cause was threatened by division between the reformers of Saxony and Switzerland, and by the rapid spread of the Anabaptists.

SECTION III. THE SWISS REVOLT

Switzerland, though nominally a part of the empire, had long been practically independent. Its thirteen cantons were united in a loose confederacy, each being practically a self-governing republic. The land, as a whole, was deemed the freest in Europe. Its sons were in great repute as soldiers and were eagerly sought as mercenaries, particularly by the Kings of France and the Popes. Though the general status of education was low, humanism had penetrated the larger towns, and in the early decades of the sixteenth century had notably its home in Basel. The Swiss reformation was to have its sources in humanism, in local self-government, in hatred of ecclesi-

[1] Kidd, pp. 239–245.

astical restraint, and in resistance to monastic exactions, especially where the monasteries were large landowners.

Huldreich Zwingli, chief of the reformers of German-speaking Switzerland, was born on January 1, 1484, in Wildhaus, where his father was the bailiff of the village and in comfortable circumstances. An uncle, the dean of Wesen, started him on the road to an education, which was continued in Basel, and then in Bern under the humanist Heinrich Wölflin (Lupulus), from 1498 to 1500. For two years Zwingli was a student in the University of Vienna, where Conrad Celtes had great fame in the classics. From 1502 to 1506 he continued his studies in the University of Basel, graduating as bachelor of arts in 1504, and receiving the master's degree two years later. At Basel he enjoyed the instruction of the humanist Thomas Wyttenbach (1472–1526), whom he gratefully remembered as having taught him the sole authority of Scripture, the death of Christ as the only price of forgiveness, and the worthlessness of indulgences. Under such teaching Zwingli became naturally a humanist himself, eager to go back to the earlier sources of Christian belief, and critical of what the humanists generally deemed superstition. He never passed through the deep spiritual experience of sin and forgiveness that came to Luther. His religious attitude was always more intellectual and radical than that of the Saxon reformer.

The year of Zwingli's second graduation saw his appointment, apparently through the influence of his clerical uncle, as parish priest in Glarus. Here he studied Greek, became an influential preacher, opposed the employment of Swiss as mercenaries, save by the Pope, and in 1513 received a pension from the Pope, anxious to secure the continued military support of the Swiss. He accompanied the young men of his parish as chaplain in several Italian campaigns. He corresponded with Erasmus and other humanists. His knowledge of the world was increasing, and he touched life on many sides.[1]

Zwingli was patriotically convinced of the moral evil of mercenary service, but the French, eager to enlist Swiss soldiers, made so much trouble in his Glarus parish that, without resigning the post, he transferred his activities in 1516 to the still-famous pilgrim shrine of Einsiedeln. The change brought him enlarged reputation as a preacher and a student. To this

[1] Kidd, pp. 374–380.

Einsiedeln sojourn Zwingli, always jealous of admitting indebtedness to Luther, later ascribed his acceptance of the Evangelical position. The evidence that has survived points, however, to little then beyond the more advanced humanistic attitude. His own life at this time was, moreover, not free from reproach for breach of the vow of chastity.

His opposition to foreign military service and reputation as a preacher and scholar led to Zwingli's election by the Minster chapter in Zürich as people's priest, an office on which he entered with the commencement of 1519. He began at once the orderly exposition of whole books of the Bible, commencing with Matthew's Gospel. He now became acquainted with Luther's writings. He was brought near to death by the plague. He preached faithfully against mercenary soldiering, so that Zürich ultimately (May, 1521) forbad the practice.[1] His own spiritual life deepened, through bereavement by the death of a beloved brother in 1520, and the same year he resigned his papal pension.

Though Zwingli had thus long been moving in the reformatory direction, it was with 1522 that his vigorous reformatory work began. It is interesting to note that the question first at issue did not grow, as with Luther, out of a profound religious experience, but out of the conviction that only the Bible is binding on Christians. Certain of the citizens broke the lenten fast, citing Zwingli's assertion of the sole authority of Scripture in justification. Zwingli now preached and published in their defense. The bishop of Constance, in whose diocese Zürich lay, now sent a commission to repress the innovation. The cantonal civil government ruled that the New Testament imposed no fasts, but that they should be observed for the sake of good order. The importance of this compromise decision was that the cantonal civil authorities practically rejected the jurisdiction of the bishop and took the control of the Zürich churches into their own hands. In the August following the Zürich burgomaster laid down the rule that the pure Word of God was alone to be preached, and the road to revolution was thus fully open.[2]

Zwingli believed that the ultimate authority was the Christian community, and that the exercise of that authority was through the duly constituted organs of civil government acting

[1] Kidd, pp. 384–387.   [2] *Ibid.*, pp. 387–408.

in accordance with the Scriptures.   Only that which the Bible commands, or for which distinct authorization can be found in its pages, is binding or allowable.   Hence his attitude toward the ceremonies and order of the older worship was much more radical than that of Luther.   Really the situation in Zürich was one in which the cantonal government introduced the changes which Zwingli, as a trusted interpreter of Scripture and a natural popular leader, persuaded that government to sanction.   Zwingli now began a process of governmental and popular education, which he employed with great success. Persuaded by Zwingli, the cantonal government ordered a public discussion, in January, 1523, in which the Bible only should be the touchstone.   For this debate Zwingli prepared sixty-seven brief articles, affirming that the Gospel derives no authority from the church, that salvation is by faith, and denying the sacrificial character of the mass, the salvatory character of good works, the value of saintly intercessors, the binding character of monastic vows, or the existence of purgatory.   He also declared Christ to be the sole head of the church, and advocated clerical marriage.   In the resulting debate the government declared Zwingli the victor, in that it affirmed that he had not been convicted of heresy, and directed that he should continue his preaching.   It was an indorsement of his teaching.[1]

Changes now went rapidly.   Priests and nuns married. Fees for baptisms and burials were done away.   In a second great debate, in October, 1523, Zwingli and his associate minister, Leo Jud (1482–1542), attacked the use of images and the sacrificial character of the mass.   The government was with them, but moved cautiously.[2]   January, 1524, saw a third great debate.   The upholders of the old order were given choice of conformity or banishment.   In June and July, 1524, images, relics, and organs were done away.   December witnessed the confiscation of the monastic establishments, their property being wisely used, in large part, in the establishment of excellent schools.   The mass continued till Holy Week of 1525, when it too was abolished.   The transformation was complete.   Episcopal jurisdiction had been thrown off, the services put into German, the sermon made central, the characteristic doctrines and ceremonies of the older worship done

---

[1] Kidd, pp. 408–423.   [2] Ibid., pp. 424–441.

away.[1] Meanwhile, on April 2, 1524, Zwingli had publicly married Anna Reinhard, a widow, whom he and his friends, not without considerable unfriendly gossip, had treated as in some sense his wife since 1522. All this time the Popes had made no effective interference in Zürich affairs, largely by reason of the political value of Switzerland in the wars. The bishop of Constance had done what he could, but to no avail.

Naturally Zwingli followed with eagerness the fortunes of the ecclesiastical revolution in other parts of Switzerland and the adjacent regions of Germany, and aided it to the utmost of his ability. Basel, where the civil authority had gained large influence in churchly affairs before the revolt, was won gradually for the Evangelical cause, chiefly by Johann Œcolampadius (1482–1531), who labored there continuously from 1522. There the mass was abolished in 1529. Œcolampadius and Zwingli were warm friends. Bern, the greatest of the Swiss cantons, was won for the reform in 1528, after much preliminary Evangelical labor, by a public debate in which Zwingli took part.[2] St. Gallen, Schaffhausen, Glarus, and Mülhausen in Alsace were also won. Of even larger importance was the inclination of the great German city of Strassburg to the Zwinglian, rather than the Lutheran, point of view. In that city the Evangelical revolution, begun in 1521 by Matthew Zell (1477–1548), had been carried forward vigorously from 1523 by Wolfgang Capito (1478–1541) and by the able and peace-loving Martin Butzer (1491–1551), though not wholly completed till 1529.

Zwingli and Luther were in many respects in substantial agreement, but they were temperamentally unlike, and their religious experiences had been very different. Luther had reached his goal by a profound religious struggle, involving a transforming sense of relationship between his soul and God. Zwingli had travelled the humanists' road, though going much farther than most humanists. His emphases were unlike Luther's. When Luther thought of the *why* of salvation, which was relatively infrequently, he gave the Augustinian answer. Luther's interest was much more in the *how*. To Zwingli the will of God rather than the way of salvation was the central fact of theology. To Luther the Christian life was one of freedom in forgiven sonship. To Zwingli it was far more one of conformity to the will of God as set forth in the Bible.

---

[1] Kidd, pp. 441–450.   [2] *Ibid.*, pp. 459–464.

Zwingli's nature was intellectual and critical. In no point of Christian doctrine was his diversity from Luther more apparent than in their unlike interpretation of the Lord's Supper, and here their disagreement unfortunately ultimately sundered the Evangelical ranks. To Luther Christ's words, "This is my body," were literally true. His deep religious feeling saw in an actual partaking of Christ the surest pledge of that union with Christ and forgiveness of sins of which the Supper was the divinely attested promise. But as early as 1521 a Dutch lawyer, Cornelius Hoen, had urged that the proper interpretation is "This signifies my body." Hoen's argument came to Zwingli's notice in 1523, and confirmed the symbolic understanding of the words to which the Swiss theologian was already inclined. Henceforth he denied any physical presence of Christ in the Supper, and emphasized its memorial character and its significance as uniting a congregation of believers in a common attestation of loyalty to their Lord. By 1524 the rival interpretations had led to an embittered controversy of pamphlets in which Luther and Bugenhagen on the one side and Zwingli and Œcolampadius on the other, and their respective associates, took part. The most important work of Luther's was his [Great] Confession Concerning the Lord's Supper, of 1528. Little charity was shown on either side. To Zwingli Luther's assertion of the physical presence of Christ was an unreasoning remnant of Catholic superstition. A physical body could be only in one place. To Luther Zwingli's interpretation was a sinful exaltation of reason above Scripture, and he sought to explain the physical presence of Christ on ten thousand altars at once by a scholastic assertion, derived largely from Occam, that the qualities of Christ's divine nature, including ubiquity, were communicated to His human nature. Luther was anxious, also, to maintain that the believer partook of the whole divine-human Christ, and to avoid any dismemberment of His person. Luther declared Zwingli and his supporters to be no Christians, while Zwingli affirmed that Luther was worse than the Roman champion, Eck. Zwingli's views, however, met the approval not only of German-speaking Switzerland but of much of southwestern Germany. The Roman party rejoiced at this evident division of the Evangelical forces.

Zwingli was the most gifted of any of the reformers politically, and developed plans which were far-reaching, though in the end futile. The old rural cantons, Uri, Schwyz, Unterwalden, and Zug, were strongly conservative and opposed to the changes in Zürich, and with them stood Lucerne, the whole constituting a vigorous Roman party. By April, 1524, these had formed a league to resist heresy. To offset this effort and to carry Evangelical preaching into yet wider territories, Zwingli now proposed that Zürich enter into alliance with France and Savoy, and began negotiations with the dispossessed Duke Ulrich of Württemberg. Matters drifted along, but a more successful attempt was the organization of "The Christian Civic Alliance," late in 1527, between Zürich and Constance,[1] a league to which Bern and St. Gallen were added in 1528, and Biel, Mülhausen, Basel, and Schaffhausen in 1529. Though Strassburg joined early in 1530, the league was far less extensive than Zwingli planned. As it was it was divisive of Swiss unity, and the conservative Roman cantons formed a counter "Christian Union" and secured alliance with Austria in 1529. Hostilities were begun. But Austrian help for the Roman party was not forthcoming, and on June 25, 1529, peace was made between the two parties at Kappel, on terms very favorable to Zürich and the Zwinglians.[2] The league with Austria was abandoned.

Zürich was now at the height of its power, and was widely regarded as the political head of the Evangelical cause. Yet the peace had been but a truce, and when, in 1531, Zürich tried to force Evangelical preaching on the Roman cantons by an embargo on shipment of food to them, war was once more certain. Zürich, in spite of Zwingli's counsels, made no adequate preparation for the struggle. The Roman cantons moved rapidly. On October 11, 1531, they defeated the men of Zürich in battle at Kappel. Among the slain was Zwingli himself. In the peace that followed[3] Zürich was compelled to abandon its alliances, and each canton was given full right to regulate its internal religious affairs. The progress of the Reformation in German-speaking Switzerland was permanently halted, and the lines drawn substantially as they are to-day. In the leadership of the Zürich church, not in his political ambitions, Zwingli was succeeded by the able and conciliatory Heinrich Bullinger (1504–1575). The Swiss movement, as a

[1] Kidd, p. 469. [2] *Ibid.*, p. 470. [3] *Ibid.*, pp. 475–476.

whole, was to be modified and greatly developed by the genius of Calvin; and to the churches which trace their spiritual parentage to him, and thus in part to Zwingli, the name "Reformed," as distinguished from "Lutheran," was ultimately to be given.

SECTION IV. THE ANABAPTISTS

It has been said, in speaking of Karlstadt, that some who once worked with Luther came to feel that he was but a halfway reformer. Such was even more largely Zwingli's experience. Among those who had been most forward in favoring innovations in Zürich were Conrad Grebel and Felix Manz, both from prominent families of the city. They and others soon came to feel that Zwingli's leadership in the application of the Biblical test to Zürich practices was far too conservative. This element first came into evidence at the second great debate, in October, 1523 (*ante*, p. 362), where it demanded the immediate abolition of images and of the mass—steps for which the cantonal authorities were not as yet fully ready. An abler participant in that debate was Balthasar Hubmaier (1480?–1528), once a pupil, then colleague and friend of Luther's opponent, Eck, but now preacher in Waldshut, on the northern edge of Switzerland. Led to Evangelical views by Luther's writings in 1522, he was successfully urging reform in his city. As early as May, 1523, he had come to doubt infant baptism, and had discussed it with Zwingli, who, according to his testimony, then sympathized with him. His criticisms were based on want of Scriptural warrant for administration to infants.[1] By 1524 Grebel and Manz had reached the same conclusion,[2] but it was not till early in 1525 that they or Hubmaier translated theory into practice.

Their criticisms led, in January, 1525, to a public debate with Zwingli, as a consequence of which the cantonal authorities of Zürich ordered all children baptized—there had evidently been delay on the part of some parents—and in particular directed Grebel and Manz to cease from disputing, and banished the priest of Wytikon, Wilhelm Röubli.[3] To these men this seemed a command by an earthly power to act counter to the Word of God. They and some of their friends

---

[1] Kidd, p. 451. [2] *Ibid.*, p. 452. [3] *Ibid.*, pp. 453, 454.

gathered in a private house in Zollicon, near Zürich, on February 7, 1525, and there Manz, or Georg Blaurock, once a monk, instituted believers' baptism by sprinkling. A few weeks later a case of immersion occurred, and after Easter, Hubmaier was baptized in Waldshut by Röubli.[1]

These acts constituted the groups separate communions. By their opponents they were nicknamed "Anabaptists," or rebaptizers. Really, since they denied the validity of their baptism in infancy, the name was inappropriate, and "Baptists" would be the truer designation; but as a title consecrated by long usage to a remarkable movement of the Reformation age, the more common name is convenient. The Zürich government, in March, 1526, ordered Anabaptists drowned, in hideous parody of their belief, and a few months later Manz thus suffered martyrdom.[2] Zwingli opposed them with much bitterness, but with little success in winning them from their position.[3]

In Waldshut Hubmaier soon gathered a large Anabaptist community, and was even more successful in propagating his opinions by his pen. In his view the Bible is the sole law of the church, and according to the Scriptural test the proper order of Christian development is, preaching the Word, hearing, belief, baptism, works—the latter indicating a life lived with the Bible as its law. Waldshut, however, was soon involved in the peasant revolt—in how far through Hubmaier is doubtful—and shared the collapse of that movement. Hubmaier had to fly, and the city was once more Catholic. Imprisoned and tortured in Zürich, he fled to Moravia, where he propagated the Anabaptist movement with much success.

These persecutions had the effect of spreading the Anabaptist propaganda throughout Germany and the Netherlands. The movement soon assumed great proportions, especially among the lower classes, when the miserable failure of the peasant revolt had caused deep distrust of the Lutheran cause, now wholly associated with territorial princes and aristocratic city magistrates. In the still Catholic parts of the empire the Anabaptist propaganda practically superseded the Lutheran. On the other hand, Anabaptist rejection of princely control but strengthened the hostility of the Lutheran and Roman authorities. In February, 1527, a meeting of Anabaptist leaders was

[1] Kidd, pp. 454, 455.   [2] *Ibid.*, p. 455.   [3] *Ibid.*, pp. 456–458.

held in Schlatt, where seven articles of faith were drawn up by Michael Sattler, an earnest and worthy former monk. In them believers' baptism was asserted. The church is regarded as composed only of local associations of baptized experiential Christians—united as the body of Christ by common observance of the Lord's Supper; its only weapon is excommunication. Absolute rejection of all "servitude of the flesh," such as the worship of the Roman, Lutheran, and Zwinglian Churches, is demanded. Each congregation is to choose its own officers and administer through them its discipline. While civil government is still a necessity in this imperfect world, the Christian should have no share in it, nor should he take any form of oath. Here were ideas which were to be represented, in varying proportions, by later Baptists, Congregationalists, and Quakers, and through them to have a profound influence on the religious development of England and America.

The Anabaptist ideal implied a self-governing congregation, independent of state or episcopal control, having the Bible as its law, and living a rather ascetic life of strict conformity to a literal interpretation of supposedly Biblical requirements. The sources of these opinions are still in dispute. By some the Anabaptists are regarded as the radicals of the Reformation period; by others as the fruit of new interest in Bible reading by the literal-minded; by still others as revivals of mediæval anti-Roman sects. There is truth in all these theories. The Anabaptists themselves had no consciousness of connection with pre-Reformation movements; they made the Bible literally their law, but many of their characteristics are undoubtedly pre-Reformation. Such is their view of the Bible as a new law in church and state, through obedience to which God's favor is to be preserved. They had as little sympathy with Luther's conception of the Gospel as summed up in the forgiveness of sins, as with the Roman conception of salvation through the sacraments. Pre-Reformation is their ascetic view of the Christian life. So is their conception of the state as a concession to sin, and unworthy of the participation of a Christian in its administration. Such, also, are their strong apocalyptic and mystical tendencies.

The views which have been indicated were those of the overwhelming majority of Anabaptists; but a radical movement attracts extremists, and there were not a few who went much further, but cannot be regarded as representative of the Anabaptists as a whole. Such was the learned humanist Johann Denk (?–1527), who taught an inner light superior to all Scripture, saw in Christ only the highest human example of love, and held that the Christian may live without sin. Associated with Denk in these opinions, was the learned Ludwig Haetzer, to whom was due, with Denk's aid, a translation of the Old Testament prophetical books, but who was beheaded for adulteries at Constance in 1529. The radical preacher, Hans Hut, to whose work much of the rapid spread of Anabaptist views among the working classes of south Germany and Austria was due, declared himself a prophet, affirming that persecution of the saints would be immediately followed by the destruction of the empire by the Turks, following which event the saints would be gathered, and by them all priests and unworthy rulers destroyed, whereupon Christ would visibly reign on earth. In Hubmaier, Hut had a vigorous opponent, but Hut's preaching ended only with his death, in 1527 in Augsburg, through burns received in an attempt to escape from the prison by setting it afire. Some of the more radical Anabaptist leaders taught community of goods and social revolution.

Everywhere the hand of the authorities, Catholic and Evangelical, was heavy on the Anabaptists—though most Protestant territories used banishment rather than the death penalty. Their leaders were martyred. In 1527 Manz met death by drowning in Zürich, while Sattler was burned and his wife drowned near Rottenburg. The next year Hubmaier was burned in Vienna and his wife drowned. Blaurock was burned in the Tyrol in 1529. With these leaders perished great numbers of their followers. Yet the movement continued to spread, and by 1529 was exceedingly perilous for the Protestant cause, being looked upon by the Catholics as the legitimate outcome of revolt from Rome, dividing the forces of reform, and to the thinking of the Lutherans bringing the Evangelical cause into discredit. There can be no doubt that one important effect of the Anabaptist movement was to attach the Lutherans more strongly to the conception of prince and magistrate ruled territorial churches as the only guarantee of good order and of effective opposition to Rome.

SECTION V.   GERMAN PROTESTANTISM ESTABLISHED

The successful conclusion of the great war with France and reconciliation with Pope Clement VII had left the Emperor free, in 1529, to interfere at last effectively in German affairs. The Reichstag of Speier, of that year, alarmed at Lutheran progress and the spread of the Anabaptists, and conscious of the change in the Emperor's prospects, had forbidden further Lutheran advance, and practically ordered the restoration of Roman episcopal authority.   The Lutheran minority had protested.   In this threatening situation Philip of Hesse had attempted to secure a defensive league of all German and Swiss Evangelical forces.   The chief hindrances were the doctrinal differences between the two parties, but Philip hoped that they might be adjusted by a conference, and though Luther was opposed, consent was at last secured, and October 1, 1529, saw Luther and Melanchthon met face to face with Zwingli and Œcolampadius, in Philip's castle in Marburg.   With them were a number of the lesser leaders of both parties.   During the succeeding days the Marburg colloquy ran its course.   Luther was somewhat suspicious of the soundness of the Swiss on the doctrines of the Trinity and original sin, but the real point of difference was the presence or absence of Christ's physical body in the Supper.   Luther held firmly to the literal interpretation of the words: "This is My body."   Zwingli urged the familiar argument that a physical body could not be in two places at the same time.   Agreement was impossible. Zwingli urged that both parties were, after all, Christian brethren, but Luther declared: "You have a different spirit than we." [1]

Yet Philip would not let the hope of a protective league thus vanish, and he persuaded the two parties to draw up fifteen articles of faith.   On fourteen there was agreement. The fifteenth had to do with the Supper, and here there was unanimity on all save the one point as to the nature of Christ's presence, where the differences were stated.   These Marburg Articles both sides now signed with the provision that "each should show Christian love to the other as far as the conscience of each may permit." [2]   Luther and Zwingli each left Marburg with the conviction that he was the victor.   On the way

[1] Kidd, pp. 247–254.   [2] *Ibid.*, pp. 254, 255.

home Luther prepared a somewhat more pointed series of articles—the Schwabach Articles—on the basis of those of Marburg.[1] Their greatest significance for the development of Lutheranism is, perhaps, the declaration that "the church is nothing else than believers in Christ who hold, believe, and teach the above enumerated articles." The original Lutheran conception of a church composed of those justified by their faith, had become transformed into that of those who not only have faith but accept a definite and exact doctrinal statement. These Schwabach Articles were now made by the Elector of Saxony and the margrave of Brandenburg-Ansbach the test of political confederacy. Only Nuremberg of the great south German cities would accept them. The defensive league of Evangelicals which Philip had hoped, was impossible. The Lutherans and the Swiss each went their own way, for the division was permanent.

In January, 1530, the Emperor sent the call from Italy, where he was about to be crowned by the Pope, for a Reichstag to meet in Augsburg. With unexpected friendliness, while declaring the adjustment of religious differences to be a main object of its meeting, he promised a kindly hearing for all representations. That demanded of the Protestants a statement of their beliefs and of their criticisms of the older practice, and these they now set about to prepare.[2] Luther, Melanchthon, Bugenhagen, and Jonas drew up their criticisms of Roman practices, which, as worked over by Melanchthon, constitute the second, or negative, part of the *Augsburg Confession;* and a little later Melanchthon prepared its affirmative articles, which form the first part. On June 25, 1530, it was read to the Emperor in German. It bore the approving signatures of Elector John of Saxony, his heir, John Frederick, Margrave George of Brandenburg-Ansbach, Dukes Ernst and Franz of Brunswick-Lüneburg, Landgrave Philip of Hesse, Wolfgang of Anhalt, and of the representatives of Nuremberg and Reutlingen. Before the close of the Reichstag the cities of Heilbronn, Kempten, Weissenburg, and Windsheim also signified their approval of this *Augsburg Confession.*[3]

The *Augsburg Confession* was chiefly the work of the mild and conciliatory Melanchthon. Though kept informed of the

[1] Kidd, p. 255. [2] *Ibid.*, pp. 257–259.
[3] *Ibid.*, pp. 259–289; in Eng. tr. Schaff, *Creeds of Christendom*, 3 : 3–73.

course of events, Luther, as under imperial ban, could not come to Augsburg and remained in Coburg. Melanchthon modified his draft and made concessions, till checked by his fellow Protestants. Nor was it wholly conciliation that moved Melanchthon. His purpose was to show that the Lutherans had departed in no vital and essential respect from the Catholic Church, or even from the Roman Church, as revealed in its earlier writers. That agreement is expressly affirmed, and many ancient heresies are carefully repudiated by name. On the other hand, Zwinglian and Anabaptist positions are energetically rejected. The sole authority of Scripture is nowhere expressly asserted. The papacy is nowhere categorically condemned. The universal priesthood of believers is not mentioned. Yet Melanchthon gave a thoroughly Protestant tone to the confession as a whole. Justification by faith is admirably defined, the Protestant notes of the church made evident; invocation of saints, the mass, denial of the cup, monastic vows, and prescribed fasting rejected.

To the Emperor Zwingli sent a vigorous expression of his views, which received scanty attention. A more significant event was the presentation of a joint confession by the Zwinglian-inclined south German cities, Strassburg, Constance, Memmingen, and Lindau—the *Confessio Tetrapolitana*—largely from the pen of Butzer, in which a position intermediate between that of the Zwinglians and Lutherans was maintained.

The papal legate, Cardinal Campeggio, advised[1] that the confession be examined by Roman theologians present in Augsburg. This the Emperor approved, and chief among these experts was Luther's old opponent, Eck. Melanchthon was willing to make concessions that would have ruined the whole Lutheran cause,[2] but fortunately for it the Evangelical princes were of sterner stuff. The Catholic theologians prepared a confutation, which was sent back to them by the Emperor and Catholic princes as too polemic, and was at last presented to the Reichstag in much milder form on August 3.

The Emperor still hoped for reconciliation, and committees of conference were now appointed; but their work was vain—a result to which Luther's firmness largely contributed.[3] The Catholic majority voiced the decision of the Reichstag that the Lutherans had been duly confuted, that they be given

---

[1] Kidd, pp. 289–293.   [2] *Ibid.*, pp. 293, 294.   [3] *Ibid.*, p. 296.

till April 15, 1531, to conform; that combined action be had against Zwinglians and Anabaptists, and that a general council be sought within a year to heal abuses in the church. The reconstituted imperial law court should decide, in Catholic interest, cases of secularization.[1] The Lutherans protested, declared their confession not refuted, and called attention to Melanchthon's *Apology*, or defense of the confession, which he had hastily prepared when the vanity of concessions was at last becoming apparent even to him. That *Apology*, rewritten and published the next year (1531), was to be one of the classics of Lutheranism.

Such a situation demanded defensive union. Even Luther, who had held it a sin to oppose the Emperor by force, now was willing to leave the rightfulness of such resistance to the decision of the lawyers. At Christmas the Lutheran princes assembled in Schmalkalden and laid the foundations of a league. Butzer, whose union efforts were unremitting, persuaded Strassburg to accept the *Augsburg Confession*—an example which had great effect on other south German cities. Finally, on February 27, 1531, the Schmalkaldic league was completed. Electoral Saxony, Hesse, Brunswick, Anhalt, and Mansfeld stood in defensive agreement with the cities Strassburg, Constance, Ulm, Reutlingen, Memmingen, Lindau, Isny, Biberach, Magdeburg, Bremen, and Lübeck.[2]

Strong as the position of Charles V appeared on the surface it was not so in reality in the face of this united opposition. The Catholic princes were jealous of one another and of the Emperor. The Pope feared a general council. France was still to be reckoned with. The fatal day—April 15, 1531—therefore passed without the threatened result. In October, 1531, the death of Zwingli at Kappel (*ante*, p. 365) deprived Swiss Evangelicalism of its vigorous head, and inclined south German Protestantism to closer union with that of Wittenberg. The spring of 1532 brought a new danger to the empire as a whole, that of Turkish invasion. In 1529 the Turks had besieged Vienna, and before their advance religious differences had, in a measure, to give way. On July 23, 1532, the Emperor and the Schmalkaldic league agreed to the truce of Nuremberg, by which all existing lawsuits over secularizations should be dropped and peace was assured to the Protestants until a

[1] Kidd, pp. 298–300.   [2] *Ibid.*, p. 301.

general council, or at least a new Reichstag, should assemble.[1]
Shortly after Charles V left Germany for Italy and Spain, not
to return till 1541. Though still precarious, the Protestant
outlook had greatly improved.

Protestantism now rapidly won new territories. By 1534
Anhalt-Dessau, Hanover, Frankfort, and Augsburg had been
gained. Of even greater moment was the conquest for Protestantism of Württemberg by Philip of Hesse, from the Emperor's brother, Ferdinand, and the restoration of its Duke
Ulrich—a result greatly aided by Catholic jealousy of the power
of the house of Habsburg. The death of Duke George, in 1539,
was followed by the triumph of Protestantism in ducal Saxony,
and the same year a cautious adhesion to the Reformation was
won from electoral Brandenburg.

This growing victory of Lutheranism was aided by a tragic
episode of 1533–1535, which robbed Anabaptism of its influence in Germany—the Münster revolution. The Anabaptists
in general were peaceable, if rather ignorant, people, of great
religious earnestness, and patient endurance in persecution.
The Münster episode was not typical of them as a whole.
Yet there were among them many radicals of whom Hans Hut
(*ante*, p. 369) was an early example. Such a leader was Melchior Hoffmann. At first a devoted Lutheran, he became an
equally earnest Anabaptist, with added claims to prophetic
inspiration. His great success was in Friesland. He declared
that Strassburg had been divinely designated as the new
Jerusalem, where he, as the prophet of the new dispensation,
should suffer imprisonment for six months, but with 1533 the
end of the world would come, and all who opposed the "saints"
be destroyed. In this faith he went to Strassburg, and his
prophecy was so far fulfilled that he was there imprisoned, and
in prison he remained till his death in 1543.

Hoffmann's apocalyptic preaching won many disciples in
the Netherlands. One of these, Jan Mathys, a baker of Har-
lem, gave himself forth as the prophet Enoch, and soon spread
a fanatical propaganda widely through the Netherlands and
adjacent parts of Germany. Unlike Hoffmann, who would
wait for the power of God to bring in the new age, Mathys
would inaugurate it by force. Popular democratic discontent
gave him his opportunity.

[1] Kidd, pp. 302–304.

Nowhere was this new teaching more influential than in Münster, where Bernt Rothmann, the Evangelical preacher, was won for radical views in January, 1534. Thither came Mathys soon after, and a tailor of Leyden, Jan Beukelssen. It was now asserted that God had rejected Strassburg by reason of its unbelief, and chosen Münster as the new Jerusalem in its stead. Radicals flocked thither in large numbers. In February, 1534, they gained the mastery of the city, and drove out those who would not accept the new order. The bishop of Münster laid siege to the city. Mathys was killed in battle. Jan Beukelssen was proclaimed King. Polygamy was established, community of goods enforced, all opponents bloodily put down. The struggle, though heroically maintained, was hopeless. The bishop, aided by Catholic and Lutheran troops, captured the city on June 24, 1535, and the surviving leaders were put to death by extreme torture. For German Anabaptism it was a catastrophe. Such fanaticism was popularly supposed to be characteristic of the Anabaptists, and the name became one of ignominy. For Lutheranism it was a gain. It freed the Lutheran cause from the Anabaptist rivalry, but it made Lutheranism even more positively than before a party of princely and middle-class sympathies. As for the Anabaptist movement itself it came, especially in the Netherlands, under the wise, peace-loving, anti-fanatical leadership of Menno Simons (1492–1559), to whom its worthy reorganization was primarily due, and from whom the term "Mennonite" is derived.

Charles V had never ceased to hope and to labor for a general council, by which the divisions of the church could be healed and administrative reforms effected. From Clement VII he could not secure it. Paul III (1534–1549), who succeeded Clement, though by no means a single-hearted religious man, had much more appreciation than Clement of the gravity of the situation caused by the Reformation. He promptly appointed as cardinals Gasparo Contarini (1483–1542), Jacopo Sadoleto (1477–1547), Reginald Pole (1500–1558), and Giovanni Pietro Caraffa (1476–1559), all men desirous of reform in morals, zeal, and administration, who laid before the Pope, in 1538, extensive recommendations for ecclesiastical betterments.[1] By Paul III a general council was actually called

[1] Kidd, pp. 307–318.

to meet in Mantua in 1537.   Before the date set the new war between Charles V and Francis I of France (1536–1538) had made its assembly impossible.   Charles had set his heart on the council, and before the time that it should have opened he demanded of the Protestant leaders assembled in Schmal-kalden, in February, 1537, that they agree to take part.   The imperial order put them in a difficult position.   They had long talked of a general council.   Luther had appealed to such a gathering as early as 1518.   But they saw clearly that they would be outvoted, and they refused to share in the council as in an Italian city, and under the dominance of the Pope.

Charles saw that a council was impossible for the time, and he now tried the experiment of reunion discussions.   Such were actually held in Hagenau in June, 1540, in Worms later in the same year, and in Regensburg in April, 1541.   Melanchthon, Butzer, Calvin, and others took part in one or more of the colloquies on the Protestant side ; Eck, Contarini, and others on the Catholic.   It was in vain, however.   The differences were too vital for compromise.

It was evident to Charles V that the pathway of conciliation was hopeless, and that the Protestants would not share in a general council unless their military and political strength could first be reduced.   That union of Protestant interests was no less a peril to imperial authority in political concerns. It was breaking hopelessly what little unity was left in the empire.   Charles, therefore, slowly and with many hesitations, developed his great plan.   He would have a general council in being.   He would so reduce the strength of Protestantism by force that the Protestants would accept the council as a final arbiter ; and the council could then make such minor concessions as would be needful for the reunion of Christendom, and correct such abuses as Protestants and Catholics alike condemned.   To realize this plan he must secure three preliminary results.   He must, if possible, divide the Schmalkaldic league politically ; he must ward off danger of French attack ; and the ever-threatening peril of Turkish invasion must, for a time at least, be minimized.

The Emperor's purpose of dividing the Protestants was aided by one of the most curious episodes of Reformation history. Landgrave Philip of Hesse, the political genius of the Schmal-kaldic league, though sacrificial in devotion to the Protestant

cause, was, like most princes of that age, a man of low personal morality. Though married early to a daughter of Duke
George of Saxony, who bore him seven children, he had no affection for her. His constant adulteries troubled his conscience
to the extent that, from 1526 to 1539 he partook of the Lord's
Supper but once. He grew anxious as to his soul's salvation,
without improving his conduct. For some years he entertained the thought of a second marriage as a solution of his
perplexities. The Old Testament worthies had practised
polygamy. The New Testament nowhere expressly forbad it.
Why should not he? This reasoning was strengthened by
acquaintance with Margarete von der Sale, an attractive seven-
teen-year-old daughter of a lady of his sister's little court.
The mother's consent was won on condition that the Elector
and the duke of Saxony, and some others should be informed
that it was to be a real marriage. Philip's first wife also consented. Philip was fully persuaded himself of the rightfulness
of the step, but for the sake of public opinion, he desired the
approval of the Wittenberg theologians. He therefore sent
for Butzer of Strassburg, whom he partly persuaded, partly
frightened with threats of seeking dispensation from the Emperor or the Pope, into full support of his plan. Butzer now
became Philip's messenger to Luther and Melanchthon, and
to the Saxon Elector, though the matter was presented as an
abstract question, without mention of the person with whom
marriage was contemplated. On December 10, 1539, Luther
and Melanchthon gave their opinion. Polygamy they declared
to be contrary to the primal law of creation, which Christ had
approved; but a special case required oftentimes treatment
which did not conform to the general rule. If Philip could not
reform his life, it would be better to marry as he proposed
than to live as he was doing. The marriage should, however,
be kept absolutely a secret, so that the second wife should appear to be a concubine. The advice was thoroughly bad,
though the Wittenberg reformers seem to have been moved
by a sincere desire to benefit Philip's soul.

Philip was more honorable than the advice. On March 4,
1540, he married Margarete in what, though private, cannot be
called secret fashion. A court preacher performed the ceremony, and Melanchthon, Butzer, and a representative of the
Saxon Elector were among the witnesses. Though an attempt

was made to keep the affair private, that soon proved impossible. Luther could only advise "a good strong lie"; but Philip was manly enough to declare: "I will not lie."

The scandal was great, both among Protestants and Catholics. The other Evangelical princes would not defend Philip's act or promise protection from its results. The Emperor saw in it his opportunity. On June 13, 1541, he secured an agreement from Philip, as the price of no worse consequences, that the landgrave would neither personally, nor as representative of the Schmalkaldic league, make alliances with foreign states. The hopeful negotiations with France, England, Denmark, and Sweden, which would have greatly strengthened the power of the Schmalkaldic league against the Emperor had to be dropped. Worse than that, Philip had to promise not to aid the Evangelically inclined Duke Wilhelm of Cleves, whose rights over Gelders Charles disputed. As the Saxon Elector was Wilhelm's brother-in-law, and determined to support him, a serious division in the Schmalkaldic league was the result, which showed its disastrous consequences when the Emperor defeated Wilhelm, in 1543, took Gelders permanently into his own possession, and forced Wilhelm to repudiate Lutheranism. This defeat rendered abortive a hopeful attempt to secure the great archbishopric of Cologne for the Protestant cause.[1]

Fortune favored Charles in the rest of his programme. Paul III was persuaded to call the General Council to meet in Trent, a town then belonging to the empire, but practically Italian, in 1542. War caused a postponement, but in December, 1545, it at last actually began its sessions, which were to run a checkered and interrupted course till 1563. By vague, but indefinite, promises Charles secured, at the Reichstag in Speier in 1544, the passive support of the Protestants, and some active assistance, for the wars against France and the Turks. The campaign against France was brief. The Emperor, in alliance with Henry VIII of England, pushed on nearly to Paris, when, to the surprise of Europe he made peace with the French King, without, apparently, gaining any of the advantages in his grasp. Really, he had eliminated French interference in possible aid of German Protestantism for the immediate future.[2] The Turks, busy with a war in Persia, and internal quarrels, made a truce with the Emperor in

---

[1] Kidd, pp. 350–354.   [2] *Ibid.*, p. 354.

October, 1545. All seemed to have worked together for his blow against German Protestantism.

It was while prospects were thus darkening that Luther died on a visit to Eisleben, the town in which he was born, on February 18, 1546, in consequence of an attack of heart-disease or apoplexy. His last years had been far from happy. His health had long been wretched. The quarrels of the reformers, to which he had contributed his full share, distressed him. Above all, the failure of the pure preaching of justification by faith alone greatly to transform the social, civic, and political life about him grieved him. He was comforted by a happy home life and by full confidence in his Gospel. The work which he had begun had passed far beyond the power of any one man, however gifted, to control. He was no longer needed; but his memory must always be that of one of the most titanic figures in the history of the church.

Before actually entering on the war, Charles succeeded yet further in dividing the Protestants. Ducal Saxony had become fully Protestant under Duke Heinrich (1539–1541), but his short reign had been followed by the accession of his young son, Moritz (1541–1553). Of great political abilities, Moritz was a character difficult to estimate, because in an age dominated by professed religious motives, however in reality oftentimes political, he cared nothing for the religious questions involved and everything for his own political advancement. Though son-in-law of Philip of Hesse and cousin of Elector John Frederick of Saxony (1532–1547), Moritz had quarrelled with the Elector and was not on very good terms with Philip. The Emperor now, in June, 1546, secured his support secretly, by the promise of the transfer to Moritz of his cousin's electoral dignity in case of successful war, and other important concessions. Thus at length prepared, the Emperor declared John Frederick and Philip under ban for disloyalty to the empire—Charles desired the war to seem political rather than religious. The Schmalkaldic league had made no adequate preparations. Moritz's defection was a great blow. Though at first the campaign went well for the Protestants, electoral Saxony was crushed at the battle of Mühlberg on the Elbe, on April 24, 1547, in which John Frederick was captured. Philip saw the cause was hopeless and surrendered himself to the Emperor. Both princes were imprisoned. Moritz received

the electoral title and half his cousin's territories. Politically
Protestantism was crushed. Only a few northern cities, of
which Madgeburg was the chief, and a few minor northern
princes still offered resistance.

Yet, curiously enough, the Emperor who had just crushed
Protestantism politically had never been on worse terms with
the Pope. Paul III had aided him early in the war, but had
drawn back fearing that the successful Emperor might grow too
powerful. Charles wished the Council of Trent to move slowly
till he had the Protestants ready to recognize it. He would
have it make such minor concessions as might then seem to
allay Protestant prejudice. The Pope wished the council
to define Catholic faith quickly and go home. It had already,
by April, 1546, made agreement difficult by defining tradition
to be a source of authority in matters of faith.[1] To minimize
imperial influence the Pope declared the council adjourned to
Bologna in March, 1547. This transfer the Emperor refused
to recognize and declined to be bound by the Tridentine decisions already framed. Some method of religious agreement
must be reached under which Germany could live till the healing of the schism which Charles expected from the council.
The Emperor, therefore, had an ecclesiastical commission
draft an *Interim*. This was essentially Roman, while granting
the cup to the laity, permitting clerical marriage and limiting
slightly the powers of the Pope. The Catholic princes refused
to accept it as applying to them. The Pope denounced it.
Charles had to abandon hope of making it a temporary reunion
programme, but secured its adoption on June 30, 1548, by the
Reichstag in Augsburg as applying to the ex-Protestants. This
Augsburg Interim he now proceeded to enforce with a heavy
hand. Moritz of Saxony had done such service to the imperial
cause that a modification, known as the *Leipzig Interim* was
allowed in his lands. It asserted justification by faith alone,
but re-established much of Roman usage and government. To
it Melanchthon reluctantly consented, regarding its Roman
parts as "adiaphora," or non-essential matter. For this weakness he was bitterly denounced by the defiant Lutherans of
unconquered Magdeburg, notably by Matthias Flacius Illyricus (1520–1575) and Nikolaus von Amsdorf (1483–1565).
Flacius, especially, did much to maintain popular Lutheranism

[1] Kidd, pp. 355, 356.

in this dark time; but the bitter quarrels among Lutheran theologians had begun.

Yet, superficially, it seemed as if Charles was nearing his goal. Pope Paul III died in 1549, and was succeeded by Julius III (1550–1555), who proved more tractable to the Emperor. The new Pope summoned the council to meet once more in Trent, and Protestant theologians actually appeared before it in 1552. Really, Germany was profoundly disaffected, the Protestants groaning under the imperial yoke, and the Catholic princes jealous of Charles's increased power and of his apparently successful attempt to secure the imperial succession ultimately for his son, later to be famous as Philip II of Spain. Moritz of Saxony was dissatisfied that his father-in-law, Philip of Hesse, was still imprisoned; he felt, moreover, that he had secured all he could hope for from the Emperor, that his subjects were Lutheran, and that only as a Lutheran leader against the Emperor, could his boundless ambition be further gratified.

The reduction of defiant Magdeburg, in the name of the Emperor, gave Moritz excuse for raising an army. Agreements were made with the Lutheran princes of northern Germany. The aid of King Henry II of France (1547–1559) was secured at the price of the surrender to France of the German border cities of Metz, Toul, and Verdun. Charles knew the plot, but took no adequate steps to meet it. The blow came swiftly. Henry invaded Lorraine and took the coveted cities. Moritz marched rapidly southward, almost capturing the Emperor, who escaped by flight from Innsbruck. The whole structure that Charles had so laboriously built up toppled like a card house, not so much before the power of Lutheranism as before the territorial independence of the princes. On August 2, 1552, the Treaty of Passau brought the brief struggle to an end.

By the Treaty of Passau the settlement of the religious question was referred to the next Reichstag. That body was not able to meet till three years later. Princely rivalries distracted Germany. Moritz lost his life in warfare against the lawless Margrave Albrecht of Brandenburg in 1553. Charles, conscientiously unwilling to tolerate Protestantism, but seeing such toleration inevitable, handed over full authority to treat to his brother Ferdinand, though the latter was not to be chosen Emperor till 1558. The Reichstag met in Augsburg. The

Lutherans demanded full rights, and possession of all ecclesiastical property, heretofore or hereafter secularized. They asked toleration for Lutherans in all Catholic territories, but proposed to grant none to Catholics in their own. These extreme demands were naturally resisted, and the result was a compromise, the Peace of Augsburg, of September 25, 1555.[1] By its provisions equal rights in the empire were extended to Catholics and Lutherans—no other Evangelicals were recognized. Each lay prince should determine which of the two faiths should be professed in his territory—no choice was allowed his subjects—and but one faith should be permitted in a given territory. This was the principle usually defined as *cujus regio, ejus religio.* Regarding ecclesiastical territories and properties, agreement was reached that the time of the Treaty of Passau should be the norm. All then in Lutheran possession should so remain, but a Catholic spiritual ruler turning Protestant thereafter should forfeit his position and holdings, thus insuring to the Catholics continued possession of the spiritual territories not lost by 1552. This was the "ecclesiastical reservation." To the common man, dissatisfied with the faith of the territory where he lived, full right of unhindered emigration and a fair sale of his goods was allowed —a great advance over punishment for heresy, but his choice was only between Catholicism and Lutheranism.

So Lutheranism acquired full legal establishment. Germany was permanently divided. Luther's dream of a purification of the whole German church had vanished, but so had the Catholic conception of visible unity.

The older leaders were rapidly passing. Luther had died nine years before. Melanchthon was to live till 1560. Charles V was to resign his possession of the Netherlands in 1555, and of Spain a year later, and seek retirement at Yuste in Spain till death came to him in 1558.

SECTION VI. THE SCANDINAVIAN LANDS

Denmark, Norway, and Sweden had been nominally united under one sovereign since the union of Kalmar, in 1397. Since 1460, Schleswig-Holstein had also been under Danish control. In none of these lands was the crown powerful. In all, the great

[1] Kidd, pp. 363. 364.

ecclesiastics were unpopular as oppressive, and often foreign-born, and in all they were in rivalry with the nobility. In no portion of Europe, not even in England, was the Reformation to be more thoroughly political. At the dawn of the Reformation the Danish throne was occupied by Christian II (1513–1523), an enlightened despot of Renaissance sympathies. He saw the chief evil of his kingdom in the power of the nobles and ecclesiastics, and to limit that of the bishops by introducing the Lutheran movement he secured a Lutheran preacher in the person of Martin Reinhard, in 1520, and an adviser in Karlstadt for a brief time in 1521. Partially at least through the latter's counsels, a law of 1521 forbad appeals to Rome, reformed the monasteries, limited the authority of the bishops, and permitted priestly marriage. Opposition prevented its execution, and the hostility of the privileged classes, which Christian II had roused in many ways, drove him from his throne in 1523, and made his uncle, Frederick I (1523–1533), King in his stead.

Though inclined to Lutheranism, Frederick was forced by the parties which had put him on the throne to promise to respect the privileges of the nobles and prevent any heretical preaching. Yet Lutheranism penetrated the land. In Hans Tausen (1494–1561), a one-time monk and former Wittenberg student, it found a preacher of popular power from 1524 onward. The year before, a Danish translation of the New Testament had been published. By 1526, King Frederick took Tausen under protection as his chaplain. The same year the King took the confirmation of the appointment of bishops into his own hands. A law of 1527 enacted this into statute, granted toleration to Lutherans, and permitted priestly marriage.[1] These changes were aided by the support of a large section of the nobility won by the King's countenance of their attacks on ecclesiastical rights and property. In 1530, the same year as the *Augsburg Confession*, Tausen and his associates laid before the Danish Parliament the "Forty-three Copenhagen Articles." No decision was reached at the time, but Lutheranism made increasing progress till Frederick's demise in 1533.

The death of Frederick left all in confusion. Of his two sons, most of the nobles favored the elder, Christian III (1536–1559), a determined Lutheran, while the bishops supported the

[1] Kidd, p. 234.

younger, Johann.　A distracting period of civil conflict followed, from which Christian III emerged the victor in 1536.　The bishops were imprisoned, their authority abolished, and church property confiscated for the crown.[1]　Christian now called on Wittenberg for aid.　Johann Bugenhagen, Luther's associate, came in 1537, and seven new Lutheran superintendents, named by the King, but retaining the title "bishop," were ordained by the German reformer, who was himself a presbyter.　The Danish church was now reorganized in fully Lutheran fashion.[2]

Norway was a separate kingdom, but by election under the Danish King.　The Reformation scarcely touched the land during the reign of Frederick I.　In the struggles that followed Archbishop Olaf Engelbrektsson of Trondhjem, the head of the Norwegian clergy, led a temporizing party and fled the land on Christian III's success.　Norway was made a Danish province, and the new Danish Lutheran religious constitution was nominally introduced.　Effective preaching and superintendence in Norway was, however, largely neglected by Christian III with the result that the Reformation, imposed from above, was long in taking effective possession of popular sympathies.

Much the same story may be told of the far-away Danish possession, Iceland.　The Reformation travelled slowly thither. Bishop Gisser Einarsen of Skalholt, educated in Germany and of Lutheran sympathies, began a conservative Lutheran reformation in 1540, and the same year an Icelandic New Testament was published.　In 1548 a strong Catholic reaction, led by Bishop Jon Aresen of Holum, attempted to throw off the Danish yoke.　By 1554 the rebellion was suppressed and Lutheranism forcibly established, though long with little popular approval.

The reformation of Sweden was largely bound up with a national struggle for independence.　Christian II of Denmark found bitter resistance to his efforts to secure the Swedish throne.　His chief supporter was Gustaf Trolle, archbishop of Upsala.　Gustaf procured from Pope Leo X approval of the excommunication of his opponents, though that opposition was purely political.　In 1520 Christian II captured Stockholm and followed his coronation as King of Sweden by a deed of the utmost cruelty.　He had the unsuspecting nobles, gathered

---

[1] Kidd pp. 322–328.　　　　　　　[2] *Ibid.*, pp. 328–335.

for the ceremony, executed, nominally as excommunicated heretics. The Stockholm Bath of Blood roused Sweden to a rebellion against Christian II; which soon found an energetic leader in Gustaf Vasa. The Danes were expelled and, in 1523, Gustaf was chosen King (1523–1560).

Meanwhile Lutheran doctrine was being taught by two brothers, who had returned in 1519 from studies in Wittenberg —Olaf (1497–1552) and Lars Petersson (1499–1573), who labored in Strengnäs, and soon won the archdeacon, Lars Andersson (1482–1552). By 1524 King Gustaf was definitely favoring these leaders. Andersson became his chancellor, and Lars Petersson professor of theology in Upsala. On December 27, 1524, a discussion in Upsala between Olaf Petersson, now preacher in Stockholm, and the Roman champion, Peter Galle, seemed a victory for the reformers.[1] Part of the support of the King was probably due to religious conviction, but no small portion was owing to the dire poverty of the crown, which Gustaf thought could be remedied only by extensive confiscation of church property. In June, 1527, the King struck the blow. At the Diet of Westerås Gustaf demanded and obtained by threat of resignation, the assignment to the crown of all episcopal or monastic property which the King should deem not needed for proper religious work, the surrender to the heirs of the original owners of all lands exempt from taxes acquired by the church since 1454, and "pure" preaching of "God's Word." Provision was made for the reconstitution of the church under royal authority.[2] Though master of the Swedish church, and now possessor of a large part of its property, Gustaf used his power in religion conservatively. Most of the old prelates left the land. The bishop's office was retained, though its holders were now appointed by the King. New bishops were consecrated, with the old rites, in 1528, at the hands of Bishop Peter Magni, of Westerås, who had received his office in Catholic days, and through whom apostolical succession was believed to be transmitted to the Swedish Lutheran episcopate. Further reform measures were taken by the synod of Orebro in 1529.[3] A Swedish service was issued in 1529, and the "Swedish Mass" in 1531. In the year last named Lars Petersson was made archbishop of Upsala, though without jurisdiction over his fellow bishops—that remained in

[1] Kidd, pp. 155–164.   [2] *Ibid.*, pp. 234–236.   [3] *Ibid.*, pp. 236–239.

the hands of the King. Most of the lower clergy accepted the
Reformation and kept their places, but such changes by royal
power were far from winning immediate popular approval, and
it was long before Sweden became thoroughly Evangelical.
Its type of Lutheranism in doctrine and practice was strongly
conservative. The reform of Sweden carried with it that of
Finland, then part of the Swedish monarchy. The Swedish
church was to pass through a period of Romanizing reaction,
especially under the reign of Gustaf's son, Johan III (1569–
1592); but it was ended in 1593, when the synod of Upsala
formally adopted the *Augsburg Confession* as the creed of
Sweden.

SECTION VII. REVOLT IN FRENCH SWITZERLAND AND GENEVA BEFORE CALVIN

Zürich was the strongest power in northern Switzerland,
Bern in the south. The latter was in constant rivalry with
the dukes of Savoy, especially for possession of French-speaking territories in the neighborhood of Lake Geneva. The acceptance of Evangelical views by Bern on February 7, 1528
(*ante*, p. 363), led the Bernese government to further the introduction of the Reformation into these dependent districts
by encouraging the preaching of Guillaume Farel (1489–1565).
Farel was a native of Gap, in the French province of Dauphiné.
As a student in Paris he came under the influence of the humanistic reformer, Jacques Le Fèvre, of Etaples, and by 1521
was preaching under the auspices of the moderately reformatory
Guillaume Briçonnet, bishop of Meaux. An orator of fiery ve-
hemence, intense feeling, and stentorian voice, he soon was so
preaching the Reformation that he had to leave France. By
1524 he was urging reform in Basel, but his impetuosity led
to his expulsion.

The next months were a period of wandering, during which
Farel visited Strassburg and won Butzer's friendship; but, in
November, 1526, his work in French-speaking Switzerland
began in Aigle, where the Bernese government defended him,
though not yet itself fully committed to the Reformation.[1]
With the complete victory of the newer views in Bern, Farel's
work went faster. In 1528 Aigle, Ollon, and Bex adopted the

[1] Kidd, pp. 477–481.

Reformation, destroying images and ending the mass.[1] After vainly attempting to invade Lausanne, he began a stormy attack in Neuchâtel, in November, 1529, which ultimately secured the victory of the Reformation there.[2] Morat followed in 1530;[3] but in Grandson and Orbe, which, like Morat, were under the joint overlordship of Protestant Bern and Catholic Freiburg, he could secure only the toleration of both forms of worship.[4] A visit by invitation in September, 1532, to a synod of the Waldenses in the high valleys of the Cottian Alps resulted in the acceptance of the Reformation by a large section of the body,[5] and was followed in October by an attempt, at first unsuccessful, to preach reform in Geneva.[6] Everywhere Farel faced opposition with undaunted courage, sometimes at the risk of life and at the cost of bodily injury, but no one could be indifferent in his strenuous presence.

Geneva, at Farel's coming, was in the struggle of a revolutionary crisis. Situated on a main trade route across the Alps, it was an energetic business community, keenly alive to its interests and liberties, of rather easy-going moral standards, in spite of its extensive monasteries and ecclesiastical foundations. Genevan liberties were being maintained with great difficulty against the encroachments of the powerful duke of Savoy. At the beginning of the sixteenth century three powers shared the government of the city and its adjacent villages— the bishop; his *vicedominus,* or temporal administrator; and the citizens, who met annually in a General Assembly and chose four "syndics" and a treasurer. Besides the General Assembly, the citizens were ruled by a Little Council of twenty-five, of which the "syndics" of the year and of the year previous were members. Questions of larger policy were discussed by a Council of Sixty appointed by the Little Council, and in 1527 a Council of Two Hundred was added, its membership including the Little Council and one hundred and seventy-five others chosen by that inner body. The aggressive dukes of Savoy had appointed the *vicedominus* since 1290, and had controlled the bishopric since 1444. The struggle was therefore one for freedom by the citizens against Savoyard interests, represented by the bishop and the *vicedominus.*

In 1519 the Genevan citizens made a protective alliance with

---

[1] Kidd, pp. 481, 482.   [2] *Ibid.*, pp. 483–489.   [3] *Ibid.*, p. 489.
[4] *Ibid*, pp. 489–491.   [5] *Ibid.*, pp. 491, 492.   [6] *Ibid.*, pp. 492–494.

Freiburg, but Duke Charles III of Savoy won the upper hand, and the Genevan patriot Philibert Berthelier was beheaded. Seven years later Geneva renewed the effort, this time entering into alliance with Bern as well as Freiburg. In 1527 the bishop, Pierre de la Baume, left the city, which he could not control, and fully attached himself to the Savoyard interests. The authority of the *vicedominus* was repudiated. Duke Charles attacked the plucky city, but Bern and Freiburg came to its aid in October, 1530, and he had to pledge respect to Genevan liberties.[1] Thus far there was little sympathy with the Reformation in Geneva, but Bern was Protestant and was anxious to see the Evangelical faith there established. Placards criticising papal claims and presenting reformed doctrine were posted on June 9, 1532, but Geneva's ally, Freiburg, was Catholic, and the Genevan government disowned any leanings toward Lutheranism.[2] In October following Farel came, as has been seen, but could get no footing in the city. Farel sent his friend Antoine Froment (1508–1581) to Geneva, who found a place there as a schoolmaster, and propagated reformed doctrine under this protection. On January 1, 1533, Froment was emboldened to preach publicly, though the result was a riot. By the following Easter there were enough Protestants to dare to observe the Lord's Supper, and in December Farel effectively returned. The Genevan government was in a difficult position. Its Catholic ally, Freiburg, demanded that Farel be silenced. Its Protestant ally, Bern, insisted on the arrest of Guy Furbity, the chief defender of the Roman cause.[3] Farel and his friends held a public disputation, and on March 1, 1534, seized a church. Under Bernese pressure the government broke the league with Catholic Freiburg. The bishop now raised troops to attack the city. His action greatly strengthened Genevan opposition, and on October 1, 1534, the Little Council declared the bishopric vacant, though Geneva was still far from predominantly Protestant.[4]

With the following year Farel, emboldened by the successful result of a public debate in May and June, proceeded to yet more positive action. On July 23, 1535, he seized the church of La Madeleine, and on August 8 the cathedral of St. Pierre itself. An iconoclastic riot swept the churches. Two days

[1] Kidd, pp. 494–500.
[3] *Ibid.*, pp. 504–508.
[2] *Ibid.*, pp. 500–504.
[4] *Ibid.*, pp. 508–512.

later the mass was abolished, and speedily thereafter the monks and nuns were driven from the city. On May 21, 1536, the work was completed by the vote of the General Assembly, expressing its determination "to live in this holy Evangelical law and word of God."[1] Meanwhile the duke of Savoy had been pressing Geneva sorely, but Bern came at last powerfully to its aid in January, 1536. Geneva saw the peril from Savoy removed, only to have danger arise of falling under Bernese control. Yet the courage of its citizens was equal to the situation, and on August 7, 1536, Bern acknowledged Genevan independence.[2] The courageous city was now free, and had accepted Protestantism, more for political than for religious reasons. Its religious institutions had all to be formed anew. Farel felt himself unequal to the task, and in July, 1536, he constrained a young French acquaintance passing through the city to stay and aid in the work. The friend was John Calvin.[3]

SECTION VIII. JOHN CALVIN

John Calvin was born in Noyon, a city of Picardy, about fifty-eight miles northeast of Paris, on July 10, 1509. His father, Gérard Cauvin, was a self-made man, who had risen to the posts of secretary of the Noyon bishopric and attorney for its cathedral chapter, and possessed the friendship of the powerful noble family of Hangest, which gave two bishops to Noyon in his lifetime. With the younger members of this family John Calvin was intimately acquainted, and this friendship earned for him a familiarity with the ways of polite society such as few of the reformers enjoyed. Through the father's influence the son received the income from certain ecclesiastical posts in and near Noyon, the earliest being assigned him before the age of twelve. He was never ordained. Thus provided with means, Calvin entered the University of Paris in August, 1523, enjoying the remarkable instruction in Latin given by Mathurin Cordier (1479–1564), to whom he owed the foundation of a style of great brilliancy. Continuing his course with special emphasis, as was then the custom, on philosophy and dialectics, Calvin completed his undergraduate studies early in 1528. As a student he formed a number of warm friendships,

---

[1] Kidd, pp. 512–519.   [2] *Ibid.*, pp. 519–521.   [3] *Ibid.*, p. 544.

notably with the family of Guillaume Cop, the King's physician, and an eager supporter of humanism.

Calvin's father had designed him for theology, but by 1527 Gérard Cauvin was in quarrel with the Noyon cathedral chapter and determined that his son should study law. For that discipline Calvin now went to the University of Orléans, where Pierre de l'Estoile (1480–1537) enjoyed great fame as a jurist, and in 1529 to the University of Bourges, to listen to Andrea Alciati (1493–1550). Humanistic interests, also, strongly attracted him, and he began Greek in Bourges with the aid of a German teacher, Melchior Wolmar (1496–1561). He graduated in law; but the death of his father, in 1531, left Calvin his own master, and he now took up the study of Greek and Hebrew in the humanist Collège de France, which King Francis I had founded in Paris in 1530. He was hard at work on his first book—his *Commentary on Seneca's Treatise on Clemency*—which was published in April, 1532. It was a marvel of erudition, and marked no less by a profound sense of moral values; but in it Calvin displayed no interest in the religious questions of the age. He was still simply an earnest, deeply learned humanist.

Yet it was not for want of opportunity to know the new doctrines that Calvin was still untouched by the struggle. Humanism had done its preparatory work in France as elsewhere. Its most conspicuous representative had been Jacques Le Fèvre of Etaples (1455?–1536), who made his home in the monastery of St.-Germain des Prés in Paris, from 1507, for some years, and gathered about him a notable group of disciples. Le Fèvre never broke or wished to break with the Roman Church, but in 1512 he published a commentary on Paul's epistles, which denied the justifying merit of good works, declared salvation the free gift of God, and held to the sole authority of Scripture. It was the study of a quiet scholar and aroused no sensation at the time. Eleven years later, in 1523, he put forth a translation of the New Testament. Among his pupils were Guillaume Briçonnet (1470–1534), from 1516 bishop of Meaux; Guillaume Budé (1467–1540), to whose persuasions the establishment of the Collège de France by royal authority was due; François Vatable (?–1547), Calvin's teacher of Hebrew on that foundation; Gérard Roussel (1500?–1550), Calvin's friend, later bishop of Oloron; Louis de Berquin (1490–1529), to die at the stake for his Protestantism; and Guillaume Farel, whose fiery reformatory career has already been noted. With these men of reformatory impulse, none of whom, save the two last mentioned, broke with the Roman Church, many humanists sympathized, such as the family of Cop, whose friendship Calvin enjoyed in Paris. They had powerful support in King Francis's gifted and popular sister, Marguerite d'Angoulême (1492–1549), from 1527 Queen of Navarre, who was ultimately an unavowed Protestant. Luther's books early penetrated into France and were read in this circle. Few of its members realized, however, the gravity of the situation or were ready to pay the full price of reform; but there was no ignorance of what the main questions were in the scholarly circle in which Calvin moved. They had not as yet become important for him.

Between the publication of his *Commentary on Seneca's Treatise on Clemency* in the spring of 1532 and the autumn of 1533 Calvin experienced a "sudden conversion." [1] Of its circumstances nothing is certainly known, but its central experience was that God spoke to him through the Scriptures and God's will must be obeyed. Religion had henceforth the first place in his thoughts. How far he even yet thought of breaking with the Roman Church is doubtful. He was still a member of the humanistic circle in Paris, of which Roussel and his intimate friend Nicolas Cop were leaders. [2] On November 1, 1533, Cop delivered an inaugural address as newly elected rector of the University of Paris, in which he pleaded for reform, using language borrowed from Erasmus and Luther. [3] That Calvin wrote the oration as has often been alleged, is improbable, but he undoubtedly sympathized with its sentiments. The commotion aroused was great, and King Francis enjoined action against the "Lutherans." [4] Cop and Calvin had to seek safety, which Calvin found in the home of a friend, Louis du Tillet, in Angoulême. Calvin's sense of the necessity of separation from the older communion was now rapidly developing, and forced him to go to Noyon to resign his benefices on May 4, 1534. Here he was for a brief time imprisoned. Though soon released, France was too perilous for him, especially after Antoine Marcourt posted his injudicious theses against the

[1] Kidd, pp. 523, 524.   [2] *Ibid.*, pp. 524, 525.
[3] *Ibid.*, pp. 525, 526.   [4] *Ibid.*, pp. 526–528.

mass in October, 1534,[1] and by about New Year's following Calvin was safely in Protestant Basel.

Marcourt's placards had been followed by a sharp renewal of persecution, one of the victims being Calvin's friend the Parisian merchant, Estienne de la Forge. Francis I was coquetting for the aid of German Protestants against Charles V, and therefore, to justify French persecutions, issued a public letter in February, 1535, charging French Protestantism with anarchistic aims such as no government could bear. Calvin felt that he must defend his slandered fellow believers. He therefore rapidly completed a work begun in Angoulême, and published it in March, 1536, as his *Institutes*, prefacing it with a letter to the French King. The letter is one of the literary masterpieces of the Reformation age. Courteous and dignified, it is a tremendously forceful presentation of the Protestant position and defense of its holders against the royal slanders. No French Protestant had yet spoken with such clearness, restraint, and power, and with it its author of twenty-six years stepped at once into the leadership of French Protestantism.[2]

The *Institutes* themselves, to which this letter was prefixed, were, as published in 1536, far from the extensive treatise into which they were to grow in Calvin's final edition of 1559; but they were already the most orderly and systematic popular presentation of doctrine and of the Christian life that the Reformation produced. Calvin's mind was formulative rather than creative. Without Luther's antecedent labors his work could not have been done. It is Luther's conception of justification by faith, and of the sacraments as seals of God's promises that he presents. Much he derived from Butzer, notably his emphasis on the glory of God as that for which all things are created, on election as a doctrine of Christian confidence, and on the consequences of election as a strenuous endeavor after a life of conformity to the will of God. But all is systematized and clarified with a skill that was Calvin's own.

Man's highest knowledge, Calvin taught, is that of God and of himself. Enough comes by nature to leave man without excuse, but adequate knowledge is given only in the Scriptures, which the witness of the Spirit in the heart of the believing reader attests as the very voice of God. These Scriptures teach that God is good, and the source of all goodness every-

---

[1] Kidd, pp. 528–532. [2] *Ibid.*, pp. 532, 533.

where. Obedience to God's will is man's primal duty. As originally created, man was good and capable of obeying God's will, but he lost goodness and power alike in Adam's fall, and is now, of himself, absolutely incapable of goodness. Hence no work of man's can have any merit; and all men are in a state of ruin meriting only damnation. From this helpless and hopeless condition some men are undeservedly rescued through the work of Christ. He paid the penalty due for the sins of those in whose behalf He died; yet the offer and reception of this ransom was a free act on God's part, so that its cause is God's love.

All that Christ has wrought is without avail unless it becomes a man's personal possession. This possession is effected by the Holy Spirit, who works when, how, and where He will, creating repentance; and faith which, as with Luther, is a vital union between the believer and Christ. This new life of faith is salvation, but it is salvation unto righteousness. That the believer now does works pleasing to God is the proof that he has entered into vital union with Christ. "We are justified not without, and yet not by works." Calvin thus left room for a conception of "works" as strenuous as any claimed by the Roman Church, though very different in relation to the accomplishment of salvation. The standard set before the Christian is the law of God, as contained in the Scriptures, not as a test of his salvation but as an expression of that will of God which as an already saved man he will strive to fulfil. This emphasis on the law as the guide of Christian life was peculiarly Calvin's own. It has made Calvinism always insistent on character, though in Calvin's conception man is saved to character rather than by character. A prime nourishment of the Christian life is by prayer.

Since all good is of God, and man is unable to initiate or resist his conversion, it follows that the reason some are saved and others are lost is the divine choice—election and reprobation. For a reason for that choice beyond the will of God it is absurd to inquire, since God's will is an ultimate fact. Yet to Calvin election was always primarily a doctrine of Christian comfort. That God had a plan of salvation for a man, individually, was an unshakable rock of confidence, not only for one convinced of his own unworthiness, but for one surrounded by opposing forces even if they were those of priests and Kings

It made a man a fellow laborer with God in the accomplishment of God's will.

Three institutions have been divinely established by which the Christian life is maintained—the church, the sacraments, and civil government. In the last analysis the church consists of "all the elect of God"; but it also properly denotes "the whole body of mankind . . . who profess to worship one God and Christ." Yet there is no true church "where lying and falsehood have usurped the ascendancy." The New Testament shows as church officers, pastors, teachers, elders, and deacons, who enter on their charges with the assent of the congregation that they serve. Their "call" is twofold, the secret inclination from God and the "approbation of the people." Calvin thus gave to the congregation a voice in the choice of its officers not accorded by any other Reformation party except that of the Anabaptists, though circumstances at Geneva were to compel him to regard that voice there as expressed by the city government. Similarly Calvin claimed for the church full and independent jurisdiction in discipline up to the point of excommunication. Further it could not go; but it was a retention of a freedom which all the other leaders of the Reformation had abandoned to state supervision. Civil government has, however, the divinely appointed task of fostering the church, protecting it from false doctrine, and punishing offenders for whose crimes excommunication is insufficient. It was essentially the mediæval theory of the relations of church and state.

Calvin recognized only two sacraments—baptism and the Lord's Supper. Regarding the burning question of Christ's presence in the Supper, he stood, like Butzer, part way between Luther and Zwingli, nearer the Swiss reformer in form, and to the German in spirit. With Zwingli he denied any physical presence of Christ; yet he asserts in the clearest terms a real, though spiritual presence received by faith. "Christ, out of the substance of His flesh, breathes life into our souls, nay, diffuses His own life into us, though the real flesh of Christ does not enter us." [1]

On the publication of the *Institutes* in the spring of 1536, Calvin made a brief visit to the court of Ferrara, in Italy, doubtless intending to advance the Evangelical cause with his liberal-minded and hospitable fellow countrywoman, the Duch-

---

[1] The quotations in these paragraphs are from the edition of 1559.

ess Renée. His stay was short, and a brief visit to France followed, to settle his business affairs and to proceed to Basel or Strassburg with his brother and sister. The perils of war took him to Geneva in July, 1536, and there Farel's fiery exhortation, as has been seen (*ante*, p. 389), induced him to remain.

Calvin's work in Geneva began very modestly. He was a lecturer on the Bible, and was not appointed one of the preachers till a year later. Over Farel, however, he exercised great influence. Their first joint work was to aid the Bernese ministers and civil authorities in the effective establishment of the Reformation throughout Vaud and in Lausanne, which had just come under Bernese control.[1] In Lausanne, Pierre Viret (1511–1571) was appointed pastor, an office which he was to hold till 1559. With him Calvin was to enjoy close friendship. Calvin and Farel now undertook to accomplish three results in Geneva itself. In January, 1537, they laid before the Little Council a series of recommendations from Calvin's pen.[2] These proposed monthly administration of the Lord's Supper. For better preparation, the city government should appoint "certain persons" for each quarter of the city, who, in connection with the ministers, might report the unworthy to the church for discipline up to excommunication. This was Calvin's first attempt to make Geneva a model community, and likewise to assert the independence of the church in its own sphere. A second effort was the adoption of a catechism composed by Calvin, and a third the imposition on each citizen of a creed, probably written by Farel.[3] These recommendations the Little Council adopted with considerable modification.

The success of Calvin's work was soon threatened. He and Farel were unjustly charged with Arianism by Pierre Caroli, then of Lausanne. They vindicated their orthodoxy easily, but not till great publicity had been given to the matter.[4] In Geneva itself the new discipline and the demand for individual assent to the new creed soon aroused bitter opposition. This was strong enough to secure a vote of the Council of Two Hundred, in January, 1538, that the Supper should be refused to no one, thus destroying Calvin's system of discipline.[5] The next month the opposition won the city election, and determined to force the issue. The Bernese liturgy differed some-

---

[1] Kidd, pp. 548–558.   [2] *Ibid.*, pp. 560–567.   [3] *Ibid.*, pp. 568–572.
[4] *Ibid.*, pp. 573–575.   [5] *Ibid.*, p. 577.

what from that now established in Geneva. Bern had long wished it adopted in Geneva, and the opposition now secured a vote that it be used. Calvin and Farel regarded the differences in Bernese and Genevan usage as of slight importance, but an imposition by civil authority, without consulting the ministers, they viewed as robbing the church of all freedom. Calvin and Farel refused compliance, and on April 23, 1538, were banished.[1] Their work in Geneva seemed to have ended in total failure.

After a vain attempt at restoration to Geneva by the intervention of Swiss Protestant authorities, Farel found a pastorate in Neuchâtel, which was thenceforth to be his home; and Calvin, at Butzer's invitation, a refuge in Strassburg. The three years there spent were in many ways the happiest in Calvin's life. There he was pastor of a church of French refugees and lecturer on theology. There he was honored by the city and made one of its representatives in Charles V's reunion debates between Protestants and Catholics (*ante*, p. 376), gaining thereby the friendship of Melanchthon and other German reformers. There he married, in 1540, the wife who was to be his faithful companion till her death in 1549. There he found time for writing, not merely an enlarged edition of the *Institutes*, and his *Commentary on Romans*, the beginning of a series that put him in the front rank of exegetes among the reformers, but his brilliant *Reply to Sadoleto*, which was justly regarded as the ablest of vindications of Protestantism generally.[2]

Meanwhile a political revolution occurred in Geneva for which Calvin was in no way responsible. The party there which had secured his banishment made a disastrous treaty with Bern in 1539, which resulted in its overthrow the next year and the condemnation of the negotiators as traitors. The party friendly to Calvin was once more in power, and its leaders sought his return. He was with difficulty persuaded, but in 1541 was once more in Geneva, practically on his own terms.[3]

Calvin promptly secured the adoption of his new ecclesiastical constitution, the *Ordonnances*, now far more definite than the recommendations accepted in 1537. In spite of his successful return, however, he could not have them quite all that he

---

[1] Kidd, pp. 577–580. [2] *Ibid.*, pp. 583–586.
[3] *Ibid.*, pp. 586–589.

wished. The *Ordonnances*[1] declare that Christ has instituted in His church the four offices of pastor, teacher, elder, and deacon, and define the duties of each. Pastors were to meet weekly for public discussion, examination of ministerial candidates, and exegesis, in what was popularly known as the *Congrégation*. The teacher was to be the head of the Geneva school system, which Calvin regarded as an essential factor in the religious training of the city. To the deacons were assigned the care of the poor and the supervision of the hospital. The elders were the heart of Calvin's system. They were laymen, chosen by the Little Council, two from itself, four from the Sixty, and six from the Two Hundred, and under the presidency of one of the syndics. They, together with the ministers, made up the *Consistoire*, meeting every Thursday, and charged with ecclesiastical discipline. To excommunication they could go; beyond that, if the offense demanded, they were to refer the case to the civil authorities. No right seemed to Calvin so vital to the independence of the church as this of excommunication, and for none was he compelled so to struggle till its final establishment in 1555.[2]

Besides this task, Calvin prepared a new and much more effective catechism,[3] and introduced a liturgy, based on that of his French congregation in Strassburg, which, in turn, was essentially a translation of that generally in use in that German city. In formulating it for Genevan use Calvin made a good many modifications to meet Genevan customs or prejudices.[4] It combined a happy union of fixed and free prayer. Calvin had none of the hostility against fixed forms which his spiritual descendants in Great Britain and America afterward manifested. It also gave full place to singing.

Under Calvin's guidance, and he held no other office than that of one of the ministers of the city, much was done for education and for improved trade; but all Genevan life was under the constant and minute supervision of the *Consistoire*. Calvin would make Geneva a model of a perfected Christian community. Its strenuous Evangelicalism attracted refugees in large numbers, many of them men of position, learning, and wealth, principally from France, but also from Italy, the Netherlands, Scotland, and England. These soon became a

---

[1] Kidd, pp. 589–603.   [2] *Ibid.*, p. 647.
[3] Extracts, Kidd, pp. 604–615.   [4] Kidd, pp. 615–628.

very important factor in Genevan life. Calvin himself, and all his associated ministers, were foreigners. Opposition to his strenuous rule appeared practically from the first, but, by 1548, had grown very serious. It was made up of two elements, those to whom any discipline would have been irksome; and much more formidable, those of old Genevan families who felt that Calvin, his fellow ministers, and the refugees were foreigners who were imposing a foreign yoke on a city of heroic traditions of independence. That there was a party of religious *Libertins* in Geneva, is a baseless tradition.

Calvin's severest struggle was from 1548 to 1555, from the time that some of the older inhabitants began to fear that they would be swamped politically by the refugees, till the refugees, almost all of whom were eager supporters of Calvin, achieved what had been dreaded, and made Calvin's position unshakable. Constantly increasing in fame outside of Geneva, Calvin stood in imminent peril, throughout this period, of having his Genevan work overthrown.

The cases of conflict were many, but two stand out with special prominence. The first was that caused by Jérôme Hermès Bolsec, a former monk of Paris, now a Protestant physician in Veigy, near Geneva. In the *Congrégation* Bolsec charged Calvin with error in asserting predestination. That was to attack the very foundations of Calvin's authority, for his sole hold on Geneva was as an interpreter of the Scriptures. If he was not right in all, he was thoroughly discredited. Calvin took Bolsec's charges before the city government in October, 1551. The result was Bolsec's trial. The opinions of other Swiss governments were asked, and it was evident that they attached no such weight to predestination as did Calvin. It was with difficulty that Calvin procured Bolsec's banishment, and the episode led him to a more strenuous insistence of the vital importance of predestination as a Christian truth than even heretofore.[1] As for Bolsec, he ultimately returned to the Roman communion and avenged himself on Calvin's memory by a grossly slanderous biography.

Calvin was thus holding his power with difficulty, when in February, 1553, the elections, which for some years had been fairly balanced, turned decidedly in favor of his opponents. His fall seemed inevitable, when he was rescued and put on

[1] Kidd, pp. 641–645.

the path to ultimate victory by the arrival in Geneva of Miguel Servetus, whose case forms the second of those here mentioned. Servetus was a Spaniard, almost the same age as Calvin, and undoubtedly a man of great, though erratic, genius. In 1531 he published his *De Trinitatis Erroribus*. Compelled to conceal his identity, he studied medicine under the name of Villeneuve, being the real discoverer of the pulmonary circulation of the blood. He settled in Vienne in France, where he developed a large practice. He was working secretly on his *Restitution of Christianity*, which he published early in 1553. To his thinking, the Nicene doctrine of the Trinity, the Chalcedonian Christology, and infant baptism were the chief sources of the corruption of the church. As early as 1545, he had begun an exasperating correspondence with Calvin, whose *Institutes* he contemptuously criticised.

Servetus's identity and authorship were unmasked to the Roman ecclesiastical authorities in Lyons, by Calvin's friend, Guillaume Trie, who, a little later, supplied further proof obtained from Calvin himself. He was condemned to be burned; though, before sentence, he had escaped from prison in Vienne. For reasons hard to understand he made his way to Geneva, and was there arrested in August, 1553. His condemnation now became a test of strength between Calvin and the opposition, which did not dare come out openly in defense of so notorious a heretic, but made Calvin all the difficulties that it could. As for Servetus, he had much hope for a favorable issue, and demanded that Calvin be exiled and Calvin's goods adjudged to him. The trial ended in Servetus's conviction and death by fire on October 27, 1553. Though a few voices of protest were raised, notably that of Sébastien Castellio (1515–1563) of Basel, most men agreed with Melanchthon that it was "justly done." However odious the trial and its tragic end may seem in retrospect, for Calvin it was a great victory. It freed the Swiss churches from any imputation of unorthodoxy on the doctrine of the Trinity, while Calvin's opponents had ruined themselves by making difficult the punishment of one whom the general sentiment of that age condemned.

Calvin's improved status was soon apparent. The elections of 1554 were decidedly in his favor, those of 1555 yet more so. In January, 1555, he secured permanent recognition of the right of the *Consistoire* to proceed to excommunication with-

out governmental interference.[1] The now largely Calvinist
government proceeded, the same year, to make its position
secure by admitting a considerable number of the refugees to
the franchise. A slight riot on the evening of May 16, 1555,
begun by Calvin's opponents, was seized as the occasion of
executing and banishing their leaders as traitors. Henceforth
the party favorable to Calvin was undisputed master of Geneva.
Bern was still hostile, but the common danger to Bern and
Geneva when Emmanuel Philibert, duke of Savoy and victor
for Spain over the French at St.-Quentin in 1557, was enabled
to lay claim to his duchy, then mostly in possession of the
French, brought about a "perpetual alliance," in January, 1558,
in which Geneva stood for the first time on a full equality with
its ally, Bern. Thus relieved of the most pressing perils, at
home and abroad, Calvin crowned his Genevan work by the
foundation in 1559 of the "Genevan Academy"—in reality,
as it has long since become, the University of Geneva.[2] It became immediately the greatest centre of theological instruction
in the Reformed communions, as distinguished from the
Lutheran, and the great seminary from which ministers in
numbers were sent forth not only to France but in less degree to the Netherlands, England, Scotland, Germany, and
Italy.

Calvin's influence extended far beyond Geneva. Thanks to
his *Institutes*, his pattern of church government in Geneva, his
academy, his commentaries, and his constant correspondence,
he moulded the thought and inspired the ideals of the Protestantism of France, the Netherlands, Scotland, and the English
Puritans. His influence penetrated Poland and Hungary, and
before his death Calvinism was taking root in southwestern
Germany itself. Men thought his thoughts after him. His
was the only system that the Reformation produced that could
organize itself powerfully in the face of governmental hostility,
as in France and England. It trained strong men, confident
in their election to be fellow workers with God in the accomplishment of His will, courageous to do battle, insistent on character, and confident that God has given in the Scriptures the
guide of all right human conduct and proper worship. The
spiritual disciples of Calvin, in most various lands, bore one common stamp. This was Calvin's work, a mastery of mind over

[1] Kidd, p. 647.   [2] *Ibid.*, p. 648.

mind, and certainly by the time of his death in Geneva, on May 27, 1564, he deserved the description of "the only international reformer."[1]

Calvin left no successor of equal stature. The work had grown too large for any one man to direct. But in Geneva, and to a considerable extent in his labors beyond its borders, his mantle fell on the worthy shoulders of Theodore Beza (1519–1605), a man of more conciliatory spirit and gentler ways, but devoted to the same ideals.

SECTION IX. THE ENGLISH REVOLT

In England the stronger Kings had long practically controlled episcopal appointments, and such as were made directly by the Pope were usually on some basis of agreement with the sovereign. The chief political posts were filled by churchmen, partly because few laymen could vie with them in learning or experience, and partly because the emoluments of high churchly office made such appointments inexpensive for the royal treasury. Naturally, in such appointments, ability and usefulness in the royal service were apt to be more valued than spiritual fitness. Such was the state of affairs when Henry VIII (1509–1547) began his reign. Some Wyclifianism existed in humble circles and occasionally came under churchly censure. Humanism had entered England and had found supporters in limited groups among the educated. John Colet (1467?–1519), ultimately dean of St. Paul's in London, had lectured in Oxford on Paul's epistles, in full humanistic spirit, as early as 1496, and refounded St. Paul's school in 1512. Erasmus had taught in Cambridge from 1511 to 1514, having first visited England in 1499, and he made many friends there. One of these was the excellent John Fisher (1469?–1535), bishop of Rochester, and another, the famous Sir Thomas More (1478–1535). Yet there was little in the situation at the beginning of Henry VIII's reign that made a change in the existing ecclesiastical situation seem possible. One trait of the national life was conspicuous, however, which was to be the basis of Henry VIII's support. That was a strongly developed national consciousness—a feeling of England for Englishmen—that was easily aroused to opposition to all foreign encroachment from whatever source.

[1] Kidd, p. 651.

Henry VIII, who has been well described as a "tyrant under legal forms," was a man of remarkable intellectual abilities and executive force, well read and always interested in scholastic theology, sympathetic with humanism, popular with the mass of the people, but egotistic, obstinate, and self-seeking. In the early part of his reign he had the support of Thomas Wolsey (1475–1530), who became a privy councillor in 1511, and in 1515 was made lord chancellor by the King and cardinal by Pope Leo X. Thenceforth he was Henry's right hand. When Luther's writings were received in England their use was forbidden, and Henry VIII published his *Assertion of the Seven Sacraments* against Luther in 1521, which won from Leo X the title "Defender of the Faith." At the beginning of his reign Henry had married Catherine of Aragon, daughter of Ferdinand and Isabella of Spain, and widow, though the marriage had been one in name only, of his older brother, Arthur. A dispensation authorizing this marriage with a deceased brother's wife had been granted by Julius II in 1503. Six children were born of this union, but only one, Mary, survived infancy. By 1527, if not earlier, Henry was alleging religious scruples as to the validity of his marriage. His reasons were not wholly sensual. Had they been, he might well have been content with his mistresses. A woman had never ruled England. The Wars of the Roses had ended as recently as 1485. The absence of a male heir, should Henry die, would probably cause civil war. It was not likely that Catherine would have further children. He wanted another wife, and a male heir.

Wolsey was induced to favor the project, partly from his subservience to the King, and partly because, if the marriage with Catherine should be declared invalid, he hoped Henry would marry the French princess, Renée, afterward duchess of Ferrara, and thus be drawn more firmly from the Spanish to the French side in continental politics. Henry, however, had other plans. He had fallen in love with Anne Boleyn, a lady of his court. A complicated negotiation followed, in which Wolsey did his best to please Henry, while Catherine behaved with dignity and firmness, and was treated with cruelty. Probably an annulment of the marriage might have been secured from Pope Clement VII had it not been for the course of European politics, which left the Emperor Charles V victor in war, and forced the Pope into submission to the imperial policy (*ante*, p. 358).   Charles was determined that his aunt, Cathe-rine, should not be set aside.   Henry, angered at Wolsey's want of success, turned on him, and the great cardinal died, November 30, 1530, on his way to be tried for treason.

Henry now thought well of a suggestion of Thomas Cranmer (1489–1556), then teaching in Cambridge University, that the opinions of universities be sought.   This was done in 1530, with only partial success; but a friendship was begun between the King and Cranmer that was to have momentous con-sequences.

Favorable action from the Pope being now out of the ques-tion, Henry determined to rely on the national feeling of hos-tility to foreign rule, and his own despotic skill, either to break with the papacy altogether, or to so threaten papal control as to secure his wishes.   In January, 1531, he charged the whole body of clergy with breach of the old statute of *Præmunire* of 1353 for having recognized Wolsey's authority as papal legate —an authority which Henry himself had recognized and ap-proved.   He not only extorted a great sum as the price of par-don, but the declaration by the convocations in which the clergy met, that in respect to the Church of England, he was "single and supreme Lord, and, as far as the law of Christ allows, even supreme head."   Early in 1532, under severe royal pressure, Parliament passed an act forbidding the pay-ment of all annates to Rome save with the King's consent.[1] In May following, the clergy in convocation agreed reluctantly, not only to make no new ecclesiastical laws without the King's permission, but to submit all existing statutes to a commission appointed by the King.[2]   About January 25, 1533, Henry secretly married Anne Boleyn.   In February Parliament for-bad all appeals to Rome.[3]   Henry used the conditional prohibi-tion of annates to procure from Pope Clement VII confirmation of his appointment of Thomas Cranmer as archbishop of Can-terbury.   Cranmer was consecrated on March 30; on May 23, Cranmer held court and formally adjudged Henry's marriage to Catherine null and void.   On September 7, Anne Boleyn bore a daughter, the princess Elizabeth, later to be Queen.

While these events were occurring Clement VII had prepared

---

[1] Gee and Hardy, *Documents Illustrative of English Church History*, pp. 178–186.

[2] *Ibid.*, pp. 176–178.   [3] *Ibid.*, pp. 187–195.

a bull threatening excommunication against Henry on July 11, 1533. Henry's answer was a series of statutes obtained from Parliament in 1534, by which all payments to the Pope were forbidden, all bishops were to be elected on the King's nomination, and all oaths of papal obedience, Roman licenses, and other recognitions of papal authority done away.[1] The two convocations now formally abjured papal supremacy.[2] In November, 1534, Parliament passed the famous Supremacy Act, by which Henry and his successors were declared "the only supreme head in earth of the Church of England," without qualifying clauses, and with full power to redress "heresies" and "abuses."[3] This was not understood by the King or its authors as giving spiritual rights, such as ordination, the administration of the sacraments and the like, but in all else it practically put the King in the place of the Pope. The breach with Rome was complete. Nor were these statutes in any way meaningless. In May, 1535, a number of monks of one of the most respected orders in England, that of the Carthusians, or Charterhouse, were executed under circumstances of peculiar barbarity, for denying the King's supremacy. In June and July the two most widely known subjects of the King, Bishop John Fisher and Sir Thomas More, distinguished alike for character and scholarship, were beheaded for the same offense.

For his work, Henry had found a new agent in Thomas Cromwell (1485?–1540), a man of very humble origin, a soldier, merchant, and money-lender by turns, of whom Wolsey had made much use as business and parliamentary agent. By 1531 Cromwell was of the privy council; in 1534 master of the rolls; and in 1536, layman that he was, viceregent for the King in ecclesiastical affairs. Henry was hungry for ecclesiastical property, both to maintain his lavish court and to create and reward adherents—the Reformation everywhere was marked by these confiscations—and late in 1534 he commissioned Cromwell to have the monasteries visited and report on their condition. The alleged facts, the truth or falsity of which is still a disputed matter, were laid before Parliament, which in February, 1536, adjudged to the King, "his heirs and assigns forever, to do and use therewith his and their own wills," all

---

[1] Gee and Hardy, pp. 201–232.   [2] *Ibid.*, pp. 251, 252.
[3] *Ibid.*, pp. 243, 244.

monastic establishments having an income of less than two hundred pounds annually.[1] The number thus sequestered was three hundred and seventy-six.

Meanwhile Henry had been in part relieved from the danger of foreign intervention by the death in January, 1536, of Catherine of Aragon. He seems now to have wished to contract a marriage not open to the criticisms of that with Anne Boleyn, of whom he was, moreover, tired. She was accordingly charged with adultery, in May, 1536, whether rightly or wrongly is impossible to decide, though the accusation seems suspicious, and on the 19th was beheaded. Two days before Cranmer had pronounced her marriage to Henry null and void. Eleven days later Henry married Jane Seymour, who bore him a son, Edward, on October 12, 1537, and died twelve days thereafter. Henry's deeds, especially the suppression of the monasteries, aroused much opposition, notably in northern England, with the result that a formidable insurrection, known as the Pilgrimage of Grace, broke out in the summer of 1536, but by the early part of the following year was effectually crushed.

Though these changes in England were primarily those of ecclesiastical politics rather than religious conviction, the disturbed state of the country gave opportunity for a real, though as yet not numerous, Protestant party. In origin it seems to have been more indigenous than imported, and to have followed more at first the pathway shown by Wyclif than by Luther. Like Wyclif, it looked to the state to reform the church, and viewed the riches of the church as a hindrance to its spirituality. Hence this party had little fault to find with Henry's assertions and confiscations. Like Wyclif, it valued the circulation of the Bible, and came more and more to test doctrine and ceremony by conformity to the Scriptures. As the German revolt developed, it came to feel more and more continental influences. A conspicuous leader was William Tyndale (1492?–1536). Eager to translate the New Testament, and unable to have it published in England, he found refuge on the Continent in 1524, visited Luther, and published a really admirable translation from the Greek in 1526. Churchly and civil authorities tried to suppress it, but it was a force in spreading the knowledge of the Scriptures. Tyndale himself died a martyr in Vilvorde,

[1] Gee and Hardy, pp. 257–268.

near Brussels, in 1536. Tyndale's friend, John Frith (1503–1533), found refuge in Marburg, and thence returned to England, only to be arrested and burned in London in 1533 for denying the doctrines of purgatory and transubstantiation. In sympathy with these doctrinally reformatory views, though varying in outward expression, were Cranmer, Nicholas Ridley (1500?–1555), Hugh Latimer (1490?–1555), and John Hooper (?–1555), all to be bishops, and all to die by fire for their faith. As Henry's opposition to Rome developed, Protestant feeling spread among laymen of influence, a conspicuous instance being the Seymour family, from which Henry had taken his third Queen.

Henry's own religious attitude was that of Catholic orthodoxy, save on the substitution of his own authority for that of the Pope. His only departures from it were when dangers of attack from abroad compelled him to seek possible political support from the German Protestants, and he did not then go far. Such an occasion occurred in the years 1535 and 1536. He sent a commission to discuss doctrine in Wittenberg, though it came to little. In 1536 Henry himself drafted Ten Articles in which he made his utmost concession to Protestantism. The authoritative standards of faith are the Bible, the Apostles', Nicene, and Athanasian creeds, and the "four first councils." Only three sacraments are defined: baptism, penance, and the Lord's Supper; the others are not mentioned either in approval or denial. Justification implies faith in Christ alone, but confession and absolution and works of charity are also necessary. Christ is physically present in the Supper. Images are to be honored, but with moderation. The saints are to be invoked, but not because they "will hear us sooner than Christ." Masses for the dead are desirable, but the idea that the "bishop of Rome" can deliver out of purgatory is to be rejected.

A more influential act of this time, instigated by Cranmer, was that an English translation of the Bible, made up in large part of Tyndale's version, but in considerable portion from the inferior work of Miles Coverdale, was allowed sale in 1537, and was ordered by Cromwell in 1538 to be placed accessible to the public in each church.[1] The Lord's Prayer and the ten commandments were to be taught in English, the litany was

[1] Gee and Hardy, p. 275.

translated; but otherwise worship remained substantially unchanged in the Latin language and form while Henry lived.

Henry's work during these years had been free from foreign interference, because Charles V and Francis I were at war from 1536 to 1538. With the arrival of peace his dangers greatly increased. The Pope demanded a joint attack by France and Spain on the royal rebel. Henry's diplomacy and mutual jealousies warded it off; but he took several steps of importance to lessen his peril. He would show the world that he was an orthodox Catholic save in regard to the Pope. Accordingly, in June, 1539, Parliament passed the Six Articles Act.[1] It affirmed as the creed of England a strict doctrine of transubstantiation, denial of which was to be punished by fire. It repudiated communion in both bread and wine, and priestly marriage. It ordered the permanent observation of vows of chastity, enjoined private masses, and auricular confession. This statute remained in force till Henry's death. It was not enough, however, that Henry should show himself orthodox. He was a widower, and Cromwell was urgent that he strengthen his position by a marriage which would please the German Protestants, and unite him with those opposed to the Emperor Charles V. Anne of Cleves, sister of the wife of John Frederick, the Saxon Elector, was selected. The marriage took place on January 6, 1540.

Meanwhile Henry had completed the confiscations of all the monasteries in 1539.[2] He was stronger at home than ever. Francis and Charles were evidently soon to be again at war, and the Emperor was beginning to court Henry's assistance. German Protestants looked askance at his Six Articles, and he now no longer needed their aid. Henry had regarded the marriage with Anne of Cleves as a mere political expedient. An annulment was obtained in July, 1540, from the bishops on the ground that the King had never given "inward consent" to the marriage, and Anne was handsomely indemnified pecuniarily. For Cromwell, to whom the marriage was due, he had no further use. A bill of attainder was put through Parliament, and the King's able, but utterly unscrupulous, servant was beheaded on July 28, 1540. These events were accompanied by increasing opposition to the Protestant element, and this Catholic inclination was evidenced in Henry's

[1] Gee and Hardy, pp. 303–319.   [2] *Ibid.*, pp. 281–303.

marriage to Catherine Howard, niece of the duke of Norfolk, shortly after his separation from Anne of Cleves; but the new Queen's conduct was open to question, and in February, 1542, she was beheaded. In July, 1543, he married Catherine Parr, who had the fortune to survive him. On January 28, 1547, Henry died.

At Henry's death England was divided into three parties. Of these, that embracing the great body of Englishmen stood fairly with the late King in desiring no considerable change in doctrine or worship, while rejecting foreign ecclesiastical jurisdiction. It had been Henry's strength that, with all his tyranny, he was fairly representative of this great middle party. There were, besides, two small parties, neither fairly representative—a Catholic wing that would restore the power of the papacy, and a Protestant faction that would introduce reform as it was understood on the Continent. The latter had undoubtedly been growing, in spite of repression, during Henry's last years. It was to be England's fortune that the two smaller and unrepresentative parties should be successively in power during the next two reigns, and that to religious turmoil agrarian unrest should be added, owing to the great changes in property caused by monastic confiscations, and even more to enclosures of common lands by greedy landlords, and the impoverishment of humbler tenants by the loss of their time-honored rights of use.

Edward VI was but nine years of age. The government was, therefore, administered in his name by a council, of which the earl of Hertford, or, as he was immediately created, duke of Somerset, was chief, with the title of Protector. Somerset was the brother of the young King's mother, the short-lived Jane Seymour. He was a man of Protestant sympathies, and of excellent intentions—a believer in a degree of liberty in religious and political questions in marked contrast to Henry VIII. He was, also, a sincere friend of the dispossessed lower agricultural classes. Under his rule the new comparative freedom of religious expression led to many local innovations and much controversy, in which the revolutionary party more and more gained the upper hand. In 1547 Parliament ordered the administration of the cup to the laity.[1] The same year the last great confiscation of church lands occurred—the dissolution of

---

[1] Gee and Hardy, pp. 322–328.

the "chantries," that is, endowed chapels for saying masses. The properties of religious fraternities and guilds were also sequestered.[1] The Six Articles were repealed. Early in 1548 images were ordered removed from the churches. The marriage of priests was made legal in 1549.[2]

The confusion soon became great, and as a means at once of advancing the reforms and securing order, Parliament, on January 21, 1549, enacted an Act of Uniformity,[3] by which the universal use of a Book of Common Prayer in English was required. This book, known as the First Prayer Book of Edward VI, was largely the work of Cranmer, based on the older English services in Latin, with some use of a revised Roman breviary, published in 1535 by Cardinal Fernandez de Quinones, and the Lutheranly inclined tentative *Consultation* of Hermann von Wied, archbishop of Cologne, issued in 1543. In its larger feature it is still the Prayer Book of the Church of England, but this edition preserved much of detail of older worship, such as prayers for the dead, communion at burials, anointing and exorcism in baptism, and anointing the sick, which was soon to be abandoned. In the Eucharist the words used in handing the elements to the communicant were the first clause of the present Anglican form, implying that the body and blood of Christ are really received.

Meanwhile, Somerset was beset with political troubles. To counteract the growing power of France in Scotland he urged the union of the two countries by the ultimate marriage of King Edward with the Scottish Princess Mary, to be "Queen of Scots," and supported his efforts by an invasion of Scotland in which the Scots were terribly defeated, on September 10, 1547, at Pinkie, but by which his main purpose was frustrated. The angered Scottish leaders hastened to betroth Mary to the heir of France, the later Francis II, an event of prime significance for the Scottish reformation.

Somerset's fall came about, however, through causes creditable to himself. He realized the agrarian discontent, and believed that efforts should be furthered to check enclosures. In this he had the bitter opposition of the landowning classes, of whom none were more greedy than the recent purchasers of monastic property. Extensive risings took place in 1549. They were put down with difficulty, largely by the efficiency of

[1] Gee and Hardy, pp. 328–357.   [2] *Ibid.*, pp. 366–368.   [3] *Ibid.*, pp. 358–366.

the earl of Warwick. Thus in favor with the propertied classes, Warwick headed a conspiracy which thrust Somerset from his protectorate in October, 1549.

Warwick, or the duke of Northumberland as he later became, though never assuming the title Protector, was now the most powerful man in England. The religious situation underwent rapid change. Somerset had been a man of great moderation, anxious to conciliate all parties. Northumberland was without religious principles himself, but he pushed forward the Protestant cause for political reasons, and the movement now took on a much more radical character. Though apparently reconciled to Somerset, he distrusted the former protector's popularity, and had Somerset beheaded in 1552. His own greed, tyranny, and misgovernment made him cordially hated.

The Prayer Book of 1549 was not popular. Conservatives disliked the changes. Protestants felt that it retained too much of Roman usage. These criticisms were supported by a number of foreign theologians of prominence, driven from Germany by the *Interim*, who found welcome in England, of whom the most influential was Butzer of Strassburg. This hostility was now able to be effective under the more radical policy of Northumberland, and led to the revision of the Prayer Book, and its reissue under a new Act of Uniformity in 1552.[1] Much more of the ancient ceremonial was now done away. Prayers for the dead were now omitted, a communion table substituted for the altar, common bread, instead of a special wafer, used in the Supper, exorcism and anointing set aside, the priests' vestments restricted to the surplice, and what is now the second clause of the Anglican form of the delivery of the elements substituted, implying a doctrine looking toward the Zwinglian conception of the Supper.

Cranmer had been engaged in the preparation of a creed, which was submitted by order of the Council of Government in 1552 to six theologians, of whom John Knox was one. The result was the Forty-two Articles, which were authorized by the young King's signature, June 12, 1553, less than a month before his death. Though moderate for the period, they were decidedly more Protestant in tone than the Prayer Book.

Unpopular as he was, Northumberland was determined to

---

[1] Gee and Hardy, pp. 369–372.

maintain his power. Edward VI was visibly frail in body, and Northumberland feared for his own life should Mary succeed to the throne. The plan that he now adopted was desperate. He induced the youthful King to settle the succession on Lady Jane Grey, wife of Northumberland's fourth son, Guilford Dudley, and granddaughter of Henry VIII's sister Mary. Edward VI had no legal right so to do. He passed by the claims of his half-sisters, Mary and Elizabeth, and of Mary "Queen of Scots," whose genealogical title was better than that of Lady Jane. To this wild plan Cranmer gave reluctant consent. On July 6, 1553, Edward VI died.

Northumberland's plot failed completely. His unpopularity was such that even the most Protestant portions of England, such as the city of London, rallied to Mary. She was soon safely on the throne and Northumberland was beheaded, declaring on the scaffold that he was a true Catholic. Mary proceeded with caution at first, guided by the astute advice of her cousin the Emperor Charles V. Parliament declared her mother's marriage to Henry VIII valid. The ecclesiastical legislation of Edward VI's reign was repealed, and public worship restored to the forms of the last year of Henry VIII.[1] Cranmer was imprisoned. The Emperor saw in Mary's probable marriage an opportunity to win England, and now proposed his son Philip, soon to be Philip II of Spain, as her husband. The marriage took place on July 25, 1554, and was exceedingly unpopular, as threatening foreign control.

Reconciliation with Rome had thus far been delayed, though bishops and other clergy of reformatory sympathies had been removed, and many of the more earnest Protestants had fled to the Continent, where they were warmly received by Calvin, though coolly treated by the Lutherans as heretical on the question of Christ's physical presence in the Lord's Supper. The reason of this delay was fear lest the confiscated church properties should be taken from their present holders. On intimation that this would not be the papal policy, Cardinal Reginald Pole (1500–1558) was admitted to England. Parliament voted the restoration of papal authority, and on November 30, 1554, Pole pronounced it and the nation was absolved of heresy. Parliament now proceeded to re-enact the ancient laws against heresy[2] and to repeal Henry VIII's ecclesiastical legislation,

---

[1] Gee and Hardy, pp. 377–380.   [2] *Ibid.*, p. 384.

thus restoring the church to the state in which it had been in 1529, save that former church property was assured by the statute to its present possessors.[1]

Severe persecution at once began.   Its first victim was John Rogers, a prebendary of St. Paul's, who was burned in London on February 4, 1555.   The attitude of the people, who cheered him on the way to the stake, was ominous for this policy; but before the end of the year, seventy-five had suffered by fire in various parts of England, of whom the most notable were the former bishops, Hugh Latimer and Nicholas Ridley, whose heroic fortitude at their deaths in Oxford, on October 16, created a profound popular impression.   Another conspicuous victim of this year was John Hooper, former bishop of Gloucester and Worcester.   Mary was determined to strike the highest of the anti-Roman clergy, Archbishop Cranmer.   Cranmer was not of the heroic stuff of which Latimer, Ridley, Hooper, and Rogers were made.   He was formally excommunicated by sentence at Rome on November 25, 1555, and Pole was shortly after made archbishop of Canterbury in his stead.   Cranmer was now in a logical dilemma.   He had asserted, since his appointment under Henry VIII, that the sovereign is the supreme authority in the English church.   His Protestantism was real, but that sovereign was now a Roman Catholic.   In his distress he now made submission declaring that he recognized papal authority as established by law.   Mary had no intention of sparing the man who had pronounced her mother's marriage invalid.   Cranmer must die.   But it was hoped that by a public abjuration of Protestantism at his death he would discredit the Reformation.   That hope was nearly realized. Cranmer signed a further recantation denying Protestantism wholly; but on the day of his execution in Oxford, March 21, 1556, his courage returned.   He repudiated his retractions absolutely, declared his Protestant faith, and held the offending hand, which had signed the now renounced submissions, in the flame till it was consumed.   His dying day was the noblest of his life.

Philip had left England in 1555, and this absence, coupled with her own childless state, preyed on Mary's mind, inducing her to feel that she had not done enough to satisfy the judgment of God. Persecution therefore continued unabated till her

[1]Gee and Hardy, pp. 385–415.

death on November 17, 1558. In all, somewhat less than three hundred were burned—a scanty number compared with the toll of sufferers in the Netherlands. But English sentiment deeply revolted. These martyrdoms did more for the spread of anti-Roman sentiment than all previous governmental efforts had accomplished. It was certain that the accession of the next sovereign would witness a change or civil war.

Elizabeth (Queen 1558–1603) had long passed as illegitimate, though her place in the succession had been secured by act of Parliament in the lifetime of Henry VIII. Of all Henry's children she was the only one who really resembled him in ability, insight, and personal popularity. With a masculine force of character she combined a curious love of personal adornment inherited from her light-minded mother. Of real religious feeling she had none, but her birth and Roman denials of her mother's marriage made her necessarily a Protestant, though under Mary, when her life had been in danger, she had conformed to the Roman ritual. Fortunately her accession had the support of Philip II of Spain, soon to be her bitterest enemy. That favor helped her with English Catholics. Earnest Roman as he was, Philip was politician enough not to wish to see France, England, and Scotland come under the rule of a single royal pair, and if Elizabeth was not Queen of England, then Mary "Queen of Scots," wife of the prince who was in 1559 to become King Francis II of France, was rightfully entitled to the English throne. In her first measures on accession Elizabeth enjoyed, moreover, the aid of one of the most cautious and far-sighted statesmen England has ever produced, William Cecil (1521–1598), better known as Lord Burghley, whom she at once made her secretary and who was to be her chief adviser till his death. For Elizabeth it was a great advantage also that she was thoroughly English in feeling, and deeply sympathetic with the political and economic ambitions of the nation. This representative quality reconciled many to her government whom mere religious considerations would have repelled. No one doubted that she put England first.

Elizabeth proceeded cautiously with her changes. Parliament passed the new Supremacy Act,[1] with much opposition, on April 29, 1559. By it the authority of the Pope and all pay-

---

[1] Gee and Hardy, pp. 442–458.

ments and appeals to him were rejected.   A significant change
of title appeared, however, by Elizabeth's own insistence.
Instead of the old "Supreme Head," so obnoxious to the
Catholics, she was now styled "Supreme Governor" of the
church in England—a much less objectionable phrase, though
amounting to the same thing in practice.   The tests of heresy
were now to be the Scriptures, the first four General Councils,
and the decisions of Parliament.   Meanwhile a commission
had been revising the Second Prayer Book of Edward VI (*ante*,
p. 410).   The prayer against the Pope was omitted, as was the
declaration that kneeling at the Supper did not imply adoration, while the question of Christ's physical presence was left
intentionally undetermined by the combination of the forms
of delivery in the two Edwardean books (*ante*, pp. 409, 410).
These modifications were designed to render the new service
more palatable to Catholics.   The Act of Uniformity[1] now
ordered all worship to be conducted, after June 24, 1559, in
accordance with this liturgy, and provided that the ornaments
of the church and the vestments of its ministers should be
those of the second year of Edward VI.

The oath of supremacy was refused by all but two ob-
scurer members of the Marian episcopate, but among the lower
clergy generally resistance was slight, the obstinate not amounting to two hundred.   New bishops must be provided, and
Elizabeth directed the election of her mother's one-time chaplain, Matthew Parker (1504–1575), as archbishop of Canterbury.   His consecration was a perplexing question; but there
were those in England who had received ordination to the
bishopric under Henry VIII and Edward VI.   Parker was now
consecrated, on December 17, 1559, at the hands of four such—
William Barlow, John Scory, Miles Coverdale, and John Hodgkin.   The validity of the act, on which the apostolic succession
of the English episcopate depends, has always been strongly
affirmed by Anglican divines, while attacked by Roman theologians, on various grounds, and declared invalid by Pope Leo
XIII in 1896, for defect in "intention."   Thus inaugurated,
a new Anglican episcopate was speedily established.   A definition of the creed, other than implied in the Prayer Book, was
purposely postponed; but in 1563 the Forty-two Articles of
1553 (*ante*, p. 410) were somewhat revised, and as the famous

---

[1] Gee and Hardy, pp. 458–467.

Thirty-nine Articles, became the statement of faith of the Church of England.[1]

Thus, by 1563 the Elizabethan settlement was accomplished. It was threatened from two sides: from that of Rome, and, even more dangerously, from the earnest reformers who wished to go further and soon were to be nicknamed Puritans. The remarkable feature of the English revolt is that it produced no outstanding religious leader—no Luther, Zwingli, Calvin, or Knox. Nor did it, before the beginning of Elizabeth's reign, manifest any considerable spiritual awakening among the people. Its impulses were political and social. A great revival of the religious life of England was to come, the earlier history of which was to be coincident with Elizabeth's reign, but which was to owe nothing to her.

SECTION X.   THE SCOTTISH REVOLT

At the dawn of the sixteenth century Scotland was a poor and backward country. Its social conditions were mediæval. The power of its Kings was small. Its nobles were turbulent. Relatively its church was rich in land, owning about one-half that of the country, but churchly positions were largely used to supply places for younger sons of noble houses, and much clerical property was in the hands of the lay nobles. The weak monarchy had usually leaned on the church as against the lay nobility. Education was backward, though universities had been founded in the fifteenth century in St. Andrews, Glasgow, and Aberdeen. Compared with continental seats of learning they were weak.

The determining motive of most of Scottish political history in this period was fear of dominance or annexation by England, persuading it to link the fortunes of the land with those of France. Three grievous defeats by the English—Flodden (1513), Solway Moss (1542), and Pinkie (1547)—strengthened this feeling of antagonism, but showed that even English superiority in force could not conquer Scotland. On the other hand, Scotland in alliance with France was a great peril for England, the more serious when England had broken with the papacy. Therefore England and France both sought to build up parties and strengthen factions favorable to themselves in Scotland.

[1] Schaff, *Creeds of Christendom*, III: 487–516.

On the whole the powerful family of Douglas was inclined toward England, while that of Hamilton favored France. France also had strong supporters in Archbishop James Beaton (?–1539) of St. Andrews, the primate of Scotland, and his nephew, Cardinal David Beaton (1494?–1546), his successor in the same see. Though King James V (reigned 1513–1542) was nephew of Henry VIII, and his grandson, James VI, was to become James I of England in 1603 and unite the two crowns after the death of Elizabeth, James V threw in his fortunes with France, marrying successively a daughter of Francis I, and, after her death, Mary of Lorraine, of the powerful French Catholic family of Guise. This latter union, so important in the history of Scotland, was to have as its fruit Mary "Queen of Scots."

Some Protestant beginnings were early made in Scotland. Patrick Hamilton (1504?–1528), who had visited Wittenberg and studied in Marburg, preached Lutheran doctrine, and was burned on February 29, 1528. The cause grew slowly. In 1534 and 1540 there were other executions. Yet, in 1543 the Scottish Parliament authorized the reading and translation of the Bible. It was but a temporary phase, due to English influence, and by 1544 Cardinal Beaton and the French party were employing strong repression. Chief of the preachers at this time was George Wishart (1513?–1546), who was burned by Cardinal Beaton on March 2, 1546. On May 29 Beaton himself was brutally murdered, partly in revenge for Wishart's death and partly out of hostility to his French policy. The murderers gained possession of the castle of St. Andrews and rallied their sympathizers there. In 1547 a hunted Protestant preacher, apparently a convert and certainly a friend of Wishart, of no considerable previous conspicuity, took refuge with them and became their spiritual teacher. This was John Knox, to be the hero of the Scottish reformation.

Born in or near Haddington, between 1505 and 1515, Knox's early career was obscure. He was certainly ordained to the priesthood, but when Wishart was arrested he was with that martyr, and prepared to defend him. French forces sent to reduce the rebels in St. Andrews castle compelled its surrender, and Knox was carried to France to endure for nineteen months the cruel lot of a galley-slave. Released at length, he made his way to England, then under the Protestant government ruling in the name of Edward VI, became one of the royal chap-

lains, and in 1552 declined the bishopric of Rochester. The
accession of Mary compelled his flight, in 1554, but the English
refugees whom he first joined in Frankfort were divided by
his criticisms of the Edwardean Prayer-Book,[1] and he soon
found a welcome in Geneva, where he became an ardent disciple of Calvin, and labored on the Genevan version of the
English Bible, later so valued by the English Puritans.

Meanwhile the English had alienated Scotland more than
ever by the defeat of Pinkie, in 1547. Mary "Queen of Scots"
had been betrothed to the heir to the French throne and sent
to France for safety in 1548, while her mother, the Guise,
Mary of Lorraine, became regent of Scotland in 1554.

To a large portion of the Scottish nobles and people this
full dependence on France was as hateful as any submission
to England could have been. Protestantism and national independence seemed to be bound together, and it was in this
double struggle that Knox was to be the leader. Knox now
dared to return to Scotland, in 1555, and preached for six
months; but the situation was not yet ripe for revolt, and
Knox returned to Geneva to become the pastor of the church
of English-speaking refugees there. He had, however, sowed
fruitful seed. On December 3, 1557, a number of Protestant
and anti-French nobles in Scotland entered into a covenant
to "establish the most blessed Word of God and His congregation"—from which they were nicknamed "The Lords of the
Congregation." [2] Additional fuel was given to this dissent
by the marriage of Mary to the French heir on April 24, 1558.[3]
Scotland now seemed a province of France, for should there
be a son of this union he would be ruler of both lands, and the
French grip was made doubly sure by an agreement signed by
Mary, kept secret at the time, that France should receive
Scotland should she die without heirs. Before 1558 was ended
Elizabeth was Queen of England, and Mary "Queen of Scots"
was denouncing her as an illegitimate usurper, and proclaiming
herself the rightful occupant of the English throne.

Under these circumstances the advocates of Scottish independence and of Protestantism rapidly increased and became
more and more fused into one party. Elizabeth, moreover,
could be expected to assist, if only for her own protection.
Knox saw that the time was ready. On May 2, 1559, he was

[1] Kidd, p. 691.   [2] *Ibid.*, p. 696.   [3] *Ibid.*, p. 690.

back in Scotland. Nine days later he preached in Perth. The mob destroyed the monastic establishments of the town.[1] This action the regent naturally regarded as rank rebellion. She had French troops at her disposal, and both sides promptly armed for combat. They proved fairly equal, and the result was undecided. Churches were wrecked and monastic property sacked, to Knox's disgust, in many parts of Scotland. On July 10, 1559, Henry II of France died, and Mary's husband, Francis II became King in his stead. French reinforcements were promptly sent to the regent in Scotland. Matters went badly for the reformers. At last, in January, 1560, English help came. The contest dragged. On June 11, 1560, the regent died, but her cause perished with her. On July 6 a treaty was made between France and England by which French soldiers were withdrawn from Scotland, and Frenchmen were debarred from all important posts in its government. The revolution had triumphed through English aid, but without forfeiting Scottish national independence, and its inspirer had been Knox.[2] In this contest the Scottish middle classes had first shown themselves a power, and their influence was for the newer order.

The victorious party now pushed its triumph in the Scottish Parliament. On August 17, 1560, a Calvinistic confession of faith, largely prepared by Knox, was adopted as the creed of the realm.[3] A week later the same body abolished papal jurisdiction, and forbad the mass under pain of death for the third offense.[4] Though the King and Queen in France refused their approval, the majority of the nation had spoken.

Knox and his associates now proceeded to complete their work. In December, 1560, a meeting was held which is regarded as the first Scottish "General Assembly," in January following the *First Book of Discipline* was presented to the Parliament.[5] It was a most remarkable document, attempting to apply the system worked out by Calvin to a whole kingdom, though the Presbyterian system was far from thoroughly developed as yet. In each parish there should be a minister and elders holding office with the consent of the congregation. Minister and elders constituted the disciplinary board—the

---

[1] Kidd, p. 697. [2] *Ibid.*, pp. 698–700.
[3] *Ibid.*, pp. 700, 704–707; Schaff, *Creeds of Christendom*, 3: 437–479.
[4] *Ibid.*, pp. 701, 702. [5] *Ibid.*, p. 707.

later "session"—with power of excommunication. In the larger towns were to be meetings for discussion, out of which "presbyteries" were to grow; over groups of ministers and congregations were synods, and over all the "General Assembly." The need of the times and the inchoate state of the church led to two further institutions, "readers," in places where there were no ministers or the work was large, and "superintendents," without spiritual authority, but with administrative right to oversee the organization of parishes, and recommend ministerial candidates. Besides these ecclesiastical features, the *Book* sketched out notable schemes of national education and for the relief of the poor. Knox would have church, education, and poor supported from the old church property; but here the *Book* met the resistance of Parliament, which did not adopt it, though many of the body approved. The ecclesiastical constitution gradually came into force; but the nobles so possessed themselves of church lands that the church from relatively to the means of the country one of the richest became one of the poorest in Christendom. This relative poverty stamped on it a democratic character, however, that was to make the church of Scotland the bulwark of the people against encroachments by the nobles and the crown.

All observances not having Scriptural authority were swept away. Sunday was the only remaining holy day. For the conduct of public worship Knox prepared a *Book of Common Order*, sometimes called "Knox's Liturgy," which was approved by the "General Assembly," in 1564.[1] It was largely based on that of the English congregation in Geneva, which in turn was modelled on that of Calvin. It allowed, however, even more use of free prayer, the forms given being regarded as models, the strict employment of which was not obligatory, though the general order and content of the service were definite enough.

Knox was soon obliged to defend what he had gained. King Francis II of France died on December 5, 1560, and in the following August Mary returned to Scotland. Her position as a youthful widow was one to excite a sympathy which her great personal charm increased. She was no longer Queen of France, and that element which had supported Protestantism not by reason of religion but from desire of national in-

[1] Kidd, pp. 708–715.

dependence might well think that the pressing danger of French domination which had induced acquiescence in the religious revolution had passed. Mary behaved, at first, with great prudence. While she made no secret of her own faith, and had mass said in her chapel to the furious disapproval of Knox, who was now minister of St. Giles in Edinburgh, and admired by the burghers of that city, she did not interfere in the religious settlement effected in 1560. She strove to secure recognition as Elizabeth's heir to the English throne, a thing which Elizabeth had no mind to grant. Mary had the sage advice of her half-brother, James Stewart, later to be earl of Moray (1531?-1570), who had been a leader of the "Lords of the Congregation." She tried by personal interviews of great skill to win Knox, but he refused any overture and remained the soul of the Protestant party. Still the prospect darkened for him. Mary won friends. The Protestant nobles were divided. The mass was increasingly being used. Knox had good reason to fear that Mary would give a Catholic King to Scotland by marrying some great foreign prince. A marriage with the son of Philip II of Spain was seriously discussed. Even more alarming for the Protestant cause in Scotland and England was Mary's actual marriage on July 29, 1565, to her cousin, Henry Stewart, Lord Darnley (1545-1567), with whom she had fallen in love. Darnley's claim to the English throne stood next to that of Mary herself. He was popular with English Catholics, and though he had passed as a Protestant in England, he now avowed himself a Catholic. The marriage increased Elizabeth's danger at home and strengthened the Catholic party in Scotland. Moray opposed it, was driven from court, and soon into exile, and Mary made much progress in subduing, one after another, the Protestant lords who sympathized with Moray. She thus lost her wisest adviser.

Thus far Mary had acted fairly shrewdly, but Scottish Protestantism was now saved by Mary's mistakes and want of self-control. Darnley was certainly disagreeable and vicious. Her feelings for him changed. On the other hand, his jealousy was roused by the favor which Mary showed to David Riccio, an Italian whom Mary employed as a foreign secretary, and who was looked upon by the Protestant lords as their enemy. Darnley and a number of Protestant nobles, therefore, entered into a plot by which Riccio was dragged from Mary's presence and murdered in the palace of Holyrood, on March 9, 1566. Mary behaved with great cunning. Dissembling her anger at the weak Darnley, she secured from him the names of his fellow conspirators, outlawed those who had actually participated in the deed, and took the others back into favor, of course with the knowledge on their part that they were received on sufferance. On June 19, 1566, Mary and Darnley's son was born, the future James VI of Scotland and James I of England. Mary never seemed surer on the Scottish throne.

In reality Mary had never forgiven her husband, and she was now thrown much with a Protestant noble, James Hepburn, earl of Bothwell (1536?–1578), a rough, licentious, but brave, loyal, and martial man, whose qualities contrasted with those of her weak husband. Bothwell now led in a conspiracy to rid Mary of Darnley, with how much share on the part of Mary herself is still one of the disputed questions of history. Darnley, who was recovering from smallpox, was removed by Mary from Glasgow to a house on the edge of Edinburgh, where Mary spent part of the last evening with him. Early on the morning of February 10, 1567, the house was blown up, and Darnley's body was found near it. Public opinion charged Bothwell with the murder, and it widely believed, probably with justice, that Mary also was guilty of it. At all events she heaped honors on Bothwell, who succeeded in securing acquittal by a farce of a trial. On April 24, Bothwell met Mary on one of her journeys and made her captive by a show of force—it was generally believed with her connivance. He was married, but he was divorced from his wife for adultery on May 3, and on May 15 he and Mary were married by Protestant rites.

These shameless transactions roused general hostility in Scotland, while they robbed Mary, for the time, of Catholic sympathy in England and on the Continent. Protestants and Catholics in Scotland joined forces against her. Just a month after the wedding Mary was a prisoner, and on July 24, 1567, she was compelled to abdicate in favor of her year-old son, and appoint Moray as regent, while she was herself imprisoned in Lochleven Castle. On July 29 John Knox preached the sermon at James VI's coronation. With Mary's fall came the triumph of Protestantism, which was now definitely established by Parliament in December. Mary herself escaped from

Lochleven in May, 1568, but Moray promptly defeated her supporters, and she fled to England, where she was to remain, a centre of Catholic intrigue, till her execution for conspiracy against Elizabeth's life, in February, 1587.

Knox's fiery career was about over. On November 24, 1572, he died, having influenced not merely the religion but the character of the nation more than any other man in Scottish history. Knox's work was to be taken up by Andrew Melville (1545–1623), who had taught as Beza's colleague in Geneva, from 1568 to his return to Scotland in 1574. He was the educational reformer of the Universities of Glasgow and St. Andrews and even more distinguished as the perfecter of the Presbyterian system in Scotland and its vigorous defender against the royal and episcopal encroachments of James VI, who compelled him to spend the last sixteen years of his life in exile from his native land.

SECTION XI. THE ROMAN REVIVAL

It has already been noted (*ante*, pp. 321–325) that a generation before Luther's breach with Rome, Spain was witnessing a vigorous reformatory work led by Queen Isabella and Cardinal Ximenes. It combined zeal for a more moral and intelligent clergy, abolition of glaring abuses, and Biblical studies for the learned, not for the people, with unswerving orthodoxy, judged by mediæval standards, and repression of heresy by the inquisition. It was this movement that was to give life and vigor to the Roman revival, often, though rather incorrectly, called the Counter-Reformation. Outside of Spain it had very little influence when Luther began his work. Indeed, the decline of the Roman Church was nowhere more evident than in the feebleness with which Protestant onslaughts were met by the contemporaries of the first quarter century of the great revolt, and the incapacity of the Popes themselves to realize the real gravity of the situation, and to put their interests as great churchmen above their concerns as petty Italian princes. Though Adrian VI (1522–1523) exhibited a real, though utterly ineffective, reformatory zeal, in the Spanish sense, during his brief and unhappy pontificate, neither his predecessor, Leo X (1513–1521), nor his successor, Clement VII (1523–1534), was in any sense a religious leader, and the politi-

cal ambitions of the latter contributed materially to the spread
of Protestantism.

Yet there were those, even in Italy, who were anxious for
reform, though not for revolution.   Such a group founded in
Rome about 1517 the "Oratory of Divine Love."   Among its
leaders was Giovanni Pietro Caraffa (1476–1559), later to be
Pope Paul IV (1555–1559), of distinguished Neapolitan parentage, who had lived for a number of years in Spain, and had
brought from there an admiration for the Spanish reformation,
though no love for the Spanish monarchy.   Another member
was Jacopo Sadoleto (1477–1547); and in close sympathy,
though not one of the Oratory, was Senator Gasparo Contarini
(1483–1542) of Venice, who was still a layman.   Of these,
Caraffa was of unbending devotion to mediæval dogma, while
Contarini had much sympathy with Luther's doctrine of justification by faith alone, though not with his rejection of the
ancient hierarchy.   Pope Paul III (1534–1549), more alive
than his predecessors to the gravity of the situation, made
Contarini, Caraffa, Sadoleto, and the English Reginald Pole
(1500–1558) cardinals early in his pontificate, and appointed
them, with others, a commission on the betterment of the
church, which made a plain-spoken, but resultless, report in
1538.[1]

These men were far removed from really Protestant views.
But there were a considerable number whose sympathies led
them much further.   In Venice they were particularly numerous, though they produced no real leader there.   In that city
Bruccioli's Italian translation of the New Testament was
printed in 1530, and of the whole Bible in 1532.   Ferrara's
hospitality, under Duchess Renée, has already been noted in
connection with Calvin (*ante*, p. 394).   The most remarkable
of these groups was that gathered in Naples about Juan Valdés,
(1500?–1541), a Spaniard of high rank, employed in the service of Charles V and a man of devout, Evangelical mysticism.
From his disciple, Benedetto of Mantua, came about 1540 the
most popular book of this circle, *The Benefits of Christ's Death*.
Among his adherents were Pietro Martire Vermigli (1500–
1562), whose father had been an admirer of Savonarola, himself
prior of the monastery of St. Peter in Naples, destined to be
professor of Protestant theology in Strassburg and Oxford;

[1] Kidd, pp. 307–318.

and Bernardino Ochino (1487–1564), vicar-general of the Capuchin order, later Protestant prebendary of Canterbury, pastor in Zürich, and ultimately a wanderer for erratic opinions. Another friend of this group was Caraffa's own nephew, Galeazzo Caraccioli, marquis of Vico, later to be Calvin's intimate associate in Geneva. These Italian Evangelicals were, however, unorganized and without princely support, save very cautiously in Ferrara, nor did they gain following among the common people. In Italy they were an exotic growth; and the same may be said of the very few Protestants who were to be found in Spain.

Pope Paul III wavered for a time between the method of conciliation advocated by Contarini, who took part in the re-union discussions in Regensburg (*ante*, p. 376) as papal legate, and that of Caraffa, who urged stern repression of doctrinal divergence, while advocating administrative and moral reform. Eventually he decided for the latter, and his decision became the policy of his successors. On Caraffa's urgent appeal Paul III, on July 21, 1542, reorganized the inquisition, largely on the Spanish model, on a universal scale,[1] though of course its actual establishment took place only where it had the support of friendly civil authority. Before it, the feeble beginnings of Italian Protestantism rapidly disappeared. One of the main weapons of the Catholic Counter-Reformation was thus forged.

Much more important was a revival of missionary zeal which the fresh genius of Spain contributed to kindle Catholic enthusiasm. Viewed from any standpoint, Ignatius Loyola is one of the master figures of the Reformation epoch. Inigo Lopez de Recalde was born of a noble family in northern Spain in 1491. After serving as a page at the court of Ferdinand, he became a soldier. His intrepid firmness was exhibited when Pamplona was besieged by the French in 1521, but he received there a wound that made further military service impossible. During his slow recovery he studied the lives of Christ, St. Dominic, and St. Francis. Chivalrous ideals still lingered in Spain, and he determined that he would be a knight of the Virgin. Recovered, in a measure, he journeyed to Monserrat, and hung his weapons on the Virgin's altar. Thence he went to Manresa, where, in the Dominican monastery, he began those directed visions which were afterward to grow into his *Spiritual Ex-*

[1] Kidd, pp. 347–350.

ercises. The year 1523 saw him a pilgrim in Jerusalem, but the Franciscans who were there maintaining the cross with difficulty, thought him dangerous and sent him home.

Convinced that if he was to do the work he desired he must have an education, Ignatius entered a boy's class in Barcelona, and went rapidly forward to the Universities of Alcalá and Salamanca. A born leader, he gathered like-minded companions with whom he practised his spiritual exercises. This aroused the suspicion of the Spanish inquisition and his life was in danger. In 1528, he entered the University of Paris, just as Calvin was leaving it. There he made no public demonstration, but gathered round himself a handful of devoted friends and disciples—Pierre Lefèvre, Francis Xavier, Diego Lainez, Alfonso Salmeron, Nicolas Bobadilla, and Simon Rodriguez, mostly from the Spanish peninsula. In the church of St. Mary on Montmartre, in Paris, on August 15, 1534, these companions took a vow to go to Jerusalem to labor for the church and their fellow men, or, if that proved impossible, to put themselves at the disposition of the Pope. It was a little student association, the connecting bond of which was love to God and the church, as they understood it.

The year 1536 saw them in Venice; but Jerusalem was barred by war, and they now determined to ask the Pope's direction. Ignatius was beginning to perceive what his society might become. Italy had seen many military companies in earthly service. His would be the military company of Jesus, bound by a similar strictness of obedience, and a like careful, though spiritual, exercise of arms, to fight the battle of the church against infidels and heretics. In spite of ecclesiastical opposition, Paul III was induced by the favorable attitude of Contarini and the skill of Ignatius to authorize the company on September 27, 1540.[1] The constitution of the society was as yet indefinite, save that it was to have a head to whom full obedience was due, and should labor wherever that head and the Pope should direct. In April, 1541, Ignatius was chosen the first "general"—an office which he held till his death, July 31, 1556.

The constitution of the Jesuits was gradually worked out, indeed it was not completed till after Ignatius's death, though its main features were his work. At the head is a "general,"

---

[1] Kidd, pp. 335-340.

to whom absolute obedience is due; but who, in turn, is watched
by assistants appointed by the order, and can, if necessary,
be deposed by it. Over each district is a "provincial," appointed by the "general." Each member is admitted, after a
careful novitiate, and pledges obedience to the fullest extent in
all that does not involve sin. His superiors assign him to the
work which they believe him best fitted to do. That that
work may be better accomplished the Jesuits are bound to no
fixed hours of worship or form of dress as are monks. Each
member is disciplined by use of Ignatius's *Spiritual Exercises*,
—a remarkable work, in accordance with which the Jesuit is
drilled in a spiritual manual of arms, by four weeks of intense
contemplation of the principal facts of the life and work of
Christ, and of the Christian warfare with evil, under the guidance of a spiritual drill-master. It was a marvellous instrument that Ignatius constructed, combining the individualism of
the Renaissance—each man assigned to and trained for his
peculiar work—with the sacrifice of will and complete obedience
to the spirit and aims of the whole. It stands as the very
antithesis of Protestantism.

Though the Jesuit society spread rapidly in Italy, Spain,
and Portugal, it was slower in gaining strong foothold in France
and Germany, but by the latter half of the sixteenth century
it was the advance-guard of the Counter-Reformation. Its
chief agencies were preaching, the confessional, its excellent
schools—not for the multitude, but for the well-born and
well-to-do—and its foreign missions. Under Jesuit influence
more frequent confession and communion became the rule in
Catholic countries; and, to aid the confessional, the Jesuit
moral practice was gradually developed, chiefly after Ignatius's
death, and especially in the early part of the seventeenth century, in a fashion that has aroused the criticism not only of
Protestants but of many Catholics. In estimating them
aright it should be remembered that these moral treatises do
not represent ideals of conduct, but the *minima* on which absolution can be given; and, also, that the Jesuit morality emphasized the universal Latin tendency to regard sin as a series
of definite acts rather than as a state.

The nature of sin itself was minimized. That only is sin
which is done with a clear knowledge of its sinfulness and a full
consent of the will. Personal responsibility was undermined

by the doctrine of "probabilism," by which a man could choose what seemed to him the worse course if it had for it accepted authority. "Mental reservation," also, taught that men, for ends that seemed good, were not bound to give the whole truth on oath, or even a correct impression—a doctrine that more than any other produced the common Anglo-Saxon Protestant feeling that Jesuits were unscrupulous and untrustworthy.

Naturally a society thus international in character, the members of which were bound to their officers by constant letters and reports, speedily became a force in political life.

With the establishment of the world-wide inquisition and the foundation of the Company of Jesus, the Council of Trent must be classed as an important agency of the Counter-Reformation. That council had a checkered history. Earnestly desired by Charles V, and reluctantly called by Paul III, it actually met in Trent in December, 1545. In March, 1547, the Italian majority transferred it to Bologna; but in May, 1551, it was back in Trent, where the Spanish minority had all along remained. On April 28, 1552, it adjourned in consequence of the successful Protestant uprising under Moritz of Saxony against the Emperor (*ante*, p. 381). Not till January, 1562, did it meet again, and it completed its work on December 4, 1563. The voting was confined to bishops and heads of orders, without division by nations, as at Constance (*ante*, p. 308). The majority was therefore in Italian hands. That represented the papal wish that definition of doctrine should precede reform. On the other hand, the Spanish bishops, equally orthodox in belief, stood manfully for the Emperor's desire that reform should precede doctrine. It was agreed that doctrine and reform should be discussed alternately, but all decisions had to have the approval of the Pope, thus strengthening the papal supremacy in the church. No voices were more influential in the council than those of the Pope's theological experts, the Jesuits Lainez, and Salmeron, and at a later stage, that of the earliest German Jesuit, Peter Kanis, and their influence steadily supported the anti-Protestant spirit.

The doctrinal decrees of the Council of Trent[1] were clear and definite in their rejection of Protestant beliefs, while often indecisive regarding matters of dispute in mediæval controversies. Scripture and tradition are equally sources of truth.

[1] Schaff, *Creeds of Christendom*, 2: 77–206.

The church alone has the right of interpretation. Justification is skilfully defined, yet so as to leave scope for work-merit. The sacraments are the mediæval seven and defined in the mediæval way. The result is ably expressed, but the church had shut the door completely on all compromise or modification of mediæval doctrine.

Though the reforms effected by the council were far from realizing the wishes of many in the Roman Church, they were not inconsiderable. Provision was made for the public interpretation of Scripture in the larger towns. Bishops were bound to preach and the parish clergy to teach plainly what is needful for salvation. Residence was required and pluralities restrained. Seminaries for clerical training were ordered, and better provision for the moral supervision of the clergy. Regulations were enacted to prevent clandestine marriages. A less praiseworthy step was the approval of an index of prohibited books, to be prepared by the Pope, following the example set by Paul IV in 1559. It resulted in 1571 in the creation by Pius V (1566–1572) of the Congregation of the Index, at Rome, to censure publications.

From a Spanish theologian, influential at Trent, Melchior Cano (1525–1560), came the ablest defense of the Roman position that had yet appeared, in his *De Locis Theologicis Libri XII*, published three years after his death. Theology, he taught, is based on authority. The authority of Scripture rests on the sifting and approving power of the church, which determines what is Scripture and what not; but as by no means all of Christian doctrine is contained in the Scripture, tradition, handed down and sifted by the church, is another authoritative basis.

The middle of the sixteenth century witnessed a change in the prime interest of the holders of the papacy. They were still Italian temporal princes, but the concerns of the church had now assumed the first place. With Paul IV (Caraffa, 1555–1559) the Counter-Reformation reached the papal throne, with the result that many of the abuses of the curia were done away. Rome was a more sombre, a much more ecclesiastical, city than in the Renaissance, but the Popes were now prevailingly men of strict life, religious earnestness, and strenuous Catholicism.

The result of all these influences was that by 1565 Catholic earnestness had been revived. A new spirit, intense in its opposition to Protestantism, mediæval in its theology, but ready to fight or to suffer for its faith, was wide-spread. Against this renewed zeal Protestantism not merely ceased to make new conquests, its hold on the Rhineland and in southern Germany was soon shaken in considerable measure. Catholicism began to hope to win back all that it had lost.

This Catholic revival was also characterized by a large development of mystical piety, in which, as in so much else, Spain was the leader. The chief traits of this religious life were self-renouncing quietism—a raising of the soul in contemplation and voiceless prayer to God—till a union in divine love, or in ecstasy of inner revelation, was believe to be achieved. Often ascetic practices were thought to aid this mystic exaltation. Conspicuous in this movement were Teresa de Jesus (1515–1582) of Avila and Juan de la Cruz (1542–1591) of Ontiveros, in Spain. François de Sales (1567–1622), nominally bishop of Geneva, to whose efforts the winning for Catholicism of the portions of Savoy near Geneva was due, represented the same type of piety, and it was spread in France by his disciple, Jeanne Françoise Frémyot de Chantal (1572–1641). It was combined with extreme devotion to the church and its sacraments. It satisfied the religious longings of more earnest Catholic souls, and the church, in turn, recognized it by enrolling many of its exemplars among the saints.

Catholic zeal went forth, in full measure, also, in the work of foreign missions. These were primarily the endeavor of the monastic orders, notably the Dominicans and Franciscans, with whom from its foundation the Company of Jesus eagerly shared in the labor. To the work of these orders the Christianity of Southern, Central, and large parts of North America is due. They converted the Philippines. Most famous of these Roman missionaries was Ignatius's original associate, Francis Xavier (1506–1552). Appointed by Ignatius missionary to India, at the request of King John III of Portugal, he reached Goa in 1542 and began a career of marvellous activity. In Goa he founded a missionary college, he preached throughout southern India, in 1549 he entered Japan and began a work which had reached large dimensions, when its severe repression was undertaken by the native rulers in 1612. Xavier died, in 1552, just as he was entering China. His work was superficial, an exploration rather than a structure, but his example was a contagious influence of far-reaching force. In China the labor which Xavier had attempted was begun, in 1581, by the Jesuit Matteo Ricci (1552–1610), but his desire to be "all things to all men," led him to compromise with ancestor-worship, a relaxation which missionaries of other Catholic orders strongly opposed. In India the converts were almost entirely from outcasts or low-caste ranks. The Jesuit, Roberto de' Nobili (1576?–1656), began a work for those of high caste in Madura, in 1606, recognizing caste distinctions and otherwise accommodating itself to Indian prejudices. Its apparent success was large, but its methods aroused criticism and ultimate prohibition by the papacy. Probably the most famous experiment of Jesuit missions was that in Paraguay. Their work there began in 1586. In 1610, they commenced gathering the natives into "reductions," or villages, each built on a similar plan, where the dwellers were kept at peace and taught the elements of religion and industry, but held in strict and semi-childlike dependence on the missionaries, in whose hands lay the administration of trade and agriculture. Greatly admired, the system fell with the expulsion of the Jesuits, in 1767, and has left few permanent results.

The rivalries of the several orders, and the more effective supervision of missionary labors, induced Pope Gregory XV (1621–1623) to found, in 1622, the *Congregatio de Propaganda Fide,* by which the whole field could be surveyed and superintended from Rome.

SECTION XII. THE STRUGGLE IN FRANCE, THE NETHERLANDS, AND ENGLAND

The rivalries of France and Spain, with their political and military consequences, had made the growth of the Reformation possible, and had facilitated the division of Germany between Lutherans and Catholics recorded in the Peace of Augsburg of 1555. Henry II (1547–1559) had succeeded Francis I in France, and Charles V had transferred to his son Philip II (1556–1598) the sovereignty of Spain, the Netherlands, and of the Spanish territories in Italy; but the old rivalry continued. In war, however, Philip II at first proved more successful than his father had been, and the battles of St. Quentin in August,

1557, and Gravelines in July, 1558, forced France to the Treaty of Cateau-Cambrésis of April 2, 1559. That treaty was a reckoning point in the history of Europe. France abandoned the long struggle for Italy. Spanish leadership was evidently first in Europe, and had largely bound France to follow, or at least not to oppose, its interests. Protestantism was confronted by a much more politically united Catholicism than it had yet met. The political head of that Catholicism was Philip II of Spain, methodical, industrious, patient, and inflexibly determined, who saw as his God-appointed task the extirpation of Protestantism, and bent every energy to its accomplishment. The next thirty years were to be the time of chief peril in the history of Protestantism.

The point of highest danger was, perhaps, in the year 1559, when after the death of Henry II, in July, the crown passed to Francis II, whose wife was Mary "Queen of Scots," and by her own claim Queen of England also. Yet even Philip's ardent Catholicism was not willing to see a combination so dangerous to Spain as that of France, Scotland, and England under a single pair of rulers. He therefore helped Elizabeth, an action which he must afterward have regretted (*ante*, p. 413).

Calvin's influence had increasingly penetrated France, and French Protestants, or Huguenots, as they were known from 1557, multiplied in spite of severe persecution. By 1555 there was a congregation in Paris. Four years later the number of Huguenot Churches in France was seventy-two. That year, 1559, they were strong enough to hold their First General Synod in Paris, to adopt a strongly Calvinistic creed prepared by Antoine de la Roche Chandieu,[1] and a Presbyterian constitution drawn from Calvin's ecclesiastical principles. Popular estimate credited them with 400,000 adherents. Besides these Huguenots of religion, most of whom were from the economically oppressed and discontented artisan classes, the party was soon strengthened by the accession of political Huguenots.

The death of Henry II and the accession of Francis II left the family of Guise, uncles of Francis's Queen, all powerful in his court. The Guises were from Lorraine, and were looked upon by many of the French nobility as foreigners. Strenuously Catholic, the two brothers, Charles (1524–1574), the

[1] Schaff, *Creeds of Christendom*, 3 : 356–382.

"cardinal of Lorraine," was head of the French clergy as archbishop of Rheims, while Francis (1519–1563), duke of Guise, was the best soldier of France. Opposed to the Guise family were the family of Bourbon, of whom the chief in rank was Antoine of Vendôme, titular King of Navarre, a man of weak and vacillating spirit, and his much abler brother, Louis, prince of Condé. Of the house of Châtillon, also opposed to the Guise brothers, the leader was Gaspard de Coligny, known as Admiral Coligny, a man of sterling character and devoted to Calvinism. These high nobles were moved in large part by opposition to the centralization of power in the King. They represented thus the hostility of the old feudal nobility to royal encroachment. Their interests and those of the humbler middle-class Calvinists coincided in a desire that things in France should not continue as they were. The first step toward a revolution was taken when the badly planned "Conspiracy of Amboise" in March, 1560, failed in its attempt to capture the young King and to transfer the government to the Bourbons. Condé would have been executed had it not been for the death of Francis II on December 5, 1560.

The succession of Charles IX (1560–1574), brother of the late King, brought a new party into the confused struggle. The Guises lost much of their power at court, but were regarded still as the head of Catholic interests in France, and were in constant communication with Philip II of Spain. The chief influence about the new sovereign, who was not yet eleven, was now that of his mother, Catherine de' Medici (1519–1589), able and unscrupulous, determined to maintain the rights of the crown by playing off the two great noble factions of France against each other. She was aided by a statesman of broad and conciliatory views, Michel de l'Hôpital (1505–1573), who became chancellor of France in 1560. Catherine now sought a reconciliation of the factions, released Condé from prison, permitted a public discussion between Catholic and Protestant theologians in Poissy, in September, 1561—in which Beza took part—and followed it, in January, 1562, with an edict permitting the Huguenots to assemble for worship except in walled towns.

Rather than submit, the Catholic party determined to provoke war. On March 1, 1562, the body-guard of the duke of Guise attacked a Huguenot congregation worshipping in

Vassy. Three savage wars followed between the Huguenots and Catholics, 1562–1563, 1567–1568, and 1568–1570, with short truces between. Duke Francis of Guise was murdered by a Protestant assassin. Antoine, King of Navarre, and Condé died of wounds. Coligny was left the head of the Huguenot cause. On the whole, the Huguenots held their own, and jealousy of Spanish influence helped their cause, so that in August, 1570, peace was made at St. Germain-en-Laye, by which nobles were given freedom of worship, and two places for services were permitted to the Huguenot common people in each governmental division of France, while four cities were put in Huguenot control as a guarantee.

The situation at this juncture was greatly complicated by the course of events in the Netherlands. The sources of unrest in that region were even more political and economic than religious in their origin, though in the struggle religion assumed a constantly increasing prominence. The Netherlands, which had come to Philip II of Spain from his father, Charles V, in 1555, were a group of seventeen provinces, tenacious of local rights, predominantly commercial and manufacturing, and disposed to resent all that interfered with existing customs or disturbed trade. Lutheranism had early entered, but had been largely displaced by Anabaptism among the lowest stratum of the population, while by 1561 when the Belgic Confession was drafted by Guy de Bray,[1] Calvinism was winning converts among the middle classes. The nobility was as yet hardly touched, and in 1562 the total number of Protestants was reckoned at only 100,000.

Charles V, though strenuously resisting the inroads of Protestantism, had largely respected Netherlandish rights and jealousies. Not so Philip II. He determined to secure political and religious uniformity there similar to that in Spain. In 1559 he appointed his sister, Margaret of Parma, regent, with an advisory committee of three, of which the leading spirit was his devoted supporter, Cardinal Granvella (1517–1586), bishop of Arras. This committee practically usurped the power of the old councils of state, in which the high nobles had shared. The next year Philip secured from the Pope a reconstitution of the ecclesiastical geography of the Netherlands, which had merit in that it freed the Netherlandish

---

[1] Schaff, *Creeds of Christendom*. 3 : 383–436.

bishoprics from foreign ecclesiastical supervision, but aroused jealousy, since the new prelates were Philip's nominees and had places in the Parliament, or "States General," thus greatly strengthening Spanish influence. Philip, moreover, used every power to crush "heresy"—a course that was disliked by the middle classes, because it hurt trade and drove workmen to emigration. Nobles and merchants were, therefore, increasingly restive.

Chief among the opponents of these changes were three eminent nobles, William of Nassau, Prince of Orange (1533–1584), born a Lutheran, but now, nominally at least, a Catholic, to be the hero of Dutch independence; and the Catholic counts of Egmont and Horn. They forced Granvella's dismissal in 1564. Philip now saw in them the chief hindrance to his plans. He demanded the enforcement of the decrees of the Council of Trent and a stricter punishment of heresy. A petition of protest was circulated and presented to the regent on April 5, 1566—the nickname "Beggars" given to its signers on that occasion becoming the name of the party of Netherlandish freedom. Popular excitement was intense. Protestant preaching was openly heard, and in August, 1556, iconoclastic riots, opposed by such men as William of Orange, wrecked hundreds of churches.

To Philip these events were rebellion in politics and religion. He therefore sent the duke of Alva (1508–1582), an able Spanish general, to Brussels with a picked Spanish army and practically as governor. His arrival in August, 1567, was followed by hundreds of executions, among them those of Egmont and Horn. William of Orange escaped to Germany, and organized resistance, but it was beaten down by Alva's skill. Alva, however, completed the alienation of the mercantile classes, in 1569, by introducing the heavy Spanish taxes on sales. Meanwhile William of Orange was commissioning sea-rovers, who preyed on Spanish commerce and found an uncertain refuge in English harbors, where the English Government had been driven into a more strenuous attitude of hostility to all Catholic forces, of which Philip was chief, by the bull of deposition, issued against Elizabeth by Pope Pius V on February 25, 1570.

In April, 1572, these sea-rovers captured Brill. The northern provinces rose. William of Orange put himself at the head of the movement.   On July 15, the leading towns of Holland, Zealand, Friesland, and Utrecht recognized him as Stadholder. Meanwhile, since the peace of 1570, the Huguenots and the opponents of Spain in France had been working for a revival of the older political policy, which made France the rival instead of the ally of Spain.   Immediate assistance to the Netherlandish rebels, to be rewarded by accession of some territory to France, was planned, and none favored it more than Coligny, whose influence over Charles IX was now great.   To emphasize the reconciliation of parties in France, a marriage was arranged between Henry of Navarre, the Protestant son of the late Antoine of Bourbon, and Charles IX's sister, Marguerite of Valois.   For the wedding, on August 18, 1572, Huguenot and Catholic nobles and their followers gathered in the fanatically Catholic city of Paris.

Catherine de' Medici had come to look with fear on the influence now exerted by Coligny over her son, the King. Whether the cause was jealousy regarding her own influence, or fear that the war into which Coligny was leading the King would be disastrous to the French crown, is uncertain.   Apparently all that she wanted at first was Coligny's removal by murder.   In this she had the hearty sympathy of Henry, duke of Guise (1550–1588), the son of the murdered Francis, who wrongly charged Coligny with responsibility for his father's death.   On August 22 an attempt on Coligny's life failed, and its ill-success carried panic to Catherine.   The Huguenots had been alienated without being deprived of their leader.   She and her supporters now suddenly decided on a general massacre, for which the Guise party and the fanatical people of Paris furnished abundant means.   On August 24, St. Bartholomew's day, the bloody work began.   Coligny was killed, and with him a number of victims that has been most variously estimated, reaching not improbably 8,000 in Paris, and several times that number in the whole of France.   Henry of Navarre saved his life by abjuring Protestantism.

The news was hailed with rejoicing in Madrid and in Rome, and rightly, if its moral enormity could be overlooked.   It had saved the Catholic cause from great peril.   The policy of France was reversed.   Plans for interference in the Netherlands were at an end.   The desperate struggle for Netherlandish freedom was the consequence.   Yet the Catholics did not gain in France what they hoped. The fourth, fifth, sixth, and seventh Huguenot Wars, 1573, 1574–1576, 1577, 1580, ran their course of destruction and misery, but the Huguenots were not crushed. Charles IX died in 1574 and was succeeded as King by his vicious brother, Henry III (1574–1589).

A division among the Catholics themselves was developing. There had long been a considerable element which, while Catholic in religion, felt that the protracted wars were ruining the land and permitting foreign, especially Spanish, intrigue. They believed that some basis of peace with the Huguenots should be reached, and were known as the *Politiques*. On the other hand, those who put religion first and were willing to see France become a mere appanage of Spain, if thereby Catholicism could triumph, had been for some time organizing associations in various parts of France to maintain the Roman Church. In 1576 these were developed into a general "League," led by Henry of Guise and supported by Spain and the Pope. Its existence drove the *Politiques* more and more into alliance with the Huguenots, who found their political head in Henry of Navarre, he having reasserted his Protestant faith in 1576.

The massacre of St. Bartholomew shattered the hopes of William of Orange for the speedy expulsion of Spain from the Netherlands. The two years following were those of intensest struggle, of which William was the soul. Alva's generalship seemed at first irresistible. Mons, Mechlin, Zutphen, Naarden, and Haarlem fell before the Spanish forces; but Alkmaar they failed to take, in October, 1573. Alva was recalled at his own request, and was succeeded, in November, by Luis de Requesens (1525?–1576), under whom the Spanish policy was substantially unchanged. But October, 1574, saw the successful end of the defense of Leyden, and it was evident that the northern Netherlands could not be conquered by the forces then available for Spain. In 1576 Requesens died, and the Spanish troops sacked Antwerp, an event which roused the southern provinces to resistance. The new Spanish commander, John of Austria (1545–1578), was able to effect little. Elizabeth aided the revolted Netherlands from 1576. In September, 1577, William was able to make a triumphal entry into Brussels. John of Austria died, a disappointed man, in October, 1578; but he was succeeded by his nephew, Alexander Farnese, duke of Parma (1545–1592), a general and a statesman of commanding talents.

Matters went better for the Spanish cause. Parma played on the jealousies of the Catholic south and the Calvinist north. The former united in the League of Arras for the protection of Catholicism in January, 1579; the latter replied the same month by the Union of Utrecht. Protestants left the south for the north by the thousands, many Catholics went southward. Ultimately the ten southern provinces were saved by Parma for Spain, and modern Belgium is his monument. The seven northern states declared their independence of Spain in 1581, and though much remained to be done before all dangers were passed, their freedom was so strongly intrenched that not even the murder of William of Orange, on July 10, 1584, by a fanatic encouraged by Parma, could overthrow it.

During this struggle the Calvinistic churches of the Netherlands had been shaping. The First National Synod had been held outside of Netherlandish territory, in Emden, in 1571. William of Orange had accepted Calvinism two years later. In 1575 a university was established in Leyden, soon to be famed for its learning in theology and the sciences. The Reformed Church of the Netherlands was, like the Huguenot Church of France, Presbyterian in constitution, though its degree of independence of state control was long a matter of controversy, and varied with the different provinces. The severity of the struggle for national independence, the wish to secure the aid of all who were friendly to it, and the mercantile spirit led the Protestant Netherlands to a larger degree of toleration than elsewhere at the time in Christendom. Catholics were not, indeed, allowed public worship or political office, but they had right of residence and employment. To the Anabaptists William of Orange granted in 1577 the first protection in rights of worship that they anywhere received. This degree of toleration, partial as it was, soon made the Netherlands a refuge for the religiously oppressed and added to the strength of the nation.

Yet the death of their wise leader, William of Orange, brought great peril to the revolted Netherlands. They did not feel able to stand alone, and offered their sovereignty first to Henry III of France and then to Elizabeth of England. Both refused; but Elizabeth sent her favorite, the earl of Leicester, in 1585, with a small army. He now became governor-general, but his rule was a failure, and he returned to England in 1587. It looked as if Parma's skilful generalship might reduce the rebellious provinces; but, fortunately, Philip demanded his attention for a larger enterprise. The Spanish King had determined on nothing less than the conquest of England.

At the beginning of her reign Philip had aided Elizabeth for political reasons (*ante,* p. 413) but those reasons soon ceased to apply, and Philip became her enemy, seeing in Elizabeth the head of that Protestantism that it was his chief desire to overthrow. The early part of Elizabeth's reign had been surprisingly free from actual trouble from her Catholic subjects. Mary "Queen of Scots" was the heir to the throne, however, and a constant centre of conspiracy. In 1569 a Catholic rebellion broke out in the north of England, aided by Spanish encouragement. It was put down. In 1570 there followed the papal bull declaring Elizabeth excommunicate and deposed. In 1571, a wide-spread plot—that of Ridolfi—aiming at Elizabeth's assassination was uncovered. Elizabeth was saved by the new turn of French affairs just before the massacre of St. Bartholomew (*ante,* p. 435) and the outbreak of the Netherlands rebellion. Parliament answered by making attacks on Elizabeth's person, orthodoxy, or title to the throne high treason. For the immediate present, however, England had comparative peace.

During Elizabeth's early years the English Catholics had been left by Rome and their fellow believers on the Continent with surprisingly little spiritual aid or leadership. To remedy this situation, William Allen (1532–1594), an able English exile who became a cardinal in 1587, established a seminary in Douai, in 1568, for training missionary priests for England. His students were soon flocking to England. Their work was almost wholly spiritual, but was looked upon with great hostility by the English authorities. The situation was intensified when, in 1580, the Jesuits began a mission under the leadership of Robert Parsons (1546–1610) and Edmund Campion (1540–1581). Campion was seized and executed, though he seems to have intended no political movement. Not so Parsons. He escaped to the Continent, won Allen for his plans, and began a course of intrigue to bring about a Spanish invasion of England, a Catholic rising there, and the death or dethronement of Elizabeth. His work was most unfortunate for his fellow Catholics. Most of the priests laboring in England are now known to have been free of traitorous designs; but it was not so under-stood, and the English authorities looked upon them all as public enemies, and executed such as its spies could discover. Their work preserved a Roman Church in England, but it was carried on at frightful cost. Elizabeth now sent an army to the Netherlands, in 1585 (*ante*, p. 437), while she encouraged a semipiratical expedition under Sir Francis Drake, the same year, which burned and plundered Spanish settlements on the Caribbean and Gulf of Mexico.

In 1586, a new scheme was hatched against Elizabeth's life— the Babington Plot—in which English spies discovered that Mary "Queen of Scots" was personally involved. As a con-sequence, she was executed, on February 8, 1587, after a good deal of wavering on the part of Elizabeth. Philip now deter-mined on an invasion of England. Its conquest would estab-lish Catholicism and his own mastery there, and make hopeful the reduction of the rebellious Netherlands. For the work he would collect a great fleet which could hold the North Sea, while Parma brought over his seasoned soldiers from the Netherlands. After infinite trouble, the "Great Armada" got away from Spain on July 12, 1588. The enterprise had appealed to the religious zeal of the nation and men of dis-tinction in unusual numbers had enlisted for it. In the estimate of Europe generally it was believed invincible; but, in reality, it was badly equipped and the sailors inefficient. Moreover, the battle in which it was about to engage was a contest be-tween old and new naval tactics. The Spanish plan of battle was that of grappling and boarding. Their guns were light and few, their vessels slow, though large. England had developed swifter ships, armed with far heavier guns, able to avoid grap-pling, and to punish the unwieldy Spaniards frightfully. On July 21 the battle was joined off Plymouth. Then followed a week of running fight up the Channel. culminating in a great battle off Gravelines on the 28th. The Spanish fleet, hopelessly defeated, fled north, to escape home around Scotland and Ire-land. Any crossing by Parma was impossible. While it is a legend that the Armada was defeated by storms, it really fell before the English gunnery and seamanship, though a week later, on its retreat storms completed its wreck. England was the rock on which Philip's plans of a victorious Catholicism had shattered, and they had shattered for a cause which he could scarcely have understood. In the contest, instead of the Catholic rising which he had anticipated in England, and which men like Allen and Parsons had predicted, Catholics and Protestants had stood shoulder to shoulder as Englishmen against Spain.

While Philip's larger hopes were thus crushed in 1588, he held as tenaciously as ever to the plan of uprooting Protestantism in France. The death of Henry III's brother, the duke of Anjou, in 1584, left the Huguenot Henry Bourbon of Navarre prospective heir to the throne. To prevent this succession, Philip and the League entered into a treaty, in January, 1585, by which the crown should go to Henry of Navarre's uncle, Charles, Cardinal Bourbon, on Henry III's death. In July, 1585, Henry III was forced by the League to withdraw all rights from the Huguenots, and in September a bull of Sixtus V (1585–1590) declared Henry of Navarre incapable of succeeding to the throne. The eighth Huguenot War was the result—that known as the "War of the Three Henrys," from Henry III, Henry of Guise, the head of the League, and Henry of Navarre. Paris was entirely devoted to Henry of Guise. On May 12, 1588, its citizens compelled Henry III to leave the city. The weak King saw no way to resist the demands of the League and its imperious head and, on December 23, had Henry of Guise treacherously murdered. Thirteen days later Catherine de' Medici closed her stormy life.

Henry of Guise was succeeded in the leadership of the League by his brother Charles, duke of Mayenne. Henry III now made terms with Henry of Navarre, and the two were jointly laying siege to Paris, when Henry III was murdered by a fanatic monk, dying on August 2, 1589. But Henry of Navarre, or as he now became, Henry IV of France (1589–1610), was still far from secure on his new throne. A brilliant victory at Ivry, in March, 1590, defeated the League, but Spanish troops under Parma's able generalship prevented his capture of Paris that year, and of Rouen in 1592. Not till after the death of Parma, on December 3, of the year last named, was Henry IV really master. And now, for purely political reasons, Henry IV declared himself a Catholic, being received into the Roman Church on July 25, 1593, though terms were not concluded with the Pope till more than two years later. However to be criticised morally—and Henry's life, whether as a Protestant or as a Catholic, showed that religious principles had little influence over his conduct—the step was wise. It gave peace to the distracted land. It pleased the vast majority of his subjects. Nor did Henry forget his old associates. In April, 1598, the Edict of Nantes was issued, by which the Huguenots were admitted to all public office, public worship was permitted whereever it had existed in 1597, save in Paris, Rheims, Toulouse, Lyons, and Dijon, and children of Huguenots could not be forced to receive Catholic training. Certain fortified towns were placed in Huguenot hands as guarantees.

The same year (1598), Philip II died, on September 13, convinced to the end that what he had done was for the service of God, but having failed in his great life effort to overthrow Protestantism.

The Huguenot Churches now entered on their most prosperous period. Their organization was completed, and their schools at Sedan, Saumur, Montauban, Nîmes, and elsewhere flourished. They were a political corporation within the state. As such, they were opposed by the centralizing policy of Richelieu, Louis XIII's great minister. In 1628, Rochelle was taken from them, and their political semi-independence ended. By the Edict of Nîmes, in 1629, their religious privileges were preserved, but they suffered increasing attack from Jesuit and other Catholic influences as the century went on, till the revocation of the Edict of Nantes, by Louis XIV, in 1685, reduced them to a persecuted, martyr church, to be proscribed till the eve of the French Revolution, and drove thousands of their numbers into exile, to the lasting gain of England, Holland, Prussia, and America.

SECTION XIII.   GERMAN CONTROVERSIES AND THE THIRTY YEARS'
WAR

It was the misfortune of Lutheranism that it had no other bond of union between its representatives in its several territories than agreement in "pure doctrine," and that differences in apprehension were regarded as incompatible with Christian fellowship. The original Lutheran conception of a faith which constitutes a new personal relationship between God and the believing soul tended to shade off into a belief which, as Melanchthon once defined it, is "an assent by which you accept all articles of the faith." The result was a new Protestant scholasticism.

Melanchthon, influenced by humanistic thought, gradually moved from his original agreement with Luther to some emphases different from those of his greater colleague. By 1527 he had lost sympathy with Luther's denial of human freedom and had reached the conclusion that salvation is only possible through the co-operant action of the will of man—a view to which the name "synergism" is usually given. By 1535 he was emphasizing good works, not as the price of salvation, but as its indispensable evidence. Regarding the Lord's Supper he came to feel that Luther had overemphasized Christ's physical presence and, without quite reaching Calvin's position (*ante*, p. 394), to hold that Christ is given "not in the bread, but with the bread," that is, to lay stress on the spiritual rather than the physical reception. These differences never made a breach with Luther, partly because of Luther's generous affection for his younger friend, and partly because of Melanchthon's caution in their expression, though they made Melanchthon uncomfortable at times in Luther's presence during that reformer's later years. They were to cause trouble enough in the Lutheran communions.

One chief cause of bad feeling was Melanchthon's reluctant consent to the *Leipzig Interim*, in 1548. To Melanchthon many Roman practices then reintroduced were "non-essentials." To Matthias Flacius Illyricus and Nikolaus von Amsdorf, in the security of Magdeburg, nothing could be "non-essential" in such a time (*ante*, p. 380). They attacked Melanchthon bitterly, and perhaps he deserved some of their blame. This strain was soon increased by the feeling of the princes of the old deprived Saxon electoral line that Melanchthon by remaining in Wittenberg, which now belonged to their successful despoiler, Moritz, was guilty of desertion of a family which had faithfully supported him; and they magnified the school in Jena, making it a university in 1558, and appointing Flacius to one of its professorships.

Other theological disputes arose. Andreas Osiander (1498–1552) roused the opposition of all other Lutheran parties by declaring, with Paul, that the sinner receives actual righteousness from the indwelling Christ, and is not simply declared righteous. Georg Major (1502–1574) affirmed, in essential agreement with Melanchthon, the necessity of good works as evidences of salvation. In 1552 he was bitterly assailed by Amsdorf, who went so far as to assert that good works are a hindrance to the Christian life. The same year saw a fierce attack on Melanchthon's doctrine of the Lord's Supper by Joachim Westphal (1510?–1574), as crypto-Calvinism, or Calvinism surreptitiously introduced. It is not surprising that shortly before his death, which occurred on April 19, 1560, Melanchthon gave as a reason for his willingness to depart, that he might escape "the rage of the theologians."

The Protestant situation in Germany was soon after further turmoiled by the victorious advance of Calvinism into the southwest. Frederick III (1559–1576), the excellent Elector Palatine, was led by studies of the discussions regarding the Lord's Supper to adopt the Calvinist position. For his territories the young theologians, Kaspar Olevianus (1536–1587), and Zacharias Ursinus (1534–1583) prepared the remarkable Heidelberg Catechism in 1562—the most sweet-spirited and experiential of the expositions of Calvinism.[1] It was adopted by the Elector in 1563. But Calvinism had no protection under the Peace of Augsburg, of 1555, and not only Catholics but Lutherans were soon protesting against its toleration.

The disputes in Lutheranism continued with great intensity. In 1573, Elector August of Saxony (1553–1586), having assumed guardianship over the young princes of ducal Saxony, where the foes of Melanchthon were supreme, drove out their more radical representatives. Thus far electoral Saxony, with its Universities of Wittenberg and Leipzig, had followed the Melanchthonian or "Philippist" tradition. Now, in 1574, the same Elector August, influenced by his wife, and by an anonymous volume, believed he had discovered a heretofore unsuspected Calvinist propaganda regarding the Lord's Supper, in his own dominions. He had some of his principal theologians imprisoned, and one even put to torture. "Philippism" was vigorously repressed.

Yet this struggle gave rise, in 1577, to the last great Lutheran creed—the *Formula of Concord*.[2] Prepared by a number of theologians, of whom Jakob Andreæ (1528–1590) of Tübingen, Martin Chemnitz (1522–1586) of Brunswick, and Nikolaus

[1] Schaff, *Creeds of Christendom*, 3 : 307–355.
[2] *Ibid.*, 3 : 93–180.

Selnecker (1530–1592) of Leipzig were chief, it was put forth, after infinite negotiation, in 1580, on the fiftieth anniversary of the *Augsburg Confession*, with the approving signatures of fifty-one princes, thirty-five cities, and between eight and nine thousand ministers. A number of Lutheran princes and cities refused their approval; but it undoubtedly represented the decided majority of Lutheran Germany. Not as extreme as Flacius and Amsdorf, it represents the stricter Lutheran interpretation. It is minute, technical, and scholastic in marked contrast to the freshness of the *Augsburg Confession* half a century before. The period of Lutheran high orthodoxy had begun, which was to have its classic exposition in 1622, through the *Loci Theologici* of Johann Gerhard (1582–1637) of Jena. Its scholasticism was as complete as any in the Middle Ages. Under this repression, the Philippists turned increasingly to Calvinism, and Calvinism made larger inroads in Germany. To the Palatinate, Nassau was added in 1577, Bremen by 1581, Anhalt in 1597, and part of Hesse in the same period. The electoral house of Brandenburg, from which the present German imperial line is descended, became Calvinist in 1613, though most of the inhabitants of Brandenburg remained Lutheran. This transformation was often accompanied by the retention of the *Augsburg Confession*. Yet though these German "Reformed" churches became Calvinist in doctrine and worship, Calvin's characteristic discipline found little foothold among them.

Protestantism in Germany reached its flood-tide of territorial advance about 1566. From that time it began to ebb. The revived Catholicism of the Counter-Reformation became increasingly aggressive, led by the Jesuits and supported by earnest Catholic princes like the dukes of Bavaria. Divided Protestantism could not offer united resistance. In Bavaria, Duke Albert V (1550–1579) vigorously applied the principle *cujus regio, ejus religio*, to crush his Protestant nobility and people. The abbot of Fulda similarly attempted the repression of Protestantism in his territories in 1572. Successfully opposed for a time, he effected his task in 1602. Similar Catholic restorations were effected in the Protestantized territories belonging to the archbishoprics of Mainz and Trier. Under Jesuit leadership similar Catholic advances were made in other bishoprics, the inhabitants of which had embraced Evangelical views. The archbishop of Cologne, Gebhard Truchsess, one of the seven Electors, proposed to marry, in 1582, and embraced Protestantism. Little help came to him. He was forced from his strategically situated see, and the territory fully restored to Catholicism. In Austria and Bohemia the situation became steadily more unfavorable for Protestantism; and there as well as elsewhere in the empire the Jesuit propaganda gained many individual converts. It was aggressive and confident of ultimate victory. The situation between Protestants and Catholics was constantly strained.

An event of the years 1606–1607 markedly increased this bitterness. The city of Donauwörth was overwhelmingly Protestant, yet Catholic monasteries had been there allowed. A Catholic procession of 1606 was stoned. On imperial command, Maximilian, the able Catholic duke of Bavaria (1597–1651) occupied the city and began a repression of its Evangelical worship. At the Reichstag of 1608 the Catholics demanded the restitution of all ecclesiastical property confiscated since 1555. For this claim they had the strict letter of the law in the Peace of Augsburg; but many of these districts had become, in the two generations that had elapsed, solidly Protestant in population.

Under these circumstances a number of Protestant princes formed a defensive "Union" on May 4, 1608, headed by the Calvinist Elector Frederick IV of the Palatinate. To it Catholic princes, led by Maximilian of Bavaria, opposed a "League," on July 10, 1609. The strong Lutheran states of northern Germany were unwilling to join the "Union," nor was the Emperor in the "League." Had Henry IV of France lived, war would probably have broken out at this time; but his assassination in 1610 and the uncertainty of the imperial succession in Germany delayed it for a time.

Besides the bitter disputes between Catholics and Lutherans, the condition of Germany was, in many ways, one of unrest. Business was bad. The debased coinage caused great suffering, the country was growing impoverished. The enforcement of unity of belief in Protestant and Catholic territories alike was damaging to the intellectual life of the people; while the witchcraft delusion which cost thousands of lives, and was equally entertained by Catholics and Protestants, was at its worst between 1580 and 1620.

The actual outbreak of the Thirty Years' War came from Bohemia. That then largely Protestant land had wrung from its King, the Emperor Rudolf II (1576–1612), in 1609, a charter—the *Majestätsbrief*—granting a high degree of toleration. Rudolf was succeeded, both as Emperor and King, by his feeble brother Matthias (King, 1611–1619; Emperor, 1612–1619), but he was childless, and in 1617 his cousin, Ferdinand of Styria, a strenuous representative of the Counter-Reformation, succeeded in securing recognition as Matthias's successor from the Bohemian estates. Catholic influences were augmented, and in May, 1618, a party of disaffected Protestants flung the two Catholic regents representing the absent Matthias from a high window in Prague. This act put Bohemia into rebellion and began the war. Its commencement was favorable for the Bohemian insurgents, and in 1619, after the death of Matthias, they elected the Calvinist, Frederick V (1610–1632), Elector Palatine, their King. The same week Ferdinand of Styria was chosen Emperor as Ferdinand II (1619–1637).

Frederick found little support outside of Bohemia, and now Maximilian of Bavaria and a Spanish force from the Netherlands came to Ferdinand's assistance. Under the command of a Walloon general, Jan Tzerklas, Baron Tilly (1559–1632), this Catholic combination overwhelmed the Bohemian forces, near Prague, on November 8, 1620. Frederick fled the land. The *Majestätsbrief* was annulled, the property of Bohemian Protestants largely confiscated, to the great financial advantage of the Jesuits, and the Counter-Reformation enforced with a high hand in Bohemia, Moravia, and Austria. Among those enriched by the acquisition of confiscated property was one destined to play a great part in the further history of the war, Albrecht von Wallenstein (1583–1634). The "Union" was dissolved. A similar repression of Protestantism now took place in Austria.

Meanwhile Spanish troops, under Spinola, had invaded the Palatinate in 1620, and thither Tilly and the army of the "League" soon followed. The land was conquered, Catholicism enforced, and Frederick's electoral title with a good share of the Palatinate transferred to Maximilian of Bavaria in 1623.

Northwestern Germany, where many bishoprics had become Protestant possessions since the Peace of Augsburg, was now threatened with war, and the disasters to Protestantism which had already happened aroused Protestant foreign powers. Nothing effective was done, however, except by Christian IV of Denmark, to whom England and the Protestant Netherlands sent some slight aid. To the Emperor Ferdinand the enmity of the Danish King seemed formidable, and he therefore turned to Wallenstein to raise a new army as imperial commander-in-chief. This remarkable adventurer, born a Protestant, was nominally a Catholic, and now the richest noble of Bohemia. A natural leader of men, he raised an army in which he asked no questions of race or creed, but simply of capacity to fight, and loyalty to himself. He soon had a force of great efficiency.

On April 25, 1626, Wallenstein defeated the Protestant army under Ernst of Mansfeld, at the Dessau bridge over the Elbe, following the beaten forces to Hungary, whither they retreated in the vain hope of making effective stand in conjunction with the Emperor's enemy, Bethlen Gabor, prince of Transylvania. On August 27, 1626, Christian IV of Denmark was beaten by Tilly and the army of the "League" at Lutter. These successes were followed up by the Catholics in 1627 and 1628. Hanover, Brunswick, and Silesia were conquered, then Holstein, Schleswig, Pomerania, and Mecklenburg. Wallenstein found it impossible to capture the Baltic seaport of Stralsund, which was aided by the Swedes, and thought it wise to make peace before the able Swedish King, Gustavus Adolphus (1611–1632), might interfere. Accordingly, Christian IV was allowed, by a treaty of May, 1629, to keep his territories on condition of no further share in German politics.

The Catholics had determined to reap the fruits of their great victories. On March 6, 1629, an imperial "Edict of Restitution" ordered the restoration to Catholic possession of all ecclesiastical property which had come into Protestant hands since 1552, the expulsion of Protestants from territories ruled by Catholics, and no recognition of any Protestants save Lutherans, thus depriving the Calvinists of any rights whatever. The events of the next few years prevented its full execution, but five bishoprics, a hundred monasteries, and hundreds of parish churches were, for a time, thus transferred. Many more would have been had Catholic success continued, and had not the Catholics themselves quarrelled over the spoils. These disputes, and the jealousy of the "League," headed by Maximilian of Bavaria, by reason of the great increase in imperial power which Wallenstein had effected, now led to a successful demand by the "League" that Wallenstein be dismissed. In September, 1630, the Emperor was compelled to part with his able general.

Even before Wallenstein's dismissal an event of prime importance had occurred, though its consequences were not immediately apparent. Gustavus Adolphus of Sweden with a small army had landed on the German coast on June 26, 1630. Two motives induced his interference in the war. He came undoubtedly as a champion of the Protestant faith; but he also desired to make the Baltic a Swedish lake, and he saw in the imperial attacks on the German Baltic seaports an immediate danger to his own kingdom. Should they be held by a hostile power, Sweden would be in great peril. Gustavus soon succeeded in driving the imperial forces out of Pomerania; but he moved slowly, since he had no adequate allies. In January, 1631, however, he entered into a treaty with France, then under the masterful leadership of Louis XIII's great minister, Armand du Plessis, Cardinal Richelieu (1585–1642), by which considerable financial subsidies were granted. Richelieu had resumed the historic hostility of France to the Habsburgs of Spain and Austria, and the ancient French policy of aiding their enemies for the political advantage of the French monarchy, even if those enemies were Protestants. Gustavus's next important and difficult work was to secure the alliance of Brandenburg, which, though Protestant, had been imperialist, and of Saxony, which had been neutral. On May 20, 1631, Tilly captured Magdeburg, the inhabitants being treated with brutal ferocity.

This loss of a great Protestant stronghold was followed by an alliance in June between Gustavus and the Elector of Brandenburg, and in August Saxony threw off its neutrality and joined the Swedes. On September 17, 1631, Gustavus, with little real help from the Saxons, won a great victory over Tilly at Breitenfeld, close by Leipzig. The imperial power in northern Germany crumbled, and the Swedish King marched victoriously to the Rhine, establishing himself in Mainz, while the Saxons took Prague. In his extremity, the Emperor called on Wallenstein once more to raise an army, and in April, 1632, that general was at the head of a redoubtable force.

Gustavus now marched against Maximilian of Bavaria, defeating Tilly in a battle near Donauwörth, in which that commander was mortally wounded. Munich, the Bavarian capital, had to surrender to the Swedish King. Meanwhile Wallenstein had driven the Saxons out of Prague, and marched to meet Gustavus. For some weeks the two armies faced each other near Nuremberg, but the fighting was indecisive, and Wallenstein marched northward to crush Saxony. Gustavus followed him, and defeated him at Lützen, near Leipzig, on November 16, 1632, in a fierce battle in which Gustavus was slain. His work was enduring. He had made the Edict of Restitution a dead letter in northern Germany, and his memory is deservedly cherished by German Protestantism.

The control of Swedish affairs passed to the able chancellor, Axel Oxenstjerna, though the most capable Protestant general was now Bernhard of Saxe-Weimar (1604–1639). In November, 1633, Bernhard captured the important south German city of Regensburg, and opened the line of the Danube to Protestant advance. Meanwhile Wallenstein had remained comparatively inactive in Bohemia, partly jealous of large Spanish forces which had been sent to southern Germany, and partly intriguing with Saxony, Sweden, and France. Just what he had in mind is uncertain, but the most probable supposition is that he aimed to secure for himself the crown of Bohemia. His failure to relieve Regensburg was the last straw in rousing the suspicious hostility of the Emperor, and on February 25, 1634, he was murdered by his own soldiers as a result of imperial intrigue.

On September 5 and 6, 1634, Bernhard and the Swedish troops were badly defeated at Nördlingen, by combined imperial and Spanish forces. In its way the battle was as decisive as Breitenfeld nearly three years before. That had shown that northern Germany could not be held by the Catholics; this that southern Germany could not be conquered by the Protestants. The war ought now to have ended; on June 15, 1635, peace was made at Prague between the Emperor and Saxony. November 12, 1627, was taken as the normal date. All ecclesiastical properties should remain for forty years in the hands of those who then held them, and their ultimate fate should be decided by a court composed equally of Catholic and Protestant judges. No mention was made of privileges for Calvinists.

To this peace most of Protestant Germany agreed in the next few weeks.

Yet no peace was to be had for the wretched land. For thirteen years more the war continued as savagely as ever. Its original aims were practically lost, and it became a struggle, fought out on German soil with the aid of German parties, for the aggrandizement of Spain, France, and Sweden, in which France gained most. Ferdinand II was succeeded by his son, Ferdinand III (1637–1657), but the change brought no real alteration of the situation. Germany lacked men of real leadership, the only conspicuous exception being Frederick William the "Great Elector" (1640–1688) of Brandenburg, but though he succeeded in enlarging his territorial possessions, he was too young largely to affect the course of the war.

At last, after infinite negotiation, the "Peace of Westphalia" was made on October 27, 1648. Sweden was firmly settled on the German shore of the Baltic. Most of Alsace went to France. The long-existing independence of Switzerland was formally acknowledged. Brandenburg received the archbishopric of Magdeburg and the bishoprics of Halberstadt and Minden as compensation for surrender of its claims on part of Pomerania to the Swedes. Maximilian of Bavaria kept his title of Elector and part of the Palatinate, while the rest of the Palatinate was restored to Karl Ludwig, son of the unfortunate Frederick V, for whom a new electoral title was created. More important was the religious settlement. Here the ability of the "Great Elector" secured the inclusion of the Calvinists who, with the Lutherans, were regarded as one party as over against the Catholics. German Calvinists at last secured full rights. The Edict of Restitution was fully abandoned and the year 1624 taken as the norm. Whatever ecclesiastical property was then in Catholic or Protestant hands should so remain. While the power of a lay sovereign to determine the religion of his subjects still remained, it was modified by a provision that where divided religious worship had existed in a territory in 1624, each party could continue it in the same proportion as then existed. Between Lutherans and Calvinists it was agreed that the norm should be the date of the Peace, and that a change of the lay ruler to one or the other form of Protestantism thereafter should not affect his subjects. On the other hand, by the insistence of the Emperor, no privileges were accorded to Protestants in Austria or Bohemia.

Neither side liked the Peace. The Pope denounced it. But all were tired of the war, and the Peace had the great merit of drawing the lines between Catholicism and Protestantism roughly, but approximately, where they really stood. As such, it proved essentially permanent, and with it the period of the Reformation on the Continent may be considered closed.

To Germany the Thirty Years' War was an unmitigated and frightful evil. The land had been ploughed from end to end for a generation by lawless and plundering armies. Population had fallen from sixteen millions to less than six. Fields were waste. Commerce and manufacturing destroyed. Above all, intellectual life had stagnated, morals had been roughened and corrupted, and religion grievously maimed. A century after its close the devastating consequences had not been made good. Little evidence of spiritual life was manifested in this frightful time of war; yet to it, in large part, and reflecting the trust of heartfelt piety in its stress, belongs the work of perhaps the greatest of Lutheran hymn-writers, Paul Gerhardt (1607–1676). In its earlier years, also, lie the chief activities of that strange and deep Protestant mystic, Jakob Böhme (1575–1624), of Görlitz.

SECTION XIV. SOCINIANISM

The Reformation age exhibited a number of departures from traditional orthodoxy regarding the person and work of Christ. Though not characteristic of Anabaptists, in general, their earliest manifestation is to be found among such Anabaptists as Denk and Haetzer (*ante*, p. 369). Servetus's radical opinions and tragic fate have already been noted (*ante*, p. 399), but this ingenious thinker founded no school of disciples. The chief anti-Trinitarians of the age came from Italy, where reformed opinions took often radical form, and where the scepticism of the Renaissance and the criticism of the later schoolmen often blended with Anabaptist readiness to see in the meaning of Scripture other than the traditional interpretations. Such Italian radicals were Matteo Gribaldi (?–1564), once professor of law in Padua, whom Calvin drove from Geneva in 1559; and Giovanni Valentino Gentile (1520?–1566), who came to Geneva about 1557, fled from punishment for his views there, and, after a wandering career, was beheaded in Bern in 1566. Of greater importance was Giorgio Biandrata (1515?–1588?), who spent a year in Geneva, but found it wise to leave for Poland in 1558, serving as physician to the ruling families of that land and of Transylvania, helping to found a Unitarian communion in the latter region, which ultimately obtained legal standing.

Those who were destined to give their name to the movement were the two Sozzinis, uncle and nephew. Lelio Sozzini (Socinus, 1525–1562) was of a prominent Sienese family and a student of law. His opinions were at first Evangelical, and he lived for a year, 1550–1551, in Wittenberg, enjoying Melanchthon's friendship. Among other Swiss cities, he was well received in Geneva, and settled in Zürich, where he died. Servetus's execution turned his attention to the problem of the Trinity, but his speculations were not made public in his lifetime. His more distinguished nephew Fausto (1539–1604) was in Lyons in 1561 and Geneva in 1562. Although already a radical and influenced, though less than has often been represented, by his uncle's notes and papers, Fausto conformed outwardly to the Roman Church and lived from 1563 to 1575 in Italy. Thence he removed to Basel, till he went to Transylvania, in 1578, at the instance of Biandrata. The next year saw him in Poland, where he lived till his death in 1604.

Thanks to the labors of Fausto Sozzini and others in Poland the party gained considerable foothold, and expressed its belief effectively in the Racovian Catechism, on which Fausto had labored, published in 1605, in Rakow, the city from which it took its name and in which these "Polish Brethren" had their headquarters. The catechism is a remarkable combination of rationalistic reasoning and a hard supernaturalism. The basis of truth is the Scriptures, but confidence in the New Testament is based primarily on the miracles by which its promulgation was accompanied and especially by the crowning miracle of the resurrection. The New Testament, thus supernaturally attested, guarantees the Old Testament. The purpose of both is to show to man's understanding the path to eternal life. Though there may be in them matters above reason, there is nothing of value contrary to reason. The only faith that they demand is belief that God exists and is a recompenser and a judge. Man is by nature mortal and could not find the way to eternal life of himself. Hence God gave him the Scripture and the life and example of Christ. Christ was a man, but one who lived a life of peculiar and exemplary obedience, filled with divine wisdom, and was therefore rewarded with a resurrection and a kind of delegated divinity, so that He is now a hearer of prayer. The Christian life consists in joy in God, prayer and thanksgiving, renunciation of the world, humility and patient endurance. Its consequences are forgiveness of sins and eternal life. Baptism and the Lord's Supper are to be retained as commanded by Christ and possessing a certain symbolic value. Man's essential freedom is asserted, and original sin and predestination denied.

The most successful portion of the Socinian polemic was its attack on the satisfaction theory of the atonement, which the reformers had universally accepted. Satisfaction is no demand of God's nature. Forgiveness and satisfaction are mutually exclusive conceptions. It is absolute injustice that the sins of the guilty be punished on the person of the innocent. Christ's death is a great example of the obedience which every Christian should, if necessary, manifest; but that obedience was no greater than He owed for Himself, and He could not transfer its value to others. Could it be so transferred, in so far as a man felt himself thereby relieved from moral effort for righteousness, character would thereby be weakened.

The relation of Socinianism to the later Scholasticism, especially that of Scotus, is undoubted; but unlike that mediæval system, it rejected all authority of the church and found its source in the Scriptures, interpreted by reason. It rebelled against the prevailing views of human inability and total depravity. It did not a little to free religion from the bondage of dogma and to favor the unprejudiced study of Scripture; but it had almost no conception of what religion meant to Paul, Augustine, or Luther—a new, vital personal relationship between the believing soul and God through Christ.

Suppressed, largely through the efforts of the Jesuits in Poland, Socinianism found some supporters in the Netherlands and even more in England, where it was to have no little influence.

SECTION XV. ARMINIANISM

The rigor of Calvinism produced a reaction, especially in Holland, where humanistic traditions had never died out and where Anabaptism was widely spread. It manifested itself in an emphasis on the more practical aspects of religion, a disinclination toward sharp creedal definitions, and a more tolerant attitude. Such a thinker was the Dutch scholar Dirck Coornhert (1522–1590); but it came to its fullest expression in the work of Jacobus Arminius (1560–1609) and his disciples.

Arminius, whose relatives were killed in the Netherland struggle for independence, was educated by friends at the University of Leyden, from 1576 to 1582. He was then sent to Geneva at the expense of the merchant's guild of Amsterdam. In 1588, he entered on a pastorate in Amsterdam, winning distinction as a preacher and pastor of irenic spirit. In 1603 he was chosen to succeed the eminent Franz Junius (1545–1602), as professor of theology in Leyden, where he remained till his death. Though indisposed to controversy, he was appointed in 1589 to reply to Coornhert and to defend the "supralapsarian" position against two ministers of Delft. The discussion last named had to do with the order of the divine purposes. Did God "decree" election and reprobation, and then permit the fall as a means by which the decree could be carried out (*supra lapsum*)? Or did He foresee and permit that man would fall, and then decree election as the method of saving some (*infra lapsum*)? As he studied the questions involved, Arminius came to doubt the whole doctrine of unconditional predestination and to ascribe to man a freedom, which, however congenial to Melanchthon (*ante*, p. 442), had no place in pure Calvinism. A bitter controversy sprang up between Arminius and his supralapsarian colleague in the university, Franz Gomarus (1563–1641), and soon the Protestant Netherlands were widely involved.

After Arminius's death, in 1609, the leadership of the party was taken by the court preacher Johan Wtenbogaert (1557–1644) and by Simon Episcopius (1583–1643), Arminius's friend and pupil, and soon to be professor of theology in Leyden. By them "Arminian" views were systematized and developed, and both opposed the current emphasis on minutiæ of doctrine, viewing Christianity primarily as a force for moral transformation. In 1610, they and other sympathizers to the number of forty-one, at the instance of the eminent Dutch statesman, Johan van Oldenbarneveldt (1547–1619), a lover of religious toleration, drew up a statement of their faith called the "Remonstrance," [1] from which the party gained the name "Remonstrants." Over against the Calvinist doctrine of absolute predestination, it taught a predestination based on divine foreknowledge of the use men would make of the means of grace. Against the doctrine that Christ died for the elect only, it asserted that He died for all, though none receive the benefits of His death except believers. It was at one with Calvinism in denying the ability of men to do anything really good of themselves—all is of divine grace. Hence the Arminians were not Pelagians (*ante*, p. 185). In opposition to the Calvinist doctrine of irresistible grace, they taught that grace may be rejected, and they declared uncertainty regarding the Calvinist teaching of perseverance, holding it possible that men may lose grace once received.

All the Protestant Netherlands were speedily filled with conflict. The vast majority of the people were Calvinists, and that view had the support of the Stadholder Maurice (1588–1625). The Remonstrants were favored by Oldenbarneveldt, the leader of the province of Holland, and by the great jurist and historian, the founder of international law, Hugo Grotius (1583–1645). The dispute soon became involved in politics. The Netherlands were divided between the supporters of "states rights," which included the wealthier merchant classes and of which Oldenbarneveldt and Grotius were leaders, and the national party of which Maurice was the head. The national party now wished a national synod to decide the controversy. The province of Holland, under Oldenbarneveldt, held that each province could decide its religious affairs and resisted the proposal. Maurice, by a *coup d'état* in July, 1618, overthrew the "states-rights" party. Oldenbarneveldt, in spite of his great services, was beheaded on May 13, 1619, and Grotius condemned to life imprisonment, from which he escaped in 1621.

Meanwhile a national synod, called by the states-general, held session in Dort from November 13, 1618, to May 9, 1619. Besides representatives from the Netherlands, delegates from England, the Palatinate, Hesse, Bremen, and Switzerland shared in its proceedings. By the synod of Dort, Arminianism was condemned and "canons," aggressively Calvinistic in tone, adopted, which, together with the Heidelberg Catechism, and

---

[1] Schaff, *Creeds of Christendom*, 3 : 545–549.

the Belgic Confession (*ante*, pp. 433, 443) became the doctrinal basis of the Dutch Church.[1] Not so extreme as individual Calvinists—it did not adopt Gomarus's supralapsarian views —the synod of Dort reached the high-water mark of Calvinistic creed-making.

Immediately after the synod of Dort the Remonstrants were banished, but on the death of Maurice, in 1625, the measures against them became dead letters. They returned, though they were not to receive official recognition till 1795. In the Netherlands the party grew slowly, and still exists. Its type of piety in the home land was prevailingly intellectual and ethical, and was somewhat affected by Socinianism. Arminianism was to have even greater influence in England than in its home land, and was to prove, in the person of John Wesley, its possibility of association with as warm-hearted and emotional a type of piety as any interpretation of Christian truth can exhibit.

Out of this controversy there emerged from the pen of Grotius, in 1617, an important theory of the atonement. The view of Anselm had looked upon Christ's death as the satisfaction of the injured divine honor (*ante*, p. 263). The reformers had viewed it as the payment of penalty for sin to outraged divine justice on behalf of those for whom Christ died, and had represented the exaction of penalty as a fundamental demand of God's nature, who may be merciful but must be just. To Calvinistic conception, Christ's sacrifice was sufficient for all, but efficient only for the elect in whose behalf He died. The Socinians had subjected these views to a radical criticism, denying that God's nature demanded punishment, or that the penalty due to one could justly be met by the sufferings of another (*ante*, p. 453). To the Socinian criticism Grotius now replied. God is a great moral ruler. Sin is an offense against His law. Like a wise earthly governor He may pardon if He chooses; but to pardon without making evident the regard in which He holds His law would be to bring that law into contempt. Hence Christ's death was not a payment for man's sin —that is freely forgiven—but a tribute to the sanctity of the divine government, showing that while God remits the penalty, He vindicates the majesty of His divine government. In that sense the sacrifice of Christ is no injustice. It is the divine

---

[1] Schaff, *Creeds of Christendom*, 3 : 550–597.

tribute to offended law. Like a wise earthly ruler, God may offer pardon to all who will receive it on such terms as He chooses, for example, on condition of faith and repentance. The ingenuity of this theory is undeniable. It relieved the embarrassment of the Arminians caused by their assertion that Christ died for all. If that sacrifice was for all, and not for the elect only, and was a payment of the penalty for sin, why then were not all saved? Grotius gave answer by denying the payment of penalty. He also gave, in reply to the Socinians, a definite reason for the great sacrifice. Yet, of all the theories of the atonement this is the most theatrical and least satisfactory, for the message of the Gospel is that in some true sense Christ died, not for general justice, but for *me*.

SECTION XVI. ANGLICANISM, PURITANISM, AND CONGREGATION-ALISM IN ENGLAND. EPISCOPACY AND PRESBYTERIANISM IN SCOTLAND

Queen Elizabeth's relations to the Catholics have been elsewhere considered (*ante*, p. 438). Her position, at the beginning of her reign, was one of exceeding difficulty. With her people far from united in religious belief, with plots at home and enemies abroad, it was only by political manœuvring of extreme skilfulness that she was able to steer a successful course. Her difficulties were increased by the divisions which appeared, soon after the beginning of her reign, among those who accepted her rejection of Rome. These were augmented, as that reign advanced, by the quickened popular religious life which was transforming a nation that had been previously rather spiritually apathetic during the changes under Henry VIII, Edward VI, and Mary.

Elizabeth purposely made the acceptance of her religious settlement as easy as possible. The church, in its officers and services, resembled the older worship as fully as Protestant sentiment would tolerate. All but a fragment of its parish clergy conformed, and Elizabeth was well satisfied to leave them undisturbed in their parishes, provided they remained quiet, though their hearty acceptance of Protestantism was often doubtful and their capacity to preach or spiritual earnestness often dubious. From a political point of view her policy was wise. England was spared such wars as devastated France and Germany.

From the first, the Queen was faced, however, by a more aggressive Protestantism. Many who had been exiles under Mary had come under the influence of Geneva or Zürich and returned filled with admiration for their thoroughgoing Protestantism. They were men prevailingly of deep religious earnestness, upon whom Elizabeth must depend in her conflict with Rome, yet who, if they could introduce the changes which they desired, the Queen believed would turmoil a situation kept at peace at best with difficulty. Yet the desires of these men are easily understandable from a religious point of view. They would purge from the services what they believed to be remnants of Roman superstition, and procure in every parish an earnest, spiritual-minded, preaching minister. In particular, they objected to the prescribed clerical dress as perpetuating in the popular mind the thought of the ministry as a spiritual estate of peculiar powers, to kneeling at the reception of the Lord's Supper as implying adoration of the physical presence of Christ therein, to the use of the ring in marriage as continuing the estimate of matrimony as a sacrament, and the sign of the cross in baptism as superstitious. Because they thus desired to purify the church, this party, by 1564, was popularly called the "Puritans."

Led by Laurence Humphrey (1527–1590), president of Magdalen College, Oxford, and Thomas Sampson (1517–1589), dean of Christ Church, Oxford, both Marian exiles, the earliest Puritan discussion was over the use of the prescribed garments —the "Vestiarian Controversy." Cambridge University sympathized largely with the Puritans. But in this matter the Queen's policy was strongly opposed to modification, and in 1566 Archbishop Parker issued his "Advertisements," [1] by which all preachers were required to secure fresh licenses from the bishops, controversial sermons forbidden, kneeling at communion required, and clerical dress minutely prescribed. Under these regulations a number of Puritan clergy were deprived of their positions.

Among men who had learned in Zürich and Geneva to feel that any worship for which Biblical warrant could not be found

[1] Gee and Hardy, *Documents Illustrative of English Church History*, pp. 467–475.

is an insult to the divine majesty, this led to a further position—
a question whether an ecclesiastical system which deposed
ministers who refused to use vestments and ceremonies not
capable of Scriptural demonstration was that which God intended for His church. Furthermore, as they read their New
Testament through Genevan spectacles, they saw there a
definite pattern of church government quite unlike that existing in England, in which effective discipline was maintained by
elders, ministers were in office with the consent of the congregation, and there was essential spiritual parity between those
whom, as Calvin said, the Scriptures in describing them as
"bishops, presbyters, and pastors," "uses the words as synony-
mous." [1]   It was the same conviction as to the essential equality
of those in spiritual office that nerved Scottish Presbyterianism
to its long fight with "prelacy."

The representative and leader of this second stage of Puritanism was Thomas Cartwright (1535?–1603). As Lady Margaret professor of divinity in Cambridge University in 1569, he
advocated the appointment of elders for discipline in each
parish, the election of pastors by their people, the abolition of
such offices as archbishops and archdeacons, and the reduction
of clergy to essential parity. That was practical Presbyterianism, and the more radical Puritans moved henceforth in the
Presbyterian direction. The more moderate of the party continued their opposition to ceremonies and vestments without
joining with Cartwright in a demand that the constitution of
the English Church be altered. Cartwright's arguments
aroused the opposition of the man who was to be the chief
enemy of the early Puritans, John Whitgift (1530–1604).
Against Cartwright's assertion of *jure divino* Presbyterianism,
Whitgift was far from asserting a similar authority for episcopacy. To him it was the best form of church government, but
he denied that any exact pattern is laid down in the Scriptures,
and affirmed that much is left to the judgment of the church.
By Whitgift's influence, Cartwright was deprived of his professorship in 1570, and the next year driven from the university.
He lived thenceforth a wandering and persecuted life, much
of the time on the Continent, but laboring indefatigably to
further the Presbyterian Puritan cause.

The changes advocated by Cartwright were presented in an

[1] *Institutes*, 4: 3, 8.

extreme but popularly effective pamphlet entitled *An Admonition to the Parliament*, written by two London ministers, John Field (?–1588) and Thomas Wilcox (1549?–1608), in 1572. To it Whitgift replied, and was answered, in turn, by Cartwright. Presbyterian Puritanism was growing. To those more moderate than Cartwright, it seemed that it would require relatively little alteration of the existing churchly constitution. The obnoxious ceremonies could be discarded, the Prayer Book revised, elders instituted in parishes, and the bishops preserved as presiding officers of the churches of each diocese organized as a synod, *primi inter pares*. A voluntary local classis, a kind of presbytery, was organized by Puritan ministers in Wandsworth, near London, in 1572; and similar organizations sprang up elsewhere. Meeting of ministers for preaching and discussion—the so-called "prophesyings"—were begun about the same time. The radical Puritan cause was advanced by the *Declaration of Ecclesiastical Discipline*, published by a young Cambridge scholar, Walter Travers (1548?–1635), in 1574. This soon became, in a sense, the Puritan standard. All this was aided by the succession to the archbishopric of Canterbury, on Parker's death, in 1576, of Edmund Grindal (1519?–1583), who sympathized with the Puritans and was suspended for his conscientious objections to the Queen's orders to forbid "prophesyings."

Cartwright and his fellow Puritans opposed all separation from the Church of England. Their thought was to introduce as much of Puritan discipline and practice as possible, and wait for its further reformation by the government. Such a hope did not seem vain. Within a generation, the constitution and worship of the church of the land had been four times altered. Might it not soon be changed for a fifth time into what the Puritans deemed a more Scriptural model? They would agitate and wait. This remained the programme of the Puritans generally. Naturally, there were some to whom this delay seemed unjustifiable. They would establish what they conceived to be Scriptural at once. These were the Separatists or early Congregationalists.

On June 19, 1567, the authorities in London seized and imprisoned the members of such a Separatist congregation, assembled for worship ostensibly to celebrate a wedding. This company had rejected the Church of England and had chosen at least two officers—Richard Fitz, minister, and Thomas Bowland, deacon. It was evidently moving in the Congregational direction. Whether remnants of this congregation maintained a subsequent corporate existence is not known.

The first really conspicuous advocate of Congregational principles in England was Robert Browne (1550?–1633), a student in Cambridge in the troublous time of Cartwright's brief professorship, and a graduate there in 1572. At first an advanced Presbyterian Puritan, he came to adopt Separatist principles by about 1580, and in connection with a friend, Robert Harrison, founded a Congregational Church in Norwich in 1581. As a result of his preaching he found himself speedily in prison. He and the majority of his congregation sought safety in Middelburg, in the Netherlands. Here in Middelburg Browne had printed, in 1582, a substantial volume containing three treatises. One, directed against the Puritans who would remain in the Church of England, bears its burden in its title: *A Treatise of Reformation without Tarying for anie, and of the Wickednesse of those Preachers which will not reforme . . . till the Magistrate commaunde and compell them.* Another, *A Booke which sheweth the Life and Manners of all true Christians*, presented the fundamental principles of Congregationalism.

According to Browne, the only church is a local body of experiential believers in Christ, united to Him and to one another by a voluntary covenant. Such a church has Christ as its immediate head, and is ruled by officers and laws of His appointment. Each is self-governing and chooses a pastor, a teacher, elders, deacons, and widows, whom the New Testament designates; but each member has responsibility for the welfare of the whole. No church has authority over any other, but each owes to other brotherly helpfulness. The system thus outlined was essentially democratic—far more so than early Congregationalism in general was actually to be in its practice.

Browne's system so closely resembles the views of the Anabaptists (*ante*, p. 368) that some connection in thought at least seems well-nigh certain. Norwich, also, was largely populated by Dutch refugees. Yet Browne displayed no conscious indebtedness to the Anabaptists, and did not reject infant baptism. His emphasis on the covenant as the constitutive element in the church is much more positive than among the Anabaptists. The probable conclusion is that Browne owed much to a somewhat widely diffused Anabaptist way of thinking, rather than borrowed directly from any Anabaptist source. Browne's own stay in Holland was brief. His church was turmoiled, and after a period in Scotland he returned to England, where he conformed, outwardly at least, to the Established Church in October, 1585, and spent his long remaining life, from 1591 to 1633, in its ministry. With such a record of abandonment of early principles it is no wonder that early Congregationalists resented the name "Brownists"; yet Congregationalism has never been more clearly enunciated than by him.

Under Grindal's archbishopric many of the Puritan ministers ceased to use the Prayer Book in whole or in part, and the establishment of the "Holy Discipline," as that set forth in Traver's *Declaration of Ecclesiastical Discipline* was called, went on apace. Grindal was succeeded, however, from 1583 to 1604, in the see of Canterbury by Whitgift. A thorough Calvinist in theology, he was a martinet in discipline, and in this had the hearty support of the Queen. He promptly issued articles enjoining full approval and use of the Prayer Book, prescribing clerical dress, and forbidding all private religious meetings.[1] Thenceforth the hand of repression rested heavily on Puritans and Separatists. This hostility was embittered by the secret publication of a telling satire against the bishops, coarse and unfair, but extremely witty and exasperating, plainly of Puritan origin, though disliked by the Puritans generally. Issued in 1588–1589, and known as the "Martin Marprelate Tracts," their authorship has never been fully ascertained, though probabilities point to Job Throckmorton (1545–1601), a Puritan layman.

Puritan and Separatist assertion of the divine character of their systems was now rapidly producing a change of attitude in the leaders of their opponents, who may be called Anglicans. In his sermon at Paul's Cross, in London, in 1589, Richard Bancroft (1544–1610), to be Whitgift's successor as archbishop, not merely denounced Puritanism, but affirmed a *jure divino* right for episcopacy. Adrian Saravia (1531–1613), a Walloon theologian domiciled in England, advocated the same view a year later, as did Thomas Bilson (1547–1616), soon to be bishop of Winchester, in his *Perpetual Government of Christ's Church*, in 1593. Less extreme was the learned Richard

---

[1] Gee and Hardy, pp. 481–484.

Hooker (1553?–1600), in his *Laws of Ecclesiastical Polity,* of 1594. Though episcopacy is grounded in Scripture, his chief argument in its favor is its essential reasonableness, over against the extreme Biblicism of the Puritans. The foundations of a high-church party had been laid.

The repression of Puritanism and Separatism was greatly aided by the court of the High Commission. From Henry VIII's time it had been a favorite royal expedient to control ecclesiastical affairs or persons by commissions appointed to investigate and adjudicate without being bound by the ordinary processes of law. The system was a gradual growth. Elizabeth developed it, and made it more permanent; but it did not become a thoroughly effective ecclesiastical court till Bancroft had become one of its members in 1587. By 1592 it had fully attained its powers. The presumption of guilt was against the accused, and the nature of proof was undefined. It could examine and imprison anywhere in England, and had become the right arm of episcopal authority.

Meanwhile, Congregationalism had reappeared. In 1587 Henry Barrowe (1550?–1593), a lawyer of London, and John Greenwood (?–1593), a clergyman, were arrested for holding Separatist meetings in London. From their prison they smuggled manuscripts which appeared as printed treatises in Holland, attacking Anglicans and Puritans alike, and explaining Congregational principles. A number were won, including Francis Johnson (1562–1618), a Puritan minister. In 1592 a Congregational Church was formed in London with Johnson as its "pastor" and Greenwood as its "teacher," and on April 6 of the next year Barrowe and Greenwood were hanged for denying the Queen's supremacy in ecclesiastical matters. The same year Parliament passed a statute proclaiming banishment against all who challenged the Queen's ecclesiastical authority, refused to go to church, or were present at some "conventicle" where other than the lawful worship was employed.[1] Under its terms most of the London Congregationalists were compelled to seek refuge in Amsterdam, where Johnson continued their pastor and Henry Ainsworth (1571–1623?) their teacher.

The closing years of Elizabeth's reign also saw the beginnings of a reaction from the dominant Calvinism. By 1595 a controversy broke out in Cambridge, where Peter Baro (1534–

[1] Gee and Hardy, pp. 492–498.

1599) had been advocating views that would later have been called Arminian. This discussion led to the publication, under Whitgift's auspices of the strongly Calvinistic "Lambeth Articles";[1] but the tendency to criticise Calvinism, thus started, increased, and through opposition to Puritanism, in part, was to become more and more characteristic of the Anglican party.

Elizabeth closed her long reign on March 24, 1603, and was succeeded by Mary "Queen of Scots's" son, James I (1603–1625), who had already held the Scottish throne since 1567, as James VI. All religious parties in England looked with hope to his accession, the Catholics because of his parentage, the Presbyterian Puritans by reason of his Presbyterian education, and the Anglicans on account of his high conceptions of divine right and his hostility to Presbyterian rule, which had developed in his long struggles to maintain the power of the crown in Scotland. Only the Anglicans read his character correctly. "No bishop, no King," was his favorite expression. In claim and action he was no more arbitrary than Elizabeth; but the country would bear much from a popular and admired ruler which it resented from a disliked, undignified, and unrepresentative sovereign.

On his way to London, in April, 1603, James I was presented with the "Millenary Petition,"[2] so-called because it was supposed to bear a thousand signatures, though really unsigned. It was a very moderate statement of the Puritan desires. As a consequence, a conference was held at Hampton Court, in January, 1604, between bishops and Puritans, in the royal presence—the leading Anglican disputant, besides the King himself, being Bancroft, now bishop of London. No changes of importance desired by the Puritans were granted, except a new translation of the Bible, which resulted in the "Authorized Version" of 1611. They were ordered to conform. This Anglican victory was followed by the enactment by convocation, with royal approval, in 1604, of a series of canons elevating into church law many of the declarations and practices against which the Puritans had objected. The leading spirit here was Bancroft, who was soon to succeed Whitgift in the see of Canterbury (1604–1610). The Puritans were now thoroughly alarmed, but Bancroft was more considerate in government

---

[1] Schaff, *Creeds of Christendom*, 3 : 523.
[2] Gee and Hardy, pp. 508–511.

than his declarations and previous conduct would have prophesied, and only a relatively small number of ministers, estimated variously from forty-nine to three hundred, were actually deprived. Anglicanism was gaining strength, also, from a gradual improvement in the education and zeal of its clergy, which Whitgift and Bancroft did much to foster—a conspicuous example being the learned, saintly, and eloquent Lancelot Andrewes (1555–1626), who became bishop of Chichester in 1605.

Bancroft's successor as archbishop was George Abbot (1611–1633), a man of narrow sympathies and strong Calvinism, unpopular with the mass of the clergy, and himself in practical disgrace in the latter part of his episcopate. The loss of such strong hands as those of Whitgift and Bancroft was felt by the Anglicans, and under these circumstances, not only Puritanism but Separatism made decided progress.

A Separatist movement of far-reaching ultimate consequences had its beginnings probably about 1602, in the work of John Smyth (?–1612), a former clergyman of the establishment, who had adopted Separatist principles and now gathered a congregation in Gainsborough. Soon adherents were secured in the adjacent rural districts, and a second congregation gathered in the home of William Brewster (1560?–1644), at Scrooby. Of this Scrooby body William Bradford (1590–1657) was a youthful member. From about 1604 it enjoyed the leadership of the learned and sweet-tempered John Robinson (1575?–1625), like Smyth a former clergyman of the Puritan party in the Church of England, and like him led to believe Separatism the only logical step. The hand of opposition being heavy upon them, the Gainsborough congregation, led by Smyth, were self-exiled to Amsterdam, probably in 1607. That centred in Scrooby, under Robinson and Brewster's leadership, followed the same road to Holland, in 1607 and 1608, but established itself in 1609 in Leyden.

At Amsterdam Smyth came into contact with the Mennonites, and by his own study was convinced that their position rejecting infant baptism was that of primitive Christianity. In 1608 or 1609 he therefore baptized himself by pouring, and then the others of his church. Of unstable disposition, Smyth soon after quarrelled with his flock, but two of its members, Thomas Helwys (1550?–1616?), and John Murton (?–1625?), led the return of a considerable portion to England, and established in London, in 1611 or 1612, the first permanent Baptist congregation on English soil. In the contemporary Dutch controversies they had adopted the Arminian position, and were therefore known as "General Baptists." Apparently some remnants of the exiled Congregational Church of Johnson and Greenwood (*ante*, p. 463) kept up an organization in London, but the effective permanent replanting of Congregationalism in England was when Henry Jacob (1563–1624), who had been of Robinson's congregation in Leyden, established a church in Southwark in 1616. From this church a portion seceded in 1633, on Baptist principles. They were Calvinists, and hence named "Particular Baptists." By them immersion was practised about 1641, and thence spread to all English Baptists.

The chief event in the history of the Leyden Congregational Church was the decision to send its more active minority to America. Robinson reluctantly stayed with the majority. In 1620, after infinite negotiation, the "Pilgrim Fathers" crossed the Atlantic in the *Mayflower*, under the spiritual leadership of their "elder," William Brewster, and on December 21 laid the foundations of the colony of Plymouth, of which William Bradford was soon to be the wise and self-forgetful governor. Congregationalism was thus planted in New England.

Meanwhile under Abbot's less vigorous government Puritanism was establishing "lectureships," the successors of the old-time "prophesyings." In parishes where the legal incumbent was hostile, or unwilling, or unable to preach—sometimes with the consent of the incumbent himself—Puritan money was financing afternoon preachers, of strongly Puritan cast. Puritanism had always laid stress on a strict observance of Sunday. Its Sabbatarian tendencies were augmented by the publication, in 1595, by Nicholas Bownde (?–1613) of his *Doctrine of the Sabbath*, urging the perpetuity of the fourth commandment in Jewish rigor. Much Puritan hostility was, therefore, roused—and that of Archbishop Abbot also—when James I issued his famous *Declaration of Sports*, in 1618, in which he commended the old popular games and dances for Sunday observance. To the Puritan it seemed a royal command to disobey the will of God. Puritanism was steadily growing as a political force all through James's reign. The

King's arbitrary treatment of Parliament, his failure to support effectively the hard-pressed Protestants of Germany in the opening struggles of the Thirty Years' War, and above all, his ultimately unsuccessful attempts to procure marriage with a Spanish princess for his heir, were increasingly resented, and drove the Commons into a steadily growing political sympathy with Puritanism, the more that the Anglicans were identified largely with the royal policies. By the end of his reign, in 1625, the outlook was ominous.

Nor was James's policy in his northern kingdom less fraught with future mischief. During James's childhood the Regent Morton, in 1572, had secured the nominal perpetuation of the episcopate largely as a means of getting possession of church lands. There were, therefore, bishops in name in Scotland. Their power was slight. In 1581, under the lead of Andrew Melville, the General Assembly had given full authority to presbyteries as ecclesiastical courts, and had ratified the Presbyterian *Second Book of Discipline*. In spite of James's opposition, the King and the Scottish Parliament had been compelled to recognize this Presbyterian system as established by law in 1592.

Yet James was determined to substitute a royally controlled episcopacy for this largely self-governing Presbyterianism. He had the means at hand in the nominal bishops. By 1597 he was strong enough to insist that he alone had the right to call general assemblies, and his encroachments on Presbyterianism steadily grew. Melville and other leaders were exiled. The year 1610 saw a notable royal advance. James established two high commission courts for ecclesiastical cases in Scotland, similar to that of England, and each with an archbishop at its head; and he procured from English bishops episcopal consecration and apostolical succession for the hitherto irregular Scottish episcopate. A packed Parliament, in 1612, completed the process by giving full diocesan jurisdiction to these bishops. Thus far there had been no changes in worship, but nine years later the King forced through a cowed General Assembly, and then through Parliament, kneeling at communion, confirmation by episcopal hands, the observation of the great church festivals, private communion and private baptism. Scotland was seething with religious discontent when James died.

James I was succeeded, in England and Scotland, by his son

Charles I (1625–1649).   A man of more personal dignity than his father, of pure family life, and of sincere religion, he was quite as exalted as James in his conceptions of the divine right of Kings, arbitrary in his actions, and with no capacity to understand the drift of public sentiment.   He was also marked by a weakness that easily laid him open to charges of double-dealing and dishonesty.   From the first he enjoyed the friendship and support of one of the most remarkable men of the time, William Laud (1573–1645).

Laud had been, under James, a leader among the younger Anglicans.   A vigorous opponent of Calvinism, he had argued as early as 1604 "that there could be no true church without bishops."   In 1622, in contest with the Jesuit, Fisher, he had held that the Roman Church was a true church, and a branch of the Catholic Church universal, of which the Church of England was the purest part.   In many respects he was a founder of the "Anglo-Catholic" position; but it is not to be wondered that both the Puritans and the Roman authorities, to whom that view was then novel, believed him a Roman Catholic at heart.   Twice he was offered a cardinalate.   So to class him was, however, to do him a great injustice.   Laud was a martinet, intent on uniformity in ceremony, dress and worship, with a rough tongue and overbearing manner that made him many enemies.   At bottom, with all his narrowness of sympathy, he had a real piety of the type, though not of the winsomeness, of Lancelot Andrewes.   In 1628 Charles made Laud bishop of the strongly Puritan diocese of London, and in 1633 archbishop of Canterbury.   To all intents he was Charles's chief adviser also in political affairs after the murder of the duke of Buckingham in 1628.

The country gentry, who formed the backbone of the House of Commons were strongly Calvinist in their sympathies, and disposed politically to resent the arbitrary imposition of taxes without parliamentary consent.   Charles soon put himself in disfavor in both respects.   Under Laud's guidance he promoted Arminians to church preferments.   To prevent Calvinistic discussion, in 1628, he caused a declaration to be prefixed to the Thirty-nine Articles, that no man shall "put his own sense," on any Article, "but shall take it in the literal and grammatical sense." [1]   Parliament resented these actions. [2]

[1] Gee and Hardy, pp. 518–520.   [2] *Ibid.*, pp. 521–527.

Charles had proceeded to forced taxation, imprisoning some who refused to pay. Roger Manwaring (1590–1653), a royal chaplain, preached in 1627, arguing that as the King ruled as God's representative, those who refused taxes imposed by him were in peril of damnation. Parliament condemned Manwaring, in 1628, to fine and imprisonment, but Charles protected him by pardon and rewarded him by ecclesiastical advancement, ultimately by a bishopric. Questions of royal right to imprison without statement of cause, and of taxation, as well as of religion, embittered the relations of King and Parliament, and after dismissing that of 1629, Charles determined to rule without parliamentary aid. No Parliament was to meet till 1640. The weakness of the Anglican party was that it had identified itself with the arbitrary policy of the King.

Laud, with the support of the King, enforced conformity with a heavy hand. Lectureships were broken up. Puritan preachers silenced. The *Declaration of Sports* was reissued. Under these circumstances many Puritans began to despair of the religious and political outlook, and to plan to follow the Separatists across the Atlantic. It was no abstract religious liberty that they sought, but freedom to preach and organize as they desired. By 1628, emigration to Massachusetts had begun. In 1629, a royal charter for Massachusetts was secured, and a church formed in Salem. The year 1630 saw the arrival of many immigrants under the leadership of John Winthrop (1588–1649). Soon there were strong churches about Massachusetts Bay, under able ministerial leaders, of whom John Cotton (1584–1652) of Boston, and Richard Mather (1596–1669) of Dorchester, were the most conspicuous. Connecticut colony was fully established in 1636, with Thomas Hooker (1586–1647) as its chief minister at Hartford; and New Haven colony in 1638, under the spiritual guidance of John Davenport (1597–1670). These men were clergy of the English establishment. They had no fondness for Separatism. But, like the Separatists, they looked on the Bible as the sole law of church organization, and they read it in the same way. Their churches were organized, therefore, on the Congregational model. Till 1640, the Puritan tide to New England ran full, at least twenty thousand crossing the Atlantic.

Charles's period of rule without Parliament was a time of considerable prosperity in England, but taxes widely believed to be illegal, such as the famous "ship-money," and enforced religious uniformity, kept up the unrest. It was in Scotland, however, that the storm broke. James I had succeeded in his overthrow of Presbyterianism largely by securing the support of the nobles by grants of church lands. At the beginning of his reign Charles, by an act of revocation that was just, though impolitic, ordered the restoration of these lands, to the lasting advantage of the Scottish church, though the command was imperfectly executed. Its political effect, however, was to throw the possessors of church lands and tithes largely on the side of the discontented Presbyterians. There was now a relatively united Scotland, instead of the divisions which James had fomented to his profit.

Great as were the changes effected by James I, he had not dared alter the larger features of public worship (*ante*, p. 467). But now, in 1637, in a fatuous desire for uniformity, Charles, inspired by Laud, ordered the imposition of a liturgy which was essentially that of the Church of England. Its use, on July 23, in Edinburgh, led to riot. Scotland flared in opposition. In February, 1638, a National Covenant to defend the true religion was widely signed. In December, a General Assembly deposed the bishops, and repudiated the whole ecclesiastical structure which James and Charles had erected since 1597. This was rebellion, and Charles raised forces to suppress it. So formidable was the Scottish attitude that an agreement patched up a truce in 1639; but in 1640 Charles determined to bring the Scots to terms. To pay the expenses of the war in prospect Charles was at last compelled to call an English Parliament in April, 1640. The old parliamentary grievances in politics and religion were at once presented, and Charles speedily dissolved the "Short Parliament." In the brief war that followed the Scots successfully invaded England. Charles was forced to treat, and to guarantee the expenses of a Scottish army of occupation till the treaty should be completed. There was no help for it. The English Parliament must again be summoned, and in November, 1640, the "Long Parliament" began its work. It was evident at once that Presbyterian Puritanism was in the majority. Laud was cast into prison. In July, 1641, the High Commission was abolished. In January, 1642, the attempt of the King to seize five members of the Commons, whom he accused of treason, precipitated the civil war. In general, the North and West stood for the King, the South and East for Parliament.[1]

Parliament abolished episcopacy in January, 1643. Provision must be made for the creed and government of the church, and therefore, Parliament, quite in the spirit of Elizabeth, as sovereign, called an assembly of one hundred and twenty-one clergymen and thirty laymen, named by it, to meet in Westminster on July 1, 1643, to advise Parliament, which kept the power of enactment in its own hands. The Westminster Assembly, thus convened, contained a few Congregationalists and Episcopalians, but its overwhelming majority was Presbyterian Puritan. Meanwhile the war had begun ill for Parliament, and to secure Scottish aid the Solemn League and Covenant, pledging the largest possible uniformity in religion in England, Scotland, and Ireland, and opposing "prelacy," was accepted by the Scottish and English Parliaments between August and October, 1643, and was soon required of all Englishmen over eighteen years of age. Scottish commissioners, without vote, but with much influence, now sat in the Westminster Assembly. The Assembly presented to Parliament a *Directory of Worship* and a thoroughly Presbyterian system of church government in 1644. In January following, Parliament abolished the Prayer Book and substituted the *Directory*, which provided an order of worship substantially that used in conservative Presbyterian and Congregational Churches to the present day, without liturgical prayer, though with suggestions of appropriate subjects of petition. Parliament looked askance at the establishment of Presbyterian government, though finally ordering it in June, 1646. The work was, however, very imperfectly set in operation. The same month that witnessed the abolition of the Prayer Book, saw the execution of Laud under a bill of attainder—an act which must be judged one of vindictiveness. The Assembly next prepared its famous confession,[2] which it laid before Parliament late in 1646. Adopted by the General Assembly of Scotland on August 27, 1647, it remains the standard of Scottish and American Presbyterianism. The English Parliament refused approval till June, 1648, and then modified some sections. In 1647, the Assembly completed two

---

[1] For important documents illustrative of this period, see Gee and Hardy, pp. 537–585.

[2] Schaff, *Creeds of Christendom*, 3 : 598–673.

catechisms, a Larger, for pulpit exposition, and a Shorter,[1] for the training of children. Both were approved by the English Parliament and the Scottish General Assembly in 1648.

The *Westminster Confession* and catechisms have always ranked among the most notable expositions of Calvinism. In general, they repeat the familiar continental type. On the question of the divine decrees they are infralapsarian (*ante*, p. 454). One of their chief peculiarities is that in addition to the familiar derivation of original sin from the first parents as "the root of all mankind," they emphasize a "covenant of works" and a "covenant of grace." In the former, Adam is regarded as the representative head of the human race, to whom God made definite promises, which included his descendants, and which he, as their representative, forfeited by his disobedience for them as well as for himself. The "covenant of works" having failed, God offered a new "covenant of grace" through Christ. This covenant doctrine is to be traced to Kaspar Olevianus (*ante*, p. 443), though its fullest exposition was to be in the work of Johann Coccejus (1603–1669), professor in Franeker and Leyden. It was an attempt to give a definite explanation of sin as man's own act, and to show a real human responsibility for his ruin. Another peculiarity of these symbols is an emphasis on the Sabbath consonant with the Puritan development of this doctrine (*ante*, p. 466).

While these theological and ecclesiastical discussions were in progress the civil war had run its early course. On July 2, 1644, the royal army had been defeated on Marston Moor near York, largely by the skill of a member of Parliament of little military experience, Oliver Cromwell (1599–1658), whose abilities had created a picked troop of "religious men." Not quite a year later, on June 14, 1645, Cromwell cut to pieces the last field army of the King near Naseby. The next year Charles gave himself up to the Scots, who, in turn, surrendered him to the English Parliament. The army, as created by Cromwell, was a body of religious enthusiasts, in which little question was raised of finer distinctions of creed. So long as they opposed Rome and "prelacy," Baptists, Congregationalists, and Puritans were welcome in it. The rigid Presbyterianism of the parliamentary majority was as distasteful to the army as the older rule of bishops, and Cromwell fully shared this

[1] *Ibid.*, pp. 676–703.

feeling.   The army was soon demanding a large degree of toleration.

This attitude of the army prevented the full establishment of Presbyterianism which Parliament sanctioned. It displeased the Scots. Charles now used this situation to intrigue with the Scots to invade England in his interest, inducing them to believe that he would support Presbyterianism. On August 17–19, 1648, the invading Scottish army was scattered by Cromwell near Preston. This victory left the army supreme in England. On December 6 following, "Pride's Purge" expelled from Parliament all opposed to the army's wishes. Charles I was then tried and condemned for his alleged treasons and perfidies, and beheaded on January 30, 1649, bearing himself with great dignity. Cromwell then subjugated Ireland in 1649, reduced Scotland the next year, and overthrew Charles's son, the later Charles II (1660–1685) near Worcester in 1651. Opposition had been everywhere put down.

Cromwell, though not identified wholly with any denomination, was practically a Congregationalist, or Independent, and under his Protectorate a large degree of toleration was allowed.[1] Since the beginning of the war, however, about two thousand Episcopal clergymen had been deprived, and had suffered great hardship. Then as in earlier and later changes it is evident, nevertheless, that the great majority of the clergy either were undisturbed or managed to adjust themselves to the new state of affairs. Able, conscientious, and statesmanlike as Cromwell was, his rule was that of military authority, and was, as such, disliked, while the bickerings of rival religious bodies were equally distasteful to a great majority of the people of England who could, as yet, conceive of only one established form of faith. Till his death, on September 3, 1658, Cromwell suppressed all disaffection.

Oliver Cromwell was succeeded by his son, Richard, as Protector; but the new ruler was a man of no force, and practical anarchy was the result. Royalists and Presbyterians now combined to effect a restoration of the monarchy. On April, 14, 1660, Charles II issued a declaration "of liberty to tender consciences," from Breda,[2] and on May 29 was in London. But if the Presbyterians had just hopes of being included in the

---

[1] Gee and Hardy, pp. 574–585.
[2] *Ibid.*, pp. 585–588.

new religious settlement, they were doomed to bitter disappointment.

Charles II may have intended some comprehension of Presbyterians in the national church. Edward Reynolds (1599–1676), heretofore a decided Puritan, was made bishop of Norwich. The saintly Richard Baxter (1615–1691), one of the most eminent of the Presbyterian party, was offered a bishopric, but declined. A conference between bishops and Presbyterians was held by government authority at the Savoy Palace in 1661,[1] but led to little result. Charles II was thoroughly immoral, weak, and indifferent in religion, and little reliance could be placed on his promises. Had he been a better or a stronger man, it is doubtful whether he could have stemmed the tide of national reaction against Puritanism. The first Parliament chosen after his restoration was fiercely royalist and Anglican. The Convocations of Canterbury and York met in 1661, and some six hundred alterations were made in the Prayer Book, but none looking in the Puritan direction, and in May, 1662, the new Act of Uniformity received the royal assent. By it[2] the use of any other service than those of the revised Prayer Book was forbidden under heavy penalties, and each clergyman was required, before August 24, to make oath of "unfeigned assent and consent to all and everything contained and prescribed" therein; and also, "that it is not lawful, upon any pretense whatsoever, to take arms against the King."

These provisions were intended to bar the Puritans from the church, and as such they were effectual. From fifteen hundred to two thousand ministers gave up their places rather than take the prescribed oaths. The Puritan party was now, what it had never been before, one outside the Church of England. Non-conformity had been forced to become Dissent. Severer acts soon followed, induced in part by fear of conspiracy against the restored monarchy. By the First Conventicle Act, of 1664, fine, imprisonment, and ultimate transportation were the penalties for presence at a service not in accordance with the Prayer Book, attended by five or more persons not of the same household. The "Five Mile Act," [3] of the next year, forbad any person "in Holy Orders or pretended Holy Orders," or who had preached to a "conventicle," and did not take the

---

[1] Gee and Hardy, pp. 588–594.   [2] *Ibid.*, pp. 600–619.
[3] *Ibid.*, pp. 620–623.

oath condemning armed resistance to the King, and pledging no attempt at "any alteration of government either in church or state," to live within five miles of any incorporated town or within the same distance of the former place of his ministry. Such persons were also forbidden to teach school—about the only occupation readily open to a deprived minister. The Second Conventicle Act,[1] of 1670, made penalties for such unlawful attendance less severe, but ingeniously provided that the heavy fines on preacher and hearers could be collected from any attendant, in case poverty prevented their payment by all. Yet, in spite of this repression, Dissenting preaching and congregations continued.

Charles II, though a man of no real religion, sympathized with the Roman faith, which he professed on his death-bed, and his brother, the later James II, was an acknowledged and earnest Catholic from 1672. Moreover, Charles was receiving secret pensions from the strongly Catholic Louis XIV of France. On March 15, 1672, with a design of aiding the Catholics and securing Dissenting favor to that end, Charles issued, on his own authority, a Declaration of Indulgence, by which Protestant Dissenters were granted public worship, the penal laws against the Catholics remitted, and their worship permitted in private houses. To Parliament this seemed an unconstitutional favor to Rome. It forced the withdrawal of the Indulgence, in 1673, and passed the Test Act,[2] which, though aimed at Catholics, bore hard on Protestant Dissenters. All in military or civil office, with few minor exceptions, living within thirty miles of London, were required to take the Lord's Supper according to the rites of the Church of England or forfeit their posts. This statute was not to be repealed till 1828. The repression of Dissent, therefore, continued unchanged till the death of Charles II, in 1685.

For James II (1685–1688) it must be said that he saw in the establishment of Catholicism his chief aim, and his measures, though unwise, were courageous. He ignored the Test Act, and appointed Catholics to high office in military and civil service. He brought in Jesuits and monks. He secured from a packed Court of the King's Bench, in 1686, an acknowledgment of his right "to dispense with all penal laws in particular cases." He re-established a High Commission Court. On

---

[1] Gee and Hardy, pp. 623–632.   [2] *Ibid.*, pp. 632–640.

April 4, 1687, he issued a Declaration of Indulgence,[1] granting complete religious toleration. In itself it was a well-sounding, and from the modern standpoint, a praiseworthy act. Yet its motives were too obvious. Its ultimate aim was to make England once more a Roman Catholic country, and all Protestantism was alarmed, while lovers of constitutional government saw in it a nullification of the power of Parliament by arbitrary royal will. The vast majority of Dissenters, though relieved thereby from grievous disabilities, refused to support it, and made common cause with the churchmen. When, in April, 1688, James II ordered the Indulgence read in all churches, seven bishops protested. They were put on trial and, to the delight of the Protestants, acquitted. James had taxed national feeling too greatly. William of Orange (1650–1702), the Stadholder of the Netherlands, who had married Mary, James's daughter, was invited to head the movement against James. On November 5, 1688, he landed with an army. James fled to France. The Revolution was accomplished, and on February 13, 1689, William (III) and Mary were proclaimed joint sovereigns of England.

The clergy of the Restoration had asserted too long the doctrines of the divine right of Kings and of passive obedience to royal authority to make this change palatable. Seven bishops, headed by William Sancroft (1616–1693), refused the oath of allegiance to the new sovereigns, and with them about four hundred clergy. To them James II was still the Lord's anointed. They were deprived, as Anglicans and Dissenters had been before, and they bore themselves with equal courage. Many of them were men of earnest piety. They formed the Nonjuror party, which gradually died out.

Under the circumstances of the Revolution of 1688, toleration could no longer be denied to Protestant Dissenters. By the Toleration Act[2] of May 24, 1689, all who swore, or affirmed, the oaths of allegiance to William and Mary, rejected the jurisdiction of the Pope, transubstantiation, the mass, the invocation of the Virgin and saints, and also subscribed the doctrinal portions of the Thirty-nine Articles, were granted freedom of worship. It was a personal toleration, not a territorial adjustment as in Germany at the close of the Thirty Years' War. Diverse forms of Protestant worship could now exist side by

---

[1] Gee and Hardy, pp. 641–644.   [2] Ibid., pp. 654–664.

side. The Dissenters may have amounted to a tenth of the population of England, divided between Presbyterians, Congregationalists, Baptists, and Quakers. They were still bound to pay tithes to the establishment, and had many other disabilities, but they had won essential religious freedom. No such privileges were granted to deniers of the Trinity or to Roman Catholics. The effective relief of the latter did not come till 1778 and 1791, and was not completed till 1829.

In Scotland, the Restoration was a time of great turmoil and suffering. The Parliament of 1661 annulled all acts affecting religion passed since 1633. Episcopacy was, therefore, restored as in the time of Charles I. In September, 1661, four bishops were appointed, chief of them James Sharp (1618–1679) as archbishop of St. Andrews. Consecration was obtained from England. Sharp had been a Presbyterian minister, but had betrayed his party and his church. All officeholders were required by Parliament to disown the covenants of 1638 and 1643. In 1663 Parliament enacted heavy fines for absence from the now episcopally governed churches, though even it did not dare introduce a liturgy. Many Presbyterian ministers were now deprived, especially in southwestern Scotland. When their parishioners absented themselves from the ministration of the new appointees, they were fined, and if payment was not forthcoming, soldiers were quartered on them. In 1664 a High Commission Court was added to the instruments of repression. Two years later some of the oppressed supporters of the covenants of 1638 and 1643, or Covenanters, engaged in the Pentland Rising. It was ruthlessly crushed, and the Presbyterian element treated with increasing severity. On May 3, 1679, in belated retaliation, Sharp was murdered. This crime was speedily followed by an armed rising of Covenanters; but on June 22 the revolt was crushed at Bothwell Bridge and the captured insurgents treated with great cruelty. Six months later the King's brother, James—the later James II of England—was practically put in charge of Scottish affairs. The extremer and uncompromising Presbyterians were now a proscribed and hunted folk, known as Cameronians—from one of their leaders, Richard Cameron.

The accession of James II, or VII, as he was numbered in Scotland, but intensified at first the repression of the Cameronians. His first year was the "killing time"; and the Parliament of 1685 made death the punishment for attendance at a "conventicle." James, however, soon pursued the same course as in England. He filled his council with Catholics, and in 1687 issued Letters of Indulgence granting freedom of worship. As in England, this release of Catholics from penalty aroused the hostility of all shades of Protestants. Episcopalians and Presbyterians were alike opposed; and when William and Mary mounted the throne of England they had many friends in the northern kingdom. Scotland was more divided than England, however. The Stewarts were Scotch, and though Episcopalians disliked the Catholicism of James they distrusted the Calvinism of "Dutch William," whom the Presbyterians favored. The Revolution triumphed, however, and on May 11, 1689, William and Mary became rulers of Scotland. In 1690 Parliament restored all Presbyterian ministers ejected since 1661, ratified the Westminster Confession (*ante*, p. 472), and declared Presbyterianism the form recognized by the government. This legal establishment of Presbyterianism was opposed by the Cameronian laity, who continued their hostility to any control of the church by civil authority and condemned the failure to renew the covenants, and by the Episcopalians, who were strong in northern Scotland. The latter, however, though in the status of a "dissenting" body, were permitted by a toleration act of 1712, to use the English liturgy. In both England and Scotland the long quarrels between Protestants were, therefore, adjusted in similar fashion by toleration.

SECTION XVII.   THE QUAKERS

One of the most remarkable products of the period of the civil wars in England was the Society of Friends, or Quakers. George Fox (1624–1691) was one of the few religious geniuses of English history. Born in Fenny Drayton, the son of a weaver, he grew up earnest and serious-minded, having "never wronged man or woman." At nineteen a drinking bout, to which he was invited by some nominal Christians, so disgusted him by the contrast between practice and profession that he was set on a soul-distressing search for spiritual reality. Shams of all sorts he detested. His early associates had been to some extent Baptist, and many of his later peculiarities are to be found among the Anabaptists of the Continent or were represented by the irregular sects of the English civil-war period. These were but the outward trappings. His transforming and always central experience came to Fox in 1646. He felt that Christianity is not an outward profession, but an inner light by which Christ directly illuminates the believing soul. Revelation is not confined to the Scriptures, though they are a true Word of God—it enlightens all men who are true disciples. The Spirit of God speaks directly through them, gives them their message, and quickens them for service.

In 1647 Fox began his stormy ministry. Since God gives inner light where He will, the true ministry is that of any man or woman that He deigns to use. A professional ministry is to be rejected. The sacraments are inward and spiritual verities. The outward elements are not merely unnecessary but misleading. Oaths are a needless corroboration of the truthful word of a Christian. Servility in speech or behavior is a degradation of the true Christian respect of man to man. Artificial titles are to be rejected—Fox did not deny legal titles like King or judge. War is unlawful for a Christian. Slavery abhorrent. All Christianity to be true must express itself in a transformed, consecrated life. Such a protest as that of Fox against tendencies to confine all divine revelation to the Scriptures or to the Fathers of early centuries was a wholesome and needed corrective to a one-sided interpretation of Christianity. Nor was its insistence on spiritual honesty less beneficial.

The sincerity and spiritual earnestness of Fox's beliefs, his hatred of all that savored of formalism, and his demand for inward spiritual experience were immensely attractive forces. By 1652 the first Quaker community was gathered in Preston Patrick in northern England. Two years later the Friends had spread to London, Bristol, and Norwich. Fox's most eminent early convert was Margaret Fell (1614–1702), whom he married after she became a widow, and her home, Swarthmore Hall, furnished a headquarters for his preachers.

In the circumstances of English life such a movement met with fierce opposition. Before 1661 no less than three thousand one hundred and seventy-nine, including Fox himself, had suffered imprisonment. A missionary zeal was early manifested which sent Quakers to proclaim their faith to as far distant points as Jerusalem, the West India Islands, Germany, Austria, and Holland. In 1656, they entered Massachusetts, and by

1661 four had been hanged. There was some explanation, though no justification, for this severity in the extravagant conduct of a good many of the early Quakers, which would have aroused police interference in any age.

These extravagances were made possible by the early want of organization, as well as belief in the immediate inspiration of the Spirit. Fox saw the necessity of order, and by 1666 the main features of the Quaker discipline were mapped out, though in the face of considerable opposition. In that year "Monthly Meetings" were established, by which strict watch could be kept over the life and conduct of the membership. Before Fox died, in 1691, the body had taken on the sober characteristics which have ever since distinguished it.

The laws against Dissenters at the Restoration bore with peculiar severity on the Quakers, since they, unlike the Presbyterians and Congregationalists, made no effort to conceal their meetings, but defiantly maintained them in the face of hostile authority. About four hundred met their deaths in prison, and many were ruined financially by heavy fines. To this period, however, belongs their most eminent trophy and their great colonial experiment. William Penn (1644–1718), son of Admiral Sir William Penn, after inclinations toward Quakerism as early as 1661, fully embraced its beliefs in 1666 and became at once one of the most eminent preachers and literary defenders of the faith. He determined to find in America the freedom denied Quakers in England. After aiding in sending some eight hundred Quakers to New Jersey in 1677–1678, Penn obtained from Charles II the grant of Pennsylvania, in 1681, in release of a debt due from the crown to his father. In 1682 Philadelphia was founded, and a great colonial experiment begun.

The Toleration Act of 1689 (*ante*, p. 476) relieved the Quakers, like other Dissenters, of their more pressing disabilities, and granted them freedom of worship.

PERIOD VII. THE TRANSITION TO THE MODERN RELIGIOUS SITUATION

SECTION I. THE TURNING POINT

THE question has been much controverted whether the Reformation is to be reckoned to the Middle Ages or to modern history. Not a little may be urged in support of either position. Its conceptions of religion as to be maintained by external authority, of the dominance of religion over all forms of educational and cultural life, of a single type of worship as alone allowable, at least within a given territory, of original sin and the essential worthlessness of the natural man, of evil spirits and witchcraft, of the immediacy and arbitrariness of the divine relations with the world, and of the other-worldliness of religious outlook, all link the Reformation to the Middle Ages. So, too, the problems primarily discussed, however different their solution from that characteristic of the Middle Ages, were essentially mediæval. Sin and grace had been, since the time of Augustine, if not rather of Tertullian, the very heart problems of Latin theology. They were so of the Reformation. However Luther himself might reject Aristotle, the older Protestant philosophy was thoroughly Aristotelian. Nor, though monasticism was repudiated, was the ascetic view of the world rejected, least of all by Calvinism.

On the other hand, the Reformation broke the dominance of the sacramental system which had controlled Christianity East and West certainly since the second century. Baptism and the Lord's Supper were preserved and highly valued, but they were now regarded as seals to the divine promises, not as exclusive channels of grace. The Holy Spirit, who works when and how and where He will, uses them for His gracious purposes doubtless, but not to the exclusion of other means. Salvation is, therefore, a direct, individual, and personal relationship, wrought by God, bringing the soul into union with Him, needing no saintly or priestly intervention. Furthermore, man's relation to God is not one of debt and credit, of evil acts

481

to be purged and merit to be acquired, but a state of reconciliation of which good works are the natural fruits. Nor was the Protestant estimate of the normal relations and occupations of life as the best fields for service to God a less radical departure from the Middle Ages. These characteristics link the Reformation with the modern world. Yet if one strikes a balance, and remembers, also, how largely the worldly tendencies of humanism were suppressed by the Reformation, the movement in its first century and a half must be reckoned in great measure a continuance of the Middle Ages. Though great religious bodies still use Reformation formulas, and bear names then originating, they no longer move in its atmosphere, but in various measure indeed in that of modern Christianity.

To assign an exact line of demarcation for this change is impossible. The alteration was not due to a single leader or group of leaders. It has modified Christian thought very unequally. The transformation has not yet been completed, after more than two centuries, if the Christian world as a whole is taken into view. It has been aided by a great variety of causes. One of these has been the steady secularization of government since the close of the seventeenth century. Even more important has been the rise of the professional,—other than clerical,—mercantile, and laboring classes to constantly increasing education and political influence. In the Reformation age leaders of thought and sharers in government were few. Their number and independence have been steadily expanding. This growth has helped to bring about, and, in turn, has been aided by, an increasing toleration on the part of the state, which has made easy the enormous subdivision of Protestantism and the rise of many groups of thinkers not directly associated with, or opposed to, organized religion.

Yet the most potent instruments in effecting this change of atmosphere have been the rise of modern science and philosophy, with the immense consequent transformations in outlook upon the universe and upon man's position in it; and the subsequent development of the historic method of examining and interpreting thought and institutions.

SECTION II.   THE BEGINNINGS OF MODERN SCIENCE
AND PHILOSOPHY

The early Reformation period conceived of the universe in
Ptolemaic fashion.   This earth was viewed as the centre about
which sun and stars revolve.   The Renaissance had revived in
Italy Greek speculations of a heliocentric system, and these
were elaborately developed by Nicolaus Copernicus (1473–
1543), of Thorn in Poland, and published in the year of his
death.   At the time, they excited slight attention and that
mostly unfavorable.   But astronomic science made progress.
Tycho Brahe (1546–1601), though but partially accepting the
Copernican system, multiplied observations.   Johann Kepler
(1571–1630), a Copernican, developed these into brilliant
generalizations.   Both were pursuing, though uninfluenced
directly by him, the new method of Sir Francis Bacon (1561–
1626), by which inductive experiment was made the basis of
hypothetical generalization.   Galileo Galilei (1564–1642), of
Pisa, gave to the world the thermometer, developed the pen-
dulum, put mechanical physics on a new basis by experiment,
and, above all, applied the telescope to the study of the heavens.
To him the real triumph of the theory of Copernicus was due.
But its explication, especially in his *Dialogue* of 1632, led to
bitter philosophical and ecclesiastical opposition, and he was
compelled to abjure it by the inquisition the year following.
The real popular demonstration of the Copernican theory was,
however, the work of Sir Isaac Newton (1642–1727).   His
Principia of 1687 made a European sensation, showing as it
did by mathematical demonstration that the motions of the
heavenly bodies are explainable by gravitation.   The effect
of Newton's conclusions was profound.   To thinking men, the
physical universe no longer appeared a field of arbitrary divine
action, but a realm of law, interpretable, such was the conclusion of the science of that age, in strict terms of mechanical
cause and effect.   This earth was no longer the centre of all
things, but a mere speck in a vast realm of bodies, many of
infinitely greater size, and all moving in obedience to unchangeable law.

While science was thus revealing a new heaven and a new
earth, philosophy was no less vigorously challenging the claims
of authority in the name of reason.   René Descartes (1596–

1650), a native of France and a Catholic, spent most of his active intellectual life in the Netherlands. There he wrote his *Discourse on Method* of 1637, his *First Philosophy* of 1641, and his *Principia* of 1644. To his thinking, only that is really knowledge which the mind fully understands. Mere erudition is not intelligence. The objects and ideas which present themselves to the mind are so involved and so dependent one on another that they must be analyzed and separated into simplicity to be really understood. Hence the beginning of all knowledge is doubt; and no real progress can be made till a basis, or point of departure, can be found which cannot be doubted. That Descartes found, with Augustine, in his own existence as a thinking being. Even in doubting, "I think, therefore I am." If we examine the contents of this thinking I, we find in it ideas greater than it could of itself originate, and since nothing can be without an adequate cause, there must be a cause great enough and real enough to produce them. Hence we are convinced of the existence of God, and His relation to all our thinking. In God thought and being are united. Our ideas are true and Godlike only as they are clear and distinct with a logical clarity like the demonstrations of geometry. Matter, though equally with mind having its source in God, is in all things the opposite of mind. In the last analysis it has only extension and the purely mechanical motion imparted to it by God. Hence animals are merely machines, and the relations between human bodies and minds caused Descartes great perplexities.

Yet, influential as the Cartesian philosophy was, it was not its details which profoundly affected popular thought, but its assertion that all conceptions must be doubted till proved, and that any adequate proof must have the certainty of mathematical demonstration. These two principles were to have momentous consequences.

Much less influential in his own age though far more logical than their author in carrying Descartes's principles to their logical development, was the Netherlandish Hebrew, Baruch Spinoza (1632–1677). A pantheist, all is an infinite substance, all is God or nature, for with him the terms are equivalent, known in two modes or attributes, thought and extension, of which all finite persons or attributes are the expression. As to Descartes, to Spinoza clearness is the test of truth.

But *how* do men know?   One influential answer came from
the German mathematician, historian, statesman, and philosopher, Gottfried Wilhelm Leibnitz (1646–1716), for the last
forty years of his life librarian in Hanover, and an earnest seeker
of the reunion of Catholicism and Protestantism.   Unlike
Spinoza, who saw in the universe one substance, Leibnitz believed substances infinite in number.   Each is a "monad,"
an indivisible centre of force.   Each mirrors the universe,
though the degree of consciousness in differing monads varies
from practical unconscious to the highest activity.   The
greater and clearer the consciousness, the nearer the monad
approaches the divine.   God is the original monad, to whose
perception all things are clear.   All ideas are wrapped up in the
monad, are innate, and need to be drawn out to clearness.
Here again is the characteristic test of truth, which Descartes
and Spinoza had presented.   No monad influences another;
but all that seems mutual influence is the working of pre-
established harmony, like perfect clocks pointing to the same
hour.   Nor do the aggregations of monads which constitute
bodies really occupy space.   Each monad is like a mathematical
point, and time and space are simply the necessary aspects
under which their groupings are perceived.   God created the
world to exhibit His perfection, and therefore, of all possible
worlds, chose the best.   What seems evil is imperfection,
physical pain, and limitation, or moral wrong, which is nevertheless necessary in the sense that God could not have made a
better world.   Leibnitz's answer was, therefore, that men know
by the elucidation of their innate ideas.

Very different was the answer given by the most influential
English thinker of the close of the seventeenth and opening of
the eighteenth centuries, John Locke (1632–1704).   In his famous *Essay Concerning Human Understanding* of 1690 Locke
denied the existence of innate ideas.   The mind is white paper,
on which sensation writes its impressions, which the mind combines by reflection into ideas, and the combination of simple
ideas gives rise to more complex ideas.   Locke's purpose was to
show that all that claims to be knowledge is justly subject to
criticism as to its reasonableness judged by reason based on
experience.   Thus tested, he finds the existence of God demonstrated by the argument from cause and effect; morality
is equally demonstrable like the truths of mathematics.   Re-

ligion must be essentially reasonable. It may be above reason—beyond experience—but it cannot be contradictory to reason. These views Locke developed in his *Reasonableness of Christianity* of 1695; the Scriptures contain a message beyond the power of unaided reason to attain, attested by miracles; but that message cannot be contrary to reason, nor could even a miracle attest anything essentially unreasonable. Hence, though sincerely Christian, Locke had little patience with mystery in religion. For him it was enough to acknowledge Jesus as the Messiah, and practise the moral virtues which He proclaimed, and which are in fundamental accord with the dictates of a reason which is hardly distinguishable from enlightened common sense.

Locke was no less influential as an advocate of toleration and opponent of all compulsion in religion. Religion's only proper weapon is essential reasonableness. Nor was Locke less formative of political theory in England and America. He had indeed been preceded in this field, in various directions, by Grotius (1583–1645), Hobbes (1588–1679), and Pufendorf (1632–1694). In his *Treatises on Government* of 1690 Locke urged that men have natural rights to life, liberty, and property. To secure these, government has been established by the consent of the governed. In such a state the will of the majority must rule, and when that will is not carried out, or fundamental rights are violated, the people have the right of revolution. The legislative and executive functions should be carefully discriminated. The legislative is the superior. However inadequate and fanciful this may be as a historic explanation of the origin of the state, its influence in the development of English and American political theory can hardly be overestimated.

Of considerable significance in the theory of morals was the view developed by the earl of Shaftesbury (1671–1713) in his *Characteristics of Men* of 1711. Hobbes had attempted to find the basis of morality in man's constitution, but had discovered there nothing but pure selfishness. To Locke the basis which reason discovers is the law of God. Though entirely reasonable, morality is still positive to Locke, a divine command. Shaftesbury now taught that, since man is a being having personal rights and social relationships, virtue consists in the proper balancing of selfish and altruistic aims. This harmony is achieved, and the value of actions determined, by an inward "moral sense." Shaftesbury thus based right and wrong on the fundamental constitution of human nature itself, not on the will of God. This gave a reason why even one who rejected the divine existence—which was not the case with Shaftesbury—was nevertheless bound to maintain moral conduct. It removed the hope of reward or fear of punishment as prime motives for moral conduct. Atheist and rejector of morality could no longer be considered, as they had generally been, equivalent terms. Nor was it difficult for Bishop Joseph Butler (1692–1752) to preserve Shaftesbury's "moral sense," while giving to it the theistic interpretation of "conscience," a divinely implanted monitor and judge of conduct.

SECTION III. DEISM AND ITS OPPONENTS. SCEPTICISM

Locke's test of truth was reasonableness, in the sense of conformity to common sense. He viewed morality as the prime content of religion. The Newtonian conception of the universe was of a realm of law, created by a "first cause," and moving in unchangeable mechanical order. The new knowledge of foreign nations of long-established civilization and other religions like the Chinese, enlarged men's horizons and made familiar other than Christian culture. All these influences led to a radical departure in English religious thought, that known as Deism. As early as 1624 Edward Herbert of Cherbury (1583–1648) had enumerated the articles of belief alleged to constitute natural religion, held by all mankind in primitive unspoiled simplicity, as: God exists; He is to be worshipped; virtue is His true service; man must repent of wrong-doing; and there are rewards and punishments after death. To the later Deists these seemed a statement of the content of natural, universal reasonable religion. In 1696 came John Toland's (1670–1722) *Christianity not Mysterious;* 1713 saw Anthony Collins's (1676–1729) *Discourse of Freethinking;* in 1730 was published Matthew Tindal's (1653?–1733) *Christianity as Old as Creation.* In these works the main features of the Deistic position were set forth. All that is acknowledged beyond or above reason is held on belief without proof. What is believed without proof is superstition. To be rid of superstition is to be free, hence the only rational thinker is a freethinker. The worst enemies

of mankind are these who have held men in bondage to superstition, and the chief examples of these are "priests" of all
sorts. All that is valuable in revelation had already been given
men in natural reasonable religion, hence "Christianity"—
that is, all that is of worth in Christianity—is "as old as creation." All that is obscure or above reason in so-called revelation is superstitious and worthless or worse. Miracles are no
real witness to revelation; they are either superfluous, for all
of value in that to which they witness reason already possesses;
or they are an insult to the perfect workmanship of a Creator
who has set this world running by most perfect mechanical
laws and does not now interfere with its ongoing. Deism thus
seemed to destroy all historic Christianity and authoritative
revelation. It was widely denounced as atheism, yet destructive as it was, not justly. In the thought of its advocates it
was a rescue of religion from bondage to the superstitious and
a return to primitive rational simplicity and purity.

From a modern standpoint the weakness of Deism is evident.
Its primitive universal, rational religion is as much a figment of
the imagination as the primitive unspoiled social and political
state of the unspoiled child of nature so dear to the eighteenth
century. Its assertion that "whatever is," that is, whatever is
natural, "is right," is shallow optimism. It had no sense of
the actual facts of the historic religious development of the race.
Its God was afar off, a being who once for all established certain religious principles, essentially rules of morality, and set
a wonderfully contrived mechanical world in motion with which
He has nothing now to do. Its merit was that it forced consideration of the fundamental reasonableness and moral worthiness of religious claims. So to criticise and to estimate it is
to measure it by a standard entirely foreign to its age. Neither
its supporters nor its critics could have viewed it from the
standpoint here indicated.

Deism called out many replies, and the chief proof of its
power is that, relatively mediocre men as most of the Deists
were, most of its opponents attempted to meet it by rational
argument, often admitting a considerable share of its method,
though not its results. Some few met it by a flat denial of
any power of reason in the realm of religion. Such was the
answer of the excellent Nonjuror William Law (1686–1761)
in his reply to Tindal, entitled *The Case of Reason* (1732).

Reason, Law argued, not merely does not find truth in religion; "it is the cause of all the disorders of our passions, the corruptions of our hearts." God is above the power of man to comprehend, "His own will is wisdom and wisdom is His will. His goodness is arbitrary."

Less directly designed as an answer to Deism but believed by himself to be destructive of all "atheism" was the philosophy of George Berkeley (1685–1753), a man of most generous impulses, who attempted to found a missionary college in Bermuda for the evangelization of the American Indians, lived for a time in Rhode Island, and in 1734 became bishop of Cloyne in Ireland. To Berkeley's thinking nothing really exists but minds and ideas. There is no other knowledge of what is called matter but an impression in our minds, and since like can only affect like, our minds must be affected only by other minds. Since ideas are universal and constant, they must be the product in our minds of a universal, eternal, and constantly working mind. Such a mind is God, and to Him all our ideas are due. But ideas exist not merely subjectively in our minds. In some sense what we call nature is a range of ideas in the divine mind, impressed in a definite and constant order on our minds, though their reality to us is only in our perception of them in our own minds. By thus denying the reality of matter Berkeley would destroy that whole conception of the world as a huge mechanism—a magnified watch—made once for all by an all-wise Maker, who has nothing now to do with its ongoing, which Deism had held. For it he would substitute a universal constant divine spiritual activity. Though this conception of Berkeley has always enjoyed high philosophic respect, it is too subtle and too contrary to the evidences of his senses for the average man.

More famous in its own time, yet of far less philosophic ability or permanent value, was a work of Joseph Butler (1692–1752), a Presbyterian by descent who had early entered the Church of England and become bishop of Bristol in 1738, and of Durham in 1750. His *Analogy of Religion* of 1736 was a work of immense labor, candor, and care. In answer to the Deists he starts from the premises, held equally by the Deists and their opponents, that God exists, that nature moves in a uniform course, and that human knowledge is limited. God is admittedly the author of nature: if the same difficulties can be raised against the course of nature as against revelation, the probability is that both have the same author. Their positive resemblances also lead to the same conclusion. Immortality is at least strongly probable. As present happiness or misery depend on conduct, it is probable that future will also. Every man is now in a state of "probation" as regards his use of this life; it is probable that he is also now on "probation" as to his future destiny. Our limited knowledge of nature does not warrant a declaration that revelation is improbable, much less impossible, and whether there has actually been a revelation is a historic question to be tested by its attestation by miracles and fulfilment of prophecy. Believed widely in its time an unanswerable answer to Deism, and as such long required in English and American universities, Butler's cautious balance of probabilities utterly fails to meet modern questions, and has been well criticised as raising more doubts than it answers. Its most attractive feature is its moral fervor in its exaltation of the divine regnancy of conscience over human action.

A noteworthy attack alike on Deism and on much of the current defenses of Christianity against it was made by the acutest British philosopher of the eighteenth century, David Hume (1711–1776). Born in Edinburgh, he died in that city. He lived in France for some years, saw some public employment, wrote a popular but highly Tory *History of England,* and won deserved fame as a political economist. During his last years he was regarded as the friendly, kindly head of the literary and intellectual circles of his native city. His philosophical system was ably set forth in his *Treatise of Human Nature* of 1739; but this rather youthful publication attracted little notice. Very different was it when the same ideas were recast in his *Philosophical Essays* of 1748 and his *Natural History of Religion* of 1757. Philosophically, Hume was one of the keenest of reasoners, standing on the basis of Locke, but with radical and destructive criticism of Locke's theories and with most thoroughgoing religious scepticism. Experience gives us all our knowledge, but we receive it as isolated impressions and ideas. All connection between our mental impressions as related by cause and effect, or as united and borne by an underlying substance, are simply the inveterate but baseless view-points of our mental habit. They are the ways in which our minds are accustomed to act. What we really perceive is that in our limited observation certain experiences are associated. We jump to the conclusion that there is a causal relation between them. So, too, substance is "feigned." If therefore cause and effect are ruled out, the argument for a God founded thereon is baseless. The denial of substance leaves no real permanent I behind my experiences, and leaves no philosophical basis for immortality. Hume, in whom a dawning of historic criticism manifested itself, also held that history shows that Polytheism preceded Monotheism in human development, and thus history gives no support to the doctrine of the one originally recognized God of Deism, or to the existence of the simple primitive, rational religion of nature which Deists claimed. Most of Hume's criticisms were too subtle and too radical to be very fully understood by either Deists or their orthodox opponents in his day, against whom they were equally directed.

Hume's greatest sensation was his criticism of miracles, then looked upon as the main defense of revelation and Christianity. His argument was twofold. Experience is the source of all our knowledge. Our experience witnesses to the uniformity of nature much more strongly than to the infallibility of human testimony. Hence the probability that error, mistake, or deception has led to the report of a miracle is vastly greater than that the uniform course of nature has really been interrupted. Yet, granted that testimony may prove that unusual events have occurred, that would not prove that they established anything, unless it could be further proved that they were wrought for that special purpose by divine power, which is an even more difficult task. The positions here assumed have had lasting effect. Few who now affirm miracles view them, as the eighteenth century did, as the prime proofs of Christianity. Rather, the revelation is regarded as carrying faith in the miracles far more than their lending support to it. Those who accept miracles now largely regard the revelation as so supernatural and divine as to render miracles not unfitting as its accompaniment. Since Hume's criticism, the question of miracles has been increasingly felt to be one of peculiar difficulty.

Deism, though soon a good deal weakened in England, still continued, and extended strongly beyond its borders. It aided not a little in the development of rationalism in Germany; but its most powerful influence was in France, where it had many advocates and became fashionable. Chief of these French supporters was François Marie Arouet, or, as he called himself, Voltaire (1694–1778), who had become familiar with its tenets during a sojourn in England from 1726 to 1729. In Voltaire eighteenth-century France had its keenest wit. No philosopher, vain, self-seeking, but with genuine hatred of tyranny, especially of religious persecution, no one ever attacked organized religion with a more unsparing ridicule. Such a contest was, of necessity, more sharply drawn in France than in Great Britain. In the latter country a certain degree of religious toleration had been achieved, and great divergence of religious interpretation was practically allowed. In France dogmatic Roman Catholicism was dominant. The contest was, therefore, between Deism or Atheism, on the one hand, and a single assertive type of Christianity, on the other. Voltaire was a true Deist in his belief in the existence of God and of a primitive natural religion consisting of a simple morality; also in his rejection of all that rested on the authority of Bible or church. Of the extent and significance of his work in influencing the French mind in directions that were to appear in the French Revolution there can be no question. Deism affected the eighteenth century widely. It was substantially the creed of Frederick the Great of Prussia (1740–1786); of Joseph II, the Holy Roman Emperor (Austria, 1765–1790); and of the marquis of Pombal (1699–1782), the greatest of Portuguese statesmen of the century. Nor was Deism less influential on this side of the Atlantic. Benjamin Franklin (1706–1790) and Thomas Jefferson (1743–1826) were its adherents.

Deism had powerful popular presentation in the brutal, savage work of Thomas Paine (1737–1809), the son of an English Quaker, whose *Common Sense* of 1776 did great service to the American Revolution; nor was his *Rights of Man* of 1791 less effective in defense of the principles underlying the French Revolution. In 1795 came his *Age of Reason*, in which Deism was presented in its most aggressive form. Though unsparingly denounced, it left a series of followers, and represented a type of criticism of the morality of the traditional representation of the divine nature and dealings, on the basis of an uncritical and unhistoric treatment of the Scriptures, which found a belated echo in Robert G. Ingersoll (1833–1899).

A sceptical criticism on the early history of Christianity advanced by the historian Edward Gibbon (1737–1794) in the fifteenth and sixteenth chapters of his great *History of the Decline and Fall of the Roman Empire* (1776) deserves notice, not for its inherent importance, but for the controversy that it aroused, and the light that it throws on the thought of the time. In accounting for the spread of Christianity, Gibbon gave as reasons its zeal inherited from the Jews, its teaching of immortality, its claim to miraculous gifts, its strict morality, and its efficient organization. No modern historian would probably object to any of these explanations, as far as they go. What would impress him is their absolute want of comprehension of the nature of religion, whether Christian or other, and of the forces by which religion makes conquests. But that was an ignorance equally shared by Gibbon's critics in the eighteenth century. The usual orthodox explanation had been that the first disciples had been so convinced of the truth of the Gospel by miracles that they were willing to hazard their lives in its behalf. The excitement roused by Gibbon's rather superficial explanation was that it supplied other causes, less directly supernatural, for the spread of Christianity. Its one permanent result was to aid, with other influences, toward the historical investigation of the Scriptures and Christian origins, which was to be so largely the work of the nineteenth century.

The general attitude of the period, and also the general rationalizing of even orthodox Christian presentation in England, at the close of the eighteenth century is best illustrated in the work of William Paley (1743–1805). His *View of the Evidences of Christianity* of 1794 and *Natural Theology* of 1802 were written with remarkable clearness of style and cogency of reasoning, and long enjoyed high popularity. From a watch, he argues, we infer a maker, so from the wonderful adaptation of the human body, the eye, the hand, the muscles, we infer an almighty Designer. These arguments, therefore, prove the existence of God. God has made His will the rule of human action and revealed it to men. The purpose of revelation is "the proof of a future state of rewards and punishments." That revelation was given by Christ, and its convincing force to the first disciples was in the miracles by which it was accompanied. "They who acted and suffered in the cause acted and suffered for the miracles." Paley then proceeds to defini-

tion. "Virtue is the doing good to mankind, in obedience to
the will of God, and for the sake of everlasting happiness."
This prudential and self-regarding estimate of virtue is characteristic of Paley's age, as were his emphases on the evidential
character of miracles and on a mechanical demonstration of
the divine existence which the theory of evolution has since
largely robbed of force. Yet it is pleasant to note that Paley's
thought of "doing good to mankind" led him to strenuous
opposition to human slavery.

SECTION IV.   ENGLISH UNITARIANISM

It has already been pointed out that on the Continent anti-
Trinitarian views were represented by some Anabaptists (*ante*,
p. 369) and by the Socinians (*ante*, pp. 451–453). Both types
penetrated into England. Under Elizabeth "Arian Baptists"
from the Netherlands were burned in 1575. Under James I
Bartholomew Legate and Edward Wightman, of similar views,
have the distinction in 1612 of being the last Englishmen
burned for their faith. With the controversies of the civil-war
period anti-Trinitarian views became more evident. In John
Biddle (1615–1662), an Oxford graduate, Socinianism had a
more learned representative, who suffered much imprisonment. The great Puritan poet, John Milton (1608–1674), inclined to Arianism in his later years. Biddle's chief convert
was Thomas Firmin (1632–1697), a London layman, who furthered the publication of anti-Trinitarian tracts.

With the dawn of the eighteenth century, with its rationalizing impulses both in orthodox and Deistic circles, and its inclination to see in morality the essence of religion, these anti-
Trinitarian tendencies were greatly strengthened. The Presbyterian minister Thomas Emlyn (1663–1741) published his
widely read *Inquiry into the Scripture Account of Jesus Christ*
in 1702. In 1712 Samuel Clarke (1675–1729), rector of St.
James, Westminster, and deemed the most philosophical of the
Anglican clergy, published his *Scripture Doctrine of the Trinity*,
in which he sought to demonstrate Arian views by a painstaking
examination of the New Testament. It was, however, among
the Dissenters, especially the Presbyterians and General Baptists, that anti-Trinitarian views won the largest following.
In 1717 Joseph Hallet and James Peirce, Presbyterian minis-

ters in Exeter, adopted Arianism. The movement spread widely. The most learned of eighteenth-century Dissenters, Nathaniel Lardner (1684–1768), was its representative. On the whole, the Congregationalists and the Particular Baptists were little affected, and in consequence grew in numbers as the century went on, surpassing the Presbyterians, who at the time of the Toleration Act had been the most numerous Non-Conformist body.

Arianism changed to Socinianism. A further impulse was given to the movement when a clergyman of the establishment, Theophilus Lindsey (1723–1808), who was already a Socinian, circulated a petition which received some two hundred and fifty signatures asking that clergymen be relieved from subscription to the Thirty-nine Articles, and pledge their fidelity to the Scriptures alone. Parliament in 1772 refused to receive it. In 1773 Lindsey withdrew from the establishment, and the next year organized a Unitarian Church in London. Closely associated with Lindsey was Joseph Priestley (1733–1804), a Dissenting clergyman, an eminent chemist, the discoverer of oxygen, a sympathizer with the American and French Revolutions, who spent the last ten years of his life in Pennsylvania. Parliament in 1779 amended the Toleration Act by substituting profession of faith in the Scriptures for the required acceptance of the doctrinal part of the Thirty-nine Articles, and removed all penal acts against deniers of the Trinity in 1813. This older English Unitarianism was formal and intellectual, clear in its rejection of "creeds of human composition," and insistence on salvation by character. It was often intellectually able, but had little influence on popular religious life. Its effect in producing a similar movement in New England was considerable, though that grew also out of the general rationalizing tendencies of the eighteenth century, and was on the whole less dryly intellectual than its counterpart in England.

SECTION V. PIETISM IN GERMANY

The development of a scholastic Lutheranism has already been noted (*ante,* pp. 441–444). Though nominally based on the Scriptures, it was practically a fixed dogmatic interpretation, rigid, exact, and demanding intellectual conformity.

Emphasis was laid on pure doctrine and the sacraments, as constituting the sufficient elements of the Christian life. In some respects the field had grown narrower than that of Roman Catholicism, for if Catholicism was equally dogmatic regarding belief and sacraments, it also laid an emphasis on good works, which dogmatic Lutheranism rejected. For that vital relationship between the believer and God which Luther had taught had been substituted very largely a faith which consisted in the acceptance of a dogmatic whole. The layman's rôle was largely passive, to accept the dogmas which he was assured were pure, to listen to their exposition from the pulpit, to partake of the sacraments and share in the ordinances of the church, these were the practical sum of the Christian life. Some evidences of a deeper piety, indeed, existed, of which the hymns of the age are ample proof, and doubtless many individual examples of real and inward religious life were to be found, but the general tendency was external and dogmatic. It was the tendency often, though only partially justly, called "dead orthodoxy."

Pietism was a breach with these tendencies, an assertion of the primacy of the feeling in Christian experience, a vindication for the laity of an active share in the upbuilding of the Christian life, and the assertion of a strict ascetic attitude toward the world. Many sources have been assigned to it, Anabaptist influences, Roman Catholic mystical piety, the example of the Reformed ecclesiastical life of Holland or England. The subject is a difficult one. All these may have contributed something, but so far as a definite cause for Pietism can be given it is to be found in the teaching and example of one of the most notable religious figures of the seventeenth century, Philipp Jakob Spener.

Spener was born on January 13, 1635, in Rappoltsweiler, in Alsace. The *True Christianity* of the German ascetic mystic, Johann Arndt (1555–1621) roused him, and its impressions were deepened by translations of some of the edificatory treatises of the English Puritans. His student years in Strassburg familiarized him with Biblical exegesis, and he saw there a church discipline and a care in catechetical instruction far beyond what was customary in most Lutheran circles. Further studies in Geneva deepened these impressions without weaning him from Lutheranism. In 1666 he became chief pastor in the

prosperous commercial city of Frankfort. He felt the need
of church discipline, but found himself hindered, because all
authority was in the hands of the city government. Under
such leadership as was permitted him, catechetical instruction
speedily improved. His first considerable innovation occurred
in 1670, when he gathered in his own house a little group of
like-minded people for Bible reading, prayer, and the discussion of the Sunday sermons—the whole aiming at the deepening of the individual spiritual life. Of these circles, to which
the name *collegia pietatis* was given (hence Pietism), the first
was that in Spener's home.

These plans for cultivating a warmer Christian life Spener
put forth in his *Pia desideria* of 1675. The chief evils of the
time he pictured as governmental interference, the bad example
of the unworthy lives of some of the clergy, the controversial
interpretation of theology, and the drunkenness, immorality, and
self-seeking of the laity. As measures of reform he proposed
the gathering within the various congregations of circles—
ecclesiolæ in ecclesia—for Bible reading; and since all believers
are priests—a Lutheran contention which had been practically
forgotten—for mutual watch and helpfulness. Christianity
is far more a life than an intellectual knowledge. Controversy
is unprofitable. Better training for the clergy is desirable.
An experimental knowledge of religion, and a befitting life
should be demanded of them. A new type of preaching should
be practised, designed to build up the Christian life of the
hearers, not primarily controversial or exhibitory of the argu-
mentative abilities of the preacher. That only is genuine Christianity which shows itself in the life. Its normal beginning is
a spiritual transformation, a conscious new birth. Spener also
showed certain ascetic tendencies, like the English Puritans,
inculcating moderation in food, drink, and dress, and rejecting
the theatre, dances, and cards, which contemporary Lutheranism regarded as "indifferent things." Spener's efforts encountered bitter opposition, and aroused enormous controversy. He was accused of heresy. Falsely so, as indicating
any intentional departure from Lutheran standards; but rightly
so in the sense that his spirit and ideals were totally unlike
those of contemporary Lutheran orthodoxy. His work involved
a going back to the Scriptures from the creeds and theological
interpretations of dogmatism. Spener's feeling that, if "the

heart" was right, differences of intellectual interpretation were relatively unimportant, was not merely opposed to the Lutheran emphasis on "pure doctrine," it was destructive of it. The two points of view were mutually exclusive. Spener undoubtedly greatly popularized familiarity with the Bible, and undermined the authority of confessional standards, as giving in final logical form what the Scriptures had to teach. A result of this Biblical study was to prepare the way for, rather than to effect, an investigation of the nature and history of the Scriptures themselves. Spener greatly improved the religious instruction of youth, and achieved his purpose of introducing a more strenuous, Biblically fed, and warmer popular Christian life.

At Frankfort some of Spener's disciples, in spite of his protests, withdrew from church worship and the sacraments. Spener's meetings consequently met with police opposition, and he was glad, in 1686, to accept a call to Dresden as court preacher.

Meanwhile, the Pietist movement had spread to the University of Leipzig. In 1686 one of the younger instructors, August Hermann Francke (1663–1727), and a few associates, founded there a *collegium philobiblicum* for the study of the Scriptures. Its members were at first instructors, its method scientific, and it had the approval of the university authorities. But in 1687 Francke experienced what he regarded as a divine new birth while in Lüneburg and engaged in writing a sermon on *John* 20[31]. A couple of months' stay with Spener, in Dresden, completed his acceptance of Pietism. In 1689 Francke was back in Leipzig, lecturing to the students and to the townspeople with great following. Leipzig was soon in a good deal of turmoil. An electoral edict soon forbad the meeting of citizens in "conventicles." Undoubtedly Francke's lectures led some students to neglect other studies and to assume a critical attitude. Under the leadership of the Leipzig professor of theology, Johann Benedict Carpzov (1639–1699), the university authorities limited Francke's work. Carpzov became one of the most unwearied of Spener's opponents. Francke's position became so uncomfortable that he was glad, in 1690, to accept a call to Erfurt as "deacon."

Meanwhile Spener's path in Dresden was not easy. The Saxon clergy looked upon him as a stranger; the two Saxon universities, Leipzig and Wittenberg, opposed him. His meetings for spiritual upbuilding developed criticism. The Elector, John George III (1647–1691), took offense at Spener's pastoral reproof of his drunkenness. When, therefore, an invitation to Berlin came from the Elector of Brandenburg, Frederick III (1688–1701), who was to become King Frederick I of Prussia (1701–1713), Spener willingly accepted it in 1691. Though Spener never won his new sovereign for personal Pietism, he had much support from Frederick, and his years in Berlin, to his death, on February 5, 1705, were his happiest and most successful.

While in Berlin Spener was able to do his greatest service to Pietism. Christian Thomasius (1655–1728), a rationalist in the sense of Locke, a critic of the theological hair-splitting of the day, a creator of German jurisprudence, the first to substitute German for Latin as the language of the university instruction, a defender of religious toleration, a sceptic regarding witchcraft, the opponent of the judicial use of torture, had been driven from Leipzig in 1690 by the hostility of the theologians. His popularity in the student body was great. Thomasius was no Pietist, though he disliked the persecution of the Pietists, and had done his utmost to aid Francke in the contest with the Leipzig authorities. The Elector of Brandenburg, long desirous of having a university of his own, improved the exile of Thomasius to found a university in Halle, in 1691, which was formally opened in 1694, and in which Thomasius was to lead the faculty of law till his death.

Meanwhile Francke had many difficulties in Erfurt. His energetic introduction of Pietistic measures roused the opposition of the clergy of the city. Carpzov's hostility pursued him, and in 1691 he was expelled by the authorities. Spener now procured for him from the Elector appointment to a professorship in Halle, and the pastorate of the neighboring village of Glaucha, and also the appointment of colleagues of Pietistic sympathies. From the first Francke dominated the theological methods and instruction in Halle, though he did not become formally a member of the theological faculty till 1698. Till his death, in 1727, Francke made and kept Halle a centre of Pietism.

Francke was a man of unbounded energy and organizing genius. His parish of Glaucha was a model of pastoral faithfulness. His lectures in the university were largely exegetical and experiential; and his combination of the classroom and parish practice was highly helpful for his students. In 1695 he began a school for poor children, and such was its fame that children from outside were offered to him in such numbers that in 1696 he established his famous fitting school, the *Pædagogium*. To these, in 1697, he added a Latin school. These educational foundations were soon renowned, and all were managed in the spirit of Pietism. At his death two thousand two hundred children were under instruction. In 1698 he established his famous Orphan House, which numbered a hundred and thirty-four inmates when he died. All these foundations, most of which have continued to the present, were begun almost without means, and Francke sincerely believed were maintained in answer to prayer. Gifts flowed in from all parts of Germany. Without doubting Francke's faith, it is but just to note that he understood the art of honorable publicity, and of enlisting friends. The number of nobles who were patrons of his foundations was really remarkable. One further foundation may be called almost his own. That was the Bible Institute, established in 1710 by his friend, Karl Hildebrand, Freiherr von Canstein (1667–1719), for the publication of the Scriptures and their circulation in inexpensive form. The institute has done a noble work to the present day.

One notable feature of these activities in Halle was the zeal for missions there aroused. At a time when Protestants generally still failed to recognize the missionary obligation, Francke and his associates were awake to it. When Frederick IV (1699–1730), of Denmark, wished to send the first Protestant missionaries to India, in 1705, establishing them in 1706 in Tranquebar, then belonging to Denmark, he found them among Francke's students in Halle, Bartholomäus Ziegenbalg and Heinrich Plütchau. During the eighteenth century not less than sixty foreign missionaries went forth from the University of Halle and its associated foundations, of whom the most famous was Christian Friedrich Schwartz (1726–1798), who labored, from 1750 to his death, in India. Certainly Francke's name deserves high place on the roll of missionary leadership.

By the time of Francke's death, in 1727, Pietism had passed its high-water mark. It produced no further leaders equal in ability to Spener and Francke. It continued to spread in Germany, notably in Württemberg. A statistical estimate is difficult, as Pietists did not separate from the Lutheran Churches; but Pietism undoubtedly affected Germany very widely and for good. It fostered a more vital type of piety. It greatly improved the spiritual quality of the ministry, preaching, and the Christian training of the young. It increased the share of the laity in the life of the church. It greatly augmented familiarity with the Bible, and the devotional study of the Scriptures. Its shadows were its insistence on a conscious conversion through struggle as the only normal method of entrance into the kingdom of God, its ascetic attitude toward the world, illustrated in Francke's severe repression of play among the children in his foundations, its censorious judgments on those who were not Pietists as irreligious, and its neglect of the intellectual elements in religion. It produced very few intellectual leaders. But, on the whole, the judgment on Pietism must be predominantly favorable. It did a service of great value for the religious life of Protestant Germany.

One fruit of Pietism deserves notice in a contribution of value made to the interpretation of church history by one of the most radical of the Pietists, Gottfried Arnold (1666–1714), a friend of Spener, for a short time a professor in Giessen, and thenceforward living in comparative retirement in Quedlinburg. Since the Reformation church history had been polemic and had regarded all thinkers as to be rejected whom the church of their own age rejected. In his *Unparteiische Kirchen und Ketzer-Historie* of 1699 and 1700 Arnold introduced a new conception. He had read much of the ancient heretics. No man is to be deemed a heretic because his own age so deemed him. He is to be judged on his own merits, and even the views of so-called heretics have their place in the history of Christian thought. As is always a danger to a man who has conceived a fruitful idea, Arnold pushed his interpretation rather to the conclusion that there had been more truth with the heretics than with the orthodox. Yet he gave to church history a forward step of decided importance.

SECTION VI. ZINZENDORF AND MORAVIANISM

One of the most notable results of the Pietistic awakening, though far from approved by the Pietists in general, was the reconstitution of the Moravian Brethren, under the leadership of Zinzendorf. Nicolaus Ludwig, Graf von Zinzendorf, was born in Dresden, on May 26, 1700. His father was a high official of the Saxon electoral court and a friend of Spener. Zinzendorf's father died shortly after his son's birth, the mother married again, and the boy was brought up, rather solitary and introspective, by his grandmother, the Pietistic Katherine von Gersdorff. Even as a boy he was marked by the two traits which always characterized his religious life— passionate personal devotion to Christ and the conviction that God is only known as Christ, at least in Christianity. From the time he was ten till his seventeenth year he studied in Francke's *Pædagogium* in Halle. Its rigor repelled him, but he gradually came to appreciate Francke's zeal, and his religious nature was quickened in 1715 in connection with his first communion. The insistence of his family that he should enter public employment sent him to Wittenberg from 1716 to 1719 to study law. Though a decided Pietist, his experiences in Wittenberg gave him a kindlier feeling than before toward orthodox Lutheranism. In 1719 and 1720 he took a long journey to Holland and France, forming the acquaintance of many distinguished men, and making his religious principles clearly, though tactfully, evident. On his return journey through Castell he fell in love with his cousin, but he thought Graf Heinrich XXIX, of Reuss, a more favored suitor, and resigned his pretensions, believing that God thereby had indicated some work for him to do. He ultimately married, in 1722, Graf Heinrich's sister, Erdmute Dorothea, who made him a most sympathetic wife.

The wishes of his relatives led him to enter the electoral service in Dresden in 1721. Yet he was primarily interested in cultivating the "heart-religion," in the Pietistic sense, among his friends in Dresden, and even more on his estate of Berthelsdorf, about seventy miles east of Dresden, where as patron he appointed his like-minded friend, Johann Andreas Rothe, to the pastorate. Here in wholly unlooked-for fashion his life-work was to meet him.

The old Hussite church of Bohemia had fallen on evil days. Part had found refuge in Poland, where it had long maintained its episcopal constitution, but finding the difficulties increasing, had preserved it by persuading Frederick III's Calvinistic court preacher in Berlin, Daniel Ernst Jablonski, of the

Polish Hussite church by ancestry and training, to accept ordination to the bishopric in 1699. The consequences of the Thirty Years' War to Bohemian Protestantism had been destructive, and it had persisted in Bohemia and the neighboring province of Moravia only in concealment and under persecution. As early as 1722 the German-speaking Moravians began to seek a refuge in Saxony under the leadership of the carpenter, Christian David. Zinzendorf allowed them to found a village on his Berthelsdorf estate, which they named Herrnhut, and where they collected in considerable numbers. Zinzendorf at first paid little attention to these immigrants besides allowing them a refuge, but by 1727 he began their spiritual leadership. The task was hard at first. The refugees were divided, their aim was a separate church, while that of Zinzendorf and Rothe was incorporation in the Saxon Lutheran state church, though with special additional meetings as in Spener's plan of *collegia pietatis*. On the other hand, local customs permitted an organized village to give itself a secular organization and make its own rules. Under these customs Herrnhut chose "elders" for its secular direction in 1727. Zinzendorf, as lord of the estate, had a certain indefinite right of leadership, and all this was sealed by a communion service of such spiritual power in Berthelsdorf on August 13, 1727, that that date has generally been reckoned that of the rebirth of the Moravian Church.

Out of these institutions for the leadership of the village of Herrnhut, originally secular, a spiritual organization soon grew. An executive committee of four developed from the eldership, and by 1730 was regarded as exercising ministerial functions. A general eldership was formed, of which the first holder, in 1733, was Leonhard Dober. To Zinzendorf the Herrnhut society soon seemed a body of soldiers of Christ, to advance His cause at home and abroad—a new Protestant monasticism without vows or celibacy, but bound to their Lord by daily prayer and worship. The young men and the young women were separated from ordinary family life by 1728, and each class placed under strict superintendence. Children were brought up away from their parents—after the manner of the Halle Orphan House. The community even attempted to regulate choices in marriage. The ideal was that of a community separate from the world, yet ready to send forces to work anywhere for Christ's kingdom. Yet two tendencies confused this development. The Moravian element would gladly have seen the establishment of a separate denomination, a full revival of the ancient Moravian Church. Zinzendorf clung firmly to the Pietistic idea of an *ecclesiola in ecclesia*. He would keep them part of the Lutheran state church, only a special group within it, where a warmer spiritual life, a "heart-religion," should be fostered. The movement soon met much opposition, not merely from orthodox Lutherans, but from Pietists, both by reason of Herrnhut's peculiarities, and as separatist. On the whole, the separatist tendencies slowly won the upper hand.

The Moravian willingness to go anywhere in the service of Christ soon gave a noble missionary development to the movement which it has never lost. No Protestant body had been so awake to the duty of missions, and none is so consecrated to this service in proportion to its numbers to the present day. A journey to Copenhagen to attend the coronation of Christian VI (1730–1746) of Denmark brought Zinzendorf into contact with natives of the Danish West India Islands and of Greenland. Zinzendorf returned to Herrnhut aflame with missionary enthusiasm. As a result Leonhard Dober and David Nitschmann began a mission to the West Indies in 1732, and Christian David and others to Greenland in 1733. Two years later a considerable party, led by August Gottlieb Spangenberg (1704–1792), began labors in Georgia. For this outreaching work Nitschmann was ordained a bishop—the first of the modern Moravian succession—by Jablonski in 1735.

Meanwhile Zinzendorf's relations with the Saxon government were becoming strained. The Austrian authorities complained, without ground, that he was enticing their subjects. Ecclesiastical complaints were renewed, and on March 20, 1736, he was banished from Saxony. Zinzendorf found opportunity to carry on his work in Ronneburg in western Germany and in the Baltic provinces. In 1737 he was ordained bishop by Jablonski in Berlin. In 1738–1739 he journeyed to the West India Islands; in 1741 he was in London, where Moravian work had been several years in progress. By December, 1741, Zinzendorf was in New York, and on Christmas he named the settlement which Moravians from Georgia were beginning to effect in Pennsylvania, Bethlehem—a town destined to become the American headquarters of the movement. Zinzendorf's sojourn in America was full of activities. He made great efforts toward a union of all the scattered German Protestant forces in Pennsylvania, he began missions to the Indians, he organized seven or eight Moravian congregations and planted schools. Itineracy was established under the superintendence of Peter Böhler. In January, 1743, Zinzendorf sailed for Europe, and in December, 1744, Spangenberg was put in charge of all the American work as bishop. Its most famous Indian missionary was David Zeisberger (1721–1808), who worked among the Creeks of Georgia from 1740, and from 1743 to his death in labor for the Iroquois.

Herrnhut thus became a hive of missionary activity. Missions were begun in Surinam, Guiana, Egypt, and South Africa. In 1771, after repeated attempts, a permanent mission was established in Labrador. The names of its early mission fields show one characteristic of Moravian effort. They were prevailingly hard places, requiring peculiar patience and devotion, and this trait characterizes Moravian missionary labors to the present.

Meanwhile, in spite of Zinzendorf's dislike of separatism, Moravianism was becoming more fully a church. In 1742 it was so recognized in Prussia by the government. By 1745 the Moravian Church was thoroughly organized with bishops, elders, and deacons, though its government was, and still is, more Presbyterian than Episcopal. The English Parliament by a law of 1749 recognized it as "an ancient Protestant Episcopal Church." Yet Zinzendorf did not give up his theory of an *ecclesiola in ecclesia*. Negotiations with the Saxon authorities resulted in his recall from banishment in 1747, the acceptance of the Augsburg Confession by the Moravian body the next year, and its recognition in 1749 as a portion of the Saxon state church, with its own special services. By this time Moravianism was developing a liturgy of much beauty and a hymnody of large fulness.

During the time of his banishment Zinzendorf and some of the Moravians developed certain theological and cultural peculiarities that were the source of deserved criticism. His emphasis on relation to Christ as the heart of religion took on sometimes a sentimental expression in word and hymn. Since Christ, to his thinking, was the Creator, our relation to God the Father is as to the Father of Christ. Since the Holy Spirit effects the new birth, the designation "Mother" seemed to him appropriate. Zinzendorf always made much of the sufferings of Christ, and brought Christian experience into connection with His wounds in a way that was at once fanciful and sentimental. Peculiarly was this the case with His wounded side. Zinzendorf pictured the church as drawn from the side of Christ as Eve from that of Adam. Zinzendorf's insistence that Christians must become as little children to enter the kingdom of God led to much puerility of expression. These peculiarities were at the height of their manifestation between 1747 and 1749, but in large measure they corrected themselves. This period was called by the Moravians themselves "the sifting time." Zinzendorf himself ultimately largely turned away from them. Yet, at the most, they must be regarded as but blemishes on the character of one who could say of his devotion to Christ, as few can: "I have one passion. It is He."

Zinzendorf's life from 1749 to 1755 was spent mostly in England. His property had been spent unstintedly for the Moravians, and he now found himself almost bankrupt. His debts were assumed, as was fitting, by the Moravian body, and gradually discharged. This financial need led to a growth in Moravian constitutional development. A collegiate directorate was established, which soon became a board of control, by which Moravian affairs were superintended, and the taxes paid by the several congregations soon led to their representation in a general synod, meeting at regular intervals.

Zinzendorf's last few years were spent chiefly in pastoral activities. His strength had been lavishly spent, and he was bereaved of his wife and only son. On May 9, 1760, he died in Herrnhut.

The Moravian Church, which Zinzendorf had done so much to renew and inspire, was firmly grounded, so that his death made no serious breach. It was fortunate, however, that its practical leadership fell to Spangenberg, who was called back from America to Herrnhut in 1762, and continued his guidance to his death, thirty years later. Not a man of genius and enthusiasm like Zinzendorf, he was marked by equal devotion, great practical sense, and high organizing abilities. Under his strong, wise guidance Moravianism strengthened and grew; its criticised peculiarities were generally discarded. His work was quiet and unpicturesque but wholly useful. The Moravian Church took its accredited place among the families of Christendom. It gained increasing good-will in Germany, though sufficient of Zinzendorf's *ecclesiolæ in ecclesia* remained to prevent a rapid numerical growth in that land.

SECTION VII. WESLEY AND METHODISM

The condition of religion in England in the early part of the eighteenth century has already been described (*ante,* pp. 485–491). The end of the struggles of the seventeenth century had been marked by a general spiritual lethargy in the establishment and among Dissenters alike. Rationalism had penetrated all classes of religious thinkers, so that even among the orthodox Christianity seemed little more than a system of morality supported by divine sanctions. Butler (*ante,* pp. 489, 490) may stand as typical. His frigid probabilities may have convinced some intellects, but they can have led few men to action. There were able preachers, but the characteristic sermon was the colorless essay on moral virtues. Outreaching work for the unchurched was but scanty. The condition of the lower classes was one of spiritual destitution. Popular amusements were coarse, illiteracy wide-spread, law savage in its enforcement, jails sinks of disease and iniquity. Drunkenness was more wide-spread than at any other period in English history.

Furthermore, Great Britain stood on the eve of the industrial revolution that was to transform it in the last third of the eighteenth century from agriculture to manufacture. James Watt (1736–1819) patented the first really effective steam-engine in 1769. James Hargreaves (?–1778) patented the spinning-jenny in 1770. Richard Arkwright (1732–1792) brought out the spinning-machine in 1768. Edmund Cartwright (1743–1823) invented the power-loom in 1784. Josiah Wedgwood (1730–1795) made the Staffordshire potteries effective from 1762 onward. The industrial and social changes, and problems consequent upon the changes, were of the widest importance, and of themselves involved readjustments of immense practical religious consequence.

There were not wanting men and movements, early in the eighteenth century, looking toward better things. Bishop Berkeley's missionary zeal has already been seen (*ante,* p. 489).

William Law was not only a vigorous opponent of Deism (*ante*, p. 488) but his *Serious Call to a Devout and Holy Life* of 1728 profoundly influenced John Wesley, and remains one of the monuments of English hortatory literature, though it is to be feared now seldom read. The Congregationalist, Isaac Watts (1674–1748), long since forgotten as a theologian, has well been called "the founder of modern English hymnody." His *Hymns* of 1707 and *The Psalms of David, Imitated in the Language of the New Testament* of 1719 broke down the prejudice on both sides of the Atlantic then existing in non-prelatical English-speaking circles against the use of all but rhymed passages of Scripture. They express a deep and vital piety.

Some combined efforts of significance were being made for a warmer religious life. Such were the "societies," the earliest of which was formed by a group of young men in London about 1678, for prayer, reading the Scriptures, the cultivation of a religious life, frequent communion, aid to the poor, soldiers, sailors, and prisoners, and encouragement of preaching. They spread rapidly. By 1700 there were nearly a hundred in London alone, and they were to be found in many parts of England and even in Ireland. One of these societies was formed by John Wesley's father, Samuel Wesley, in Epworth in 1702. In many ways they resembled Spener's *collegia pietatis* (*ante*, p. 497), but they had no Spener to further them. They were composed almost exclusively of communicants of the establishment. Many of the clergy looked upon the movement as "enthusiastic," or as would now be said fanatical, and after 1710 it measurably declined, though the "societies" were to continue and be of importance in the beginnings of Methodism. These "societies" gave the pattern to a more outreaching work, initiated by Thomas Bray (1656–1730). Bray was appointed commissary of Henry Compton, bishop of London (1675–1713), in Maryland in 1696, and in 1699 and 1700 was in that colony strengthening Anglican churches. Impressed with the need of Bibles, libraries, and religious literature, he founded the Society for Promoting Christian Knowledge, on March 8, 1699. Convocation supported it, and led to the foundation on June 27, 1701, of the Society for the Propagation of the Gospel in Foreign Parts, which was to develop into a great missionary society. Both have carried on their work in increasing measure to the present. Both were strictly Anglican and to the work of the latter-named the establishment of Episcopacy in New England and its development in the American colonies were primarily due.

Yet these efforts were at best local and partial in their influence. The mass of the people of England was in spiritual lethargy, yet blindly conscious of sin and convinced of the reality of future reward and retribution. Emotions of loyalty to Christ, of salvation through Him, of a present transforming faith had not been aroused. It needed the appeal of vivid spiritual earnestness—directed to conviction of the heart rather than to considerations of prudence or cold logical argument. That a profound transformation was effected in England, the results of which flowed in beneficent streams to all English-speaking lands, was primarily the work of three men—the brothers John and Charles Wesley and George Whitefield—whose labors were to make England and America vastly different spiritually, and have put those lands permanently into debt to them.

The parents of the Wesley brothers were of Non-Conformist ancestry. Both grandfathers had been among the ejected clergy of 1662. Their father, Samuel Wesley (1662–1735), had preferred the ministry of the establishment, and was, from 1695 to his death, rector of the rough country parish of Epworth. A man of earnest religious disposition, he was somewhat unpractical, a writer of a *Life of Christ in Verse* and of a commentary on the book of *Job*. Their mother, Susanna (Annesley), was a woman of remarkable strength of character, like her husband a devoted Anglican. The sons took much from either parent, but perhaps more of force from the mother. In a household of nineteen children, even if eight died in infancy, hard work and stringent economy were perforce the rule. Of this large brood John was the fifteenth and Charles the eighteenth.

John Wesley was born on June 17, 1703, Charles on December 18, 1707. Both were saved with difficulty from the burning rectory in 1709, an event that made an ineffaceable impression on the mind of John, who thenceforth regarded himself as literally "a brand snatched from the burning." In 1714 John entered the Charterhouse School, in London, and Charles the Westminster School two years later. Both boys distinguished themselves for scholarship. In 1720 John entered

Christ Church College, Oxford, whither Charles followed him six years after, and such was John's intellectual attainment that, in 1726, he was chosen a Fellow of Lincoln College. To become a candidate for that honor John must be in holy orders, and therefore, on September 25, 1725, he was ordained a deacon. With his ordination the spiritual struggles began which were to last till his conversion, in 1738, and perhaps in a sense beyond that time.

From 1726 to 1729 John Wesley was for the most part his father's assistant. On September 22, 1728, he was ordained a priest. During his absence from Oxford, in the spring of 1729, Charles Wesley and two fellow students, Robert Kirkham and William Morgan, formed a little club, primarily for progress in their studies, but which soon engaged in reading helpful books and frequent communion. On his return to Oxford in November, 1729, John Wesley became the leader of the group, which soon attracted other students. Under his guidance it sought to realize William Law's ideals of a consecrated life.   Under Morgan's influence it began visitation of the prisoners in the Oxford jail in August, 1730. The members fasted. Their ideals were high-churchly. They were derided by the university. They were called the "Holy Club," and finally some student hit upon a nickname that stuck, the "Methodists"—though the name had been in currency in the previous century. They were very far as yet from what Methodism was to be. They were still a company painfully bent on working out the salvation of their own souls. As matters then were, they more resembled the Anglo-Catholic movement of the nineteenth century than the Methodism of history.

An important accession to the club, early in 1735, was George Whitefield. Born in Gloucester on December 16, 1714, the son of an inn-keeper, he had grown up in poverty, entering Oxford in 1733. A severe illness in the spring of 1735 brought a crisis in his religious experience, from which he emerged in joyous consciousness of peace with God. In June, 1736, Whitefield sought and received episcopal ordination, and at once, young as he was, began his marvellous career as a preacher. No Anglo-Saxon of the eighteenth century showed such pulpit power. A man absolutely without denominational feeling, in an age when such feelings were usually intense, he was ready to preach anywhere, and in any pulpit open to him. Sometimes censorious as to the genuineness of religious experiences unlike his own, his nature was in the highest degree simple and un-self-seeking. His message was the Gospel of God's forgiving grace, and of peace through acceptance of Christ by faith, and a consequent life of joyful service. His few printed sermons give little sense of his power. Dramatic, pathetic, appealing, with a voice of marvellous expressiveness, the audiences of two continents were as wax melted before him. A large part of his active ministry was spent in America. In 1738 he was in Georgia. In 1739 he was back in America, and his preaching in New England in 1740 was accompanied by the greatest spiritual upheaval ever there witnessed, the "Great Awakening"; nor was his success less in the middle colonies, though there and in New England there was great division of feeling as to the permanent spiritual value of his work. The years 1744 to 1748 saw him again on this side of the Atlantic, once more in 1751 and 1752; again in 1754 and 1755. His sixth visit was from 1763 to 1765. In 1769 he came for his last preaching tour, and died in Newburyport, Mass., on September 30, 1770. He had given himself unstintedly to the service of the American churches of every Protestant family. He was no organizer. He left no party to bear his name, but he awakened thousands.

None of the leaders of the Methodist Club was destined long to remain in Oxford, nor did their movement have much influence on the university, which was then in scholastic and religious ebb. The death of their father on April 25, 1735, whom John Wesley would gladly have succeeded, if possible, in Epworth, left the Wesleys less bound to home, and both now gained employment as missionaries to the new colony of Georgia, the settlement of which had been begun by General Oglethorpe, in 1733. They sailed in October, 1735. On the voyage they were unremitting in religious exercises and efforts for their fellow passengers; but in the ship was a company of twenty-six Moravians, headed by Bishop David Nitschmann. The cheerful courage of this company in a storm convinced John Wesley that the Moravians had a trust in God that was not yet his. From them he learned much. Soon after reaching Savannah he met Spangenberg (*ante*, pp. 504–506), who asked him the embarrassing question: "Do you know Jesus Christ?"

Wesley answered: "I know He is the Saviour of the world."
Spangenberg responded: "True, but do you know He has saved
you?"

The Wesleys' labors in Georgia were strenuous, yet most unsuccessful. Charles Wesley returned home in disgust and ill
health in 1736. John continued. He showed his marvellous
linguistic abilities by conducting services in German, French,
and Italian. In May, 1737, he founded a little society in
Savannah for cultivating the warmer religious life. He worked
indefatigably, yet with little peace of mind or comfort to others.
He was a punctilious high-churchman. He lacked tact. A
conspicuous case was that of Sophy Hopkey, a woman in every
way suitable to be his wife. He gave her and her friends every
encouragement to believe his intentions earnest, but he see-
sawed up and down between clerical celibacy and possible
matrimony. A vein of superstition always present in Wesley,
which led him to decide important questions by the first verse
of Scripture to which he should open, or by drawing lots, led
him now to the latter method of decision as to the marriage.
The lot fell adverse, and Wesley naturally aroused the resentment of the young woman and of her relatives. In a pique she
married hastily another suitor. The husband objected to her
continuance in attendance on Wesley's intimate religious discussions. Wesley now felt that she was not making proper
preparation for communion, and refused her the sacrament.
No wonder her friends charged that this was the act of a dis-
gruntled suitor. Wesley's influence in Georgia was at an end.
Suits were started against him. He decided to leave the colony
for home. On February 1, 1738, John Wesley was back in
England. As on his outward voyage, he had feared death. In
his bitterness of disappointment he could only say: "I have a
fair summer religion." Yet he was a preacher of marked power,
he had labored unsparingly. He had made a good many mistakes, but they were not those which show lack of Christian
consecration.

Fortunately for their distressed state of mind, within a week
of John Wesley's return both brothers were in familiar intercourse with a Moravian, Peter Böhler, delayed in London till
May on his way to Georgia. Böhler taught a complete self-
surrendering faith, an instantaneous conversion, and a joy in
believing. But though before sailing Böhler organized a

"society," later to be known as the "Fetter-Lane Society," of which John Wesley was one of the original members, neither brother was as yet at peace. That experience, his "conversion," came to Charles Wesley, then suffering from a serious illness, on May 21, 1738. On Wednesday, May 24, the transforming experience came to John. That evening, as he recorded, he went unwillingly to an Anglican "society" in Aldersgate Street, London, and heard Luther's preface to the *Commentary on Romans* read. "About a quarter before nine, while he [Luther] was describing the change which God works in the heart through faith in Christ, I felt my heart strangely warmed. I felt I did trust in Christ, Christ alone, for salvation; and an assurance was given me, that He had taken away my sins, even mine, and saved me from the law of sin and death." Of the far-reaching significance of this experience there can be no question. It determined thenceforth Wesley's estimate of the normal mode of entrance on the Christian life. It was the light of all his theologic insight. Yet it was in some measure gradually, even after it, and by preaching and observing a similar work in others and by communion with God, that he entered into full freedom from fear and complete joy in believing.

John Wesley determined to know more of the Moravians, who had helped him thus far. Less than three weeks after his conversion he was on his way to Germany. He met Zinzendorf in Marienborn, spent two weeks in Herrnhut, and in September, 1738, was back in London. It was a happy visit for Wesley. He saw much to admire. Yet he was not pleased with all. He felt that Zinzendorf was treated with too great deference, and that Moravian piety was not without its subjective limitations. Much as he owed to the Moravians, Wesley was too active in religious attitude, too little mystical, too outreaching to men in their wider needs, to be fully a Moravian.

John and Charles Wesley now preached as opportunities offered, finding many pulpits closed to their "enthusiasm," and speaking chiefly in the "societies" in and about London. Early in 1739 Whitefield was developing a great work in Bristol, and there on February 17 he began preaching in the open to the coal miners of Kingswood. He now entered into friendly relations with Howel Harris (1714–1773), who had been working with great success, since 1736, as a lay preacher in Wales. Whitefield now invited John Wesley to Bristol. Wesley hesitated about field-preaching; but the opportunity to proclaim the Gospel to the needy was irresistible, and on April 2 he began in Bristol what was thenceforth to be his practice for more than fifty years, as long as strength permitted. Charles Wesley soon followed his example. While without Whitefield's dramatic power, John Wesley was a preacher with few equals in popular effectiveness—earnest, practical, fearless. Thenceforward he was to tour England, Scotland, and Ireland. Attacked, especially in the early part of his ministry, in peril from mob violence, no danger could daunt him, or interruption could check him. Under his preaching, as under that of Whitefield, remarkable exhibitions of bodily excitement were frequent. Men and women cried out, fainted, were torn with convulsions. To both preachers these seemed the working of the Spirit of God, or the visible resistance of the devil. They are the frequent accompaniments of great religious excitement among the ignorant and uncontrolled, and the disfavor with which they were regarded accounts for much of the opposition which these preachers encountered from the regular clergy.

John Wesley's gifts as an organizer were pre-eminent. Yet the creation of Methodism was a gradual work—an adaptation of means to circumstances. In Bristol he founded in 1739 his first really Methodist "society," and began the erection of the first chapel there on May 12, 1739. Late that year he secured in London an old "foundery," which became the first chapel there.

Thus far, in London, the Methodists had also joined in the Moravian Fetter-Lane Society, which Peter Böhler had founded in 1738 (ante, p. 513). Wesley's ideals were leading him away from Moravianism. This separation was increased when, in October, 1739, Philipp Heinrich Molther, just come from Zinzendorf, asserted in Fetter-Lane, that if any man had doubts he had no true faith, and should absent himself from the sacraments and prayer, awaiting in silence till God should renew his religious hope. Such teaching found little sympathy from Wesley's strenuous activity. The Fetter-Lane Society was divided. Wesley and his friends withdrew and founded a purely Methodist "United Society" in the Foundery, on July 23, 1740. Wesley continued on friendly terms with some of the Moravians, but thenceforth the movements were independent of each other.

Wesley had no desire or intention of breaking with the Church of England. He did not, therefore, found churches, but took up into service the device of the long-existing "religious societies," but these should now consist only of converted persons. These "societies" were from the first divided into "bands," or groups, within the society, for mutual cultivation of the Christian life. This was a Moravian device; but experience soon showed Wesley something more efficient. Soon after the Bristol society was formed Wesley hit on the plan of giving "society tickets" to those whom he found sufficiently grounded to be full members, and receiving others on trial. These tickets were renewable quarterly, and furnished a ready means of sifting the society. The debt on the Bristol chapel led to a yet more important arrangement. On February 15, 1742, the members were divided into "classes" of about twelve persons, each under a "class leader," charged to collect a penny weekly from each member. This system was introduced in London on March 25. Its advantages for spiritual oversight and mutual watch were soon even more apparent than its financial merits. It soon became one of the characteristic features of Methodism, though the older "bands," also, long continued.

Wesley would have preferred to have all preaching by ordained men, but few of the clergy were sympathetic with the movement. A lay preacher, Joseph Humphreys, was helping him as early as 1738; but extensive use was not made of this agency till 1742, when Thomas Maxfield became regularly the earliest of what soon became a considerable company. The growth of the movement developed other lay officers, "stewards," to care for property, teachers for schools, "visitors of the sick," for the duties which their names implied. At first Wesley visited all "societies," which were chiefly in the regions of London and Bristol, but the task soon became too great. In 1744 he had the preachers meet him in London—the first of the "Annual Conferences." Two years later the field was divided into "circuits," with travelling preachers and more stationary leaders to "assist chiefly in one place." Soon an "assistant," later called a "superintendent," was placed in charge of each "circuit." Wesley endeavored by suitable publications to aid the intellectual development of his lay preachers and secured study as far as possible. He tried in vain to obtain episcopal ordination for them; but would not allow the sacraments to be administered by unordained men.

While Wesley stood theologically on the common basis of Evangelical doctrinal tradition and regarded his "societies" as part of the Church of England, two disputes led to considerable controversy. One was regarding perfection. Wesley believed it possible for a Christian to attain right ruling motives—love to God and to his neighbor—and that such attainment would free from sin. To Wesley's cautious and sober judgment this was an aim rather than a frequently completed achievement—however it may have appeared to some of his followers. No man was ever more positive than he that salvation evidences itself in a life of active, strenuous obedience to the will of God.

A second dispute was regarding predestination. Wesley, like the Church of England generally of his time, was Arminian, but he had derived a special parental hostility to Calvinism, which seemed to him paralyzing to moral effort. Whitefield was Calvinistic. A hot interchange of letters took place between the two Evangelists in 1740 and 1741. Their good personal relations were soon restored in large measure. Whitefield found a supporter, in 1748, in Selina, countess of Huntingdon (1707–1791), a wealthy widow, a convert to Methodism, but far too dominant a character to yield to Wesley's insistent leadership. She would be her own Wesley, and, like Wesley, founded and superintended "societies" and chapels—the first in Brighton in 1761—thus beginning the "Lady Huntingdon's Connection." She made Whitefield her chaplain. Her "Connection" was Calvinist. In 1769 the predestinarian controversy broke out with renewed intensity. At the "Conference" of 1770, Wesley took a strongly Arminian position. Whitefield died that year, but Wesley was fiercely attacked by Augustus Toplady (1740–1778), author of the hymn "Rock of Ages." Wesley was defended by his devoted disciple, the Swiss John William de la Flechère (1729–1785), who had settled in England and accepted a living in the establishment in 1760 (Fletcher of Madeley), where he was to do notable work. The effect of these discussions was to confirm the Arminian character of Wesleyan Methodism. Yet "Lady Huntingdon's Connection" and these Calvinistic Dissenters must be regarded as parallel rather than as hostile movements. Their fundamental spirit was essentially the same as that of Wesley.

The Methodist movement grew enormously. John Wesley had many friends and assistants, but few intimates who shared his responsibilities. His brother Charles long had part in his constant travels, but Charles had not the iron constitution of John. After 1756 Charles itinerated seldom. He labored in Bristol, and from 1771 to his death on March 29, 1788, he preached in London. He was always more conservative than John, and more Anglican. His great service was as the hymn-writer, not merely of Methodism, but of all English-speaking Christianity. John's unwise marriage to a widow, Mrs. Mary Vazeille, in 1751, was unhappy. He devoted himself all the more unreservedly to his work. Over all the multitudinous concerns of Methodism he exercised a wise but absolute authority. Naturally, as the "societies" grew and preachers multiplied pressure rose for authority to administer the sacraments, this Wesley resisted long; but episcopally ordained men were few, and the force of events made the pressure irresistible in spite of Wesley's insistence that his movement was within the establishment.

Methodism was carried to America by Philip Embury (1728–1773), who began work in New York in 1766, and Robert Strawbridge (?–1781), who was laboring in Maryland about the same time. A vigorous early preacher was Captain Thomas Webb (1724–1796) of the British army. So promising was the work that, in 1771, Wesley sent over Francis Asbury (1745–1816)—a most wise choice. These were all lay preachers. By 1773 the first American "Conference" was held in Philadelphia. Then came the storm of the Revolutionary War, but Methodism grew in spite of it. With peace, in 1783, dependence on England was no longer desirable, and the sacramental question was even more pressing than in England, as in many regions of the United States there were no Episcopal Churches to which the Methodists could resort. Wesley had tried in vain, in 1780, to procure ordination for clergymen for America from the bishop of London. He had long been convinced that bishops and presbyters in the ancient church were one order. He therefore, as a presbyter, felt empowered to ordain in case of necessity. At Bristol, on September 1, 1784, he and his intimate disciple, Thomas Coke (1747–1814), like Wesley a presbyter of the establishment, ordained Richard Whatcoat and Thomas Vasey as presbyters for America; and the next day, "assisted by other ordained ministers" "set" Coke "apart as a superintendent" for the same work. This was, indeed, a breach with the Church of England, though Wesley did not then see it as such. His brother Charles disliked the act. The necessity was great, and no non-prelatical believer can blame Wesley. Regret has often been expressed that Wesley and the church of his affections were thus compelled to separate. It would have been of infinite advantage if some solution other than division could have been found; but in the existing state of ideals and organization it seems well-nigh impossible to conceive what adjustment could then have been proposed with success.

Under date of September 10, 1784, Wesley notified his action to the American Methodists, and also informed them that he had appointed Asbury as well as Coke "superintendents." In December, 1784, Wesley's newly consecrated ministers held a "conference" in Baltimore, at which Asbury was ordained "elder" and "superintendent," and it was "agreed to form a Methodist Episcopal Church." By 1788 Coke and Asbury were called "bishops," and that title thenceforth supplanted "superintendent" in America. Once begun, Wesley in the course of the next few years ordained ministers for Scotland, Antigua, Newfoundland, and finally England.

Another event of 1784 was of great importance. Wesley had been thus far the controlling force in Methodism. By a "Deed of Declaration," of February 28, he now provided that those who should preach in the chapels should be such as the "Conference" should recognize, and otherwise defined the powers of that body. It was a great step toward the self-government of Methodism.

Wesley's strength and activities continued unabated almost to the end. On March 2, 1791, he died in London, having done a work which had largely revolutionized the religious condition of the English lower and middle clasess, and was even more largely to affect America.

SECTION VIII.   SOME EFFECTS OF METHODISM

The great Wesleyan revival was felt beyond the range of its nominal adherents. Its influence on the older Non-Conformist bodies was stimulating though very unequal. Their condition in the first half of the eighteenth century was one of decay.

Their leaders looked askance at Wesley and Whitefield at first; but as the revival continued the younger men caught its zeal. This was especially the case among the Congregationalists, who profited most of all. Their preaching was quickened, their zeal revived, their numbers rapidly increased. Many accessions came to them from those awakened by Methodism to whom the Methodist discipline was irksome. Many came to them from parishes of the establishment. By 1800 the Congregationalists occupied a very different position in England from that of 1700. The Particular Baptists also shared in this growth, though to less extent, since their Calvinism was intense and antagonistic to Wesleyan Arminianism. The General Baptists, in spite of a considerable leaven of Socinianism, also gained by the revival. They were divided—the General Baptist New Connection of 1770, being Evangelical. The Presbyterians, on the other hand, were almost unaffected. Arianism and Socinianism were dominant among them. Their numbers dwindled. Nor were the Quakers much moved. Their noble humanitarian zeal was never more manifest, but the revival methods were too foreign to their spirit to make much impression.

Wesley won many sympathizers in the establishment. These men were generally in agreement with his religious emphases, on conversion, a confident faith, a religious life manifested in active work for others. On the other hand, they adopted few of his peculiar methods, and in general were marked theologically by an extremely moderate Calvinism rather than by his aggressive Arminianism. Whitefield was the spiritual father of many. They were never a body. They were rather a way of thinking, and to it the name Evangelical or low-church was given. Conspicuous among these Evangelicals were John Newton (1725–1807), once a slave-dealing shipmaster. Converted, he became one of the most helpful of preachers, first in Olney and then as rector of St. Mary Woolnoth in London. His hymns express his cheerful, confident faith.

Thomas Scott (1747–1821), Newton's successor in Olney, was best known for his *Family Bible with Notes*—a commentary of immense popularity on both sides of the Atlantic. Richard Cecil (1748–1810) in later life was one of the most influential preachers in London. Joseph Milner (1744–1797) made Hull an Evangelical stronghold and won much influence through his

History of the Church of Christ, continued after his death by his brother, Isaac, in which he emphasized the development of Christian biography rather than the disputes of Christianity. Isaac Milner (1750–1820), was long a professor in Cambridge and aided in making the tone of that university largely Evangelical, a work which was continued there in power by Charles Simeon (1759–1836).

Several not in clerical ranks were instrumental in the spread of Evangelical opinions. Such was William Cowper (1731–1800), the greatest English poet of the latter half of the eighteenth century, and Newton's warm friend. In Hannah More (1745–1833) Evangelicalism had a supporter personally acquainted with the literary, artistic, and theatrical circles of London, a writer of tracts and stories of unbounded popularity and herself of generous and self-denying philanthropy. Zachary Macaulay (1768–1838), father of the historian, was a determined opponent of the slave trade. That evil had received John Wesley's severest condemnation. It had been vigorously opposed by the Quakers. Its most effective enemy was one of the most eminent of Evangelical laymen, William Wilberforce (1759–1833). Wealthy, popular, and a member of Parliament, he was "converted" in 1784 through the instrumentality of Isaac Milner. In 1797 he published his *Practical View of the Prevailing Religious System of Professed Christians in the Higher and Middle Classes in this Country Contrasted with real Christianity*. It proved one of the most popular of Evangelical treatises. In 1787 he began his lifelong battle with slavery, resulting in the abolition of the slave trade in 1807, and of slavery itself throughout the British dominions in 1833.

The Methodist movement was forward-looking in its philanthropic sympathies, and the Evangelicals shared this trait. Methodism, under Wesley's leadership, sought to aid its poorer members financially, to provide work, to care for the sick, to furnish schools and cheap reading, and to overcome the coarseness and brutality of the lower classes.

The awakening of the new spirit of humanitarianism had one of its noblest illustrations in John Howard (1726–1790), a quiet, religious, country landlord, interested in schools and model cottages, a worshipper in Congregational and Baptist congregations; Howard was chosen high sheriff of Bedford in 1773. He was inexpressibly shocked at the moral and physical filth of the jails, their officers supported by what they could wring from the prisoners, not by salaries; no proper separation of prisoners, no release for those acquitted till their fees were discharged. Thorough in all that he did, Howard visited practically all the jails of England, and laid the horrible results before Parliament in 1774. He then did a similar work for Scotland, Ireland, and the Continent. Much remained to be done, but he deserves the title of the "father of prison reform." His last years were devoted to equally self-sacrificing efforts to ascertain methods to prevent the spread of the plague. His devotion cost him his life in southern Russia.

The Society for Promoting Christian Knowledge had been founded in 1699 (*ante*, p. 508), but the revival movement gave a great impulse to the diffusion of Christian literature. Wesley made that one of his chief agencies, publishing constantly. In 1799 the interdenominational Religious Tract Society was formed in London. Even earlier, in 1789, the Methodist Book Concern had been founded on this side of the Atlantic. The New York Religious Tract Society, which was to be merged with other local organizations into the American Tract Society, was begun in 1812. Pietism had set the example of extensive and cheap publication of the Bible through Baron Canstein's great foundation in Halle, in 1710 (*ante*, p. 500). In 1804 the British and Foreign Bible Society was founded in London through the efforts of Evangelicals. Ireland and Scotland soon followed; in 1808 the first of a series of local societies was organized in Philadelphia, and out of consolidation the American Bible Society came into existence in 1816. By their work the present enormous diffusion of the Scriptures has been made possible.

Some form of religious teaching of children is probably as old as organized religion, and the Reformation age made much of catechetical instruction. Though attempts were made even earlier, the first systematic and successful efforts to reach the poor and unschooled with a Christian training on a large scale were in the Sunday schools, founded in 1780 by Robert Raikes (1735–1811), an Evangelical layman of the establishment, of Gloucester. In the absence of public education, he sought to give the ignorant training in the three "R's," and in Christian fundamentals by means of paid teachers, on the only day, Sunday, when the children were free. Attendance at church was also required. Raikes was proprietor of the *Gloucester Journal*, which published accounts of these activities. The work spread with great rapidity. Wesley and the Non-Conformists favored them. A Society for Promoting Sunday Schools throughout the British Dominions, was organized in London in 1785. A similar society was formed in Philadelphia in 1791. Though the growth of the movement was as rapid as it was permanent, it was not without clerical opposition, partly on account of its novelty and partly as a desecration of Sunday. The secular instruction rapidly decreased, and the paid teacher gave place to the voluntary leader. No Christian agency has become more fully part of normal modern church life.

SECTION IX. THE MISSIONARY AWAKENING

The development of Roman Catholic missions in the Reformation age was rapid and fruitful (pp. 429, 430, 565). Lack of geographical contact with heathen lands and internal problems prevented any equivalent Protestant efforts. With Dutch conquests work was begun in Ceylon, Java, and Formosa in the seventeenth century. The first English foreign missionary organization, the Society for the Propagation of the Gospel in New England, came into existence by act of Parliament in 1649, in response to the efforts among the Massachusetts Indians of John Eliot (1604–1690). At its expense his Indian Bible and other works, were printed. The Society for the Propagation of the Gospel in Foreign Parts was organized in 1701 (*ante*, p. 508). German Pietism produced the Halle-Danish missions from 1705 onward (*ante*, p. 500). In 1732 the notable missionary career of the Moravians began (*ante*, p. 504). Quakers had made some missionary efforts.

Interest in non-Christian peoples was aroused in Great Britain by the voyages of discovery in the Pacific, under government auspices, conducted by Captain James Cook (1728–1779), from 1768 to his death. These discoveries awakened the missionary zeal of William Carey (1761–1834), a shoemaker, then a Baptist preacher, and who was to show himself a man of remarkable talents as a linguist and a botanist, as well as of unquenchable missionary devotion. The result of his thought was his *Enquiry into the Obligation of Christians to use Means for the Conversion of the Heathens* of 1792. In October of that year this book and Carey's sermon on *Isaiah* 54[2, 3] induced the organization of the Baptist Society for Propagating the Gospel among the Heathen.   Carey was its first missionary, and his letters from India proved a powerful stimulus to other missionary endeavor.   In 1795 the London Missionary Society was formed, as an interdenominational enterprise, largely through the efforts of David Bogue (1750–1825), a Congregational minister of Gosport, and of Thomas Haweis (1734–1820), the Evangelical rector of Aldwinkle.   Its first missionaries were sent in 1796 to Tahiti.   It has long been Congregational. The growing sense of missionary obligation led in 1799 to the organization of the Church Missionary Society, representative of the Evangelical wing of the establishment, through the agency of John Venn (1759–1813), rector of Clapham, and Thomas Scott, editor of the *Family Bible*.

This deepening of English missionary obligation roused interest widely in other lands.   In the United States news of these efforts aroused the zeal of a group of students in Williams College, among whom Samuel J. Mills, Jr. (1783–1818), was leader, and resulted in the formation in 1810 of the American Board of Commissioners for Foreign Missions—originally interdenominational, but long since essentially Congregational. Its first missionaries were sent to India in 1812.   In 1814 the American Baptist Missionary Union came into being.   The Wesleyan Methodist Missionary Society of England was founded in 1813, and its American Methodist counterpart in 1819. The Dutch Reformed and Presbyterian Churches of the United States, which had co-operated with the American Board, formed their own organizations in 1835 and 1837.   After small local beginnings in Scotland, as early as 1796, the Church of Scotland Mission Boards came into being in 1825.

On the Continent the Basel Evangelical Missionary Society dates from 1815 ; the Danish Missionary Society from 1821 ; the Berlin Society from 1824 ; and that of Paris from the same year.

The nineteenth century witnessed a constant extension of missionary activities, Protestant and Catholic, a more pervading sense of missionary obligation, and a constant increase in the number of those men and women who thus consecrate themselves to the spread of the Gospel.   No greater change has taken place in the religious life of the last century and a half than the general diffusion of the spirit of missions.

England had well advanced in its Deistic, rationalistic, and Unitarian development before the rise of Methodism. There the two streams long ran parallel. If Methodism, theologically, was a return to older doctrinal conceptions, it was even more an appeal to the strong, deep religious feelings of the nation. In Germany Pietism, with its emphasis on feeling, preceded the Enlightenment (Aufklärung), though continuing to run parallel to the latter movement when that developed. The Enlightenment in Germany was sure to come. Pietism had broken the grasp of confessional orthodoxy, but it had raised up no theological leaders to take the intellectual place of the older dogmatic theologians. The eighteenth century, with its critical rationalistic spirit; the works of the English Deists and their opponents; and the radical popular modification of Deism in France, necessarily invaded Germany and found the intellectual field vacant, through the discrediting of confessional orthodoxy and the constructive inefficiency of Pietism. The result was the rapid growth of the Enlightenment, as it styled itself. To call it rationalism is not quite just, though that it largely became. It represented many shades. Its chief importance is that, more than in England or in France, by its critical and constructive work it prepared the way for a great reconstruction in theology, which, in the nineteenth century, was to spread widely throughout Protestant lands.

Leibnitz's speculations (*ante*, p. 485) were too deep to produce a profound impression on his own age, though later they were of powerful effect. Thomasius (*ante*, p. 499) spread a rationalistic spirit, without working out a system. His influence was marked in developing an attitude of mind, so that he has not untruly been described as the "road-breaker of the Enlightenment." Its great protagonist, however, was Christian Wolff (1679–1754). Not a creative genius, it was Wolff's fortune so to embody and give expression to the unformed and inarticulate thought of his age, as to become the philosophical and theological leader of two generations of his countrymen. Skilled in mathematics, like most of the philosophers of his and the preceding century, he began lecturing on mathematics in Halle in 1707. Here his philosophy rapidly developed, in close connection with that of Leibnitz, whose deeper thoughts, however, he never grasped. That alone is true, Wolff held, which can be demonstrated by logical certainty akin to mathematics. Truth must thus rationally be deduced from the innate contents of the mind—the "pure reason." All that comes by experience is merely contingent and confirmatory. The world is composed of an infinite multitude of simple substances, each endowed with force, though not with all the qualities of Leibnitz's monads (*ante*, p. 485). Bodies are aggregations of these substances. The world is a huge machine, ruled by mechanical laws. The soul is that in us which is conscious of itself and of other objects. It is endowed with capacities of knowledge and desire. Their completeness of fulfilment is pleasure, their incompleteness, pain.

Since the world is contingent, it must have a cause. Hence God exists and has made the world. The laws of all rational thinking and acting give us the divine attributes. Since completeness is the highest aim of all being, all that aims at the completeness of ourselves and other men must be virtue. Hence the principles of right action are embodied, as with the Deists, in the fundamental divinely appointed constitution of man. Wolff did not deny that there might be revelation, though, if so, it could contain nothing not in agreement with reason; nor are miracles impossible, though improbable, and each would imply two acts of equal power, the interruption of the order of nature and its restoration after the event. Wolff's view of man was optimistic. He is going on individually, and socially, to larger completeness. Here was a breach with the older theology, both of orthodoxy and of Pietism, and one that came to its age with the conclusiveness of a logical demonstration. God, natural religion, originally implanted morality, and progress toward individual and racial perfection, not supernatural revelation or supernatural rescue from sin and ruin, are the proper objects of religious regard, even if Wolff allows a little standing room to revelation and miracle. Nor is man the hopeless or incapable being of the older theology.

Wolff's views aroused the hostility of his Pietistic colleagues in Halle. They procured from King Frederick William I (1713–1740) his removal. The royal sentence was even to them surprisingly strenuous. Wolff was ordered, in 1723, to leave the university within forty-eight hours, or be hanged. He found a refuge in Marburg, and was honorably restored to

Halle in 1740 by Frederick the Great. His work had, however, become common property, and he added little to his achievements during the fourteen years in Halle till his death. His thought had become that of a large section of Germany. The sway of Pietism in Halle was over.

Less radical, but influential in aiding the new attitude of German thought, was Johann Lorentz von Mosheim (1694?–1755), professor in Helmstädt and finally in Göttingen. The most admired preacher of his time, master of a style of brilliancy in Latin or in German, his influence was essentially latitudinarian. He had no sympathy with the dogmatism of the orthodox. The emphases of the Pietists awakened no response in him; nor could he support the extreme rationalism of Wolff. He touched most fields of religious thought, and his influence, on the whole, favored the spread of the Enlightenment. His chief service was in the field of history. His *Institutiones*, first issued in 1726 and in final form in 1755, embraced the whole story of the church. In his *Commentarii de rebus Christianorum ante Constantinum* of 1753, he treated the earlier centuries in ampler fashion. Mosheim well deserves the name of "the father of modern church history." He desired to be free of all partisan bias, and succeeded in remarkable measure at the expense of some colorlessness. His is the first church history which aimed to tell events exactly as they happened, without a cause to defend. As such, and by reason of its learning and style, his work long survived his death.

More extreme rationalism soon found its representatives in Germany. Hermann Samuel Reimarus (1694–1768), long a highly reputed professor of Oriental languages in Hamburg, and the leader in scholarly circles there, had travelled in England in early life, and had there adopted Deist views, in defense of which he wrote much, though his works were not issued till after his death, when they were put forth by Lessing between 1774 and 1778 as fragments found in the library of Wolfenbüttel—hence *Wolfenbüttel Fragments*, the publication of which aroused immense discussion. As with the Deists, all that is true is that natural religion which teaches the existence of a wise Creator, a primitive morality, and immortality—all ascertainable by reason. The world itself is the only miracle and the only revelation—all others are impossible. The writers of the Bible were not even honest men, but were moved by fraud

and selfishness. It is a curious commentary on the condition
of thought in Germany that Reimarus's writings, though widely
criticised, were no less valued by others as a defense of religion
against materialism and atheism.

Gotthold Ephraim Lessing (1729–1781), to whom the publication of Reimarus's religious writings was due, eminent as a
dramatist and a literary and artistic critic, himself ranking as
a German classic writer with Goethe and Schiller, though not
agreeing wholly with Reimarus, presented in his *Education of
the Human Race* of 1780 a theory of much plausibility. As the
individual passes through the successive stages of childhood,
youth, and manhood, so does the race. The Scriptures have
been given by God to meet these needs. Childhood is moved
by immediate rewards and punishments. For men in that
condition the Old Testament is a divine book of training, with
its promises of long life and temporal blessings for obedience.
Youth is ready to sacrifice present ease and lesser goods for
future success and happiness. For it, or for men in that state,
the New Testament with its present self-surrender and eternal
rewards is a fitting guide. But manhood is ruled by duty,
without hope of reward or fear of punishment as its motives.
Its guide is reason, though perhaps God may yet send some
further revelation as its aid. Lessing's work spread wide the
feeling in educated Germany that the historic Christian religion belonged to a past or to an inferior present stage of
human development.

The effect of the Enlightenment was a wide diffusion of the
views that what alone were valuable in the Scriptures were the
truths of natural religion and its morality, divested of miracle
or the supernatural. Jesus was a moral teacher rather than a
personal centre of faith. This was rationalism, and was characteristic of much of the strongest theological thinking of Germany by 1800, and was to continue powerful in the nineteenth
century. Side by side with it, confessional orthodoxy and
Pietism continued, though with decreasing intellectual appeal,
and much, also, which may be called semi-rationalism. Yet
the age was characterized, also, by vigorous polemic against
superstitions, and a large development of voluntary and
popular beneficence, and provision for popular education.

The eighteenth century was also marked, and nowhere more
than in Germany, by the development of textual and historical

studies of the Bible which initiated the modern period of criticism. The English scholar, John Mill (1645–1707), published a Greek Testament, based on a careful collation of manuscripts, in the year of his death. Jean le Clerc (1657–1736), brought up in Geneva, later an Arminian in Amsterdam from 1684 to his death, won fame as an exegete, through his attempts to explain the teaching of the Scriptures without dogmatic prepossessions—approaching them not to discover proof texts, but their actual meaning. Johann Albrecht Bengel (1687–1752), long head of the theological seminary in Denkendorf, in Württemberg, a man of Pietistic leanings, was the first to recognize that New Testament manuscripts may be grouped in families, and to establish the generally accepted critical canon that a more difficult reading is to be preferred. His *Gnomon*, or Index, of the New Testament, of 1742, was the most remarkable commentary thus far produced. Nothing, he declared, should be read into the Scripture, and nothing there contained omitted, which could be drawn out by the most rigid application of grammatical principles. Wesley made it the basis of his *Notes upon the New Testament* of 1755. Contemporaneously Johann Jakob Wettstein (1693–1754), of Basel and Amsterdam, spent nearly a lifetime of labor on his *Greek New Testament with Various Reading*, published in 1751–1752. Textual criticism and sound exegesis were thus given a great advance.

To Jean Astruc (1684–1766), royal professor of medicine in Paris, was due the announcement, in his *Conjectures* of 1753, of the composite character of *Genesis*. The theory won essential support in 1781 from Johann Gottfried Eichhorn (1752–1827), later the rationalistic professor in Göttingen, often called "the founder of Old Testament criticism," but it is only in the latter part of the nineteenth century that Astruc's discovery won extensive recognition.

In Johann August Ernesti (1707–1781), professor in Leipzig from 1742, Germany had a teacher who not only aided greatly that awakening of classical thought and ideals which affected German intellectual life in the closing years of the eighteenth century, but one who carried to New Testament interpretation the same principles which he applied to classical literature. The meaning is to be ascertained by the same grammatical and historical methods in the one field as in the other. Reimarus (*ante*, p. 526), in his seventh Fragment, published by Lessing in 1778, for the first time subjected the life of Christ to rigid historic methods, like those applied to secular history. His total rejection of the supernatural, the mythical, or the legendary left his results barren enough, but he raised questions of method and conclusion which have constituted the problems of this investigation, in large measure, ever since. Johann Salomo Semler (1725–1791), professor in Halle from 1752, was of Pietistic training, though in manhood a conservative rationalist. His importance was in the paths he indicated rather than in the results he achieved. He distinguished between the permanent truths in Scripture and the elements due to the times in which the several books were written. He denied the equal value of all parts of Scripture. Revelation, he taught, is in Scripture, but all Scripture is not revelation. The creeds of the church are a growth. Church history is a development. In particular he made a distinction between Petrine, Judaizing parties, in the early church, and Pauline, anti-Judaic, that was to play a great rôle in later discussions.

SECTION XI. ROMANTICISM

Nothing seemed more characteristic of the earlier half of the eighteenth century than the dominance of "reason," or common sense. The age was unemotional, intellectual. It did a remarkable work in questioning that which had been accepted on tradition, in sweeping away ancient superstitions and abuses, and demanding the rightfulness of that which claimed authority. But it was cold and one-sided. It was met, as the eighteenth century went on, by an immense opposition. The claims of feeling asserted themselves, voiced in a "return to nature," that was too often a nature conjured up by the imagination, but accompanied by a renewed appreciation of the classical and the mediæval, and the revival of a sense of the supernatural in religion, often vague and obscure, but creating a totally different atmosphere in which man's claims as a feeling, rather than as a purely thinking, being were asserted.

Its most effective apostle was Jean Jacques Rousseau (1712–1778); but the movement was manifested throughout Europe. Nowhere was it more evident than in Germany. Lessing shared it. Its most conspicuous literary representatives there were Johann Wolfgang von Goethe (1749–1832) and Johann Christoph Friedrich von Schiller (1759–1805). The older rationalism was not, indeed, swept from the field, but a totally different habit of thought contended on more than equal terms for the mastery—that of Romanticism.

Philosophy, in the eighteenth century, had seemed to lead to no thoroughfare. Leibnitz had taught that all knowledge was an elucidation of that which was wrapped up innate in the monad. Wolff had affirmed the power of "pure reason" to give the only certainties. On the other hand, Locke had taught that all comes by experience, and though Hume had pushed to scepticism all conclusion based on cause and substance, he had viewed, like Locke, all knowledge as founded on experience. The British and the German tendencies were apparently mutually destructive. It was to be the work of Kant to combine and supersede both, on a new basis which should be the starting-point of modern philosophy, and to give a value to feeling which neither earlier parties had recognized.

Immanuel Kant (1724–1804) was a native of Königsberg, where all his life was spent. His paternal ancestry, he believed, was Scotch. His earliest influences were Pietist. In 1755 Kant became a teacher in the University of Königsberg. His development was slow. He held at first to the school of Leibnitz-Wolff. Study of Hume awakened doubts as to its adequacy, though he did not become Hume's disciple. Rousseau profoundly influenced him with the "discovery of the deep hidden nature of man." In 1781 came Kant's epoch-making work, the *Critique of Pure Reason*—a blow struck primarily at the then dominant philosophy of Wolff. His formative treatises rapidly followed, and his thought was soon powerful in Germany. By 1797 his mental and physical powers had begun a decline which was to end in pitiful ruin. A little man in physical stature, never married, of strict moral uprightness, he devoted himself to his task with singular simplicity and fidelity.

Kant's system is in many respects a theory of knowledge. With the school of Locke and Hume he held that in our knowledge something, or some stimulus—the content—comes to the mind from without. With Leibnitz and Wolff he maintained that the mind has certain innate qualities, transcendent in the

sense that they do not come by experience, which condition
and give form to that which comes from without. Time and
space are subjective conditions under which perception is possible. The mind classifies what comes to it from without
under its own laws. These are the categories. Knowledge is,
therefore, the product of two elements—a content from without,
to which form is given by the laws of the mind. These two elements give us experience; but they do not give us knowledge
of what things are in themselves, only of what our minds make
of what has come into them from without. Such a demonstration from "pure reason," as Wolff had attempted of God,
natural religion, and the constitution of the universe, is intellectually impossible. We cannot thus demonstrate the nature of
these existences as they are in themselves. Nature may be
studied as the realm of exact law, but the law is simply that
of our own thinking.

While absolute knowledge of that beyond experience is,
therefore, unattainable by purely intellectual processes, man
is conscious of a feeling of moral obligation when he asks what
ought he to do? This subject was developed in Kant's *Critique
of the Practical Reason* of 1788. When man answers the question as to conduct, he feels within the "categorical imperative"
—an imperative because a command; and categorical because
without conditions. It is so to act that the principles of action
may become those of universal law—in a phrase, do your duty.
That moral law within is the noblest of man's possessions,
it shows him as a personality and not as a machine. With
this "categorical imperative" three postulates, or inseparable
thoughts, are united. The most evident is, that if man ought to
do his duty, he can. Hence man must have freedom. And
freedom gives us a glimpse of a supersensuous realm of moral
purpose—of a sphere of moral order. A second postulate is that
of immortality. If life should be subjected to the categorical
imperative it must last long enough for that result to be accomplished. Closely connected is the third postulate. Virtue
should result in happiness. Experience does not give that
union. Hence its accomplishment demands a power that can
unite the two. The third postulate is, therefore, God. His
existence is in the "pure reason" only a hypothesis; but in the
postulates of the practical reason it becomes a conviction.

Kant's religious ideas were set forth in his *Religion Within the*

Bounds of Reason Only of 1793. Emphasizing morality as the prime content of the practical reason, he reduces religion practically to theistic ethics. Evil and the categorical imperative contest for the obedience of man. One ruled by this principle of moral good—the categorical imperative—is pleasing to God, is a son of God. Of this sonship Christ is the highest illustration. The invisible church is the ideal union of all those obedient to moral law. The visible church is a union to develop this obedience. Its complete achievement will be the kingdom of God. Kant's contribution to Christian theology was not his rationalizing interpretation of doctrines, but his vindication of man's profoundest feelings as bases of practical religious conviction and moral conduct.

A decided impulse to the historical interpretation of the Bible was given by Johann Gottfried von Herder (1744–1803), in early life an intimate with Goethe, influenced by personal contact with Kant, and an eager supporter of the romantic movement. From 1776 to his death he was court preacher in Weimar. His *Spirit of Hebrew Poetry* appeared in 1782–1783. His *Philosophy of the History of Mankind* in 1784–1791. Religion, especially Christianity, is the embodiment of that which is deepest in the feelings of mankind. The Scriptures are to be understood in the light of the views and feelings of the times in which the several books were written. They are, therefore, essentially a religious literature. What is true and permanent in them must be distinguished from the temporary and local.

Out of this romantic movement came the most influential German theologian of the opening nineteenth century, and one whose work has moulded religious thought far outside the borders of his native land—Friedrich Daniel Ernst Schleiermacher (1768–1834). The son of a Prussian army chaplain, he was educated by the Moravians, fell under the influence of the views of Wolff and Semler, and was then greatly impressed by Plato, Spinoza, Kant, and Romanticism. In 1796 he became hospital chaplain in Berlin, then a centre of the Enlightenment, and there published in 1799 his remarkable *Addresses on Religion*, directed to a rationalistic circle. In these his fundamental thoughts were set forth. From 1804 to 1807 he was professor in Halle. In the year last named he settled once more in Berlin, becoming a little later pastor of the Trinity Church. In 1810, on the founding of the University of Berlin, he was appointed professor of theology, a post which he occupied till his death in 1834. In 1821–1822 he set forth his mature views in his *Christian Belief According to the Principles of the Evangelical Church.*

Schleiermacher's prime significance is that he took up into his own system the results of previous tendencies, and gave to theology a new basis, and to the person of Christ a meaning largely ignored in his age. Orthodoxy and rationalism had both made religion essentially acceptance of an intellectual system and an externally authoritative rule of conduct. To the orthodox religion was based on assent to the truths of revelation and obedience to the will of God. To the rationalists it was acceptance of natural theology and of universal morality ascertained by the reason. Both parties in the eighteenth century looked upon religion and morality as primarily means for securing a happy immortality. To Schleiermacher the sole basis of religion is inward, in the feeling. In itself religion is neither a body of doctrines, revealed or rationally certified, nor a system of conduct, though both belief and conduct flow from religion.

Schleiermacher took much from Spinoza, Leibnitz, and Kant. In our experience we perceive the antithesis of the manifold and changing over against a principle of unity and permanency. These antitheses give us the Absolute and eternal—God—without whom all would be chaos; and the world, without which all would be empty. The Absolute is throughout all. God is therefore immanent in His world. Man is, in himself, as with Leibnitz, a microcosm, a reflection of the universe. As contrasted with that which is universal, absolute, and eternal, he feels himself finite, limited, temporary—in a word, dependent. This feeling of dependence is the basis of all religion. To bridge over the gulf between the universal and the finite, to bring man into harmony with God, is the aim of all religions. Hence the worth of each religion is to be measured by the degree in which this result, which is the aim of all, is accomplished. Hence religions are not to be divided into true and false, but into relative degrees of adequacy. All advances in religion throughout history are in a true sense revelations, a fuller manifestation to human consciousness of the immanent God. Of all religions thus far known to men, Christianity is the best, since it most fully accomplishes what it is the aim of all religions to achieve.

Its problems are those most fundamental to all religion, sin and pardon, separation and reconciliation. And in the Christian religion the person of Christ is the central element. He is Himself the reconciliation of the finite with the universal, the temporal with the eternal, the union of God and man. He is, therefore, the Mediator of this reconciliation to others. Hence Schleiermacher was strongly Christocentric. The life thus uniting the temporal and the eternal—man and God—is now immortal. An immortality in duration is a great hope, but true immortality is a quality of life rather than a mere question of duration.

Doctrines are these fundamental religious experiences defining and interpreting themselves intellectually; but these explanations have only a relative and secondary value. They have changed and may change. They are simply the forms in which abiding truth from time to time expresses itself.

In Schleiermacher's view, morality is the result of the proper understanding of that of which man is a part, the family, the community, the state, the world. Such an enlarging view of his real place in these relations will drive out selfishness and self-centering. Morality is not religion, nor religion morality; but religion is the main aid to morality. It asks the question insistently, what ought to be, in the light of the Christian consciousness.

Schleiermacher was condemned by the orthodox of his day as too radical, by the rationalists as too visionary; but no one has influenced modern religious thinking in Protestant circles more, or more variously.

Kant's system contained two evident points of difficulty. It denied the power of intellectual processes to give knowledge of things as they are in themselves, and it did not explain how mental processes are necessarily the same in all individuals. Philosophy was developed in the clarification of both these difficulties, under the influence of Romanticism, into idealism, by Johann Gottlieb Fichte (1762–1814) and Friedrich Wilhelm Joseph von Schelling (1775–1854); but in more consistent form and with a stricter realism, though predominantly idealistically, by Hegel.

Georg Wilhelm Friedrich Hegel (1770–1831) was a native of Stuttgart, educated at Tübingen. He taught in Jena, with scanty following, from 1801 to 1807. From 1808 to 1816 he was the head of the gymnasium school in Nuremberg. The year 1818 saw his appointment to a professorship in Berlin, where his fame rapidly rose to that of the first philosopher of his day in Germany. He died of cholera, at the height of his reputation and activity, in 1831. This distinction was in spite of his uninteresting and obscure manner of presentation in the classroom.

To Hegel the universe is a constant development of the Absolute, that is, God, through struggle and effort. The Absolute is spirit, and its development is in accordance with the laws by which mind thinks itself out logically. These always involve three stages, a movement in one direction—a thesis. This proceeds till it encounters its opposition or its limitation —the antithesis. But the two are but aspects of the one Absolute, and both thesis and antithesis unite in a higher union, the synthesis. Over against the "idea," the thesis, as its antithesis, is nature—but the two unite in higher synthesis in man, who is the union of both mind and matter. Since all is the Absolute developing in accordance with the laws of all thought, the laws of thought are the laws of things; and since our thinking is a fragment of that of the Absolute, in so far as it is true, it gives us true knowledge of the things outside our minds, and is the same in all minds since a part of the one Absolute. Since we are portions of the Absolute come to consciousness, a prime duty of the finite spirit is to realize its relation to the Absolute— such realization is religion. Religion may, indeed, begin, as with Schleiermacher, in feeling; but to be true it must become real knowledge. Every religion is an attempt thus to know God, of which Christianity is the most complete realization. God is always striving to reveal Himself; yet this outworking must always be through the three necessary stages of development. Thus the Father is the divine unity—the thesis. He objectifies Himself in the Son—the antithesis. The uniting love is the Holy Spirit—the synthesis. The whole process gives the Trinity. So regarding the incarnation. God is the thesis. He is distinguished from finite humanity, the antithesis. Both unite in the higher synthesis, the God-man. Hegel's system did much to substitute for the older sharp distinction between the divine and the human, the sense of their fundamental unity so prevalent in modern Protestant theology.

The profundity, power, and ingenuity of Hegel's views

cannot be questioned. Yet they were too procrusteanly phil-osophical not to lead to reaction. Though their reign in Ger-many was comparatively short, they had much following in Great Britain throughout the latter half of the nineteenth cen-tury, and have long been influential in America.

SECTION XII. FURTHER GERMAN DEVELOPMENTS

Hegel's theory of development had a significant application to New Testament criticism in the work of Ferdinand Christian Baur (1792–1860), professor in Tübingen from 1826 to his death, and founder of the new Tübingen school in theology. The essential features of his interpretation were sketched by Baur in his account of the parties in the Corinthian Church, published in 1831, and were thenceforward developed in a series of bril-liant studies, which won many disciples. All historical progress, Baur felt, with Hegel, must be through the three stages of thesis, antithesis, and synthesis. Semler (*ante*, p. 529) had already taught the existence of Petrine (Judaizing) and Pauline parties in the early church. These gave the elements of the Hegelian triad. Christianity, so Baur taught, began as essentially a Messianic Judaism. This—the thesis—was the position of all the original Apostles. The necessary antithesis inevitably arose and was Pauline Christianity. Petrine and Pauline views struggled far into the second century; but the inevitable syn-thesis came eventually, in the Old Catholic Church, which hon-ored both Peter and Paul, and was unconscious that they had ever stood in serious opposition.

The most debated use made by Baur of this reconstruction of the early history of the church was a redating of the books of the New Testament. They must display the biases of the various aspects of this development—that is, they must show "tendencies." Applying this test, Baur found only *Romans*, *Galatians*, and the *Corinthian* epistles genuinely Pauline, since they alone showed traces of the conflict. The others did not reveal the struggle, and hence must be dated later, when it had become a forgotten story. *Revelation* was early and Juda-izing. In 1847 Baur turned to the investigation of the Gospels by the same methods. *Matthew* reveals Judaizing tendencies, and is the oldest. *Luke* is probably a reworking of Marcion's (*ante*, p. 57) gospel. *Mark* sought to hide the conflict, an̈

is later, while *John* is not only irenic but betrays familiarity
with controversies of the later half of the second century.
The greater part of the New Testament was, therefore, written
in the second century.

Baur's discussion aroused advocates and opponents in great
numbers. Its ultimate effect on New Testament investigation
was most beneficial. These debates immensely enlarged the
knowledge of the early church and of its literature. Their results have been, however, the best answer to Baur's own theories. He had no adequate conception of the significance of
Christ in the development of the early church. There were
important differences between Judaic and Pauline Christianity;
but to reduce the intellectual reactions of nascent Christianity
to these only is far too simple. There were many other shades
of unlikeness. Above all, an increasing knowledge of the second century, and an appreciation of its atmosphere impossible
in Baur's time, makes it inconceivable that the books which
he assigns to it could, for the most part, have been then written.
They are not of that age and outlook.

By the time that Baur began his work, and for the next generation, German theologians were divided into three main
groups. On one extreme stood the rationalists, the continuation of the type of the closing eighteenth century. Among
them none was of greater influence than Heinrich Eberhard
Gottlob Paulus (1761–1851), professor from 1789 in Jena, who
spent the latter part of his long life (1811–1844) as professor
in Heidelberg. An opponent of all supernaturalism, his *Life
of Jesus* of 1828 is typical of the woodenness of the rationalism
of his period. Christ's walking on the water, he explains as
a misunderstanding of the disciples, viewing Christ through
the mist as He walked on the shore. The feeding of the five
thousand was accomplished by the generous freedom with
which Christ bestowed the little food He had, thus awakening
the generosity of those in the throng who had a larger supply.
Christ's death was no real event. He revived in the tomb,
aroused by the earthquake, and returned to His disciples.

Confessional orthodoxy of the most uncompromising pattern
had a notable representative in Ernst Wilhelm Hengstenberg
(1802–1869), professor in Berlin from 1826 to his death.

Between the two extremes stood a "mediating" school,
largely influenced by Schleiermacher, sharing his warmth of

Christian feeling, perhaps generally intensified, strongly devoted, like him, to the personal Christ, but disposed to accept many of the results of criticism, especially regarding the Biblical inspiration and narratives.

Most influential of these "mediating" theologians was Johann August Wilhelm Neander (1789–1850). Of Hebrew parentage, originally David Mendel, he took the name by which he is known at baptism in 1806, to signify his new birth. A student under Schleiermacher in Halle, it was his teacher's influence that secured for him a professorship in Berlin in 1813, which he filled with distinction till his death in 1850. Neander turned his attention to church history with a series of remarkable monographs, and in 1826 published the first volume of his *History of the Christian Religion and Church*, at which he labored for the rest of his life. Distinguished by thorough use of the sources, Neander's conception of the history of the church was that of a divine life gaining increasing control over the lives of men. That life is manifested in individuals. Hence, Neander's work was a series of striking biographical portraits. Its weakness was its over-emphases on the influence of individuals, and its scanty appreciation of the institutional or corporate life of the church. Yet it put church history on a new plane of achievement. Quite as significant as his writings were the influence of Neander's personal intercourse with his students, and his childlike, unaffected Christian trust. "The heart makes the theologian," was frequently on his lips, and expresses his character. Few men have been more personally helpful or more beloved.

A similar personal influence was exercised by Friedrich August Gottreu Tholuck (1799–1877), who became a professor in Berlin in 1823, but held a chair in Halle from 1826 to his death. A man of Pietistic sympathies, yet with acceptance of the critical views in many features, he turned Halle from the rationalism which had dominated since the time of Wolff to the Evangelicalism which still characterizes it. As a preacher he was distinguished. His kindness to English and American students was unwearied.

A third important representative of the "mediating" school was Isaac August Dorner (1809–1884), a student in Tübingen from 1827 to 1832, and an instructor there in 1834. After service in a number of German universities he closed his career as professor in Berlin from 1862 to his death in 1884. Dorner's most important early publication was his *Doctrine of the Person of Christ* of 1839. His completed theology was formulated in fulness, late in life, in his *System of the Doctrines of Faith* of 1879–1880. Theology and philosophy are truly akin, but both embody themselves in a progressive historic development. Christian belief thus finds its attestation in the Christian consciousness, which in turn recognizes the validity of the spiritual experience recorded in the Scriptures, and has had its growing clarification in Christian history. The central doctrine of Christianity is the incarnation in which Christ is the revelation of what God is, and of what man may be—the Head of humanity. Dorner had much influence in Great Britain and America. A comparatively minor feature of his system, that man's moral status is not finally determined till he has been brought, here or hereafter, to the knowledge of the historic Christ, adopted by the theologians of Andover Seminary, and popularly known as "continued probation," led to the heated "Andover controversy" in America in the eighties of the nineteenth century.

This "mediating school," by reason of its warm Christian faith, and its partial, though cautious, acceptance of critical positions, had no little following in lands essentially theologically conservative like the United States; but like all compromising parties its influence was temporary, and in Germany has hardly survived its principal leaders.

The most epoch-making book in German theological development came not from any of these schools, but from a young scholar of twenty-seven at the University of Tübingen, in 1835, David Friedrich Strauss (1808–1874). Strauss had made himself at home in the Hegelian philosophy. He was familiar with the earlier positions of Baur. He was, also, acquainted with the interpretation as mythical which the historian and statesman Barthold Georg Niebuhr (1776–1831) had made of the early story of Rome. These principles he now applied to the life of Christ. He was far from denying that much could be known of Jesus' earthly career; it must be viewed, however, as moving wholly in the realm of the human, like other historical events. Of the Gospel sources, he regarded that bearing the name of *John* as most removed in time and of the least historical worth, thus differing from much of the scholarship immediately before him which, notably that of Schleiermacher, had preferred *John* to the others. Strauss gave the first place to *Matthew*, but none of the Gospels were by eye-witnesses. Miracles are inherently impossible; but the Gospels are full of them. The ordinary rationalistic interpretations, like those of Paulus (*ante*, p. 537), are ridiculous; the assertions of the ultra-rationalists, like Reimarus (*ante*, p. 526), that they were recounted with intent to deceive, are impossible. The only adequate explanation is that the simple, natural facts of Christ's life are covered over with myth. The men of that time were expecting a Messiah who would be a wonder-worker; they were looking for the fulfilment of Old Testament prophecy; they had great true ideas, such as that the race is partly divine and partly human, that it rises above death by union with God. These were attributed to, or regarded as impersonated in, Christ. Jesus lived; but the Christ of the New Testament is therefore, essentially, in all His superhuman characteristics a creation of myth.

Strauss's book aroused an enormous controversy. He had attacked the views of every party in contemporary Germany, the orthodox, the rationalists of all shades, the "mediating" theologians. He met unsparing denunciation. He was debarred all further theological employment, and lived an embittered existence. Yet, looking back from the lapse of nearly three-quarters of a century, it is evident that his work placed the investigation of the life of Christ on a new plane, that he answered conclusively the older rationalists, and that the discussions which he inaugurated have been of immense service. Though the legend, that is, the transformation of the actual facts by retelling and accretion, is generally preferred to the myth, such explanation of much otherwise perplexing in the Gospels is widely accepted. Strauss's estimate of the relative low historic value of the Johannine Gospel, though not undisputed, is very generally entertained. His preference for *Matthew* has almost universally given place, especially since the labors of Heinrich Julius Holtzmann (1832–1910), to a view that sees in *Mark* the oldest narrative, and posits by its side, as the other main source of *Matthew* and *Luke*, an early collection of Christ's sayings.

Granting the services of Strauss's youthful work in the development of New Testament scholarship, two fundamental criticisms of his method as a whole remain. Either the church

created that which is important in the figure of Christ, albeit
unconsciously; or Christ is the source of the church.   If Strauss
and those who share his essential position were right, the
former conclusion is true; but it seems much more difficult of
acceptance than the latter.   Nor has the purely human historical interpretation of the life of Christ, though largely developed to the present, led to the construction of a really plausible picture that could long be maintained.   As one of the
ablest living students of the history of the investigation of the
life of Christ has asserted, its results have been essentially failure.[1]   The sayings of Jesus Himself, and the beliefs of the early
church as witnessed by the Pauline letters, demand, as Friedrich Loofs (1858–) of Halle contends,[2] a Being impossible of
classification merely in the categories of humanity.

Strauss's work was the inspiration, in large measure, of the
French scholar, Ernst Renan (1823–1892).   His *Life of Jesus*,
of 1863, was indebted, though in less measure, also to the work
of other German students.   The literary skill, the charm with
which Renan's marvellous pen depicted the purely human life
of a Galilean peasant prophet, gave Renan's work enormous
and permanent popularity.   Yet it was sentimental, theatrical,
and, in its use of the sources, fundamentally insincere.   Infinitely superior to Strauss in literary art, in other respects
Renan's work stood on a far lower level.

The most potent influence alike in the interpretation of the
history of the early church and of theology in Germany during
the last half-century has been that of Albrecht Ritschl (1822–
1889).   A disciple at first of the school of Baur, he broke with
its main contentions when he published the second edition of
his *Origin of the Old Catholic Church* in 1857.   Baur's Hegelian
Petrine thesis and Pauline antithesis are not adequate explanations of the growth of the early church.   There were differences, but all parties had a greater fundamental unity in owning the mastery of Jesus.   Nor are the unlikenesses of early
Christianity resolvable into two sharply antagonistic parties.
There were many shades of opinion.   Christianity came into
no empty world, but one filled with religious, philosophical, and
institutional ideas.   By them, especially on Gentile soil, the

[1] Albert Schweitzer (1875–), *The Quest of the Historical Jesus*, 1910.
[2] *What is the Truth about Jesus Christ*, 1913; also *Wer war Jesus Christus*,
1916.

simple, primitive truths of Christianity were profoundly modified, resulting in the theology and institutions of the Old Catholic Church. This fertile and illuminating interpretation is that most widely accepted by modern Protestant scholars.

Ritschl began teaching in the University of Bonn in 1846. In 1864 he became professor in Göttingen, where he remained till his death. Here he published, in 1870–1874, his chief theological work, *The Christian Doctrine of Justification and Reconciliation*. Ritschl had few personal disciples, but the propagating influence of his writings was great.

Ritschl was much influenced by Kant's assertion of moral feeling as the basis of practical certainty and denial of absolute intellectual knowledge, and by Schleiermacher's affirmation of religious consciousness as the foundation of conviction. Yet Schleiermacher's assertion of the normative value of religious consciousness was, to his thinking, too individual. The real consciousness is not that of the individual, but that of the Christian community, the church. Nor is that consciousness a source of abstract speculative knowledge. It has to do with eminently practical, personal relationships—those of God and the religious community—sin and salvation. Hence "natural" or speculative philosophic theology is valueless. Philosophy may give, as with Aristotle, a "first cause"; but that is far from a loving Father. Such a practical revelation is made to us only through Christ. That revelation is mediated to us through the consciousness of the first disciples. Hence the Old Testament, as revealing their religious background, and especially the New Testament, as recording their consciousness of Christ and His Gospel, are of supreme value. To ascertain the religious consciousness recorded in the Old and New Testaments, no theory of inspiration is necessary, only normal historical investigation.

Though Ritschl thus rejected metaphysics as an aid to Christian truth, he made much use of a theory of knowledge advocated by the philosopher Rudolf Hermann Lotze (1817–1881). While it is true, Lotze held with Kant, that things as they are in themselves cannot be known, he affirmed that they are truly known in their attributes or activities. A brick pavement is known, and truly known, to me as a sidewalk. To the ants whose mounds of sand rise between the bricks it may be a home. What it is abstractly or in itself I have no means of knowing. If that knowledge in its attributes is one affecting my conduct it is a "value judgment." So Ritschl held that to those who came in contact with Him in the first Christian community, Christ was truly a revelation of what God is in love, the pattern of what man may be, the bearer of God's moral authority over men, and the Founder of the kingdom of God. As such He was truly known; but to ask whether He was pre-existent, was of two natures, or was one person of a Trinity, is to ask what the experience of the early church could not answer, and what only metaphysics could assert or deny. This recognition of what Christ is and signifies, arouses faith in men, that is trust and love toward God through Christ. This new attitude is accompanied by the forgiveness and removal of sin, which constituted the barrier between man and God—justification—and the new relationship expresses itself in desire to do the will of God and to live the life of the kingdom—reconciliation. The Christian life is essentially social, hence Redeemer, redeemed, and the redeemed community are inseparable conceptions. These ideas of salvation Ritschl believed have never been more clearly formulated, in later church history, than by Luther.

Ritschl's spiritual disciples have been by no means blind followers, and much variety of interpretation may be found among them. Their influence among those in leadership in German religious thinking is great. Among them may be mentioned the prince of church historians, Adolf von Harnack, of Berlin (1851–), his eminent younger contemporary, Friedrich Loofs of Halle (1858–); and of theologians, Ferdinand Kattenbusch of Halle (1851–) and Wilhelm Herrmann of Marburg (1846–). In general, the Ritschlians have been marked by an earnest, vital religious life, and a contagious warmth of piety.

In spite of the spread of Ritschlianism the school of Baur was continued in modified form, with Hegelian outlook in metaphysics, by Otto Pfleiderer of Berlin (1839–1908).

More conservative than the Ritschlian school, yet with much influence from modern problems, is Reinhold Seeberg (1859–) of Berlin, who presents "a modern positive theology."

Yet a reaction from the emphasis of Ritschl was almost inevitable. His rejection of metaphysics, his assertion of the fundamental uniformity of religious experience now and in the days of primitive Christianity, were sure to arouse question.

Especially the rise of the study of comparative religions was certain to awake inquiry whether that principle of growth under the influence of external religious and philosophical ideas which Ritschl himself had applied so brilliantly to the development of Christian doctrine, when once that was planted in the world, was not to be applied, as he had not, to the beginnings of Christianity itself. The result is the rising, though as yet far from dominant, *Religionsgeschichtliche* school which counts such representatives as William Wrede (1859–1906) of Breslau, Wilhelm Bousset (1865–) of Göttingen, and especially Ernst Troeltsch (1865–) of Heidelberg.

It is evident that German theological development is still in progress.

SECTION XIII.   ENGLAND IN THE NINETEENTH CENTURY

English religious life in the opening years of the nineteenth century was dominated by the spiritual awakening of the great Methodist revival, which was leading to large separation from the establishment (*ante*, pp. 518, 519). In the establishment that revived zeal was represented by the Evangelical, or low-church party, like the Methodists, keenly alive to works of practical and missionary activity (*ante*, pp. 519–523); yet it was far from dominating the Church of England as a whole. Its enterprise and its good works were in contrast to the apathy of the establishment in general. Intellectually, all parties in the Church of England stood on the basis of the rather provincial discussions of the eighteenth century. Theology was looked upon in the same rationalistic fashion—a system of intellectual demonstration, or of authoritative revelation, or both combined. The stirrings of new intellectual forces were being felt however. English poetry flowered into splendid blossoming with the opening years of the nineteenth century. Romanticism, as powerfully as in Germany (*ante*, p. 529), was beginning to produce an intellectual atmosphere wholly unlike that of the preceding age. The novels of Sir Walter Scott are familiar illustrations of this new outlook. A new humanitarianism, largely due to the Methodist revival, was developing, and was to be manifested multitudinously in reformatory movements. All the tendencies were sure to affect theological thinking and religious ideals.

Probably the most stimulating force in the religious thinking of the first quarter of the nineteenth century was that of Samuel Taylor Coleridge (1772–1834), eminent as a poet, literary critic, and philosopher. A Neo-Platonist in his early sympathies, study in Germany, in 1798 and 1799, led to ultimate acquaintance not only with the masters of German literature but with the thought of Kant, Fichte, and Schelling, and a philosophical outlook then fully unfamiliar in England. Coleridge never worked out a rounded system. His most significant volume was his *Aids to Reflection* of 1825. Over against the rationalizing of Paley he held to a distinction between "reason" and "understanding." To Coleridge "reason" was a power of intuitive perception, an "inward beholding," by which religious truths are directly perceived. This "moral reason" has, as its associate "conscience," which is an unconditional command, and has as its postulates the moral law, a divine lawgiver, and a future life. Religious certainty is thus based not on external proofs but on religious consciousness. Hence, he has been called the "English Schleiermacher." In most respects Coleridge was the forerunner of the broad-church way of thinking; but in his emphasis on the church as a divine institution, higher and nobler than anything "by law established," he prepared the way for the high-church party.

The work of Coleridge in its religious aspects was continued by Thomas Arnold (1795–1842), who began his famous mastership of Rugby in 1828. A man of profound and simple Christian faith, his helpfulness to his pupils was great. His views much resembled those of Herder (*ante*, p. 532). The Bible is a literature, to be understood in the light of the times in which it was written, but its divine truth finds us.

Biblical criticism was furthered, in a very moderate fashion, by Henry Hart Milman (1791–1868), dean of St. Paul's, London, from 1849, by his *History of the Jews* of 1829, in which he applied critical methods to the Old Testament. His most valuable work was his *History of Latin Christianity* of 1855.

Not willing to be reckoned to the broad-church school, yet contributing much to its spread, was John Frederick Denison Maurice (1805–1872). The son of a Unitarian minister, he conformed to the establishment, and became chaplain of Guy's Hospital in London. In 1840 he was appointed to a chair in King's College, of which he was deprived for his opinions in 1853. The year after he founded the Working Men's College, and was instrumental in inaugurating a Christian socialist movement. In 1866 he was appointed to a professorship in Cambridge. To Maurice's thinking, Christ is the Head of all humanity. None are under the curse of God. All are sons, who need no other reconciliation than a recognition by them of their sonship, with the filial love and service to which such recognition will naturally lead. All will ultimately be brought home to God and none forever lost.

Not very unlike Maurice in his theology, but primarily a great preacher, was Frederick William Robertson (1816–1853), educated under Evangelical influences, then passing through a period of intense questioning to a broad-church position. From 1847 to his early death he was minister in Brighton. No English sermons of the last century have been so influential on both sides of the Atlantic as those of Robertson. Spiritual truth must be spiritually discerned rather than intellectually proved. The nobility of Christ's humanity attests and leads to faith in His divinity.

Much influence in the spread of broad-church opinions was wielded by Charles Kingsley (1819–1875), rector of Eversley, the novelist, and by Alfred, Lord Tennyson (1809–1892), whose *In Memoriam* of 1850 was fully a broad-church poem. Similarly to be reckoned were Arthur Penrhyn Stanley (1815–1881), dean of Westminster, and Frederic William Farrar (1831–1903), dean of Canterbury. Great commotion was caused in 1860 by the *Essays and Reviews,* in which a group of Oxford scholars tried to present Christianity in the light of contemporary science and historical criticism, and by the trial of Bishop John William Colenso (1814–1883) of Natal for his Pentateuchal criticism published in 1862. The broad church was, however, never, strictly speaking, a party. Its numbers were relatively few, but its influence on English religious thought, in varying degrees, wide-spread. In the last half-century England, like other Protestant lands, has witnessed the steady advance of Biblical criticism, championed conspicuously by Samuel Rolles Driver (1846–1914) and Thomas Kelly Cheyne (1841–1915), both of Oxford.

The Evangelical or low-church party has remained largely represented in the Church of England, especially among the laity.

By far the largest movement within the Church of England in the nineteenth century in numerical, and in many respects in spiritual, significance has been the development of the high-church, or Anglo-Catholic party. The early years of the second quarter of the nineteenth century saw several significant breaches in the exclusive privileges of the establishment. The Test (*ante*, p. 475) and Corporation Acts were repealed in 1828. Roman Catholics were made eligible to the House of Commons and to most public offices in 1829. The July Revolution of 1830 in France stimulated a demand for reform in parliamentary representation, which triumphed, after heated struggles, in 1832, and transferred power largely from the landed gentry to the middle classes, thus increasing Non-Conformist influence. To many conservative churchmen it seemed that the foundations of church and state were being removed. They were disposed to raise the question of the nature of the church itself. Is it an essentially unalterable divine institution, or may it be altered, as so often since the Reformation, by government enactment? The form their answer took was to be determined largely by the romantic revival of interest in the primitive and mediæval.

During these discussions several young clergymen, mostly associated with Oriel College, Oxford, were led to take the steps that inaugurated the "Oxford movement," as it was often called, which was the birth of the Anglo-Catholic party. Probably the most influential of the group, while his brief life lasted, was Richard Hurrell Froude (1803–1836). To him the church is in possession of the truth, important elements of which primitive endowment were repudiated by the reformers. A revival of fasting, clerical celibacy, reverence for the saints and "Catholic usages" he deemed imperative. Closely associated with Froude was a man of great pulpit and intellectual abilities, whose early training had been Evangelical, but who had come to share Froude's feelings, John Henry Newman (1801–1890). A third of the Oriel group was John Keble (1792–1866), of Nonjuror ancestry, and already distinguished as the author of the most popular volume of religious poetry that was issued in the nineteenth century, *The Christian Year* of 1827. In hearty sympathy stood a Cambridge scholar, Hugh James Rose (1795–1838), who founded the *British Magazine* in 1832, to further faith in the divine authority and essential unchangeableness of the church. To all these men the course of recent political events seemed menacing. The formal beginning of the Anglo-Catholic movement is usually associated with Keble's sermon of July 14, 1833, in Oxford, on the *National Apostasy*. In September of that year Keble formulated the principles for which he and his associates stood. The way to salvation is through reception of the body and blood of Christ in the Eucharist, which is validly administered only through those in apostolical succession. This is the treasure of the church—a church which must in all ways be restored to the purity of its undivided early centuries.

The same month Newman began the publication of the famous *Tracts for the Times*, which gave to the movement they fostered the name "Tractarianism." By 1835 these associates had won the support of one who, next to Newman, and fully after Newman's defection, was to be its leader, Edward Bouverie Pusey (1800–1882). A man of great earnestness and piety, Pusey was so fully ultimately to become the head of the Anglo-Catholic movement, that it was largely called "Puseyism"—to Pusey it was the revival of primitive Christianity.

Of these *Tracts*, of which ninety were issued, Newman wrote twenty-three. Keble, Pusey, and Froude, with others, also contributed. To Newman the Church of England was the golden mean between Protestantism and Rome; but as the series went on the writers emphasized increasingly those doctrines and practices which, though undoubtedly ancient, are popularly identified with Rome. Thus, Pusey taught the regenerative nature of baptism and the sacrificial aspect of the Lord's Supper. Confession was commended. Reserve was to be practised in the use of the Bible and the proclamation of religious truth. It was the ninetieth *Tract* by Newman, in 1841, that aroused most controversy. Newman held that the Thirty-nine Articles were not to be interpreted in accordance with the intention of their authors, but in the "sense of the Catholic Church." The bishop of Oxford now forbad the continuation of the *Tracts*.

Newman was at the height of his influence when *Tract Ninety* was published. The Anglo-Catholic movement numbered hundreds of followers among the clergy. Newman was doubting, however, the catholicity of the Church of England, and on October 9, 1845, he made his submission to Rome. Several hundred clergy and laymen followed him into the Roman communion, of whom the most distinguished was Henry Edward Manning (1808–1892), who conformed to Rome in 1851, and was created a cardinal in 1875. Great excitement was caused in 1850 by the re-establishment in England by Pope Pius IX of the Roman Catholic diocesan episcopate, which had been in abeyance since the Reformation. Manning became an extreme ultramontane supporter of papal claims, unlike Newman, who was always moderate, and who, though the most eminent of English Roman Catholics, was not given a cardinalate till 1879.

These conversions to Rome were a severe blow to the Anglo-Catholic party, but it weathered the storm under Pusey's able leadership, and in a few years was stronger than ever. As its doctrinal modifications became established, it concerned itself increasingly with the "enrichment" of the liturgy, by the introduction of usages which Protestantism had discarded. These changes encountered much popular and legal opposition; but the modifications desired by the ritualists have been largely secured. In 1860 the English Church Union, now widely extended, was organized to support high-church faith and practice. The high-church movement is still a growing force in the Church of England. To a degree unparalleled in other countries, the laity of England, with conspicuous exceptions, are disposed to regard disputes between the various parties in the Church of England as clerical problems, so that lay religious life in the establishment is more uniform than might be supposed.

Any estimate of the Anglo-Catholic movement would be erroneous that failed to recognize its profound religious zeal. If it has Romanized the worship and the theology of the church —it would prefer to say Catholicized it—it has shown marvellous devotion, especially to the poor, neglected, and unchurched. It has done much to regain the hold of the church on the lower classes which seemed to have almost ceased when the movement began. Its sympathy with the destitute and delinquent has been intelligent and self-sacrificing. It has been a real awakening of religion, alike in faith and good works.

The sister Protestant state church of Ireland, always an anomaly in that it was the governmentally supported church of a minority of the population, was disestablished in 1869. It has

endured this change in its fortunes with no diminution of effectiveness.

The nineteenth century was marked by a steady diminution
of the disabilities resting on Non-Conformists. In 1813 the Unitarians obtained relief by the repeal of penal acts against deniers
of the Trinity. The Test and Corporation Acts were abolished
in 1828. Marriages were permitted in dissenting places of
worship in 1836. Non-Conformists were freed from taxes for
the benefit of the establishment in 1868. In 1871 all religious
tests, save for degrees in theology, were abolished at the Universities of Oxford, Cambridge, and Durham. In 1880 Non-
Conformist services were permitted at burials in churchyards.

Non-Conformity has steadily grown, and is supposed to embrace at least half the population of England. Its strength is
in the middle classes. It has produced preachers of great
power, and has had its scholars and its social workers, but in
scholarship and in work for the unchurched it has been less eminent than the Church of England. The tendency among the
larger Evangelical Non-Conformist bodies has been strongly
toward federation. Since 1893 England and Wales have been
organized into a complete system of local "councils," embracing Baptists, Congregationalists, Methodists, Presbyterians,
and Quakers, each local church being primarily responsible for
its own territory—thus preventing competition. These "councils" are united in "federations," and all culminating in the
National Council of Evangelical Free Churches.

Three movements of interest have taken place among English
Non-Conformists. Edward Irving (1792–1834) was a Scottish
Presbyterian minister in London, of eloquence and mystic tendencies. By 1828 he had become persuaded that the "gifts"
of the apostolic age would be restored if faith was sufficient.
Though no claimant to them himself, he believed by 1830
that his hopes had been fulfilled in others. In 1832 he was
deposed from his Presbyterian ministry. Soon after, six Apostles were believed to be designated by prophecy, which number was similarly completed to twelve in 1835. The body
thus led took the name Catholic Apostolic Church. In 1842
an elaborate ritual was adopted. The Apostles were regarded
as organs of the Holy Spirit. The speedy coming of Christ
was long expected, but the last Apostle died in 1901. The
church is represented also in Germany and the United States.

A second movement grew out of reaction against the unspirituality of the establishment in the early years of the nineteenth century. Groups of "brethren," who claimed faith and Christian love as their only bonds, gathered in Ireland and western England. Their great increase was through the labors of John Nelson Darby (1800–1882), formerly a clergyman, in the vicinity of Plymouth about 1830. They are therefore generally nicknamed "Plymouth Brethren." To their thinking all believers are priests, and hence formal ministries are to be rejected. Creeds are to be refused. The Holy Spirit guides all true believers, and unites them in faith and worship after the apostolic model. Though professedly rejecting all denominationalism, the "brethren" found themselves speedily compelled to corporate acts of discipline, and are divided into at least six groups. Darby was an indefatigable propagandist. Through his efforts the "brethren" were planted in Switzerland, France, Germany, Canada, and the United States. Among their eminent adherents have been George Müller (1805–1898), whose remarkable orphan houses in Bristol were supported, he believed, largely in direct answer to prayer; and Samuel Prideaux Tregelles (1813–1875), the eminent student of the Greek text of the New Testament.

The most important of these new organizations is the Salvation Army. Its creator, William Booth (1829–1912), was a New Connection Methodist minister, who, after successful revival work in Cardiff, began similar labors in London in 1864, out of which an organization in military form, with military obedience, developed in 1878, to which the name Salvation Army was given in 1880. Always strongly engaged in practical philanthropy as well as street evangelism, the philanthropic work was developed on a great scale from 1890 onward, when Booth published his *In Darkest England and the Way Out*. In spite of its autocratic military form, the Salvation Army is in many respects a church. Though open to the charge of occasional arbitrariness, it has done an immense and beneficent work for the defective and delinquent, and has extended to all English-speaking lands, as well as to France, Germany, Switzerland, Italy, the Scandinavian lands, and the Orient.

The most powerful impulse toward modern religious thinking, the world over, that was contributed by England in the nineteenth century came from the work of a naturalist who,

though a Christian believer in early life, was all his maturer
years a tolerant agnostic, Charles Robert Darwin (1809–1882).
A man of great keenness of investigation, remarkable powers of
generalization, and transparent honesty in his use of facts and
in his readiness to abandon all inferences which continued
observations did not warrant, his long and patient work was
done under the constant handicap of ill health.   A voyage of
nearly five years, 1831 to 1836, as naturalist of the surveying
ship *Beagle*, laid the foundations of his knowledge.   In 1859
came his *Origin of Species by Means of Natural Selection*, in which
he elaborated his theories of evolution and of the survival of
the fittest, reached practically contemporaneously by his friend,
Alfred Russel Wallace (1823–1913).   No scientific theory since
Newton's doctrine of gravitation (*ante*, p. 483) has been so
transforming in all realms of thought.   Much modified in details since promulgated, the theory of evolutionary development, though accepted with varying degrees of fulness, has
profoundly modified much theological thinking, and has to be
taken into most serious consideration even by those who deny
its applicability to the realm of religion.

SECTION XIV.   SCOTTISH DIVISIONS AND REUNIONS

Presbyterianism was established as the state church of
Scotland under William and Mary in 1690.   In 1707 England
and Scotland were united into one kingdom of Great Britain ;
but the independent rights of the Church of Scotland were
safeguarded.   Under Queen Anne, in 1712, two important acts
were passed by Parliament.   By one the status of a tolerated
communion was given to episcopacy, then strongly intrenched
in northern Scotland.   The other, destined to be the source
of infinite trouble, permitted "patrons," usually the crown or
the great landlords, to force appointments of Presbyterian
ministers on hostile parishioners.   Controversies were soon tur-
moiling the Scottish church.   In 1718 an anonymous seven-
teenth-century work, *The Marrow of Modern Divinity*, was re-
published at the instigation of Thomas Boston (1676–1732),
of Ettrick, a zealous popular preacher.   *The Marrow* seemed
antinomian to a large portion of the ministry, as so putting an
emphasis on faith in Christ as to exclude even the necessity of
repentance.   Boston won sympathy.   In 1722 the "Marrow-

men" were censured by the General Assembly. They represented unquestionably, however, a warm Evangelical spirit.

One of these "Marrowmen," Ebenezer Erskine (1680–1754), of Stirling, a preacher of power, denounced all limitation of the power of the congregation to choose its minister, in 1733. He was disciplined by his synod, and he and several associates were deposed by the General Assembly in 1740. Before these censures were completed they had founded the first Scottish free church, ultimately known as the Secession Church. It grew rapidly, but was soon turmoiled over the question whether the burgesses of the Scottish cities could properly swear to support "the true religion . . . authorized by the laws" of Scotland. In 1747 the Secession Church divided into Anti-Burgher, or Nonjuror, and Burgher sections. Further subdivisions occurred, but most of the Anti-Burghers and Burghers united, in 1820, as the United Secession Church.

The question of patronage continued divisive. Thomas Gillespie (1708–1774), of Carnock, refused to participate in the installation of a minister over an unwilling congregation, and was deposed by the General Assembly in 1752. In 1761 he and like-minded ministers founded the organization which became the Relief Church. These various secessions won large popular support, especially among the more earnest-minded. By 1765 they counted one hundred and twenty congregations, and one hundred thousand adherents. In 1847 the United Secession Church and the Relief Church combined as the United Presbyterian Church.

Under these circumstances the state church was robbed of a good deal of its spiritual strength. Rationalistic thought penetrated Scotland as the eighteenth century advanced, as contemporaneously in England and Germany. Hume's speculations (*ante*, p. 490) were not without influence. The result was the growth of what was called Moderatism, which was controlling in the latter half of the eighteenth century, and influential well into the nineteenth. To the Moderates generally Christianity was largely ethical rather than strongly experiential or doctrinal. It was believed that the patronage system favored the appointment of Moderates, where congregations would often have chosen men of more Evangelical type. With the reaction from the French Revolution, the rise of Romanticism, and the general revolt from the rationalism of the eighteenth century, a warm-hearted Evangelicalism, in sympathy also with the liberal political aspirations of the people, began to contest the field with Moderatism.

From 1815, when he entered on a memorable pastorate in Glasgow, the most eminent of the Evangelical party was Thomas Chalmers (1780–1847), distinguished as a preacher, a social reformer, a mathematician, a theological teacher, and an ecclesiastical statesman. Under his leadership, and in the changed spirit of the times, the Evangelical party rapidly grew in strength. Under Chalmers's guidance a great campaign to meet the needs of the growing population of Scotland was inaugurated, which resulted by 1841 in the erection of two hundred and twenty new churches by popular gifts. The old question of patronage still continued burning. In 1834 the growing Evangelical party secured the passage by the General Assembly of a "veto" rule, by which presbyteries were forbidden to proceed to installation where a majority of the congregation were opposed to the candidate. This rule soon involved legal controversy. The courts held that the General Assembly had exceeded its powers. Parliament was asked for relief, which was refused. Under Chalmers's leadership, therefore, some four hundred and seventy-four ministers formally withdrew from the state church in 1843 and founded the Free Church of Scotland. They gave up parishes and salaries. All had to be provided anew; but the enthusiasm and sacrifice of the new body was equal to the task. In general, it was a withdrawal of the Evangelical element from the already considerably modified but less zealous and spiritual "Moderates." A third, and that the most active part, of the state church had gone out. Yet the example of the seceders worked ultimately for a quickening of zeal in the state church itself. In 1874 the rights of patronage, the original ground of division, were abolished by law.

The older separatist bodies, combined since 1847 as the United Presbyterian Church, had long rejected connection with the state. The new Free Church of Scotland had practically to take the same position, though Chalmers and its early leaders clung to the conception of a national state church, free from hampering state dictation. This contention was rendered academic by the logic of facts. All circumstances counselled union, and therefore, on October 31, 1900, the vast majority of the Free Church of Scotland and the United

Presbyterian Church were joined in one body as the United Free Church of Scotland.

A minority of the old Free Church refused the union, in all some sixty-three congregations, mostly in the Highlands, small and strongly conservative in theology and practice. This body was popularly known as the Wee Frees. It brought legal claim to the property of the whole former Free Church. In 1904 the law judges of the House of Lords awarded to the Wee Frees their whole claim, on the ground that the Free Church majority, in combining with the professedly independent United Presbyterians, had abandoned the early Free Church belief in a purified state church. The situation created was not merely unjust, but absurd. Relief was sought from Parliament, and in 1905 the property was divided fairly equitably by a commission between the Wee Frees and their former brethren, on the basis of ability to make effective use of it. The growth of modern views in theology was also recognized by Parliament, in this act of 1905, by permission to the state church to formulate the terms of subscription to the ancient confessions as it may see fit.

The vast majority of independent Presbyterians being thus joined in the United Free Church of Scotland, and many of the grounds of contention with the state church having been removed, a union between the two in the near future is probable —foreshadowed by the merger, in 1916, of the theological schools of the established church and the United Free Church in Aberdeen and Edinburgh.

SECTION XV. ROMAN CATHOLICISM

The Counter-Reformation had spent its force by the middle of the seventeenth century. Its strength had been in the might of Spain and the zeal of the Jesuit order. Spain had emerged from the Thirty Years' War shorn of its power. The Jesuits, though more potent than ever in the counsels of the Roman Church, had become more worldly, and had kept little of their earlier spiritual zeal. None of the Popes of the seventeenth or eighteenth centuries were men of commanding force. Several, like Innocent XI (1676–1689), Innocent XII (1691–1700), or Benedict XIV (1740–1758), were of excellent character and intentions, but they were not rulers of men. The course

of the Roman Church was one of increasing feebleness in the
face of the growing claims of the Catholic civil governments.
A really effective attack upon Protestantism was no longer possible, save where it existed, as in France, in predominantly
Roman lands.

Under Louis XIV (1643–1715) the French monarchy pursued a policy dictated by the King's absolutism. As against
papal claim he asserted possession by the crown of all income
of vacant bishoprics, and favored the proclamation by the
French clergy in 1682 of the "Gallican liberties," that civil
rulers have full authority in temporal affairs, that general councils are superior to the Pope, that the usages of the French
church limit papal interference, and that the Pope is not infallible. The resulting quarrel was compromised in 1693 in
such wise that the clergy practically withdrew their assertions,
but the King kept the disputed income.

As against his own subjects, Louis XIV's policy was determined by his conception of national unity and Jesuit influence,
especially after his marriage to Madame de Maintenon in
1684. In 1685 he revoked the Edict of Nantes (*ante*, p. 441),
and made Protestantism illegal under the severest penalties.
The ultimate result was disastrous for France. Thousands of
its most industrious citizens emigrated to England, Holland,
Germany, and America. The former alliances with Protestant
Powers were ruptured, contributing much to the military failures of the latter years of Louis XIV's reign.

Jesuit influence led to equally disastrous opposition by the
King and Pope to Jansenism. Cornelius Jansen (1585–1638),
bishop of Ypres, an earnest Catholic, was a thoroughgoing
Augustinian, convinced that the semi-Pelagian Jesuit interpretations of sin and grace must be combated. His chief work,
Augustinus, was published in 1640, after his death. Jansen's
book was condemned by Pope Urban VIII (1623–1644) in 1642,
but Jansen's views found much support among the more deeply
religious Catholics of France, notably in the nunnery of Port
Royal, near Paris. The most influential opponent of the
Jesuits was Blaise Pascal (1623–1662), especially in his *Lettres
Provinciales* of 1656. Louis XIV supported the Jesuit hostility to Jansenism, and persecuted its followers. In 1710 the
buildings of Port Royal were torn down. Jansenism had found
a new leader of power in Pasquier Quesnel (1634–1719), who

had to seek safety in the Netherlands. His devotional commentary, *Moral Reflections on the New Testament*, of 1687-1692, aroused bitter Jesuit hostility, and through their efforts Pope Clement XI (1700-1721), by the bull *Unigenitus* of 1713, condemned one hundred and one of Quesnel's statements, some taken literally from Augustine. Louis Antoine de Noailles (1651-1729), cardinal archbishop of Paris, protested and appealed to a general council. Opposition was, however, vain. The Jesuits, supported by the French monarchy, ultimately triumphed.

Partly through this Jansenist controversy, and partly by reason of quarrels between the Jesuits and the older Roman clergy, a division occurred in Utrecht, in the Netherlands, from which in 1723 a small, independent, so-called Jansenist Catholic Church originated, which still exists, with an archbishop in Utrecht, and bishops in Haarlem and Deventer.

For France the expulsion of the Huguenots and the triumph of the Jesuits were great misfortunes. While much variety of religious interpretation was possible in England, Germany, and Holland, within the bounds of Christianity, in eighteenth-century France the choice was only between Romanism of the narrow Jesuit type, which many of its own noblest sons condemned, and the rapidly rising tide of the new rationalism of a Voltaire and his associates (*ante*, p. 492). Thousands preferred the latter, and the destructive results were to be obvious in the French Revolutionary treatment of the church.

The latter half of the eighteenth century brought to the Jesuits their greatest catastrophe. They had largely engaged in colonial trade, in spite of its prohibition in their own constitutions; their political influence was notorious, and they had the hostility of the radical rationalism of the age. In this latter force they found their most determined foes. The powerful minister of King Joseph of Portugal (1750-1777), the marquis of Pombal (1699-1782), was a man of rationalistic sympathies. He was angered by Jesuit resistance to his policy in Paraguay. He opposed the free-trade attitude of the Jesuits. In 1759 he enforced the deportation of all Jesuits from Portuguese territory with ruthless high hand. France contemporaneously was aroused by the scandalous bankruptcy of the Jesuit Lavelette in Martinique. The controlling force in the French Government was that of the duke of Choiseul (1719-

1785), a sympathizer with the Enlightenment. He was also aided by Madame de Pompadour, the mistress of Louis XV (1715–1774). A large part of the French clergy were also hostile to the Jesuits. In 1764 the Jesuits were suppressed in France. Spain and Naples expelled them in 1767. The rulers of these lands now forced from Pope Clement XIV (1769–1774) the abolition of the order in July, 1773. These events attested the weakness of the papacy. The Jesuits continued existence in non-Roman Russia and in Protestant Prussia.

The growth of tolerance in France is shown by the exemption from persecution accorded to Protestants by the government of Louis XVI in 1787.

The tremendous storm of the French Revolution was about to break and to sweep away the church, with the nobility, the throne, and kindred ancient institutions. The Revolutionary leaders were filled with the rationalistic spirit. They viewed the churches as religious clubs. In 1789 church lands were declared national property. In 1790 the monasteries were abolished. The same year the civil constitution of the clergy overthrew the old ecclesiastical divisions, made each "department" a bishopric, and provided for the election of all priests by the legal voters of their communities. The constitution of 1791 pledged complete religious freedom. In 1793 the Jacobin leaders procured the abolition of Christianity. Hundreds of ecclesiastics were beheaded. After the "terror" was over, in 1795, religious freedom was once more proclaimed, though the state, as such, was to be without religion. It was, in reality, strongly antichristian. This situation was extended by French conquests to the Netherlands, northern Italy, and Switzerland. In 1798 Rome was made a republic by French arms, and Pope Pius VI (1775–1799) carried a prisoner to France, where he died.

The military events of 1800 led to the election of Pius VII (1800–1823) and the restoration of the States of the Church. Napoleon, on attaining power, though himself without religious feeling, recognized that a majority of the French people were Roman Catholics, and that the church might be used by him. The result was the Concordat with the papacy in 1801 and the Organic Articles of 1802. By the former, the church surrendered all confiscated lands not still held by the government. Those in government possession were restored to it. Appointment of bishops and archbishops were to be by the Pope on nomination by the state. Lower clergy were appointed by bishops, but the state had a veto power. Clergy were to be paid from the state treasury. By the Organic Articles no papal decrees were to be published or French synods held without governmental allowance. To Protestants full religious rights were accorded, at the same time, and the pay of their ministers and control of their affairs assumed by the state. Napoleon soon quarrelled with Pius VII, annexed the States of the Church in 1809, and held the Pope a prisoner from that time till 1814. Napoleon's Concordat was to rule the relations of France and the papacy for more than a century. Intended to place the French Catholic Church under the control of the government, and accomplishing that result under Napoleon, its real effect was to make the French clergy look to the Pope as their sole aid against the state. By ignoring all ancient local rights, it really ruined all Gallican claims to partial freedom, and opened the door to that Ultramontane spirit characteristic of French Catholicism throughout the nineteenth century.

The wars of the republican and Napoleonic periods resulted in far-reaching changes in Germany. The old ecclesiastical territories practically ceased to exist in 1803, and were divided between the secular states. In 1806 Francis II (1792–1835) resigned the title Holy Roman Emperor. He had already assumed that of Emperor of Austria. It was the passing of a venerable institution, the Holy Roman Empire, which had, indeed, been long but a shadow, but which was bound up with mediæval memories of the relations of church and state.

Napoleon's downfall was followed by universal reaction. The old seemed of value by its antiquity. It was to be years before the real progress effected by the Revolutionary age was to be manifest. This reaction was aided by the rise of Romanticism with its new appreciation of the mediæval and rejection of that spirit of the eighteenth century which had been dominant in the Revolution. The papacy profited by all these impulses and soon developed a strength greater than it had shown for a hundred years. A characteristic evidence of this new position of the papacy was the restoration, by Pius VII, in August, 1814, of the Jesuits, who speedily regained their old ascendancy in papal counsels, and their wide extended activities, though not their former political power. They have, in turn, been fore-

most in the development and support of papal authority.   At
the same time the restoration of the power of the Roman
Church was accompanied and made possible by a real revival
of piety that has continued to characterize it to the present
day.

Roman development during the nineteenth century has
been in the direction of the assertion of papal supremacy, that
called Utramontanism—*i. e.*, beyond the mountains from the
point of view of northern and western Europe—that is Italian.
To this Ultramontane tendency to exalt the papacy above all
national or local ecclesiasticism the Jesuits have powerfully
contributed.   Pius VII's successor, Leo XII (1823–1829), was
reactionary, condemning, like his predecessor, the work of
Bible societies.   Gregory XVI (1831–1846) was a patron of
learning, but reactionary toward modern social and political
ideals.   This essentially mediæval outlook and refusal to make
terms with the modern world led to the formation, in the first
half of the nineteenth century, of clerical and anticlerical
parties in Catholic countries, whose contests have largely determined the politics of those lands to the present.

The Ultramontane tendencies found their conspicuous illustration in the papacy of Pius IX (1846–1878).   Beginning his
pontificate at a time when the States of the Church were on
the edge of revolt because the leading political offices were held
by the clergy, he was at first a political reformer; but the task
proved too much for him and he adopted a reactionary political
policy which made it necessary to seek the support of foreign
soldiery and rendered the people dissatisfied with his political
rule.   In religion he was sincerely convinced that in the papacy
is a divinely appointed institution to which the modern world
can appeal for the decision of its vexed religious problems.
He desired to make this evident.   In December, 1854, after
consultation with the bishops of the Roman Church, he proclaimed the immaculate conception of the Virgin—that is, that
Mary shared in no taint of original sin.   The question had been
in discussion since the Middle Ages, though the balance of
Catholic opinion in the nineteenth century was overwhelmingly
in favor of the view approved by the Pope.   He elevated it,
by his own act, into a necessary dogma of faith.

In 1864 a Syllabus of Errors, prepared under papal auspices,
condemned many things which most Christians oppose; but

also repudiated much which is the foundation of modern states, like the separation of church and state, non-sectarian schools, toleration of varieties in religion, and concluded by condemning the claim that "the Roman Pontiff can and ought to reconcile himself to, and agree with, progress, liberalism, and civilization as lately introduced."

The crowning event of Pius IX's pontificate was the Vatican Council. Opened on December 8, 1869, with a remarkably large attendance from all over the Roman world, its most important result was the affirmation, on July 18, 1870, of the doctrine of papal infallibility by a vote of five hundred and thirty-three to two. It was far from asserting that all papal utterances are infallible. To be so the Pope must expound, in his official capacity, "the revelation or deposit of faith delivered through the Apostles." "The Roman pontiff, when he speaks *ex cathedra*, that is, when in discharge of the office of pastor and doctor of all Christians, by virtue of his supreme apostolic authority, he defines a doctrine regarding faith or morals to be held by the universal church, by the divine assistance promised to him in blessed Peter, is possessed of that infallibility with which the divine Redeemer willed that His church should be endowed." Thus the Vatican Council sealed the triumph of Ultramontanism. It was the completion of the absolute papal monarchy, and the overthrow of that doctrine of the supremacy of a general council which had loomed so large in the fifteenth century (*ante*, pp. 306–312), and had not been without its representatives since.

Though undoubtedly the logical outcome of centuries of papal development, this doctrinal definition encountered considerable opposition, especially in Germany. The most eminent refuser of conformity was the distinguished Munich historian, Johann Joseph Ignaz von Döllinger (1799–1890), but though excommunicated, he declined to initiate a schism. What he refused, others achieved, and the result was the organization of the Old Catholics, who received episcopal ordination from the Jansenist Church of Utrecht (*ante*, p. 557). Their chief spread has been in Germany, Switzerland, and Austria, where they number still more than a hundred thousand adherents. They have even, though very feebly, reached the United States. Yet the Old Catholic movement would seem to have little future. Its departures from Rome, though important, were not vital enough to serve as a long-continuing basis of a branch of the Christian Church.

Meanwhile the tide of Italian national unity had been rising. The war carried on jointly by the kingdom of Sardinia, under Victor Emmanuel II (1849–1878), and France, under Napoleon III (1852–1870), against Austria, supplemented by Italian enthusiasm led by Giuseppe Garibaldi (1807–1882), resulted in the establishment of the kingdom of Italy under Victor Emmanuel in 1861, and the inclusion in it of the greater part of the old States of the Church. Rome and its vicinity were preserved to the Pope by the Ultramontane policy of Napoleon III. On the outbreak of the war between France and Germany in 1870, the French troops were withdrawn. On September 20, 1870, Victor Emmanuel captured Rome, and the inhabitants of the district voted one hundred and thirty-three thousand to one thousand five hundred for annexation to Italy. To the Pope the Italian Government guaranteed the privileges of a sovereign, and absolute possession of the Vatican, the Lateran, and Castel Gandolfo. Thus came to an end the States of the Church, the oldest continuous secular sovereignty then existing in Europe. Pius IX protested, declared himself a prisoner, and excommunicated Victor Emmanuel. The papacy has continued to desire the restoration of its temporal possessions; but to a non-Roman this sacrifice seems to have been an advantage. It removed from the papacy a secular task which it was ill adapted to meet, and the attempted accomplishment of which laid it open to well-grounded charges of maladministration. It gave to the papacy unhindered scope for the development of its spiritual functions. It is no accident that in the forty-seven years that have elapsed since the loss of its territorial possessions the papacy has been more influential and has enjoyed the general respect of mankind in higher measure than at any period since before the Reformation.

Pius IX was succeeded by a statesman Pope, Leo XIII (1878–1903). He concluded the conflicts between the papacy and the imperial government of Germany. He urged French Catholics to support the republic. With Italy he was less successful, owing to insistence on the restoration of the States of the Church. He declared Aquinas (*ante*, p. 270) the standard of Roman instruction, thus returning to the best period of mediæval religious thought. He urged the study of the Scriptures. He opened the treasures of the Vatican to historical scholars. The relations of labor and capital and the interests of working men enlisted his attention. He sought the reunion of the Roman and the Oriental Churches; but he pronounced Anglican orders invalid in 1896. In 1878 he restored the Roman Catholic episcopate in Scotland. A man of scholarly tastes and wide sympathies, he was far removed from any countenance of Protestantism, but won deserved admiration for the skill, wisdom, Christian zeal, and religious earnestness with which he administered his great office.

Pius X (1903–1914) was, in many ways, a contrast to Leo XIII. The latter was of noble birth. Pius X was of humble origin. Leo XIII was of great diplomatic ability and far-sighted vision. Pius X was a faithful parish priest whose parish had become world-wide. He was called to handle two questions of great difficulty. The first had to do with the relations of church and state in France. In spite of the efforts of Leo XIII, the majority of French Catholics were regarded as luke-warm toward the republic. Relations had long been growing strained. In 1901 religious orders not under state control were forbidden to engage in instruction. The refusal of conformity by some was followed in 1903 by the suppression of many monasteries and nunneries, and the confiscation of their properties. In 1904 President Loubet of France paid a state visit in Rome to the King of Italy. Pius X, regarding the Italian sovereign as in wrongful possession of Rome, protested. France withdrew its ambassador from the papal court, and soon after broke off all diplomatic intercourse. In December, 1905, the French Government decreed the separation of church and state. All governmental aid was withdrawn from Catholics and Protestants. All churches and other church property were declared the possession of the state, to be rented for use by state-responsible local associations for worship, preference being given to those representative of the faith by which the property had last been employed. Though many French bishops were ready to form such organizations, Pius X forbade. The result was a deadlock, which still continues, though the French Government has allowed worship to go on as before. Catholics and Protestants have since had to provide the cost of their services by voluntary gifts. The adjustment has been difficult; but the task, which has been successfully accomplished, seems by its perplexities to have served to arouse the religious interest of the nation.

The second problem was occasioned by the rise of the Modernists. In spite of growing Ultramontanism, modern historical criticism, Biblical investigation, and scientific conceptions of growth through development, have found a foothold, though scanty, in the Roman communion. To some earnest and thoughtful men some reinterpretation of Catholicism in terms of the modern intellectual world seemed imperative. Such were Hermann Schell (1850–1906) in Germany, Alfred Loisy (1857–) in France, George Tyrrell (1861–1909) in England, and quite a group in Italy. Modernism was confined to no country. Against this movement Pius X set his face. By a "syllabus," and an "encyclica," in 1907, Modernism was condemned, and stringent measures taken for its repression. These have apparently been successful, but whether such tendencies can be permanently crushed only the future can determine. Pius X interested himself in many administrative reforms with effect.

The present Pope, Benedict XV (1914–), is of scholarly spirit and peace-loving nature, but the brevity of his pontificate and the overshadowing interests of the great world war have, as yet, rendered an estimate of his pontificate difficult.

SECTION XVI.   AMERICAN CHRISTIANITY

American Christianity is primarily an importation from the Old World. As the colonization of America represented many races of Europe, so the various types of European Christianity were reproduced on the new continent. Where, as in South and Central America, the immigration was of a single race, imposing its civilization on the natives, a single type of Christianity—the Roman Catholic—is dominant to-day, however extensively its control may have been contested by secularist influences. Where, as in North America, many stocks have contributed to the population, though one form of Christianity was here and there dominant in colonial beginnings, the result has been great variety and religious freedom, as a consequence of necessary mutual toleration. America has produced certain indigenous religious types, but they have been relatively insignificant; but in North America, where contact between various types has been acute, and where the principle of independence from state control has been dominant for more than a century, there had been much modification from European forms, especially in church government—what may be called an Americanization.

The conversion of South and Central America was largely the work of the monastic orders, strongly supported by the Spanish Government. By 1508 the Franciscans were laboring in Venezuela. By 1529 they were numerous enough to hold a provincial synod in Mexico. In 1535 they had constituted Peru a province. Four years later they had begun work in Argentina. They were the first to enter Brazil. By 1597 they had founded Christian communities in what is now part of the United States—New Mexico. In 1700 they were in Texas. Their mission period in California was from 1769 to 1843.

The Franciscans found worthy competitors in the Dominicans. By 1526 they were in Mexico. Soon after they were laboring in Colombia. In 1541 they were Christian pioneers in Chile.

Even more extensive was the activity of the Jesuits. From 1549 they developed an extensive work in Brazil. Colombia soon proved one of their most successful fields. They were in Peru by 1567, and in Paraguay by 1586. In the country last named, in 1610, they established their much discussed paternally controlled Indian villages (*ante*, p. 430). The seventeenth century witnessed their extensive activities in Ecuador, Bolivia, and Chile. By 1572 they began a great work in Mexico. No brighter page of missionary sacrifice is to be found than that written by the Jesuits in Canada, beginning in 1611. Though aided by other orders, the strongly Roman province of Quebec is their monument to this day. In 1673 a Jesuit missionary, Jacques Marquette (1637–1675), discovered the Mississippi. A series of mission stations through the Mississippi valley, as far south as Louisiana, followed.

Florida was missionary land for Dominicans, Franciscans, and Jesuits from 1568, but proved difficult. The flourishing period of Roman missions there was from 1625 to 1700.

Universities were founded in Mexico City in 1551, and in Lima in 1557, which are the most venerable institutions of higher learning in the New World.

The Church of England was introduced into the oldest Eng-

lish colony in what is now the United States—that of Virginia—
at its planting in 1607, and remained established by law till
1776. Though it retained the affections of many of the noblest
of the colonists, even the establishment of William and Mary
College, in 1693, failed to provide an adequate supply of native
clergy. Throughout the colonial period Virginia was dependent
on clerical appointments by the distant bishop of London.
The result was too often the selection of the incompetent and
sometimes of the unworthy, while the parishes which were
bound by law to furnish the minister's support revenged themselves by a grudging acquiescence. The attempts of the clergy
to collect their dues by law, supported by the home government,
was one of the causes of disaffection leading to the Revolution.
On the whole, Virginia episcopacy, in colonial days, led a
troubled and scantily fruitful existence.

Virginia's northern neighbor, Maryland, the first English
proprietary colony in what is now the United States, was
chartered to Lord Baltimore in 1632. Himself a Roman
Catholic, to secure freedom under the sovereignty of England
for his fellow believers, Baltimore established full religious
toleration. Under these conditions the Protestant Dissenters
in Maryland, by the close of the seventeenth century, outnumbered the Roman Catholics and Anglicans. In 1691 Maryland
was created a royal colony, and the next year the Church of
England was by law established. During the remainder of
the colonial period its livings were the most valuable of any in
the colonies; but it suffered from the inefficiency of the clergy,
like Virginia. Quakers, Presbyterians, and Methodists grew
numerous. The establishment practically ended in the turmoil of the Revolution. A bright spot in the religious history
of these two colonies was the efficient labor of Thomas Bray
(1656–1730), commissary of the bishop of London, who secured
the foundation of the Society for the Propagation of the Gospel
in Foreign Parts in 1701 (*ante*, p. 508).

North and South Carolina both saw the Church of England
legally established till the contests of the Revolution. The
mixed religious character of their population, including Huguenots, Scotch-Irish Presbyterians, Baptists, and Quakers, rendered this establishment ineffective, though these colonies were
well served, in the eighteenth century, by missionaries of the
society founded by Bray, and Charleston had a distinguished

succession of rectors. Georgia was founded on the basis of toleration for all save Roman Catholics; but not a little work was done by the missionaries of the Society for the Propagation of the Gospel, and something has been said of the experiences of the Wesleys and of Whitefield (*ante*, pp. 511, 512). In general, it may be said that in the southern colonies in the period preceding the Revolution the condition of religion was low, and the existence of an establishment did little to improve it.

The settlement of English Separatists and Puritans in New England, beginning in 1620, and the steps which led to the erection, between then and 1638, of the Congregational colonies of Plymouth, Massachusetts, Connecticut, and New Haven have already been noted (*ante*, pp. 466, 469). Founded in religious enthusiasm, possessing an educated ministry, these colonies made provision for its maintenance from their own sons by the founding of Harvard College in 1636 and of Yale College in 1701. Nor was effort neglected for the conversion of the Indians. The work of John Eliot (1604–1690), begun in 1646, led to the formation, in 1649, of the first missionary society in England (*ante*, p. 522). The early Congregationalists of New England did not differ theologically from their Puritan and Presbyterian brethren in Great Britain. For their first century their controversies were regarding the developments of polity rather than concerning questions of doctrine. By 1631, in Massachusetts, and speedily in the other adjacent colonies Congregationalism was established by law. A religious establishment there continued longer than elsewhere in the United States, in Connecticut till 1818, and in Massachusetts till 1834. Dissent from the established order appeared. There were occasional Baptists in the Massachusetts colony almost from the beginning, and in spite of governmental repression they organized a church in Boston in 1665. By 1705 there was a Baptist Church in Groton, in Connecticut. Quakers arrived in Massachusetts in 1656, and within the next five years four were hanged in Boston. They continued, however, to increase. Church of England worship was established in Boston, in 1687, and gained a footing at Stratford, in Connecticut, in 1707. Freedom of Protestant worship was granted by the Massachusetts charter of 1691, and by Connecticut law in 1708, and exemption from taxation for the support of Congregational Churches was granted to Baptists, Episcopalians,

and Quakers, under somewhat onerous conditions, in both
colonies, between 1727 and 1729.   At the Yale Commencement
of 1722 the rector, or president, of the college, Timothy Cutler
(1683–1765), and Samuel Johnson (1696–1772), later (1754) to
be the first president of what is now Columbia University in New
York City, with one of the tutors at Yale, declared for episcopacy.   The event was important, not in the college, which
deposed them, but as establishing a native episcopal ministry
in New England, especially in Connecticut, where its labors
were supported by the English Society for the Propagation of
the Gospel in Foreign Parts.

In general it may be said, however, that, though New England
remained a religious land, the zeal of its founders had burned
low by the opening of the eighteenth century, and isolation,
wars with the Indians, and frontier conditions brought their
inevitable provincialism.

A highly individual development in New England was the
settlement of Rhode Island.   Providence was begun, in 1636,
by Roger Williams (1604?–1684?), then under banishment from
Massachusetts and an opponent of coercion in matters of religion.   Rhode Island became a refuge for those seeking freedom of religious expression.   In 1639 the first Baptist Church
in America was established, of which Williams was for a short
time a member, spending his later life as a "seeker."   In spite
of many internal troubles from an intense individualism, the
broad principles of religious toleration on which Rhode Island
was founded were well and honorably maintained.   The
Quakers, in particular, found in it a home.

New York was permanently founded as a Dutch trading
colony in 1624.   By 1628 its first Dutch Reformed Church,
the earliest representative of the Presbyterian polity in America,
was formed.   New York soon asserted, however, its cosmopolitan character.   By 1644 the future city included in its inhabitants Dutch Reformed, Lutherans, Mennonites, English-
speaking Puritans, and Roman Catholics.   From 1652 onward
an attempt was made by the colonial authorities to prevent
any other worship than that of the Reformed Church of Holland.   The Quakers were specially objects of repression.   Dutch
control ceased in 1664, when New York passed to the English,
whose possession was finally confirmed ten years later.   The
English governors attempted to construe the Church of Eng-

land as established. The majority of inhabitants, especially as represented in the legislative assembly, offered successful opposition. In the foundation of Trinity Church, in 1697, the Church of England was effectively planted in New York City, though the Dutch Reformed and French Huguenots were then even more strongly represented. In 1709 a large German Reformed immigration from the Palatinate came into the colony. In 1720 the Dutch Reformed Church received a notable accession in the arrival from Holland of Theodorus Jacobus Frelinghuysen (1691–1747), whose remarkable ministry was exercised in New Jersey, but was to extend its quickening and organizing influence to New York also.

Of what was to become New Jersey, East Jersey saw the establishment of Congregational settlers from New Haven colony, at Newark, in 1666, of the Dutch Reformed in the region of New Brunswick, and of Scotch Presbyterians. West Jersey received a large Quaker immigration in 1677–1678.

Mention has already been made of the grant of Pennsylvania to William Penn, in 1681, and its settlement by Quakers in the following year (*ante*, p. 480). The Quaker policy of toleration attracted representatives of other forms of faith. Hence no other colony presented such a variety of religious bodies as Pennsylvania. Baptists from Wales and Ireland were soon more strongly represented than elsewhere in the colonies. Mennonites from Germany and Holland settled Germantown, in 1683. Dunkards and other German bodies soon followed. The Church of England was planted in Philadelphia in 1695, but was long feeble. The first half of the eighteenth century saw a great influx of German Lutherans and German Reformed (Calvinists). The beginnings of the Moravians have already been noted (*ante*, p. 504).

After the Stewart restoration of 1660 a new element, destined to be of great economic and political importance, the Scotch-Irish, came from the Scottish settlements in Ulster. They were devotedly Presbyterian. They found a missionary and an organizer in Francis Makemie (?–1708), who labored, certainly from 1691 onward, from New York to South Carolina. To his initiative the organization of the first American presbytery, that of Philadelphia, in 1705, was due. From 1713 nearly to the American Revolution the Scotch-Irish were pouring in like a flood. They settled much of Maine and New

Hampshire in New England, where, however, they were mostly absorbed by the Congregational Churches. In New York they constituted a large fraction of the population. Nowhere were they more strongly represented than in Pennsylvania, and by 1764 were able practically to wrest the political control of the colony from the Quakers. They sought prevailingly the frontier, and to this energetic race the settlement of what is now West Virginia, western North Carolina, and ultimately Kentucky, Tennessee, as well as large sections of South Carolina, Georgia, and Alabama, was due. By 1717 a synod was formed, including the presbyteries of New York and New Jersey, Pennsylvania, Delaware, and Maryland. In general the Scotch-Irish were long in a period of religious destitution, through lack of ministers and organized churches.

Religion in America during the period till the second quarter of the eighteenth century was essentially the propagation of European bodies. Save in New England, it was relatively feeble, and there had suffered a serious decline of its original enthusiasm. No one religious body was dominant in the colonies as a whole. While particular denominations were intrenched in particular colonies, no church could become that of all the colonies. The way was thus made ready for that religious freedom which was to become the characteristic of the United States as a nation.

The most far-reaching and transforming event of the eighteenth-century religious life of America was the revival known as the Great Awakening. It was not only a tremendous quickening of the Christian life, it changed the conceptions of entrance on that life in a way that profoundly affects the majority of American churches to this day. In this respect it was the analogue of Pietism in Germany or Methodism in Great Britain. It emphasized the conception of a transforming regenerative change, a "conversion," as the normal method of entrance into the kingdom of God. It gave general diffusion to the Baptist or Congregational view of the church as a company of experiential Christians. It laid little weight on Christian nurture. It promoted an ascetic theory of the Christian life.

Some premonitions of the revival were to be seen under the preaching, in the vicinity of Raritan, New Jersey, of Theodorus Jacobus Frelinghuysen after 1720 (*ante*, p. 569). He had come under Pietistic influences in Holland. Near him, and impressed

by him, was Gilbert Tennent (1703–1764), the young Presbyterian minister of New Brunswick, New Jersey, whose powerful,
though often injudicious, revival preaching began to show large
fruitage in 1728. A remarkable revival began, in 1734, in Northampton, Massachusetts, under the ministry of Jonathan Edwards (1703–1758). But all these manifestations of religious
feeling were local compared with the general interest aroused
by the first Evangelistic tour throughout the English-speaking
colonies in 1739 and 1740 by George Whitefield, then in the
height of his youthful enthusiasm (*ante*, p. 511). Everywhere
throngs hung upon his words, faintings and outcries attended
his sermons. Hundreds were permanently changed. The spiritual condition of many communities was transformed.

Unfortunately the Great Awakening, with all its unquestionable benefits, brought division in its wake. When Whitefield
himself was denunciatory of those who did not agree with
him as unconverted, it is not surprising that his followers and
imitators were even more censorious and uncharitable. The
Congregationalists of New England were soon divided into
New Lights, who saw in the revivals a work of God, and the
Old Lights, who disliked their method. A similar schism into
Old Side and New Side occurred among the Presbyterians of
the middle colonies. Harvard and Yale were Old Light in sentiment. Many of the revivalistic ministers of the New Side
party had been trained in the Log College, founded in 1728 by
Gilbert Tennent's father, William Tennent (1673–1746). Some
of these, with much New Light sympathy from New England,
and under the auspices of the synod of New York, founded in
1746 the institution now known as Princeton University. While
the revivals affected American religious ideals profoundly, two
bodies, which had always emphasized Christian nurture, were
relatively unaffected by them, the Lutherans and the Church
of England—the latter proving, in New England, at least, a
home for some of those who disapproved the revival methods.

Intense as was the Great Awakening, and permanent as
was its moulding effect upon American religious conceptions,
its active period was brief. Men's minds were turned from
strenuous interest in religion by a long series of military and
political events of absorbing concern. The struggle begun in
1755, resulting in the conquest of Canada, had scarcely ter-
minated in 1763 when it was followed by the controversies

aroused by the Stamp Act, and by increasing friction with the mother country, resulting in the outbreak of the Revolution in 1775; the Declaration of Independence in 1776; the destructive war till 1783; and the protracted discussions of the framework of the nation which did not terminate till the establishment of government under the Constitution in 1789. For more than a generation men's thoughts were absorbed in these questions, and religion in America was at low ebb. Many of the trusted political leaders were influenced by the Deism of England or France (*ante*, p. 492). The most significant religious force arising during this period was the planting of American Methodism, beginning in 1766 (*ante*, pp. 517–518)— a sowing destined to a mighty harvest.

Out of the discussions of the Great Awakening there emerged in New England the most considerable contribution that eighteenth-century America had to make to theology—in the work of Jonathan Edwards and his school. Born in a pastor's home in what is now South Windsor, Connecticut, in 1703, Edwards graduated at Yale in 1720. From 1727 to his dismissal, after a painful controversy, in 1750, he was pastor in Northampton, Massachusetts; then missionary to the Indians at Stockbridge, in the same Commonwealth, till his removal to undertake the presidency of Princeton, a few weeks before his death in 1758. A leader in the great revival, his was also the keenest philosophical intellect that colonial America produced. A Calvinist, emphasizing the absolute divine sovereignty in conversion against all Arminian modifications, in his *Enquiry into . . . Freedom of Will* of 1754 he held that while all men have natural ability to turn to God, they lack moral ability—that is, the inclination—so to do. This determining inclination is the transforming gift of God; though its absence is no excuse for sin. To Edwards's thinking virtue is love to intelligent being in proportion to the amount of being each possesses. Hence God, the greatest of all beings, justly seeks His own glory, while man by the same test must place the service of God and his fellows before his own advantage. Sin is, therefore, selfishness, and virtue disinterested benevolence.

Edwards's views were developed by his disciples, Joseph Bellamy (1719–1790), Samuel Hopkins (1721–1803), Timothy Dwight (1752–1817), Edwards's son and namesake, Jonathan

(1745–1801), and Nathanael Emmons (1745–1840). All of these insisted on a conscious conversion, involving a transformation from selfishness to "disinterested benevolence," as the method of entrance into the kingdom of God. To Hopkins this "benevolence" was not complete in self-sacrifice unless it involved a willingness to be damned, should that seem best to divine wisdom. The younger Jonathan Edwards, believing that Christ died for all and not for the elect only, was driven by the rise of Universalism to substitute the Grotian conception of Christ's death as a sacrifice to "general justice" (*ante*, p. 456), rather than a penal satisfaction for individual sins. This "governmental" theory of the atonement largely dominated New England thinking till after the middle of the nineteenth century. This Edwardean school was strongly missionary in spirit, and from it most of the early New England foreign missionaries came.

Meanwhile there developed in eastern Massachusetts, under the leadership of such men as Charles Chauncy (1705–1787) and Jonathan Mayhew (1720–1766), both of Boston, partly in opposition to revival methods, and also through the influence of contemporaneous English Dissent, a "liberal" movement of a decidedly Arian tendency, though its separation and full development as Unitarianism was not to come till the beginning of the nineteenth century.

The attainment of American independence thrust upon those religious fellowships that had heretofore been branches of European communions the problem of separate American organization. In the condition of the new national life this must be organization independent of the state. As already independent of their European progenitors, such a task was not laid upon the Congregationalists or the Presbyterians.

The Roman Catholics were still scantily represented within the bounds of the United States. They were under the superintendence of the vicar apostolic of London. In 1784 the much-respected John Carroll (1735–1817) of Maryland was appointed prefect apostolic for the United States by Pius VI (1775–1799). Six years later Carroll was consecrated bishop of Baltimore. In 1791 the first Roman Catholic synod of the United States was held in Baltimore. In 1808 Baltimore, under Carroll, was made the seat of an archbishopric, while bishoprics were established in New York, Boston, Philadelphia, and Bardstown (Kentucky). By Carroll's death the foundations of Roman Catholicism in the United States had been strongly established, and the priesthood numbered more than a hundred, though the immigration which was so enormously to augment this communion was yet in the future.

No communion in America suffered so severely from the Revolution as the Church of England. Its ministry and congregations were largely sympathetic with the mother country, and it emerged from the struggle in ruins. Its very name seemed unpatriotic, and that of "Protestant Episcopal" was adopted by a conference of clergy and laity of Maryland in November, 1780. Two years later William White (1748–1836), rector of Christ's Church in Philadelphia, and a hearty supporter of American independence, sketched out the plan under which the American Protestant Episcopal Church was essentially to be organized, in independence of the state and of English ecclesiastical control, with representative bodies composed not only of clergy but of laymen. He believed the prospect of securing an American episcopate remote. In accordance with White's suggestions, a voluntary convention, representative of eight states, met in New York City in October, 1784, and called the First General Convention to gather in Philadelphia in September, 1785.

Meanwhile, the Episcopal clergy of Connecticut had held aloof and had chosen Samuel Seabury (1729–1796) as bishop, and he had gone to England for ordination in June, 1783. Finding it impossible to receive consecration from the English episcopate in the absence of action by Parliament, Seabury procured it at the hands of the Nonjuror Scottish bishops in Aberdeen in November, 1784.

The General Convention of 1785 adopted a constitution for the Protestant Episcopal Church in the United States, largely the work of William White. It also appealed to the English bishops for the ordination of bishops for America. Seabury's Scottish ordination might be valid, but the derivation of orders from the parent English body was desired. The local Episcopal conventions of the several states were asked to name bishops. The General Convention reconvened in 1786 was able to report that the English bishops had procured an enabling act from Parliament, and that William White had been chosen bishop of Pennsylvania and Samuel Provoost (1742–1815) of

New York. On February 4, 1787, they were consecrated by the archbishop of Canterbury.

Bishop Seabury and Bishops White and Provoost, representing different lines of consecration, looked upon each other at first with antagonism. Connecticut had not yet been represented in the General Convention; but these difficulties were adjusted, and in the General Convention of 1789 all parties united, the Prayer Book was revised and adapted to American needs, and the foundation of the American Protestant Episcopal Church fully laid.

Separation from the mother country made a similar independent organization for American Methodism imperative. The result was the ordination by John Wesley in September, 1784, of Thomas Coke, Richard Whatcoat, and Thomas Vasey, for work in America; the Conference in Baltimore, the formation of a Methodist Episcopal Church in the United States, and the ordination of Francis Asbury the same year (*ante*, pp. 517, 518).

The year 1792 saw the abandonment by the (Dutch) Reformed Church, and 1793 by the (German) Reformed Church, of a dependence on Holland which had long been weakening, but which now ended in complete self-government.

One now very extensive American communion, the Lutheran, though not directly affected by the Revolutionary struggle to the degree characteristic of the bodies just mentioned, now developed its organization on American lines. The earlier German immigration of the eighteenth century was prevailingly other than Lutheran. By the middle of that century Lutheranism was pouring in a flood, especially into Pennsylvania, though of course in numbers far smaller than the great immigration of the nineteenth century. Religiously, the transition was difficult. The institutions of a state church could not be transplanted, and little help came from Germany, save from the Pietists of Halle. Great disorganization and scarcity of ministers were the results. Some improvement was effected by Zinzendorf (*ante*, p. 505); but the great organizer of American Lutheranism was Heinrich Melchior Mühlenberg (1711–1787), who reached Philadelphia in 1742. Under his leadership the first Lutheran synod, or ministerium, was formed in Philadelphia in 1748. Quite as important for the future development of American Lutheran polity was the constitution prepared by

Mühlenberg for his Philadelphia congregation in 1762, by which all officers were chosen by the congregation itself. The two essential features of American Lutheranism were thus sketched—Congregational in respect to the local congregation, Presbyterian in respect to the standing of ministers in the synod. The synodical system spread slowly. The ministerium of New York was organized in 1786. A third synod was soon after formed in North Carolina. In 1821 a general synod, intended to be representative of all local synods, was formed, but only a portion of the Lutherans supported it, and this willingness of the rapidly multiplying local synods to group themselves as they choose has continued till recently characteristic of American Lutheranism. Steps taken in connection with the four hundredth anniversary of the Reformation, in 1917, promise the union of all American Lutheran bodies.

One further religious body that developed during the period of struggle for national independence was that of the Universalists. Belief in the salvation of all occasionally appeared in eighteenth-century America as elsewhere as a sporadic speculation. The father of organized Universalism was John Murray (1741–1815), who had been touched by Whitefield's preaching in his native England, and by the writings of James Relly (1722?–1778), who had passed from the status of one of Whitefield's preachers to that of an advocate of universal salvation. It was as a disciple of Relly that Murray came to America in 1770, and began an itinerating ministry, chiefly in New England. A strict Calvinist, Murray believed that Christ had made full payment not for the sins of a restricted group of the elect, but for all men, and immediate blessedness would be theirs at the judgment, when all unbelief in God's mercy would vanish. For those who fully believe, the divine promised blessedness begins now.

A further impulse was given to Universalism when in 1780 Elhanan Winchester (1751–1797), a Baptist minister of Philadelphia, independently of Murray, adopted Universalist views, which he advocated with eloquence. Unlike Murray, his general opinions were Arminian. Salvation is based on the ultimate free submission of all to God; but will not be achieved in the case of the unrepentant till their spirits have been purified by protracted, but not eternal, suffering. Even more influential was Hosea Ballou (1771–1852), long a pastor in Boston. Murray and Winchester had been Trinitarians. Ballou was an Arian, and in this Unitarian direction American Universalism has followed him. The purpose of the atonement was moral— to set forth God's love to men. Sin brings punishment, here or hereafter, till men turn from it to God.

By 1790 the Universalists were sufficiently numerous to hold a convention in Philadelphia. Three years later a New England convention was organized which in 1803 met in Winchester, New Hampshire, and adopted a brief creed which, though modified in 1900, is the historic basis of American Universalism. The early converts to Universalism were prevailingly, though not always, from the humbler walks of life.

Unitarianism, on the other hand, won the allegiance of some of the oldest Congregational Churches and eminent men of eastern Massachusetts. The growth of a "liberal" party before the Revolution has already been noted (ante, p. 573). Theological discussion in that region was overshadowed by the momentous events of the struggle for independence. In 1785, however, the proprietors of King's Chapel, the ancient Church of England place of worship in Boston, excluded from the Prayer Book all references to the Trinity, thus becoming the first Unitarian congregation in America. Similar views spread, and criticism of the doctrine of original sin, of the Calvinistic theory of predestination, and an insistence on salvation by character were even more characteristic of the "liberal" movement than denial of the Trinity. With the incoming of the revival impulse at the close of the eighteenth century, of which mention will soon be made, and the consequent strengthening of the conservative element, a cleavage was soon evident between the "liberal" and "orthodox" parties. A struggle between the two over the theology of the Hollis professor of divinity in Harvard University resulted in 1805 in the victory of the "liberals" by the choice of Henry Ware (1764–1845).

Meanwhile, in 1803, William Ellery Channing (1780–1842) had begun a greatly respected and widely influential pastorate in Boston, and was preaching a high Arian Christology. Increasing division, and attacks by the "orthodox," led in 1815 to the adoption by the "liberals" of the Unitarian name. A sermon by Channing in 1819 at the installation of Jared Sparks (1789–1866) in Baltimore was widely regarded as the authoritative statement of the party, and gave to Channing henceforth an unofficial leadership in American Unitarianism. In 1825 the American Unitarian Association was formed. Though largely confined to eastern New England, the roll of Unitarian men of letters, philanthropists, and public servants is of eminent distinction.

The periods of the Revolutionary contest and of the discussions resulting in the adoption of the Constitution of the United States were epochs of great religious depression. The last decade of the eighteenth century saw a marvellous transformation initiated. Without the aid of any single outstanding personality, like that of Whitefield in the "Great Awakening," a mighty reawakening of religious interest began. Felt in New England by 1792, within the next four years it was strongly manifested in the Middle States, whence it swept through the South, and by the dawn of the nineteenth century was in triumphant progress in the new West beyond the Alleghanies. In Kentucky it was felt with peculiar power. There the "camp-meeting" began in 1800; and there the revival was often accompanied, as had been the "Great Awakening," by outcries and bodily manifestations. As a whole, this new revival period was far less marked than the earlier by these symptoms of over-wrought excitement. Its effects were none the less profound, and the new religious interest was long continued and transforming. Indeed, the revivals may be said to have continued, with less frequency and diminishing intensity till 1858, as the predominant feature of American religious life.

Led as was this revival movement, on its human side, by men who fully shared the Pietistic and Methodist traditions of the eighteenth century, it emphasized the relation of the individual soul to God, and regarded a conscious conversion as the normal entrance into the Christian life. It was disposed to view that as scarcely religion for which some account of a transforming change in feeling could not be given. All American religious bodies except the Roman Catholics, Lutherans, Protestant Episcopalians, Quakers, and Unitarians shared these convictions. Presbyterians and Congregationalists, Methodists and Baptists, were in these respects essentially at one. But the Methodists and Baptists, to whom this type of piety was most native, found the largest popular following, aided by their willingness to use such ministerial instrumentalities, whether educated or not, as were available. They speedily reached that numerical leadership which they have since maintained among American Protestants. The fidelity of Congregationalists and Presbyterians to the tradition of an educated ministry made them founders of schools and colleges, but rendered their appeal less widely popular; but all grew amazingly in numbers and power.

Under the impulse of the new religious spirit American Christian life blossomed with new activities. The Sunday school, first introduced from England (*ante*, p. 522) into Philadelphia in 1791, now became well-nigh universal. The prayer-meeting, heretofore only sporadic, became general. Foreign missions, inaugurated by the Congregationalists in 1810, by the formation of the American Board, with which the Presbyterians and (Dutch) Reformed co-operated, were adopted by the Baptists through the establishment of the General Missionary Convention of the Baptist Denomination in 1814. The Methodists followed with their Missionary Society in 1819. The Protestant Episcopal Church took similar action in 1821. Nor was the progress of home-missionary effort in the United States less remarkable. The circuit-rider and the pastor kept pace with the progress of population westward, and state and national organizations in the larger denominational bodies energetically supported the work.

Ministerial training was greatly stimulated by the religious awakening. A prime purpose in the foundation of Harvard (1636), Yale (1701), and Princeton (1746) had been pastoral preparation. The ordinary curriculum had at first been deemed adequate, but it was supplemented at Harvard by the foundation of a professorship of divinity in 1721, and at Yale in 1755. More popular training throughout the eighteenth century was instruction in the home of some active pastor. In 1784 the (Dutch) Reformed Church instituted ministerial training ultimately removed to New Brunswick, New Jersey, which has often been called the oldest American theological seminary. More like a modern theological seminary was the school established in Baltimore in 1791 by Bishop John Carroll, with the aid of French Sulpitians, for training for the Roman Catholic priesthood. The United Presbyterians were beginning theological instruction later to find a home in Xenia, Ohio, in 1794. In 1807 the Moravians established a theological school in Nazareth, Pennsylvania.

The most elaborately equipped theological seminary, and in many ways the inaugurator of a new era, was that opened by the Congregationalists in Andover, Massachusetts, in 1808. Four years later the Presbyterians inaugurated a similar seminary at Princeton, New Jersey. In 1815 a Lutheran theological school was established in Hartwick, New York. The Divinity School of Harvard University was opened under Unitarian auspices the same year. Bangor Theological Seminary, in Maine, was founded by Congregationalists in 1816. The Baptists inaugurated Hamilton (New York) Theological Seminary in 1819. Two years later the Presbyterian School in Auburn, New York, was established, and in 1822 the Congregationalists opened the Divinity School of Yale University. These institutions for ministerial training multiplied rapidly, and by 1860 had increased to fifty, a number since greatly augmented. The whole character of pastoral preparation was broadened, deepened, and systematized.

Out of these religious awakenings there grew many divisions. One such of importance was the rise of the Cumberland Presbyterian Church. The Cumberland region in Tennessee and Kentucky was powerfully stirred by the revival in 1800. Churches were rapidly multiplied, and in 1802 the Cumberland Presbytery was formed. The need of preachers was great, and the presbytery desired ministerial standing for some earnest young men who lacked the educational qualifications demanded by Presbyterianism generally. The revival preaching had produced a conviction that the doctrines that Christ died for the elect only, and that any portion of the race is reprobate save by its own personal acts, were hindrances rather than helps. The Kentucky synod viewed these departures with disfavor, and in 1806 ordered the Cumberland Presbytery dissolved. In 1810 the Cumberland Presbytery reconstituted itself as an independent body. Its growth was rapid. In 1813 a synod was organized, and in 1816 it took the name Cumberland Presbyterian Church, though it was soon represented vastly more widely than the region from which the title was derived.

The older Presbyterians and Congregationalists worked in harmony in home missions in what have long been the northern central states under the plan of union formed in 1801 by the General Association of Connecticut and the Presbyterian General Assembly, till it was repudiated by the Old School wing of the Presbyterians in 1837, and by the Congregationalists in 1852. In general, however, denominational rivalries were keen and controversy bitter, especially in the extension work of the developing West.

Out of an earnest conviction of the evils of these divisions a movement of much importance grew. Thomas Campbell (1763–1854) was a minister of the Secession Presbyterian Church (*ante*, p. 553) of the north of Ireland, who came to America in 1807, and began work in western Pennsylvania. Here his freedom in welcoming Presbyterians of all parties to communion aroused criticism, and he was disciplined by the Secession Presbytery of Chartiers. Campbell felt it his duty to protest against such sectarianism, and to assert as the standard of all Christian discipleship the literal terms of the Bible alone, as he understood it. Thomas Campbell now broke with the Secession Presbyterians, but continued to labor in western Pennsylvania, announcing as his principle: "Where the Scriptures speak, we speak; and where the Scriptures are silent, we are silent." It was not a new denomination that he planned, but a union of all Christians on this Biblical basis, without added tests of creed or ritual. In August, 1809, Thomas Campbell organized The Christian Association of Washington— so-called from the Pennsylvania county of its origin—and for it he prepared the "Declaration and Address" which has since been regarded as a fundamental document of what was to be known as the Disciples movement. The same year Thomas Campbell's son, Alexander (1786–1866), emigrated to America, and was soon to outstrip his father in fame as an advocate of the former's views.

In spite of their deprecation of sectarianism, the Campbells organized a church in Brush Run, Pennsylvania, in May, 1811. The Lord's Supper was observed each Sunday from the beginning. But doubts now arose as to the Scriptural warrant of infant baptism. In 1812 the Campbells and a number of their associates were immersed. A year later the Brush Run church became a member of the Redstone Association of Baptist Churches. Points of disagreement with the Baptists developed. The Campbells disliked the Baptists' strenuous Calvinism. To the Campbells the Old Testament was far less authoritative than the New. To the Baptists baptism was a privilege of the already pardoned sinner; to the Campbells it was a condition of forgiveness. Moreover, the Campbells, without being in any sense Unitarians, refused to employ other than Scriptural expressions regarding the Father, Son, and Holy Spirit. The result was a withdrawal from the Baptists, which may be said to have been completed by 1827. From this time onward the followers of the Campbells were practically a denomination, known popularly as Disciples of Christ. They are Congregational in polity. Their growth has been remarkable, and has constituted the Disciples an important factor in American religious life.

A peculiar development of prophetical interpretation was that of William Miller (1782–1849), a Baptist farmer of Low Hampton, New York. From 1831 onward he preached widely, asserting on the basis of calculations from the book of *Daniel* that the second coming and the inauguration of the millennial reign of Christ would occur in 1843–1844. He won thousands of followers. In spite of the failure of his prediction, his disciples held a general conference of Adventists, as they styled themselves, in 1845, and have persisted to the present, some holding to the observance of the seventh day. Their belief that the coming of Christ is near, though at a date not determinable, is widely diffused among many who do not bear the Adventist name.

A remarkable perversion of Christianity is Mormonism, founded by Joseph Smith (1805–1844), who claimed to have dug up, near Manchester, New York, in 1827, a volume of gold plates, the *Book of Mormon*, supplementary to the Bible, written in mysterious characters which he was able to translate by means of a pair of magic spectacles, but the original of which was removed by angelic agency. In this book Smith is proclaimed a prophet. The first Mormon Church was organized in 1830, in Fayette, New York. It was soon largely recruited in the neighborhood of Kirtland, Ohio. Here Brigham Young (1801–1877) became a member. In 1838 the Mormon leaders removed to Missouri, and in 1840 founded Nauvoo, Illinois. In spite of the monogamy enjoined by the *Book of Mormon*, Smith claimed to have received a revelation, in 1843, establishing polygamy. Popular hostility led to his murder by a mob the next year. The church now came under the leadership of Brigham Young, an organizer and leader of the highest ability. Under him the Mormons marched to Salt Lake, in Utah, and a community of great material prosperity was inaugurated. After protracted conflict with the United States Government, Wilford Woodruff (1807–1898), then head of the Mormon Church, declared against polygamy in 1890.

The Mormons have been indefatigable missionaries, and their numbers have been largely recruited from Europe. Their system of economic and social supervision has been remarkable and has produced a large degree of material prosperity. They hold that God was revealed as Adam, and that Christ, Mohammed, Joseph Smith, and Brigham Young were also manifestations of deity. By these divine beings souls are created, for whom the faithful should provide bodies. At their deaths the righteous will share in divinity. Salvation is through the atonement of Christ, by faith, repentance, and baptism by immersion; though baptism by proxy is of avail for the dead. Their numbers are such that the Mormons bid fair long to be an element in American religious life.

The religious activity of the first half of the nineteenth century was accompanied by efforts for social righteousness. The death of Alexander Hamilton by the hand of Aaron Burr, in 1804, led to a wide-spread and largely successful attack by the religious forces on duelling, in which an extensively circulated sermon by Lyman Beecher (1775–1863) was of much influence.

Temperance aroused the efforts of the Presbyterian General Assembly and of the Congregational Associations of Connecticut and Massachusetts in 1811. Lyman Beecher's sermons against drunkenness, of 1813, attracted great attention. The American Society for the Promotion of Temperance was formed in 1826. The result was a great and permanent change in the drinking habits of professed Christians by 1830. Effort then turned toward a promotion of temperance among those not actively of the church. The Washingtonian movement of 1840 sought the reformation of drunkards. Prohibition by legislation was enacted in Maine in 1846. Its history has been checkered, but legislative prohibition has made great strides since the opening of the twentieth century throughout the United States, and has had the constantly increasing support of the actively Christian elements of American population.

Slavery also aroused the hostility of Christian people, North and South, from the dawn of the nineteenth century. A great change came over the Southern attitude soon after 1830, partly by reason of the supposedly industrial necessity of the system and partly through resentment by reason of the injudicious attacks of Northern Abolitionists on the character of all slaveholders. The question thenceforth was to be profoundly divisive, but with ever-increasing sensitiveness of the Northern religious consciousness to the evils of human bondage.

The fourth and fifth decades of the nineteenth century were a period of controversy and division. The Presbyterian Church had been recruited from two main elements—the descendants of Scotch-Irish parentage and those of New England ancestry. The latter were inclined to greater doctrinal and administrative freedom. At the General Assembly of 1837 the Presbyterian Church was rent into two nearly equal bodies, the "Old School" and the "New School."

Controversies of nearly equal intensity, though with less divisive results, turmoiled the Congregationalists of New England. Hartford Theological Seminary was founded in 1834 to offset the supposed errors of the Yale Divinity School, then under the leadership of Nathaniel W. Taylor (1786–1858). Horace Bushnell (1802–1876), of Hartford, Connecticut, influenced by Samuel Taylor Coleridge (*ante*, p. 545), attacked the conception of Christian doctrine as based primarily on demonstration to the intellect, then almost universal in America, and would substitute for such logical proof an appeal to the witness of the religious feeling. Bushnell's most influential publication was his *Christian Nurture*, of 1847, in which he urged the quiet unfolding of the Christian nature of the child, under appropriate influences, as the normal method of entrance in the kingdom of God, instead of the struggling conversion which Pietist and Methodist tradition had considered the only legitimate experience.

The Protestant Episcopal Church was turmoiled by disputes between the high-church and Evangelical parties.

The most extensive separations were caused, however, by the contests anticipatory of or accompanying the Civil War. Growing antipathy to slavery led to the organization, in 1843, of the Wesleyan Methodist Church of America on the basis of no slaveowning membership. The question was thus in the foreground when the General Conference of the Methodist Episcopal Church met in 1844, and an immediate struggle arose over the retention of a slaveholding bishop. Northern and

Southern sentiment was hopelessly divided. The Conference adopted a report permitting the division of the church, with the result that the Methodist Episcopal Church, South, was constituted, in 1845.

Contemporaneously a similar division separated the Baptists of North and South. The Alabama State Convention of Baptists demanded, in 1844, that the Foreign Mission Board make no discrimination against slaveholders in missionary appointments. The board declared that it would take no action implying approval of slavery. The result was the formation of the Southern Baptist Convention in 1845 and the cleavage of the churches.

The rupture of the Old School Presbyterian body and the formation of the Presbyterian Church, South, did not occur till 1861, after the outbreak of the war between the states.

These divisions, unhappily, still continue, though signs are abundant of reunion in the not distant future.

The Protestant Episcopal Church was divided only during the Civil War, and was reunited at its close.

A pleasing illustration of an opposite tendency was the reunion, after much effort, of the Old School and New School Presbyterian Churches of the North, voted in 1869 and completed in 1870.

The last great revival, nation-wide in its scope, occurred in 1858, though many similar, though more local, movements have been felt to the present. Though the Pietist conception of religion has still continued predominant in American Protestantism, Christian nurture has won increasing allegiance, especially among Congregationalists and Presbyterians since the Civil War, and has greatly favored the growth of the Protestant Episcopal Church, which has always championed it.

The Roman Catholic Church grew enormously in the United States throughout the nineteenth century, chiefly through immigration from Ireland and southern Germany, and since 1890 from Italy and eastern Europe. These races have been prolific in their new home. Bitter Protestant opposition was encountered between 1840 and 1860; but since the date last named relations between Protestants and Roman Catholics have been increasingly tolerant. The Roman Church has accomplished an enormous task of building churches, parochial schools, convents, hospitals, and institutions of higher learning through the gifts and sacrifices of a relatively scanty financial ability. National councils have been held in 1852, 1866, and 1884. Long under the superintendence of the *Congregatio de Propaganda Fide* in Rome, Pius X (1903–1914) granted to the Roman Church in the United States in 1908 the same degree of autonomy enjoyed in European lands.

An outstanding feature of American religious life since the war between the states is the steady increase in the demand for an educated ministry in those bodies which formerly laid little stress on training. This demand has been met by constantly increasing provision, and the older theological seminaries have steadily enlarged their facilities by augmented faculties and extension of the curriculum.

The period has witnessed an ever-enlarging recognition of the work of women in the Protestant Churches. A Woman's Board of Foreign Missions was founded among the Congregationalists in 1868. The Methodist Episcopal Church, North, followed in 1869; the Northern Presbyterians in 1870; and the Protestant Episcopal Church in 1871. Similar organizations for home and foreign missions are now well-nigh universal in American Protestantism. Women have long been eligible to the representative conventions of the Baptist and Congregational Churches. They won the right of election to the Methodist Episcopal General Conference in 1900. They have been ordained to the ministry by Baptists, Congregationalists, Disciples, Unitarians, and Universalists.

The last half-century, especially the last twenty-five years, has witnessed a great theological change in American Protestantism, the exact extent of which it is difficult to estimate, so silently and unequally has it come. Certain outstanding evidences have attracted wide attention. Such were the controversies aroused among the Congregationalists by the "progressive orthodoxy" of Andover Theological Seminary between 1885 and 1892. Such was the deposition of Professor Charles Augustus Briggs (1841–1913) by the Presbyterian General Assembly in 1893. These tangible evidences have been few. Yet even in bodies officially bound by confessional statements of the Reformation age, the characteristic doctrines are proclaimed with little of their ancient satisfaction. The newer Biblical criticism, especially of Germany, and the evolutionary view of development, have found large acceptance in many of the most influential schools of ministerial training, and have wide following among the ministry, especially in the northern and eastern portion of the United States.

Equally marked, during the recent period, but as impossible of exact estimate, has been the growth of the conviction that the message of the Gospel is social. Not a rescue by individual salvation only, but the establishment of a reign of righteousness among men, has become increasingly the ideal. Christian outlook, without ceasing to be other-worldly, has become this-worldly also. Emphasis is placed on service in preventative and reformatory effort. The duty of the church to share in civic betterment is emphasized. A great enlargement has come in the conception of the church's mission. Adjustment has been awkward and has been but partially accomplished, since the organization of the churches has been adapted to the older and more limited vision. To find organs for the work of the new has not been easy. This difficulty has led to a large relinquishment to secular organizations, manned, indeed, chiefly by members of the churches and infused with the spirit of Christian helpfulness, of much social service with which the church should have a more direct relation. The sense of obligation in the churches is undeniably rapidly augmenting. A patent evidence was seen at the outbreak of the world war, in 1914, when the question was widely asked whether that catastrophe did not demonstrate the failure of Christianity. The question implies a vastly altered vision. To the thought of a century earlier the war would have been but another evidence of a world lying in wickedness, from which individuals might be rescued by the Gospel. To those who asked it the Gospel implied a transforming power for righteousness which ought to banish war and kindred evils from mankind in this present world. The same enlargement of conception of the scope of Christianity is evident on the mission field. The feeling animating early American missionaries was that their task was to save a few individuals of the millions of hopelessly lost from their eternal doom. As recently as thirty years ago the proclamation of any other conception was widely declared to "cut the nerve of missions." The aim of missions has not been so much changed as immensely enlarged. The missionary seeks necessarily individual converts, but he strives, as his larger work,

to plant Christian civilization, to sweep away hoary superstitions and oppressions, and to foster a native Christianity which
may be a transforming force to whole peoples.   Never have
gifts to missions been larger or missionary candidates more
numerous than they now are.

An outstanding feature of the existing religious situation
in the United States and Canada is the decline of denominational rivalries, and the increase of co-operation in religious
work.   Voluntary associations for co-operate Christian endeavor have developed remarkably.   Conspicuous have been
the Young Men's Christian Association, founded by George
Williams (1821–1905) in London in 1844, and since spread
throughout the world, and its sister society, the Young Women's
Christian Association, organized in England in 1855, and both
peculiarly successful in the United States.   They have never
been more useful than during the world war.   Less directly
co-operant but uniting in similar aims have been the Young
People's Society of Christian Endeavor, formed by Francis E.
Clark in 1881; and the similar Baptist Young People's Union,
the Epworth League, the Luther League, and the Brotherhood
of St. Andrew.

It is from missions that the strongest impulses to co-operation
have come.   A powerful force in this direction has been the
Student Volunteer Missionary Movement, launched in 1886.
The manifest impropriety of transferring denominational divisions to the mission field has led to large association of similar
groups of Christians into single bodies in China, India, and
Japan.   The essential unity of missionary endeavor was manifest at the World Missionary Conference, held in Edinburgh
in 1910, the influence of which has been potent.   The evils of
religious rivalries led, in the United States, to the establishment
of the Home Missions Council in 1908, composed of representatives of societies engaged in similar work.   This has been
followed by the Foreign Missions Conference of North America,
the Council of Women for Home Missions, and the Federation
of Women's Boards of Foreign Missions.

These associations are voluntary.   A federation of a more
organic character was created, after considerable preliminary
negotiation, by the formation in 1908 of the Federal Council
of the Churches of Christ in America, composed of official delegates from its co-operating churches.   Its functions are ad-

visory, not legislative or judicial. Its objects are: "To express the fellowship and catholic unity of the Christian Church. To bring the Christian bodies of America into united service for Christ and the world. To encourage devotional fellowship and mutual counsel concerning the spiritual life and religious activities of the churches. To secure a larger combined influence for the churches of Christ in all matters affecting the moral and social condition of the people, so as to promote the application of the law of Christ in every relation of human life." The Federal Council now has the support of thirty denominations, including such important bodies as the Northern Baptists, Congregationalists, Disciples, Lutherans (under the General Synod), Methodists, North and South, Presbyterians, North and South, Protestant Episcopalians, and the (Dutch and German) Reformed.

A movement even more ambitious in its plans was inaugurated by the General Convention of the Protestant Episcopal Church in the United States in 1910, aiming at an ultimate world conference on faith and order, which may effect the reunion of Christendom. The object has received the support of a majority of American Protestant bodies to the extent of official representation in several preliminary conferences which have been held, and an American delegation has urged cooperation in Great Britain with success. The world war has delayed the progress in other countries that was hoped.

In Canada a movement for the organic union of Congregationalists, Methodists, and Presbyterians has every prospect of success.

The long story of the Christian Church is a panorama of lights and shadows, of achievement and failure, of conquests and divisions. It has exhibited the divine life marvellously transforming the lives of men. It has also exhibited those passions and weaknesses of which human nature is capable. Its tasks have seemed, in every age, almost insuperable. They were never greater than at present when confronted by a materialistic interpretation of life, and when the furnace of almost universal war bids fair to transform the whole fabric of European and American civilization. Yet no Christian can survey what the church has done without confidence in its future. Its changes may be many, its struggles great. But the good hand of God which has led it hitherto will guide it to larger usefulness in the advancement of the kingdom of its Lord, and toward the fulfilment of His prediction that if He be lifted up He would draw all men unto Him.

BIBLIOGRAPHICAL SUGGESTIONS

No attempt is made to do more than indicate what volumes **the** reader of this History, especially if unacquainted with any language besides English, will find most useful.

An encyclopædia should be at hand. The following are especially serviceable: *The New Schaff-Herzog Encyclopedia of Religious Knowledge*, New York, 1908–12; *Encyclopædia of Religion and Ethics*, Edinburgh and New York, 1908–17 (nine volumes **to** "Phrygians" thus far issued); *The Catholic Encyclopædia*, New York, 1907–12; *The Encyclopædia Britannica*, eleventh edition, Cambridge and New York, 1910.

SOURCE BOOKS.—The following source books are indispensable: Philip Schaff, *The Creeds of Christendom*, New York, fourth edition, 1905; Joseph Cullen Ayer, Jr., *A Source Book for Ancient Church History, from the Apostolic Age to the Close of the Conciliar Period*, New York, 1913; Ernest F. Henderson, *Select Historical Documents of the Middle Ages*, London, 1912; James Harvey Robinson, *Readings in European History*, Boston and New York [1904, 1906]; Henry Gee and William John Hardy, *Documents Illustrative of English Church History*, London, 1896. The selections in the volumes just enumerated are in English translation. For those who can read Latin and French the following work is of high worth: B. J. Kidd, *Documents Illustrative of the Continental Reformation*, Oxford, 1911. All these source books are cited in this history. To any who can read Latin, Carl Mirbt, *Quellen zur Geschichte des Papsttums*, Tübingen and Leipzig, 1911, is invaluable for papal development.

SOURCES.—The following sources are readily available in English translation: J. B. Lightfoot and J. R. Harmer, *The Apostolic Fathers*, London, 1898; Kirsopp Lake, *The Apostolic Fathers*, two volumes, New York, 1913. *The Ante-Nicene Fathers . . . Down to A. D. 325*, ten volumes, New York, 1896. The translations are of varying excellence. This series is continued in the *Nicene and Post-Nicene Fathers*. The First Series, fourteen volumes, New York, 1886–94, embraces the works of Augustine and Chrysostom. The Second Series, twelve volumes, New York, 1890–95, **contains** the whole or selections from the principal writers from Eusebius to Gregory the Great. The first volume of this Second Series, Eusebius's *Ecclesiastical History*, translated and annotated by A. C. McGiffert, is indispensable. For those who read Greek and Latin much ampler sources are provided by J. P. Migne in his two great series, *Patrologia Latina*, two hundred and twenty-one volumes, Paris, 1844–64, extending to Innocent III; and *Patrologia Græca*, one hundred and sixty-six volumes, Paris, 1857–66. The texts are often uncritically given. Of highest critical excellence for the early portion of the field covered by Migne are the *Corpus scriptorum ecclesiasticorum latinorum*, in course of publication since 1866 by the Vienna Academy; and *Die griechischen christlichen Schriftsteller*, issued since 1897 by the Prussian Academy. For the acts of councils the new edition (Paris, 1901–) of J. D. Mansi, *Sacrorum conciliorum nova et amplissima collectio*, extending to the present, may be consulted. Papal letters and decrees may be found to 1304 in P. Jaffé, *Regesta pontificum Romanorum*, and his continuers, Leipzig, 1881–88; Berlin, 1874. The relations of the papacy and mediæval empire may be studied in the great collection by G. H. Pertz and successive editors, *Monumenta Germaniæ historica*, Hanover, 1826– to the present.

John Huss's *The Church* is accessible in translation by David S. Schaff, New York, 1915.

Luther's fundamental writings are translated by H. Wace and C. A. Buchheim, *First Principles of the Reformation*, Philadelphia, 1885; enlarged as *Luther's Primary Works together with His Shorter and Larger Catechisms*, London, 1896. Luther's *Works* are in process of publication in English, vols. I and II., Philadelphia, 1915. Much of Luther's table-talk is accessible in Preserved Smith and H. P. Gallinger, *Conversations with Luther*, Boston, 1915. Lutheran symbolics may be studied in H. E. Jacobs, *The Book of Concord: or, The Symbolical Books of the Evangelical Lutheran Church*, two volumes, Philadelphia, 1882–83. For those who read German and Latin the definitive edition of Luther's writings is the *Werke*, in process of publication in Weimar since 1884, of which more than fifty volumes have been issued.

The writings of Zwingli are accessible in S. M. Jackson, *The Latin Works and Correspondence of Huldreich Zwingli*, two volumes, New York, 1912, 1917.

Most of Calvin's writings are translated into English, as *The Works of John Calvin*, fifty-two volumes, Edinburgh, 1843–55.

The student will find the *Institutes* indispensable. They are best translated by Henry Beveridge, in the series just cited, 3 volumes, Edinburgh, 1845–46. For those who read Latin and French the edition of the Strassburg editors, *Joannis Calvini Opera*, fifty-nine volumes, Braunschweig, 1863–1900, is a storehouse.

The *Works of James Arminius* are available in English translation by James Nichols and W. R. Bagnall, three volumes, London, 1825 and 1828, Buffalo, 1853. Hugo Grotius's *Defence of the Catholic Faith Concerning the Satisfaction of Jesus Christ* was translated by F. H. Foster, Andover, 1889.

The *Racovian Catechism* is a prime source for Socinianism. English translation, London, 1818.

The general student will find much regarding the English Reformation in Henry Gee and W. J. Hardy, *Documents Illustrative of English Church History*, London, 1896, already cited under Source Books; and in Charles Hardwick, *A History of the Articles of Religion*, Cambridge, 1859; and in Francis Procter and W. H. Frere, *A New History of the Book of Common Prayer*, London and New York, 1901. Puritan wishes can be studied in W. H. Frere, *Puritan Manifestoes, a Study of the Origin of the Puritan Revolt*, London, 1907; and S. R. Gardiner, *Constitutional Documents of the Puritan Revolution*, Oxford, 1899. The aims of Congregationalists are manifest in Williston Walker, *The Creeds and Platforms of Congregationalism*, New York, 1893; and W. J. McGlothlin, *Baptist Confessions of Faith*, Philadelphia, 1911, does a similar service for the Baptists.

Any who would make a special study of the English Reformation will need to consult the *Letters and Papers, Foreign and Domestic, of the Reign of Henry VIII*, twenty-one volumes, London, 1862–1910; and *Calendar of State Papers, Domestic Series, of the Reigns of Edward VI, Mary, Elizabeth, James I*, twelve volumes, London, 1856–72. The writings of the leading English reformers were published by the Parker Society, *Works of the English Reformers*, fifty-four volumes, Cambridge, 1841–54. Many documents of prime importance may be found in E. Cardwell, *Documentary Annals of the Church of England*, two volumes, Oxford, 1844; Gilbert Burnet, *History of the Reformation of the Church of England*, Pocock's edition, seven volumes, Oxford, 1865; and John Strype, *Complete Works*, twenty-seven volumes, Oxford, 1822–40.

A collection of much importance for Scotland is [William Dunlop] *A Collection of Confessions of Faith, Catechisms . . . of Public*

Authority in the Church of Scotland, two volumes, Edinburgh, 1719–22. Further study should be made of the *Calendar of State Papers Relating to Scotland* (1547–1603), six volumes, Edinburgh, 1898–1910. The works of Knox and other Scottish Presbyterian leaders were published by the Wodrow Society, twenty-four volumes, London, 1842–. A similar service for the leaders of Scottish episcopacy was performed by the Spottiswoode Society, sixteen volumes, Edinburgh, 1844–.

HISTORIES OF DOCTRINE AND CHRISTIAN THOUGHT.—The following brief volumes will constitute a good introduction: Charles A. Briggs, *History of the Study of Theology,* two volumes, New York, 1916; H. B. Workman, *Christian Thought to the Reformation,* New York, 1911; A. C. McGiffert, *Protestant Thought before Kant,* New York, 1911; and E. C. Moore, *History of Christian Thought Since Kant,* New York, 1912. A more comprehensive work is George P. Fisher, *History of Christian Doctrine,* New York, 1896. A work of great value reaching to the Reformation, and with the quotations in English translation as well as the text, is Reinhold Seeberg, *Text-Book of the History of Doctrines,* two volumes, Philadelphia, 1905. For any who can read German the best work (to the close of the Reformation) is Friedrich Loofs, *Leitfaden zum Studium der Dogmengeschichte,* fourth edition, Halle, 1906. For the advanced student an indispensable work (to the close of the Reformation) is Adolf von Harnack, *History of Dogma,* English translation, seven volumes, Boston, 1896–1900. An illuminating treatment is that of Henry Osborn Taylor, *The Mediæval Mind,* two volumes, London and New York, 1914. Julius Köstlin, *The Theology of Luther,* English translation, two volumes, Philadelphia [1897], is to be commended. For later development, I. A. Dorner, *History of Protestant Theology, Particularly in Germany,* English translation, two volumes, Edinburgh, 1871. A very useful work is A. C. McGiffert, *The Rise of Modern Religious Ideas,* New York, 1915. The development of the modern situation may be further studied in Ernst Troeltsch, *Protestantism and Progress,* New York, 1912; W. E. H. Lecky, *The History of the Rise and Influence of Rationalism in Europe,* London, 1867; Andrew D. White, *A History of the Warfare of Science with Theology,* New York, 1896; Leslie Stephen, *History of English Thought in the Eighteenth Century,* two volumes, New York, 1876; John Tulloch, *Movements of Religious Thought in Britain During the Nineteenth Century,* New York, 1901. The best work in its field is Frank H. Foster, *A Genetic History of the New*

England Theology, Chicago, 1907. A work of great suggestiveness is William James, *Varieties of Religious Experience,* New York, 1902.

MISSIONS.—The following works will initiate the student into the story of Christian missions. Adolf von Harnack, *The Mission and Expansion of Christianity in the First Three Centuries,* English translation, two volumes, New York, 1908; George F. Maclear, *A History of Christian Missions During the Middle Ages,* London, 1863; Gustav Warneck, *Outline of the History of Protestant Missions,* English translation, Edinburgh, 1906; Charles H. Robinson, *History of Christian Missions,* New York, 1915; W. H. P. Faunce, *The Social Aspects of Foreign Missions,* New York, 1914.

THE PREPARATION.—Three small volumes will serve as an introduction to the Jewish situation. Charles F. Kent, *A History of the Jewish People During the Babylonian, Persian, and Greek Periods,* New York, 1899; James S. Riggs, *A History of the Jewish People During the Maccabean and Roman Periods,* New York, 1900; Shailer Mathews, *A History of New Testament Times in Palestine,* London and New York, 1913. The more advanced student will consult Emil Schürer, *History of the Jewish People in the Time of Jesus Christ,* English translation, five volumes, Edinburgh, 1885–90, New York, 1896; A. B. Davidson, *The Theology of the Old Testament,* New York, 1904; R. H. Charles, *The Apocrypha and Pseudepigrapha of the Old Testament,* two volumes, Oxford, 1913.

For the situation outside of Judaism, Wilhelm Windelband, *A History of Philosophy,* English translation, New York, 1901; Eduard Zeller, *History of Greek Philosophy,* English translation, two volumes, London, 1881; and his *Stoics, Epicureans, and Sceptics,* London and New York, 1892; Franz Cumont, *Oriental Religions in Roman Paganism,* Chicago, 1911; T. R. Glover, *The Conflict of Religions within the Roman Empire,* London, 1909; Samuel Dill, *Roman Society from Nero to Marcus Aurelius,* London, 1904.

THE BEGINNINGS.—S. J. Case, *The Evolution of Early Christianity,* Chicago, 1914; Paul Wernle, *The Beginnings of Christianity,* English translation, two volumes, New York, 1903–04. The history and present status of investigation regarding the life of Christ can be learned from Albert Schweitzer, *The Quest of the Historical Jesus,* English translation, London, 1910; William Sanday, *The Life of Christ in Recent Research,* New York, 1907; S. J. Case, *The Historicity of Jesus,* Chicago, 1912. The life of Paul is well treated in B. W. Bacon, *The Story of St. Paul,* Boston, 1904. The history of Pauline investigation is discussed in Albert Schweitzer, *Paul and His Interpreters*, English translation, London, 1912; see also H. A. A. Kennedy, *St. Paul and the Mystery Religions*, London and New York [1913].

Excellent general discussions of the apostolic period are A. C. McGiffert, *History of Christianity in the Apostolic Age*, second edition, New York, 1910; J. H. Ropes, *The Apostolic Age*, New York, 1906. A more elaborate treatment is Carl von Weizsäcker, *The Apostolic Age of the Christian Church*, English translation, two volumes, London and New York, 1897.

The following works will aid in initiation into the present status of New Testament discussion: H. S. Nash, *The History of the Higher Criticism of the New Testament*, New York, 1900; Edward C. Moore, *The New Testament in the Christian Church*, New York, 1904; James Moffatt, *Introduction to the Literature of the New Testament*, New York, 1911.

THE CHURCH IN THE ROMAN EMPIRE.—The best introductory work is Louis Duchesne, *The Early History of the Christian Church from Its Foundation to the End of the Fifth Century*, English translation, two volumes, New York, 1909, 1912. A good sketch is that of Robert Rainy, *The Ancient Catholic Church*, New York, 1902. A larger work on the early period is H. M. Gwatkin, *Early Church History to A. D. 313*, two volumes, London, 1909. Indispensable is Adolf von Harnack, *The Mission and Expansion of Christianity in the First Three Centuries*, second edition, two volumes, New York, 1908. An elaborate work for the more advanced student is Wilhelm Moeller and Hans von Schubert, *History of the Christian Church*, First Volume to A. D. 600, English translation, London and New York, 1892. A readable collection of biographies is Frederic W. Farrar, *Lives of the Fathers*, two volumes, New York, 1889. A suggestive volume is J. Estlin Carpenter, *Phases of Early Christianity*, New York, 1916.

Early Christian life is admirably treated by Ernst von Dobschütz, *Christian Life in the Primitive Church*, English translation, New York, 1904. For the persecutions see H. B. Workman, *Persecution in the Early Church*, London, 1906; L. H. Canfield, *The Early Persecutions of the Christians*, New York, 1913; W. M. Ramsay, *The Church in the Roman Empire before A. D. 170*, London and New York, 1893.

For the Apostles' Creed see A. C. McGiffert, *The Apostles' Creed*, New York, 1902

For the organization of the early church, Edwin Hatch, *The Organization of the Early Christian Churches*, London, 1895; Walter Lowrie, *The Church and Its Organization*, London and New York, 1904; T. M. Lindsay, *The Church and the Ministry in the Early Centuries*, London and New York, 1902; Adolf von Harnack, *The Constitution and Law of the Church in the First Two Centuries*, English translation, London and New York, 1910. For the High Anglican view see Charles Gore, *The Ministry of the Christian Church*, London, 1889; and his *Orders and Unity*, New York, 1909.

A good guide to the non-canonical literature of early Christianity is Gustav Krüger, *History of Early Christian Literature in the First Three Centuries*, English translation, London and New York, 1897. The student who can read German will have recourse to the monumental work by Adolf von Harnack, *Geschichte der altchristlichen Litteratur bis Eusebius*, three volumes, Leipzig, 1893–1904.

A good brief introduction to Christian archæology is Walter Lowrie, *Monuments of the Early Church*, New York, 1901.

For the church in the empire after the conversion of Constantine the student will find much of value in *The Cambridge Mediæval History*, vol. I, *The Christian Roman Empire*, New York, 1911. Good manuals on this period are A. H. Hore, *Students' History of the Greek Church*, London and New York, 1902; and W. F. Adeney, *The Greek and Eastern Churches*, New York, 1908. Monasticism is discussed by H. B. Workman, *The Evolution of the Monastic Ideal*, London, 1913; and Adolf von Harnack, *Monasticism; Its Ideals and Its History*, English translation, New York, 1895. A mine of information for the German reader is Max Heimbucher, *Die Orden und Kongregationen der Katholichen Kirche*, two volumes, Paderborn, 1896–97.

A compact sketch of the councils is that of W. P. DuBose, *The Ecumenical Councils*, New York, 1896. Much fuller is K. J. Hefele, *A History of the Christian Councils*, English translation, five volumes, Edinburgh, 1871–96.

Two special studies of unusual value are J. B. Bury, *The Life of St. Patrick and His Place in History*, London and New York, 1905; and F. H. Dudden, *Gregory the Great: His Place in History and Thought*, two volumes, London, 1905.

THE CHURCH IN THE MIDDLE AGES AND TO THE REFORMATION. —The earlier portion of this period is well treated in *The Cambridge Mediæval History*, vol. II, *The Rise of the Saracens and the Foundation of the Western Empire*, New York, 1913. A classic exposition of the relations of the mediæval church to the state is James Bryce, *The Holy Roman Empire*, new edition, London, 1904. A work of wealth of information regarding the ecclesiastical life and institutions is André Lagarde, *The Latin Church in the Middle Ages*, English translation, New York, 1915. A classic treatment especially of the mediæval papacy is Ferdinand Gregorovius, *History of the City of Rome*, English translation, eight volumes, London, 1894–1902. For the latter part of the period (1049–1517) a fresh and suggestive treatment is that of D. S. Schaff in continuation of his father, Philip Schaff's *History of the Christian Church*, viz., vol. V, Parts I and II (each an ample volume), New York, 1907, 1910. A general history of the period for the advanced student is Wilhelm Moeller, *History of the Christian Church*, vol. II, *The Middle Ages*, English translation, London, 1893.

Special treatises of value are Gustav Krüger, *The Papacy: the Idea and Its Exponents*, English translation, New York, 1909; and Paul Sabatier, *Life of St. Francis of Assisi*, New York, 1894.

Compact volumes of service are M. R. Vincent, *The Age of Hildebrand*, New York, 1896; J. M. Ludlow, *The Age of the Crusades*, New York, 1896; R. L. Poole, *Illustrations of the History of Mediæval Thought*, London, 1884.

For English church history the student will find the following of use: William Hunt, *The English Church from Its Foundation to the Norman Conquest*, London and New York, 1899; W. R. W. Stephens, *The English Church from the Norman Conquest to the Accession of Edward I*, London and New York, 1901; W. W. Capes, *The English Church in the Fourteenth and Fifteenth Centuries*, London and New York, 1900; G. M. Trevelyan, *England in the Age of Wycliffe*, London and New York, 1899. For an unsympathetic treatment see James Gairdner, *Lollardy and the Reformation in England*, vol. I, London, 1908.

For Huss, David S. Schaff, *John Huss, His Life, Teachings and Death, After Five Hundred Years*, New York, 1915; and Schaff's translation of Huss's *The Church*, New York, 1915.

For Savonarola, P. Villari, *Life and Times of Girolamo Savonarola*, English translation, two volumes, New York, 1888.

Most valuable and extensive treatments of the period preceding the Reformation are given in Mandell Creighton, *History of the Papacy from the Great Schism to the Sack of Rome*, six volumes, London and New York, 1892. From a Roman point of view, Ludwig Pastor, *History of the Popes from the Close of the Middle Ages*,

English translation, twelve volumes, London, 1891–1912. Gregorovius, *History of the City of Rome*, already cited, continues of great worth for this period. The same may be said of *The Cambridge Modern History*, vol. I, *The Renaissance*, London and New York, 1902.

THE REFORMATION.—The student will find the best introduction T. M. Lindsay, *A History of the Reformation*, two volumes, New York, 1906, 1907. A succinct treatment is Williston Walker, *The Reformation*, New York, 1900. A more elaborate work of great value by Wilhelm Moeller and Gustav Kawerau is *History of the Christian Church*, vol. III, *Reformation and Counter-Reformation*, English translation, London, 1900. Volumes of great wealth of detail are: *The Cambridge Modern History*, London and New York, 1904–06, vol. II, *The Reformation;* vol. III, *The Wars of Religion;* vol. IV, *The Thirty Years' War.* For the Roman point of view see Johannes Janssen, *History of the German People After the Close of the Middle Ages*, English translation, sixteen volumes, London, 1896–1910. A good brief sketch is A. W. Ward, *The Counter-Reformation*, London, 1889.

The life of Luther is well told in the following: A. C. McGiffert, *Martin Luther, the Man and His Work*, New York, 1911; Preserved Smith, *The Life and Letters of Martin Luther*, Boston, 1911; H. E. Jacobs, *Martin Luther*, New York, 1898. A study of great value is H. Boehmer, *Luther in the Light of Recent Research*, English translation, New York, 1916. A Roman estimate of Luther is that of Hartmann Grisar, *Luther*, English translation, London, 1913.

Other biographies of Reformation leaders are: J. W. Richard, *Philip Melanchthon*, New York, 1898; Ephraim Emerton, *Desiderius Erasmus*, New York, 1899; S. M. Jackson, *Huldreich Zwingli*, New York, 1901; Williston Walker, *John Calvin*, New York, 1906; H. Y. Reyburn, *John Calvin, His Life, Letters and Work*, London and New York, 1914; H. M. Baird, *Theodore Beza*, New York, 1899.

For German conditions, Henry C. Vedder, *The Reformation in Germany*, New York, 1914. For France, H. M. Baird, *History of the Rise of the Huguenots*, second edition, five volumes, New York, 1895–1907. For the Netherlands, P. J. Blok, *History of the People of the Netherlands*, English translation, five volumes, New York, 1898–1912; Ruth Putnam, *William the Silent*, two volumes, New York, 1895.

For the Anabaptist movement, A. H. Newman, *A History of*

Anti-Pædobaptism, Philadelphia, 1897; Henry C. Vedder, *A Short History of the Baptists*, Philadelphia [1907]; Henry C. Vedder, *Balthasar Hubmaier*, New York, 1903; J. Horsch, *Menno Simons, His Life, Labours and Teaching*, Scottdale, Pa., 1916.

For contemporary and later developments in the Greek, Russian, and other Oriental Churches: A. H. Hore, *Student's History of the Greek Church*, London and New York, 1902; W. F. Adeney, *The Greek and Eastern Churches*, New York, 1908.

GREAT BRITAIN IN THE REFORMATION AND SINCE.—The English Reformation is carefully treated by James Gairdner, *The English Church . . . from the Accession of Henry VIII to the Death of Mary*, London and New York, 1902; and by W. H. Frere, *The English Church in the Reigns of Elizabeth and James I*, London and New York, 1904. Learned but unsympathetic is James Gairdner, *Lollardy and the Reformation in England*, four volumes, London, 1908–14. The Roman point of view is given by F. A. Gasquet, *The Eve of the Reformation*, London, 1905. Two biographies of high value are those of A. F. Pollard, *Henry VIII*, London, 1905; and *Thomas Cranmer*, New York, 1904. See also R. W. Dixon, *History of the Church of England from the Abolition of the Roman Jurisdiction*, five volumes, London, 1878–92.

An excellent introduction not merely to the Scottish Reformation but to the whole religious history of Scotland is that of P. Hume Brown, *History of Scotland*, three volumes, Cambridge, 1902–09. A good sketch is D. Hay Fleming, *The Scottish Reformation*, London, 1910. For Knox see Henry Cowan, *John Knox*, New York, 1905.

For the rise and history of Non-Conformity valuable introductions are: Henry W. Clark, *History of English Non-Conformity*, two volumes, London, 1911, 1913; Champlin Burrage, *The Early English Dissenters in the Light of Recent Research*, two volumes, Cambridge, 1912; William Pierce, *An Historical Introduction to the Marprelate Tracts*, London, 1908; R. W. and A. W. W. Dale, *History of English Congregationalism*, London, 1907.

A work presenting the Anglican point of view effectively for the latter part of Elizabeth's reign and the early years of James I is Roland G. Usher, *The Reconstruction of the English Church*, two volumes, London and New York, 1910. A general sketch from the same standpoint is W. H. Hutton, *The English Church from the Accession of Charles I to the Death of Anne*, London and New York, 1903.

A mine of information regarding religious movements in sixteenth-century England, and especially the Quakers, is Robert Barclay, *The Inner Life of the Religious Societies of the Commonwealth*, London, 1879. For Fox see Thomas Hodgkin, *The Life of George Fox*, London and New York, 1896; and the extracts from Fox's Journal, edited by Rufus M. Jones, *George Fox, an Autobiography*, two volumes, Philadelphia, 1903.

For the Methodist movement and its leaders see W. J. Townsend, H. B. Workman, and George Eayrs, *A New History of Methodism*, two volumes, London, 1909. Much relating to the religious condition of England is to be found in W. E. H. Lecky, *History of England During the Eighteenth Century*, eight volumes, London, 1878–90. See also Henry W. Clark, *History of English Non-Conformity*, already cited.

For the high-church movement see R. W. Church, *The Oxford Movement*, London, 1891; J. H. Overton, *The Anglican Revival*, London, 1897; J. H. Newman, *Apologia pro vita sua*, London, 1864; J. T. Coleridge, *A Memoir of John Keble*, Oxford, 1869; H. P. Liddon, *Life of Edward Bouverie Pusey*, five volumes, London, 1893–99.

GERMANY.—For Pietism and Rationalism see J. A. Dorner, *History of Protestant Theology, Particularly in Germany*, English translation, two volumes, Edinburgh, 1871; H. E. Guericke, *Life of A. H. Francke*, English translation, London, 1837. Moravians, see John Holmes, *History of the Protestant Church of the United Brethren*, two volumes, London, 1825, 1830; A. G. Spangenberg, *The Life of Nicholas, Count Zinzendorf*, English translation, London, 1838; Augustus C. Thompson, *Moravian Missions*, New York, 1895.

For Rationalism, the following work, though unsympathetic, is of value in the absence of much literature in English: J. F. Hurst, *History of Rationalism Embracing a Survey of the Present State of Protestant Theology*, revised edition, New York, 1901. See also K. R. Hagenbach, *German Rationalism*, English translation, Edinburgh, 1864.

For later developments see F. A. Lichtenberger, *History of German Theology in the Nineteenth Century*, English translation, Edinburgh, 1889; Otto Pfleiderer, *The Development of Theology Since Kant and Its Progress in Great Britain since 1825*, London and New York, 1893; Friedrich Paulsen, *Immanuel Kant, His Life and Doctrine*, English translation, New York, 1902; F. D.

E. Schleiermacher, *On Religion*, English translation, London, 1902; W. B. Selbie, *Schleiermacher: A Critical and Historical Study*, New York, 1913; A. T. Swing, *The Theology of Albrecht Ritschl*, New York, 1901; R. Mackintosh, *Albrecht Ritschl and His School*, London, 1915.

AMERICA.—The most accessible and, on the whole, the most valuable outlines of the history of the principal religious denominations in the United States are those in the series entitled *American Church History*, thirteen volumes, New York, 1893–97. Vol. XIII of this series, by L. W. Bacon, *A History of American Christianity*, is a compendious sketch of the religious life of the United States. See also Daniel Dorchester, *Christianity in the United States*, New York, 1895.

Denominational histories of value, besides those in the "American Church History" series, are: Abel Stevens, *History of the Methodist Episcopal Church*, four volumes, New York, 1864–67; Charles A. Briggs, *American Presbyterianism, Its Origin and Early History*, New York, 1885; S. D. McConnell, *History of the American Episcopal Church*, New York, 1890; W. T. Moore, *A Comprehensive History of the Disciples of Christ*, New York [1909].

A sketch of the religious life of New England is that of G. L. Walker, *Some Aspects of the Religious Life of New England*, Boston, 1897.

A wealth of biographical information regarding American ministers of many denominations, to the middle of the nineteenth century, may be found in W. B. Sprague, *Annals of the American Pulpit*, nine volumes, New York, 1857–69. Typical American religious leaders are commemorated by Williston Walker, *Ten New England Leaders*, Boston, 1901; A. V. G. Allen, *Jonathan Edwards*, Boston, 1889; J. W. Chadwick, *William Ellery Channing*, Boston, 1903; T. T. Munger, *Horace Bushnell*, Boston, 1899; J. O. Murray, *Francis Wayland*, Boston, 1891; George Prentice, *Wilbur Fisk*, Boston, 1890; J. W. Chadwick, *Theodore Parker*, Boston, 1901; W. W. Newton, *Dr. [William A.] Muhlenberg*, Boston, 1890; Lyman Abbott, *Henry Ward Beecher*, Boston, 1903; A. V. G. Allen, *Phillips Brooks*, New York, 1907.

The following among many other volumes may be cited as illustrative of recent tendencies in American religious thought: W. N. Clarke, *An Outline of Christian Theology*, New York, 1898; W. A. Brown, *Christian Theology in Outline*, New York, 1906; Henry C. King, *Theology and the Social Consciousness*, London and New

York, 1902; his *Reconstruction in Theology*, London and New York, 1901; his *Fundamental Questions*, London and New York, 1917; F. G. Peabody, *Jesus Christ and the Social Question*, London and New York, 1901; his *Jesus Christ and the Christian Character*, London and New York, 1905; G. A. Gordon, *Through Man to God*, Boston, 1906; Walter Rauschenbusch, *Christianity and the Social Crisis*, London and New York, 1907; his *Theology for the Social Gospel*, London and New York, 1917; Shailer Mathews, *The Gospel and the Modern Man*, London and New York, 1910; and his *The Church and the Changing Order*, London and New York, 1913.

The present tendencies to co-operation between American communions, especially as illustrated in the Federal Council of the Churches of Christ are discussed by C. S. Macfarland, *The Churches of Christ in Council*, New York [1917].

INDEX

Abbot, George, archbishop of Canterbury, 465, 466.
Abelard, schoolman, 264–266; *also* 267, 273, 275.
Abyssinia, church of, 157, 158.
Acacius, patriarch of Constantinople, 135, 154.
Acolytes, 90, 91.
Act, the Conventicle, 474, 475.
Act, the Five-Mile, 474.
Act, the Test, 475, 547.
Act, the Toleration, 476, 480, 495.
Adaldag, missionary, 236.
Ademar, bishop and Crusader, 240.
Adeodatus, Augustine's son, 176, 178.
Adrian VI, Pope, 351, 354, 422.
Adventists, the, 582.
Æthelberht, King of Kent, 198.
Aetius, count of Italy, 132.
Agape, the, 23, 43, 92.
Agatho, Pope, 161.
Agnes, Empress, 221, 225–227.
Agricola, Rudolf, humanist, 327.
Aidan, missionary, 197, 199.
Aigulf, King, 192.
Ailli, Pierre d', theologian, 307, 308, 338, 345.
Ainsworth, Henry, Congregationalist, 463.
Aistulf, King, 203, 204.
Alaric, Visigoth, 131, 184.
Alberic, ruler of Rome, 215.
Albert, count of Mansfeld, 325.
Albert V, duke of Bavaria, 444.
Albert, duke of Prussia, 355, 357.
Albertus Magnus, schoolman, 256, 269.
Albigenses, *see* Cathari.
Albornoz, cardinal, 296, 297.
Albrecht, archbishop of Mainz, 340, 341.
Albrecht, margrave of Brandenburg, 381.
Alciati, Andrea, jurist, 390.
Alcuin, scholar, 207, 210, 261.
Aleander, Girolamo, nuncio, 346, 347.
Alexander, bishop of Alexandria, 114, 115, 117, 146.
Alexander, Popes, II, 227, 228, 276 (*see* Anselm of Lucca); III, 251–253, 285, 286; V, 303, 304, 308; VI, 318, 320.
Alexander, the Great, 5, 11, 76.
Alexander Farnese, duke of Parma, 436–440.

Alexander, of Hales, schoolman, 269, 276.
Alexander Severus, Emperor, 85.
Alexandria, school of, 76, 77.
Alexius, Emperors, I, 239, 240; III, 243.
Alfonso IX, King of Leon, 287.
Alfred, the Great, King of England, 211.
Allemand, Louis d', cardinal, 312.
Allen, William, cardinal, 438, 440.
Alogoi, the, 72.
Alva, the duke of, general, 434, 436.
Alypius, 176, 178.
Amadeus, duke of Savoy, *see* Felix V.
Amalrich, of Bena, mystic radical, 282, 283.
Amboise, conspiracy of, 432.
Ambrose, bishop of Milan, 140, 141; monasticism, 138; hymns, 167; preacher, 168; and Augustine, 176, 178; mentioned, 128, 165, 173, 190, 330.
Amsdorf, Nikolaus von, reformer, 340, 349, 380, 442, 443.
Anabaptists (*see also* Baptists), 366–373; beliefs, 368, 369; Münster, 374, 375; toleration, 457; Anti-Trinitarian, 369, 451; *see also* 433, 437, 453, 461.
Anacletus II, Pope, 247.
Anastasius, Emperor, 135.
Anaxagoras, philosopher, 3.
Andersson, Lars, reformer, 385.
Andover controversy, the, 539, 586.
Andreæ, Jakob, theologian, 443.
Andrews, Lancelot, bishop, 465.
Angelico, Fra, painter, 316.
Angels, worship of, 171.
Anglo-Catholic movement, the, 547–549.
Anicetus, bishop of Rome, 64.
Anne, of Cleves, Queen of Henry VIII, 407.
Anne, Queen of Great Britain, 552.
Anno, archbishop of Cologne, 227, 228.
Anselm, bishop of Lucca, 225, 226.
Anselm, theologian and archbishop of Canterbury, 233, 263, 264; on the atonement, 263, 264, 456; *see also* 267, 271, 272, 338.
Ansgar, missionary, 213, 214, 236, 237.
Anthony, monastic founder, 137.